Introduction to Business

William H. Cunningham
Dean, College and Graduate School
of Business Administration
University of Texas at Austin

Ramon J. Aldag
Professor of Management and Organization
Graduate School of Business
University of Wisconsin at Madison

Christopher M. Swift
Graduate School of Business Administration
University of Texas at Austin

G90

Published by
SOUTH-WESTERN PUBLISHING CO.

CINCINNATI   WEST CHICAGO, ILL.   DALLAS
PELHAM MANOR, N.Y.   PALO ALTO, CALIF.

Copyright © 1984

by South-Western Publishing Co.

Cincinnati, Ohio

All Rights Reserved

The text of this publication, or any part thereof, may not be reproduced or transmitted in any form or by any means, electronic or mechanical, including photocopying, recording, storage in an information retrieval system, or otherwise, without the prior written permission of the publisher.

ISBN: 0-538-07900-2
Library of Congress Catalog Card Number: 83-50770

2 3 4 5 6 7 8 9 D 1 0 9 8 7 6 5

Printed in the United States of America

PREFACE

The 1980s are very exciting years for business. Corporations and other business concerns are experiencing evolutionary and revolutionary change. Fifteen years ago, computers were used mostly for accounting purposes; today, they are an integral part of decision making in all facets of business. Computers have even found their way into the home. Many other examples of social, economic, and technological change are evident in the business world.

Why is the study of business important? Everyone in our society interacts with business—through the products we buy; the advertisements we see and hear; and the money we invest in stocks, bonds, and other securities. We are all inextricably woven into the fabric of our economic and business systems. Moreover, the vast majority of us, at one time or another, will work for private businesses and maybe even run them. It is critically important that we understand what the role of business is in our society, how businesses operate, and what types of decisions businesses make. The objectives of this book are to introduce students to the world of business and to help prepare them for a more meaningful and beneficial interaction with business.

Text Organization

The book is divided into seven parts. The first part introduces the student to business in America. It takes a wide-reaching look at such fundamental concerns as the free enterprise system; the U.S. economy today; economic and social forces (inflation, high energy costs, population shifts, and others) affecting the business environment; and the social responsibility of business. The analysis of business concepts and methods really begins in the second section, where business ownership and business law are examined. The section also includes a chapter on small business and the franchise system.

The next four parts of the text discuss the important functional areas of business: management, marketing, finance and insurance, and business information. Each part contains several chapters which together offer a comprehensive view of all major topics in the functional area. The business information section pulls together a diversity of material: accounting principles and financial statements, management information systems, basic statistical analysis, business information sources, data processing, and computer applications in business.

In the seventh and last part of the text, the focus again widens. The first chapter here deals with international business—an increasingly important topic in today's world of interdependent national economies, transnational capital flows, and intense competition for global markets. The next chapter in this section, dealing with the future of American business, offers possible answers to the question, Where are current social, economic, and technological trends taking us? The final chapter serves as a bridge between the text and the student's personal life and career. It explores the fundamentals of career planning, offers guidelines on choosing a job and a career, and provides salary and availability information about various careers in business.

We believe the sequencing of sections and chapters in the text is concise and logical, and that it represents a natural progression. However, each part can stand alone, and instructors are encouraged to develop their own course outlines to suit their particular purposes.

Special Chapters

Writing a textbook such as this one involves many choices as to what to include and what not to include. Still other decisions concerning topic emphasis must be made. Certain traditional topics, of course, merit entire chapters—for example, forms of business ownership, product management, or the securities markets. We also devote whole chapters to the contemporary social and economic environment of business, small business management, computers and data processing, international business, and the future of business, because of the increasing importance of these topics. The decisions regarding other topics are not so easily handled, since even a survey text cannot possibly discuss everything. The discussion of statistics and research methods appears in an appendix, since it is believed that this material is ancillary rather than essential to the text narrative. Similar reasoning governed the division of the career material into a chapter and a career appendix.

Chapter Organization

INTRODUCTION TO BUSINESS will be the first formal look at the world of business for many students. The more students learn in this initial encounter with business, the greater their advantage in the years ahead. Accordingly, each chapter contains several special teaching devices. Their purpose is to facilitate learning by clarifying and reinforcing basic concepts, principles, and analytic methods. These devices include:

- A list of learning objectives at the start of each chapter.
- Many tables, graphs, and schematics to present information and relationships in a visually appealing way.
- Extensive use of headings to organize the chapter narrative.
- Key terms and concepts printed in boldface type in the text narrative and listed at the end of the chapter.
- A comprehensive, enumerated chapter summary.
- Review questions to test recall and understanding.
- Discussion questions to encourage further thought on selected topics and to stimulate class discussion.
- A short vignette entitled "From the File" which depicts a business person in the midst of a typical decision situation.
- Two in-depth cases to give students opportunities to apply chapter concepts and methods to real-world business problems.

Contemporary Topics

The world of business has changed dramatically over the last decade or so. We know that change will certainly continue to be a fact of life in the years ahead. The fundamental principles of business stay the same from year to year; but recent social, economic, technological, and regulatory developments have introduced new ideas and methods into business practice and, therefore, into the study of business. We have integrated many of the more significant of these developments into the discussion of business principles. Often the topics are presented through examples. A sampling of these exciting new topics is as follows: robotics, bioengineering, kanban, computer assisted manufacturing, Japanese approaches to management, financial deregulation, microcomputers, quality circles, and the Protean career.

Special Features

First and foremost, the objective of any textbook is to inform and instruct. How much students learn from a text depends upon how much energy they devote to the task of learning. We believe that the full-color design of this text encourages student interest in the material and invites greater participation. Reading a text should be a pleasurable experience. In addition to its design features and many captioned photographs, the text contains examples about current business problems. These examples illustrate text principles and enliven class discussions.

As a society, we have entered the computer era, and formal business education should include a discussion of computers alongside the discussion of more traditional topics. Accordingly, six of the parts of the text feature a Computer Awareness section intended to introduce the student to the logic of computer programs and the ways computers help to solve business problems. Each Computer Awareness section contains a short program which can be run on either a personal computer or a mainframe computer.

Each chapter of the text also features a Controversial Issue. Examples of such issues include robots and job loss in the workplace, the ethics of advertising, and the prospects for national health insurance. Each Controversial Issue is presented as a debate, beginning with a statement or proposition followed by a "pro" argument and a "con" argument. This structure was chosen to encourage student thought on the issue and to avoid the pitfall of author editorializing.

It is people who make business decisions, and INTRODUCTION TO BUSINESS profiles a diverse group of these individuals in a section of each chapter called "Profile." The women and men chosen for the profiles represent many different industries and types of businesses. All of their careers are success stories. The profile for each chapter, in one way or another, demonstrates the successful application of the principles or concepts discussed in the chapter.

Finally, many of the chapters feature boxed discussions on such topics as the causes of the Great Depression, labor legislation, financial leverage, and "dumping" products on foreign markets. The topics chosen are thought to be of interest to instructors and students alike. The aim of these discussions is to develop awareness of topics not dealt with directly in the text narrative.

Supplementary Materials

We have prepared a student Study Guide to accompany INTRODUCTION TO BUSINESS. It was designed to aid student learning by affording direct interaction with text material through multiple-choice questions, completion exercises, true-false questions, and short case exercises. The Study Guide follows the sequence of chapters in the text. Besides the questions and exercises already listed, each chapter of the Study Guide begins with a narrative summary of text material and a listing of key terms and concepts to facilitate vocabulary building.

The complete teaching/learning package accompanying INTRODUCTION TO BUSINESS includes:

- **Instructor's Manual**—provides answers to end-of-chapter questions, suggested solutions to the text cases, and answers to the experimental exercises in the Study Guide.
- **Test Bank**—contains approximately 1,500 multiple-choice and true-false questions. The Test Bank is available in both printed and computerized form.
- **Chapter Outlines/Teaching Notes**—provides overview outlines of each text chapter and a suggested lecture for each chapter including many examples not discussed in the text.
- **Film/Business Organization Guide**—lists current films available for classroom use and business and professional organizations of interest to students of business.
- **Business Forms**—provides examples of documents commonly used in the operation of a business.
- **Transparencies**—includes 100 professionally prepared acetate transparencies.

Acknowledgments

The development of a textbook requires the efforts of many people. We would like to express our deep gratitude and appreciation to several who assisted with INTRODUCTION TO BUSINESS. Without their hard work, good ideas, and insightful comments, this book might not have been possible. In particular we would like to thank Carla Williams, Betty Lane, and Linda Rice, who typed the manuscript and offered invaluable comments and suggestions for improvement. Lane DeCamp, a principal researcher for the text who had a knack for finding lively and appropriate examples to include, also contributed significantly to the preparation of all supplementary materials. Beth Conley and Rick Siegl were also priceless as researchers. Rita Wright of the Bureau of Business Research of the University of Texas at Austin often led us successfully through government data sources in search of a needed document or piece of information.

The following individuals reviewed part or all of the manuscript. We are especially appreciative of their assistance.

W. G. Bacon (North Lake College)
Alec Beaudoin (Triton College)
Leonard S. Bethards (Miami-Dade Community College)
Robert M. Fishco (Middlesex County College)
Norma N. Givens (Fort Valley State College)
David A. Keys (Macon Junior College)

Dedication

For their patience, understanding, forbearance, and constant encouragement, we are truly grateful to the members of our families. We therefore dedicate this text to Isabella, John, Holly, Elizabeth, Lyn, Bill, and Andy.

William H. Cunningham
Ramon J. Aldag
Christopher M. Swift

CONTENTS

Part 1   The American Business Environment

Chapter 1 • Free Enterprise in America   2

What is a Business? • Objectives of a Business • The Private Enterprise System • The U.S. Economy

Cases   WD-40 • Weis Markets

Chapter 2 • Environmental Forces Affecting Business   23

Inflation • Energy • Pollution • Demographic Shifts • The Changing Role of Women • Consumerism

Cases   The Decker Hotel • Global Marine, Inc.

Chapter 3 • Social Responsibility of Business   46

Social Responsibility Defined • Some Views on Social Responsibility • Interested Groups • Benefits and Costs of Social Actions • The Social Audit • Business Ethics

Cases   Ford Foundation • Manville Corporation

Contents ix

Part 2 Business Organization and Government

Chapter 4 • Forms of Ownership 62

An Overview of Business Ownership • Sole Proprietorships • Partnerships • Corporations • Merger and Acquisition

Cases   Softsel Computer Products • The Mississippi Band of Choctaw Indians

Chapter 5 • Small Business and the Franchise System 79

How Small is Small Business? • How Big is Small Business? • Types of Small Businesses • Is Small Business for You? • Buying a Small Business • Starting a Small Business • Franchising

Cases   Jan Stuart Natural Skin Care for Men • Plenum Publishing Company

Chapter 6 • Legal Aspects of Business 99

The Law: What It Is and Where It Comes From • Contracts: More Than Just a Handshake • Regulation of Competition • Regulation of Promotion • Employee Protection • Computer Awareness

Cases   Aluminum Company of America (ALCOA) • Loeb & Company, Inc. v. Schreiner

Part 3 Management of the Enterprise

Chapter 7 • Management and the Organization 120

What is Management? • Organizational Design • Functions of Managers •

Managerial Decision Making • Managing Organizational Change

Cases   Nestlé • Panaeros Airlines

Chapter 8 • Motivating Employees   139

Early Perspective on Job Motivation • Motivation Theory Today • Rewarding Employees • How Can Management Motivate Employees?

Cases   Banquet Foods Corporation • Control Data Corp. (CDC)

Chapter 9 • Human Resources Management   155

Staffing the Firm • Training and Development • Appraising Performance • Compensating Employees

Cases   Smith Pipe and Supply, Inc. • Gala Cosmetics, Inc.

Chapter 10 • Labor-Management Relations   175

Labor Unions • When It's Time to Organize • Collective Bargaining • Settling Disputes • Sources of Negotiating Strength • New Developments in Labor-Management Relations

Cases   General Motors Work Rules • Louisville, Kentucky

Chapter 11 • Production Management   194

The Management Task in Production • Modern Manufacturing • Materials Purchasing and Inventory

Contents   xi

                   Control • Production Planning and Control • Maintenance Policies • Computer Awareness

Cases   Lubella Furniture Company • Williams Greenhouses

Part 4   Marketing Management

Chapter 12 • Marketing: The Strategic Input   216

Macromarketing—The Forest • Micromarketing—The Trees • The Marketing Concept • Market Segmentation • Marketing Research

Cases   Budweiser • Marshall Field & Company

Chapter 13 • Product Management   234

Product Classification • Product Life Cycle • Branding • New Product Development • What Makes a Product Successful?

Cases   Firestone Tires • Atari

Chapter 14 • Channels of Distribution   252

Channels of Distribution • Wholesaling Retailing • Physical Distribution

Cases   John Deere • Revco

Chapter 15 • Pricing   270

The Meaning of Price • Pricing Objectives • Setting Price • Pricing Policies

Cases   Paper Plates • Wham-O

Chapter 16 • Promotion 288

Developing a Communication Strategy • Advertising • Personal Selling • Sales Promotion • Computer Awareness

Cases   Mendel's Book Stores • Prince Tennis Rackets

Part 5   Financial Management

Chapter 17 • Short-Term Financing—The Banking System 312

Why Borrow Short Term? • Sources of Short-Term Funds • Commercial Banking • Federal Reserve System

Cases   Nike, Inc. • Grinberg Telecommunications Systems, Inc.

Chapter 18 • Long-Term Financing—The Capital Markets 335

Uses and Sources of Long-Term Funds • Retained Earnings • Bonds • Common Stock • Preferred Stock • Which Source of Financing Is Best?

Cases   Trammel Crow Co. • Genentech

Chapter 19 • The Securities Markets 357

Perspective of the Firm • Perspective of the Investor • The Stock Exchanges • How Stocks Are Bought and Sold • Speculative Trading Tactics • Mutual Funds: A New Way to Shop Wall Street • Stock Market Indicators

Cases   General Electric • Cessna Aircraft Company

Chapter 20 • Risk Management and Insurance   378

Risk Management • Principles of Insurance • Sources of Insurance • Types of Insurance • Computer Awareness

Cases   Interminco • Safety-Deposit Boxes

Part 6   Management Control and Information Systems

Chapter 21 • Accounting and Financial Statements   402

Role of the Accountant • Two Accounting Concepts • Balance Sheet • Income Statement • Inventory Valuation • Interpreting Financial Statements

Cases   Mississippi Power Company • Texaco

Chapter 22 • Information Management and Computers   428

Information and Management • Computers • Computer Hardware • Computer Software • Business Applications of the Computer • Computer-Assisted Decision Making • Problems with Computers

Cases   Computer Courses • Computers on the New York Stock Exchange

Statistical Appendix   450

Gathering Information • Descriptive Statistics • Displaying Information • Do Statistics Lie? • Computer Awareness

Part 7 The Challenge of the Future

Chapter 23 • International Business—A Growing Sector 464

Why Study International Business? • Barriers to International Trade • Entering Foreign Markets • One International Marketing Strategy? • International Corporations: Saints or Sinners? • International Economic Communities

Cases The Soviet Trade Balance • Thompson International Education, Inc.

Chapter 24 • The Future of American Business 484

Forecasting and Prediction • Into the Next Century • Industrial Outlook • The Future and You

Cases The Genetic Revolution in Agriculture • The Sardine Industry

Chapter 25 • You and Your Career 500

What Is a Career? • Employment Opportunities • How to Obtain a Position in Business • Career Stages • Success Chess

Cases The Recession and Your Career • How Executives See Women in Management

Careers Appendix 517

What Do Bosses Want? • Jobs in Business • Suggestions for Additional Reading • Sources of Additional Career Information • Computer Awareness

Chapter 20 • Risk Management and Insurance 378

Risk Management • Principles of Insurance • Sources of Insurance • Types of Insurance • Computer Awareness

Cases Interminco • Safety-Deposit Boxes

Part 6 Management Control and Information Systems

Chapter 21 • Accounting and Financial Statements 402

Role of the Accountant • Two Accounting Concepts • Balance Sheet • Income Statement • Inventory Valuation • Interpreting Financial Statements

Cases Mississippi Power Company • Texaco

Chapter 22 • Information Management and Computers 428

Information and Management • Computers • Computer Hardware • Computer Software • Business Applications of the Computer • Computer-Assisted Decision Making • Problems with Computers

Cases Computer Courses • Computers on the New York Stock Exchange

Statistical Appendix 450

Gathering Information • Descriptive Statistics • Displaying Information • Do Statistics Lie? • Computer Awareness

Part 7 The Challenge of the Future

Chapter 23 • International Business—A Growing Sector 464

Why Study International Business? • Barriers to International Trade • Entering Foreign Markets • One International Marketing Strategy? • International Corporations: Saints or Sinners? • International Economic Communities

Cases   The Soviet Trade Balance • Thompson International Education, Inc.

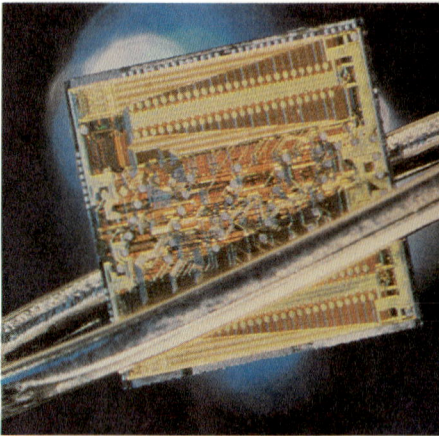

Chapter 24 • The Future of American Business 484

Forecasting and Prediction • Into the Next Century • Industrial Outlook • The Future and You

Cases   The Genetic Revolution in Agriculture • The Sardine Industry

Chapter 25 • You and Your Career 500

What Is a Career? • Employment Opportunities • How to Obtain a Position in Business • Career Stages • Success Chess

Cases   The Recession and Your Career • How Executives See Women in Management

Careers Appendix 517

What Do Bosses Want? • Jobs in Business • Suggestions for Additional Reading • Sources of Additional Career Information • Computer Awareness

1 The American Business Environment

1

Free Enterprise in America

After studying this chapter, you should be able to:

- Describe what a business is and does, as well as how profits provide the incentive for a private enterprise system to work.
- Explain the objectives of a business from the perspective of owners, employees, and society in general.
- Discuss the basic freedoms of a private enterprise system, the operation of supply and demand forces, and four market structures.
- Describe the status of the U.S. economy today in terms of growth, the service sector, international trade, and consumer sovereignty.

The cornerstone of the American economic system is private enterprise. **Private enterprise** means that business is free to organize and operate for a profit, that it is free to function in a competitive system, and that government intervention will be limited to a regulatory role. The production of goods and services in this country—the clothes we wear, the cars we

drive, the food we eat—is the responsibility of private enterprise, not the government. All of the nation's 14 million businesses are privately owned. The economy of a private enterprise system is driven by the decisions of individuals and private organizations acting on behalf of themselves. Fair competition within the system is the best guarantee of economic efficiency.

In the first chapter, we will take a broad look at business today. We will view the business world as if from atop New York's World Trade Towers. On the crowded streets below, we see the private enterprise system at work, with all its achievements and all its flaws. We see how the desire to make money makes the system more efficient. We see many people with ideas about what the objectives of business should be. We see the laws of supply and demand operating under many different market conditions. And we see an economy that is changing rapidly in a changing world. We'll go down for a closer look in later chapters.

WHAT IS A BUSINESS?

A **business** is an individual or a group of people whose goal is to make a profit by selling products or services. A business can be as small as the local radiator repair shop or as large as the Exxon Corporation.

The Role of Profit in a Competitive Economy

Profit is the money left over after all costs have been paid. The **profit motive** (the desire to make money) is what makes a private enterprise economy work. A business, whether a gift shop or a worldwide conglomerate, can't survive unless it makes money—or takes in more money than it spends.

What happens when a firm cannot turn a profit? The answer may be seen in the failure of the W.T. Grant Corporation. In the early 1970s, Grant operated 1,200 discount department stores around the country. When Grant ceased to make a profit, the company went out of business. Its owners lost their entire investment; its bankers lost $234 million in unpaid loans; its suppliers lost $100 million in unpaid bills; and more than 80,000 people lost their jobs.

Not all business failures are as dramatic as Grant's or the more recent bankruptcy of Braniff Airlines, but all of them are the result of inadequate profit. Without a steady stream of profit, a business won't be able to pay for needed expansion of its plant capacity or additions to its fleet of cars or trucks. Nor will there be much incentive for its managers and workers to give their best.

The Scoop on Profits

Many people think that most companies, especially the large ones, make huge profits. The truth is that they do not. Figure 1-1 shows profits as a percentage of sales, as a percentage of **gross national product** (GNP is the value of all goods produced in the United States in a year), and as a percentage return on their stockholders' investment. The percentage return on sales averages only 4.9 percent. At 6.1 percent, corporate profits as a percentage share of GNP aren't much better. Finally, total profits turn out to be only 13.9 percent of the total amount of money invested in U.S. corporations. The profit percentages are about equal to the yield on some savings accounts.

Key Activities of a Business

A profitable business is efficient in performing at least eight separate activities. Figure 1-2 lists these activities. Each is discussed briefly here, and in more detail in later chapters.

Hire and Train Employees. Many businesses employ only a few people, but others, as Figure 1-3 (page 5) shows, employ thousands. All companies need a good system for finding talented people and persuading them to work for the company.

Figure 1-1

The Scoop on Profits

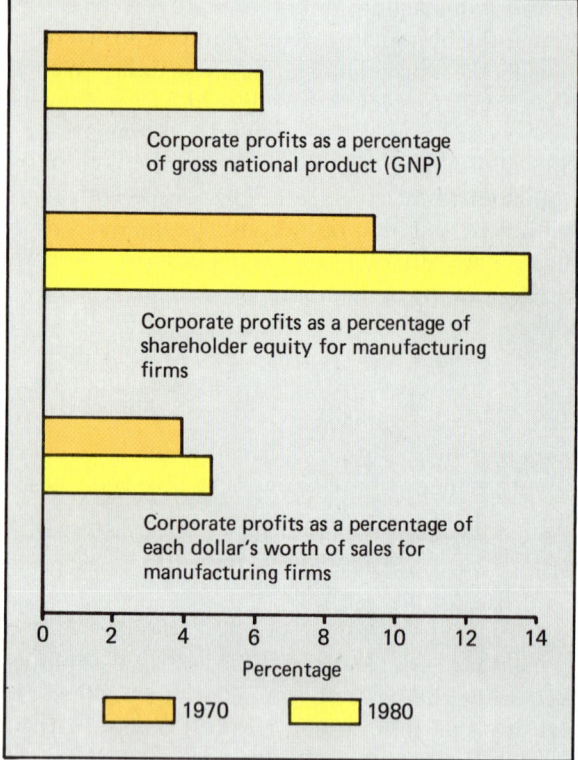

Source: U.S. Department of Commerce, Bureau of Economic Analysis, *The National Income and Product Accounts of the United States*; U.S. Federal Trade Commission, *Quarterly Financial Report for Manufacturing, Mining and Trade Corporations*.

Effective training programs develop employee confidence and prepare employees for higher paying positions. This helps keep valuable people from going to other companies. The personnel department is usually in charge of both hiring and training new employees.

Buy Goods and Services. Businesses buy goods and services for their own use and for resale. Whirlpool Corporation makes refrigerators: It buys steel, rubber, and other materials for use as inputs in its production process. It also buys services, such as advertising time on television, in order to promote its refrigerators to the public. Obtaining the right goods and services at the right prices is essential for effective cost control. By keeping costs down, Whirlpool is able to keep the selling price of its refrigerators down. In so doing, it is able to stay competitive in the marketplace. Buying the best goods and services at the lowest prices is so important that most larger firms employ a staff of professionally trained purchasing agents to do this job.

Raise Money. Businesses borrow money so that they can make money. They borrow from local banks for short-term cash needs. Before the start of the Christmas selling season, for example, merchants usually take out a bank loan to pay for their large Christmas merchandise inventories. They repay the loan with the profits from the Christmas sales.

When a business needs money for a longer period of time, such as a loan to finance an expansion program involving several manufacturing plants around the country, it may borrow from a bank, issue bonds, or sell stock. It is the job of the company's finance department to find the best way to raise the needed money.

Maintain Accounting Records. Firms must also maintain accounting records. The single most important number in these records is the one at the bottom—the "bottom-line" net profit or loss. To compute this number, it is necessary for the firm to keep track of the number of products sold and the amount of money spent on production, salaries, rent, insurance, interest on loans, building repairs, and other items.

Figure 1-2

Key Business Activities

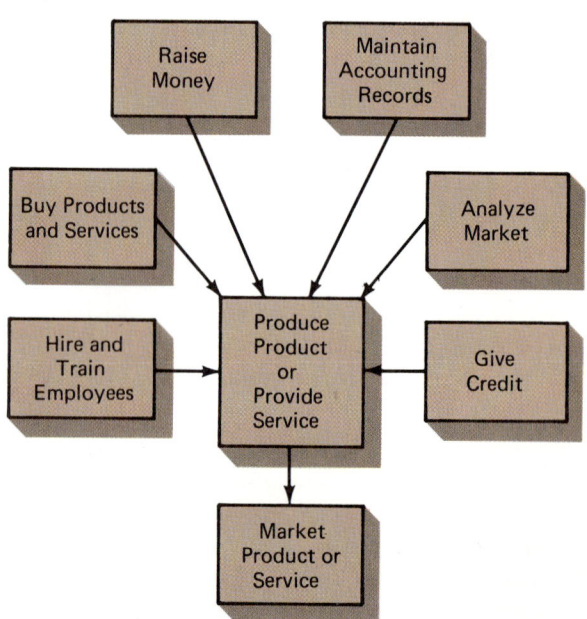

Figure 1-3

Ten Largest U.S. Industrial Corporations Ranked in Terms of Number of Employees, 1981

Source: *Fortune* (May 3, 1982), p. 261.

Rank	Company	Number of Employees
1	General Motors	741,000
2	Ford Motor	408,000
3	General Electric	404,000
4	International Business Machines	355,000
5	International Telephone & Telegraph	324,000
6	Mobil	206,000
7	United Technologies	190,000
8	Exxon	180,000
9	E.I. Du Pont de Nemours	177,000
10	Western Electric	168,000

Study Markets. All businesses need to know about their market(s) and the products currently in demand. One source of this information is the company's sales force, which is in daily contact with the marketplace. Test markets, discussed in Part 4, are also useful to see how customers respond to a new product or to a new way of selling an old product.

Give Credit. Businesses lend money as well as borrow it. When, as customers, we buy a set of tires at Sears with credit, we are borrowing money from the store to pay for the purchase. We probably will not have to pay interest if we pay off the loan in 30 days, but we will pay a finance charge if we make payments over several months.

Similarly, when one company sells something to another company, the seller usually gives the buying company 30 days to pay for its purchase. Like bankers, business people are careful in this regard; they don't want to offer credit if there is a good chance they won't be repaid. Credit decisions are usually the responsibility of the accounting department.

Produce a Product or Provide a Service. The real business of a business is to produce some sort of good or to provide some sort of service. The business does this by manufacturing products, buying them for resale, or providing services to other firms or to the public. The manufacturer has all the problems of doing business—raising money, finding good people, keeping track of sales and costs—plus the special problems involved in manufacturing a product. The reseller, such as a department store, drugstore, or appliance mart, must offer the right selection of goods at prices customers can afford. The service firm, such as an advertising agency or neighborhood dry cleaner, must rely primarily on a reputation for quality or competence.

Market the Product or Service. The final activity is marketing the product or service. Many businesses spend as much as 30 to 40 percent of their budgets on selling and marketing. Industrial firms spend most of their marketing money on first-rate salespeople. Makers of consumer goods spend heavily on advertising. In 1981, for example, Procter and Gamble, the maker of such well-known products as Tide detergent, Crest toothpaste, Ivory soap, and Sure deodorant, spent $521 million on television advertising. Why? To encourage people to buy its products.

OBJECTIVES OF BUSINESS

A business represents different things to different people. Each individual or group associated with the business expects certain things from it; that is to say, each has certain objectives in relation to the business. The owners have their objectives; the employees have their objectives; and members of society have still other objectives.

Owners' Objectives

The owners of a business must make a profit on their investment. As we said earlier, the survival of a firm depends upon its profitability. One kind of owner is someone who owns all of a business. Another is a person who simply buys stock in a business. The objectives of these two types of owners differ.

The Private Owner. The basic objective of the private owner is to produce a reliable stream of cash income. The owner of a local paint supply store cannot pay the mortgage on a home or buy new clothes for the family unless enough paint is sold. Besides the need for income, the owner of a small business has several other objectives.

Independence. Many owners of small businesses do not make as much money as they would if they worked for someone else. Being their own boss, however, is more important to them than making more money.

Family Jobs. A small business often serves as a place where the owner's children can work while growing up. The children earn extra money and the owner has a dependable source of employees. One or more of the children may even take over the business when their parents retire.

Retirement Security. Many people sell their businesses when they are ready to retire. The cash from the sale will offer some amount of security in their later years.

The Stockholder. Owning stock means owning a part of a business and its profits. It does not mean that an individual stockholder has the right to tell management how to run the company. Nor does it mean that an individual stockholder can claim ownership of any specific part of a company, such as an assembly machine or a wall of an office building. Rather, stock ownership is the ownership of an undivided interest in the company. Stockholders are concerned with cash dividends and the value of their investments. Table 1-1 suggests the importance of these objectives to stockholders. Stocks and stockholders will be discussed further in Chapter 18.

Employees' Objectives

Ideally, employees should have the same objectives as the firm for which they work. Sometimes the longer people work for a company, the more their objectives tend to resemble those of the owners. These objectives may be to make a

How is American business represented in the photographs below?

Table 1-1

Returns on Investments for Ten Large Companies in the United States in 1980 and 1981*

	1980			1981		
	Dividend as a Percentage of January 1, 1980, Stock Selling Price	Percent Change in the Price of Stock for 1980	Total Return for 1980	Dividend as a Percentage of January 1, 1981, Stock Selling Price	Percent Change in the Price of Stock for 1981	Total Return for 1981
Exxon	5.0	49.9	54.9	7.4	−23.0	−15.6
Mobil	3.4	57.1	60.5	4.9	−40.9	−36.0
General Motors	6.0	−8.7	−2.7	5.3	−15.6	−10.3
American Telephone and Telegraph	9.6	−8.3	1.3	11.1	20.3	31.4
Texaco	8.8	71.4	80.2	5.7	−32.8	−27.1
Standard Oil of California	3.3	83.4	86.7	4.4	−13.9	−9.5
Ford	8.2	−36.7	−28.5	5.9	−19.0	−13.1
Standard Oil of Indiana	5.2	105.9	111.1	3.4	−34.6	−31.2
IBM	5.5	8.5	14.0	5.0	−17.9	−12.9
Gulf	7.2	32.7	39.9	5.9	−21.7	−15.8
Averages	6.2	35.5	41.7	5.9	−19.9	−14.0

*Ten largest companies were selected based on 1981 sales.

profit, to produce a high-quality product which is sold at a reasonable price, to contribute to society by developing new technology, and to avoid abusing the environment. Employees may also have their own personal objectives.

Income. The employees' basic objective is to make enough money to support themselves and their families. They expect the company to provide them with employment and income. Without the steady flow of income, why work for the company?

Security. Another objective of employees is to feel secure—to believe that they will have a job in the future. They expect the company to offer this security. When a company closes down permanently, it can be a terrible shock to employees, especially to those who have worked there most of their lives.

Personal Growth. A third employee objective is personal growth as the employee continues with the company. Most people want to be promoted, to take on more responsibility, and to grow in self-esteem. Without these opportunities, many of a company's employees would prefer to work somewhere else.

Society's Objectives

A few years ago, society did not pay much attention to how businesses operated. Businesses were considered only to be sources of employment and prosperity; they brought jobs to the community and channeled money into the local economy. While this is still true, society now expects more. Society is concerned about how businesses operate—about whether they act fairly and responsibly.

Profile—
Fred Smith

His professors must be proud of him. Fred Smith's company earned about $79 million in its fiscal year 1982. His own personal stake in the company is estimated to be $115 million.

Fred Smith was a business student. He wrote a paper for a business class, describing a novel overnight package delivery service. His professor didn't think much of the idea, but Fred did, and he later created Federal Express. From every business class, he drew innovative approaches for developing a successful and lucrative corporate style.

Smith realized that *reliable* overnight delivery was crucial to his company, and that it was dependent on his transport system and on his labor. To solve transportation problems, Smith centralized his operations in Memphis, where the airport was closed for weather only ten hours a year; remained open all night; and had modern radar, plenty of hangar space, and available runway access. Then he bought a fleet of planes so he wouldn't have to rely on scheduled airlines, as Emery and Airborne Freight had chosen to do.

Smith decided to staff the company's sorting facility in Memphis by hiring local college students. Federal Express hires college students to sort packages and documents at rates that are (for students) quite lucrative. Students work at night so they can take classes during the day, and Federal Express pays most of their tuition bills. Consequently, Federal Express employees value their jobs and, since they know they will move on when they graduate, they find no appeal in unionization.

Federal Express, founded in 1973, was breaking even by 1976. This was because Smith made sure that Federal Express had paid for its major capital investments early on, at a time when no one took Federal too seriously or tried to edge it out of the market. Since 1976, Federal's earnings have increased annually, while its competitors have been heavily burdened with startup costs.

As its delivery network has broadened, Federal Express has consistently sought new and more profitable business techniques and markets. Federal now delivers overnight letters, competing with the U.S. Postal Service and surpassing the capabilities of its competitors. Federal has even leased a transponder—an electronic relay system in a communications satellite—and applied for operation permits for low-powered television transmitters that will send mail by television.

Company couriers soon will have computers installed in their pick-up and delivery vans. These computers will be linked to company offices by radios, which will continually update the drivers on pickups and deliveries and direct them in the most economical manner.

Competitors? Federal Express has left them by the side of the road. The United States Postal Service even considered hiring Federal to make its overnight deliveries. Only United Parcel Service has the potential to challenge Federal successfully, but Fred Smith has remembered his professors' advice and has created an operation with sufficient flexibility, financial strength, and innovation to handle any newcomers. UPS is getting into the market against Federal, but Fred Smith has dealt the cards so that a win for UPS would be very, very costly.

A Good Corporate Citizen. Businesses should be good citizens. They are expected to pay their fair share of local taxes and to support important local causes. Today businesses not only contribute to charities such as the United Fund, but also collect money for these charities from their employees who wish to donate. In addition, local businesses are expected to show some concern for the environment.

A Conscientious Seller. The quality of a product should reflect the dollar spent. Not all products must be of high quality, but low-quality products should sell for less than higher quality products. If there are any hazards or dangers associated with the use of a product, people expect the manufacturer to so inform them. Too, a company should stand behind its products. If a product is defective, the company should repair or replace it.

THE PRIVATE ENTERPRISE SYSTEM

Although the United States operates under a private enterprise or free market system, the country's businesses are not totally free to do whatever they choose. Businesses are not free to fire employees because of the employees' religious beliefs. We'll learn in Chapter 6 that firms cannot discriminate in hiring or promoting because of race, sex, national origin, or age. Firms are not free to market their products regardless of safety considerations or the truthfulness of advertising.

So just how free are businesses in the United States? We will answer this question by looking at businesses' "basic freedoms." We will then examine the law of supply and demand and discuss four different market structures.

Basic Freedoms

There are three basic business freedoms in this country. They are the freedom to own property, the freedom to make a profit, and the freedom to go out of business.

Private Property. Businesses are generally free to buy and sell land and buildings and to use such property holdings to generate income. For instance, a real estate development firm may own an apartment building which generates income in the form of tenant rental payments. Businesses may own the factories in which they manufacture their products. This also applies to other physical assets, such as office machines and delivery trucks, used in the production of goods and services. Businesses may even buy and sell the "right" to take certain actions. Examples include oil-drilling rights on a given parcel of land, motion picture rights to a best-selling novel, or the team owner's rights to the services of a baseball player.

There are a great number of governmental limitations on the ownership of private commercial property. Cities often have zoning laws that prohibit some types of buildings and businesses in certain areas of town. The aim of most zoning laws is to protect residential areas. Many federal environmental laws place restrictions on the use of private property. A business may own a factory with a smokestack so long as the smokestack does not emit pollutants exceeding a level set by law.

Profit. The second basic freedom is the freedom to make a profit. As important as this freedom is, it is governed and restricted by many rules. The

An athlete's contract is a business asset that can be bought or sold.

government may require firms to install modern pollution-control equipment. Such equipment is expensive and buying it reduces the firm's profits—at least in the short run.

Government also controls profits through corporate tax laws; usually, the more money a company makes, the more taxes it should pay. Table 1-2 lists the ten most profitable companies in the United States for 1981 and the federal income tax each paid in that year. These companies together were responsible for more than $22 billion in federal income tax. They also paid social security taxes and state and local taxes. To illustrate, besides the $3.7 billion that American Telephone & Telegraph (AT&T) paid in federal income tax in 1981, it paid $460 million in state and local income taxes. These taxes reduce corporate profits.

Bankruptcy. Companies are free to go out of business. The government does not force people to stay in business if they can't make money.

If a firm is forced into **bankruptcy**, it will often sell its remaining assets (liquidate) to pay off its creditors. But what happens if, after liquidation, a business is still not able to pay all of its lenders and suppliers? Are the shareholders in the failed firm required to meet the firm's unsatisfied debts? The answer is no. The liability of the owners of a corporation is limited by law: The most shareholders can lose when a firm closes is the amount of their stock investment. The unpaid creditors in this situation remain unpaid.

Sometimes the government steps in to prevent a company from going out of business, especially when the company employs a great many people. A recent beneficiary of such intervention was the Chrysler Corporation. To most auto industry observers, it was apparent in 1979 that Chrysler would fail without massive government assistance. The U.S. Department of Transportation estimated that a Chrysler failure would cost 430,000 people their jobs—150,000 Chrysler employees, 180,000 supplier employees, and 100,000 dealer employees. The price in lost jobs was too high. As a result, Congress guaranteed $1.5 billion in new loans to the company. Chrysler did not lose its "right" to go bankrupt; Congress just decided it would have been against the national interest for it to do so.

Table 1-2

Profits and Federal Income Taxes for the Ten Most Profitable United States Businesses in 1981

	1981 Profits Before Subtracting Federal Income Taxes	**Federal Income Taxes**
1. American Telephone and Telegraph (AT&T)	$10,629,700,000	$3,741,600,000
2. Exxon	8,301,243,000	4,006,000,000
3. International Business Machines (IBM)	5,988,000,000	2,680,000,000
4. Mobil Oil	5,399,000,000	2,966,000,000
5. Standard Oil of Ohio	4,022,298,000	2,075,400,000
6. Standard Oil of California	3,996,000,000	1,616,000,000
7. Texaco	3,912,000,000	1,602,000,000
8. Standard Oil of Indiana	3,459,000,000	1,537,000,000
9. Shell	3,018,000,000	1,317,000,000
10. Atlantic Richfield	2,940,866,000	1,269,576,000

Source: 1981 Annual Reports

Supply and Demand

The prices of products are affected by many factors which may be grouped under two headings: supply factors and demand factors. **Supply** refers to the quantity of a product that a firm or industry is willing to produce at a specified price. As the selling price increases, firms will produce more of the product because higher prices mean greater profits. **Demand** refers to the quantity of a product that buyers are willing to buy at a specified price. As the selling price increases, people will buy less of the product because higher prices take more of their income.

The market for sugar provides an excellent example of how supply and demand jointly determine the price of a good. A few years ago, bad weather reduced the size of the spring sugar crop. The price of sugar rose from 10.75¢ per pound in January to 54.5¢ per pound in November. This increase occurred because consumers and industrial buyers still wanted sugar even though the supply was down. Whenever a product is in scarce supply, its price increases. However, the record-high price of sugar had two effects. First, it encouraged many farmers who had never before planted sugar to do so. Second, people cut back on sugar consumption by 8 percent. This new combination of high sugar output and reduced demand forced the price of sugar down to 11.5¢ per pound by the following May.

It is important to realize that supply and demand work simultaneously. As the price of a product goes up, suppliers produce more of it *and* consumers buy less of it. As the price of a product goes down, firms supply less of it and consumers demand more of it.

Market Structure

A private enterprise, or free market, economy consists of four basic types of competitive market structures. A **market**, in the sense considered here, is the sum total of all sales for a given kind of good among all buyers and sellers. The market for toothpaste, for example, consists of all makers of toothpaste and all buyers of it. The four market structures differ in the ways buyers and sellers interact and in the degrees of competition involved. Imagine a scale on which perfect competition is at one end and monopoly is

In some markets the consumer is not the buyer.

at the other. Figure 1-4 summarizes the differences among the four market structures.

Perfect Competition. **Perfect competition** requires a market of many small buyers and sellers. None of them is big enough to have any effect at all on the price of the product traded in the market. The product of one seller is identical to the products of all other sellers. In this structure, there is a lack of government regulation and complete freedom of movement of buyers and sellers in and out of the market. There is perfect information. This means that price changes are communicated instantaneously to all buyers and sellers. There are a few markets in this country which are quite close to perfect competition, but most economists would say that perfect competition is more of an ideal than a reality.

The markets for many agricultural commodities come close to meeting the assumptions of perfect competition. In the case of corn, one farmer's produce is essentially like any other farmer's produce. Most farm operations are small enough that if one were to withhold its harvest from the market, the price of the crop would not change at all.

Monopolistic Competition. A second type of market structure is **monopolistic competition**. We reserve this name for markets in which sellers are able to achieve some measure of product differentiation through branding, advertising, or quality improvements. Monopolistic competition

Figure 1-4

Differences Among the Four Market Structures

	Perfect Competition	Monopolistic Competition	Oligopoly	Monopoly
Existence	Does Not Exist in a Pure Form	Exists in Many Markets	Exists in Some Markets	Exists in a Few Markets
Number of Buyers and Sellers	Many Small Buyers and Sellers	Many Buyers and Sellers	Many Buyers and Few Sellers	Many Buyers and One Seller
Products	Identical Products	Similar But Not Identical Products	Similar But Not Identical Products	Only One Product is Available.
Government Regulation	No Government Regulation	Some Government Regulation	Government Closely Watches	Highly Regulated
Market Entry	Complete Freedom for Buyers and Sellers	Some Barriers to Entry for Sellers	Difficult for New Competitors to Enter Markets	Nearly Impossible for New Firms to Enter Market
Information	Perfect Information	Imperfect Information	Competitors Know What The Others are Doing	Government Requires Some Information From the Monopolists
Examples	Agricultural Products	Soft Drinks, Toothpaste, and Appliances	Automobiles and Steel	Telephone, Local Utility Companies

is like perfect competition in that it is characterized by many buyers and sellers. Under monopolistic competition, however, firms sell similar but not identical products. This means that firms, through their marketing strategies, are able to carve out market niches for themselves with selected customer groups. For example, if a firm offers a better product than its competitors, or if it advertises to a certain group of buyers, or even if it just provides faster delivery, then it has established a niche for itself. The firm has developed a "little monopoly" position in the market.

Another feature of monopolistic competition is imperfect information. Buyers do not know the prices and features of all competing products. And even when buyers are aware of price differences, they may remain loyal to a preferred brand. Finally, unlike perfect competition, monopolistic competition is controlled to a degree by government regulation.

The majority of products today, especially branded consumer products, are of this type. Cameras, household detergents, soft drinks, appliances, and stereos are all sold in markets in the monopolistic competition structure.

Oligopoly. An **oligopoly** is characterized by a few large firms selling similar products to many small buyers. When one firm in an oligopolistic industry lowers its prices or introduces a new product, other firms in the industry usually do the same. The problem with oligopolies is that they tend to limit competitive freedom and efficiency. Specifically, the high cost of building manufacturing plants and obtaining other productive assets

CONTROVERSIAL ISSUES

Can the Soviet Union and other communist countries manage their economies more efficiently than the United States? Can an economy run more efficiently when guided by government than when guided by free enterprise?

Communist Economy More Efficient than Free Enterprise Economy.

Pro

The Soviet Union points with pride to its increase in industrialization over the past few years. In addition, it boasts an impressive rate of economic growth and efficiency. From 1945 to the late 1960s, the Soviet Union's total production (known as its Gross National Product, or GNP) has increased at an annual average of 5.7 percent compared to only 3.3 percent for the United States over the same period. In just 20 years, the Soviet Union has become one of the great industrial powers of the modern world.

A socialist economy increases its efficiency by eliminating the "frills" that consume valuable portions of a country's total production without giving anything in return. In America, luxury goods contribute to our GNP (Gross National Product) without making any contribution to further development of the country. In the Soviet Union, programs monitor what is produced to be sure that correct amounts of each needed item are made and that all production serves a useful purpose in the Soviet economy. Since 1945, the Soviet Union has built its military into one of the most powerful in the world, while America, coming out of World War II with a huge military and industrial complex nearly intact, has allowed its military to deteriorate. In the process, America has encountered massive inflation and economic instability.

If the American economy were run as efficiently as the Soviet's communist economy is run, it would be more stable and far more productive.

Con

The Soviet Union had highly efficient production schedules as long as it had Joseph Stalin to send those who failed to meet schedules to Siberian camps. Says Zbigniew Brzezinski, foreign policy adviser in the Carter administration, "Today in the Soviet Union no one is working hard because they are neither ideologically motivated as they were at times, certainly during the early industrial era, nor are they terrorized into working hard as they were under Stalin." Today, a sense of alienation is widespread in the Soviet Union. Corruption and malingering by farm and factory workers have crippled output. Many workers are rewarded by moonlighting on high-priority (and therefore high-paying) construction projects that are behind schedule. Incentives to work no longer exist. Alcoholism is such a problem that the Soviet citizen's average life span is decreasing.

When Soviet planners try to organize their production schemes, they find a peculiar paradox. In America, the free enterprise market identifies a demand for a product, and the manufacturer simply has to meet that demand and price its product so it will sell for a reasonable profit. In the Soviet Union, planners not only have to set production schedules, but also they must generate the appropriate demand so that what they make is bought. This two-sided planning breaks down, however. Soviet consumers don't buy many Soviet-made products, but instead spend the money on alcohol, food, and limited quantities of more highly desired Western imports. Soviet inability to match demand with supply means that goods are not manufactured efficiently enough to meet needs in the country.

Furthermore, the Soviet Union and China both have wide ranges of ethnic groups (just as America does). Byelorussians and Ukranians hold most of the power in the Soviet Union. Islamic, Buddhist, Mongolian, and other segments of the population are frustrated by lack of participation in the economy and fail to work at all for the government. As this trend spreads, fewer people will be contributing to production goals, and efficiency will continue to decrease. Already the Soviet Union has dropped to barely half the annual GNP growth rate the United States currently shows, even though the United States is in the throes of some of the worst economic instability in its history. If the United States can still outperform the Soviet Union in these times, a strong blow is struck for the superiority of free enterprise economies.

FROM THE FILE

Clifford is a pricing executive for the fifth largest steel company in the country. At the current low market price for sheet steel, his company is not able to cover its costs. Clifford knows that the steel industry is oligopolistic.

Should Clifford recommend a price increase or a price decrease to top management? A higher price for steel would enable the company to cover production costs and thus to start making a profit again. But how would other steel producers respond to a price increase? Would they raise prices too, or would they hold the line? And what effect would either move have on the sales of steel for Clifford's company? A price decrease, Clifford reasoned, might attract many new customers, resulting in greater total sales. But how would competitors respond to a price cut? Clifford wondered what to do.

---

makes it very difficult for new firms to enter the industry. The federal government watches oligopolies to guard against illegal price fixing and to prevent one firm from becoming too powerful.

The automobile industry is a good example of an oligopoly. The U.S. automobile market has historically been dominated by three firms—General Motors, Ford, and Chrysler. From 1950 to 1970 these firms made 95 percent of all new cars sold in the United States; General Motors alone averaged 52 percent of the new car market. The Justice Department watched GM during this period to see whether it was taking over the industry.

Today, the government is no longer so worried about the market strength of General Motors. Foreign car makers have made strong gains in the U.S. market. Table 1-3 shows that because of the increased popularity of imports, GM's market share fell from 45.2 percent in 1971 to 44.5 percent in 1981; the market share declines for Ford and Chrysler were much greater. Altogether, imports now account for nearly 29 percent of the U.S. new car market.

Monopoly. The last form of market structure involves little or no competition. The market is made up of only one selling firm, called a **monopoly**, and many smaller buyers. Monopolies are illegal in the United States except in special circumstances. For example, the market for local telephone service is organized as a monopoly but is strictly regulated by the government. An unregulated monopoly is considered undesirable because of its overwhelming market power. Operating without effective restraint from competitive forces or governmental control, it can charge almost any price it wants for its products.

THE U.S. ECONOMY TODAY

More complaints are uttered about the economy than about any other subject, except perhaps the weather. Inflation is too high. Unemployment is too high. Interest rates and government spending are too high. Productivity and investment are too low. Many of the complaints are justified. But before we pronounce the economy a hopeless case, let's take another look at its operation. We'll see that in many ways it has performed quite well, indeed.

Table 1-3

Market Share of U.S. Auto Makers and All Imports, 1971 and 1981*

Auto Maker	1971	1981
General Motors	45.2%	44.5%
Ford	23.5	16.3
Chrysler	13.7	8.8
American Motors	2.5	1.6
Total for U.S. Car Makers	84.9	71.2
Total for Imports	15.1	28.8
Total for All Cars	100.0	100.0

*Percentage of new car registrations

Source: Reprinted by permission from Automotive News. Copyright, 1982.

The Economy Still Delivers the Goods . . .

The best single measure of the size and growth of the U.S. economy is gross national product. Earlier in the chapter, we defined GNP as the total value of all goods and services produced by the economy in a year. It represents the total gross output available for distribution to business users and consumers. When **real GNP** (the gross national product with the effect of price increases removed) increases faster than the rate of population growth, most of us get richer.

Figure 1-5 shows the growth of GNP and real GNP for the period 1950-1981. Notice that both GNP and real GNP increased during this period but that GNP increased much faster. The reason is inflation, which, by itself, pushes up the total dollar value of production.

Rising GNP is associated with rising family income. As shown in Figure 1-6, average family income soared from $3,319 in 1950 to more than $21,000 in 1980. Some of this gain was because of inflation, but much of the increase still represents a gain in real family wealth. In practical terms, this increased wealth means better paying jobs and more real purchasing power for the average American family. Figure 1-7 shows that the economy still "delivers the goods."

. . . and the Services, Too

Industrial activity is typically represented as a huge factory stamping out an endless stream of products and spewing smoke into the atmosphere through tall smokestacks. Is this your image of the U.S. economy?

One of the most remarkable features of the U.S. economy is its gradual transformation from a producer of goods to a producer of services. Many experts now believe that we live in a postindustrial society. This means that the provision of

Figure 1-5

Gross National Product, 1950-1981

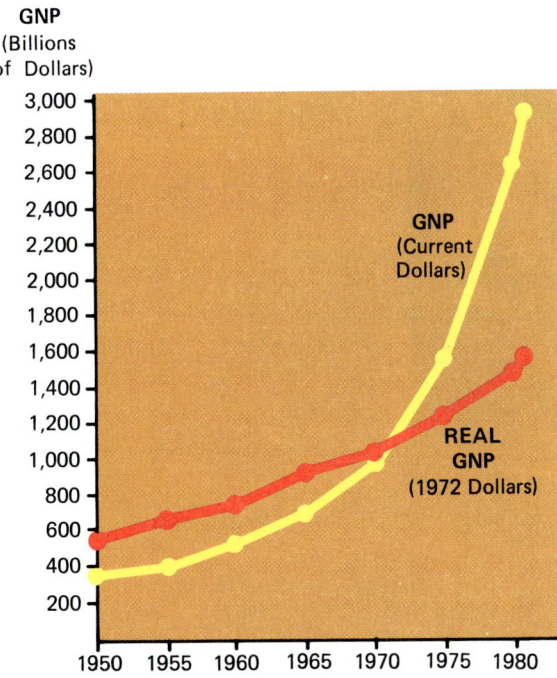

Source: U.S. Department of Commerce, Bureau of Economic Analysis, *The National Income and Product Accounts of the United States, 1929-76;* and *1976-1979;* and *Survey of Current Business* (March, 1982).

Figure 1-6

Median Family Income

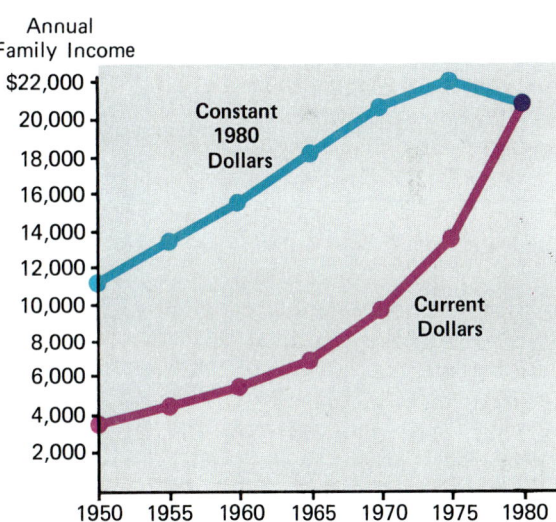

Median is a measure of central tendency; it is an "average" figure. Specifically, for 1980, the number of families earning less than $21,023 a year is equal to the number of families earning more than $21,023 a year. Thus, $21,023 is the middle value in a data series beginning with the value for the poorest family and ending with the value for the wealthiest family.

Source: U.S. Department of Commerce, Bureau of the Census, *Money Income of Households, Families, and Persons in the United States: 1980*, Series P-60, No. 132 (July, 1982).

Figure 1-7

An Economy That Still Delivers the Good Life

For all its problems, this nation's economic system in recent decades has performed well for the vast majority of Americans. For a look at some of the accomplishments that stem at least in part from economic progress since the days of the Korean War—

Buying Power
Income per person after taxes, in 1981 dollars to discount inflation's impact—

| 1951 | $4,682 |
| 1981 | $8,770 |

Up 87%

Automobile Ownership

Proportion of households owning a car—

| 1951 | 60% |
| 1981 | 84% |

Up 40%

Jobs (civilian)
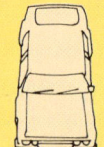

| 1951 | 59,961,000 |
| 1981 | 100,397,000 |

Up 67%

Personal Wealth

Average net worth per person (1981 dollars)—

| 1951 | $21,300 |
| 1981 | $39,600 |

Up 86%

National Output

Gross national product (1981 dollars)—

| 1951 | $1,123 bil. |
| 1981 | $2,926 bil. |

Up 161%

Homeownership
Proportion of housing units occupied by owner—

| 1951 | 55% |
| 1981 | 66% |

Up 20%

Life Expectancy at Birth
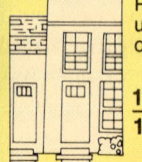

| 1951 | 68.4 years |
| 1981 | 73.6 years |

Up 8%

Average Workweek

| 1951 | 42.2 hours |
| 1981 | 35.2 hours |

Down 17%

Education

Median years of schooling (ages 25 and above)—

| 1951 | 9.3 years |
| 1981 | 12.5 years |

Up 34%

Note: Some figures are for 1950 or 1980 or latest available year.

USN&WR—Basic data: U.S. Depts. of Commerce, Labor, and Health and Human Services; Motor Vehicle Manufacturers Association, Federal Reserve Board

Source: Reprinted from "U.S. News & World Report" (April 26, 1982), p. 38. Copyright 1982, U.S. News & World Report, Inc.

services, rather than the production of goods, is now the country's chief economic activity.[1] Figure 1-8 shows the origin by industry of each dollar of goods and services produced. As of 1980, the service sector of the economy accounted for 66.4¢ of each dollar of U.S. production, up from 55.7¢ in 1950. Manufacturing industries now employ fewer than one worker out of four in the entire American work force. The importance of the service sector is illustrated by the following statistics:

- More than two thirds of all U.S. workers were employed in service-related jobs in 1982.
- More than 70 percent of all college graduates employed by private business work in the service sector.
- In this decade, more than two thirds of all newly created jobs for college students will be in the service sector.

One of the big reasons for this transformation is the creation of a large middle class (based on amount of income). In the past, only a small percentage of society could afford to spend money on services beyond vitally needed medical

[1] Eli Ginzberg and George J. Vojta, "The Service Sector of the U.S. Economy," *Scientific American*, Vol. 244 (March, 1981), pp. 48-55.

The provision of services is now America's primary economic activity.

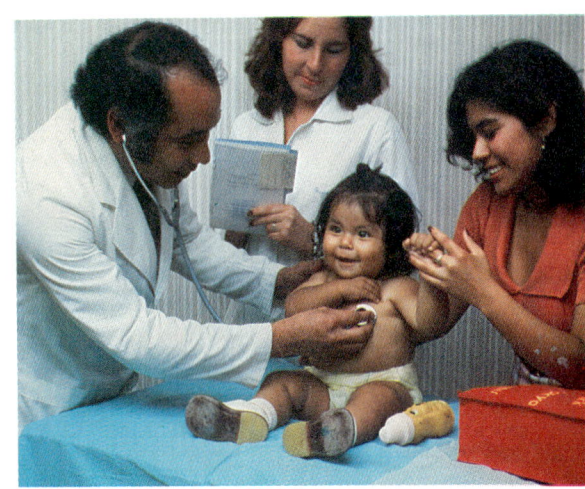

care or legal assistance. Today, middle-class people spend a great deal of money on such services as insurance, hairstylists, travel agencies, and accountants.

A second reason why the service sector has grown so much is the increase in the number of working women. Very often in families today, the

Figure 1-8

Changing Composition of the Nation's Output, 1950-1980
(Percentage of Gross National Product)

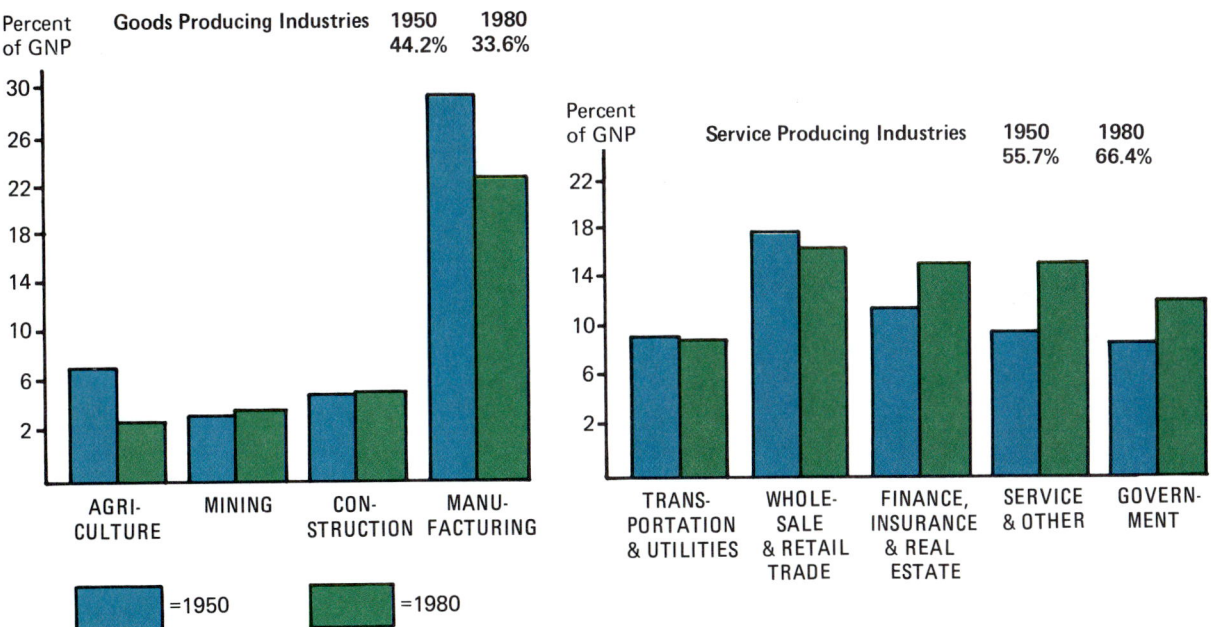

Source: *Economic Report of the President*, transmitted to the Congress, February, 1982, p. 244.

husband and wife both work outside the home. These couples, as well as single women and men, do not have the time, interest, nor willingness to do many everyday chores. People now hire service firms to clean their houses, cater their parties, and take care of their preschool children.

Internationalization of the Economy

Another major development in the U.S. economy is our growing dependence on other countries for many of the goods and services we consume. By the same token, more and more of the goods made by U.S. manufacturers are being shipped abroad. This development is called **internationalization**. The total value of American-made products shipped to foreign countries between 1950 and 1981 increased from $14.4 to $367.3 billion. The value of imported products climbed from $12.2 to $341.3 billion during the same period of time. Table 1-4 shows the ten biggest imports and exports for 1981 by product category.

This trend toward internationalization has at least two implications. First of all, it means that many products found around the home are made outside the country. Shoes, clothing, small kitchen appliances, cutlery, portable typewriters, and stereo receivers are just a few of the products that foreign manufacturers sent to the United States in large quantities. While this is not in itself a cause for alarm, it is certainly a change from just 25 years ago. Second, and perhaps not so obvious, this trend means that many U.S. jobs depend on the skill of our companies in opening new markets in other countries. The greater the demand for U.S. products there, the more jobs in this country.

The Consumer Rules the Roost

No goods or services are produced and sold unless business managers believe that consumers are willing to pay for them. Knowing what consumers want is not always an easy task. Introducing a new product to the market is a gamble in today's economy because consumers are more value conscious than they were a few years ago. Consumers want smaller houses, more fuel-efficient cars, better quality food products, and longer lasting appliances.

Table 1-4

What We Buy and Sell

10 Biggest Imports in 1981 . . .	
Petroleum	$78.5 bil.
Motor vehicles, parts	$27.4 bil.
Iron, steel	$12.1 bil.
Electrical machinery, parts	$ 9.4 bil.
TV, radio, sound products	$ 9.2 bil.
Clothing	$ 8.0 bil.
Nonferrous metals	$ 7.1 bil.
Natural gas	$ 5.8 bil.
Chemicals	$ 5.6 bil.
Special-purpose machinery	$ 5.3 bil.
. . . And 10 Biggest Exports	
Motor vehicles, parts	$16.2 bil.
Aircraft, parts	$14.7 bil.
Industrial machinery	$11.5 bil.
Electrical machinery	$11.5 bil.
Office machinery, computers	$ 9.8 bil.
Power-generating machinery	$ 9.5 bil.
Chemicals	$ 9.2 bil.
Corn	$ 8.0 bil.
Wheat	$ 7.8 bil.
Soybeans	$ 6.2 bil.

Source: Reprinted from "U.S. News & World Report" (April 26, 1982), p. 57. Copyright 1982, U.S. News & World Report, Inc.

In this new market environment, advertising executives have been forced to modify their sales pitches. Many ads now stress product quality more than image. Advertising messages are becoming more informative because the public is more discriminating and better educated. As one advertising executive put it, "there are no more 12-year-old minds, except in 12-year-olds."

When we say that "consumers rule the roost," we mean that it is consumers who decide which goods and services are produced. They do this through the decisions they make in the marketplace, that is, by which goods and services they choose to buy or not to buy. Economists call this **consumer sovereignty**. Profitable businesses closely watch changing consumer tastes. Those businesses which fail are those which cannot meet the challenge of the marketplace. Without the discipline imposed by a competitive market, inefficient and poorly managed firms would survive. But with this discipline, new ideas, new products, and new companies develop to meet the changing tastes of the consumer.

The Great Depression

The U.S. economy collapsed during the Great Depression. The Depression began in 1929, and the nation did not fully recover from it until the start of World War II.

It is hard for us today to realize the magnitude of this collapse and its effect on Americans. The production of durable goods declined 80 percent from 1929 to 1933. Wholesale prices fell by one third and consumer prices by one fourth. At least one quarter of the civilian work force was out of work. Another 25 percent was working only part-time. Tables A and B show the unemployment and inflation rates for 1926 to 1940. Notice how high unemployment was in the early 1930s, the worst of the Depression years. Prices dropped by as much as 10 percent in 1932.

What caused the Depression? Even after 50 years it is difficult to name all the reasons. Two, however, are cited by many economists. The first reason is the stock market crash of 1929, which wiped out many investors. A speculative fever in the late 1920s sent the prices of many stocks soaring. These rapid price increases created the right conditions for a collapse of investor confidence. When investors lost confidence, they sold their stock. With just about everyone selling, the price of stocks fell dramatically.

During September and October of 1929 the average price per share of stock listed on the New York Stock Exchange dropped nearly 40 percent; by 1933, it had dropped 75 percent. This price decline nearly destroyed the capital markets; investors would not buy stock anymore. Thus, there was no money to build factories and to buy manufacturing equipment. Table C shows the stock price declines for several especially hard-hit companies.

A second major cause was bank failure. Before the Depression, bank deposits were not insured as they are today. When a bank went out of business, the bank's depositors lost all their money. The situation was so unstable that even a rumor of bank failure could *cause* a bank to fail. As a rumor of a bank failure started, panic spread, people in town rushed to the bank and demanded their money. But where was the money? It was not in the vault, of course; it was loaned out. The bank quickly ran out of cash for withdrawals, closed its doors, and declared bankruptcy. Depositors not able to withdraw their money in time were out of luck.

The failure of many banks across the country, along with the stock market crash, stopped the economy in its tracks. No one had money to invest. Factory owners had no money for plant expansion nor jobs for workers. People had no money to spend. The economy stood still.

Table A

Unemployment During the Great Depression

Year	Unemployment Rate*
1926	1.8
1927	3.3
1928	4.2
1929	3.2
1930	8.7
1931	15.9
1932	23.6
1933	24.9
1934	21.7
1935	20.1
1936	16.9
1937	14.3
1938	19.0
1939	17.2
1940	14.6

*Percentage of civilian labor force unemployed, annual average

Source: U.S. Department of Commerce, Bureau of the Census.

Table B

Price Changes During the Great Depression

Year	% Change in Consumer Price Index
1926	1.0
1927	−1.9
1928	−1.3
1929	0
1930	−2.5
1931	−8.8
1932	−10.3
1933	−5.1
1934	3.4
1935	2.5
1936	1.0
1937	3.6
1938	−1.9
1939	−1.4
1940	1.0

Source: U.S. Department of Labor, Bureau of Labor Statistics.

Table C

Prices of Selected Common Stocks, 1929 and 1933 (Dollars)

	Stock Prices 1929	Stock Prices 1933
Consolidated Cigar	100	3.5
General Foods	82	20
General Motors	91	8
U.S. Steel	261	21
New York Central Railroad	256	9

Source: Gordon U. Axon, *The Stock Market Crash of 1929* (New York: Mason and Lipscomb, 1974), p. 93.

SUMMARY POINTS

1. A business is an individual or a group of people with a common goal, namely, to make a profit by selling goods or services.
2. Profit is the money left over after all costs have been paid. A firm cannot stay in business unless it earns a profit.
3. Eight key activities of a business are: hire and train employees, buy goods and services, raise money, maintain accounting records, study markets, give credit, produce a product or provide a service, and market the product or service.
4. The main objective of the owners of a business is to make a profit on their invested cash. Private owners look for a reliable income stream, whereas stockholders are concerned with cash dividends and the value of their investments.
5. The objectives of the employees of a company center on income, security, and personal growth.
6. Society's objectives for a business are that the business act responsibly in the community and sell products that are a good value for a dollar.
7. The basic freedoms of a private enterprise system are the freedom to own property, the freedom to make a profit, and the freedom to go out of business.
8. In a market economy the selling price of goods and services is affected by supply and demand.
9. Four types of market structures under a private enterprise economy are perfect competition, monopolistic competition, oligopoly, and monopoly.
10. Three important characteristics of our economy today are growing industrial output, the increasing dominance of the service sector, and expanding international trade.
11. In the U.S. economy it is the consumer who ultimately determines which goods and services are produced.

KEY TERMS AND CONCEPTS

private enterprise
business
profit
profit motive
gross national product
private property
bankruptcy
supply
demand
market structure
market
perfect competition
monopolistic competition
oligopoly
monopoly
real GNP
internationalization
consumer sovereignty

REVIEW QUESTIONS

1. Define the term private enterprise.
2. What are the eight key activities that each business must perform?
3. What are the objectives of most owners of small businesses?
4. Analyze the company's objectives from the perspective of its employees.
5. Describe the three basic freedoms that each business enjoys in our economy.
6. As the price of a product increases, will firms produce more or less of it? Explain.
7. Does perfect competition exist in the real world? If so, give examples.
8. What is meant by "real GNP"? Has the real GNP grown in recent years?
9. What does the trend toward internationalization mean for the average consumer?
10. Why do we say that the consumer "rules the roost"?

DISCUSSION QUESTIONS

1. Explain the role of profit in our economy.
2. Are profits too high in the U.S.?
3. Do you think that people should invest their money in the stock market? Would you be willing to put your money in the stock market?

Chapter 1 • Free Enterprise in America 21

4. Should a company such as Chrysler have the right to go bankrupt? What are the implications for society when a major firm goes bankrupt?
5. Why are some monopolies allowed to exist in the United States?
6. Why has the service sector of our economy grown so rapidly?

CASE 1-1

WD-40

In the 1950s, a chemist at the Rocket Chemical Company discovered "Water Displacement Formula 40," a spray lubricant and water repellent. Rocket quickly realized that the lubricant was a perfect general-purpose chemical that could be used to lubricate, prevent rust, clean metal, and repel water. The company began to market the new chemical in blue and yellow cans under the name "WD-40."

Sales weren't great at first. But when the Vietnam War started, the Rocket Chemical Company (by then renamed the WD-40 Company) supplied thousands of cans of WD-40 to service personnel all over Southeast Asia. Soldiers had found that none of the lubricants offered by the Army kept their guns from rusting in the extreme heat, grime, and humidity of Vietnam. WD-40, however, worked.

The Vietnam veterans continued to buy WD-40 after they returned to the United States. If it lubricated well and stopped rust in the jungle and rain forest, it had to be good. WD-40 sells in incredible volume and its customers remain loyal to it.

The WD-40 Company dropped all its other products in order to make only WD-40. It mixes its secret formula in one large vat, packages it in drums, and then contracts with a distributor to repackage it in the familiar spray cans and market it. The company could conduct all operations itself, and even begin marketing new products, but it has chosen not to do so. The company knows the size it wants to be, and it knows the degree of complexity that best suits its operations. WD-40 makes 17¢ profit on each sales dollar after taxes and shows no sign of peaking out in its climb in sales.

1. Why do you think WD-40 Company chose not to expand its factory? to diversify into other products? to conduct all steps of its production (including packaging and marketing) itself?
2. What advantages did WD-40 Company find for developing its product that are peculiar to a free enterprise economy?
3. Suggest possible futures for WD-40 Company in a free enterprise economy.

CASE 1-2

Weis Markets

Weis Markets is a supermarket chain of 109 stores in Pennsylvania which has been somewhat of a mystery in the grocery industry. It is only one twentieth the size of Safeway (the largest supermarket chain in America), yet its revenues are one third those of Safeway. Furthermore, Weis' profits on sales are more than twice those of Safeway and other major supermarket chains.

Weis points to two key factors, both arising from flexibility present in the free enterprise economy, in explaining its unique profitability. First, Weis Markets is family owned, so command decisions are made quickly and, judging from its success, correctly. Second, all Weis stores maintain very tight controls on product quality and inventory. To avoid errors and fraud, special methods are used for recording and checking incoming shipments.

Although its workers are not unionized, Weis pays wages equal to the wages of unionized workers at other stores. Employees are promoted according to their talents rather than their length of service. Consequently, most workers are productive and happy with their jobs.

Weis Markets is always one of the first supermarket chains to implement new accounting procedures that decrease tax obligations. It manages its finances to take full advantage of both federal and Pennsylvania tax laws. Weis also pays fewer and smaller dividends to its stockholders. This means that more funds are left for reinvestment in new stores and in new technologies such as optical scanners and computer inventory systems.

Weis Markets has profited greatly from its long-standing tradition of buying stores instead of leasing them as most other supermarket chains do. Weis Markets can obtain lower interest rates when loans are necessary because it has such good collateral. Weis is so stable financially, in fact, that it seldom has to borrow money to build new stores.

All in all, Weis Markets is an outstanding example of a company using the free enterprise system to create a business that could not succeed under any other conditions.

1. Could Weis Markets realize such success if it had to buy its labor in a totally unionized labor market? if it had to pay the same dividends that other supermarkets pay?
2. Why do you think it is crucial in a free enterprise economy for companies to have the right to choose how to reinvest profits?
3. Why do you think Safeway doesn't perform as well as Weis Markets? What do they do wrong? Do they fail to take advantage of the free enterprise system?

Environmental Forces Affecting Business

2

After studying this chapter, you should be able to:

- Describe the relationship between uncontrollable variables and business decision making.
- Identify some of the major causes of inflation.
- Discuss the current energy situation from the point of view of demand and supply.
- Identify the major environmental protection laws and some of the economic issues involved in pollution control.
- Describe the population, employment, and age shifts occurring in the United States today.
- Explain the changing role of women in business.
- Discuss the reasons behind the rise of consumerism.

Business managers must make decisions in an ever-changing environment. They are confronted daily with uncertainties from various forces in that business environment. Managers must choose investment programs, set prices for their products, or design advertising programs in spite of these uncertainties. Some of the uncertain forces, or **uncontrollable variables** as they are called, are rising inflation, dwindling energy supplies, new pollution laws, demographic shifts, the changing role of women, and the consumer movement. Business firms have no control over these economic and social forces; all they can do is adjust their business strategies in response to them. In this chapter we will see how they affect business.

INFLATION

For the past 15 years, the United States has experienced a new and highly unsettling problem—runaway inflation. By **inflation** we mean a rise in prices. Inflation itself is not new: The Romans complained about it during the time of Diocletian, as did the Europeans in the 16th Century when gold, arriving from the New World by shipload, sent prices soaring. Historically, prices have increased during times of war or periods of social and economic upheaval and then have leveled off during times of peace. What's new about current inflation is its persistence. Traditionally, an increase in unemployment was seen as the cure for inflation.[1] Today, we have both high rates of inflation and high rates of unemployment.

Inflation in Post-World-War-II America

Inflation is measured by the annual percentage change in the consumer price index. The **consumer price index** (CPI) refers to the average price changes of a group of goods and services that make up the typical consumer's budget. Figure 2-1 charts the course of inflation through the post-World-War-II period. Notice the stability of the consumer price index through the 1950s and early 1960s, except for the Korean War years of 1950 and 1951. The index began to surge upward during the Vietnam War—a time of great military spending—and has not returned to its pre-1960 levels. Peaks of the index in 1974 and 1980 coincided with dramatic increases in the price of imported oil.

Causes of Inflation

It is not difficult to list the reasons why the United States and most other Western nations have experienced so much inflation lately. Let's take a look at a few of the major causes of inflation.

High Wages and Low Productivity. One major cause of inflation is the relationship between wages and productivity. **Productivity** is defined as output per worker-hour. When wages increase faster than productivity, the result is inflation. The amount of any product we can consume depends on the amount we produce. If wages go up but output does not, we have more money income but not more purchasing power. This is because the total supply of goods available for purchase has not changed. The combination of rising wages and constant or sagging output logically exerts an upward push on prices.[2]

Wage Parity. Wage increases in one industry often put pressure on wages in other industries. When auto workers win an 11-percent pay increase, coal miners, high school teachers, and people in other occupations demand similar pay hikes, or parity. A recent example of this was the professional football players' strike. The players' union argued that football players should be paid as much as NBA basketball players and major-league baseball players.

Inflationary Expectations. Another cause of inflation is the expectation that inflation will continue in the future. Labor unions demand wage increases in anticipation of expected cost-of-living

---

[1]Robert Heilbronner and Lester Thurow, *Five Economic Challenges* (Englewood Cliffs, N.J.: Prentice-Hall, Inc., 1981), pp. 3-30.

[2]Lester Thurow, *The Zero-Sum Society* (New York: Basic Books, Inc., 1980), p. 76.

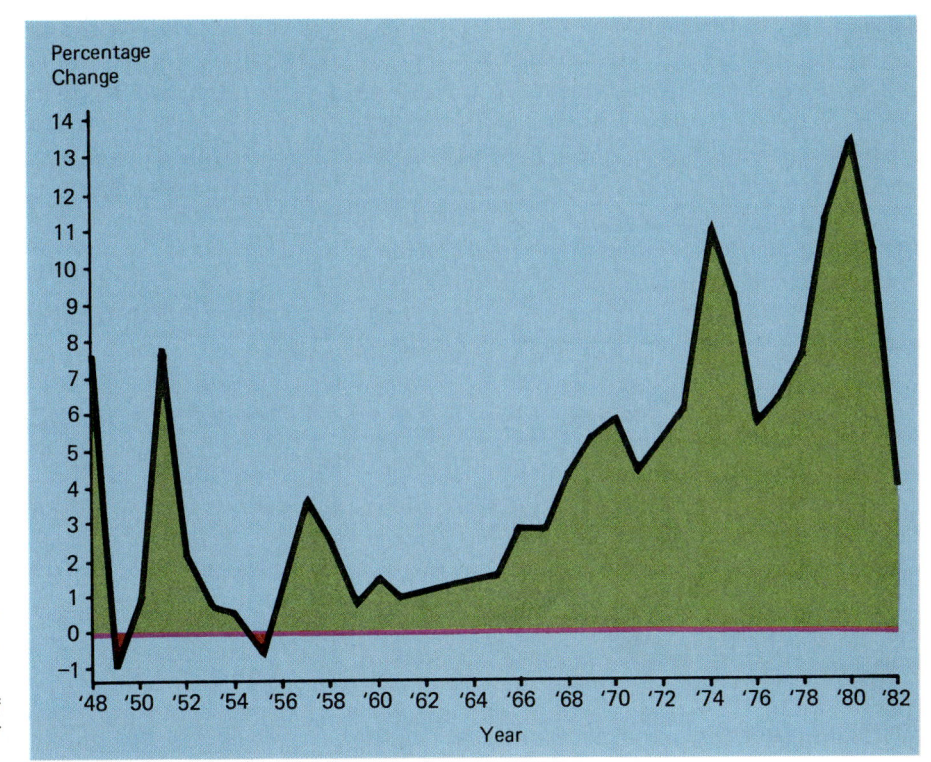

Figure 2-1

Percentage Change in Consumer Price Index, 1948-1981

Source: U.S. Department of Labor, Bureau of Labor Statistics.

increases. Manufacturers raise the prices of their products in anticipation of future labor and raw materials cost increases. And consumers borrow money to finance today's purchases in the belief that prices will be higher tomorrow. Some economists argue that inflation will subside only when people believe that it will subside.

External Shocks. What about external shocks to the economy, such as the oil price increases brought about by the Organization of Petroleum Exporting Countries (OPEC)? How much of an influence do these shocks have on inflation? Between 1973 and 1981, the price of a barrel of crude petroleum increased tenfold. These sudden price shocks work their way through the economy, and eventually the prices of new autos, tires, plastic products, textiles, and food items all begin to rise. This is because oil is an energy input in the production of nearly all products and a direct raw materials input in many others. We have already seen that the two biggest inflationary surges in recent years coincided with OPEC price squeezes.

Source: Copyright, 1983, Universal Press Syndicate. Reprinted with permission. All rights reserved.

Responses to Inflation

Both consumers and business purchasing agents have modified their buying behavior in response to high rates of inflation. Let's look at each sector separately.

Consumer Sector. Are you concerned about inflation? If you are, then you're not alone. One recent study found that 72 percent of the American people view inflation as a more serious problem than unemployment. Everyone feels the effects of inflation, but not everyone feels the effects of unemployment.

An example of an industry especially hard-hit by inflation is housing. High rates of inflation have recently been accompanied by high rates of interest. These high interest rates greatly increase the price of new housing. According to Figure 2-2, monthly average house payments of $700 now account for 36 percent of the family budget, up from 22 percent in 1970.

Consumers cope with inflation by cutting back their purchases, buying lower quality goods, and drawing upon their savings to maintain their standard of living. In many families, both husband and wife now work outside the home. Consumers have adjusted to high prices by becoming extremely price conscious. The purchase of new homes fell 40 percent when the interest rate on home loans jumped from 9 percent in 1978 to more than 15 percent in 1980. Some consumers substitute poultry for beef because poultry is less expensive, and buy store brands instead of nationally branded products. Next time you're in the supermarket, watch how often people compare the prices of competing products.

Business Sector. The purchasing agents for big companies are as concerned about inflation as consumers are. These purchasing agents now ask important questions of their suppliers. How long will the product last? How much will servicing cost? Does the warranty pay for labor and materials? Who pays for installation? Is financing available? At what interest rate? Notice that all these questions are concerned with price and value.

Industrial buyers are willing to pay more for a product if the product is durable and of good quality. For example, many trucking companies are now switching from bias-ply tires to more expensive radial tires for their 18-wheelers. Although these tires cost 40 to 50 percent more than bias-ply tires, they last much longer and can be retreaded at least twice. Radials also produce fuel savings of 2 to 6 percent and are less likely to puncture. During a time when cost control is the key to profitability, radials make more sense in terms of cost performance.

Inflation Worldwide

How does the rate of inflation in the United States compare with that in other countries? Figure 2-3 shows the percentage increase in consumer prices for the United States, the industrial nations as a group, the oil-exporting countries, the entire world, and the non-oil-developing countries for the period 1975-1980. The United

Figure 2-2

Housing Costs, 1969-1981

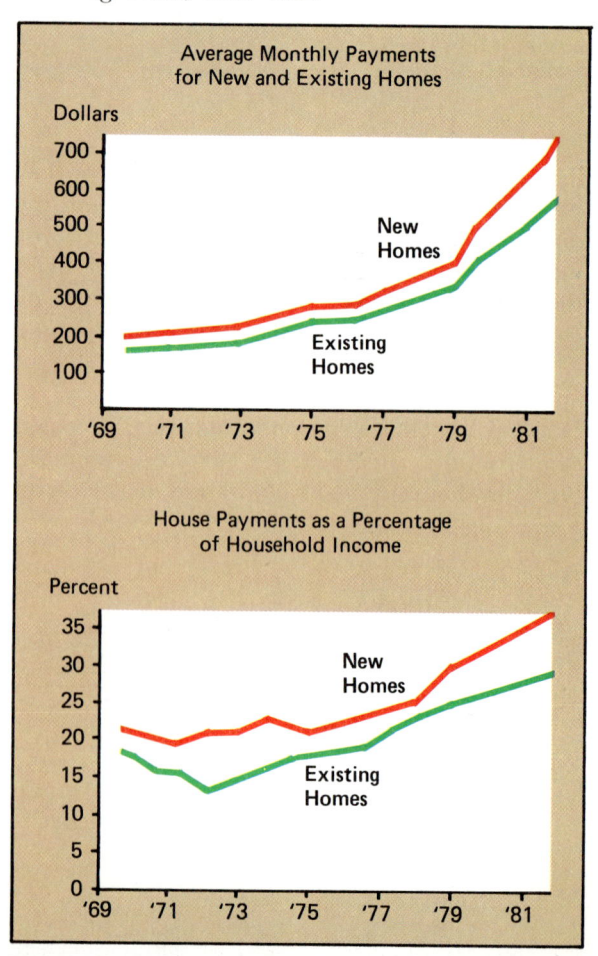

Source: Reprinted from the September 7, 1981 issue of *Business Week* by special permission, © 1981 by McGraw-Hill, Inc., New York, NY 10020. All rights reserved.

Profile—
Henry Kaufman

As chief economist to the investment banking house of Salomon Brothers, Henry Kaufman is responsible for predicting the future business environment for Salomon and for its clients. His accuracy (and hence his reputation) is so great that business people everywhere rely on his judgments.

Henry Kaufman was born in Germany in 1927, the son of a Jewish meat merchant. He spent his first few years in a Germany ravaged so badly by inflation that paper money became virtually worthless. In 1936, Kaufman's parents fled to America. After completing his education at New York University, Kaufman worked as an economist at the Federal Reserve Bank in New York, and in 1962 he joined Salomon Brothers.

His first success came in 1968, when Lyndon Johnson geared up the American economy to handle the increased demand for military supplies for the war in Vietnam. Congress and the Federal Reserve made plans to avoid high inflation and high interest rates, but Kaufman knew that what the federal government wanted often didn't come to pass. Instead, Kaufman expected the economy to heat up dramatically. Although his first estimates were wrong, Kaufman recanted his position almost immediately and achieved fame as the only accurate forecaster on Wall Street. The companies who listened to Kaufman planned correctly for inflation, higher interest rates, and other environmental problems.

In 1976, Kaufman told Salomon clients that long-term bonds issued by companies were going to drop badly. Within the month, the bond market plummeted and again, only the companies that planned for an environment predicted by Kaufman came out unscathed. The following year, he predicted that interest rates would rise substantially, and within six months his forecast was justified. In 1978, Kaufman predicted that inflation would increase to dangerously high levels, and in 1979 he predicted astronomical interest rates. In March of 1979, Kaufman admonished that America's economy had "slipped from the moorings (that) kept our behavior within reasonable limits." The federal government didn't heed his warnings. In 1980 Kaufman predicted interest rates exceeding 20 percent. Every prediction came to pass.

In 1980, Kaufman announced that a recession was inevitable; within hours, the Dow Jones average on Wall Street tumbled and the bond market soared, reflecting belief in Kaufman's predictions. Some economists were beginning to wonder if Kaufman's predictions were self-fulfilling. That is, was he so trusted that when he made a prediction, people's behavior actually caused that prediction to come to pass?

In August of 1982, Kaufman announced jubilantly that interest rates were going to drop substantially and the economy would see a marked improvement. Wall Street went wild. New records were set in trading volume and in the degree that stock prices rose. The effects spread throughout the economy. Banks continued to lower interest rates. Industrial production picked up, people were rehired, and the economy began to improve.

Kaufman is famous for his habitual reading and observation. He scans every newspaper he sees, spends hours on the telephone talking with politicians and economists about future plans, and even observes the problems faced by the local stores and shopping centers he frequents. He then applies a well-developed intuition and analytical skill to the information he has gathered in order to predict the future. His continual problem, of course, is outguessing human nature—guessing how people will react to circumstances.

Despite his upbringing in inflation-ridden Germany and his years in an unstable American economy, Kaufman still believes that endurance will pay off. As pessimistic as many of his predictions have been, Kaufman is very optimistic about the future.

Figure 2-3

Percentage Change in Consumer Prices Around the World, 1975-1980

Source: International Monetary Fund

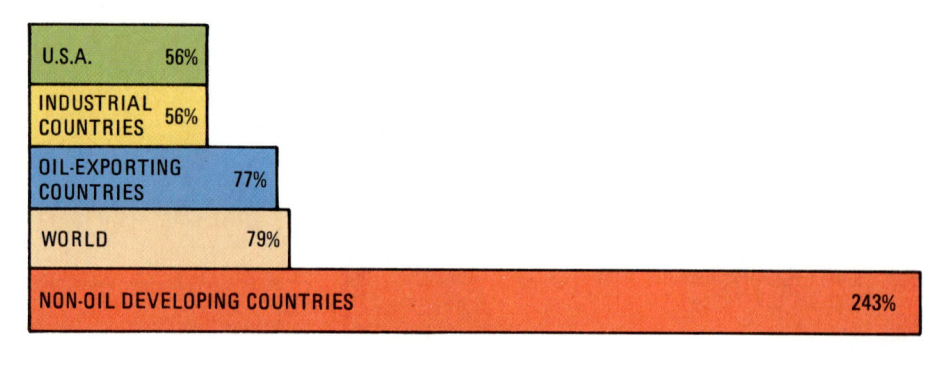

Region	%
U.S.A.	56%
INDUSTRIAL COUNTRIES	56%
OIL-EXPORTING COUNTRIES	77%
WORLD	79%
NON-OIL DEVELOPING COUNTRIES	243%

States' 56-percent rise in consumer prices compares quite favorably with the inflation record elsewhere. The rate of inflation here was 23 points lower than the worldwide rate, and it was about the same as the rate for the Western powers as a group. The developing nations without oil reserves are in the worst position. For many of them, the price level doubles every year.

ENERGY

The United States and the other nations of the world survived one energy crisis in 1973-1974 and another in 1979. Both of these energy squeezes were caused by massive oil price increases. The quadrupling of the price of a barrel of crude oil by OPEC brought about the first crisis. Then in 1978 and 1979, oil production in Iran declined dramatically in the wake of the revolution there. The result this time was a tripling of oil prices. All in all, the price of a barrel of crude rose from about $3 in 1973 to roughly $35 in 1981. Figure 2-4 shows the average price of a 40-gallon barrel of crude from four countries for the period 1970-1981. Note that between 1975 and 1979 the price of oil hardly changed at all.

Both of these crises have passed. Other short-term squeezes may be in the offing, but they are not the real problem. The real problem is how to live with the long-term consequences of dwindling energy supplies and growing energy consumption. Much of the trouble is the result of the industrialized nations' dependence on petroleum. Our response has been to look for new sources of energy and to change our pattern of energy consumption.

The Energy Balance Sheet

Energy price fluctuations can be understood in the context of supply and demand. First, let's look at the current state of energy demand, then at the status of some of our major energy sources.

Sometimes we look to the past to find new solutions.

Figure 2-4

Posted Price Per Barrel in Dollars, January 1 of Year, 1970-1981

Year	U.S.	LIBYA	IRAN	SAUDI ARABIA
1981	21.59	40.00	37.00	32.00
'80	12.64	34.67	28.50	24.00
'79	9.00	14.59	13.45	13.34
'78	8.57	14.20	12.81	12.70
'77	8.14	12.62	11.62	11.51
'76	7.56	16.06	12.50	12.38
'75	6.74	15.77	11.48	11.25
'74	3.89	9.06	5.25	5.04
'73	3.39	3.62	2.47	2.48
'72	3.39	3.40	2.27	2.29
'71	3.18	2.55	1.79	1.80
'70	3.09	2.23	1.79	1.80

Source: DeGolyer and MacNaughton, Twentieth Century Petroleum Statistics, 1981.

Energy Demand. As our economy grows, our demand for energy will also grow. Between now and the year 2000, consumption of energy in the United States will increase at an estimated average yearly rate of 1.3 percent. This rate of growth compares with a 4.1 percent figure for the period 1960-1973.[3] Some of the reduction in the rate of energy usage will be at the expense of economic growth. Increased fuel costs do act as a brake on the economy. But this reduction is also the result of more fuel-efficient production processes and slower population growth. The point is that rising energy costs do not mean the end of economic growth or prosperity.

Figure 2-5 shows the overall increase in energy demand between 1960 and the year 2000. Note first that the rate of increase before the OPEC price hike of 1973-1974 was much greater than the rate after the OPEC action. Second, note how the composition of demand is expected to change. The transportation sector, which currently accounts for about 26 percent of all energy demanded, will show the largest percentage decline. "Transportation" refers to the energy consumed by cars, trucks, boats, trains, and planes. Most of this reduction will be made up by increased industrial demand. Interestingly, in terms of total demand, transportation usage should stay fairly constant over the next decade and a half.

Energy Supply. Figure 2-6 shows the sources of our future energy supplies. In 1980 petroleum accounted for 46 percent of our energy consumption, but by 1990 it will account for only 38 percent, and by the year 2000, only 32 percent. Similarly, natural gas consumption will drop from 26 percent in 1980 to 17 percent in 2000. Which energy source is expected to pick up the slack? The answer is coal, of which this country has abundant reserves. United States coal production totaled 734 million tons in 1980; it will probably exceed 2 billion tons by the turn of the century. At that time, coal will account for 33 percent of the energy consumed in the United States.

What role will solar and nuclear technologies play in our energy future? Solar usage today is pretty much limited to a few household applications such as home heating. How soon solar power generation will play a more important role in our energy economy depends upon the pace of

---

[3]Exxon Corporation, *Energy Outlook, 1980-2000* (December, 1979), p. 8.

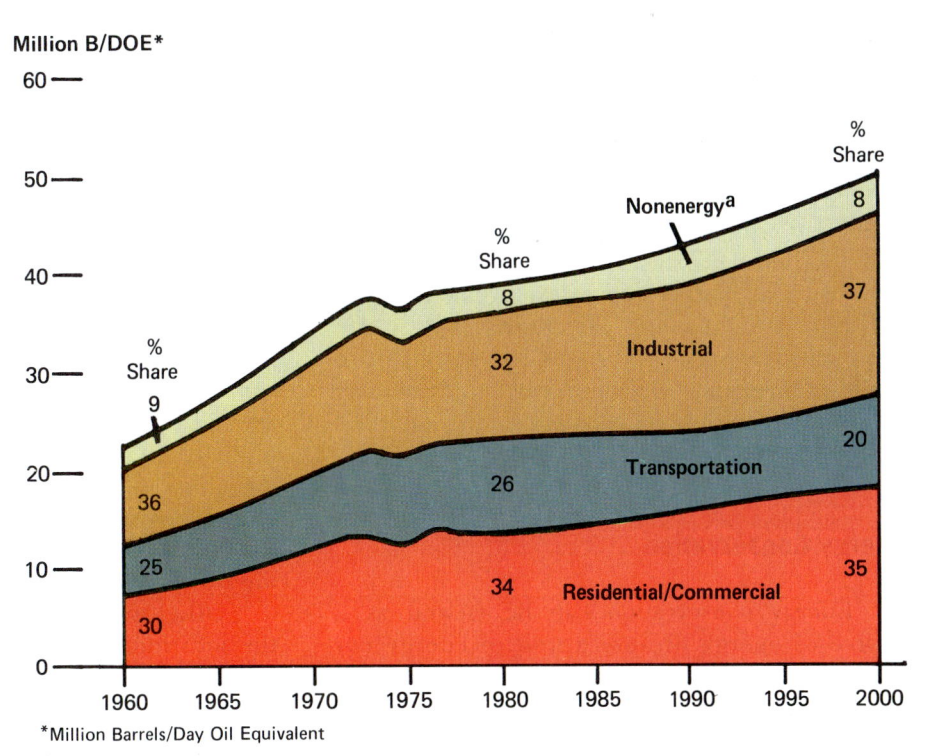

Figure 2-5

U.S. Energy Demand by Consuming Sector

*Million Barrels/Day Oil Equivalent

a Use of oil, gas or coal as a feedstock or raw material.

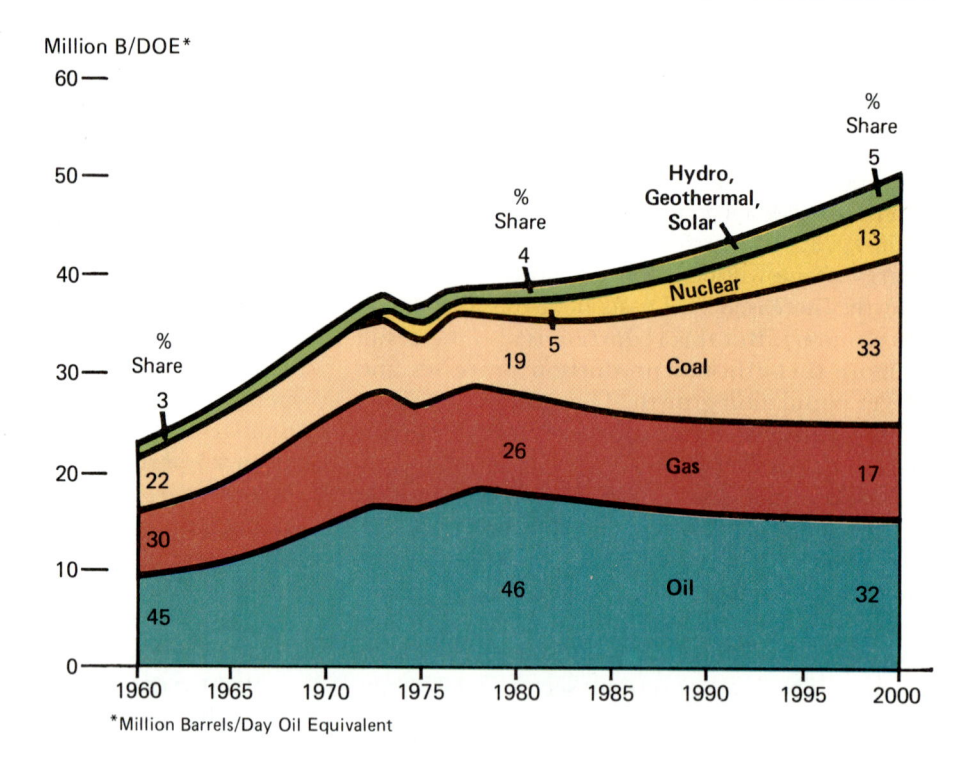

Figure 2-6

U.S. Energy Supply

*Million Barrels/Day Oil Equivalent

technological innovation. Certainly, our consumption of solar energy will increase steadily over the next 20 years. But we should not expect to see a large-scale reliance on solar energy until we are well into the twenty-first century.

Nuclear energy development may well continue to be plagued by construction delays and cost overruns. An example is the South Texas Nuclear Project, which was originally scheduled for completion in 1980 at a cost of $1 billion. By late 1982, the estimated completion date for both units of the project had been pushed back to 1989, and estimated costs had soared to $5.5 billion. Moreover, nuclear energy development is beset with regulatory and safety problems. Data in Figure 2-6 show how the annual growth rate for nuclear energy production has slowed since 1960. Still, nuclear development could account for as much as 13 percent of our energy supplies by the year 2000.

Energy Conservation

Energy conservation can be viewed as a source of energy because a unit of energy not burned wastefully is a unit of energy available for consumption later. Energy efficiency is another term for energy conservation. It has been shown that the United States in 1973 could have maintained its standard of living with 40 percent less energy consumed.

We have already said that economic growth is not necessarily tied to increased energy consumption. Likewise, company growth is not tied to increased energy consumption. Several companies have initiated programs of energy conservation while increasing their output of goods and services. Among them are General Motors, Exxon, Dow Chemical, DuPont, and AT&T. AT&T completed its ten-year energy conservation program in 1984. Between 1974 and 1984, AT&T's business grew by nearly 50 percent, and its consumption of energy remained nearly constant.

For individual consumers, the single biggest source of energy savings has been the use of more fuel-efficient automobiles. New cars in the 1973 model year averaged less than 14 miles per gallon. The law now requires new cars to average 27.5 miles per gallon by 1985. Some experts believe that by the year 2000 all cars will be averaging up to 50 miles per gallon.

Other important sources of conservation for the individual consumer include adding insulation to older homes, building smaller and more energy-efficient new homes, and using electricity more wisely. Can you think of any others?

Impacts of Energy Scarcity

The high cost of energy, which results from increasing scarcity, will cause major shifts in the ways people live and work. Already, people have begun to move back into cities. By living nearer to where they work, people can cut down on commuting costs. We've mentioned the increased fuel efficiency of new cars. One reason for this greater efficiency is a reduction in the average weight of a car from 3,000 pounds in 1979 to as low as 1,700 by the year 2000.[4] Similarly, many other products will be designed for greater fuel efficiency, especially household appliances such as microwave ovens, refrigerators, and washing machines.

An interesting example of an "old" product which can offer a solution to today's rising utility bills is the ceiling fan. Ceiling fans were a common sight in many houses and stores before the advent of air conditioning. At first, air conditioning was more convenient, more effective, and not much more expensive. But as energy costs soared in the mid-1970s, people rediscovered the ceiling fan. The Hunter Fan Company produces virtually the same style fans that it did in 1900, and they are selling as well today as they did nearly a hundred years ago.

Business will respond to the energy crunch by looking for ways to reduce energy inputs in production processes, by making their products more energy efficient for the consumer, and by developing advertising strategies that spotlight this added efficiency. For example, U-Haul advertises its "light-weight, low-profile" rental trucks as real gas savers for the consumer. Sears markets a dishwasher with a "water-miser cycle and power-miser control."

POLLUTION

One of the characteristics of an industrial society is pollution. By the late 1960s, the immensity of this problem had become clear. Our cities were blackened with soot. Our rivers and lakes were being contaminated with hazardous wastes. In response to this pollution, many environmental reforms were passed by Congress in the late 1960s and early 1970s. Foremost among these laws were the National Environmental Policy Act (1969), the Clean Air Act (1970), and the Federal Water Pollution Control Act (1972). The Environmental Protection Agency (EPA) was established to enforce the acts and to regulate polluting activities.

A Quick Look at Air Quality

The amount of pollutants poured into our air each year is truly staggering. In 1979, as shown in Table 2-1, the estimated volume of carbon monoxide emissions was 100.7 million tons. The total for sulfur oxide emissions was 27 million tons. Fortunately, the levels of these pollutants have generally dropped since 1970, when several of the major environmental laws began to take effect.

Table 2-1 also lists emissions by source for each of the five major air pollutants. Note that transportation (automobiles and trucks) accounts for most of the carbon monoxide pollution and that stationary fuel combustion (power utilities) accounts for most of the sulfur oxide pollution.

Energy Development and Environmental Protection

There is a major conflict between supporters of public energy development and supporters of environmental protection. Often, the goals of one group clash with the goals of the other. Should we allow oil exploration and drilling in our national parks or should we preserve the parks for our children? Should we build dams on our last wild rivers for hydroelectric power generation or should we leave the rivers in their natural state? Similar questions can be asked with respect to oil shale development in the rangelands of the West, pipeline construction across the Alaskan and Canadian tundra, or the burning of "dirty" coal by power utilities.

Nearly all energy development projects involve one sort of economic problem or another. An accident at an offshore oil rig can leave hundreds of miles of beach spoiled for many years. A major accident at a nuclear power plant could leave a wide area contaminated for thousands of years. Some other hazards associated with energy development and consumption are:

---

[4]Exxon Corporation, *Energy Outlook, 1980-2000* (December, 1979), p. 6.

Table 2-1

Air Pollutant Emissions, by Source, 1979
(Millions of Short Tons)

Pollutants	Total Emissions	Transportation	Stationary Fuel Combustion	Industrial Processes	Solid Waste Disposal	Other
Particulates	10.5	1.5	2.8	4.7	0.4	1.0
Sulfur Oxides	27.0	1.1	21.6	4.5	—	—
Nitrogen Oxides	24.9	10.1	13.6	0.9	0.1	0.2
Hydrocarbons	27.1	9.7	0.2	13.7	0.9	2.6
Carbon Monoxide	100.7	82.1	2.1	6.9	2.8	6.8

Source: U.S. Environmental Protection Agency, *National Air Pollutant Emission Estimates, 1970-1979*.

- Acid drainage from underground coal mining.
- Destruction of the landscape from strip mining.
- Salt water disposal from oil wells.
- Air pollution from oil refining.
- Thermal pollution from electrical generating plants.
- Marine pollution from the transportation of oil, coal, and natural gas.[5]

The disagreements between energy development groups and environmental protection groups will not go away. Any decisions in these areas involve a consideration of trade-offs. That is, achieving an energy development goal may mean not achieving an environmental protection goal, and vice versa. For example, we can reduce air pollution from automobiles by requiring better emission-control devices. But the result is fewer miles per gallon and, therefore, more gallons of gasoline consumed. In the same way, we can become less reliant on imported oil by burning more coal. Coal is mined in the United States, and it is plentiful. The problem is that much coal has a high sulfur content which presents a major air pollution problem.

Business Impacts

Environmental rules and regulations, which constitute a significant uncontrollable variable, have several effects on the economy and on business. Let's look at a few of them now.

Pollution Control Expenditures. Many companies have had to invest substantial sums of money in pollution control equipment in order to comply with the new environmental regulations. Federal, state, and local governments have spent heavily in this area, too. Roughly $274 billion was spent in the United States from 1965 through 1981 on the installation and operation of pollution control equipment. Of this total, $106 billion went for air pollution control, $121 billion went for water pollution control, and $42 billion went for solid waste management.

Table 2-2 shows these expenditures by year for air and water pollution control. These expenditures increased steadily each year through the 1970s as environmental regulations became stiffer.

It is often difficult to balance energy development and environmental protection.

---

[5] Bruce Netschert, "Energy vs. the Environment," *Harvard Business Review* (January-February, 1973), p. 26.

Table 2-2

Total U.S. Expenditures for
Air and Water Pollution Control
1972-1980
(Constant 1972 Dollars in Millions)

Year	Air Pollution Control*	Water Pollution Control*
1972	6,230	7,551
1973	7,130	8,214
1974	7,428	8,535
1975	8,544	9,298
1976	8,912	9,916
1977	9,104	9,923
1978	9,313	10,722
1979	9,648	10,581
1980	10,411	9,861

*Includes capital and operating expenditures.
Source: U.S. Department of Commerce, Bureau of Economic Analysis, *Survey of Current Business* (February, 1982).

A frequent target of criticism in recent years has been the expense of federal environmental regulation. Critics argue that funds used to implement federal law could have been invested in new manufacturing plants and facilities. The results, according to the opponents of the laws, have been higher prices, slower economic growth, and higher unemployment. However, several computer studies have shown that the economic impacts of pollution control have actually been small. It is true that stiff environmental rules have resulted in some plant closings. These closings have added to unemployment and other economic problems in local areas. But looking at the economy as a whole, the effects are not pronounced. It has been estimated that government regulation adds only about one half of one percentage point to the annual rate of inflation and slows the annual rate of growth of real GNP by only 0.1 percent. Also, the unemployment rate may even have been reduced by 0.4 percent. This is because of added employment in industries that specialize in the manufacture of pollution control equipment.[6]

The benefits of a cleaner environment are fairly obvious. The question before society is whether we are willing to shoulder the costs. How to balance the benefits and costs of environmental protection will be a heated topic of public discussion for years to come.

Project Delays. Our recent concern with environmental quality has several implications for business. For example, many building projects will be delayed by environmental impact statements. The Alaskan pipeline was delayed for years while the effects of the project were evaluated. The development of port facilities also has been slowed by environmental concerns. According to one study, it now takes more than 20 years to obtain all the necessary permits to build a new port.[7] No new permits for major port work were approved between 1976 and 1981.

New Product Opportunities. Because of the continued interest in environmental quality, the market for environmentally safe products will continue to prosper. The firms that recognize this market and promote their products accordingly will be in a good position to experience strong sales growth. This is as true of the manufacturers of pollution control equipment as it is of the makers of consumer products.

New Morality for Business. Finally, the environmental movement is indicative of a new morality for business. If firms do not act responsibly, then they can expect greater federal, state, and local regulation. But responsible behavior can have other payoffs as well. The 3M Company is an example of a business that has turned environmental protection into cost savings and higher profits. In 1975, the company introduced its 3P Program, "Pollution Prevention Pays." Its aim is to encourage 3M employees to discover cost-saving approaches for reducing or eliminating pollution from 3M products or manufacturing processes. So far, the program has produced cost savings of more than $55 million.

DEMOGRAPHIC SHIFTS

Another important uncontrollable environmental force is demographic change. **Demography** is the statistical study of the characteristics

---

[6]See Paul Portney, "The Macroeconomic Impacts of Federal Environmental Regulation," *Environmental Regulation and the U.S. Economy*, ed. Henry Peskin, Paul Portney, and Allen Kneese (Baltimore: Johns Hopkins University Press, 1981), pp. 25-54.

[7]Jean Briggs, "Shaping Up to Ship Coal," *Forbes* (February 16, 1981), p. 60.

of human populations. Business managers know that geographic shifts have an effect on the market for goods and services. In this part of the chapter we'll consider population shifts, employment shifts, and the changing age composition of the American people.

Population

The people of the United States are on the move, migrating from one part of the country to another in search of jobs, income, and a better way of life. During the next five years, two out of every five American families will move to a new residence. A full 20 percent of these moves will be to a different state.

The biggest population shifts have occurred between the Frostbelt and the Sunbelt. Each year, thousands of people leave the eastern and midwestern states and move to the southern or western parts of the country.

Figure 2-7 shows migration patterns by region. Between 1970 and 1975, and then again between 1975 and 1980, more than 1,300,000 people left the Northeast. Another one million people left the north central states. Where did they go? The figure shows that net migration to the South totaled 1,829,000 during the first half of the decade and 1,764,000 during the second half. The western states also experienced significant population growth.

Even more interesting is that this trend is likely to continue for years to come. Look at the map of the United States in Figure 2-8. United States population is expected to grow at an average annual rate of about 1 percent through the year 2000. But not all parts of the country will grow at the same rate. The figure shows that Alaska and the Rocky Mountain states will gain the most in population; the mideastern states will lose the most in population.

Employment

People migrate for a variety of reasons. One major reason is to find work. We should not be surprised to learn that the regional pattern of employment growth reflects the regional pattern of population shifts. Total employment (the number of people holding jobs) increased by 7.7 percent from 1969 to 1978 in the northeastern and Great Lakes states. Employment in the southern and western states grew by 18 percent during the same period. And, again, this pattern will probably last through the end of the century. Frostbelt employment will increase by about 15 percent and Sunbelt employment will grow by twice that amount in the 1980s and 1990s.[8]

Why have these dramatic shifts in population and employment taken place? A partial listing of the reasons for these shifts would certainly include the following:

- Manufacturing plants in the nation's northern industrial heartland have become old and outdated. It is less expensive to build new modern plants in other parts of the country than to renovate the old plants.
- The older parts of the country have many well-established special-interest groups that make economic change and redirection difficult.
- Many towns in the South and West are willing and able to attract industry by offering generous tax breaks.
- The wages paid to labor in the South and West are much lower than the wages paid in the North and Northeast. Businesses will locate new

Figure 2-7

Interregional Migration, 1970-1980

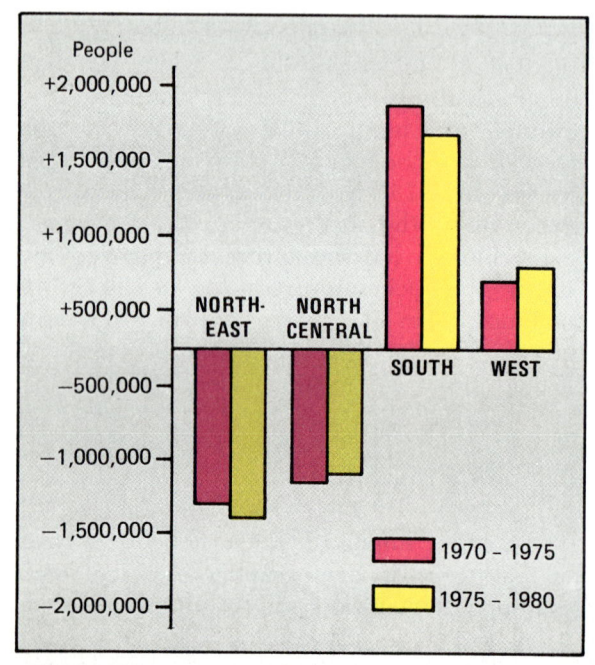

Source: U.S. Bureau of the Census, Current Population Reports, Series P-20, No. 285.

---

[8]*Survey of Current Business* (March, 1980), p. 51.

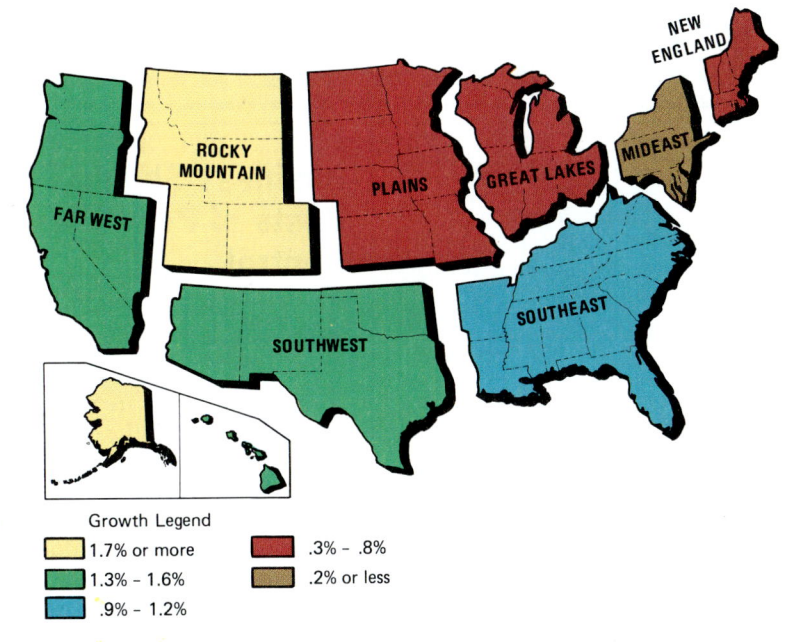

Figure 2-8

Average Annual Growth Rates in Population, 1978-2000

Source: U.S. Department of Commerce, Bureau of Economic Analysis.

Growth Legend
- 1.7% or more
- 1.3% – 1.6%
- .9% – 1.2%
- .3% – .8%
- .2% or less

offices, factories, and warehouses where labor costs are the lowest.

The cost of living is lower in the South and West than in other parts of the country. According to the 1980 census, the average value of an owner-occupied house in the United States is $47,200. For Alabama, Arkansas, and Mississippi, however, the figures are $33,900, $31,100, and $31,400, respectively. Housing is much more expensive in Connecticut ($65,000) and Maryland ($58,300).[9]

---

[9] George Sternlieb and James W. Hughes, "New Regional and Metropolitan Realities of America," *Journal of American Institute of Planners* (July, 1977), pp. 237-241.

Table 2-3 gives some indication of the effects of these employment shifts on local economies. The table shows the percentage of the labor force unemployed for cities in Michigan and Texas. These states are representative of Frostbelt and Sunbelt economies. The economy of Michigan is based on the manufacture of machine tools, automobiles, and other durable goods; the economy of Texas is based on energy development, petrochemicals, and aerospace. Through the early 1980s, the unemployment rate in the Michigan communities was at least three times as high as the rate for the Texas cities. And the problems of the Frostbelt are not expected to lessen any time

Each year, many people move in search of a better way of life.

CONTROVERSIAL ISSUES

Pollution has been a problem since the beginning of the Industrial Revolution in the middle 1800s. Society is no longer willing, however, to tolerate the pollution of the environment caused largely by businesses. Many people think business alone should pay to correct the damage caused by pollution and to prevent further pollution.

Business Should Pay Costs of Pollution Control.

Pro

Yes, businesses should pay all the costs of pollution control. For years, companies have been able to misuse power resources with no concern for the effects they have on our environment. Now it's time for them to put some of their profits to work cleaning up the mess they've created.

Because businesses haven't been held responsible for pollution in the past, they haven't cared when they made cars that pollute the countryside. They haven't cared that they overpackaged goods for sale causing garbage dumps that are now full. And most recently, they have expanded the use of nuclear power without adequate concern for safe disposal of radioactive waste.

Businesses a century ago felt free to dump their unwanted by-products. Now, such waterways as the St. Lawrence Seaway and most of the Great Lakes are nearly dead, and others, such as Love Canal, are dangerous to live near. Today, we are realizing that our world is really very small, and that we can't bury pollution in the ground, dump it in a river or an ocean, or send it into space without causing problems later on.

Businesses have to *stop* all further pollution, and they have to pay to clean up the mess they've created. The government can't afford it, and the government wasn't responsible for it. Make the businesses pay to clean it up. They caused it.

Con

You *can't* and *shouldn't* make businesses assume the cost of cleaning up pollution. After all, didn't businesses produce what consumers wanted? Aren't consumers just as responsible for the pollution? Shouldn't they help pay the cost of cleanup?

Everything that has been produced by American businesses has been produced for the American consumers. If consumers didn't like the environmental cost of a product, they could easily have signaled their feelings by refusing to buy the product. But since consumers bought large polluting cars, approved bonds for nuclear power plants, and voted for governmental representatives who proposed helping businesses which created some of today's pollution, those same Americans should be willing to pay the costs.

American businesses have invested vast amounts in research to make more pollution-free products, in new technologies that avoid pollution in the factory, and in finding ways of eliminating the pollution that can't be avoided by the current state of technology.

Businesses are doing their part. To finish the work, the government needs to chip in. If the government would give massive tax credits to companies solving pollution problems, companies would work harder. But whatever happens, the money must come from government coffers. Businesses have already done enough.

36

Table 2-3

Percentage of Labor Force Unemployed for Selected States and Localities, 1980-1982

State and City	1980 Annual Average	1981 Annual Average	March 1982
Michigan	12.4	12.3	17.0
Detroit	13.1	12.9	17.3
Flint	17.6	15.1	23.5
Saginaw	14.2	12.2	20.6
Texas	5.2	5.3	5.7
Dallas-Ft. Worth	4.5	4.7	5.2
Houston	4.2	4.3	4.9
San Antonio	6.6	6.6	6.1

Source: U.S. Department of Labor, Bureau of Labor Statistics, *Employment and Earnings*, June, 1982.

soon. One federal study estimates that 500,000 auto manufacturing jobs will be lost during the 1980s.[10]

Age

As a nation we are getting older. This development is of profound importance to the makers of consumer products and to other business planners. By "getting older," we mean that the average age of the population is increasing. As shown in Table 2-4, the median age of the U.S. population is now 30, up from 27.9 in 1970.

Population by Age Group. Table 2-4 also shows how the composition of the population has

---

[10]See Jerry Flint, "Trouble in the Heartland," *Forbes* (March 16, 1981), pp. 120-126.

What does the aging of the U.S. population mean for business?

changed. Look at the "65 Years and Over" group. This group made up 8.1 percent of the population in 1950; in 1980, its share had risen to 11.3 percent. Similarly, the 55-64 age group has increased its share of the population. The "baby boom" generation is included in the percentages for the 18-24 and 25-34 age categories. Note how dramatically these percentages have risen since 1960. Finally, the percentage share of those at the other end of the age spectrum—under 5 years—has fallen steadily since 1960.

Declining Fertility Rates. What accounts for this gradual aging of the population? One reason certainly is that people are living longer because of improved medical care and sanitation. Another reason is that, currently, fewer children are being born. Figure 2-9 shows how steeply the fertility rate, which measures the number of births per thousand women, has dropped since the late

Table 2-4

Percentage Distribution of U.S. Population by Age, 1950-1980

	Total All Ages	Under 5 Years	5-17 Years	18-24 Years	25-34 Years	35-44 Years	45-54 Years	55-64 Years	65 Years and Over	Median Age (Years)
1950	100.0	10.8	20.2	10.6	15.8	14.2	11.5	8.8	8.1	30.2
1960	100.0	11.3	24.4	8.9	12.7	13.4	11.4	8.6	9.2	29.4
1970	100.0	8.4	25.7	12.0	12.3	11.4	11.4	9.1	9.8	27.9
1980	100.0	7.2	20.9	13.3	16.4	11.3	10.0	9.6	11.3	30.0

Source: U.S. Bureau of the Census, Current Population Reports, Series P-25, Nos. 311, 519, 721, and 917.

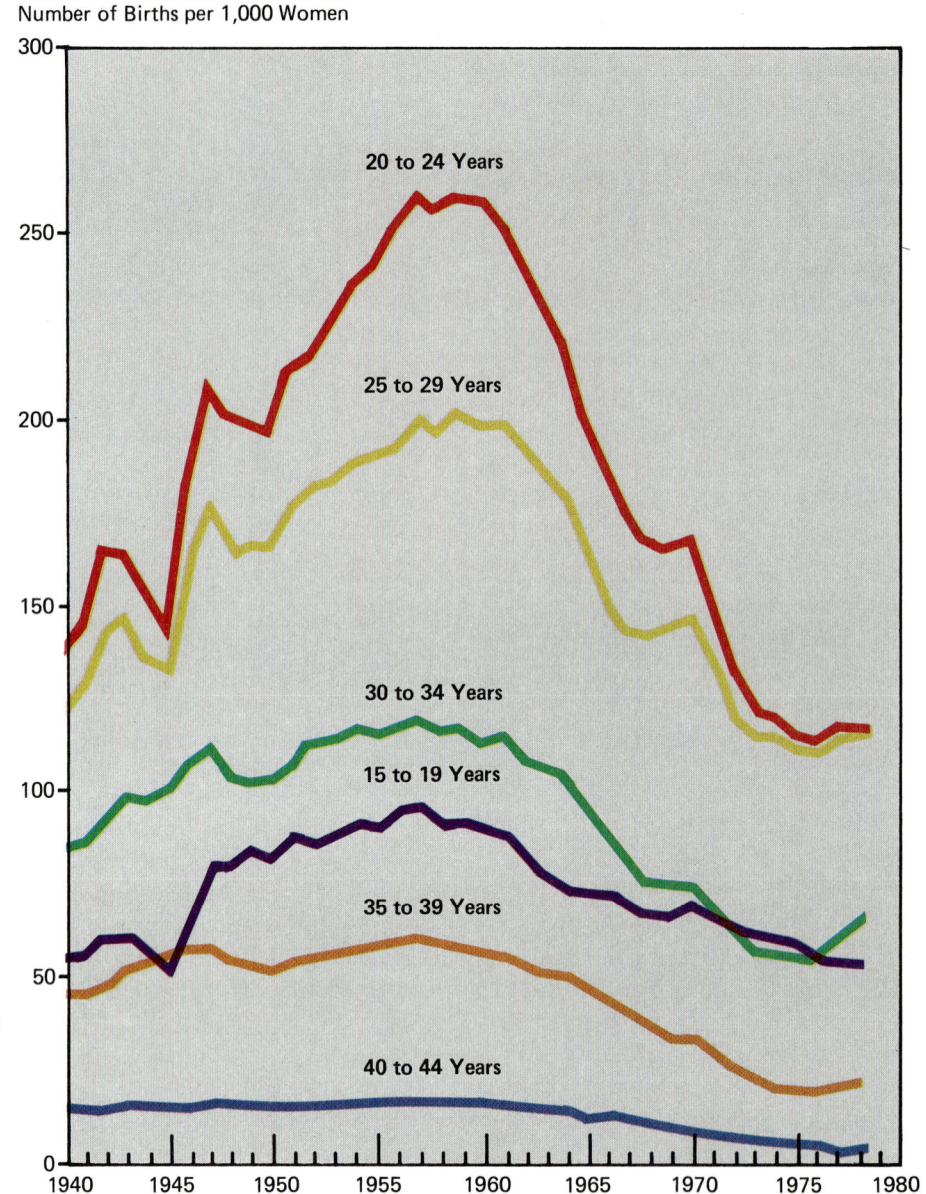

Figure 2-9

Fertility Rates, by Age of Mother: 1950-1979

Source: U.S. National Center for Health Statistics, *Vital Statistics of the United States,* annual and unpublished data.

1950s for women in the prime childbearing years of 20 to 24 and 25 to 29. How might the manufacturers of baby care products use this information?

Relevance of Demographic Changes

What is the relevance of demographic developments to product planning, investment, and other business decisions? What, in fact, do these population, employment, and age distribution changes mean?

Migration. First, let's consider the movement of people to the South and West. The rapid population growth in the Sunbelt will generate increased demand for consumer products there. Seeing this opportunity, such major retailing chains as Federated Department Stores, Allied Stores Corporation, Sears, and the May Company will build many more stores in the South and West than in the Midwest and East. These new shopping facilities will create more jobs. Location of new manufacturing plants and office headquarters in the Sunbelt in response to the lower wage scales and to the more favorable climate will also create more jobs. These shifts in employment will likely cause another migration out of the economically hard-hit Frostbelt. In the long run, population shifts will mean many new chances for growth in the service trades—from plumbing firms to advertising agencies.

Changing Age Composition. Second, what are a few of the implications of an older population? For one, the U.S. social security system will continue to face a major solvency problem because of the many people reaching retirement age. There are not enough wage earners to keep the system operating at its current level. (We will discuss this issue again in Chapter 6.) Similarly, companies will need to examine the composition of their work forces. A large number of retirements may strain company-supported retirement systems. Firms will need personnel managers who will look to the future and will recruit and train young people to fill the positions of the older company members.

Finally, changes in the age distribution of the U.S. population will force many companies to look for new product opportunities. We can expect smaller markets for baby care products, children's toys, and record albums and much larger product and service markets for the 55-and-older age group. One manufacturer of baby foods has already begun marketing its products to senior citizens. Can you think of other product and service opportunities for this age group?

THE CHANGING ROLE OF WOMEN

In 1960, fewer than 22 million women held jobs in this country; by 1982, the number had risen to 48 million. Figure 2-10 shows the number of women of working age who are employed. Notice that in 1960 only 37.8 percent of all women were jobholders, compared to more than 50 percent in the early 1980s. The Bureau of Labor Statistics estimates that, by 1995, more than 60 percent of all working-age women in the United States will be employed. The figure also shows that the percentage of employed men is dropping.

Figure 2-10

Percentage of Men and Women More Than 16 Years of Age Employed in the United States

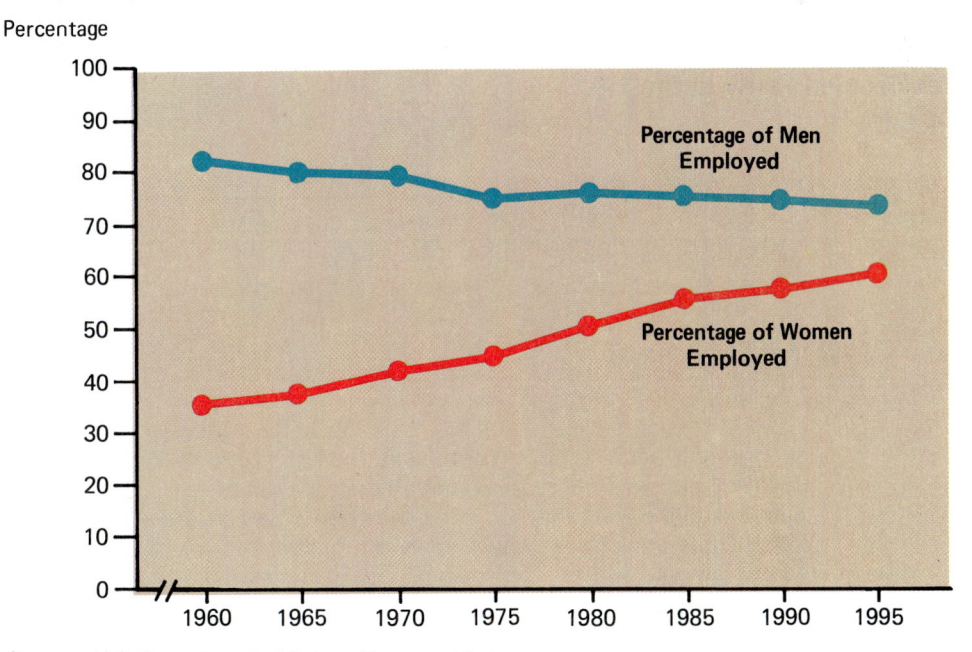

Source: U.S. Department of Labor, Bureau of Labor Statistics, *Monthly Labor Review* (December, 1980).

Why Women Work

Most women work for the same reason that men do—they need the money. The increased cost of living has forced many women into the workplace to help pay the family's bills. Other reasons that more women are working are presented in the following list:

- Today, more than 16 million women have some college education—twice as many as 20 years ago. The education gap between men and women is closing: In 1960, women accounted for only 36 percent of all college graduates; by the early 1980s, they accounted for nearly 50 percent.
- The number of jobs traditionally held by women has increased. The need for teachers, clerks, office-machine operators, and medical technicians is greater than ever before.
- High-paying, high-status jobs are now open to women. The number of women holding executive or managerial jobs is estimated at 3 million.
- One out of two marriages ends in divorce. This alone forces many women into the job market. Also, many women are staying single longer.
- Because of modern birth-control techniques, women are able to limit the size of their families. Births are planned to minimize the amount of time lost from the job. Women no longer must choose between family and career.
- The concept of the "working woman" has become socially acceptable.

Are Women Treated Fairly in the Workplace?

Most companies now understand that they have both a moral and a legal obligation to hire and promote women. Unfortunately, this attitude is not always shared by the people who make promotion and pay-raise decisions. Table 2-5 shows that in ten separate job categories, ranging from lawyer to waiter, women are paid significantly less than men for the same job.

Implications for Business

As we have said, many families today have two wage earners—the husband and the wife. The combined earnings of the two push the family into a higher income status. To illustrate, if both husband and wife worked as certified public accountants for an accounting firm, together they could earn $50,000 their first year out of college.

Business managers know that working couples have more money to spend. Even though

Table 2-5

Earnings by Occupation, 1981 Weekly Medians

	Women's Pay	Men's Pay
Clerical workers	220	328
Computer specialists	355	488
Editors, reporters	324	382
Engineers	371	547
Lawyers	407	574
Nurses	326	344
Physicians	401	495
Sales workers	190	366
Teachers (elementary)	311	379
Waiters	144	200

Source: Copyright 1982 Time Inc. All rights reserved. Reprinted by permission from TIME.

FROM THE FILE

Harold is plant manager for a lumber mill in northern Michigan. The mill employs 400 people. This represents half the local labor force. The federal government has told Harold that the mill needs new water pollution control equipment. Without this equipment, which costs $3 million, the mill will be in violation of federal law and will be shut down. Harold knows that the mill does not make enough money to justify an expense of that size. Should Harold recommend to the owners of the plant that the equipment be purchased or that the plant be closed, throwing its 400 employees out of work?

Unemployment Statistics

One of the staples of the nightly newscasts is the presentation of the latest unemployment figures. The rate of unemployment fluctuates with the "booms" and "busts" of the business cycle. The accompanying graph shows the unemployment rate during the post-World-War-II period. Besides these fluctuations, note how high the unemployment rate has been since 1974.

The unemployment rate says a great deal about the health of the economy. But it also hides as much as it reveals. Who, in fact, is out of work? What is the total number of people unemployed? How many people have given up in their search for a job? To answer these questions, it is necessary to explore unemployment data further.

In September of 1982, the unemployment rate reached 10.1 percent, the highest rate since the end of the Great Depression. The table shows the unemployment rate by race and ethnic origin, age and sex, occupation, and industry. Note how unevenly unemployment is spread across the population. Blacks are much more likely to be unemployed than whites. Construction workers are more likely to be out of work than government workers. Blue-collar workers are more likely to be laid off than white-collar workers.

An overall unemployment rate of 10.1 percent translates into a total of 11.3 million Americans out of work. And besides these people, another 6.6 million people were underemployed. That is, they were working fewer hours at their regular jobs or were working only part-time. Another 1.6 million had dropped out of the labor market altogether. These people are not even officially counted in the 10.1 percent figure. In total, therefore, 19.6 million workers were directly affected by the economic recession.

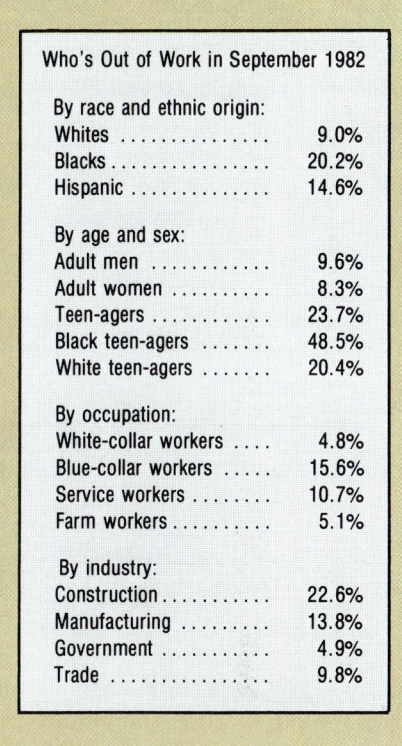

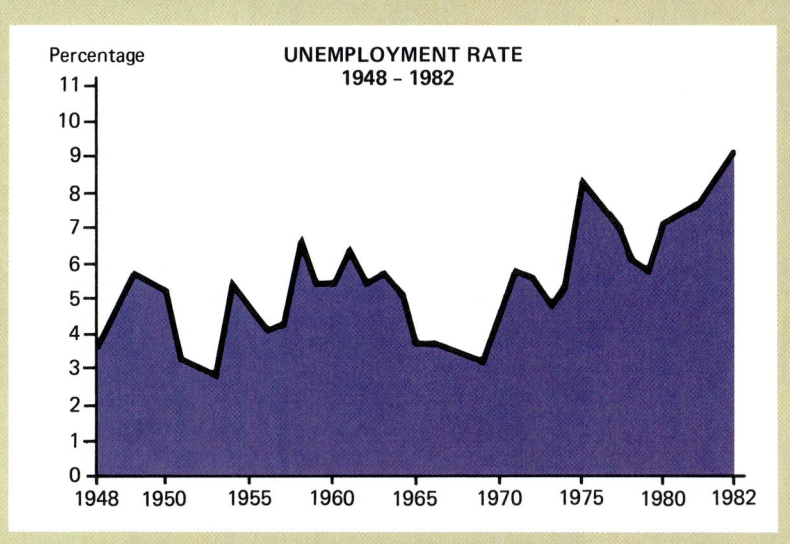

Who's Out of Work in September 1982

By race and ethnic origin:	
Whites	9.0%
Blacks	20.2%
Hispanic	14.6%
By age and sex:	
Adult men	9.6%
Adult women	8.3%
Teen-agers	23.7%
Black teen-agers	48.5%
White teen-agers	20.4%
By occupation:	
White-collar workers	4.8%
Blue-collar workers	15.6%
Service workers	10.7%
Farm workers	5.1%
By industry:	
Construction	22.6%
Manufacturing	13.8%
Government	4.9%
Trade	9.8%

Source: U.S. Department of Labor, Bureau of Labor Statistics.

---

inflation and taxes cut away some of these increased earnings, most working couples are in the market for services and labor-saving devices that make household work easier. Instead of washing clothes at home, people now send them out to the cleaners. Instead of preparing homecooked dinners, people buy convenience foods and pop them in the microwave oven.

Also, retailers have had to adjust their store hours. For example, we see many supermarkets staying open until midnight—and even all night in some cases—to accommodate the needs of working people.

CONSUMERISM

Producers and consumers interact in the marketplace through the buying and selling of goods and services. Both buyers and sellers have enjoyed certain rights in this interaction. Traditionally, the seller has been allowed to introduce virtually any product to the market as long as the product was not known to be hazardous. The seller also has had the right to design advertising strategies for its products and to price them so as to maximize profit.

Consumers have held certain rights, too. Chief among them has been the right of choice: Consumers could buy the seller's product or not. Consumers also have had the right to expect products to be safe and to be essentially what the seller represented them to be. But the consumer's best protection has always been a healthy skepticism toward product claims and promises.

Buyers and sellers have always had certain rights. But could the power of the two parties ever have been considered equal? No. In response to a series of product abuses, a movement called consumerism began to gain momentum. **Consumerism** can best be described as a reaction by consumers to what they perceive as abuses of the business system. The purpose of consumerism is to give consumers more power relative to sellers.

Why the Consumer Movement?

The consumer movement began with the great social unrest of the 1960s and 1970s. It was prompted by the sometimes irresponsible behavior of business.

Consumer dissatisfaction with defective or unsafe products, fraudulent product claims, and careless repair work contributed to the rise of consumerism and to the demand for greater business accountability. The consumer movement resulted in the establishment of the Consumer Product Safety Commission in 1972 and in the passage of a number of consumer protection laws.

Impact on Business

The consumer movement is here to stay, despite a few recent setbacks. One such setback was the defeat in 1978 of a bill in Congress to establish a federal consumer protection agency. The lasting contribution of consumerism, though, is greater fairness and frankness in the marketplace. But what specifically does consumerism mean for business?

Clean Up the Act. A month hardly passes without another major product being recalled or another cancer-causing substance being found in food products. Every time this happens, the cry goes up for more government protection of consumers. In response to such pressure, business managers have learned to look carefully at the safety of their products, the legitimacy of their advertising claims, and the sales tactics of their marketing people. Top management has no choice but to treat consumers more fairly. Without this concern, many businesses might find themselves in the position of the Ford Motor Company a few years ago. It was the target of several lawsuits because the gas tank on Ford's Pinto sometimes exploded in a rear-end collision.

Take Positive Action. Rather than simply complying with the law or avoiding lawsuits, some leading companies have taken positive steps to meet the needs of consumers. Eastman Kodak is an example of a company with a farsighted approach to the consumer movement. A few of its programs in that area are listed here:

- A product design philosophy that anticipates and eliminates consumer mistakes before they occur.
- A free photo advice service for consumers. This service handles more than 150,000 inquiries a year.
- Thirty-nine consumer service centers located across the country. Each center provides free advice and minor equipment repairs.
- A nonprofit publication program that distributes 100 different pamphlets and 25 books on photography.
- An assistant vice-president whose primary responsibility is consumer service for all divisions.
- High standards of product quality control and an easily read and understood warranty for its products.

As more businesses come to understand the importance of a good relationship with the consumer, we can expect an even greater degree of corporate accountability in the marketplace.

SUMMARY POINTS

1. Business strategies must be formulated in light of various environmental or uncontrollable variables. Six important environmental variables today are inflation, energy supply and demand, pollution control laws, demographic shifts, the changing role of women, and the consumer movement.
2. Inflation is defined as a rise in prices.
3. Four major causes of inflation are wage gains in excess of productivity gains, the tendency for wage gains in one industry to encourage the push for wage gains in others, the expectation that inflation will continue, and the rapid increase in the cost of energy.
4. Both consumers and business people have responded to inflation by showing greater concern for price and value.
5. The rate of growth in this nation's consumption of energy is falling, but the problem of living with the consequences of dwindling energy supplies still remains.
6. Coal accounts for the majority of the United States' proven reserves of energy. Solar and nuclear energy sources are not likely to play important energy roles in the near future.
7. Significant amounts of energy can be conserved without sacrificing either national economic growth or corporate sales growth.
8. Some major examples of environmental legislation are the National Environmental Policy Act, the Clean Air Act, and the Federal Water Pollution Control Act.
9. An analysis of energy development and environmental protection involves the consideration of trade-offs.
10. Compliance with environmental regulation often requires the investment of substantial sums of public and private monies in pollution control equipment.
11. However large, these pollution control expenditures do not appear to have had a big effect on the rate of inflation or growth in GNP.
12. Demography refers to the statistical study of the characteristics of human populations.
13. The biggest recent population and employment shifts have occurred between the Frostbelt states and the Sunbelt states.
14. An important development in the business environment is the increase in the median age. That is, the percentage of older people in the population is getting higher.
15. Some of the reasons for the increased number of women in the work force are inflation, job opportunities, divorce, family planning, and greater acceptance of the idea of the "working woman."
16. The chief purpose of the consumer movement is to enhance the power of the buying public relative to the power of sellers.

KEY TERMS AND CONCEPTS

uncontrollable variables
inflation
consumer price index
productivity
inflationary expectations
energy demand
energy supply
environmental protection
demography
employment
migration
consumerism

REVIEW QUESTIONS

1. What is meant by inflation? What is new about inflation today?
2. Name some of the causes of inflation.
3. Describe how wage increases in excess of productivity gains generate price increases.
4. How does inflation in this country compare to inflation elsewhere?
5. In the years ahead, which sector of the economy will experience a declining share of national energy consumption? Why do you think this will happen?
6. List the major sources of energy and briefly describe the current status of each.
7. What do we mean when we say the national economic growth is not necessarily tied to increased energy consumption?
8. What are some of the more important business impacts of environmental regulation?

9. Briefly summarize the chief population and migration flows in this country today.
10. Why is the average age of Americans increasing?
11. Why are more women working today than ever before?
12. Define consumerism. What are some of the reasons for the rise of consumerism?

DISCUSSION QUESTIONS

1. We discussed six major environmental forces in this chapter. Can you think of any others? What are their likely impacts on business today?
2. How is it that energy conservation can be viewed as a source of energy?
3. The increased cost of fuel supplies obviously affects manufacturing firms by raising production costs. The result is higher prices for finished goods. But how do you think increased fuel costs affect service firms? Give an example.
4. What are some of the economic arguments against tough environmental laws? Do you think that this country can afford the price tag for clean air and clean water?
5. The rise of the Sunbelt is one of the biggest demographic stories of the 1970s. What are some of the reasons for its sudden emergence?

CASE 2-1

The Decker Hotel

The Decker Hotel was built in the late 1800s in the downtown area of a Texas city. It was elaborately furnished with stone carvings, antique doors, valuable furniture, and a superb bar and restaurant. It operated profitably and was regarded highly by citizens and business travelers for nearly a century. Then more modern hotels began to draw business away from the Decker.

In 1955, a subsidiary of Blackwell and Greene, a construction company, purchased the Decker. For the next 15 years, attempts were made to renovate the hotel and to improve its profitability. Profits, however, continued to sag. The hotel was closed in 1968 after several years of substantial losses.

A group of local businesses and citizens banded together to form the Decker Hotel Corporation. They aimed to reopen the hotel and preserve it as a historic landmark. They planned and carried out a three-year complete renovation program and hired competent management to run the hotel. Once it was operating successfully, the hotel was sold first to an airline and then in 1980 to Lamont Hotels, a California-based investors' group. The goal of each owner was the same: to operate a luxury-class historical hotel profitably.

Like other U.S. cities, this city in Texas experienced many changes during the 1970s and early 1980s. Many people were moving there to be in the Sunbelt. Land prices rose dramatically. When new firms moved to the city, they bought land and built factories in outlying areas. The city soon became a 30-mile urban tract along the interstate highway. Stores and shopping malls followed the people who followed their employers—to the suburbs. The downtown area became rundown because the malls took the business of the central business district.

But the downtown area was still the site of many banks and government office buildings. The Hanis Hotel chain—a profitable and respected chain of luxury hotels—decided to locate a new hotel and convention center just across the river from the Decker—less than a mile away. The convention center boasted saunas, swimming pools, exercise rooms, a running trail, large convention rooms, and a wide variety of other services. The Decker faced new and tougher competition.

1. How could demographic shifts have helped the Decker?
2. How did demographic shifts actually hurt the Decker?
3. How might the Decker have avoided the problems it now faces?
4. List as many different sources of the Decker's current problems that you can find in its environment—both past and present.

CASE 2-2

Global Marine, Inc.

One of the most significant changes in the environment of business in this century has been the oil crisis of the last two decades. Starting with the first oil embargo by the OPEC countries in 1973, American oil companies began a frantic search for more domestic oil.

To serve the oil companies, a large number of oil-field suppliers sprang up. These suppliers manufactured oil-well pipe, steam generators, derricks, oil pumps, oil-transport pipeline, and countless other kinds of oil-field equipment. The richest of these companies went into the risky business of manufacturing offshore oil rigs. One such company was Global Marine, Inc.

Global Marine grew very rapidly through the first few years of the oil shortages. In 1981, Global started a $3 billion expansion program. Global decided to buy 24 jack-up rigs—or off shore rigs which settled on the ocean floor in shallow areas. These rigs were designed particularly for the Gulf of Mexico and cost $40 million apiece.

Just as Global started to sign contracts to have these rigs built, American oil companies began experiencing an oversupply of oil. Unable to sell enough oil, and forced to purchase large quantities of oil under contract from various foreign countries, the last thing they wanted to do was spend money on more oil-well exploration in the United States. Global was hard-hit.

Global now has 16 rigs that it is obligated to buy at a cost of about $1 billion. It has drilling contracts for only three of them. Plans for 1984 call for only 28 percent of Global's drilling rigs to be in use. The outlook is about the same for 1985. In particular, Global is hurt by its collection of jack-up rigs, as are many firms in the industry. As a result, even when oil companies start leasing oil rigs again, they will be able to bargain for very low prices. Consequently, profits for oil-rig companies will be depressed or nonexistent. Meanwhile, Global has $562 million in long-term debts and is worth only a bit over $400 million on paper.

Recently, oil-field suppliers have laid off workers by the thousands. Research and development has come to a standstill. All the suppliers are deep in debt, and many are failing. Global is a little better off than others, but it, too, is feeling the pinch.

1. What did Global fail to see in its environment that caused its current problems?
2. Even though energy supplies are in constant demand, why have the oil-field suppliers such as Global been so dramatically affected by their environment?
3. Explain how you would analyze energy demand and supply, were you an executive at Global, in order to predict the changes in oil company demand for offshore oil rigs.
4. Given the current attitude in the United States toward nuclear generation of energy, how do you think oil-field suppliers now see their future?

3

Social Responsibility of Business

After studying this chapter, you should be able to:

- Define social responsibility.
- Explain four views concerning the social responsibility of business.
- Identify parties to whom business may have social responsibilities.
- Identify benefits and costs of social actions.
- Explain the social audit.
- Discuss business ethics.
- Cite some notable corporate social actions.

Celanese, a chemical company, recently gave the National Audubon Society $400,000 for research on the Atlantic puffin, the California condor, and other endangered bird species. Aetna Life and Casualty, an insurance firm, provided nearly $6 million in grants in a single year for such varied purposes as publishing a bilingual community newspaper, supporting a program of legal aid for female criminal offenders, and expanding a news service for American Indians. Shell Oil contributed $2 million for testing Interferon, an antiviral drug which may be effective against cancer.

The Atlantic puffin, criminal offenders, and cancer research might seem unlikely concerns for these businesses. Undoubtedly, though, the companies saw their contributions as entirely appropriate. If pressed for a justification for such actions, they would all probably offer the same response: social responsibility. We'll begin this chapter by defining social responsibility.

SOCIAL RESPONSIBILITY DEFINED

Social responsibility of business reflects business' concern for the social and economic effects of its decisions. Socially responsible behavior is demonstrated through a company's willingness to incur a cost that does not relate directly to the company's production of goods and services. Socially responsible actions are not undertaken to improve profit performance (at least in the short run), but to meet some social need or solve some social problem. Such actions might range from voluntarily controlling smokestack emissions to building a little league baseball diamond in a neighborhood park. As we'll see, many companies now define their social responsibilities quite broadly. They are showing concern for issues and groups that traditionally fell outside their domain.

SOME VIEWS ON SOCIAL RESPONSIBILITY

Although nearly everyone agrees that business should contribute to social well-being, there is much less agreement as to *how* that can best be done. Let's examine some differing views of this complex and important question.

The Classical View

The economist Adam Smith wrote in 1776 that businesses contribute to the greater good of society when they act in their own best interest. This **classical view** of business is sometimes called the "invisible hand." According to this view, when a firm produces goods and services in the most profitable way possible, it is guided as if by an "invisible hand" to use society's material and human resources responsibly and wisely. As a result, there will be greater social welfare for all. Any action not in the self-interest of the firm works against the invisible hand and reduces the good to the community.

Arguments in Favor of the Classical View. Defenders of the invisible hand, or classical, view of business would argue first that harm will result if a business tries to achieve any end except its own well-being. Classical thinkers believe that business has an implied contract with society to use resources effectively—or to use resources to promote the business, which in turn promotes society. If a business specifically begins to spend time and money directly on some social issue, such as sponsoring a drug rehabilitation program, then business will be breaking the contract to use its resources for itself.

Second, classical thinkers believe that the voting public, not the people in business, should set social priorities. If the public wants certain social problems solved, then the public should work through the legislature for the passage of appropriate laws. Letting businesses set social priorities takes power away from the majority and gives it to the few.

Finally, the supporters of the classical view might argue that social issues are better handled by expert social planners than by companies. Business managers should stick to what they know: running businesses.

Arguments Against the Classical View. According to its many critics, the classical view of the role of business in society is based on narrow thinking and outdated assumptions. The classical view, the critics say, assumes that individual firms have no market power and no control over prices. This is nothing more than a description of perfect competition as discussed in Chapter 1. Perfect competition, you will remember, is more of an ideal than a reality.

The classical view also assumes that businesses can stay healthy in a sick society. But in reality, say critics, the pace of industrial activity places a great deal of stress on the environment and on the emotional and physical health of

Sponsoring youth activities is one way for firms to fulfill their social responsibilities.

workers. In the long run, can a firm operate profitably if clean air and water are scarce? Or if the work force deteriorates because of health problems?

The strongest argument against the classical view is that it does not acknowledge that society has certain expectations as to how businesses should act. In fact, these expectations go beyond those set down in law. Society is made up of organizations—corporations, nonprofit groups, churches—as much as it is made up of people. Just as the actions of individuals affect society, so do the actions of organizations. Therefore, if we expect socially responsible behavior from individuals, why not expect the same from organizations?

Three Current Views

Most people today don't believe that businesses should stick just to economic goals. But people do disagree as to why firms should actively consider social issues in their business planning. We can identify three views on this question. The proponents of these views are called foreboders, constrainers, and demanders.[1]

Foreboders. **Foreboders** believe that businesses must contribute to social improvement; otherwise, social problems will worsen and government will be forced to step in. Promoting such social improvement was the goal of the 51-company partnership, including the Ford Motor Company and several life insurance firms, which backed the Detroit Renaissance Center. The Renaissance Center, built in a decaying section of the Detroit waterfront, has the world's largest hotel and four massive office buildings. Foreboders would see such urban renewal as a wise and forward-thinking move.

Constrainers. **Constrainers** view business enterprises as essentially indifferent to the social consequences of their actions or feel that businesses tend to act irresponsibly unless constrained by legal and political means. This group calls for strict laws to govern product safety, advertising, pollution, and competitive practices.

Demanders. **Demanders** hold that businesses must act responsibly because of their resources and power, and that the public has a right to expect a level of social involvement that is in proportion to the amount of power held. Corporations should use some of their resources to satisfy social ends. Using company resources to protect endangered species or to further cancer research, even though these activities may not lead to increased profits, would be viewed as appropriate by demanders. Since big companies operate in our society, society can demand socially responsible behavior in return.

---

[1] R.J. Aldag and D.W. Jackson, Jr., "Assessment of Attitudes Toward Social Responsibilities," *Journal of Business Administration*, Vol. 8, No. 2 (1977), pp. 65-80.

INTERESTED GROUPS

In considering its responsibilities to society, business must weigh the interests of many groups. Some of these groups are shown in Figure 3-1 and are discussed in this section.

Shareholders

Shareholders are the owners of a firm. In light of this, we might expect that their interests are always given the highest priority. In fact, though, the managers of corporations often take actions that are not in the best interest of shareholders. Shareholders generally have little influence over the day-to-day management of their companies. Later in this chapter, the benefits and costs of social actions to shareholders will be examined separately.

Consumers

Consumers are an important societal group toward whom businesses must behave responsibly. One listing of consumer rights was expressed by President Kennedy in 1962:

- The right to choose from a range of brands of products and services.
- The right to be informed of important facts about a product or service, such as quality, health hazards, and durability.
- The right to be heard by business and government, to make complaints or suggestions, and to ask questions.
- The right to be safe when using products or services.

As discussed in Chapter 2, the **consumerism** movement sprang up in the 1960s to help guarantee these rights for consumers. The failure to consider consumer rights may be not only irresponsible, but also economically disastrous.

Johnson & Johnson showed its concern for consumer safety by recalling all of its Extra-Strength Tylenol capsules from the market. The recall was prompted by the seven poisoning deaths caused by someone introducing cyanide into Tylenol capsules. Although Johnson & Johnson was not responsible, it redesigned the Tylenol package to prevent this from happening again. The total cost to the company of the recall and the package redesign was $100 million.

Many other companies have conducted massive recall campaigns because of safety or quality considerations. Firestone Tire & Rubber, for instance, recalled 400,000 steelbelted radial tires because some tires failed high-speed tests. Firestone was later fined $500,000 because of its delay in notifying the government of the faulty tires. Procter & Gamble removed Rely tampons from the market one week after learning that the tampons had been linked with toxic-shock syndrome. It ran ads warning women not to use Rely, and it offered to buy back all Rely tampons, even those received as free samples.

Employees

Of course, firms should protect the health and safety of their employees. Occidental Petroleum closed the pesticide unit of one of its chemical plants when several male workers in the unit were found to be sterile. In a case against the Manville Corporation, maker of asbestos products, a Los Angeles Superior Court jury awarded a former shipyard worker $1.2 million in compensation. The worker had contracted asbestosis, a lung ailment caused by inhaling the asbestos fibers. Manville, as well as other firms in the same industry, is facing hundreds of other damage suits across the country.

Figure 3-1

Parties to Which Business Must Be Responsible

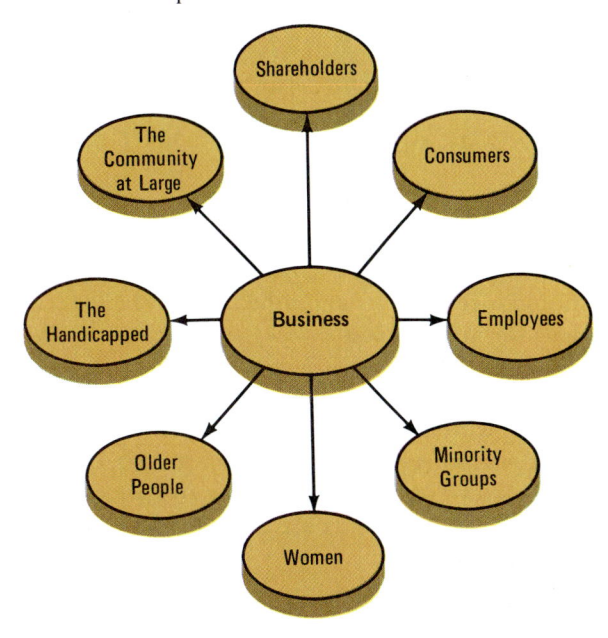

Some Notable Corporate Social Actions

A strong social conscience, when joined with the financial strength of U.S. industry, can contribute to the solution of many of our most pressing social problems. Consider the following examples:

- Time, Inc., the nation's largest magazine publisher, donated 2,138 acres of land in Texas to the Nature Conservancy for use as a nature sanctuary. The land is of great ecological significance, harboring 340 species of wildflowers.
- The Fingerhut Corporation, a Minnesota direct-mail marketing company, reimburses employees for cab fares when they take a taxi home rather than driving while intoxicated. The company also gave smoke detectors to its 2,600 employees for installation in their homes.
- New England Mutual Life Insurance Company pays all tuition costs to degree-granting institutions for its home-office employees. About two hundred, or 10 percent, of these employees are enrolled in such institutions.
- In 1980, Robert Woodruff, retired chairman of the Coca-Cola company, gave $100 million in Coca-Cola stock to Emory University in Atlanta. This was the largest single gift in the history of American philanthropy.
- Safeway Stores, the nation's largest supermarket chain, has a specially designed shopping cart for customers in wheelchairs. The cart clamps firmly to the wheelchair for easy maneuverability. There is at least one cart in each of Safeway's 2,000 stores.
- The Ore-Ida Division of the H.J. Heinz company, a major food processor, is currently testing a solar heating system for cooking french fries. The system promises to save 500,000 cubic feet of natural gas a year.

More generally, it is believed that companies should offer salaries and other employee benefits that are appropriate to the work performed as well as to the skill, knowledge, and training of the worker. Many companies also share their good fortune with their employees. When Apple Computer had an especially good quarter in 1981, it gave each of its 2,500 employees an extra week's vacation. Such benefits are a great boost for employee morale.

Minority Groups

Certain minority groups have been treated unfairly in the past. Some groups, blacks and Hispanics, for example, have been easily identifiable targets for discrimination in hiring and promotion. Several laws now help to prevent discrimination and, in some cases, attempt to make up for past discrimination. Dean Witter Reynolds, a stock brokerage firm, agreed to make payments of $1.8 million to Hispanic, black, and female brokers who applied to or worked for the company from 1976 through 1981. These people had been discriminated against in hiring and promotion decisions. The company was also required to establish a $2.8 million affirmative action program. The purpose of this program was to place minority persons in brokerage positions.

Women

Until fairly recently, most working women were employed as secretaries, nurses, teachers, receptionists, and retail sales clerks. Very few women held professional or managerial jobs. Now, more and more women are pursuing careers in these areas. Federal law requires that businesses make a serious effort to recruit and retain female employees, as well as to treat them fairly. Otherwise, the businesses risk potentially serious legal consequences. For example, the Bechtel Corporation, a California engineering firm, settled a sex discrimination case by agreeing to pay $1.3 million in damages to former and current female employees. In another case, American Airlines agreed to rehire 300 flight attendants who had been fired because of pregnancy, and to pay them a total of $2.7 million.

Older People

The average age of the U.S. work force is increasing. The reasons are quite obvious: longer life expectancy, a tapering off of the "baby boom," a greater number of middle-aged women who are working, and a relaxation of mandatory retirement rules.

The protection of the rights of older people in the workplace, therefore, is becoming more important. The Age and Discrimination Act of 1978 specifically prohibits age discrimination. But aside from the law, the attitude of employers is important. It is clear that older employees have valuable skills and abilities. Why should the firm dismiss these skills just because the employee turns 60 or 65? Doing so hurts both the worker and the company.

The Handicapped

It is also believed today that handicapped people can be productive and loyal employees. Accordingly, business firms have begun to act more responsibly in hiring and promoting the handicapped. Ability, not disability, is what matters. It is likewise the responsibility of businesses to see that curbs, stairways, and similar obstacles do not prevent handicapped people from doing their jobs properly.

The Community at Large

Many laws and watchdog groups now protect society from the potentially disruptive actions of business. One area of special concern, as we saw in the last chapter, is environmental protection. U.S. Steel settled a lengthy dispute with the Environmental Protection Agency by agreeing to spend $400 million in air and water pollution cleanup at its plants in Pittsburgh. Fines and negative publicity require that firms be especially careful about the effect of their actions on the environment and on other aspects of community life.

Businesses operate in a highly diversified society; they affect many social and economic groups and are affected by these groups in turn. It is clear that a company manager must have a wide range of abilities and an open mind to be successful in such a setting.

BENEFITS AND COSTS OF SOCIAL ACTIONS

Is social responsibility good for business? We'll approach this question from the perspective of the benefits and costs of socially responsible actions.

Benefits

A company may benefit directly and indirectly by taking socially responsible actions. One obvious benefit is improved employee motivation. Employees are likely to be more satisfied at work if they believe that their company actively contributes to community life.

Other benefits occur in the marketplace. By showing a genuine interest in social needs, a firm may become more aware of changing consumer tastes and preferences. It may spot new product opportunities in an area such as solar power generation or low-cost building materials for inner-city construction projects. The socially responsible company *may* find that its products and services are in demand simply because consumers recognize and appreciate such companies. These benefits relate directly to increased sales revenue and profitability.

Just as consumers favor the products of responsible firms, so might investors prefer the stocks of such firms. The company with a highly visible social program may find that its stock sells at a higher market price.

In the long run, socially responsible actions by business may eliminate the need for legislative controls on business activity. These controls regulate what the company can and cannot do. Such controls often cost the firm more in lost business opportunities than the socially responsible actions would have cost.

Being socially responsible also means protecting the environment.

Control Data is one company that recognizes the benefits of socially responsible actions. It has invested millions of dollars in such projects as redeveloping rundown neighborhoods, assisting small farmers, and providing computer-based education systems. According to its statement of corporate mission, Control Data is "a worldwide corporation committed to a strategy of addressing society's major needs as profitable business opportunities."

Costs

Although social responsibility may be cheaper than government controls, social responsibility is not without its costs. The most obvious cost is the money spent in support of social projects. A $50,000 grant to a community theater group is $50,000 that is no longer available for financing plant expansion. By diverting cash away from profitable investment opportunities, the company is not maximizing shareholder wealth. With goals less clearly defined, it may be difficult to distinguish between good and bad management. In the long run, therefore, the market price of the stock of socially responsible companies may just as easily fall as rise.

A second cost relates to the issue of competitive parity. A company may stay on equal footing with its competitors if all of the companies support several social projects; but a company which alone supports such projects *may* lose business if its competitors use their surplus resources to strengthen their competitive positions. One firm commissions an immense metal sculpture for the downtown civic center, while the others modernize their telemarketing systems. Who is likely to lose out in the scramble for new accounts?

Finally, it is possible that government may step in and regulate the private provision of social services and programs. Private companies traditionally have served society by providing goods, services, jobs, and a return on investment to shareholders. Venturing into this new area of social "product," well-intentioned companies may find that their actions bring forth more government regulation.

Comparing Benefits and Costs

Are the benefits of a proposed set of corporate social programs greater than the costs? How does the decision maker proceed? If we could clearly measure benefits and costs in terms of dollars, then the answer to this question would be easy: Implement the proposed programs if total benefits exceed total cost; rethink the programs if they do not. But this is an area lacking simple answers. Many factors affect the comparison of benefits and costs. Among them are the actions of competitors, possible government controls, the amount of cash on hand, and the "visibility" of the social programs themselves.

The U.S. Steel case mentioned earlier in this chapter provides a good illustration of how difficult these decisions can be. Pollution controls at the company's mills would produce an undeniable benefit of cleaner air to people living nearby. But the costs are undeniable too. Not only is there the cost of installing and operating the pollution control equipment, but also there are the costs involved in depressed output, lost jobs, and higher steel prices. If you ran U.S. Steel, what would you do? Would U.S. Steel itself be better off with the pollution control equipment in place?

THE SOCIAL AUDIT

Our discussion so far has focused on the many issues involved with corporate responsibility and on the problems of evaluating the performance of these programs. One way to think constructively about these issues and problems is to conduct a social audit.

Who benefits from company-funded scholarships?

CONTROVERSIAL ISSUES

The relationship between business and government has been a tense and unhappy compromise, in which business reluctantly accepts a governmental regulation, while government is chided by voters for failing to control what seem to be excesses by business. Should government set strict social standards for business behavior?

Pro

Yes, the government *should* set strict standards. Those who actually have to bear the final burden of corporate misbehavior are the individual citizens or consumers of America. They have a right to have their desires and demands heard. But clearly, large business won't listen, or we would have had safe cars and decreased pollution long ago. Therefore, the only recourse is government control.

Attention has focused on the dramatic increase in automobile crash deaths attributed to small late-model cars. American automakers have been blamed for delaying installation of special safety devices such as air bags, "slow-crumple" body designs, and seat belts that fasten automatically whenever a passenger is in the car. Why haven't American car manufacturers taken steps to ensure passenger safety?

They don't care, that's why! If the manufacturers are ever to be forced to feature proper safety devices, the government will have to force them. After all, did the American automakers offer to install antipollution equipment before the government required them?

The Government Should Set Strict Social Standards for Business to Obey.

No, businesses will never do the socially responsible thing. As far as they are concerned, social responsibility is an additional expense that cuts their profits. Government *has* to regulate business if the public is to be safe and satisfied.

Con

No, the government *should not* set social standards. It has already proven itself unable to respond to voter wants and has committed some incredible mistakes in the past few years. Let's consider a few examples.

The government formed OSHA, the Occupational Safety and Health Administration, to monitor and correct safety and health problems wherever people are paid to work. The original purpose was to eliminate dangers at industrial worksites and remove potential dangers in other working areas. Accident rates dropped temporarily after OSHA was created, but they have since increased at a rate even faster than before OSHA existed. OSHA makes construction-site vehicles mount beepers to warn workers when the vehicles are backing up, but it also requires the workers to wear earplugs to protect them from the sound, so they can't hear the beepers. A large chemical company had to remount literally thousands of fire extinguishers because they were located one-quarter inch too high to meet OSHA standards. And the paperwork necessary to document even the slightest workplace safety violation or injury is staggering. (One company had to file 17 pages of forms when a secretary's finger was cut on a tape dispenser.) Is this worth the effort?

Other governmental protective agencies have performed equally poorly. For example, we trust the Federal Deposit Insurance Corporation (FDIC) and the Federal Savings and Loan Insurance Corporation (FSLIC), which insure bank and savings and loan savings and checking accounts—yet the FDIC has funds to insure only 2.2 percent of all the bank accounts in the country, and the FSLIC has only enough funds to insure 1.3 percent of all savings and loan deposits. Not impressive!

For every company that is caught polluting the environment or abusing its employees or customers, there are a thousand companies that spend vast sums to improve the social welfare of their communities, and that contribute generously to local service agencies and charities. It is doubtful that most individual citizens in America are as interested in the social welfare of their towns and their people as are most businesses. And do you see a government—*any* government—serving people that well? Remember that every cent the government spends is a cent *you* earned, while the money that companies spend on their local communities and charities is money that *they* earned. So let's leave them alone.

What Is a Social Audit?

A **social audit** is a step-by-step examination of all the activities comprising a firm's social programs. The firm may evaluate its own programs in terms of goals, and it may identify new programs that it ought to pursue. Goals are then formulated for these new programs. The general aim of the social audit is to make management more aware of the impact of corporate actions on society. Figure 3-2 diagrams the social audit for a company evaluating past activities and considering new ones.

Conducting and Reporting on the Social Audit

Conducting a social audit is not easy. There are many difficult questions to be answered: What activities should be audited? How should each activity be evaluated? How should social performance be assessed? These questions generally have to be answered on a case-by-case basis.

Report to Shareholders. More and more companies are reporting on their social activities to shareholders and others. For example, Atlantic Richfield, a diversified resources company, has published three corporate social reports. They are available to anyone requesting a copy. The most recent report, "Participation III," describes Atlantic Richfield's activities in consumer affairs, human-resources management, occupational and environmental protection, energy conservation, philanthropy, and public-policy advocacy. The report presents a comprehensive and generally positive picture of the company's social activities.

Independent Critiques. An impressive aspect of the Atlantic Richfield report is that it also includes independent critiques by outside experts. Although quite favorable in regard to most of Atlantic Richfield's social activities, the critiques are often painfully candid. For example, one critique took the company to task for its all-white, all-male board of directors; its funding of memberships for company executives in private clubs discriminating against Jewish people, racial minorities, and women; and its lack of formal corporate social policies. Another critique pointed out the lack of a specific policy governing corporate donations. The company evaluated these criticisms and brought them to the attention of managers. Since publication of "Participation III," Atlantic Richfield has taken the initial step of adding a woman to its board of directors. Do you think the company will stop there?[2]

---

[2] N. B. Whaley (ed.), *Participation III: Atlantic Richfield and Society* (Los Angeles: Atlantic Richfield and Company).

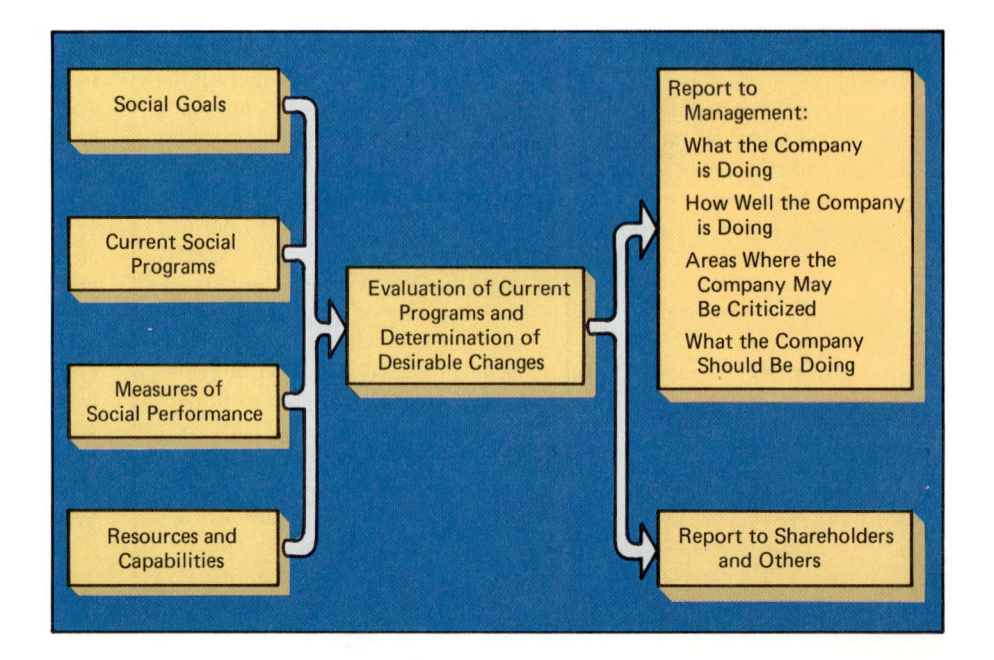

Figure 3-2
The Social Audit

How might sponsorship of the arts benefit a firm and its community?

BUSINESS ETHICS

Ethics are principles of morality or rules of conduct. **Business ethics** are rules about how businesses and their employees ought to behave. Ethical behavior conforms to these rules; unethical behavior violates them.

The Demand for Ethical Behavior

Businesses, governments, and the public are all paying more attention to business ethics. The Foreign Corrupt Practices Act of 1977 requires that companies operate ethically. When such conduct is not forthcoming, the government will use all legal means at its disposal to correct the problem.

Bribes and "kickbacks" have come under particularly close scrutiny lately. A kickback may be seen in the following example:

> A retailer hires a market researcher to find a choice location for a new retail store. The retailer does not know that the researcher has previously agreed to recommend the property of a real estate developer in return for a secret percentage of the first year's rental payment on the property.

Bribery is especially a problem in overseas dealings. The Justice Department conducted a three-year criminal investigation of the Lockheed Corporation's overseas payments. Lockheed subsequently pleaded guilty to charges of concealing payoffs to Japanese business and government officials and was fined $647,000. In another instance, the Brunswick Corporation admitted to the Securities and Exchange Commission that it had paid bribes to two Latin American countries to win contracts. And the Joseph Schlitz Brewing Company faced a 747-count federal indictment for giving kickbacks and other inducements to beer retailers and distributors in exchange for their business. It later agreed to pay a $750,000 penalty in a settlement.

Codes of Ethics

About 80 percent of U.S. companies have a **code of ethics**. Such codes set forth principles of appropriate behavior. For example, the Bank of America's "Code of Corporate Conduct" includes 77 separate items that detail the responsibilities of

FROM THE FILE

Sarah works for a U. S. company that makes household appliances. She manages one of its plants in Sao Paulo, Brazil. Because of a major equipment failure in the plant, Sarah needs to import some machine parts from the United States in a hurry. The home office of her company has a strict policy against paying bribes. But without a small bribe to a local customs official, it may take as long as three months for the needed parts to clear customs. Sarah can't wait that long. Should she pay the bribe or not?

Profile—
Myra McDaniel

When we talk about social responsibility, we often think about what we can do as employees or managers of a company. To some people, however, social responsibility is a concept that occupies their entire lives, to the extent that their jobs and lives are totally devoted to society. Myra McDaniel is such a person.

As a black woman growing up in Philadelphia, Myra was exposed through her family and school to all the influences needed to make her competitive, productive, and successful. After attending the University of Pennsylvania, she worked in the Veterans Administration and the U.S. Aviation Supply Office. In these jobs, she learned how public agencies work and how necessary good business skills are in government work.

McDaniel expanded her experience with administrative jobs at Baldwin Wallace College in Ohio and at Indiana University. She discovered, however, that she needed further education. After considering the alternatives, she decided to pursue a law degree. She graduated in 1975.

The attorney general's office in Texas hired McDaniel, respecting her combination of experience, education, and drive. McDaniel worked her way up to chief of the taxation division by 1979. She broadened her experience further with service as a counsel to the Railroad Commission, an extremely powerful and influential state agency in Texas.

For a brief time, McDaniel entered private practice in Midland, Texas, but her public management skills and her experience were too valuable to ignore. The governor of Texas offered her a position as general counsel to the governor.

In this position, McDaniel is the highest ranked black appointee in the history of Texas government. She reviews legislation, drafts executive orders, coordinates litigation, and advises the governor on recommendations for paroles and pardons and on general legal practices. She is now one of the most powerful voices speaking for social responsibility in the state of Texas.

In her spare time McDaniel, with her husband, hosts freshman athletes at the University of Texas, where she has taught courses in law. She is active in the Austin Black Lawyers Association, the Texas Bar Foundation, the Travis County Women Lawyers' Association, and other legal groups. She has received numerous awards, including a tribute from the City of Austin.

Myra is a strong believer in "putting your money where your mouth is." She welcomes the opportunity to improve life in Texas by working through the state government. Myra exemplifies the ideal of social responsibility: more than just observing its principles in her professional career, she has made it her whole life.

the company and its employees. The code prohibits bribes and kickbacks, and emphasizes the importance of full disclosure to prevent corporate misconduct. McGraw-Hill, Inc., a publishing house, has a "Code of Business Ethics" guaranteeing the privacy of employee personnel and payroll records. The Gulf Oil statement of basic business principles is shown in Figure 3-3.

Encouraging Ethical Behavior

Codes of ethics clarify the meaning of ethical behavior, but they certainly do not guarantee that people act ethically. It's easy for a company to state ethical principles, but it is quite another thing for employees to take the code seriously. Whether employees do so depends largely upon the actions and attitudes of top management. Suppose management tells its employees that bribing overseas clients is against company policy. Suppose further that winning contracts with overseas customers is of primary importance to the business. A few bribes here and there, a few big new contracts, and top management turns the other way. Do you think that the company's official policy against bribery will make much of an impression in such a situation? If management doesn't stand behind the code, who will?

Whistleblowers. Consider now the case of an employee who learns that his or her company engages in bribery or some other illegal activity. The employee can keep quiet, report the incident to top management, or even tell the press about the incident. By going outside the company, the employee is "blowing the whistle." Whistleblowers often may find that their jobs and careers are in jeopardy.[3]

Kermit Vandivier was a technical writer and data analyst at B.F. Goodrich in the 1960s. He knew that someone had tampered with the test results for an aircraft brake. He tried to get his superiors to take action to prevent an air disaster but was told to keep quiet. After finding out that he could be held legally responsible in a conspiracy to defraud, Vandivier went to the Federal Bureau of Investigation and worked undercover. The incident led to a new Department of Defense policy on contractor inspection, testing, and reporting.

Frank Camps was a senior design engineer at Ford Motor Company. He knew that certain crash tests on the Ford Pinto had been manipulated, and that they led to dangerous design changes. Camps argued that these changes made the gas tank more likely to explode in rear-end collisions. His concerns were made known to the company in 1973. A year later Ford demoted him. In 1978, he blew the whistle on Ford and went public with his criticisms. He left the company at age 55, under Ford's early-retirement program.

To some extent, government can protect employees who expose unethical behavior. Michigan has passed a Whistleblowers' Protection

Figure 3-3

The Gulf Oil Statement of Basic Business Principles

> Gulf will adhere rigorously to the highest ethical standards of business conduct. To this end the following specific principles are hereby confirmed as corporate policy, binding on all Gulf employees wherever located:
>
> 1. Gulf's business will be conducted in strict observance of both the letter and the spirit of the applicable law of the land wherever we operate.
> 2. Where a situation is not governed by statute—or where the law is unclear or conflicting—Gulf's business will be conducted in such a manner that we would be proud to have the full facts disclosed.
> 3. In cases of doubt, employees should seek competent legal and other advice, which the company is prepared to make available through regular channels.
> 4. Gulf reaffirms its conviction that in any democratic society proper and constructive participation in the political process is a continuing responsibility of individual citizens and groups of citizens, including Gulf employees and the company itself. Such participation, however, must be in full accord with the regulations, laws, and generally accepted practice of the jurisdiction involved.
>
> Strict adherence to the foregoing principles is hereby made a condition of continued employment.

---

[3] D. D. Cook, "Whistleblowers: Friend or Foe?" *Industry Week* (October 5, 1981), pp. 51-54, 56.

Source: Gulf Oil Corporation, *Human Resource Manual*.

Act. This act makes it illegal for employers in Michigan to threaten, fire, or discriminate against an employee who "reports or is about to report" a suspected violation of the law to a public body.

What Should the Company Do? If a firm is serious about maintaining ethical behavior, it must take concrete actions. First, a company needs to make its code of ethics evident—but only about half of all companies do. Can employees care much about a code that they may never have seen? In addition, companies can make sure that the codes specify procedures for handling violations and that these procedures are fairly enforced. The codes should be revised as the company's product line or competitive practices change.

Besides standing behind the code of ethics and making it available and explicit, a company can encourage ethical behavior with other positive actions. IBM has had a "Speak Up!" program for more than 20 years. This program allows an employee to appeal any supervisory action and to get a mailed response to the appeal without having the employee's name communicated to the supervisor. A meeting between the employee and management is arranged if necessary. Unfortunately, few companies have such internal programs for resolving ethical conflicts.

Other corporations have review committees made up of people specially trained to deal with ethical issues. These committees are composed of people from both inside and outside the company. The committee's role is to advise directors on sensitive ethical matters.

Ethics training is a part of some management development programs. The training usually includes discussions among the program participants of real problems that they have faced in their work. Alternative ways of dealing with each problem are then explored.

SUMMARY POINTS

1. Social responsibility reflects business' concern for the social and economic effects of its decisions.
2. The classical view of social responsibility is that the pursuit of profits results in the greatest social welfare for all.
3. Besides the classical view, there are at least three other views on the question of social responsibility. The proponents of these views are called foreboders, constrainers, and demanders.
4. Ideally, businesses should be responsible to many social groups: shareholders, consumers, employees, minority groups, women, older people, the handicapped, as well as to the community at large.
5. Socially responsible behavior means both benefits and costs for a firm. The benefits and costs of a proposed social action should be carefully weighed in the light of both economic and societal impacts.
6. Many companies now conduct social audits, which are step-by-step examinations of all activities, current and proposed, making up a firm's social program.
7. The aim of the social audit is to make management more aware of the impact of corporate actions on society.
8. Business ethics are principles of morality or rules of conduct about how businesses and their employees ought to behave.
9. U.S. corporations currently engage in a variety of socially responsible actions, ranging from energy conservation to charitable donations and consumer safety.

KEY TERMS AND CONCEPTS

social responsibility
classical view
foreboders
constrainers
demanders
shareholders
consumerism
social audit
business ethics
code of ethics
whistleblower

REVIEW QUESTIONS

1. What do we mean by "social responsibility"? Give a few examples of socially responsible actions.
2. Briefly explain the classical view of social responsibility.

3. How do foreboders, constrainers, and demanders view the question of social responsibility?
4. Name some of the social groups to whom businesses owe responsibility.
5. In what sense are businesses responsible to their employees? To minority groups? To women?
6. Give an example of a "kickback."
7. What is a code of ethics?
8. How can firms encourage ethical behavior among their employees?

DISCUSSION QUESTIONS

1. What are the chief shortcomings of the classical view of social responsibility?
2. Are the health of society and the health of individual businesses related? Explain.
3. Do you think that it is immoral for extremely profitable firms not to engage in such socially responsible actions as giving to charities and sponsoring community development projects? Support your view.
4. What are some of the potential benefits and costs of installing expensive pollution control equipment at production facilities? Consider both the company's and society's point of view.
5. Why should a firm undertake a social audit?

CASE 3-1

Ford Foundation

Edsel and Henry Ford created the Ford Foundation in 1936 and endowed it with $25,000. This money was invested and the returns on the investments were paid out to needy institutions such as charities and colleges. When Edsel and Henry died, their estates provided large amounts of money to the Ford Foundation. All their wealth had come from their ownership of the Ford Motor Company and was, in essence, a contribution from the company.

The Ford Foundation has given over $5 billion in grants to more than 7,000 schools, charities, and other organizations in the United States and in 96 foreign countries. In the last 15 years, it has supplied more than $2.6 billion for public broadcasting systems, fine arts projects, the environmentalist movement, and causes favoring America's poor.

In the 1960s, the Ford Foundation realized the danger posed by school racial segregation in the United States. It led the school desegregation fight in New York and supported civil rights issues throughout the country. When dividends on investments didn't bring in enough money to meet the needs of civil rights campaigns and other causes the Foundation championed, it actually sold its assets to keep its support going.

When the federal government began to help in many of the projects that the Ford Foundation had initially supported, the Foundation shifted its emphasis to more immediate urban problems. More attention was given to people in America who were starving or ill, to the problems of energy costs for the poor and elderly, and to programs to help the unemployed.

Ford Foundation elected its first black president, Franklin Thomas, in 1979. Thomas has been successful in working for the equality of blacks and women—the two population groups that the Foundation has tried to support most heavily in recent years. Thomas has hired more blacks and women to high posts in the Foundation, and has actively promoted higher education for them.

Throughout the world, the equality of humankind has become the goal of the Ford Foundation. In many countries, the name Ford is better known for the efforts of the Foundation than for Ford's automobile. And in the United States, almost every city owes something to the Ford Foundation. Nearly every charity, fine arts organization, and activist group has been helped by the Foundation at one time or another. It is an enviable record.

1. Why do companies like Ford want to support social organizations like the Ford Foundation? Why is it beneficial for Ford to support the Ford Foundation?
2. Write a social audit for Ford, describing the efforts of the Ford Foundation.
3. Why was it helpful to Ford to name the Ford Foundation after the company and the family behind it? Why was "Ford Foundation" a better name than, say, "American Philanthropy Union"?

CASE 3-2

Manville Corporation

Manville Corporation, once known as Johns-Manville Corporation, was the Western world's largest producer and supplier of asbestos. Asbestos was used as a crucial component of insulation for 50 years. Ships in World War II, for example, required extensive asbestos insulation around their steam pipes and boilers. Countless schools, city halls, and private homes have insulation and ceiling materials made of asbestos.

In 1964, government-sponsored studies revealed that asbestos insulation released very small quantities of asbestos fibers which could be inhaled by people. These fibers could lodge in lung tissue and cause irritation leading to serious lung disease many years later.

The Manville Corporation was financially healthy in 1981. It reported a net worth of $1.1 billion with short-term debts of only $102 million and long-term debts of only $499 million. For a company Manville's size, those figures were quite admirable. In 1981, Manville earned $60.3 million in profits after taxes.

But today, thousands of people are suing Manville on the basis of asbestos-caused lung disease. By mid-1982, Manville already faced 16,500 lawsuits. New lawsuits were arising at a rate of 500 a month. Of the lawsuits already taken to court, Manville had settled about 3,500, at about $40,000 per claim. In the cases Manville lost in court, it was having to pay an average of $616,000 per claim. Accounting standards required that a company facing a large lawsuit claim declare a liability (or debt) for the amount it expected to have to pay. Consultants estimated that the company would eventually face 52,000 lawsuits, worth about $2 billion. Manville declared bankruptcy.

Declaring bankruptcy stopped all legal action against Manville by both regular creditors and the asbestos victims suing the company. A special bankruptcy judge, appointed to handle Manville's case, would decide all further asbestos cases.

Manville was faced with an impossible situation. It felt a responsibility to its customers, to the asbestos victims, and to its stockholders. It also felt an obligation to its regular creditors, its employees, other industry corporations, and the general public.

1. Identify the interested groups in this case. How might each group have been concerned with the outcome of Manville's struggles?
2. How far do you think Manville Corporation's social responsibility extended? Do you think Manville had an obligation to sell itself out to pay the asbestos victims? Would this have been fair to its employees? its stockholders?
3. What kind of social audit would Manville write for the year of its bankruptcy? Write an audit reflecting Manville's failure to meet the claims of its asbestos victims. Write another audit reflecting Manville's attempts to be responsible to everyone, even though asbestos victims might not get the amount of compensation they desired.

2 Business Organization and Government

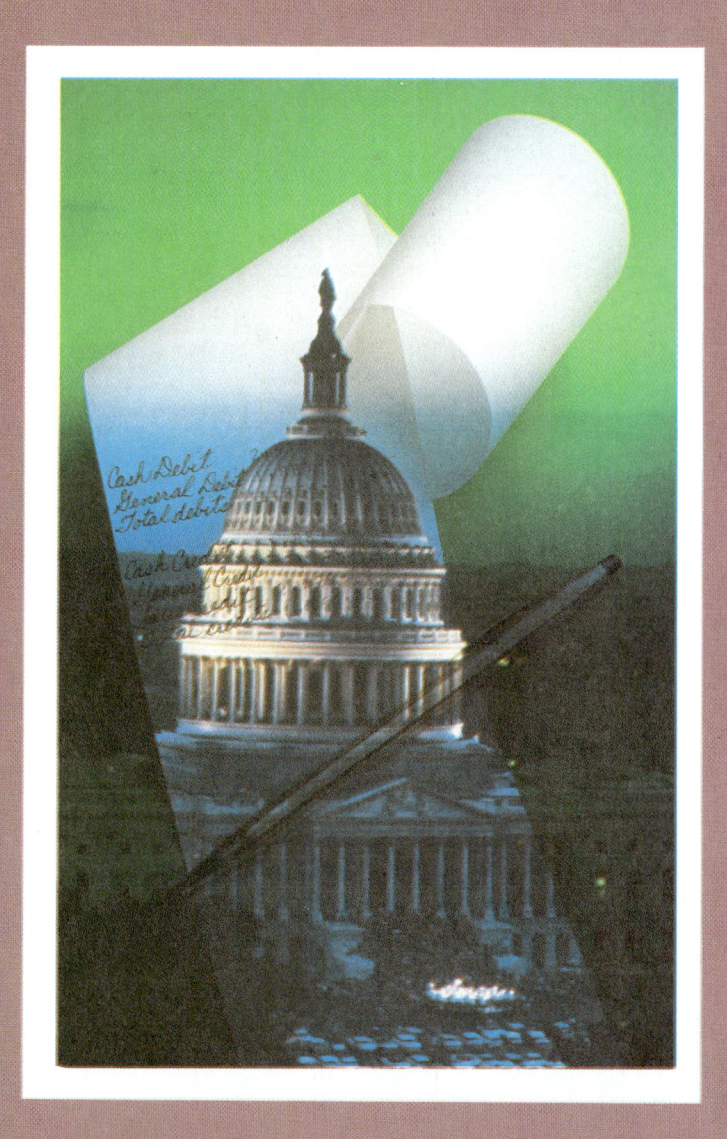

4

Forms of Ownership

After studying this chapter, you should be able to:

- Evaluate the importance of the three forms of ownership in our economy today.
- Discuss the features of a sole proprietorship as well as its advantages and disadvantages.
- Discuss the features of a partnership as well as its advantages and disadvantages.
- Discuss the features of a corporation as well as its advantages and disadvantages.
- Explain the differences among four types of mergers.

The private ownership of business is an essential characteristic of our economic system. Private commercial ownership generally takes one of three legal forms: the sole proprietorship, the partnership, or the corporation. Business enterprises range in size from a single person providing a service such as free-lance writing to a giant multinational corporation such as General Motors.

Must a business be big to provide a good product or service?

AN OVERVIEW OF BUSINESS OWNERSHIP

Figure 4-1 provides a view of the importance of each ownership form. Note that sole proprietorships make up 77 percent of all business concerns in the United States. But in terms of total earnings, proprietorships are responsible for only 18 percent. Corporations, on the other hand, account for 15 percent of business concerns, but 77 percent of all earnings!

Each year many new businesses open their doors, and many others close theirs. Figure 4-2 shows the rate of new incorporation through the 1970s. Notice how the rate increased steadily through the decade. Not surprisingly, the failure rate of business tends to be high when the economy is not performing well. To illustrate, the failure rate went up 55.2 percent in 1980 as the economy fell into a recession.

Now we're ready to look more closely at the three basic forms of ownership. We'll start with the sole proprietorship.

SOLE PROPRIETORSHIPS

Bonnie Klein graduated from St. Louis Community College, where she majored in business administration. Bonnie paid for her education by working part-time at a local McDonald's restaurant. After studying further at Washington University, she accepted an assistant manager position at a Burger King. She worked there for three years. But Bonnie wanted to be her own boss. She liked to make decisions for herself and she wanted to keep the profits of her labors. There was only one thing to do—start a business of her own.

Bonnie withdrew $4,000 from her savings account and borrowed another $5,000 from her bank. She used this money to open a hamburger stand called Bonnie's Hamburger Palace. Bonnie was set: She was owner, manager, waitress, and cook. At this point, Bonnie had a **sole proprietorship**—or a business owned by only one person.

There are no real legal obstacles to overcome in a sole proprietorship, so it was easy for Bonnie to begin. She needed a health certificate so she could serve food, a tax account number from the city so she could pay her city taxes, and a Missouri Employment Commission tax number so she could pay her unemployment compensation tax for her employees. It was so simple that Bonnie could start her business without the assistance of a lawyer.

Features of Sole Proprietorships

In most sole proprietorships, the owner also acts as manager and, as such, makes all the decisions. After all, it is the owner's money and livelihood that are at stake. In the case of Bonnie's Hamburger Palace, these decisions might include ordering food items, keeping the books current,

Figure 4-1

Ownership Structure of the U.S. Economy, 1977

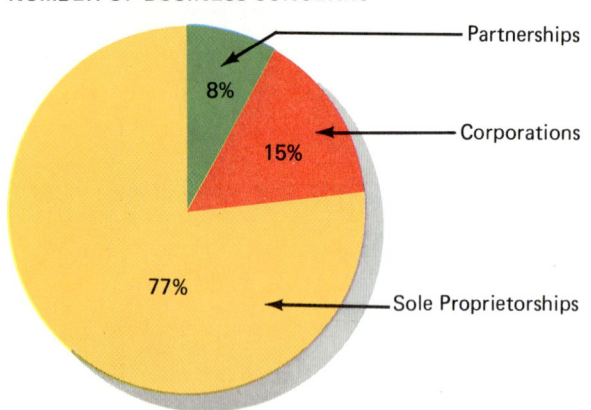

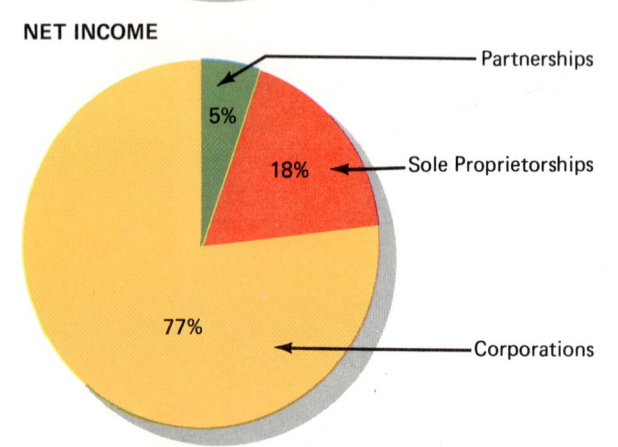

NUMBER OF BUSINESS CONCERNS

- Partnerships: 8%
- Corporations: 15%
- Sole Proprietorships: 77%

NET INCOME

- Partnerships: 5%
- Sole Proprietorships: 18%
- Corporations: 77%

Source: U.S. Department of Commerce, Bureau of the Census, *Statistical Abstract of the United States* (1981).

and supervising employees. Some sole proprietorships, however, are large enough that the owner can hire a professional manager to handle the day-to-day operations of the business.

Advantages of Sole Proprietorships

The sole proprietorship offers many advantages. Let's take a look at a few of them, noting that they are best understood when seen in relation to a partnership and a corporation, which are discussed later in more detail.

Minimal Capital Requirements. One advantage of a sole proprietorship is that it does not require much capital. This was shown in our example—Bonnie needed only $9,000 to begin operations.

Ginny's, a very successful printing and copying business in Austin, Texas, began operations with little more than a rented copying machine and one month's rent.

Control. Another advantage is that a sole owner has complete control over the business. The owner does not have to worry about whether partners or stockholders are happy. There is no one to question such decisions as staying open until midnight or closing out a particular product. The rewards of a good decision, and the losses from a bad one, belong only to the owner.

Tax Savings. The sole proprietorship also offers a tax advantage. The owner pays taxes only on the income earned from the business. If the Hamburger Palace made $12,000 after all expenses were paid, then $12,000 would be Bonnie's taxable personal income. Later in this chapter, we will see that corporations pay taxes on the income they make. Then the stockholders pay taxes on the dividends they receive. This form of double taxation does not apply to sole proprietorships.

Confidentiality. Sole proprietors, unlike stock corporations, are not required by law to disclose

Figure 4-2

New Incorporations 1970-1980

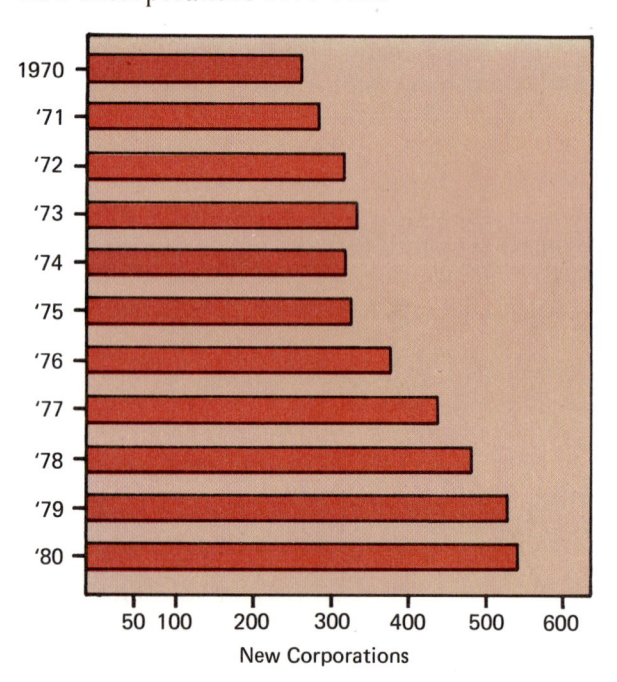

[Bar chart showing New Corporations by year from 1970 to 1980, x-axis: 50, 100, 200, 300, 400, 500, 600 New Corporations]

Source: U.S. Department of Commerce, Bureau of Economic Analysis.

financial information to the public. No one needs to know how much money Bonnie made last year except the Internal Revenue Service. However, most lenders require some sort of financial disclosure before making a loan. Without a detailed financial picture of the business, a lender has no way of knowing whether the borrower can afford to pay back the loan. When Bonnie borrowed $5,000 from her banker, she had to present a written estimate of how much money her business would make in each of the next five years. Bonnie had to show that the business could produce enough cash to repay the loan and the interest charges.

Disadvantages of Sole Proprietorships

If a sole proprietorship had no drawbacks, there would be no reason for partnerships and corporations. Let's look at a few of its disadvantages.

Unlimited Liability. **Unlimited liability** means that the business is not separate or distinct, in any legal sense, from the person who owns it. It is the owner, not the business itself, who is legally liable in the case of accident or injury involving a customer. Bonnie Klein *is* Bonnie's Hamburger Palace. The debts of the business are her debts. A customer who chokes on one of Bonnie's catfish burgers can sue Bonnie for all her business and personal assets. Unlimited liability is the most significant disadvantage of a sole proprietorship. It is the reason most entrepreneurs incorporate when their businesses get big enough.

Limited Management Talent. A second problem with sole proprietorships is that they draw upon only a limited amount of management talent or expertise. The business is successful or not depending on the skill and good judgment of the owner. Paid consultants can be helpful, but they are expensive.

Also, the fact that the owner makes all the decisions can slow the growth of the business. One person can do only so much. Often, profitable opportunities cannot be pursued because the owner is already working 12 to 15 hours a day. Only about 7 percent of all sole proprietorships in the United States ever earn more than $100,000 in profits per year.

Why do so many people wish to have their own businesses?

Credit Availability. Sole proprietorships face the problem of limited credit. Banks prefer to lend their money to big corporations since corporations are stronger financially. This makes them better credit risks. When banks lend money to sole proprietorships, they usually charge a high rate of interest. The extra few interest points act as compensation to the banker for accepting the risk involved in such a loan. The interest rate on Bonnie's loan was 21.5 percent per year; large companies at that time were paying only 15 percent. In addition, Bonnie was required to repay the loan in full within four years. A larger business ordinarily would be given a longer period of time to repay its loan.

Instability. Finally, sole proprietorships are not stable. If the owner becomes sick or dies, the business usually fails. Although some sole proprietorships are passed down from one generation of a family to the next, many others simply disappear when the owner is not able to continue.

PARTNERSHIPS

Bonnie was so successful with her Hamburger Palace that she had to expand. A second restaurant on the other side of town and a food

CONTROVERSIAL ISSUES

Corporations! Do They Hold a Bright Future for Investors?

The sheer size of major American corporations is enough to scare away many individual investors. Even those who aren't scared away feel powerless to shape company goals and performance. Many investors are asking if large corporations still provide good investment opportunities.

Pro

Yes, large corporations are good investments. They offer investors the easiest way to gain a stake in America's economy at reasonable cost and with relatively little risk. Investors know that the large company will probably have a much greater effect on America's economy as a whole than will a small new business. Furthermore, no big company is likely to put itself in a position where it faces great risks. A new business, however, almost invariably faces severe risks for its first few years of operation.

One special group of investors is a company's employees. In recent years, we have seen numerous examples of companies in which productivity is improved dramatically after employees acquire part ownership of the company. Ownership of shares in the company seems to motivate employees to want their company to succeed, so they work harder and produce more. Additionally, with labor unions and other kinds of cooperative employee programs, an employee-investor doesn't have to own a lot of stock. When all employee-investor votes are combined, the group can significantly affect corporate decisions. Companies like Lincoln Electric, for example, have shown amazing growth and success specifically because employees owned shares in the company.

Ownership—even of a very small portion—of a large company means that you own something that will probably change value as inflation occurs. Hopefully, that value will increase relative to other investments you might have made with your money.

There is much to be said for small investor ownership of large corporations. It is an important and productive form of business ownership, and it is the only way—short of starting a small business of your own—to own part of the American economy.

Con

No, buying ownership in large corporations is nothing like owning a small business. Even when you can amass voting rights with many other small owners, you still don't have many of the advantages of small businesses.

For example, small businesses are flexible and swift to change and adapt to new needs and technologies. In a marketplace that is unstable and rapidly changing, a large company is not going to be able to move rapidly when the situation demands it. You can easily become a small investor in an also-ran company like Braniff or Studebaker.

Furthermore, many new products and ideas have sprung from small companies. Products like the Apple® Microcomputer[1] very likely wouldn't have been put into production at a large company like IBM. The owner of a small business has a much better chance of successfully introducing a new product or idea.

Finally, we need those small businesses in our economy to offset the large corporations. Without the threat of small businesses, large corporations could grow complacent or could become powerful to a degree that would endanger our economic freedoms. Monopolies would thrive, prices would climb, and large companies, already too powerful in many ways, could become uncontrollable.

No, we need investment in small businesses. Don't buy ownership in large corporations. It hurts everyone when you do.

---

[1] Apple® is a registered trademark of Apple Computer, Inc. Any reference to Apple Microcomputers refers to this footnote.

distribution operation were the logical choices. She could not do it by herself, so she asked her friends Pamela Guerrero and Andy Brisbane to go into business with her. They would be partners. Pamela and Andy agreed to contribute $10,000 each and to take full-time positions in the new enterprise. A **partnership** was born. They called it BPA Enterprises.

Features of Partnerships

Bonnie, Pamela, and Andy's formation of a partnership certainly is not unusual; many thousands of partnerships are formed each year in the United States. Still, as was shown in Figure 4-1, partnerships are the least popular form of ownership.

Most partnerships have four primary characteristics. First, they usually have only two, three, or four members. It is difficult for a partnership to operate effectively with more than four partners. However, there are exceptions: Arthur Young and other "big eight" public accounting firms have hundreds of partners.

Second, all partners are expected to play an active role in the management of the business. (An exception to this is limited partnerships, which we will discuss briefly at the end of the chapter.) In BPA Enterprises, Pamela Guerrero was put in charge of the new restaurant; Andy Brisbane took over the food distribution business; and Bonnie continued to be responsible for the original Hamburger Palace.

Third, a partnership is a legal relationship between the people involved. Thus, it is usually a good idea for the partners to write and sign an agreement called **articles of partnership**. This agreement defines the role of each partner in the operation of the business. Special attention should be given to the amount of money and time that each partner is expected to invest. Figure 4-3 shows the most common provisions of partnership agreements.

Fourth, partnerships tend to be small businesses; 75 percent had total annual sales of less than $100,000 in 1977. One exception to this rule is Price Waterhouse, one of the leading public accounting firms in the country. In 1980, the total value of fees charged by Price Waterhouse for professional services was $752 million worldwide and $331 million in the United States. Total personnel employed in over 80 countries was 22,339.

Advantages of Partnerships

Bonnie Klein formed a partnership because she needed more money and management talent. Her business could not grow without it. Partnerships provide a way for entrepreneurs to obtain these resources. Let's take a closer look at the advantages of partnerships.

Access to Capital. Compared to a sole proprietorship, a partnership allows greater access to capital: All partners contribute some of their savings, and banks are more willing to extend credit.

Sears and Roebuck proved that two heads are often better than one.

Banks prefer partnerships over sole proprietorships because all partners are liable individually and jointly for the entire amount of the loan.

Management Talent. As the old saying goes, two heads are better than one. The best partner is one with money and good ideas or talent. Andy Brisbane had been an artist, so he designed all the advertisements for BPA Enterprises. Pamela Guerrero acted as the accountant for the firm.

Ease of Formation. Partnerships share ease of formation with sole proprietorships, although to a lesser degree. The most difficult task is the writing of the partnership agreement. As we said earlier, this agreement helps avoid misunderstandings that might develop later. An experienced attorney can usually draw up a partnership agreement without much trouble.

Confidentiality. Partnerships and sole proprietorships are also alike in that they are not required to make their financial records available to the public. As a rule, however, there are few secrets between a partnership and its banker.

Tax Benefits. Partners are taxed according to their percentage of ownership. For example, if BPA Enterprises cleared $99,000 in 1983, and each partner owned an equal third, then Bonnie's, Pamela's, and Andy's taxable incomes would be $33,000 each. The partnership itself does not pay taxes on its $99,000 in earned income. In a few moments we'll see how the situation is different for corporations.

Disadvantages of Partnerships

Although partnerships are a good idea in some situations, they do have major disadvantages. Some of the problems are the same as those for sole proprietorships.

Unlimited Liability. Each partner is legally responsible for all debts incurred by the partnership to the extent of that partner's personal wealth. If BPA Enterprises goes out of business, Bonnie will be liable for all the partnership's debts if Pamela and Andy cannot pay their share.

Personality Conflicts. As long as the partners are in agreement on important issues, there is no

Figure 4-3

Recommended Provisions of a Partnership Agreement

- Date of contract and length of life of the agreement.
- Nature of business, location, and name of firm.
- Names of partners and their respective investments, and distribution of profits and losses.
- Duties of each partner and hours of personal service, and provision for salaries of partners.
- Provision for paying interest on capital and drawing account balances.
- Limitation on withdrawal of funds from the business.
- Provision for an accounting system and a fiscal year.
- Method to be followed in the case of withdrawal of a partner.

problem. However, an argument over the size of the burgers or whether a fourth person should be invited into the partnership could divide BPA Enterprises.

Life of the Partnership. The partners are the partnership, so the life of the partnership is no longer than the lives of the partners. Normally, when a partner leaves the business, that partner's share is sold to one or more of the remaining partners or to a new person who is acceptable to them.

CORPORATIONS

The success of BPA Enterprises surprised its three partners. Total sales at the two Hamburger Palaces doubled within a year, and the food distribution operation had begun supplying many other restaurants around the St. Louis area. The prospect of continued growth was very strong. Bonnie talked to Pamela and Andy, and together they decided to incorporate. Such a step would make it easier for them to raise money, and it would solve the problem of unlimited liability. They filed an application form with the Secretary of State of Missouri and paid their incorporation fee. The state issued a charter, and BPA Enterprises became BPA Enterprises, *Inc.*

Corporations produce many of the products we need and enjoy.

BPA Enterprises, Inc., sold $50,000 in stock to a group of local investors and borrowed another $20,000 from a downtown bank. Then the newly appointed board of directors (Bonnie, Pamela, Andy, and three of the investors) hired Nick Love to manage its two hamburger outlets and the expanded food distribution operation. Nick had managed a nationwide chain of fast-food diners for ten years. He had built it into one of the most respected restaurant chains in the business.

Features of Corporations

The **corporation** is the most important form of business ownership in the United States today. Most of the products we buy are made by corporations. A few examples are Procter & Gamble (Tide detergent), General Foods (Maxwell House coffee), Kraft (macaroni and cheese dinners), Thomas J. Lipton (Lipton tea), and Heinz (tomato ketchup).

The first identifying feature of corporations is that they are legal entities. In the words of Chief Justice John Marshall, written in 1819:

> "A corporation is an artificial being, invisible, intangible, and existing only in contemplation of law. Being the mere creature of law, it possesses only those properties which the charter of its creation confers upon it, either expressly or as incidental to its very existence."

As such, corporations can own property, enter into contracts, and sue and be sued in court. Corporations own assets, and shareholders own the corporation, but the shareholders do not own the assets *per se*. Also, corporations, like individuals, have constitutional rights; a corporation's property cannot be taken without "due process of law."

Second, corporations usually have many owners. An exception is the Bechtel Corporation, which is owned by one family. Bechtel's revenues in 1981 were $11.4 billion. It has been largely responsible for building Hoover Dam, the San Francisco-Oakland Bay Bridge, the trans-Alaska pipeline, and the Washington subway system. In contrast, Exxon, the nation's largest industrial corporation, has nearly 790,000 shareholders. The number of shareholders for each of the five biggest U.S. companies is shown in Table 4-1.

Corporations can be classified as either closely held or publicly held. If closely held, stock is owned by only a few people. If publicly held, stock is available for purchase by anyone through a broker.

Third, corporations are characterized by professional management. That is, management and ownership are separate, especially in the case of large, publicly held corporations. The company's managers may own shares in the corporation, but their number of shares is usually small in relation to all the shares of the company. In very small corporations, one person may own all the stock and also act as the firm's manager. But even in this case, ownership is distinct from management. In effect, the owner of the corporation hires himself or herself to manage it.

Table 4-1

Number of Shareholders for Five Largest U.S. Industrial Corporations, Ranked According to 1981 Sales

Rank	Company	Number of Shareholders
1	Exxon	789,450
2	Mobil	292,422
3	General Motors	1,221,167
4	Texaco	383,640
5	Standard Oil of California	247,000

Source: Standard & Poor's *Corporation Records*. Number of shareholders of record as of February 9, 1982 (Exxon), March 8, 1982 (Mobil), December 31, 1981 (General Motors), February 23, 1982 (Texaco), and January 1, 1982 (Standard Oil of California).

Structure of Corporations

All private corporations have the same basic structure. They are made up of stockholders who own the company, a board of directors which sets policy and appoints top management, and top management which runs the company within the policies set by the board. This scheme is pictured in Figure 4-4.

Stockholders. The stockholders in most corporations really don't do much. They elect the board of directors, but in most cases this is only a ratification of the wishes of top management and the current board members. Stockholders also vote on changes in the corporate charter and on the appointment of a certified public accountant to audit the firm's books.

Board of Directors. The boards of directors for most corporations range in size from 10 to 25. Teledyne, an exception, has only 5 directors. The Enserch Corporation has 9 directors; Armco, 13; Phillips Petroleum Company, 14; and General Motors, 24.

Figure 4-4

Corporation Structure

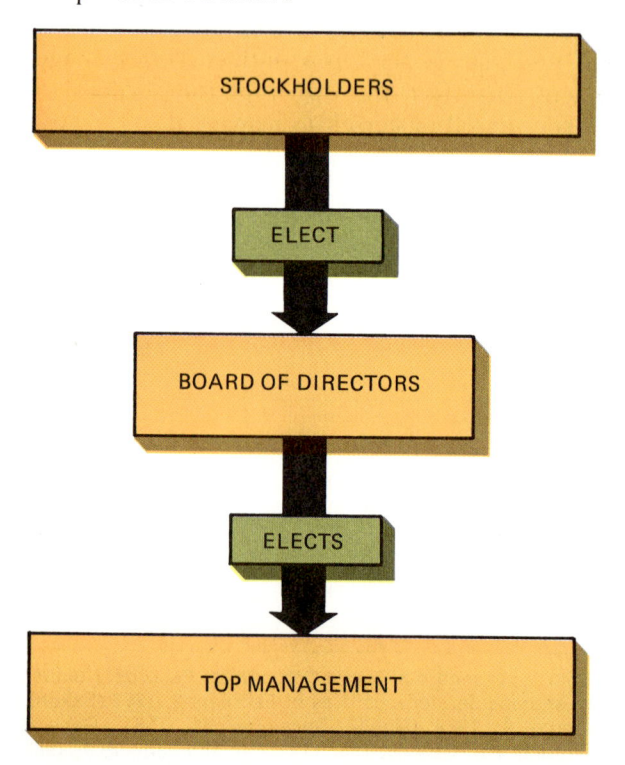

The board of directors is ultimately responsible for the management of the corporation. In the corporate structure, authority flows from the board to the firm's managers. The management powers of the board normally include the following:

- Electing the corporation's top officers, the most important of whom is the Chief Executive Officer (CEO).
- Setting corporate policy in the areas of product offerings, services, prices, wages, and labor-management relations.
- Deciding how to finance corporate expansion.
- Deciding whether to pay a cash dividend to shareholders and, if so, how much.
- Establishing salary levels and compensation packages for the firm's top officers.

Most boards of directors include a few major executives from inside the organization and several people from outside. These outside directors are usually high-ranking executives from other businesses or people from the nonprofit sector (a college president, for example). If the corporation is running smoothly, the board usually leaves its managers alone. But if the firm's fortunes begin to flounder, the board steps in and plays a more active role.

Management. As we said before, top management, or the officers of the corporation, is elected by the board of directors. These managers have the authority to act as *agents* for the firm. That is, they can sign contracts in the name of the corporation.

One particular responsibility of corporate officers is watching the marketplace. Management decides which new products to introduce, which new markets to enter, or which products to stop selling. General Motors was the first major corporation to market refrigerators (Frigidaire). A decision to sell the Frigidaire business was recommended to the board of directors by the officers of GM. The officers also researched the advantages and disadvantages of the sale. Only then was the idea presented to the board of directors for approval.

Advantages of Corporations

By now, some of the advantages of the corporate form of ownership should be apparent. Let's take a quick look at them.

Profile –
John Pierpont Morgan

Many historians have argued that John Pierpont Morgan was the greatest American business person of the 19th century. He was certainly one of the most influential.

Morgan was born in 1837 in Hartford, Connecticut and was educated at the University of Gottingen in Europe. He entered business in 1857 in New York, where he represented his father's dry goods firm. Nine years later he became a partner in Dabney Morgan and Co., which was later renamed J.P. Morgan and Co.

J.P. Morgan and Co. was influential in financing and organizing many of the nation's largest corporations. By the end of the 19th century, Morgan also played a very powerful role in the financing and managing of almost all the nation's railroads. In the early 1900s he and Andrew Carnegie organized the U.S. Steel Corporation and the International Harvester Corporation. Morgan also played an important role in organizing the General Electric Company.

Wealth and personal profit were not driving forces for J.P. Morgan. In contrast to others who were interested primarily in accumulating huge personal fortunes, Morgan was interested primarily in power and the impact of his decisions on society. As a result, he had more impact on society than much wealthier people such as John D. Rockefeller, the founder of the Standard Oil Company. Morgan was truly interested in his ability to influence the future of the nation.

On two occasions, Morgan took action to stop runs on the nation's banks. In 1895 he met with President Grover Cleveland to arrange for the purchase of gold with U.S. bonds. Although President Cleveland thoroughly disliked Morgan, he adopted Morgan's plan to save the nation's banks. Then during the money panic of 1907, the nation turned to J.P. Morgan again. Through the sheer power of his personality, he forced European bankers to send large sums of gold to the United States. This receipt of gold ended America's greatest money panic.

The greatest humiliation that J.P. Morgan ever faced came in 1912 when he testified before the House Banking and Currency Committee. The committee was investigating the control of the U.S. financial system by a small number of New York bankers. Morgan, accused by the Committee's chief attorney of being the leader of the New York bankers, resented and denied the charges brought against him and the insinuations cast upon his firm. He believed that his business had enhanced the prosperity of the nation.

When Morgan died in 1913 while vacationing in Rome, he was recognized as the founder of the greatest investment banking house in the United States. J.P. Morgan and Co. was responsible for organizing and financing many of the nation's biggest corporations.

Limited Liability. The liability of the shareholders of a corporation is limited to the extent of their stock investment. Someone who broke a jaw on one of BPA's Mystery Burgers could sue the corporation but not Bonnie, Pamela, Andy, or any of the other shareholders personally. When Braniff Airlines declared bankruptcy in 1982, its shareholders lost the value of their stock, but they did not have to sell their houses, cars, or boats to pay the company's billion-dollar debt. Strictly speaking, the liability of the shareholders is limited, but the liability of the corporation is not.

Unlimited Life. The corporation has a "life" of its own, continuing even after the original owners and managers are gone. John D. Rockefeller died in 1937, but Standard Oil is still very much in evidence.

Professional Management. The executive officers of a corporation are chosen on the basis of their managerial and decision-making skills. The board members of BPA Enterprises, Inc., selected Nick Love to manage their company because of his proven record of ability.

Disadvantages of Corporations

Starting a corporation is more involved than starting a sole proprietorship or a partnership. In addition to this problem, there are three other significant disadvantages.

Public Disclosure. The federal government requires that all publicly held corporations disclose a broad set of financial data to the Securities and Exchange Commission. This information is then made available to potential investors. The information concerns the company's earnings, financial condition, product offerings, and the qualifications of its top managers. The purpose of the disclosure is to protect investors from corporate misrepresentation of facts and conditions. But from the perspective of the firm, disclosure can be a disadvantage if it alerts competitors to the firm's financial weaknesses or to its research and development programs.

Double Taxation. One way that a corporation may reward its stockholders is by sending them a quarterly dividend. These dividends, however, are subject to double taxation. That is, a corporation pays dividends out of its after-tax income. But the dividends are taxed again as personal income for the shareholder.

To illustrate, BPA Enterprises, Inc., earned profits of $200,000 in a great year for hamburgers. It paid $80,000 in federal income taxes, leaving $120,000 in after-tax profit. A total of $60,000 was paid out in dividends. Because she held so many shares, Bonnie Klein received a check for $10,000. Her personal income tax on this amount was $3,000. The money was taxed once as corporate income and once as personal income.

Costs of Incorporation. Another disadvantage of incorporation is the cost involved. The incorporation fees with the state are not themselves that high. For example, it costs a resident $200 to incorporate in Texas—$100 in filing fees and another $100 as a deposit against payment on the first year's taxes. Out-of-state people pay $1,100, and assets of $1,000 are required as the minimum amount of capital. Also, attorney fees can become significant in the case of large ventures.

Besides sole proprietorships, partnerships, and corporations, there are a few other forms of business ownership, but they are not as popular as the three forms already discussed. Table 4-2 shows the characteristics of four of them: limited partnerships, joint ventures, cooperatives, and mutual companies.

MERGER AND ACQUISITION

Let's turn our attention now to a topic related to the forms of business ownership: merger and acquisition. Business firms grow in one of two ways—through internal expansion or through merger and acquisition. **Internal expansion** refers to the process of growing by increasing sales and capital investment each year. **External expansion** takes place when a firm purchases another company. Such a purchase is an **acquisition**. The acquired firm usually retains a separate identity. A special type of acquisition is the **merger**, in which one company buys a second one, with the latter ceasing to exist as a separate entity. For example, a playing card manufacturer could grow by purchasing one of its competitors. The merged entity would then consist of the combined assets, work forces, earnings, and markets of the two separate companies.

Bigger is Better

The trend is toward bigness in business today. In any given industry, "bigness" results in a handful of large companies dominating the industry and a few other small companies—or none at all in the case of an oligopoly—scrambling to stay in business.

Figure 4-5 presents some data on the issue of bigness. The figure shows the percentage share of all corporate assets held by the 100 and 200 largest manufacturing firms. In 1950, the 100 largest companies controlled 39.7 percent of U.S. corporate assets. By 1970, the figure had risen to 48.5 percent, falling a few percentage points to 46.7 percent in 1980. For the 200 largest corporations, the percentage share climbed from 47.7 in 1950 to 59.7 in 1980. These increasing shares indicate that the biggest companies, as a group, are getting even bigger.

The brewing industry provides a good example of the trend toward bigness. The brewing industry is currently dominated by Anheuser-Busch, Inc., and the Miller Brewing Co. These two firms together account for 53 percent of domestic beer sales. Their combined market share in 1977 was just 38 percent. In 1970, a total of 92 breweries were operating in this country. Now the number is nearing 40. The top ten producers alone account for 95 percent of all beer sales.

Why have so many small breweries disappeared? There are several reasons. First, the beer industry is intensely competitive. Unit production costs at a small brewery are too high for the product to compete against the bigger brands. These higher production costs drive up the beer's selling price to a level higher than that of the more efficiently produced national brands such as Anheuser-Busch's Budweiser. Second, only the

Table 4-2

Other Forms of Ownership

Form of Ownership	Discussion	Examples
Limited Partnership	A partnership involving one or more general partners who assume unlimited liability and act as managers of the project or business, and one or more limited partners who supply investment money but do not act as managers.	Office buildings, shopping centers, and other real estate investment syndications
Joint Venture	An agreement between two or more business concerns, usually corporations, for the joint production of a good or service. Each partner to the agreement usually supplies investment capital and management or marketing skill.	General Mills, Inc., and Justco Co., Ltd., of Japan to develop and operate jointly a chain of Red Lobster seafood restaurants in Japan
Cooperatives	An incorporated business concern owned by its user-members for the collective operation of production and/or distribution activities. Each member of the association has only one vote regardless of the amount of stock held.	The many growers who together comprise the California Fruit Grower's Exchange, producer of Sunkist oranges
Mutual Companies	A corporation owned by the users of the service provided. The owners enjoy limited liability, and, for tax purposes, dividends are treated as partial refunds on money contributed (premiums in the case of insurance companies).	Mutual of Omaha, State Farm Insurance, Mutual of New York, and some other insurance companies

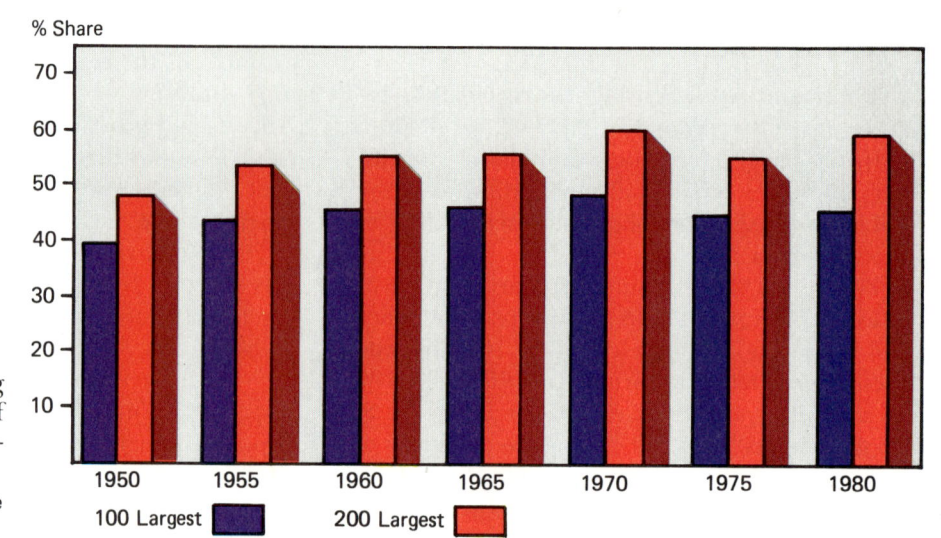

Figure 4-5

Largest Manufacturing Corporations' Share of U.S. Assets Held (Percentage), 1950-1980
Source: U.S. Federal Trade Commission.

big breweries can afford the aggressive marketing programs needed today to increase market share. Budweiser spent nearly $150 million on advertising in 1981, compared to Schlitz' $40 million and Coors' $25 million.

And third, many of the smaller breweries really don't go out of business: They are bought up by other breweries. Through mergers, the smaller companies can compete more effectively against the industry giants. Thus, we see Stroh and Schlitz agreeing to merge, Stroh buying Schaefer, Pabst seeking to acquire Olympia, and G. Heileman buying Carling National. Mergers offer the advantages of greater production efficiencies, new geographic markets, and more comprehensive advertising and distribution strategies. Keep an eye on the business press to see whether these smaller companies are able to hold their own against Budweiser and Miller.

Types of Mergers

A merger can be classified as one of four types: horizontal, vertical, congeneric, and conglomerate. Let's take a look at each of these types.

Horizontal Merger. The **horizontal merger** is a form of business combination in which one company buys another that is in the same industry and performs the same function. The recent acquisition of Continental Airlines by Texas International is a good example of a horizontal merger. By purchasing Continental, Texas International was able to expand its routes and to serve more of the country. This was a horizontal merger because both companies provided the same service—passenger air travel—on a competitive basis. The beer industry mergers just discussed are also examples of horizontal mergers.

Vertical Merger. The **vertical merger** is a business combination in which one company buys another that is in the same industry, but performs a different production or distribution activity. For example, a toy manufacturer might acquire a chain of retail stores, or a steel mill might purchase an iron ore mining company. In the first example, the retail chain gives the toy manufacturer access to consumer markets; in the second, the iron mine gives the steel maker access to raw materials. In both instances, the result is greater control over the distribution or manufacture of a product. It could be argued that Du Pont's recent purchase of Conoco is an example of a vertical merger, at least in the sense that Du Pont now has guaranteed access to petroleum supplies for its petrochemical manufacturing operations.

Congeneric Merger. A **congeneric merger** is a business combination in which one company buys another that is in a different industry, but that performs a related activity. An example of a congeneric merger is the acquisition by the Prudential Insurance Co., of the brokerage firm Bache Group Inc. Both firms have provided financial services, but they were not directly competitive before. The move allowed Prudential to broaden its range of financial services.

FROM THE FILE

Rachel is an assistant to the president of a company that designs and manufactures advanced diagnostic equipment for hospitals. This is a fast-growing industry, and Rachel's company has an aggressive attitude toward growth. Last week, top management decided that it was time for the company to enter the market for heart pacemakers. Rachel's job is to recommend to the president the best way to do this. One way is internal expansion: The company's engineers could design a new pacemaker, and a production facility could then be built. Alternatively, the company could purchase a firm that already produces pacemakers. Rachel has identified one possible acquisition, an innovative, well-staffed firm on the West Coast. Rachel knows that cost is an issue, but she also wondered what other factors are important in choosing between internal expansion and acquisition.

Conglomerate Merger. A fourth type of merger or business combination is the **conglomerate merger**, in which one company buys another that is in a different industry and performs an unrelated activity. Coca-Cola's acquisition of Columbia Pictures is an example of a conglomerate merger. Several years before that, Gulf & Western purchased the Paramount studios in a similar move. Conglomerate mergers were especially popular in the 1960s.

SUMMARY POINTS

1. The three basic forms of business ownership are sole proprietorships, partnerships, and corporations.
2. The corporation is the dominant form of business ownership today.
3. The chief advantages of a sole proprietorship are ease of formation, minimal capital requirements, managerial control, tax benefits, and confidentiality.
4. The disadvantages of a sole proprietorship are unlimited liability, limited managerial resources, and limited access to credit.
5. The advantages of a partnership are greater access to capital, extra management talent, and, again, ease of formation, tax benefits, and confidentiality.
6. The disadvantages of a partnership are unlimited liability, the potential for management conflicts, and limited life.
7. A corporation is a legal entity, with many of the rights, duties, and powers of a person. It is owned by its stockholders and directed by a board of directors. It is to be considered as separate from the people who own it and the people who manage it.
8. The chief advantages of the corporate form of ownership are limited liability for the shareholders, perpetual life, and professional management.
9. The disadvantages of a corporation are public disclosure of financial data, double taxation, and incorporation costs.
10. Four other forms of ownership are limited partnerships, joint ventures, cooperatives, and mutual companies.
11. Four types of business combination are the horizontal merger, the vertical merger, the congeneric merger, and the conglomerate merger.

KEY TERMS AND CONCEPTS

sole proprietorship
unlimited liability
partnership
articles of partnership
corporation

board of directors
limited liability
limited partnership
joint venture
cooperatives

mutual companies
internal expansion
external expansion
acquisition
merger
horizontal merger
vertical merger
congeneric merger
conglomerate merger

REVIEW QUESTIONS

1. What are the main features of a sole proprietorship?
2. What are the advantages of a sole proprietorship in relation to a partnership?
3. What is meant by unlimited liability in the context of a sole proprietorship and a partnership?
4. Why are banks generally less willing to lend money to a sole proprietorship than to a partnership? Explain.
5. What are articles of partnership? What should they include?
6. What is a corporation? In what sense does it exist apart from its owners?
7. What are the chief functions of the board of directors? Who runs a company—its managers or its stockholders?
8. List the advantages of the corporate form of ownership.
9. What is the difference between a horizontal merger and a vertical merger?
10. What is the difference between a congeneric merger and a conglomerate merger?

DISCUSSION QUESTIONS

1. If you were to start a new company, which form of ownership would you choose? Why?
2. Of all the advantages of the corporate form of ownership, which one, in your opinion, is the most important? Explain.
3. Discuss the roles of stockholders and managers in the running of a corporation. Do these roles overlap at all? Is there potential for conflict? Explain.
4. In your opinion, what are some of the advantages of growth through internal expansion as opposed to growth through merger and acquisition? Draw up a list and discuss each advantage.
5. If you were in charge of enforcing business formation guidelines for the Justice Department, which type of business combination would you look at most carefully? That is, which type of merger is most likely to stifle competition in the industry involved?

CASE 4-1

Softsel Computer Products

For several years, small and reasonably priced computers have flooded the market. Individuals and small businesses have been able to afford personal computers. The ease of operation has made virtually any owner competent at using a computer for enjoyment, running a business, or other purposes.

The major drawback to personal computers has been the programming necessary to make them work. While individuals with computer experience and a certain expertise can easily write their own programs and remove the "bugs" from them, most personal computer users don't have programming skills or don't want to be bothered by programming problems.

To meet the demand for ready-to-use programming, computer manufacturers started supplying programs tailored for their products. However, another source of programs also developed—free-lance programmers. These individuals had the expertise necessary and they enjoyed making money part-time (or sometimes even full-time) by writing programs for computer owners. Their major problem, however, was selling their programs.

Robert Leff and David Wagman were experienced programmers working for a subsidiary of a large banking company. They realized that the personal computer market needed an intermediary which could buy programs from the free-lancers and resell them to the nearly 1,500 retail computer stores which sold personal computers. For $1,300, Leff bought out one free-lancer who had sold his products from store to store. Leff then began selling programs to the retail stores himself. In a month of hard work, he earned $5,000. He quit his bank job, Wagman contributed $10,000, and they started Softsel Computer Products as a partnership.

Leff and Wagman now spend much of their time testing new programs offered by free-lancers. When they find a program they like, they include it in their offering to retail stores. Leff and Wagman make 20 percent of the retail price on each sale, splitting the rest between the retail store and the individual or small company that wrote and published the program. Their warehouse is stocked with thousands of different computer programs, including a large selection of the very popular computer games. A daily update on a company computer shows which games or programs are selling well and which need to be phased out.

So far, Leff and Wagman have not had to borrow any money to run their company. Softsel expected to have sales revenues of about $25 million in 1982, with profits of about $5 million. As partners, Leff and Wagman have done quite well.

1. Why was a partnership a better choice than a sole proprietorship by Leff? Why was a partnership a better choice than a corporation that sold its ownership in part to the public?
2. What are the advantages and disadvantages of partnership as far as Softsel Computer Products is concerned?
3. Would Leff and Wagman always want to keep their business a partnership? How might the disadvantages of a partnership become significant enough that Leff and Wagman might break up the company? How might the disadvantages of a partnership become significant enough that Leff and Wagman might form a publicly held corporation?

CASE 4-2

The Mississippi Band of Choctaw Indians

For generations, American Indians have been forced to live as wards of the federal government. They have been fed, clothed, and housed with money supplied from federal taxes. But because of cuts in government funding, many Indian reservations have begun searching for new sources of income. The Mississippi Band of Choctaw Indians, for example, decided to go into business. The Choctaws owned land which wasn't worth much because it had little valuable mineral, hunting, or lumber rights. But what they did have, they realized, was their people.

The Choctaws decided to invite manufacturing companies onto their reservation to supply sufficient jobs for all interested Choctaw Indians. American Greetings Corp., a major greeting card manufacturer, was looking for a place to build a new plant and agreed to a joint venture with the Choctaws. The Indians first needed money to help the firm finance a building. Because they didn't have money of their own to spare and because they couldn't legally issue bonds or take out large enough loans themselves, the Choctaws persuaded a nearby township to issue bonds to finance the American Greetings plant. As a result, the card company lowered the cost of building its new factory by a hefty proportion, and the Choctaws had a factory where they could find stable employment close to home. Unemployment that had run between 35 and 40 percent before the card factory opened was greatly reduced.

The American Indian National Bank in Washington, D.C., is now holding seminars for more than 65 other Indian tribes, teaching them the lessons that the Choctaws learned. Indian tribes like the Navajo and the Jicarilla Apaches have signed other joint-venture agreements modeled after the Choctaw agreements. Some tribes, such as the Salt River Pima-Maricopa tribes, which have oil or valuable timber on their land, have been able to build their own facilities without borrowing the funds. The Pima-Maricopa built a million-dollar, high-security warehouse and rented it to Motorola. This rental supplies both tribal income and employment for many Indians. Tribal lobbyists have also pushed a bill into Congress that would make it legal for tribes to issue bonds, just as cities and counties do.

1. What are the advantages of a joint venture? Why are those advantages important to the Choctaws and to American Greetings Corp.?
2. Why did the Choctaws look for a company that wanted to build a new factory, instead of building and operating their own independent factory?
3. Describe other kinds of joint ventures that Indian tribes might attempt. Identify other American population groups that might attempt such joint ventures. Why might they succeed or fail?

Small Business and the Franchise System

5

After studying this chapter, you should be able to:

- Define small business, giving some idea how the definition varies with the type of industry.
- Describe the principal functions of the Small Business Administration.
- Describe the role that small businesses play in our economy as producers, employers, and sources of new ideas.
- Explain the four major types of small businesses.
- Discuss the advantages and disadvantages of operating a small business, as well as the reasons why so many small businesses fail.
- Describe some of the factors involved in the decision whether to buy a small business.
- Explain the 12 steps in the process of starting a small business.
- Discuss how franchising offers an opportunity for operating a small business.

Small businesses are an exciting part of our economy. Although dwarfed in size by such companies as General Electric, with 404,000 employees, or American Telephone and Telegraph, with annual profits of $8

billion, small businesses provide a way for people to be their own bosses. Small businesses are often the most innovative companies, introducing new products, new management styles, and new promotional strategies.

Let's begin our discussion of small business by looking at how the government defines "small." Then we will examine just how important small businesses are in the U.S. economy.

HOW SMALL IS SMALL BUSINESS?

The Small Business Act of 1953 defines a **small business** as one "which is independently owned and operated and not dominant in its field of operation." The Small Business Administration (SBA) uses the number of employees and the sales volume as guidelines in determining whether or not a business is small. The SBA is the principal government agency concerned with the financing, operation, and management of small businesses. Depending upon the industry, the SBA has different definitions of "small." Table 5-1 shows the SBA's definition for each of the three major sectors of the economy.

How the SBA defines a small business is critical for firms applying for SBA loans. For our purposes, however, a small business typically has four characteristics:

- The boss owns the business.
- Financing is provided by one or just a few individuals.
- Most of the people working for the business live in the same community.
- The business is small compared to the dominant firms in the industry.[1]

[1] *Meeting the Special Problems of Small Business* (New York: Committee for Economic Development, 1947), p. 14.

Table 5-1

The Small Business Administration's Definition of a Small Business

Sector	Definition
Retailing and Service	Annual Sales of $2,000,000 to $7,500,000
Wholesaling	Annual Sales of $9,500,000 to $22,000,000
Manufacturing	250 or Fewer Employees

Table 5-2 shows total federal government loans to all small businesses for the period 1970 to 1980. Note that both the number of loans and the dollar value of all loans increased dramatically over the decade.

HOW BIG IS SMALL BUSINESS?

What part do small businesses play in our economy? You may be surprised at just how big the world of small business is.

Share of GNP

Small businesses are responsible for roughly 40 percent of the gross national product in the United States.[2] Large businesses contribute about 45 percent, and the federal government's share of the GNP has risen from 9 percent in 1965 to almost 15 percent in 1982.

[2] "Measuring Gross Product Originating in Small Business" (Joel Popkin and Company, September, 1980, for the SBA).

Table 5-2

Federal Loans to Small Businesses, 1970-1980

Year	Number of Loans	Dollar Value of All Loans
1970	15,100	$ 710,000,000
1972	28,000	1,574,000,000
1974	27,500	1,948,000,000
1976	26,100	2,071,000,000
1978	31,700	3,314,000,000
1980	31,700	3,858,000,000
1970-1980 Average	27,300	2,259,000,000

Source: U.S. Small Business Administration, unpublished data.

Small Businesses as Big Employers

Small businesses employ many people. Nearly 95 percent of all U.S. businesses employ fewer than 20 people; but in total, these small firms employ 22 percent of the U.S. work force. Businesses with 99 or fewer employees account for 41 percent of the work force.[3] Although big firms are also big employers, it is clear that small business, the source of nearly half the wage and salary jobs in this country, is big too. Without small business, America would be out of work.

Sources of New Ideas

Small businesses are frequently the innovators in their industries. Big business means big bureaucracy, and big bureaucracy means that decisions are made slowly. Big business is also usually interested in mass production only. As a result, without the responsiveness and low production capacities of small businesses, many products would never be made—especially products with little initial demand. Remember, all successful big businesses started as small businesses.

New ideas are the lifeblood of business. Research often provides those ideas.

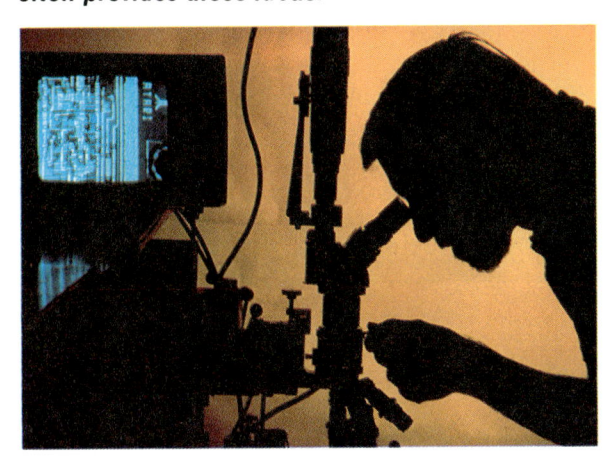

TYPES OF SMALL BUSINESSES

Small businesses operate in all parts of our economy. But as Figure 5-1 shows, the service and wholesaling sectors have much higher percentages of small businesses than does the production sector.

---

[3] U.S. Department of Commerce, Bureau of the Census, *Enterprise Statistics, Part I: General Report on Industrial Organizations* (1977).

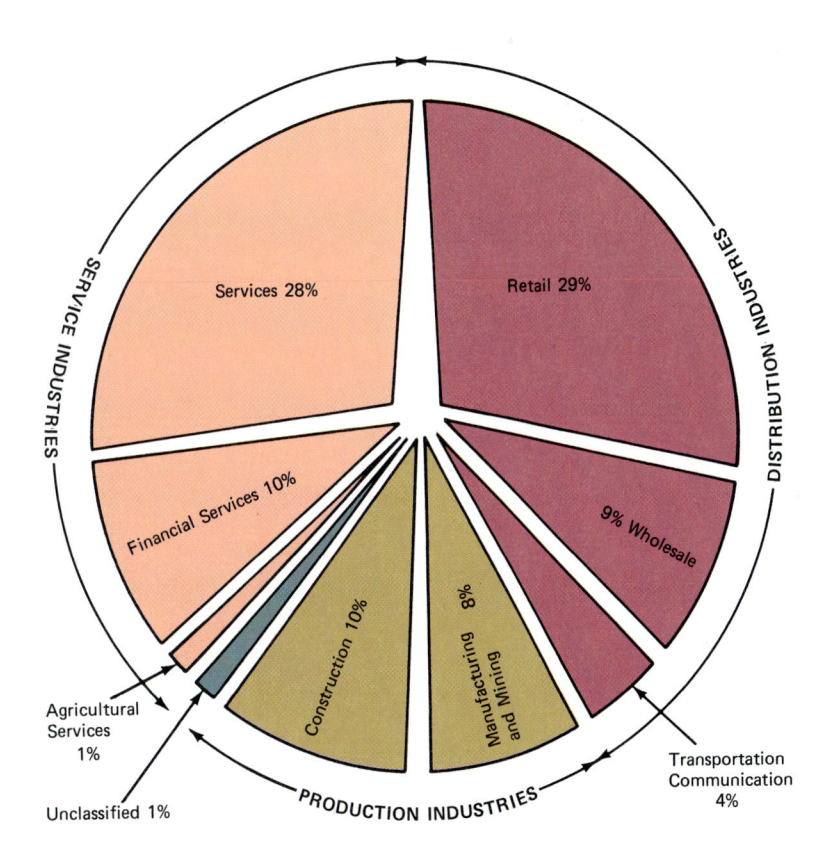

Figure 5-1

Small Business by Industry

Source: National Federation of Independent Business Research and Education Foundation, *Small Business in America*, (San Mateo, California, 1982).

SERVICE INDUSTRIES
- Services 28%
- Financial Services 10%

DISTRIBUTION INDUSTRIES
- Retail 29%
- 9% Wholesale
- Transportation Communication 4%

PRODUCTION INDUSTRIES
- Construction 10%
- Manufacturing and Mining 8%
- Agricultural Services 1%
- Unclassified 1%

Services

Some examples of service businesses are advertising agencies, travel agencies, laundries, bowling alleys, amusement parks, rock bands, and motels. The customers of these businesses buy a service—advertising time on television, a few games of bowling, three hours of music—rather than a product that they can take home with them.

One of the main features of service businesses is their small size. Only 20 percent of all service firms employ 500 or more people. More than 63 percent have fewer than 100 employees.

Wholesaling

Wholesaling is one of the few sectors of the economy that is dominated by small businesses. Figure 5-2 shows that 65.9 percent of all wholesalers have fewer than 10 employees; only 4.3 percent have more than 49. Wholesalers act as intermediaries between manufacturers and retailers or between manufacturers and industrial buyers.

Small wholesalers sell a variety of products, including groceries, farm produce, machinery, and industrial supplies. The small wholesaler can compete with a large wholesaler if it anticipates the needs of its customers.

Some businesses offer services rather than goods.

Retailing

Retailers sell products to final consumers for the consumers' own use. There are a great many small businesses in retailing. Examples include drugstores, independent supermarkets, men's

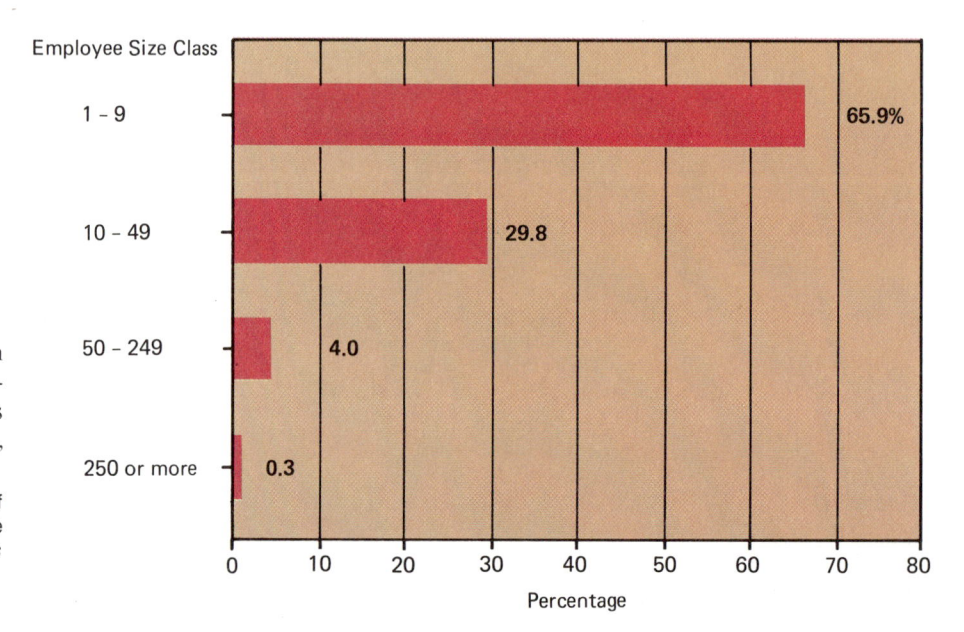

Figure 5-2

Sizes of Firms in Wholesaling — Percentages of Establishments by Employee Size Class, 1980

Source: U.S. Department of Commerce, Bureau of the Census, *County Business Patterns, 1980, United States* (September, 1982), p. 59.

Employee Size Class	Percentage
1 – 9	65.9%
10 – 49	29.8
50 – 249	4.0
250 or more	0.3

CONTROVERSIAL ISSUES

As the economy becomes more and more unstable, small businesses suffer the most from economic conditions. Is an individual contemplating a small business venture betting against the odds? Is starting a small business worth the risk?

Small Business—It's Worth the Risk.

Pro

Yes, starting a small business is definitely worth the risk! Small businesses have several advantages that make them a good choice for making money, either in good economic times or bad.

First, they allow more flexibility than large businesses do. You can trim your employee expenses more readily, you are less likely to have unionization (with long-term wage contracts, cost-of-living adjustments, and so on), and you will have less deadwood accumulated in your salaried staff at the management or operational levels. You have less paperwork to do for the government and your tax reporting problems are made much simpler by law for small businesses.

Second, the federal and some state governments have special programs, such as the Small Business Administration, which support small businesses. These programs give advice and good rates and guarantees on loans. Except in special cases, big corporations can't get money from the federal government.

Third, you usually have more freedom to develop a new product, a new service, or a new invention in a business of your own. And you have much more control over how you finance the product, how you market it, and what kind of image you develop for your firm. One of the worst experiences for many inventors or artisans is to create a high-quality product and find it cheapened to meet a large corporation's idea of what will sell best.

Con

No, small business is too risky to be worth it. Many small businesses that were started in the 1960s and early 1970s eventually became successful stable businesses. However, many were successful because they rode the peak of a long period of steady inflationary growth. Companies could invest and expand, feeling that prices would continue to rise, so money borrowed would be worth less when repaid. Everyone was buying goods, banks were lending money to everyone, and the economy was growing tremendously.

The economic stability of the past, however, has been interrupted. Consumer confidence has been shaken by escalating interest rates, high inflation, and high unemployment. Banks no longer trust economic predictions, most of which failed to anticipate the unsettled economic conditions of the '80s; consequently, they are more reluctant than in the past to make business loans. And the government has tightened its belt, eliminating many of its small business subsidies.

A firm that survives in today's economy has to meet several requirements. It must have substantial liquid assets, which means it can supply cash on short notice and in large quantities. It must also have the credit reputation to borrow money (which isn't easy any more). And, it must have almost a sixth sense when extending credit to anyone.

So what do you do if you have a business venture you really believe in? You can still turn to big business. The large corporations aren't as insensitive as they are reputed to be—they wouldn't survive if they were. In today's technological world, firms recognize research and development expenses as a necessary prelude to the sale of a product. Marketing research is often essential to avoid an embarrassing failure. And high-level corporate financing is often crucial to launching new products or new ventures.

Big business, after all, is only a matter of degree. There are nationwide corporations that franchise the sale of carnations on street corners. There are small ice cream manufacturers that, after merging with large manufacturers and distributors, now see their brands selling throughout the country.

Big business isn't necessarily bad. It's safer in today's economic conditions than taking the plunge yourself. Let big business help pay for your venture.

and women's clothing stores, bookstores, music stores, restaurants, and gasoline stations. Even though large retail chains such as Sears and Penney's dominate the larger shopping centers, nearly 35 percent of the people in retailing work for stores with fewer than 20 employees.

Production

Only 18 percent of small businesses in the United States are producers. The conversion of raw materials and other inputs into finished goods requires much expensive equipment. Small manufacturers are at a great disadvantage in raising funds for the purchase of such equipment. As a result, it is hard for them to compete with the major manufacturers.

There are, however, small producers in the construction industry. These producers build houses, small office buildings, or additions to existing structures. Construction firms do not require much equipment. Their greatest asset is their pool of skilled labor.

IS SMALL BUSINESS FOR YOU?

We have seen that small businesses offer many exciting opportunities. In deciding whether to own a small business, you need to consider carefully the advantages and disadvantages.

Advantages

First, you are the boss. Owning a small business is a way of life. The owner of a small business enjoys taking risks and making decisions. The small business entrepreneur has no organizational constraint and is not accountable to anyone else. Almost any decision is possible so long as the money is there.

Second, the potential rewards are great. Few executives of large firms ever become very wealthy. Much of their companies' profits are paid to the stockholders. In contrast, the owners of small businesses help themselves to their firms' profits. A good example of this is the owner of a California Chevrolet dealership who, in 1981, made more money than the president of General Motors. The head of GM was responsible for a firm with 741,000 employees; the Chevrolet dealer had fewer than 300 employees.

Disadvantages

Many small businesses fail each year because they are not able to pay their creditors. Business failures occur much more often when the economy is ailing. Figure 5-3 shows the failure rates for business from 1920 to 1980. Note that the failure rate of business went up during each of the major recessions.

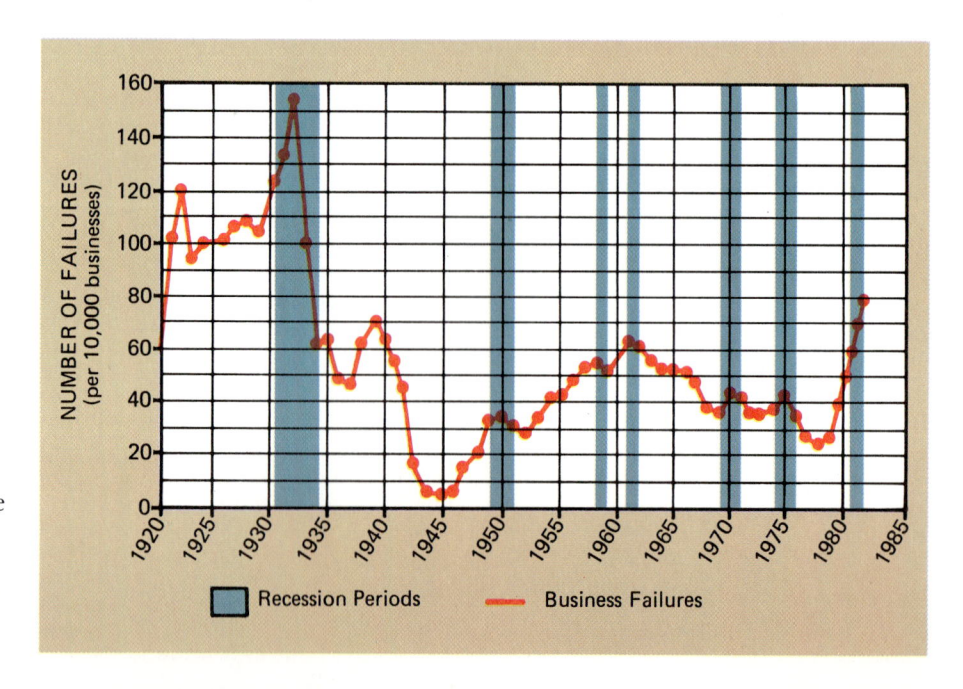

Figure 5-3

Recessions and the Rate of Business Failures 1920-1981

Source: *The Business Failure Record: 1980* (New York: Dun & Bradstreet, Inc., 1981).

Also, new businesses are more likely to fail than older businesses. Of the businesses that fail each year, nearly 55 percent are less than five years old. In contrast, fewer than 20 percent of all business failures involve firms that have been operating more than ten years.[4]

Why So Many Small Businesses Fail

There are four major reasons why small businesses fail. Let's look at these problems, and at how the small business owner can deal with them.

Lack of Management Skills. Many owners of small businesses are plagued by a lack of good management talent. Look at the information in Table 5-3. Inexperienced, incompetent management causes 94.8 percent of all business failures. Most small business owners must rely on their own managerial judgment because they can't afford to hire the best people.

How to deal with this problem? One way is occasionally to hire outside consultants for specific problems. A consultant's hourly rate is high, but the consultant may provide a great deal of useful advice.

Difficulty Keeping Good Managers. The problem of keeping good managers is closely related to the first problem. Small businesses lose talent because of low salaries. In addition, many people leave small businesses because of a lack of opportunities for advancement. One reason for this lack of opportunities is that the owner's son or daughter often ends up owning the business. In such a case, about all the owner can do is to offer different kinds of challenges to valuable employees.

Poor Financing. A stumbling block for most small businesses is a lack of capital and credit. It is particularly hard to obtain long-term financing. Banks rarely will lend money to a small business for more than ten years. When these funds are made available, they frequently carry a high interest rate. It is not unusual for banks to charge small businesses 5 to 8 percent more for borrowed money than they would charge a larger customer.

One sure source of additional funds for the successful firm is profit. The Adolph Coors Co. is a classic example of a small company that grew by reinvesting its profits in the business. A second approach is to find an outside investor to buy part of the business. The problem here is that the current owner sacrifices a certain amount of control for the needed cash.

You Against the World

The owners of small businesses carry the weight of the company alone. Their employees depend on them for regular salaries, and their families depend on them to provide for the future. The responsibility of running a small business cannot be given to someone else.

BUYING A SMALL BUSINESS

If you want to own a small business, you should decide whether you want to buy an existing business or start a new one. This part of the chapter examines the first alternative. We begin by asking an important question.

Table 5-3

Causes of Failures in 1980

Neglect	0.8%
Fraud	0.4
Inexperience/Incompetence	94.8
Inadequate Sales	59.6
Heavy Operating Expenses	28.9
Receivables Difficulties	9.4
Inventory Difficulties	9.3
Excessive Fixed Assets	3.1
Poor Location	2.0
Competitive Weakness	23.3
Other	1.3
Disaster	0.5
Reason Unknown	3.5
	100.0%

Source: The Business Failure Record, 1980 (New York: Dun & Bradstreet, Inc., 1981), p. 13. Since some failures are attributed to a combination of causes, percentages for the items in the inset column do not add to 94.8%.

---

[4] *The Business Failure Record: 1980* (New York: Dun & Bradstreet, Inc., 1981), p. 11.

Small Business Administration Functions

The **Small Business Administration** was created by Congress in 1953 to advise and assist the millions of small businesses in the United States. Its mission "is to help people get into business and to stay in business." Let's look at the functions that the SBA performs in fulfilling its mission.

LOANS. The SBA offers a variety of financial assistance programs to small business. The two most important are guaranty loans and direct loans. A **guaranty loan** is made by a private bank or other type of financial institution. The SBA guarantees up to 90 percent of the value of these loans. A **direct loan** is made directly from the SBA to a small business. Federal law prohibits the SBA from making direct loans unless private lending institutions refuse to make a loan or to take part in the guaranty loan program.

Most SBA loans are guaranty loans; the agency has relatively little money available for direct loans. The average size of an SBA guaranty loan is $115,000, and the average repayment term is eight years.

ADVOCACY. The SBA champions the cause of small business to the federal government. It serves as the focal point for complaints about how governmental actions might affect small business. It also regularly reports to Congress as to how existing law can be changed to help the owners of small business.

Assisting Women and Minorities Women and minorities are eligible for all regular SBA services and for some special services as well. Starting in 1980, the SBA designated a "women's representative" in each SBA office. Special SBA-sponsored workshops about business are held around the country to reach women. Finally, the SBA has a "mini-loan" program for women, allowing them to borrow up to an additional $20,000 easily and quickly.

The SBA has similar programs for minorities. One such program is the Capital Ownership Development Program, authorized by Congress in 1978. Its aim is to help blacks, native Americans, Hispanics, and other minority people get started in small business.

Managerial Assistance It is no secret that most small business failures are the result of poor management. Accordingly, the SBA has an active Agency's Management Assistance Program, through which SBA staff members and people from the Service Corps of Retired Executives (SCORE) and the Active Corps of Executives (ACE) provide free counseling to small business owners.

The SBA also sponsors courses, conferences, workshops, and problem clinics on a wide range of business topics. Finally, the SBA publishes a variety of booklets for small business owners. These publications are available at no charge through most SBA offices.

Procurement Assistance The Small Business Administration tries to help all small businesses, minority and nonminority, win a fair share of government contracts. It does this in three ways. First, it employs specialists in each SBA office to show small business owners how to prepare bids for government contracts. Second, it has representatives at all major military and civilian procurement centers to refer small business owners to federal contracting officers. Finally, the SBA has a computerized listing of the names and areas of expertise of many small businesses. The computer matches the skills of these businesses with specific contract requirements.

Why Is the Owner Selling the Business?

The owner may be selling the business in order to retire. If so, the buyer may have found a real opportunity. More typically, however, the owner could not make enough money to continue. The buyer's primary concern should be to find out why the business was not a success and what can be done about it. For example, a neighborhood car repair garage may have closed because it could not keep a good mechanic, or because it did not have the right equipment to test engines properly. What needs to be changed about the business depends on what went wrong in the first place.

What Does the Seller Plan to Do Next?

It is important for the person buying a small business to know what the seller is planning to do next. A small business' customers are loyal not so much to the business as they are to the owner. When the owner goes, all the customers might go too. Consider the case of Double-A Swat, a small pest-control firm. Its owner sold the business for $145,000 and invested in a building construction firm. That business went bankrupt in six months. Enough money was then borrowed from family and friends to open up a new pest-control business, Triple-A Swat. It was not long before many of Double-A Swat's customers had switched back to their old friend at Triple-A Swat. This left the new owner of Double-A Swat with a business and no customers.

Some Other Factors

The buyer of a small business should also consider five other factors: profitability, risk, reputation, buildings and equipment, and personnel. The factors are summarized in Table 5-4. Take time right now to be sure you understand why these factors are important.

STARTING A SMALL BUSINESS

Starting a small business is usually much more difficult than buying one. To make this process as trouble free as possible, the small business entrepreneur needs to follow a logical series of steps. Skipping a step can mean the difference between a successful start-up and a great deal of trouble.

Figure 5-4 shows the business start-up effort as a 12-step circular process. It is depicted as a circle because the process begins with the setting of objectives and ends with an attempt to match performance against the objectives.

Step 1: Set Objectives

The first step is to establish realistic objectives for the business. The initial objective is likely to be that the business must make money. But how much money and how quickly? The answers depend upon how well the entrepreneur wants to live—weekend vacations at the lake or three weeks on the Riviera—and whether the owner wants to leave a prosperous business to the children.

Step 2: Evaluate the Market

Which market needs are not currently being met? Can the entrepreneur meet these needs? What product or service of the new business is likely to be the most popular? The second step involves marketing research, but many small business people do not have the skills to conduct this research for themselves. Nor have they enough money to hire a professional market researcher. Many small businesses fail because there was not a market for their new product or service.

Step 3: Determine the Cost of Required Assets

In this step, the owner must determine necessary operating assets and estimate their costs. The best procedure is to list the assets and to estimate the costs by talking with suppliers. For example, a flower shop needs display materials, a large refrigerator, delivery trucks, office furniture, a cash register, as well as a stock of flowers. The cost of the assets depends on how they are obtained. For example, is leasing a building cheaper than buying one? The cost of assets must

Table 5-4

Factors to Consider When Deciding to Start or Buy a Business

Factor	Begin Your Own Business	Buy an Existing Business
Profitability	Larger Profits	Quicker Profits
Risk	More Risk	Less Risk
Reputation	No Reputation Not Easy to Establish	Established Reputation
Buildings and Equipment	No Facilities and Equipment	Facilities and Equipment in Place
Personnel	No Personnel	Personnel in Place

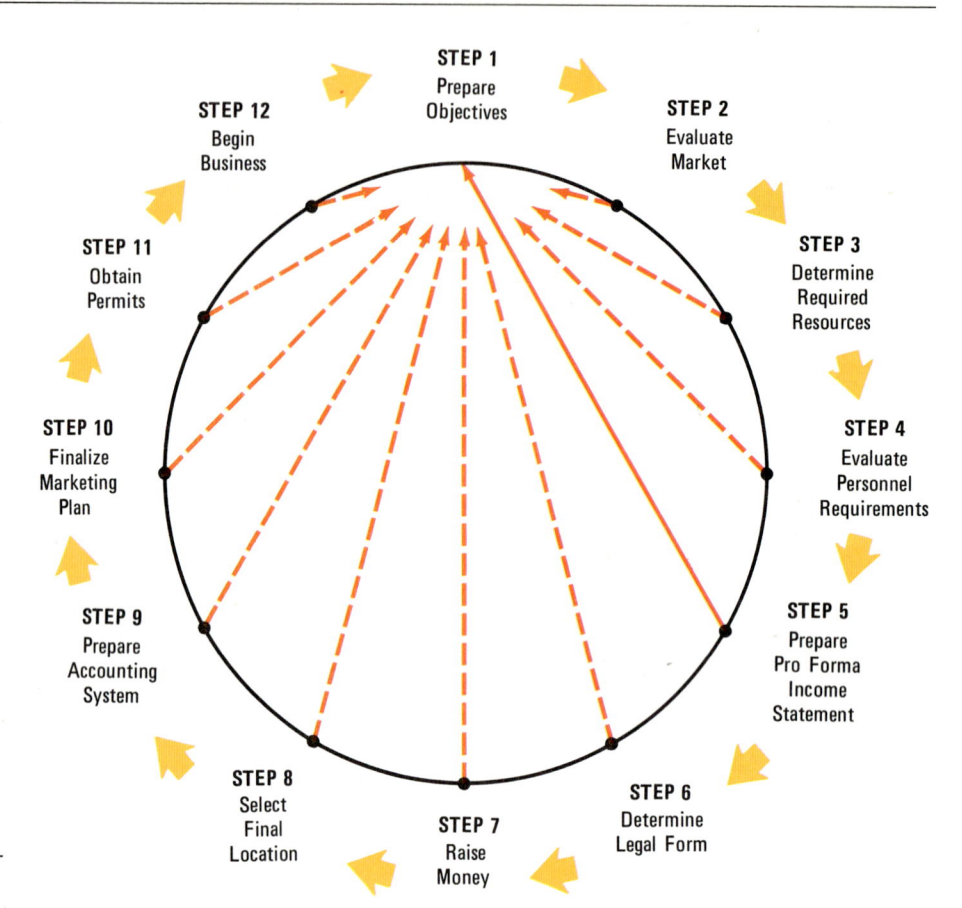

Figure 5-4

Twelve Steps for Starting a New Business

- STEP 1 Prepare Objectives
- STEP 2 Evaluate Market
- STEP 3 Determine Required Resources
- STEP 4 Evaluate Personnel Requirements
- STEP 5 Prepare Pro Forma Income Statement
- STEP 6 Determine Legal Form
- STEP 7 Raise Money
- STEP 8 Select Final Location
- STEP 9 Prepare Accounting System
- STEP 10 Finalize Marketing Plan
- STEP 11 Obtain Permits
- STEP 12 Begin Business

be accurately estimated; otherwise, the entrepreneur may find that expenses have run out of control.

Step 4: Analyze Personnel Requirements

How many people will the firm employ? Will most of the employees be part-time college students or more permanent professional people? Once again, if personnel requirements are not accurately estimated, the entrepreneur may encounter soaring costs. As we said earlier, one of the main problems of a small business is attracting and retaining good people. The way to solve the problem is to formulate explicit personnel policies dealing with the training, supervision, and promotion of employees.

Step 5: Prepare a Pro Forma Income Statement

The entrepreneur now has enough information to prepare a pro forma income statement. An estimate of future sales and expenses, the **pro forma income statement** tells the entrepreneur how much money the business is likely to make once it begins operations. In Figure 5-4, there is a heavy line between Step 5 and Step 1. This means that the owner should compare the pro forma income estimates with the profit objectives (that is, compare Step 5 with Step 1). If the comparison shows that the objectives will not be met, then the owner might need to cut expenses, to raise revenues, or to change the profit objectives. Ultimately, the entrepreneur may have to face up to the possibility that reasonable objectives cannot be reached in the area of business chosen. If this is the case, the individual should look for other small business opportunities.

Many prospective business people resist drawing up pro forma income statements because the statements are nothing more than educated guesses. However, even though forecasting is not always accurate, a pro forma income statement does give a general outline of the likely profit picture.

Step 6: Choose the Right Legal Form

Should the business be organized as a sole proprietorship, a partnership, or a corporation? Most small businesses in the United States are sole proprietorships. Before an organizational form is chosen, however, the entrepreneur should carefully consider the advantages and disadvantages of each type, as discussed in Chapter 4.

Step 7: Raise the Needed Capital

New businesses immediately face the problem of raising capital. It is apparent from Figure 5-5 that personal resources are the largest single source of funds for purchasing or starting a business. Interestingly, lenders are more generous with people buying a business than with people starting one. As the figure shows, 37 percent of the financing for purchased businesses is in the form of loans from banks and other lending institutions. Only 23 percent of the financing for beginning businesses is from these institutions. Lenders by far prefer a proven record of success.

Step 8: Pick a Good Location

Too many small businesses are located where the entrepreneur just happens to find an empty building. The result often is financial disaster. The right location is particularly critical for retail businesses.

Of key importance to small retailers is the pattern of foot and auto traffic in their community. The greater the number of people who pass by a store, the greater the store's number of customers. In a shopping mall, the best location for a small retailer is next to a large store or between two large stores. Many people will pass by the small business on their way to the large one.

Step 9: Prepare the Accounting System

The small business is now getting close to the grand opening. But before that big moment, the entrepreneur must hire an accountant to set up proper bookkeeping procedures. Without an accounting system, there is no way of knowing whether the enterprise has made a profit and whether it owes any taxes.

Step 10: Draw Up the Marketing Plan

In Step 2, the entrepreneur should have evaluated the market. Now, the task is to formulate a marketing strategy to reach the market.

Figure 5-5

Sources of Capital for Entrepreneurs

STARTED BUSINESS, PREVIOUSLY NON-EXISTENT

Source	%
Personal Resources	60%
Lending Institutions	23%
Friends, Relatives	9%
Other	4%
Investors	3%
Government	1%

PURCHASED EXISTING BUSINESS

%	Source
39%	Personal Resources
37%	Lending Institutions
11%	Friends, Relatives
7%	Other
7%	Investors
2%	Government

Source: National Federation of Independent Business Research and Education Foundation.

Profile—
Ralph Velasco, Jr.

In 1950, La Vencedora Tortilla Company was a small family-owned business engaged in the manufacture and sale of corn tortillas. Something big happened to La Vencedora in 1950, however. What happened was Ralph Velasco, Jr.

With a business degree in hand, Ralph joined the family business. He immediately realized that the Mexican food market includes a wide variety of goods and that his competitors were engaged in producing many of these products. There was no reason why La Vencedora shouldn't be doing the same. Between 1950 and 1965, Ralph added a line of wheat flour tortillas, glass-packed sauces, and other products. By adding these products, he spread the cost of distribution among more products and developed a larger market for the company.

In the late 1950s he arranged the purchase of a small canning plant, realizing that many goods La Vencedora wanted to sell needed to be canned, and La Vencedora didn't have the skills or facilities to do this. After the merger, the Velasco family renamed their company Amigos Food Company, Inc. With the canning facilities available, Ralph rapidly added a wide variety of canned Mexican foods and cooking ingredients. Improved sales of these products enabled Amigos to add more non-canned items such as tostadas and fried taco shells. When the product line was complete, consumers were able to buy Amigos tostada shells, Amigos canned refried beans, Amigos sauces and spices, and all the trimmings to make a complete Mexican meal. And as the popularity of Mexican food boomed, so did Amigos.

There were forces at work, however, that would limit Amigos' growth. Pet, a major national milk company with vast resources, entered the Mexican food market and began to compete effectively with all the companies involved. Then the U.S. Department of Agriculture changed its regulations regarding food packaging; these changes made it very difficult for the small independent Mexican food companies to package their foods at a cost low enough to permit a profit.

Ralph's response was to find new products for canning. Amigos had the facilities and the skills; it just needed products to put in the cans. Ralph discovered that Mortons Food Company of Dallas, Texas, a major potato and corn chip manufacturer, was trying to sell bean dip in zip-top aluminum cans. Ralph realized that this was a perfect product for Amigos. It didn't involve meat, which made the burden of U.S.D.A. regulations much less. Mortons was ready to do all the marketing, so Amigos had only to produce the product.

After two years of continuous product research, Amigos found a product that precisely met Mortons' needs. Ralph invested in the machinery needed to handle the zip-top cans and landed the contract. It has been a profitable relationship, and Amigos has continued to expand, adding about 40 major customers for its manufacturing operations. The company now produces six different flavors of dip, and the canning operation, now the largest part of the company, has grown more than tenfold.

While building his business, Ralph hasn't forgotten his community. Ralph has been both vice president and president of the Texas Food Processors Association, a vice president of the Texas Pepper Foundation, president of the Institute of Food Technology, and an active participant in numerous other business organizations. He serves on a variety of university advisory and service committees and councils. The Small Business Administration named Ralph its Small Businessman of the Year.

Ralph effectively combines his professional and personal lives. He understands his business, his industry, and his market. He attempts to improve his company's performance by responding to the needs of the society it serves.

How will the new business tell the public about its product or service? Which is likely to be more effective—television or newspaper advertisements? Should the business offer price discounts? Which brands and styles of products will be most desired by consumers? What pricing strategy will work best?

Step 11: Obtain the Needed Permits

Each state, county, and city has a variety of operating permits that must be obtained before a business may open its doors. For example, real estate agents and hair stylists are required to have certification from the state. In states with a sales tax, the entrepreneur will need a sales tax number. And as an employer, the entrepreneur must register with the state employment office and the Internal Revenue Service.

Step 12: Begin the Business and Match Objectives with Performance

The business is now ready to open its doors, and success depends largely on the flexibility of the entrepreneur. Earlier decisions may have to be changed as the business is forced to meet the test of the marketplace. It may be necessary to substitute television advertising for newspaper advertising, to employ four salespeople instead of three, or to stay open in the evenings. The business' assortment of products or services may need to be altered. The smart entrepreneur must adapt to changes in consumer needs and preferences. The test here is whether the business is achieving its objectives. If objectives and performance are not matched, then the small business owner needs to revise some aspect of the financial, managerial, or marketing plan.

Which elements of this restaurant's marketing strategy can you identify?

FRANCHISING

Purchasing a franchise is another way for the small business entrepreneur to get into business. Examples of successful franchises are not hard to find—just drive to the edge of almost any town and you'll see fast-food restaurants, service stations, and small retail stores, one after another. Franchise outlets are also common in the shopping malls. Before we define franchising, let's

FROM THE FILE

Akira Isobe wanted to open a consumer electronics store in a small neighborhood shopping center. He knew that he had the skill and product knowledge to operate such a store, but he had one big decision still in front of him—whether to open the store as an independent operation or to purchase a franchise from a national seller of consumer electronics. Cautious by nature, Akira made an appointment to talk over the decision with a lawyer, a banker, and three local investors. He knew that several factors were important in the decision—capital costs, access to merchandise, and management advice among them—but he thought it a good idea to prepare a list of pros and cons for each option. He didn't know where to start. Can you help Akira?

Franchises are available across the nation to provide almost any good or service.

Franchising Defined

Franchising is an ownership arrangement whereby the franchisor allows the franchisee to sell the franchisor's products under a strict set of rules, to display the franchisor's sign, and to call upon the franchisor for marketing and operating assistance. In return, the franchisee pays the franchisor a fee or royalty payment to be a part of the franchise system. Most experts agree that, even though a franchise is not perfect, the small business entrepreneur has a better chance of success if part of a franchise system.

Franchising Is Big Business Too

Franchising is not new. The first franchise system in the United States was the Singer Sewing Machine Company. In 1898, General Motors began to market its automobiles through independent franchised dealers. By 1915 franchising had become the primary way to sell and service automobiles, as well as to distribute petroleum products. Today, McDonald's Corporation sells almost $5 billion worth of hamburgers and other fast-food products annually through more than 5,000 franchise outlets. As Figure 5-6 shows, the

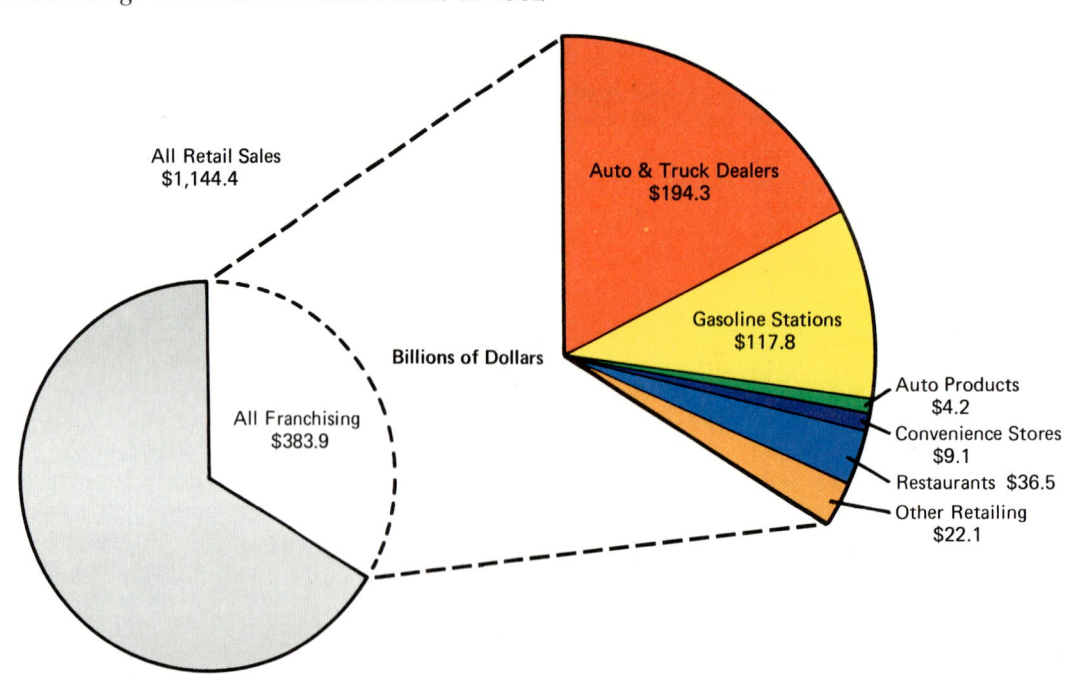

note the difference between a franchisor and a franchisee. The **franchisor** is the corporation that grants the franchise license, along with exclusive territorial distribution, use of its emblem, and whatever other benefits are offered to the franchisee. The **franchisee** is the person or group desiring to start the small business.

Figure 5-6

Franchising: 34 Percent of Retail Sales in 1982

All Retail Sales $1,144.4
All Franchising $383.9
Billions of Dollars
Auto & Truck Dealers $194.3
Gasoline Stations $117.8
Auto Products $4.2
Convenience Stores $9.1
Restaurants $36.5
Other Retailing $22.1

Source: *Franchising in the Economy 1980-1982*, U.S. Department of Commerce, Bureau of Industrial Economics (1982), p. 12.

Department of Commerce estimates that franchise retail establishments in 1982 accounted for nearly $384 billion in retail sales—well over 33 percent of total retail sales in the nation. Most of these sales still are from automobile and petroleum-related products and services.

Pros and Cons of Franchising

Franchising has several distinct advantages and disadvantages. Often, what is an advantage to the franchisor is a disadvantage to the franchisee, or vice versa. Table 5-5 outlines this situation. Let's look at franchising first from the point of view of the franchisor and then from the point of view of the franchisee.

Franchisor's Perspective. From this perspective, the big advantage of franchising is that it allows the franchisor to expand the distribution of its product without making major capital expenditures. The franchisee is usually expected not only to pay the franchisor a fee for the right to open a retail outlet, but also to raise the money needed to build and equip the facility. These requirements eliminate or greatly reduce the capital outlays required of the franchisor. In the franchisee, the franchisor also has a hardworking, highly motivated, and locally oriented person as its representative.

Another advantage for the franchisor is that several sources of revenue can be built into the franchise contract. These include an initial fee to obtain the franchise, a percentage of gross operating revenues, and profits from selling the necessary supplies to the franchisee. As an example, several successfully franchised hamburger restaurants charge more than $100,000 for the outlet, charge a fee of up to 5 percent of monthly sales, and supply the outlets with products ranging from hamburger meat to computer forms.

The main disadvantage to the franchisor is loss of control. If the franchisee does not keep the facility properly maintained, it reflects badly on the franchisor. Also, if the franchisee operates the business in an unusual manner, such as changing operating hours, there may be little the franchisor can do about it.

The franchisor sometimes gives up potential profits by franchising. This disadvantage does not apply to every business, however, since some industrious franchisees make more money for their franchisors than the latter could make for themselves.

Franchisee's Perspective. The big advantage from this perspective is the assistance provided by

Table 5-5

Advantages and Disadvantages of the Franchise System

Franchisor's Perspective	Franchisee's Perspective
Advantages	Advantages
1. Little capital required.	1. Initial training by franchisor.
2. Rapid expansion.	2. Continual advice from franchisor.
3. Local orientation.	3. Reputation of franchisor.
4. Highly motivated franchisees.	
5. Several sources of revenue.	
Disadvantages	Disadvantages
1. Lack of control over franchisee.	1. Large amount of capital required.
2. Must share profits with franchisee.	2. Too much money paid to franchisor.
	3. Franchisee finds it difficult to adapt to local market conditions.
	4. Too much control by franchisor.

the franchisor in establishing the business. Such assistance can include site-location recommendations, help in obtaining local bank financing, and instruction in the day-to-day operation of the facility. Once the franchisee is in business, the franchisor may sponsor training programs for the franchisee's staff.

The franchisee also benefits from the franchisor's reputation. Travelers may not know much about the Holiday Inn in Cincinnati, but they are aware of Holiday Inn's national reputation. As a result, they may be more likely to reserve a room at the Holiday Inn than at an independently operated motel.

One disadvantage is that the franchisee is normally expected to raise most of the capital required to begin operations. For example, as Table 5-6 indicates, buying a McDonald's restaurant costs between $250,000 and $325,000. A Burger King restaurant costs only about $150,000, whereas a Howard Johnson Motor Lodge franchise is $2.5 million.

Another disadvantage, particularly for successful franchisees, is that a big portion of their sales dollars are sent back to the franchisor. Also, the franchisor may not understand local business conditions. This problem is especially important if the franchisee is not allowed to make marketing strategy adjustments on its own.

Opportunities for Small Business Entrepreneurs

Franchising provides an opportunity for people to establish profitable businesses. But, as Table 5-6 shows, franchises are expensive. This makes it impossible for many small entrepreneurs to invest in franchises. A Chevrolet dealership (a small business by government definition) will cost more than $2 million. Not every small business entrepreneur can afford such a price.

Trend Toward Company-Owned Systems

The past few years have seen a trend away from franchised stores and toward company-owned chains. In 1960, 1.2 percent of fast-food franchises were company owned; in 1971, 11.3 percent were; and today the figure is much closer

Table 5-6

Required Investment and Number of Outlets For Ten Franchisors

Franchisor	Total Required Investment	Number of Outlets	Number of Company-Owned Outlets
McDonald's	$ 250,000–325,000	5,216	1,347
Burger King	150,000	2,900	450
Howard Johnson's Motor Lodge	2,500,000	521	131
AAMCO Transmissions	85,000	855	—
Dunkin' Donuts of America	35,000–49,000	1,055	73
Midas Muffler Shops	125,000	1,350	—
Swensen's Ice Cream	350,000	283	13
United Rent-All	160,000	130	—
H&R Block	1,000–2,000	8,000	4,000
PIP-Postal Instant Press	68,000	620	24

Source: U.S. Department of Commerce, *Franchise Opportunities Handbook, 1981*, and Edward L. Dixon, Jr., *The 1981 Franchise Annual Handbook and Directory* (Lewiston, NY, 1981).

Source: Drawing by C. Barsotti; © 1980 The New Yorker Magazine, Inc.

to 20 percent. The reason for this trend is that company-owned outlets may be more profitable than franchised outlets. John Y. Brown, Jr., past president of Kentucky Fried Chicken, has said, "We'll make more profit from three hundred company-owned stores than we will from two thousand franchised outlets."[5] Company-owned stores may be stores that were opened under company ownership, or they may be stores opened as franchises and then repurchased by the franchisor.

Thus, the franchise system may be undergoing a redefinition. A franchise may come to be viewed as a marketing research outpost for the franchisor rather than an opportunity for local businesspeople. If the franchise works out, it will be bought by the franchisor; if it does not, it will become another franchise casualty.

Fraudulent Practices

One of the biggest problem areas in franchising has been the purchase of worthless franchises by unsuspecting people. Many people have lost their entire life savings as a result of such purchases. Most of the abuses can be categorized as one or more of the following:

- Misleading information concerning profitability of the franchise.
- Refusal to show actual profit-and-loss statements for the franchise.
- Hidden charges to the franchisee.
- Improper use of celebrities' names to promote the franchise.
- Misleading promises concerning aid to the franchisee.
- Use of high-pressure sales techniques.[6]

Although several state and national laws protect the small business person from misrepresentation by fraudulent franchisors, these laws have not eliminated misrepresentation totally. The franchisee should make an effort to find out why some franchises succeed and some fail.

---

[5] See Shelby D. Hunt, "The Trend Toward Company-Operated Units in Franchise Chains," *Journal of Retailing* (Summer, 1973), p. 6.

[6] Shelby D. Hunt and John R. Nevin, "Full Disclosure Laws in Franchising: An Empirical Investigation," *Journal of Marketing* (April, 1976), pp. 53-62.

SUMMARY POINTS

1. A small business is defined as one "which is independently owned and operated and not dominant in the field of operation."
2. The Small Business Administration is the principal government agency concerned with the financing, operation, and management of small businesses.
3. Whether measured in terms of share of GNP or total employment, small business plays a major role in our economy.
4. Many small businesses operate in the service, wholesaling, retailing, and production sectors of the economy.
5. The advantages of small business ownership are freedom of operation and potentially large profits. The disadvantage is high risk of failure.
6. Small businesses most often fail because of poor financing and a lack of management skills.
7. Buyers of small businesses should ask themselves why the current owner is selling the business and whether the current owner is likely to open a competing business.
8. Other factors to consider in the purchase of a small business are profitability, risk, reputation, asset condition, and personnel.
9. The start-up of a small business involves 12 steps: (1) set objectives, (2) evaluate the market, (3) determine the cost of needed assets, (4) analyze staff requirements, (5) prepare a pro forma income statement, (6) choose the right

legal form, (7) raise the needed capital, (8) pick a good location for the business, (9) prepare the accounting system, (10) draw up the marketing plan, (11) obtain the needed operating permits, and (12) begin the business and match objectives with performance.
10. Franchising is a small business ownership arrangement whereby the franchisor contributes managerial assistance, marketing expertise, and its corporate emblem, and the franchisee contributes capital, an understanding of local business conditions, and long hours.
11. The advantages of franchising to the franchisor are minimal capital outlays and multiple sources of revenue.
12. The big advantage to the franchisee is the managerial and operating assistance provided by the franchisor.
13. The trend these days is for franchisors to own their franchise outlets.

KEY TERMS AND CONCEPTS

small business
Small Business Administration
guaranty loan
direct loan
service
wholesaling
retailing
production
pro forma income statement
franchising
franchisor
franchisee

REVIEW QUESTIONS

1. How does the federal government define a small business?
2. Do small businesses represent a major share of the nation's gross national product? Has small business's share been increasing or decreasing?
3. What sector of the U.S. economy has the fewest small businesses? Why does this sector have so few small businesses?
4. Outline the advantages and disadvantages of owning your own small business.
5. Why do so many small businesses fail?
6. What are the two most important questions that a buyer of a small business should ask the seller?
7. List the 12 steps that an entrepreneur should go through in starting a new small business.
8. What is a pro forma income statement? How can a small business person successfully use a pro forma income statement?
9. Define franchisor and franchisee.
10. What is the most important disadvantage of franchising from the franchisor's perspective?

DISCUSSION QUESTIONS

1. Do you believe that big business means big bureaucracy? Explain your answer.
2. Would you like to own your own small business? If your answer is yes, what type of small business would you like to own?
3. If you were to open a small business, would you like it to be a franchise outlet? Do the advantages of franchise outweigh the disadvantages from your own point of view?
4. Explain why franchising may really not represent an opportunity for many people.
5. Does the SBA perform a valuable function for small business? Should the average taxpayer be forced to help support the SBA through tax payments?

CASE 5-1

Jan Stuart Natural Skin Care for Men

In 1979, Jan Stuart was out of work. His mother read an article about men's cosmetics and toiletries and told him, "Develop some sensible products that men can comfortably use." The women's cosmetic industry had reached a stage of maturity, and its managers and executives had been casting about for a new kind of product or a new kind of customer. The largest possible market—half of the population—had been right under their noses. Men were ready to buy and use cosmetics. However, except for a few rare and expensive European imports, no men's cosmetics existed. Further, the European imports were scented and advertised in a manner that didn't appeal to the majority of American men.

Jan Stuart wanted a natural/organic product line. It had to satisfy the constraints of the U.S. Food and Drug Administration, which must approve most cosmetics sold in America; it had to appeal to a wide spectrum of American men; and it had to be reasonably priced and provide a good return for the stores which stocked it.

Stuart raised $60,000 and made an initial batch of his products. He first tried promoting them at New York City bathhouses and in men's magazines. His first year, Jan Stuart sold $38,000 worth of products. Meanwhile, he went after the retail outlets for men's cosmetics. He looked for the stores that sold the few successful men's cosmetics such as Aramis and Polo, and made a persistent sales pitch to their buyers. Soon several department stores, including Bloomingdale's, were carrying Jan Stuart cosmetics.

Jan Stuart currently sells over half a million dollars' worth of his cosmetics a year. He has a manufacturer do all the production, so Stuart, whose expertise lies in advertising and marketing, can stick with his specialty.

Stuart realizes that for his company to match the rapid growth of the market it serves, he must find more financing than he has had so far. He particularly needs massive advertising and sales budgets, but he cannot now afford them. Many large cosmetics manufacturers would happily buy him out, but he wants "to be fairly independent and have control of the company."

1. What kind of business is Jan Stuart's—production, wholesale, retail, or service? Is Stuart's company more than one type at once? How?
2. Given three major reasons for business failure—inadequate sales, competitive weakness, and heavy operating expenses—how could Stuart's company fail from each problem? How could he avoid each problem?
3. Using the 12 steps to forming a small business, show how Jan Stuart used good business practice to start his company.
4. If you were in Jan Stuart's position, what would you do now? Seek massive investment from outside sources? Remain a small business? Or do you have another recommendation?

CASE 5-2

Plenum Publishing Company

There has been a substantial need since World War II for communication among scientists of the Soviet Union, Western Europe, and the United States. Plenum Publishing Company was created to promote efficient written communication—especially through scholarly publications.

Plenum Publishing Company was founded by Earl Coleman shortly after the war, and it grew rapidly. Soon Plenum was translating English-language documents into Russian. The next step was to form agreements with Soviet periodicals, publishing houses, scientists, and authors. Soviet scientists who wrote for English-speaking audiences acquired great prestige in their own country and were happy to write for Plenum even though pay was very low.

Plenum's publications, with titles such as *Lithuanian Mathematical Journal, International Journal of Infrared and Millimeter Waves*, and *Hyperbaric Oxygen Review*, do not sell in large quantities. Plenum's best-selling periodical, *Digestive Diseases and Sciences*, sells only about 4,000 copies, while its best-selling book, *Monoclonal Antibodies*, sold fewer than 6,000 copies.

Plenum is not concerned over its low sales volume, however. It owns the rights to English-language translations of 95 Soviet scientific journals for the next ten years, and it has many, if not most, of the Soviet Union's top writers and scientists under contract to write and translate for the publishing company.

Plenum operates on a very tight budget. Martin Tash, who now runs the company, is financially very conservative. He realizes that ready cash is the best measure of health for a small company, so he keeps about 30 percent of the company's assets in cash or in a form readily convertible to cash. Therefore, the company never has to worry about excess debt and other financing problems that many small businesses face.

It is becoming difficult to call Plenum Publishing a small business. With careful financial planning and good management by Martin Tash, Plenum now has sales of over $26 million, and profits of nearly $4 million a year. Plenum is an excellent example of the small business that has succeeded.

1. What kind of business is Plenum—production, wholesale, retail, or service? Is it more than one kind? How?
2. How has Plenum managed to avoid the three main causes of business failure listed in Table 5-4?
3. If you were considering buying Plenum Publishing Company, how would you evaluate its profitability, risk, reputation, buildings and equipment, and personnel?
4. How might motives differ between a small business buying out Plenum and a very large publishing house buying out Plenum?

Legal Aspects of Business

6

After studying this chapter, you should be able to:

- Define statutory law, common law, and administrative law.
- Discuss the key elements in a contract.
- Describe the objectives of the major federal antitrust laws.
- Explain how the government regulates personal selling and advertising.
- Discuss the major elements of governmental protection of employees.

It's possible to go through life without being a lawyer. Millions of us do so every day. It may even be possible to go through life without ever needing the services of a lawyer. But it definitely is not possible to work in business today without knowing something about the legal environment. This chapter introduces the major areas of business law. A general understanding of the legal environment of business can keep managers from making costly mistakes.

Let's begin our study of the legal environment of business by looking at the three basic types of law in the United States and the origin of this law.

THE LAW: WHAT IT IS AND WHERE IT COMES FROM

The law of the United States can be classified in a bewildering number of ways. For the sake of simplicity, however, let us recognize three major types of law: statutory law, common law, and administrative law. We make this three-fold division on the basis of how law originates. We'll define **the law** as the standards of conduct, established and enforced by government.

Statutory Law

Statutory law refers to the legal rules and regulations enacted by legislative bodies, such as the Congress of the United States and the 50 state legislatures. Statutory law is also made by city government, such as the city council in your town when it passes a municipal ordinance. Individually, each law enacted by a legislative body is called a **statute**. Most law in this country is statutory.

Statutory law governs a wide range of business activities. It governs how a firm may issue stock and otherwise raise money, under what terms it may sell its merchandise to the public, and how it is to treat employees. The laws of each state governing the incorporation of new businesses are examples of statutory law.

Common Law

Common law is often called **unwritten law** or **case law**. Unlike statutory law, which is made by a legislative body and set forth in the text of the legislative act, common law is made by judges in reaching decisions on cases brought before them. Common law exists because the appropriate legislative body has chosen not to enact comprehensive statutes (or statutory law) in these areas.

In common law, past court decisions provide **precedents** for future decisions in the same areas of law; that is, past decisions guide the courts in settling new controversies. Normally, these precedents are established by courts of appeal, state supreme courts, and the U.S. Supreme Court. The law relating to contracts is an example of common law. The principles of contract law evolved gradually over the years through the case-by-case decisions issued by the courts. In a minute we'll look at the general principles of contract law.

Because common law is not as clearly defined as statutory law, it presents a few problems for business people. It is not always clear whether any particular action will be found to be in violation of the law. Also, many courts establish and apply common law principles. Each of the 50 states has its own body of state common law. Still, the flexibility of common law does enable the courts to apply the law in a way that makes sense in today's world.

Administrative Law

The third general type of law is administrative law. **Administrative law** refers to the rules and regulations issued by the many governmental boards, commissions, and agencies. The governmental bodies can be federal, state, or local. The National Labor Relations Board, the Securities and Exchange Commission, and the Federal Trade Commission are examples of federal agencies with rule-making powers. At present, there are more than 150 federal agencies with such powers. Figure 6-1 lists eight of the more

The availability of some products is regulated by administrative law.

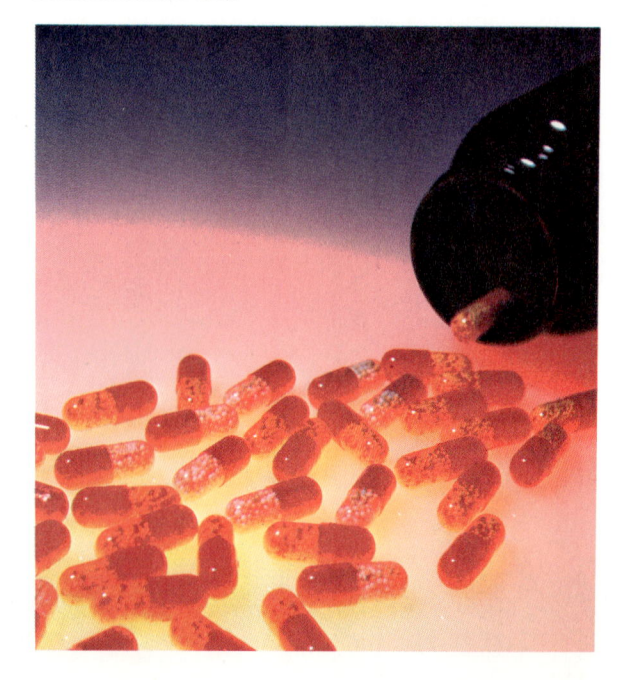

Figure 6-1

Important Federal Agencies

> **FEDERAL RESERVE BOARD**—Control money supply; supply dollar bills and coins to banks; lend money to banks; help clear and collect checks; regulate federal banks.
>
> **CONSUMER PRODUCT SAFETY COMMISSION**—Make safety standards for all consumer products.
>
> **PURE FOOD AND DRUG ADMINISTRATION**—Ensure that foods are safe and pure, ensure drugs are safe and effective, cosmetics are harmless, and products are honestly and informatively labeled.
>
> **INTERNAL REVENUE SERVICE**—Collect federal income taxes and make administrative rules as to how income and expenses must be reported by taxpayers.
>
> **FEDERAL TRADE COMMISSION**—Stop monopolies at their beginning; protect business and consumers from deceptive trade practices.
>
> **ENVIRONMENTAL PROTECTION AGENCY**—Develop and enforce rules that protect the nation's environment against all types of pollution.
>
> **SECURITIES AND EXCHANGE COMMISSION**—Regulate the nation's stock and bond markets to ensure that investors are not defrauded.
>
> **FEDERAL COMMUNICATION COMMISSION**—Regulate the nation's radio airwaves (radio, television, long-distance telephone).

important of these agencies and their primary regulatory responsibilities.

Although you may not have heard of administrative law before, instances of it are all around us. When the state public utility commission regulates the rates charged by the local power plant, it is making administrative law. When the Federal Communications Commission issues a license for the operation of a television station, it is making administrative law. When the Civil Aeronautics Board requires certain sections aboard commercial aircraft to be designated "nonsmoking areas," it is making administrative law. Each of these rules, decisions, or regulations has the force of law.

CONTRACTS: MORE THAN JUST A HANDSHAKE

Many business actions involve a contract between two or more people or companies. The purchase of raw materials, the sale of products, and the buying or leasing of land all usually involve a contract. A **contract** is an agreement between two or more people. It defines the relationship between these people in the performance of a specified action. The action might be the construction of an office warehouse or the delivery of plumbing supplies to a construction site. The agreement might be between a contractor and a group of investors or between the contractor and a plumbing supply house.

Strictly speaking, not all agreements are contracts—only those that a court is willing to enforce. An enforceable contract is one that meets certain requirements. We'll look at these requirements first and then discuss the advantages of written contracts and the Uniform Commercial Code.

Five Elements of a Contract

Figure 6-2 shows the five elements of a contract. All of these elements must be present for an agreement to be a legally enforceable contract.

Agreement. The basic element of a contract is an agreement between two or more persons. The agreement must be reasonably clear as to what the parties to the contract are expected to do. The agreement is broken down into an offer and an acceptance. An **offer** is a proposal to enter into a contractual relationship; an **acceptance** is an expression of willingness, on the part of the second party, to be legally bound by the terms of the offer. Acceptance of the offer can be signaled by signing a printed contract, by shaking hands, or by raising one's hand in agreement. The Chicago Commodity Exchange provides an example of this last type of communication: Billions of dollars of agricultural produce are bought and sold there by people who simply raise a hand to signal intent to buy.

Contractual Capacity. Not all people can enter into a legally binding contract. In most states, a person must be at least 18 years of age to do so. Other examples of people without **contractual**

Figure 6-2

Key Elements in a Contract

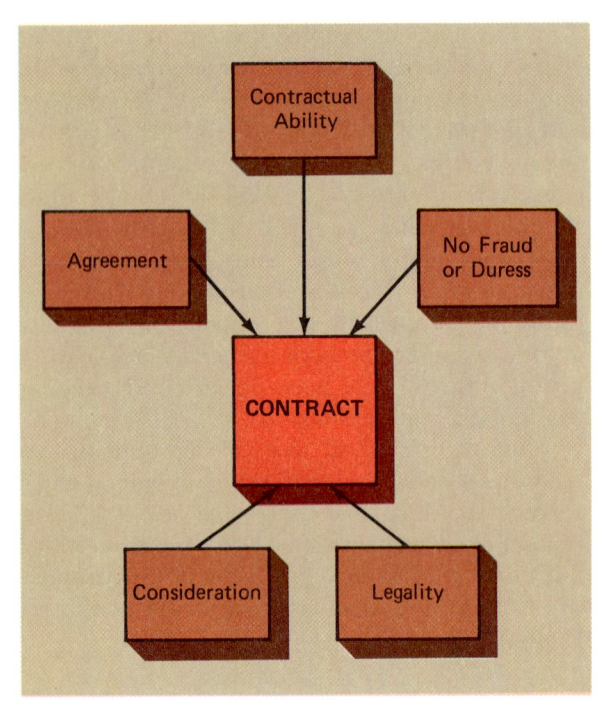

capacity, as this is called, are insane persons and persons under the influence of liquor or drugs.

No Fraud or Duress. Even if a contract met all the other requirements, it would not be legally valid if there were a willful misrepresentation of fact, or fraud, or if one party to the contract negotiated under duress.

A willful misrepresentation of fact is called **fraud**. The following is an example of fraud: Jones agrees to sell a building to Smith. Jones tells Smith that the roof on the building is two months old when, in fact, it's ten years old and about to collapse. Smith agrees to the sale, believing Jones' statement about the roof to be true. The fraud is the misleading information about the roof. Smith's deception renders the contract invalid.

A person who is *forced* to enter into an agreement is said to have negotiated under **duress**. Duress can be either physical or economic. An example of physical duress is a contract negotiated at gunpoint. An example of economic duress is a threat of great financial loss: "If you don't buy inventory from me, I'll make sure you lose your four top accounts." In the case of either physical or economic duress, the victim is not legally bound by the contract.

Consideration. Think about this situation: You offer to cut your neighbor's lawn for free next week. Your neighbor accepts. Is there a contract? No. Now consider this situation: You offer to cut your neighbor's lawn for $20 next week. Agreeing to the $20 price, your neighbor accepts the offer. Is there a contract? Yes.

What's the difference between these two situations? Consideration. In the first, your neighbor offered nothing in return for your promise to cut the lawn. Thus, even though you offered to cut the lawn for free, you are not legally bound to do so. In the second situation, your neighbor offered something of value (it does not have to be money) in return for your promise, namely, $20. You are legally bound to cut the grass and your neighbor is legally bound to pay you. That which each party agrees to give up—your time and effort and your neighbor's $20—is called **consideration**. If both parties do not give up something, there is no contract.

Legality. Finally, a contract cannot be valid if the action agreed to is itself illegal. A contract calling for the commission of a crime, therefore, is not enforceable. An agreement between a loan shark and a consumer in which the former lends money to the latter at an interest rate above the rate permitted by state law, for example, would not be a legal contract. As a result, if the consumer later refused to pay, the loan shark could not use the courts to collect the money.

Written and Oral Contracts

With few exceptions, an oral contract is just as binding as a written contract. In general, however, all contracts should be written. There are three reasons. First, a written contract assures both parties that each of the five elements of a contract is present. Do you remember all five elements? Second, each party to a written contract knows exactly what he or she is required to do. Third, a written contract makes it difficult for any party to the contract to deny having made the contract.

A few major businesses have made big mistakes by not putting a contract into writing. Several years ago, for example, the Boeing Company, the leading maker of commercial jet aircraft, contracted with the Pittsburgh-Des Moines Steel Company to build a wind tunnel for

In some situations, raising a hand may bind the parties to a contract.

airplane design testing. Pittsburgh-Des Moines subcontracted with the York-Gillespie Company to do part of the work on the project. A supplier of York-Gillespie sued Boeing because York-Gillespie would not pay for some materials it had purchased. The courts found that Boeing was indeed liable because its executives had previously assured the supplier, orally but not in writing, that the bill would be paid. The courts found that this assurance was in fact a contract between the supplier and Boeing, even though nothing had been put in writing.[1] Confused? See Figure 6-3.

Uniform Commercial Code

The Uniform Commercial Code (UCC) was drafted in 1952. It has now been adopted by 49 states, the District of Columbia, and the Virgin Islands. The only state that has not adopted the UCC is Louisiana.

The UCC deals with a number of business practices, including bank deposits, letters of credit, warehouse receipts, and investment securities. Section 2 of the UCC deals specifically with the buying and selling of merchandise. Two of the most important provisions of Section 2 are the requirements for a sales contract and the requirements for a warranty.

Sales Contracts. All contracts to which the UCC applies must meet the same requirements for a contract shown in Figure 6-2. In addition, all contracts for the sale of goods valued at $500 or more, with few exceptions, must be in writing. This does not mean that two people, simply by shaking hands, cannot agree to a sales transaction involving equipment or property valued at $500 or more. However, it does mean that the courts will not enforce such a contract.

Warranties. The UCC defines both express and implied warranties. An **express warranty** is any "fact or promise" made by the seller to the buyer concerning a product. An example is a new car warranty requiring the manufacturer to pay for

Figure 6-3

The Boeing Airplane Case

```
Boeing Company
      |
      v
Pittsburgh-Des
Moines Steel
Company
      |
      v
York-Gillespie
Company
      |
      v
Supplier to
York-Gillespie
```

———— Written Contracts
- - - - - Oral Contracts
══════ Line of Suit

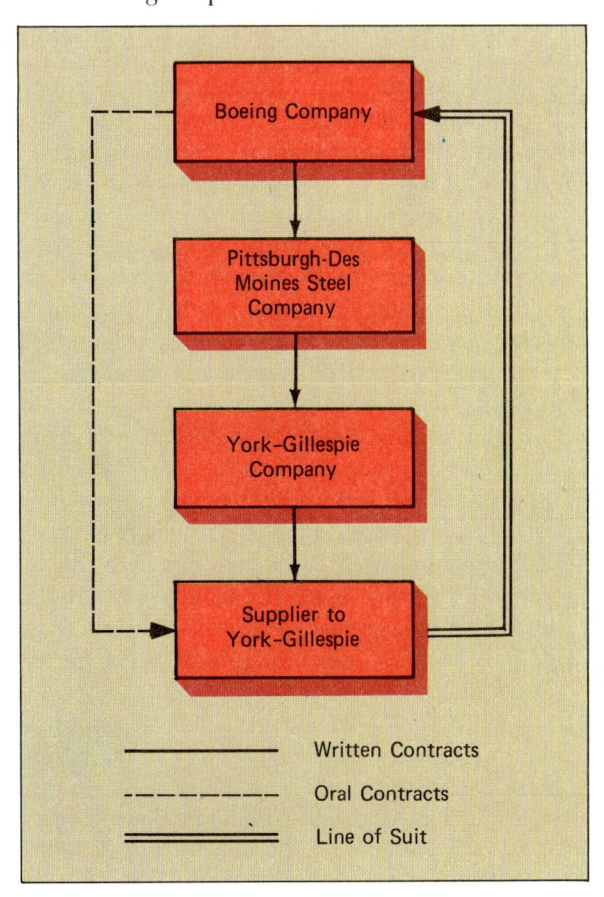

[1] Ronald A. Anderson, Ivan Fox, and David P. Twomey, *Business Law* (Cincinnati: South-Western Publishing Co., 1981), p. 204.

all parts and labor on repairs for the first 12,000 miles or 12 months, whichever comes first.

An **implied warranty** is the guarantee by the seller that the product sold is at least of "average quality" and is "adequately packaged and labeled." This protects the buyer in cases where the product turns out to be broken, spoiled, or otherwise unusable. When a dairy signs a contract to sell milk to a supermarket, there is an implied warranty that the milk delivered will be fresh.

REGULATION OF COMPETITION

We sometimes say that we have a free enterprise system—but business firms are not free to do whatever they choose. Instead, they must operate within a set of market rules. Although these rules regulate and constrain business activity, their purpose is to encourage open, vigorous, and fair competition—that is, to make our economy more competitive, more efficient, less monopolistic. Let's look at a few of these rules.

Sherman Act (1890)

This act, the first and most famous of the government's antitrust legislation, states that "every contract, combination . . . or conspiracy, in restraint of trade or commerce among the several states, or with foreign nations, is hereby declared to be illegal." Any person engaging in a monopolistic practice or conspiring to do so is guilty of a felony. The Sherman Act is enforced by the U.S. Department of Justice.

There are three types of penalties for violations of the Sherman Act. The first two are fines and prison sentences. Although the courts have generally been willing to fine individuals and companies, only recently have they shown much interest in sending executives to jail. The third type of penalty is the civil damages that the injured party can claim. If executives of General Electric, Westinghouse, and Allis Chalmers met privately to determine how much to charge customers for their electrical equipment, they would be violating the Sherman Act. An electric utility that bought such equipment from GE or Westinghouse could claim penalties of up to three times the amount of the actual damage. Therefore, if a utility paid $300,000 too much for a turbine as a result of a conspiracy to restrain trade, it could claim $900,000 in damages. This situation occurred several years ago, and General Electric alone was forced to pay nearly $600 million in penalties.

Clayton Act (1914)

The intent of the Clayton Act, passed in 1914, was to make the Sherman Act more effective. Several provisions of the Clayton Act are of special interest to us. One provision outlaws both tying agreements and exclusive agreements. In a **tying agreement**, a seller agrees to sell a product to a buyer on the condition that the buyer also purchases other, often unwanted, merchandise from the seller. In an **exclusive agreement**, the seller, as a condition of the sale, forbids the buyer from purchasing for resale the products of competing sellers.

Another provision prohibits companies from purchasing stock in competing companies if the effect would be to reduce competition in the marketplace. In addition, a person may not sit on the boards of directors of two or more competing companies if such companies each have annual sales greater than one million dollars.

Federal Trade Commission Act (1914)

The Federal Trade Commission Act was passed in the same year as the Clayton Act. This act did two things. First, it established the Federal Trade Commission (FTC) to enforce the Clayton Act. Second, it gave the commission the authority to define "unfair methods of competition" and to issue cease and desist orders. A **cease and desist order** is a ruling by the FTC requiring a company to stop an unfair business practice. If the company chooses not to obey the order, the FTC can prosecute the company in federal court for violating either the FTC Act or the Clayton Act. Note that the FTC cannot enforce its own rulings: It must work through the courts.

REGULATION OF PROMOTION

The Federal Trade Commission protects consumers from unfair promotional practices. Thus, fraud in advertising is now illegal. Let's examine in greater detail how the government regulates personal selling and advertising.

Personal Selling

Salespeople are frequently accused of using high-pressure tactics, that is, of tricking people into buying products they don't want. For example, a salesperson might use one of the aggressive sales appeals shown in Table 6-1.

To protect the consumer from such tactics, the FTC adopted the Cooling-Off Rule, and Congress passed the Truth-in-Lending Act, formally known as the Consumer Credit Protection Act.

Cooling-Off Rule (1974). The FTC's **Cooling-Off Rule** protects the consumer from making unwise purchases at home. The rule states that anyone buying a product or service for $25 or more from a door-to-door salesperson has the right to cancel the purchase within 72 hours and to receive a full refund. The seller also must inform the customer of this right of cancellation by printing the following statement on all sales contracts: "You, the buyer, may cancel this transaction at any time prior to midnight of the third business day after the date of this transaction. See the attached notice of cancellation form for an explanation of this right." In addition, the seller must give the buyer a notice form which can be used to cancel the sale. This rule has been quite effective in protecting unwary consumers from high-pressure sales tactics.

Truth-in-Lending Act (1969). Credit is part of the American way of life. Unfortunately, many consumers do not understand how interest rates are calculated. Prior to the Truth-in-Lending Act, some financial institutions and retail stores took advantage of this fact and charged customers deceptively high interest rates. Table 6-2 illustrates the problem by showing how the stated interest rate can vary depending upon how the loan is repaid and how the rate is calculated. Under the Truth-in-Lending Act, the Federal Reserve Board has the power to specify how interest rates on consumer purchases are to be calculated and reported to the consumer. In this way, it is hoped, consumers will make better purchase decisions.

Advertising

As we said before, the FTC protects consumers from misleading advertising. An advertisement is considered misleading if the overall impression given is misleading. For example, Cranberry Juice Cocktail was advertised on national television as good for you because it had a lot of "food energy." The FTC reasoned that many people might assume that food energy meant vitamins or proteins when, in fact, food energy is nothing more than calories. Why was the ad found to be in violation of the law? Because the overall impression was misleading even though the claim of more "food energy" was literally true.

Puffery. The FTC has tried to draw a line between puffery and misleading advertising. **Puffery** refers to innocent exaggerations used to sell a product. "We have the best used cars in town."

Table 6-1

High-Pressure Sales Tactics

Appeals	Statement
Timeliness	"Prices are expected to go up 5 percent next month."
	"This is the last one we have in stock. I do not know when we will be able to get any more."
Fear	"There have been a number of burglaries in this area. You really need a burglar alarm for your home."
	"This life insurance program will protect your family if you are not here."
Flattery	"Everyone in your social position has one of these."
	"You look great in this brown suit. You are a born trend setter."
Emotion	"If you do not buy six years of *Ladies Home Journal* and *Forbes*, I will not be able to go back to college."
	"For each ten new newspaper subscriptions I sell, the newspaper will donate $1 to the American Cancer Society."

Table 6-2

Differences in True Interest as a Result of Payment Schedules

	Payment at the End of One Year	Principal and Interest Paid in 12 Equal Monthly Payments
Loan	$1,000	$1,000
Interest Charges	$100	$100
Real Interest	10%	18%

Under both payment schedules, the value of the loan ($1,000) and total interest charges ($100) are the same. Under the first, however, the entire amount of the loan is borrowed for a year, but under the second, it is paid back in equal monthly installments over the year. Therefore, at the end of the sixth month, the amount of principal owed on the first is $1,000, but only about $500 on the second. As a result, the effective interest rate on the second payment schedule is higher because the average loan balance is smaller.

"No one else has better deals than we do." Both of these claims are examples of puffery.

Most consumers probably realize that such claims are intended simply to attract their attention and not to convey meaningful information. Thus, the FTC does not view puffery as either fraudulent or misleading. Figure 6-4 shows an advertisement that ran in the 1870s. It is an example of puffery in the extreme.

Corrective Advertising. When the FTC decides that an advertisement is misleading, it usually issues a cease and desist order. As mentioned earlier, this order stops the firm from running the advertisement. If the ad has already misled many people, the FTC may require the sponsoring firm to run corrective advertising.

The purpose of corrective advertising is to tell the public the truth about the product. The corrective advertisement must use the same media as the original misleading advertisement. The Ocean Spray Company, maker of Cranberry Juice Cocktail, was required to run a corrective television ad stating that "food energy" is just calories. The transcript of the original commercial for Cranberry Juice Cocktail and the corrective advertisement are shown in Figure 6-5 on page 108.

Even though the FTC does a good job of protecting consumers from deceptive trade practices, the Congress has passed a number of laws in this area. Table 6-3 on page 109 lists 11 of the more important laws.

EMPLOYEE PROTECTION

The federal government takes an active role in protecting the health and safety of working people. We begin this section of the chapter by examining some of the older federal statutes concerning employee protection. We then look at the Occupational Safety and Health Administration and at job discrimination.

From the Beginning

During the 1930s, it became generally accepted that the federal government had a responsibility to protect people in the work place. No longer was it simply assumed that businesses would treat their employees fairly and with a concern for their well-being.

Wages and Hours. The Fair Labor Standards Act of 1938 introduced both the minimum wage and the 40-hour work week. At the time of passage, the minimum wage was set at $0.40 per hour. It is now more than $3.50 an hour. The law also said that workers must receive time-and-a-half pay for time spent on the job in excess of the 40-hour standard.

Not all employees are covered by the Fair Labor Standards Act. People in managerial, professional, or sales positions, for example, are not protected by the act.

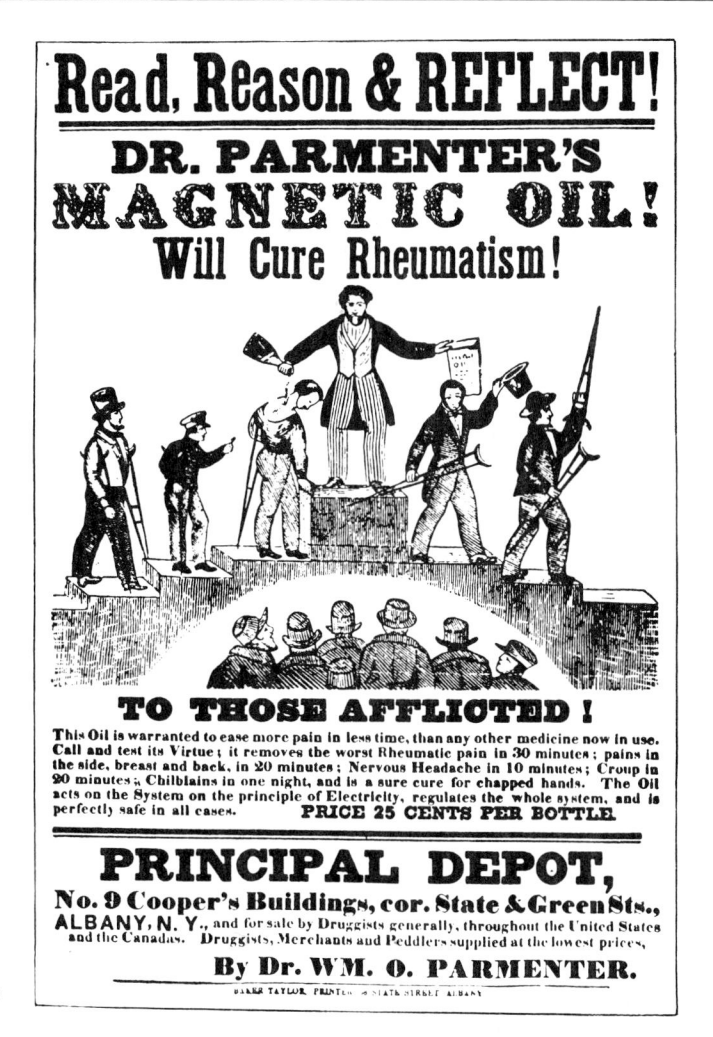

Figure 6-4

Can you spot the puffery?

Child Labor. The Fair Labor Standards Act also regulates child labor. The minimum age for most jobs is now 16. The employment of 14- and 15-year-olds is restricted to a few types of jobs, such as filing and sales. The range of jobs for children under 14 years of age is even more restricted: They may deliver newspapers, work as actors or actresses, or hold selected farm jobs.

Social Security. The Social Security Act, passed in 1935, established our social security system. The aim of the system is to provide a minimum guaranteed income to retired and disabled persons. Today, about one out of every seven people in the United States receives a social security check each month.

The social security system is funded by a tax on employees and employers. In 1983, employees were required to pay into the system an amount equal to 6.70 percent of their first $35,700 earned; employers were required to match that amount. The rate for self-employed persons was 9.35 percent on the first $35,700 earned. Currently, more than 90 percent of working people in this country pay into the social security system regularly. The average worker pays about the same amount in social security tax as in federal income tax.

An issue of great social consequence is the continued solvency of social security system. Even with an increase in the social security tax rate, there may not be enough money in the system to continue paying benefits indefinitely. The reason is that the pool of working people (those paying into the system) is growing at a slower rate than the pool of retired people (those drawing from it).

Unemployment Benefits. Each state has a program for protecting people who lose their jobs

Figure 6-5

Cranberry Juice Cocktail Advertisements

Original Advertisement

"Cranberry Juice Cocktail is more than a new taste for breakfast. Cranberry juice is good for you. Has even more food energy than orange or tomato juice. Ocean Spray—the start of something big."

Corrective Advertisement

"If you wondered what some of our earlier advertising meant when we said Ocean Spray Cranberry Juice Cocktail has more food energy than orange juice or tomato juice, let us make it clear. We didn't mean vitamins and minerals. Food energy means calories. Furthermore, food energy is important at breakfast as many of us may not get enough calories or food energy to get off to a good start. Ocean Spray Cranberry Juice Cocktail helps because it contains more food energy than most other breakfast drinks. Ocean Spray."

through no fault of their own. These programs differ in cost and coverage, but they must all meet certain federal guidelines. Under these programs, employers pay a tax to the state—usually equal to 1 percent or less of the wage of each covered employee earning $1,500 or more during any single quarter of the year. Recently unemployed workers may then draw upon these funds for the duration of their unemployment, subject to certain restrictions.

People must have worked at least 12 weeks before losing their jobs in order to be eligible for unemployment benefits. Those fired for poor performance, leaving the job voluntarily, or refusing to accept work for which they are qualified are not entitled to these benefits.

Occupational Safety and Health Act (1970)

The goal of the Occupational Safety and Health Act is to reduce the number of safety and health hazards in the work place. The law established the Occupational Safety and Health Administration (OSHA) and gave the Secretary of Labor the authority to set health and safety standards for individual industries.

HERMAN

"You'll have to move your lunchbox. It's blocking the fire exit."

Source: Copyright 1982, Universal Press Syndicate. Reprinted with permission. All rights reserved.

Table 6-3

Selected Consumer Protection Laws

Act	Description
Food and Drug Act (1906)	Established the Food and Drug Administration and prohibited unsafe and adulterated food and drug products from being sold in interstate commerce.
Federal Trade Commission Act (1914)	Established the Federal Trade Commission to guard against "unfair methods of competition."
Wheeler-Lea Act (1938)	Amended the Federal Trade Commission Act; expanded the consumer protection activities of the FTC to include "unfair or deceptive acts or practices."
Flammable Fabrics Act (1953)	Made it illegal to sell or manufacture clothing that is flammable enough to be dangerous.
Fair Packaging and Labeling Act (1966)	Regulated packaging and labeling of consumer goods; provided for the voluntary adoption, by industry, of uniform packaging standards.
Cigarette Labeling Act (1966)	Required health warning labels on cigarette packaging.
Consumer Credit Protection Act (1968) (Truth-in-Lending)	Required full disclosure of terms and conditions of finance charges in consumer credit transactions.
Child Protection and Toy Safety Act (1969)	Amended Hazardous Substance Labeling Act (1960) to ban toys and other articles used by children that pose electrical, mechanical, or thermal hazards.
Consumer Product Safety Act (1972)	Established Consumer Product Safety Commission and gave it broad authority to propose safety standards for consumer products and to levy penalties for failure to meet the standards.
Magnuson-Moss Warranty/Federal Trade Commission Improvement Act (1975)	Expanded FTC powers to include rule-making with respect to consumer product warranties and unfair or deceptive acts or practices. Also provided for consumer redress through class action suits.
Consumer Education Act (1978)	Established the Office of Consumer Education which supports consumer education research projects.

Inspections. How does OSHA find out about safety and health hazards? One way is through unannounced inspections, which may be requested by an employee or by the employee's union. Inspections may also be initiated by OSHA personnel themselves as a part of regular inspection programs.

If the OSHA inspection turns up one or more violations, the firm is issued a citation. The firm then has 15 days to appeal to an OSHA review board. In general, the severity of the penalty depends upon the nature of the violation. Fines can be as high as $10,000 for each willful violation. An employer who totally disregards an OSHA rule may be prosecuted as a criminal and sent to jail for up to one year.

Criticisms. OSHA has been one of the most widely criticized agencies of the federal government. In its first five years, OSHA put 10,000 safety rules into effect. Many of these rules were seen as trivial or unnecessary. For example, according to OSHA, ranch workers must be able to reach toilet facilities within five minutes, even when out on the range. Wall-mounted fire extinguishers must be exactly five feet from the

Profile—
Judge Learned Hand

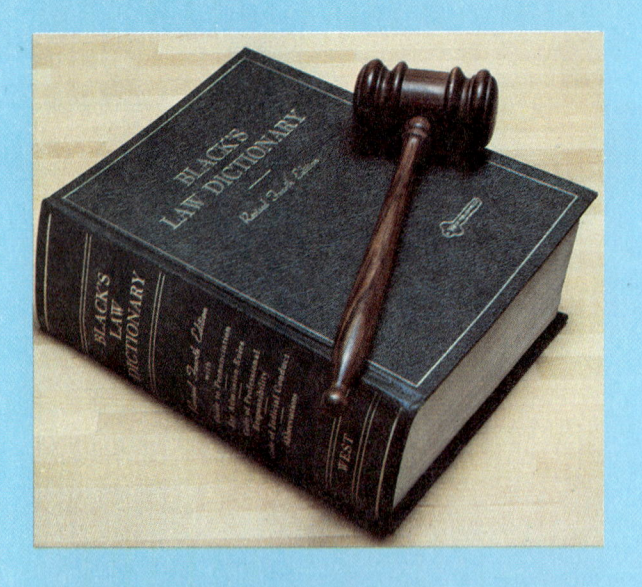

When one speaks of famous judges, the members of the Supreme Court automatically come to mind. Learned Hand was never a member of the Supreme Court, but his legal career was so far-reaching that the man is a legend unmatched by any jurist of this century.

Learned Hand was born in 1872, the son of a New York Court of Appeals judge and the grandson of a New York Supreme Court justice. He studied philosophy as an undergraduate, but decided he preferred law and obtained a law degree from Harvard. He practiced law for 12 years and then was offered a seat on the New York Southern District Court. For 15 years he occupied this position, until he advanced to the U.S. Second Circuit Court of Appeals in New York. It was when Hand became an appeals judge that he truly found his calling.

Appeals judges, unlike trial judges, must explain their decisions. They do this in "judges' decisions," written descriptions of their arguments, reasoning, and conclusions. These decisions are published and used by lawyers in trial courts to formulate arguments in their cases. The appeals judges who have achieved lasting fame are those who wrote the most influential and far-reaching decisions, and Learned Hand was certainly the best.

Learned Hand wrote more than two thousand opinions between 1924 and 1951. He was highly respected by fellow judges and clerks alike, although certainly not for his writing methods. While most judges used law clerks to write initial drafts of decisions and often paid scant attention to the decisions at all, Hand painstakingly wrote and rewrote every decision he ever signed.

Hand never believed that judges knew best, nor that there was any "best" to be known. He reasoned that American citizens are ultimately responsible for all law. If they are unhappy about the law, they must elect members of Congress who will change the law. He never accepted the common argument of his time that the courts were the defenders of the Constitution; he felt that a constitution which only a court could save could no longer be saved. He distrusted judges even more than he distrusted members of Congress, basing his arguments wherever possible on the written law.

Hand's most famous case was *U.S. vs. The Aluminum Company of America* (Alcoa). In the middle of World War II, the Supreme Court was asked to hear an antitrust suit brought by the Justice Department against Alcoa. Because of the war and political problems, the Supreme Court couldn't find a quorum of judges, so Congress passed a special act ordering Judge Hand to judge the final appeal of the Alcoa case. He had to read over 40,000 pages of testimony and evidence and listen to the arguments of more than 80 lawyers and prosecutors. The legal briefs submitted by the government and by Alcoa ran to hundreds of pages apiece. Yet, at the end of his deliberations, Judge Hand wrote a decision that was less than eight pages long and has been the clearest standard for judging monopoly cases yet written.

Long before his retirement Judge Hand was famous to lawyers and the public alike. He received honorary doctoral degrees from Columbia, Yale, Amherst, Dartmouth, Princeton, Cambridge, University of Chicago, Washington University, and several other universities. When he died in 1961, Judge Hand was eulogized by politicians and lawyers across the country. Even today, Learned Hand is one of the most quoted appeals court judges and is standard fare for any lawyer specializing in business law.

Health and safety hazards are present in many jobs. Workers must be protected.

floor—no more, no less. Backup alarms are required of all construction vehicles, yet construction workers must wear ear plugs!

The complexity of some OSHA rules has also been a source of frustration to management. As Figure 6-6 indicates, it took OSHA no fewer than 41 words to define the term "exit." It took the agency 35 pages to describe how exit signs should be designed.

But OSHA has responded to its critics. First, it eliminated much of the unnecessary paperwork that it had imposed on small businesses. Second, it dropped some 1,100 rules entirely. Third, it shifted its inspection efforts away from nonhazardous businesses, such as insurance companies and retail stores, to such hazardous industries as construction, heavy manufacturing, transportation, and petrochemicals. Fourth, it focused more on health issues, such as worker exposure to noise, lead, mercury, and asbestos. OSHA does its job: it protects the U.S. worker in the workplace.

Employment Discrimination

It has been necessary for Congress to pass several laws that directly address the problem of employment discrimination. The Civil Rights Act of 1964 and the Equal Employment Act of 1972 are two. These laws make it illegal to discriminate in hiring or promotional decisions on the basis of race, color, religion, national origin, or sex.

Enforcement Procedures. The Civil Rights Act established the Equal Employment Opportunity Commission (EEOC), which is responsible for enforcing federal law relating to job discrimination. The EEOC can take a firm to court if it violates the law. The more usual practice is to persuade the offending firm to change its policies and pay damages to any person discriminated against. When AT&T was charged by the EEOC with keeping women and minorities in low-paying jobs, the phone company agreed to change its policies and to pay 15,000 of its employees a total of $15,000,000 in damages.[2]

Major Provisions of the Law. The Civil Rights Act and the Equal Employment Act have been strengthened by other federal legislation. Let's look at the most important parts of current federal law relating to discrimination.

- Race, color, or national origin. The law clearly states that it is illegal to discriminate on the basis of race, color, or national origin. There are no exceptions.
- Sex. In only a few cases is it legal to discriminate on the basis of sex. In such cases, it is the responsibility of the firm to prove that, for example, a woman would not be able to perform the job in question. A good illustration is the case of Appellee Rawlinson. Ms. Rawlinson applied to the Alabama prison system to become a guard in a men's prison. She was turned down because she is a woman. The federal court held that Alabama had the right to require only male guards for male prisons. The court cited the fact that "violence is the order of the day" in prison and that many of the inmates had been convicted of sex offenses.

[2] Robert N. Corley, Robert L. Black, and O. Lee Reed, *The Legal Environment of Business* (New York: McGraw-Hill Inc., 1981), p. 352.

Figure 6-6

OSHA's Definition of Exit

> Exit is that portion of a means of egress which is separated from all other spaces of the building or structure by construction or equipment as required in this subpart to provide a protected way of travel to the exit discharge.

Source: OSHA.

CONTROVERSIAL ISSUES

In the late 1800s and early 1900s, large companies often merged with other firms. These mergers produced huge new companies against which there was almost no way to compete. Enraged by the greed of the firms, Congress passed laws to discourage such mergers. Recently, however, enforcement of merger laws has been relaxed and the frequency of larger mergers has increased dramatically. Should this trend be stopped and reversed?

Merger Laws—Should the Federal Government Strictly Enforce Them?

Pro

Mergers *are* dangerous. Companies merge only if they can recognize more power in their combined form than they have separately. That power must be taken from other competitors in the market. Is this *ever* fair? To be fair, each company should have the chance to act *alone* to increase its share of the market and the power that comes with that share. However, it should not be allowed to use the advantages other companies possess to gain an unfair advantage, which is what mergers permit to happen.

Consider the case of Remington shavers. In 1979, Victor K. Kiam II bought Remington Products from Sperry Corporation. On the edge of failure, Remington grew from a 19 percent market share in 1979 to a 40 percent share in 1982. Kiam's marketing genius helped restore Remington's reputation and market status, and brought consumers a better line of shavers.

Recently, however, North American Philips, whose Norelco shavers own a 55 percent share of the market, bought out Schick, Inc., which had recently discontinued its electric shaver line and was on the verge of bankruptcy. Obviously, Norelco and Remington shavers, together covering 95 percent of the market, were squared off against each other in a duel for market share. Since Philips could sell both Schick and Norelco brands, it naturally hoped to recover part of the market.

Merger statutes required that a failing company (like Schick) take bids from several companies before merging with any one of them, and that the company seek the merger that produces the least anticompetitive effect. Mr. Kiam was disappointed because he was not given an opportunity to bid competitively for Schick, so he filed suit under merger laws. Unless mergers laws are enforced more strictly, Mr. Kiam won't be able to challenge Norelco successfully.

The Justice Department has been very lenient toward mergers lately. While strict merger law enforcement can be a burden on companies, there must be protection for firms against anticompetitive mergers. If a failing company wants to merge, special provisions are written into the merger statutes to make the merger as simple and efficient as possible. With these special provisions in place to protect companies which would otherwise be harmed by merger laws, why aren't the laws enforced? They should be.

Con

No, mergers should not be stopped. Mergers are often the only way for a company to enter a market, or for an owner of a company to leave the business without severe economic loss. When a company depends on a certain supplier or a special distributor for its success, it is only natural for the company to want to minimize risk by seeking a merger with that supplier or distributor. Such was the case with North American Philips. Since shaver manufacturing technology is expensive and Schick's factories and expertise were for sale, it was understandable that North American Philips would want to get it.

The government condemns mergers because of the misbehavior of companies which merged nearly a century ago. Those companies were at fault not so much for their mergers but for how the merged companies behaved afterwards. Let's keep strict laws on business behavior, but let's not forbid mergers that might prove to be beneficial.

Since some mergers can be undesirable, the antitrust division of the Justice Department regularly publishes and revises standards and guides for firms considering a merger. Careful measurements of market power and of a merger's effect on competition are made, so no dramatically anticompetitive merger will be permitted. However, most lawyers agree that merger law is a hopelessly snarled and sticky mess of contradictory court rulings and administrative decisions.

So let's be realistic and give the market a little more freedom to act on its own, to police itself, and to cope with today's economic problems. Why hog-tie companies because of what other companies did a hundred years ago?

Bankruptcy

As we pointed out in Chapter 1, one of the basic rights of business is the right to declare bankruptcy. When a firm declares bankruptcy, it acknowledges publicly that it is not able to pay its debts.

TWO WAYS TO GO BROKE. A firm can be declared bankrupt in one of two ways. **Voluntary bankruptcy** means that the firm—the debtor—files a statement with the court indicating that it cannot pay its creditors. **Involuntary bankruptcy** is begun by one or more of the firm's creditors, who provide evidence to the court that the debtor is not able to make good on its obligations.

AIM OF BANKRUPTCY LAW. The basic aim of bankruptcy law is to ensure that the creditors of the bankrupt firm each receive a fair share of the remaining assets during the liquidation proceeding. During this proceeding, the remaining assets are sold and the money is distributed to the creditors. Today, however, the courts also try to save the bankrupt firm and the jobs of its employees.

DISTRIBUTION OF ASSETS. When a firm is declared to be bankrupt, whether voluntarily or involuntarily, the court appoints a trustee. By court order the trustee becomes the owner of all the debtor's property that is not subject to **exclusion**. Excluded property may not be sold to raise cash for payment of outstanding debts. An example of a property exclusion would be the debtor's house in a personal bankruptcy proceeding. If the firm cannot be saved, the trustee sells all assets not subject to exclusion and pays each creditor a proportionate share.

To illustrate, suppose the bankrupt firm owes the Achilles Cement Company $5,000 and the Hector Metal Works, Inc., $500,000. The total debt outstanding is $505,000. Suppose further that the firm has only $151,500 in remaining assets, or 30 percent of the total debt owed. Each creditor receives the same percentage share of the unpaid debt. The Achilles Cement Co. receives $1,500 (30% $\times$ $5,000), and the Hector Metal Works receives $150,000 (30% $\times$ $500,000).

REORGANIZATION. If the court concludes that a reorganization of the firm is possible, it will approve a formal reorganization plan. This plan is usually filed with the court by the debtor. It states how the firm expects to pay its debts and how its business practices will be changed so that it can operate profitably.

Under most corporate reorganization plans, the creditors agree to take an equity share of the business, thereby giving up all or part of the debt owed them. Taking an equity share means that the debtors become stockholders in the firm. Most creditors agree to such an arrangement because it is a way for them to minimize their losses. If the reorganized firm should become profitable, this stock may be worth as much as, or more than, the original debt.

- Appearance. Many firms want their employees to meet certain dress and grooming standards, especially employees who deal with the public, such as salespeople and receptionists. Although there have been cases of "appearance" discrimination, business firms do seem to have the right to require their employees to meet appearance standards.
- Age. It is now illegal in most cases to force employees to retire before the age 70. One exception is top executives with a planned retirement income of $27,000 a year or more. Some states now have laws prohibiting forced retirement because of age, period. President Reagan, at 71 the oldest chief executive in the history of the United States, worked hard to see that such a law was passed on a national basis. The age law also specifically protects persons between the ages of 40 and 70 from age discrimination.
- Handicapped. Every employer who has a contract with the federal government worth $2,500 or more must actively seek to hire and promote handicapped people. A handicapped person is defined as any individual with a physical or mental problem that limits the person's normal activities. However, the law does state that the handicapped person must be qualified to perform that particular job for which he or she is being considered.

Fairness In Testing. The discrimination laws are especially important in the area of testing. The government requires that any tests used for selection, transfers, promotions, or other personnel issues be fair. When the government refers to a test, it means any method used to get information. This includes interviews and application blanks.

As the government defines it, a fair test is one that does not systematically overpredict or underpredict the performance of any subgroup of employees. For instance, if a test predicted that white males would do better than black males on the job when they actually did the same, the test would be unfair.

Equal Pay and Comparable Worth. The 1963 Equal Pay Act requires that men and women receive equal pay for equal work. What is important is not whether the job *titles* are the same but that

FROM THE FILE

Veronica owned a highly profitable photography studio in Pittsburgh. She did not have the time to make sales calls herself, so she hired a part-time photographer, Ken, as an assistant and salesperson. One month later, working on his first big account, Ken agreed orally with the head of advertising of a commercial airline that Veronica's studio would handle all the airline's design and photographic needs. Veronica was furious when she found out. She had neither the equipment nor the skills to handle such a job. She would have to drop her other clients and spend heavily on equipment and assistants in order to take it on. Believing there was no other choice, she took that course. The airline declared bankruptcy a short time later. With large bills to pay and no other clients, Veronica also declared bankruptcy. Talking things over afterwards with her lawyer, Veronica wondered what mistakes she had made.

---

the *contents* of the jobs are substantially similar. If a company pays men and women differently, it must prove that the jobs differ in terms of skill, effort, responsibility, or working conditions.

Some people go further and argue that there should be equal pay not just for equal work but also for *comparable worth*. So, if a secretary's job is of equal worth to that of a carpenter, the pay should be the same.

Affirmative Action. What does **affirmative action** mean? It means that employers must actively recruit, hire, and promote members of minority groups if such groups are underrepresented in the firm. That is, if the labor pool in a community is 15 percent black and 10 percent Mexican-American, then 15 percent and 10 percent of the labor force of a firm operating in that community should be black and Mexican-American.

SUMMARY POINTS

1. Statutory law refers to the legal rules and regulations created by legislative bodies.
2. Common law is made by judges when they reach a decision in a case brought before them. Common law usually results because a legislative body has not enacted comprehensive laws in a particular area of law.
3. Administrative law refers to the rules and regulations issued by governmental boards, commissions, and agencies.
4. To be legally binding, a contract must have five elements: agreement, contractual capacity, absence of fraud or duress, consideration, and legality.
5. An oral contract is just as binding as a written contract. Oral contracts should be avoided, if possible, because they can lead to confusion.
6. The Uniform Commercial Code has been adopted by 49 states. It requires that all contracts for the sale of goods of $500 or more be in writing.
7. The Sherman Act was the first major piece of federal legislation designed to limit the power of monopolies.
8. The Clayton Act forbids tying agreements and exclusive agreements; it also prohibits firms from purchasing stock in competing companies.
9. The Federal Trade Commission Act authorized the issuing of cease and desist orders to stop unfair business practices.
10. The Cooling-Off Rule states that any person purchasing a product for $25 or more at home has the right to cancel the purchase within 72 hours.
11. The Truth-in-Lending Act gives the Federal Reserve Board the power to specify how interest rates on consumer loans are calculated and reported.
12. The Fair Labor Standards Act provides for a minimum wage and regulates child labor; the Social Security Act provides for a minimum guaranteed income for retired or disabled persons.
13. The objective of the Occupational Safety and Health Act is to reduce the number of safety and health hazards for employees.
14. The Equal Employment Opportunity Commission and the Civil Rights Act state that it is illegal to discriminate on the basis of race, color, or national origin.

Chapter 6 • Legal Aspects of Business

KEY TERMS AND CONCEPTS

- statutory law
- common law
- precedents
- administrative law
- contract
- agreement
- offer
- acceptance
- contractual capacity
- fraud
- duress
- consideration
- Uniform Commercial Code
- sales contracts
- express warranty
- implied warranty
- Sherman Act
- Clayton Act
- tying agreement
- exclusive agreement
- Federal Trade Commission
- cease and desist order
- Cooling-Off Rule
- Truth-in-Lending Act
- puffery
- corrective advertising
- Occupational Safety and Health Administration (OSHA)
- Civil Rights Act
- Equal Employment Act
- affirmative action

REVIEW QUESTIONS

1. What are the differences between administrative and statutory law?
2. What is common law? How does it originate?
3. What are the five elements of a contract? Briefly explain each element.
4. What is the Uniform Commercial Code?
5. How are the Clayton Act and the FTC Act related to each other?
6. What is meant by a cease and desist order?
7. Explain the Cooling-Off Rule.
8. What authority does the Consumer Product Safety Commission have?
9. What does the Fair Labor Standards Act say?
10. Summarize the major provisions of federal law with respect to employment discrimination.

DISCUSSION QUESTIONS

1. Is an oral contract as legally binding as a written contract? Why is a written contract usually preferable?
2. What are the three types of penalties for violating the Sherman Act? Should executives go to jail for violating the act?
3. Give an example of puffery. Should all puffery be declared illegal?
4. Do you think the minimum wage should be raised or lowered? What would happen if the minimum wage was repealed?
5. Identify and discuss some problems firms would face in establishing equal pay and comparable worth guidelines.

CASE 6-1

Aluminum Company of America (ALCOA)

In 1937, the United States government initiated a lawsuit against the Aluminum Company of America (ALCOA), charging that ALCOA had sought to produce and maintain a monopoly in the market for virgin aluminum ingot. ALCOA had obtained the first patents on the electrolytic procedures required for refining aluminum from bauxite ore, thereby creating an initial monopoly in the aluminum market. As it developed its new industry, ALCOA's vigorous research programs resulted in countless new patents in aluminum refining technology. Within a few decades, ALCOA was producing over 90 percent of the virgin aluminum ingot in America. Furthermore, because ALCOA needed large quantities of raw materials such as acids and bauxite ore, it purchased bauxite mines, chemical companies, shipping companies that transported the ore to America, and a wide variety of subsidiary industries. All in all, an outsider looking at the aluminum industry would readily admit that ALCOA owned nearly all the raw materials and processing facilities, and controlled most of the vital processes and patents in the industry.

The federal government charged that ALCOA was actively trying to create and maintain a monopoly in the market of aluminum ingot. The government claimed that ALCOA's actions were intended to prevent other firms from entering the aluminum market and competing successfully against ALCOA.

ALCOA, however, claimed that it only controlled about 33 percent of the aluminum market. ALCOA argued that two thirds of the aluminum available in the aluminum market each year was scrap that was recycled and hence not under ALCOA's control. Further, ALCOA claimed that its purchases were necessary to accommodate the rapid expansion of the metals industries in America as World War II started and also to protect its current "33 percent" market share. This lawsuit was fought from 1937 to 1945.

1. Under what law do you think the United States brought this lawsuit?
2. How is a monopoly defined? What do you have to prove to convict an accused monopolist, such as ALCOA?
3. Since monopoly is always measured within a market, why were the different market shares argued for by the government and by ALCOA so important?
4. What would have been different about this lawsuit if aluminum and steel had been perfectly substitutable (that is, had the same price, the same uses, and all the same qualities as far as aluminum users were concerned)?
5. What do you think was the result of this lawsuit?

CASE 6-2

Loeb & Company, Inc. v. Schreiner*

Loeb & Company, Inc., purchases raw cotton from farmers and then sells it, at a profit, to cotton mills. In April of 1973, Loeb & Company contacted Charles Schreiner, a cotton farmer, to buy 150 bales of cotton for several thousand dollars. Schreiner agreed orally. No written contract was signed. Loeb & Company did send Schreiner a written confirmation of the oral agreement, which Schreiner did not object to.

Shortly thereafter, and before the cotton was delivered and paid for, the OPEC oil crisis caused the cost of all synthetic fabrics produced from petroleum products to rise dramatically. The demand for cotton increased since its price and availability were not dependent on the price of oil; soon, increased demand for cotton more than doubled its market price. Schreiner decided that he could get more money for his cotton than Loeb & Company had agreed to pay. Since no written contract had been signed, he felt that no legally enforceable agreement existed. He refused to sell the 150 bales. Loeb & Company sued to enforce the sale.

A clause in Section 2 of the Uniform Commercial Code (UCC) states that if both buyer and seller are merchants, an oral agreement is legally binding as long as at least one party signs a written confirmation and the other party does not object. Loeb & Company used this argument to enforce the agreement, but Schreiner claimed that he was not a merchant. Section 2 also requires that contracts for the sale of goods valued over $500 be in writing.

1. Did agreement exist to substantiate the existence of a contract? How would you show that agreement did exist?
2. Did both potential parties have contractual capacity? Why or why not?
3. Did either party have grounds for claiming fraud or duress? Why or why not?
4. What consideration was offered by Loeb & Company? What consideration was offered by Schreiner?
5. Did a legally binding contract exist? Why or why not? What would be the effect if Loeb & Company's argument (under Section 2 of the UCC) were accepted by the court? What would be the effect if Schreiner's argument were accepted? How might Schreiner support his argument?

*Source: Loeb & Co., v. Schreiner, Supreme Court of Alabama, 320 So. 2d 199 (1975).

The Personal Budget

If you have access to a computer that uses the BASIC language, try running the program shown below. This program helps you to balance your personal budget. First, enter your monthly income and the monthly amount you want to budget for each of the five major categories. Next, tailor the budget to your particular needs by specifying up to ten categories and the amount you want to allot to each. The program then determines either the amount you have left over for savings or the amount by which you have exceeded your income and provides a complete budget summary.

Here's the Program

```
10 PRINT
20 PRINT "******PERSONAL BUDGET PROGRAM******"
30 PRINT
40 INPUT "WHAT IS YOUR NAME? ";N$
50 PRINT
60 PRINT "PROVIDE THE FOLLOWING MONTHY AMOUNTS:"
70 PRINT
80 INPUT "INCOME? ";IC
90 INPUT "HOUSING BUDGET? ";H
100 INPUT "FOOD BUDGET? ";F
110 INPUT "UTILITIES BUDGET? ";U
120 INPUT "GASOLINE AND OTHER AUTO BUDGET? ";G
130 INPUT "TOTAL INSURANCE? ";IS
140 PRINT
150 INPUT "HOW MANY OTHER ITEMS DO YOU WANT TO ADD TO YOUR BUDGET (UP TO 10)?";N
160 PRINT
170 PRINT "ENTER THOSE ITEMS BELOW. FOR EACH ITEM,"
180 PRINT "ENTER THE NAME OF THE ITEM, A COMMA, AND"
190 PRINT "THE AMOUNT BUDGETED."
200 PRINT
210 SUM=H+F+U+G+IS
220 FOR KT=1TO N
230 PRINT "ITEM ";KT;" :"
240 INPUT I$(KT),I(KT)
250 SUM=SUM+I(KT)
260 NEXT KT
270 PRINT
280 PRINT "******BUDGET RESULTS FOR  ";N$;"  ******"
290 PRINT
300 O=IC-SUM
310 IF O>0 THEN GOTO 340
320 PRINT "YOU HAVE OVERSPENT BY ";O
330 GOTO 500
340 PRINT "YOU HAVE $";O;" LEFT OVER"
350 PRINT
360 PRINT "***********STANDARD EXPENSES**********"
370 PRINT "HOUSING............";H
380 PRINT "FOOD...............";F
390 PRINT "UTILITIES..........";U
400 PRINT "GASOLINE AND AUTO...";G
410 PRINT "INSURANCE..........";IS
420 PRINT
430 PRINT "**********ADDITIONAL EXPENSES**********"
440 PRINT
450 FOR KT=1  TO N
460 PRINT I$(KT),"....";I(KT)
470 NEXT KT
480 PRINT
490 PRINT "**************************************"
500 END
```

Here's a Sample Output

A. Student's budget is shown next. A. Student has budgeted funds for a total of nine categories and should have $80 left over.

```
******BUDGET RESULTS FOR  A. STUDENT  ******

YOU HAVE $ 80  LEFT OVER

************STANDARD EXPENSES**********
HOUSING.............. 125
FOOD................. 120
UTILITIES........... 50
GASOLINE AND AUTO... 50
INSURANCE........... 25

**********ADDITIONAL EXPENSES**********
CLOTHING         .... 50
ENTERTAINMENT    .... 50
MEDICAL COSTS    .... 25
MISCELLANEOUS    .... 25
***************************************
```

Questions

1. Did your budget balance on the first try? If not, what sorts of changes did you have to make to bring it into balance?
2. Estimate your probable expenditures for each of the five major categories in the program—and for any other categories you can think of—for the first year you are out of school. Sum them up. Then estimate your expected after-tax income for that year. How do they compare? Are you pleased with the comparison?
3. Use the library or some other resource to determine values for each of the categories of expenses, as well as for the after-tax income, of the average single employed female in the United States. How do income and expenses compare? Do the same for the average single employed male in the United States.

3
Management of the Enterprise

7

Management and the Organization

After studying this chapter, you should be able to:

- Offer a definition of management and describe the three management levels.
- Discuss the principal elements of organizational design.
- Describe the management process and the five functions of management.
- Explain each stage in the decision-making process.
- Describe four types of organizational change.

The Great Pyramid of Cheops covers 13 acres and is built with more than 2 million stone blocks, each weighing an average of 5,000 pounds. Construction took 100,000 people more than 20 years. Single expeditions to find new stones and to move them back to the construction site involved as many as 8,000 people. Why discuss the building of a pyramid at the start of a management chapter? Because the pyramids of ancient Egypt are as

Chapter 7 • Management and the Organization 121

much monuments to management as they are monuments in stone. To carry out such massive efforts, careful planning, coordination, and control were necessary. These are a few of the basic functions of management. Today, General Motors, the National Aeronautics and Space Administration, and even Fraboni's Italian Restaurant perform the same basic managerial tasks.

What is management? In this chapter we'll attempt to answer this question. We'll consider some of the key elements of organizational design, as well as the steps involved in managerial decision making.

WHAT IS MANAGEMENT?

An early student of organizations defined **management** as "the art of getting things done through people." Managers achieve organizational goals by arranging for others to perform necessary tasks. What managers do depends on their position in the firm, the nature of the industry, and their own ingenuity. At Turner Construction Company, a nationally known construction firm, managers arrange for construction teams that build new office complexes and shopping centers. At Safeway stores, store managers arrange for filling shelves with merchandise, putting out new issues of magazines each week, and adjusting the air conditioning when summer arrives.

Levels of Management

As shown in Figure 7-1, managers fall into three levels: top management, middle management, and lower management. These managerial levels indicate the main functions of the various management positions in the firm's hierarchy.

Top Management. Top management is concerned with the overall direction of the firm. Managers at this level watch the environment for the kinds of developments we discussed in Chapter 2. The job of top management is to improve the company's competitive position, to lobby in government for favorable rule changes, and to develop corporate strategy. Top management at Turner Construction Company follows changing requirements for

Figure 7-1

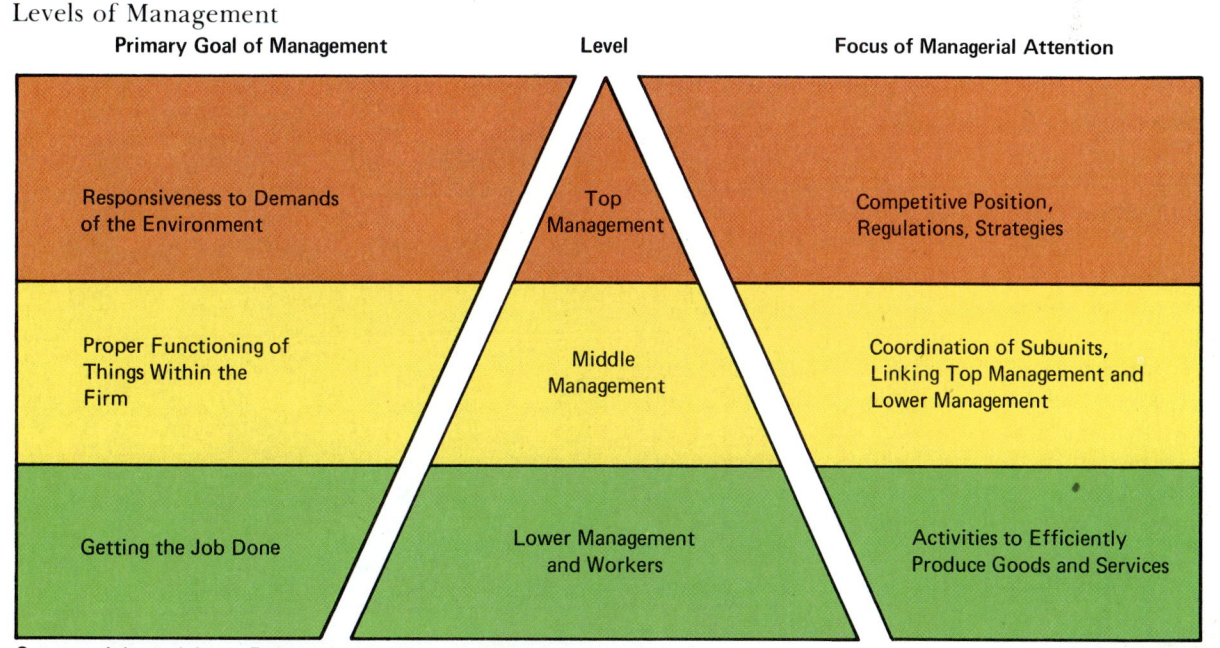

Levels of Management

Primary Goal of Management	Level	Focus of Managerial Attention
Responsiveness to Demands of the Environment	Top Management	Competitive Position, Regulations, Strategies
Proper Functioning of Things Within the Firm	Middle Management	Coordination of Subunits, Linking Top Management and Lower Management
Getting the Job Done	Lower Management and Workers	Activities to Efficiently Produce Goods and Services

Source: Adapted from Robert A. Ullrich and George F. Wieland, *Organization Theory and Design* (Homewood, Illinois: Richard D. Irwin, Inc., 1980).

office building construction and changing financial and borrowing terms. It also formulates plans for corporate growth and consolidation. Top management at Safeway headquarters makes such decisions as where to build new stores, which stores to close, and how much money to spend on renovations.

Middle Management. Middle management is concerned with the proper functioning of the organization. Middle managers coordinate activities and sub-units in the organization and act as a link between top and lower management. They are responsible for buying raw materials, selecting new employees, and planning departmental work. Middle management at Turner Construction Company may guide a large shopping mall construction project by purchasing concrete, hiring local workers, bringing in construction engineers, and keeping track of costs. Middle managers at Safeway regional offices decide how much money to spend on advertising, how to supply regional stores with less expensive produce, and so on.

Lower Management. Lower management makes sure the job gets done. Managers at this level see that machines are maintained, work is scheduled, and reports are typed. Lower management at Turner supervises the day-to-day production of concrete as well as the delivery of construction materials to workers at the site. At Safeway stores, lower management schedules work for employees, handles cash deposits at banks, and cashes checks at the store office.

Management: An Art or a Science?

The definition of management given at the start of this section said that management is an art. An art relies more on imagination, intuition, and practice than on an orderly system of facts and laws. There can be little doubt that even today management looks a lot like an art.

However, because of continued development in management theory and its practical guidelines, along with sophisticated computer applications, management is becoming more of a science. Intuition and experience in management, while still useful, will have to take a place beside more scientific approaches.

ORGANIZATIONAL DESIGN

The fundamental task of management is to structure the organization so that it meets the firm's goals and offers satisfying work to its employees. Some of the elements of organizational design are hierarchy of authority, division of labor, departmentalization, line and staff relationships, and span of control.

Hierarchy of Authority

A hierarchy is a ranking or ordering—always from top to bottom. A **hierarchy of authority**, therefore, is a ranking of people in an organization according to their authority. The value of a well-defined hierarchy is that it reduces confusion about who gives orders and who obeys them. For example, the hierarchy at American Airlines determines how orders, assignments, and responsibilities are passed downward from the chairman of the board to the president of the company and then to the finance vice-president and the assistant finance vice-president.

A firm's hierarchy is represented formally by an **organization chart**, which maps authority relationships. In Figure 7-2, for instance, manager

The military—a classic example of a hierarchy of authority.

Figure 7-2

A Simple Organization Chart

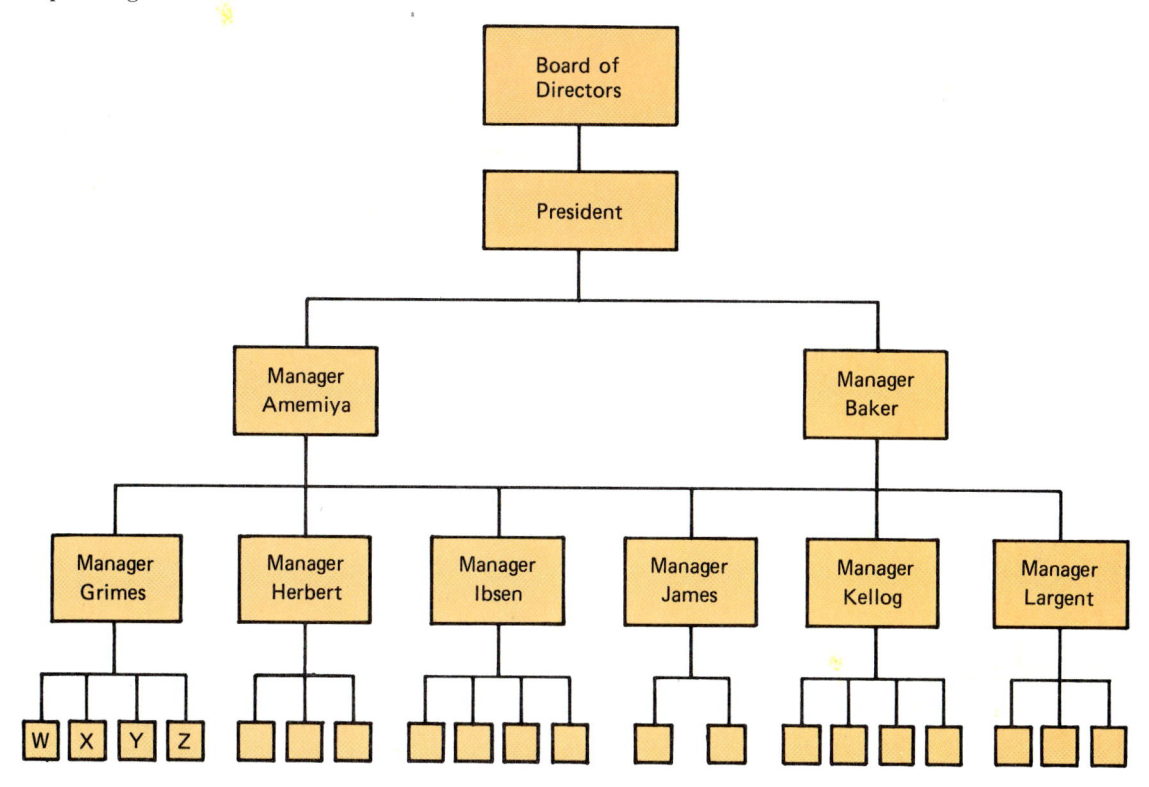

Grimes reports to manager Amemiya, who reports directly to the president. Employees W, X, Y, and Z report to Grimes. The organization chart for American Airlines establishes that the chairman of the board has authority over the president, who in turn gives orders to the finance vice-president.

Division of Labor

The term **division of labor** refers to the way big jobs, such as assembling an automobile, are broken down into many smaller jobs, such as tightening a gasket on a radiator assembly. These smaller jobs are more easily learned and mastered.

Around the turn of the century, it was believed that jobs should be divided into very small parts, with each worker doing only a tiny piece of the overall task. As we will see in the next chapter, though, many people now believe that work should be made more interesting and that employees should be given more responsibility.

Departmentalization

Any large organization, such as General Electric with 400,000 employees, must be organized into smaller units or departments. This is known as **departmentalization**. Without these smaller units, the organization would be impossible to manage. The same is often true of smaller companies. Let's take a look at three approaches to departmentalization.

Process Departmentalization. Under **process departmentalization**, departments are organized on the basis of similar skills. One type of skill is placed in one department, another in a second, and so on. The most common form of process departmentalization, as shown in Figure 7-3, is by function. For example, a firm may have separate departments for marketing, finance, and production. The Mead Paper Company features a mill products department, a packaging and distribution department, an accounting department, a sales department, and an operations and finance department. This approach is good

Figure 7-3

Departmentalization by Function

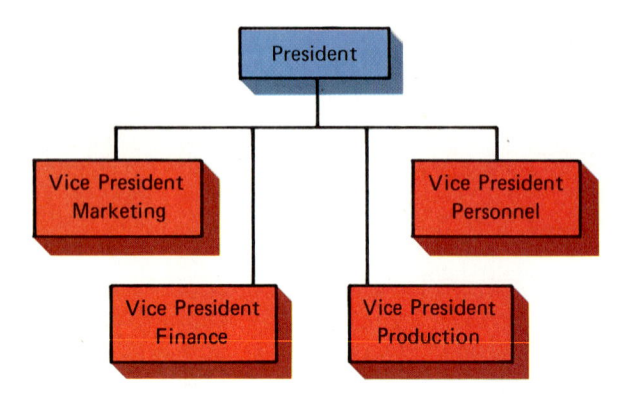

```
                President
        ┌───────────┼───────────┐
   Vice President              Vice President
     Marketing                   Personnel
   Vice President              Vice President
     Finance                     Production
```

because it minimizes the chances of functional duplication across departments. There can be a problem with coordination, however, since each function is localized in its own department.

Purpose Departmentalization. Purpose Departmentalization organizes on the basis of similarity of purpose. This purpose can refer to all activities involved in manufacturing and marketing a product in a given geographic area. For example, all operations in Europe might be organized under a European division, as illustrated in Figure 7-4(a). The firm's line of products can also serve as the basis of departmentalization. Figure 7-4(b) shows a firm with a skateboard division, a bicycle division, and a motorcycle division. Finally, the firm might be organized by customer orientation—retail operations might be in one department, wholesale operations in another, and catalog operations in a third. This variation is shown in Figure 7-4(c).

Historically, the telephone company organized its operations on the basis of geography—Southwestern Bell, New England Bell, and so on. The 3M Company has independent production and sales departments for each of its different types of products. The Ford Motor Company has separate departments for its large trucking customers, its retail passenger automobile dealers, its farm product customers, and others.

Because purpose departmentalization locates all related activities in each department, the costs of coordinating those activities are reduced. Special attention can also be paid to specific markets, products, or customer groups. And it is easier to see where profits and losses are occurring.

Matrix Departmentalization. A newer approach to organizational design, **matrix departmentalization**, is popular in rapidly changing industries such as aerospace, where organizational flexibility is needed. This approach is quite flexible but rather complicated. In essence, each employee has two bosses—one "higher up" in the organizational chart in the employee's functional area and another for the particular project being worked on.

In the matrix organization shown in Figure 7-5 on page 127, employees would report to supervisors in their functional areas of production, engineering, personnel, or accounting. They would also report to either project manager A or project manager B, depending on whether they were working on project A or project B. When the Dutch Group of the Shell Oil Company began building offshore oil rigs in the North Sea, it had the usual finance, construction, purchasing, and accounting departments. Each oil rig also had a project manager who saw to it that a particular oil rig was constructed properly, at the right cost, and with the appropriate customized features. If the rig was not finished on time or was unsatisfactory, the project manager was held responsible. All employees, again, were accountable to the project manager and to their functional area managers.

Because of their complexity, matrix organizations are not without their problems. Sometimes the lines of authority are unclear, leading to conflict and confusion. The job of the project manager is especially tough. At Lockheed, for instance, construction of advanced jet fighters required the interaction of physicists, aerospace engineers, financial analysts, government accountants, construction workers, and test pilots. The physicists and engineers had specialized training and wanted to operate independently of strict authority. The financial analysts knew nothing about aircraft design and objected to costs that the physicists thought necessary. Government accountants objected to the financial analysts' accounting procedures. Construction workers complained that test pilots were too particular, and test pilots claimed that the aerospace engineers had not designed enough speed into the jets. Matrix project managers had to deal with all these differences of opinion.

(a) GEOGRAPHIC DEPARTMENTALIZATION

- President
  - Vice President European Division
  - Vice President Asian Division
  - Vice President Latin American Division
  - Vice President North American Division

(b) PRODUCT DEPARTMENTALIZATION

- President
  - Vice President Skateboard Division
  - Vice President Bicycle Division
  - Vice President Motorcycle Division

(c) CUSTOMER DEPARTMENTALIZATION

- President
  - Vice President Retail Operations
  - Vice President Wholesale Operations
  - Vice President Catalog Operations

Figure 7-4

Departmentalization by Purpose

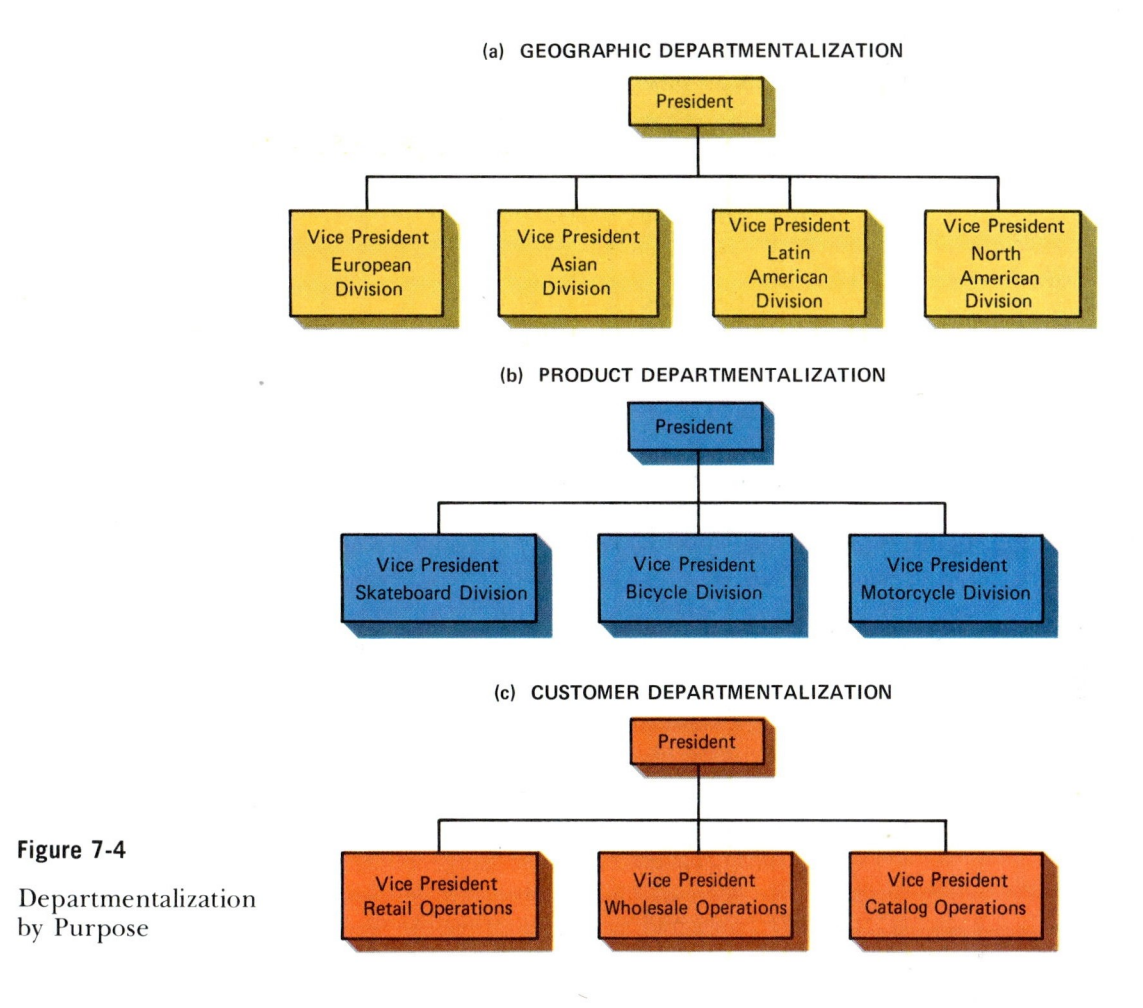

Line and Staff Relationships

One of the fundamental concepts in management is the distinction between a line position and a staff position. A **line position** is a job in the direct chain of command that begins with the board of directors and ends with the production people. Line managers, such as a supervisor of employees on the assembly line, usually have authority to give orders and to reward or punish workers. At American Airlines, the marketing vice-president may reward a district sales manager who increases sales by 30 percent.

A **staff position**, on the other hand, is ancillary to the chain of command. That is, a manager in a staff position gives advice to line managers or provides other specialized services. But a staff manager, such as an assistant to the vice-president of marketing, usually has no authority to issue work orders to production employees. Accountants at Amerian Airlines occupy staff positions. They prepare financial statements, analyze cost data, and provide information for loan applications, but they are not in the direct chain of command.

Span of Control

Span of control refers to the number of employees that a manager directly supervises. In Figure 7-6 on page 129, manager Allen has a span of control of two, whereas managers Benitez and Cohen have spans of control of five and four, respectively.

How big should the span of control be? It depends on the nature of the employees' work and their education, training, and experience. Usually, a span of control of greater than five or six is difficult to coordinate. On the other hand, a very small span of control of two or three can make workers feel that they are being closely watched.

CONTROVERSIAL ISSUES

Mechanistic organizations have highly defined and structured hierarchies of authority and control. Organic organizations are much more loosely defined and structured. Organic designs, it is claimed, can better handle the uncertainty and instability of modern business. Does that mean that mechanistic designs should be discarded?

Mechanistic Organizations Have No Place in Modern Business.

Pro

Yes, they should. It is almost impossible for a business to anticipate the problems and opportunities it will face even in the near future. Companies have to be able to respond almost instantly to changes in the marketplace. For example, companies like GM and Chrysler, using the mechanistic design, did not have the flexibility to make decisions to produce the radical change needed in responding to the oil crisis in 1973. Meanwhile, companies with organic designs like Hewlett-Packard and Bell Laboratories have done very well in coping with the influx of Japanese products. In fact, these firms may be in better shape because of good competition than they would have been without such a challenge. Their organic structures made competition a motivating force for their employees.

Furthermore, companies with an organic structure tend to adapt more quickly to new research and technology opportunities. Because a large number of managers in a mechanistic structure must first agree to venture into new research and technology, such firms are often "behind the times." In an organic company, only a few people have to agree, and the firm is more likely to use more research and new technology. American companies have reached a crossroads, with some falling seriously behind European or Japanese firms. Typically, these firms have mechanistic structures.

Another problem to consider is the satisfaction of employees working in a company. Employee desires and standards are changing. Team efforts are more important, and employees want people they can talk with as equals and can get help from without compromising their own positions in the company. These needs are best fulfilled in an organic design.

Finally, because of mergers and diversification, a firm may be involved with several unrelated kinds of business. No longer can one executive competently manage several different parts of a company's operation. Organic designs are almost essential for these companies.

Mechanistic designs have had their chance. They had their heyday when scientific management methods were popular, but today, companies and employees need something more. Let's switch to organic design.

Con

No, mechanistic designs should not be eliminated. They have very important roles in society and in business today.

First, consider IBM. This company has a strictly hierarchical, mechanistic design, and it performs very well. IBM is an example of an organization that uses mechanistic designs properly. Like organic designs, mechanistic designs can be misused. However, the fault lies with the management that misuses the design, not with the design itself. You can't write off an organizational design just because some companies can't use it.

Second, consider what would happen to GM or Ford if they implemented organic designs. The auto companies face a very potent challenge in the automobile labor unions. Most unions are highly hierarchical. The companies and the unions all send top management teams to negotiating sessions. A mechanistic structure permits such a system. If the auto companies changed to organic structures, it would be very hard to maintain a competitive stance in dealing with the labor unions, and everyone would suffer.

Consider how a company operates in the marketplace. The organic design probably *is* best suited to a company that has to float on the seas of an unstable market—it needs great flexibility to adapt to changing and uncontrollable market conditions. However, most companies *do* have market power. These companies have the power to determine at least some of the conditions of their market. To do so, they have to present a united and organized front; that is best done with a mechanistic structure. When there are market problems (such as lawsuits, needs for layoffs, opportunities for expansion, or customer complaints), there is no division or diffusion of authority and thus the company can better preserve its position and stability.

So don't knock the mechanistic design strategy. It has lots of uses, and we are going to need it for a long, long time.

Figure 7-5

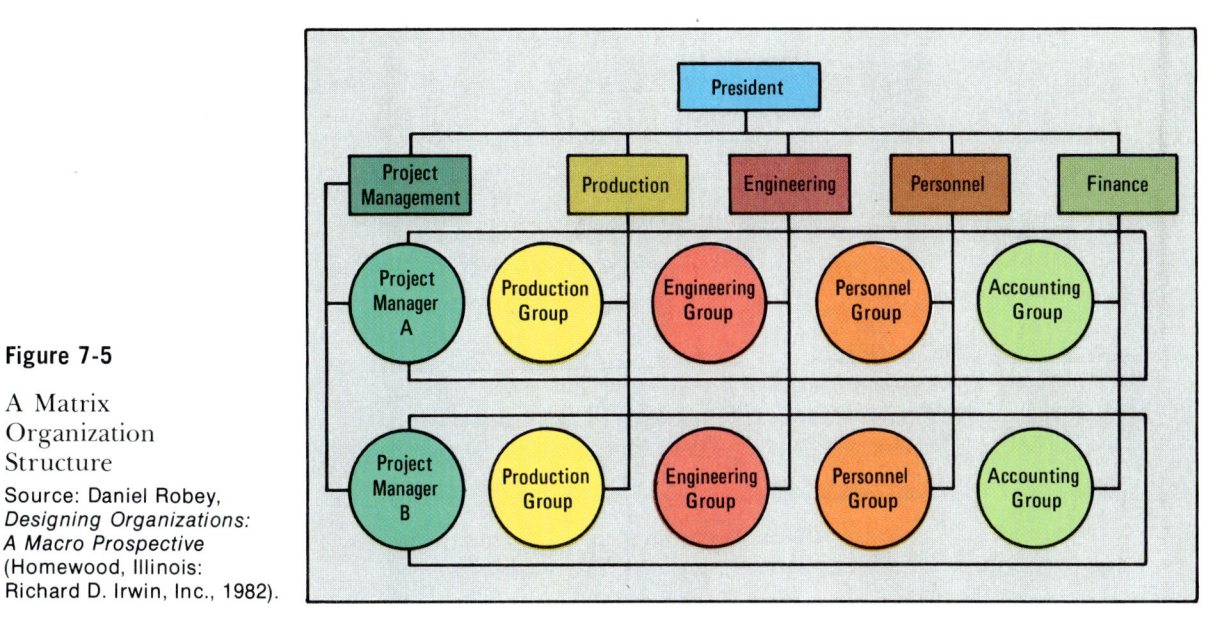

A Matrix Organization Structure

Source: Daniel Robey, *Designing Organizations: A Macro Prospective* (Homewood, Illinois: Richard D. Irwin, Inc., 1982).

Mechanistic and Organic Designs

Now that we've looked at the elements of organizational design, we can ask ourselves, "How should organizations be designed?" Most people in management approach this question from one of two points of view. Under the first, the **classical** or **mechanistic organizational design**, the organization is viewed as a complex, well-oiled machine. To make sure this "machine" runs efficiently, management relies heavily on rules and regulations. Employees follow the chain of command; that is, they communicate only with their direct superiors and immediate subordinates. Moreover, tasks are broken down into small parts and are simplified so that employees can become skilled in their jobs more easily.

The other view, the **organic organizational design**, is that organizations should be flexible and thus better able to adapt to the demands of a changing environment. One of the primary goals of management in this approach is to develop employee skills and abilities and to foster creativity as well as efficiency. Instead of behaving like a machine, the organic organization has many of the characteristics of a living organism: It senses environmental change, reacts to it, shows concern for the health of its parts, and so on.

The characteristics of each of the two approaches to organizational design are presented in Table 7-1 on page 130. As a manager, which approach would you prefer? What if you were a production worker?

FUNCTIONS OF MANAGERS

It is difficult to make generalizations about managers' duties. Managers may perform many varied tasks a day, and one manager's responsibilities may be extremely different from another manager's. For instance, imagine a manager overseeing an auto assembly plant, another managing a cosmetics sales force, and a third running a local food cooperative. What do they have in

Imagine the organizational structure necessary to make this project successful!

Profile —
R. E. (Ted) Turner

Ted Turner has been called the Mouth of the South. Turner is a man in his early forties who in less than 20 years built an overextended billboard company into a broadcasting power worth $240 million.

How did he do it? He didn't do it with his own money. Turner freely admits that he never did *anything* with his own money. His first venture into television came in 1971 when he merged his billboard company with a radio communications corporation, convinced its stockholders to buy a bankrupt independent television station in Atlanta, Georgia, and then bought the stockholders out. Channel 17 was at the bottom of the local ratings charts, unable even to compete with another independent in town. Turner challenged the network news shows with *Star Trek* reruns; won; and then bought new NBC shows that the local network affiliate had rejected. This was just the beginning.

Turner loved sports, particularly Atlanta sports. He televised professional wrestling on Channel 17 until he could afford the premiums to broadcast the Atlanta Braves. He soon added coverage of the Atlanta Hawks and the Atlanta Soccer Chiefs. Because the teams were losing so much money, the previous owners were going to move them to another city. Turner wanted them to stay in Atlanta, so he bought them.

Turner's "SuperStation," WTBS, was for lease across the country by December of 1976. By 1981, WTBS had a documented viewing audience of over 22 million homes. Net income from WTBS alone reached $15 million, and analysts calculated WTBS's worth at over $150 million. Turner Broadcasting was worth over $240 million.

In 1980 the Charlotte, North Carolina, television station, WRET, was sold to help finance the second nationwide Turner operation. Never the conservative executive, Turner decided the country needed a 24-hour cable news station; he created Cable News Network (CNN). A year and half later, he created a second news network, CNN-2. Costing at least $4 million a year to sustain, CNN was losing over $1 million a month, but Turner kept plugging. He initiated an $80 million advertising blitz for his news networks and sank $22 million into new satellite equipment.

How would he get this huge deficit off the business? Turning red ink to black ink is perhaps Turner's greatest skill. Turner sold his supersystem as a viable advertising medium and General Foods picked up $40 million in advertising space. Other advertisers are following suit. So once again, while the critics were writing Turner's obituary, he was turning a losing business into a secure and profitable investment.

Westinghouse and ABC, having seen profit in Ted Turner's madness, are entering the same market. But whether other firms have the genius to turn dogs into cash cows with Ted Turner's consistency remains to be seen. There may only be one Ted Turner.

Figure 7-6

Span of Control

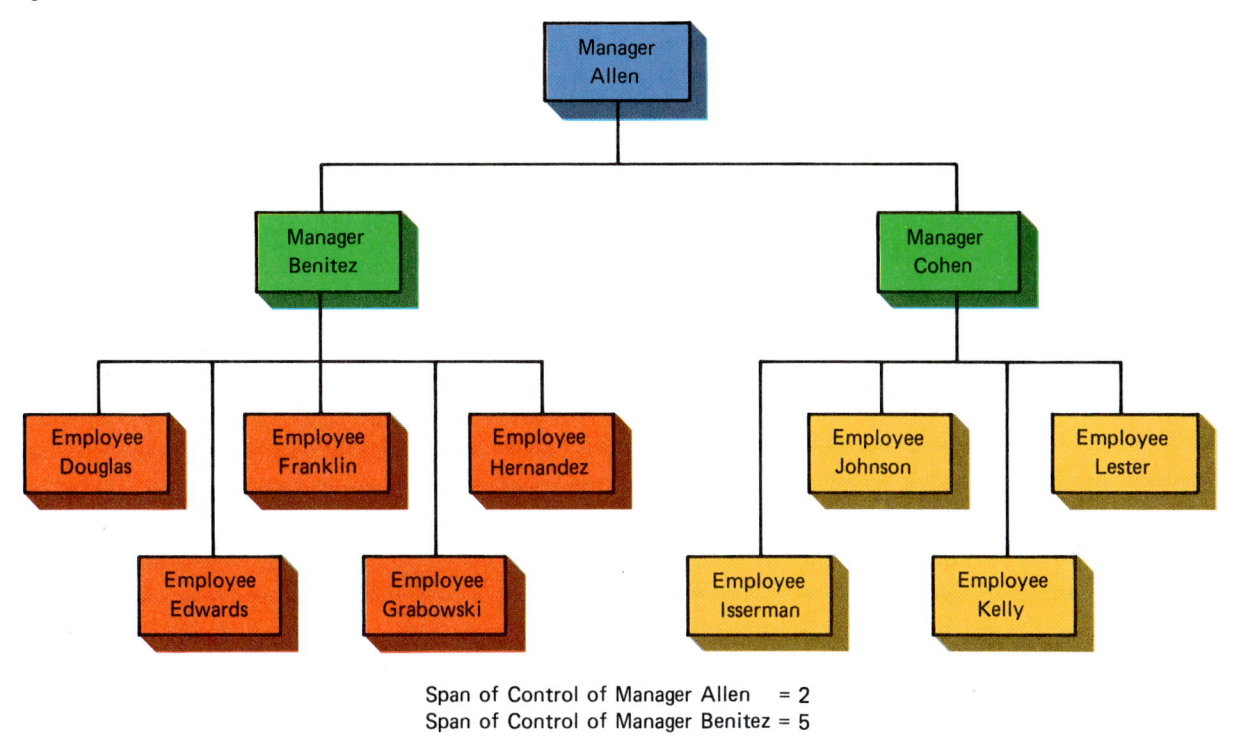

```
                        Manager
                         Allen
                    ┌──────┴──────┐
               Manager         Manager
               Benitez          Cohen
           ┌─────┬─────┐      ┌─────┬─────┐
       Employee Employee Employee  Employee Employee
       Douglas  Franklin Hernandez Johnson  Lester
          │        │                 │        │
       Employee Employee          Employee Employee
       Edwards  Grabowski         Isserman Kelly
```

Span of Control of Manager Allen   = 2
Span of Control of Manager Benitez = 5
Span of Control of Manager Cohen   = 4

common? They are all managing. They must, then, be doing some things alike.

To one degree or another, all managers perform the functions of planning, organizing, staffing, directing, and controlling. Together, these functions make up the **management process**. A process is a flow of connected activities moving toward a purpose or goal. As shown in Figure 7-7 on page 131, the five basic managerial functions are connected through the decisions made by managers. The aim of the management process is to put the firm in the strongest competitive or profit position possible.

Planning

Planning refers to determining in advance what needs to be done to achieve a particular goal. Planning decides how, when, where, and by whom a project should be done. It includes forecasting, goal setting, and selecting procedures for implementing decisions.

At K-Mart, planning is involved in storing snow tires when spring arrives, putting patio furniture into the warehouse at the start of winter, increasing floor space when a large suburban housing development is built next door, and cutting back on inventories when consumer buying falls off.

Organizing

Organizing refers to the way work is arranged and distributed among members of the firm. It involves breaking down the firm into parts and then making sure that the parts mesh. Departmentalization and division of labor are two important ways to "break down" the firm.

For a firm in a stable, relatively unchanging industry, such as the insurance industry, the coordination of its separate parts is not too difficult. Coordination can usually be accomplished through the formal hierarchy of authority. At the Metropolitan Life Insurance Company, decisions about whether to change life insurance premiums or to hire more insurance salespeople can be relayed up and down the organization. In rapidly changing industries, however, it is sometimes necessary to take extra steps to coordinate the

Table 7-1

Characteristics of the Mechanistic and Organic Organization Types

Mechanistic Organization	Organic Organization
1. Jobs are broken down into small parts and each worker does just a little of the whole job.	1. Workers are given a variety of tasks. They each do a "large" job.
2. Each worker's responsibilities are very clearly specified.	2. Responsibilities are flexible. They may change quickly as the situation demands.
3. Communications and other interactions between employees flow up and down the organizational hierarchy.	3. There are free interactions up, down, across, and throughout the organization.
4. Workers are expected to give their primary loyalty to the firms they work for.	4. Workers are primarily loyal to their professions. They tend to identify more with the profession than with the firms they work for.
5. Actions are coordinated by the organization's hierarchy.	5. Expertise, rather than formal authority, is used to coordinate.
6. There is heavy emphasis on prompt and unquestioning obedience to rules and regulations.	6. Emphasis is placed on getting the job done correctly. Rules and regulations are seen as ways to get the job done rather than as ends in themselves.

decisions of each department. The Intel Corporation makes computer chips. In this dynamic industry, it is difficult to know what will happen next. Consequently, Intel employs many people to organize the company's responses to sudden technological and market changes.

Staffing

Staffing is the management function dealing with the recruitment, selection, placement, training, development, and appraisal of the members of the firm. We will discuss this function in much greater detail in Chapter 9.

Directing

Directing refers to those activities which encourage subordinates to work toward the achievement of the company's goals. Some of these activities are leading, motivating, and communicating. How well salespeople at Mary Kay Cosmetics perform depends on how well they are led, how well they are motivated, and how well the company communicates its needs to them. See Chapter 8 for further discussion.

Controlling

Controlling refers to the set of activities which ensure that actual performance is in line with intended performance. That is, managers must see that company goals are being met. What is it that managers control in an effort to meet goals? Managers control human resources, financial resources, inventories, and communication flows.

Sometimes, control procedures put unnecessary pressure on subordinates. The subordinates may then attempt to evade controls or, at the

Figure 7-7

The Management Process

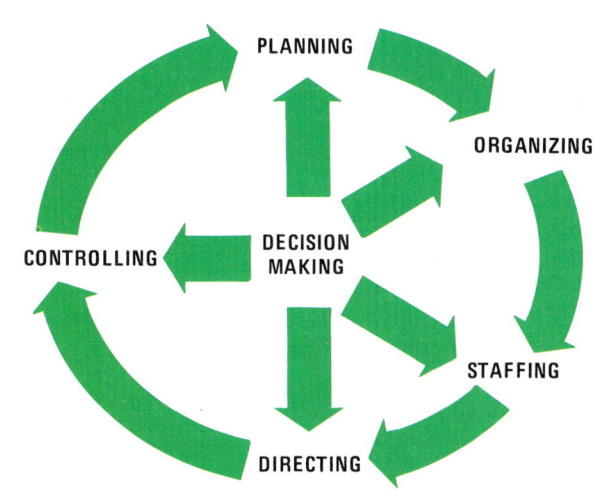

[Diagram: A circular flow showing PLANNING → ORGANIZING → STAFFING → DIRECTING → CONTROLLING around a central DECISION MAKING]

least, they may develop a very narrow point of view about company goals. At Datapoint Corporation, a maker of computer systems, people in the shipping department were told they had to improve quotas each year. As a result, they often shipped goods to empty warehouses just to meet their quotas. This burdened the company with the cost of unnecessary shipping and warehouse space. Why did the shipping department people do this? Since they were being evaluated on the basis of their quotas, they focused on filling shipping orders rather than on the real objective of the company—which was to increase sales and profits.

MANAGERIAL DECISION MAKING

Marketing, finance, accounting, management, and other areas of business all have something in common—decision making. Some decisions, such as whether to buy another company, are of great importance and involve risk. Others, such as the size of the turkey to be given as a Christmas bonus, certainly seem small. To understand what happens in organizations or to predict the behavior of employees, we must understand decision making.

Difficulties in Decision Making

Decision making is never easy, especially if the stakes are high. For one thing, we seldom have all the information we need to make a good decision. For another, we sometimes distort the information that we do have available. The president of Braniff Airlines did not believe the accountants who told him that he could not afford to expand Braniff's routes. He expanded anyway and the company failed. Finally, as human beings, we have limited memory and quantitative abilities. Because of these difficulties in decision making, we put off decisions or use simple rules of thumb to make them. The result often is a bad decision. By studying the stages in decision making, we may be able to find some clues as to how decision making can be improved.

Decision Stages

Successful decision makers recognize that there is more to a good decision than just choosing one option over another. Instead, they follow the five steps in the decision process shown in Figure 7-8.

Define the Problem. The first step is to define the problem. This step is often skipped because people assume that they know what the problem is. Or, even worse, they may define the problem in terms of its symptoms. For instance, the Translucent Glass Company experiences a big sales decline. Is that the problem? No, that is just the

Decisions must be based on adequate and accurate information.

Figure 7-8

Steps in the Decision Process

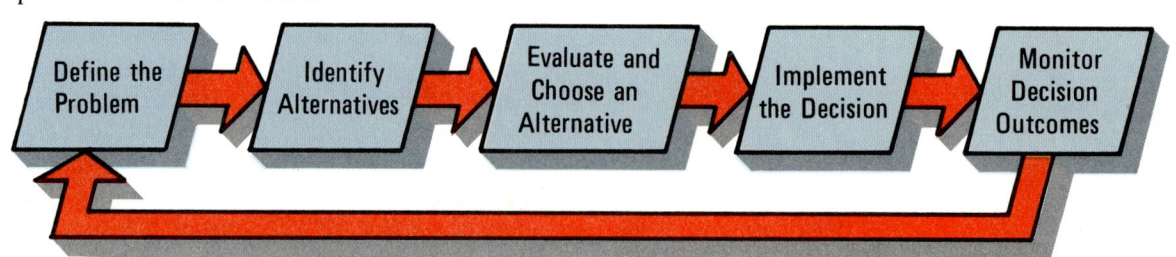

Define the Problem → Identify Alternatives → Evaluate and Choose an Alternative → Implement the Decision → Monitor Decision Outcomes → (loop back to Define the Problem)

symptom. The real problem may be a poorly motivated sales force caused by a badly structured compensation and incentive program.

Identify Alternatives. Alternatives, or options, are the various ways of solving a problem. Business problems rarely have just one solution. Managers earn their salaries, as well as promotions, by providing a range of decision alternatives for any given problem and by then choosing the best alternative. Solving problems, therefore, is largely a matter of generating creative decision alternatives.

Caterpillar, a large manufacturer of construction equipment, started to produce farm machinery in competition with John Deere, a major farm implements manufacturer. Managers at John Deere were polled for ideas on how to stop Caterpillar. The managers suggested undercutting Caterpillar on price, increasing the number of models, changing model designs frequently, forcing farm machinery retailers to carry John Deere equipment, and so on. Thus, top management identified several alternatives.

Evaluate and Choose. The alternatives are now evaluated, and the best one is selected. Generally, there are two approaches to evaluation and selection: **screening approaches** and **scoring approaches**. Under the first, each alternative in the set is identified as unsatisfactory or satisfactory. Unsatisfactory alternatives are screened out, leaving only a few satisfactory ones for further consideration and choice. The aim of scoring approaches is to assign a score to each alternative. The alternative with the highest score is then chosen.

In the John Deere and Caterpillar example, the screening approach might have narrowed the decision down to two choices. The scoring approach might have evaluated each proposal in terms of expected profitability. Management would have chosen the alternative with the greatest chance of slowing Caterpillar's entry into the market, thereby maximizing John Deere's profits.

Implement the Decision. Some managers make the mistake of assuming that the decision process is over as soon as the choice has been made. In fact, though, the decision must still be carried out. Suppose the managers at John Deere had decided to increase the number of models available. Was the decision process over? No! New research,

FROM THE FILE

Mary knew things were going to be difficult in her department at the insurance company. The secretaries she supervised were highly skilled at typing and other office duties. Now, though, computerized word processing equipment was about to be installed. Although the keyboard of the word processor looked like a typewriter keyboard, it really took a whole new set of skills to operate it. It was almost like learning a new language. Mary expected many of the secretaries to oppose the introduction of the word processors. She wondered how she should proceed.

marketing, production, and engineering would have been necessary for this plan to work.

Monitor Decision Outcomes. The final step in the decision process is monitoring decision outcomes. That is, is the decision working out as planned? Are corrective actions necessary? If the decision looks like a bad one, what other alternatives are available?

Making Creative Decisions

Managers often spend too much time choosing from among old alternatives rather than coming up with creative new alternatives. Creativity is especially important in decisions involving marketing strategy in competitive industries. In the John Deere and Caterpillar example, one John Deere manager suggested letting Caterpillar move into the farm equipment business. Then John Deere would enter the construction equipment business and compete with Caterpillar on its own turf. Caterpillar might heed the warning, the manager said, and get out of the farm implements business. If not, John Deere would match Caterpillar offensive move for offensive move. Since construction equipment was a more profitable business than farm implements, it could not hurt John Deere. Caterpillar did eventually leave the farm implements business. The manager's idea was a bold and creative one.

MANAGING ORGANIZATIONAL CHANGE

Change is a fact of life for all firms. U.S. automakers face the Japanese challenge and must respond accordingly; a corner grocery store must change how it operates when a new 7-Eleven moves across the street; new market opportunities cause cable TV system operators to redraft their business plans. In each of these instances, a change in the environment has resulted in the need for organizational change. Bringing about change within the organization is rarely easy, and sometimes it is actively resisted by employees.

Types of Change

Let's look at the four basic types of organizational change. As you read, be thinking about the difficulty of bringing change about.

Purpose or Task Change. Under a purpose or task change, the goal of the organization is changed. At one time, the goal of the March of Dimes was to conquer polio. When an effective polio vaccine was introduced, the March of Dimes changed its organizational goal to one of conquering birth defects.

Technological Change. A technological change occurs when a new means of production is used to transform resources into a product or service. The installation of robots on an automobile assembly line is a good example of a technological change. The use of this new technology helps the firm stay competitive.

Structural Change. A structural change involves an alteration of the firm's formal authority structure or an alteration of job definitions. Examples include a change in communication patterns, a change in the way rewards are given, a change in

Some management decisions may influence the lives of many people.

Creativity Enhancement Techniques

Success in business, as elsewhere in life, depends on bright ideas, creative planning, and bold moves. The day-to-day grind of the office routine, however, leaves many managers without the energy or mental flexibility to develop new solutions to old problems. Here are a few tried-and-true techniques for enhancing creativity and problem-solving skills in the workplace:

Brainstorming. Sometimes the best way to solve a problem is to come up with as many original ideas as possible—that is, to brainstorm. The key to brainstorming is to set up the right atmosphere for relaxed, creative thinking. A small group of employees with diverse backgrounds is brought together in a room, presented with the problem, and asked to propose several possible solutions. The participants are assured that their ideas will not be criticized or evaluated by others. Instead, they are encouraged to improve upon and combine other participants' ideas. Brainstorming is an especially good way to develop new product ideas and creative advertising strategies.

Retroduction. Retroduction is a big word for a rather simple—but surprisingly effective—mental exercise. It involves asking the question, "What if?" For example, "What if our firm were to diversify its line of products—how would that affect sales of our leading product?" Or, "What if we could acquire the ailing steel producer in Ohio—how would that lower the production and distribution costs for our other plants?" Retroduction helps free business managers from mental ruts.

Probably the most famous example of retroduction involved Albert Einstein. Einstein reasoned, "Our laws of physics are based on the assumption that space is flat. Instead, what if we assumed that space is curved? Where would that new assumption lead us?" In Einstein's case, that new assumption led directly to the Theory of Relativity. In business, retroduction is frequently applied to strategic planning and forecasting.

Analogies. An analogy is a similarity between two or more things that are otherwise unlike. For example, an analogy can be made between how a computer operates and how the human brain functions. By thinking in terms of analogies, it is possible to find new ways to attack problems. Alexander Graham Bell built the telephone receiver on the basis of the analogy to the human ear.

Listing. Another creativity enhancement technique is listing. It involves asking a series of questions about how we might use something that we already have. For example, "Can we put our nickel-plated gizmo to other uses?" "What would happen if we made it larger?" "Smaller?" "Would zinc-plating improve durability?"

Listing techniques were widely used by the military during World War II and were credited with saving more than six million worker-hours. These techniques were used to invent fiberglass, freeze-dried foods, tapered roller bearings, and even Spic and Span.

the way the firm is departmentalized, and a change in the number of decisions that employees are allowed to make.

At the aircraft engine factories of Rolls Royce, for instance, workshop managers were not allowed to change shop assignments or to give out rewards. Therefore, workers tended to ignore the workshop managers. The factory managers, who made the decisions and gave out the rewards, spent very little time in the workshops and could not make good decisions on giving rewards. When upper management decided to let workshop managers determine shop assignments and give out rewards, productivity and quality control increased dramatically.

Human Change. Human change is concerned with improving employee attitudes, skills, or knowledge. Persuading employees to support the United Fund, to learn how to program a computer, or to prepare for an assignment in a new department require human change.

At Hewlett-Packard, managers realized that the computer and electronics fields change so fast that everyone, from salesperson to research scientist, needs continual updating on new trends and equipment. The company started a broad program of seminars and lectures designed to better inform all types of employees within the company. Partly as a result of this forward-thinking effort, Hewlett-Packard is one of the most profitable computer companies.

Overcoming Resistance to Change

Most attempts at change are likely to meet some resistance. Change brings about doubt and may be seen as a threat to a worker's pay, relationships with others, authority, or skills. Many

Source: © King Features Syndicate, Inc. 1973

people also resist change because they think it is not needed, because they think they are being manipulated, or because they don't like the person trying to introduce the change.

Managers must learn to introduce change in the least upsetting way possible. Anticipating the resistance that may occur can help managers better prepare for dealing with that resistance.

SUMMARY POINTS

1. Management can be defined as the art and science of achieving organizational goals by arranging for others to perform the necessary tasks.
2. The three levels of management are top management, middle management, and lower management.
3. A fundamental task of management is to structure the organization so that it meets the firm's goals and offers satisfying work to its employees.
4. Five key elements of organizational design are hierarchy of authority, division of labor, departmentalization, line and staff relationships, and span of control.
5. The value of a well-defined hierarchy of authority—a ranking of people in the organization according to degree of authority—is that it reduces confusion about who gives orders and who obeys them.
6. A business firm can be departmentalized by process or function, purpose, or through a combination of both, known as matrix departmentalization.
7. A job in the direct chain of command is called a line position. A job outside the chain is called a staff position.
8. Span of control refers to the number of employees that a manager directly supervises.
9. The mechanistic organization design has characteristics of a machine, whereas the organic design is more like a living organism.
10. Five management functions are planning, organizing, staffing, directing, and controlling. These functions make up the management process.
11. Effective decisions involve at least five steps: defining the problem, identifying decision alternatives, evaluating alternatives and choosing one, implementing the decision, and monitoring decision outcomes.
12. Four important types of organizational change are purpose or task change, technological change, structural change, and human change.

KEY TERMS AND CONCEPTS

management
hierarchy of authority
organization chart
division of labor
departmentalization
process departmentalization
purpose departmentalization
matrix departmentalization
line position
staff position
span of control
mechanistic organizational design
organic organizational design
management process
planning
organizing

staffing
directing
controlling
screening approach
scoring approach

purpose or task change
technological change
structural change
human change

REVIEW QUESTIONS

1. What are the three levels of management? In general terms, briefly describe what managers do at each level.
2. Define hierarchy of authority. Why is it necessary in most firms, especially large ones, to make authority relationships explicit?
3. What is the difference between division of labor and span of control?
4. Imagine a firm with three departments: a finance department, a research department, and a West Coast sales department. Does this make sense? Why or why not?
5. What are the advantages of process departmentalization in relation to purpose departmentalization, and vice versa?
6. Describe the difference between a line position and a staff position.
7. What is the difference between a mechanistic approach to management and an organic approach?
8. What are the five functions of managers?
9. What is the distinction between planning and controlling? Are staffing and directing the same thing?
10. Identify the five stages in the decision process.
11. Describe each of the four ways in which the firm can change in response to a changing environment.

DISCUSSION QUESTIONS

1. Is management an art or a science? What do you think?
2. What are the pros and cons of the matrix approach to departmentalization? Do you feel that this approach will play a major role in business in the future?
3. Suppose you wanted to start your own business. Would you choose a mechanistic or an organic approach to organizing your company? Explain.
4. Which of the five management functions would you be best at? Explain.
5. Why is creativity important in decision making?
6. Why do many attempts to overcome resistance to change fail? What, in your opinion, can be done to reduce resistance to change?

CASE 7-1

Nestlé

Nestlé, the world's largest food company, is headquartered in Vevey, Switzerland. Several years ago, Nestlé decided to improve its American operations. By 1980, annual sales had jumped to $2.3 billion from $407 million ten years earlier. Nestlé executives wanted American sales to constitute 30 percent of total Nestlé revenues, but no matter what the executives tried, American sales never passed 20 percent.

Nestlé's managing director, Arthur Fuerer, decided to create the position of American Manager. This manager would direct and control all American operations. The position was entrusted to David E. Guerrant, the first American to make his way up through Nestlé's ranks. Guerrant was made responsible for the Nestlé Company in America, as well as for its subsidiaries which included Libby's canned foods, Beech-Nut, Stouffer, and a variety of related companies.

Guerrant's job was not easy. American operations had always been accustomed to minimal supervision by their distant Swiss directors. In addition, 11 of the firm's top managers were killed in a hotel fire. Overall, Nestlé had too little top management in the United States. Guerrant had to correct this.

At the same time, Nestlé was planning several drastic moves. For example, Libby's was dependent on the seasonal vegetable canning business for 80 percent of its $400 million sales each year. Therefore, it had not been as profitable as Nestlé wanted. Consequently, the president of Libby's, Ian Murray, began to reduce canning to 50 percent of annual revenues by moving into other kinds of foods such as spices and salad dressings. Nestlé agreed with this move. Nestlé also realized that the food industry grows in the United States at 10 to 12 percent a year, with few exceptions. Nestlé needed to move into other areas to improve growth opportunities. Deciding to stay with products related to the human body, Fuerer started to acquire pharmaceutical and cosmetics companies, such as L'Oréal, Burton, Parsons & Co., DuBarry Cosmetics, and Alcon Laboratories. Fuerer wanted to maintain a direct link with these new acquisitions from Nestlé's headquarters. As a result, Guerrant found some of the American operations under his own control, and others reporting directly to Switzerland. To top it off, Guerrant received orders to increase the number of Stouffer hotels from 20 to 50 by 1990.

1. How has hierarchy of authority been established at Nestlé?
2. How has departmentalization been established at Nestlé?
3. How did span of control change for Fuerer? for Guerrant?
4. How could an American manager have been more effective than Fuerer in each of the basic managerial functions?
5. Describe how the decision to create the post of American Manager and to name Guerrant to the position was made, using the decision stages outlined in the text.

CASE 7-2

Panaeros Airlines

In 1965, Panaeros Airlines was an obscure Spanish airline equipped almost entirely with old propeller planes and barely surviving in a highly regulated airline industry. Then along came Luis Trevino, who took over Panaeros in 1965. Trevino immediately started to buy new jets. He expanded Panaeros into South America and North Africa. He painted his terminals in exotic colors and his planes in every color of the rainbow. One plane was even gilded in 24-karat gold as a publicity ploy. He hired beauty contest winners to be stewardesses and served the very best in gourmet seafood on all flights.

By 1972, Panaeros had become the most profitable airline in Europe. By 1977, it was larger than all but the huge American airlines. But under all the apparent growth, Panaeros was dying. The problem lay in its management and, in particular, in Luis Trevino.

Today, European managers look at Trevino as an example of how not to run a business. First of all, Trevino tried to run the business alone. He had a brilliant mind and a fantastic memory for figures, so he trusted his own estimates of performance over the opinions of his executives. He was regarded as an expert salesman, even to the point of selling his ideas to his own executives; he never seemed to realize that he had only to sell the customers.

On Panaeros flights, Trevino was known as a tyrant. He often "bumped" a number of passengers to carry guests to his villa in North Africa. He had special preferences in food, which had to be specially cooked for him when he was on any Panaeros flight. He even ordered a Panaeros flight to land at the wrong airport in Paris once because it was more convenient for him; his passengers were put on an unair-conditioned bus for a two-hour drive to the correct airport.

Meanwhile, morale at Panaeros was very low. Trevino often appointed people to positions simply because he liked them. Dismissals were frequent and often without cause. Executives were actually afraid to report bad news to Trevino. Insecurity was rampant.

Even when things started to go bad, Trevino was able to go to his government and obtain large loans. However, he used the funds to build an elaborate corporate headquarters on the Costa del Sol, to acquire more planes, and to spend lavishly. High fuel costs and increased taxes hit Panaeros hard, and Panaeros died.

1. Do you think Trevino thought of management as an art or a science? Why was he wrong?
2. Does Panaeros sound like it was an organic or a mechanistic design? Was it either? Why?
3. Did a hierarchy of authority exist at Panaeros? Was it effective?
4. How would you describe Trevino's idea of span of control? How was his idea good or bad?
5. Evaluate Trevino's performance in each of the five management functions (planning, organizing, staffing, directing, and controlling).

Motivating Employees

8

After studying this chapter, you should be able to:

- Characterize the impact of Scientific Management and Hawthorn studies on motivation research.
- Describe how Maslow's need hierarchy, the need for achievement, learning theory, and expectancy theory relate to job motivation.
- Discuss reward systems and the cost to a firm of unhappy employees.
- Suggest ways to build morale in a business.

There is no question that people are important to organizations. For one thing, they are the ones who make the decisions; for another, they are expensive. Labor accounts for 25 percent of the cost of making an automobile and nearly 60 percent of the cost of publishing a book. Obviously, therefore, treating employees fairly, motivating them effectively, and designing their jobs intelligently can lead to big productivity gains. **Productivity** may be defined as output of goods and services per unit of labor over a period of time.

This chapter focuses on the roles of people within organizations. Special attention is given to the issues of job satisfaction and motivation, work rewards, and job design. We begin by looking at some of the early research on the roles of people within organizations.

EARLY PERSPECTIVES ON JOB MOTIVATION

The first major research on managing human beings was called Scientific Management. We'll examine scientific management along with what are known as the Hawthorne studies.

Scientific Management

Until the early 1900s, the human element was almost completely ignored by people writing about organizations. It was assumed that in a well-designed and well-run company, employees would act like any other pieces of machinery—they would be there when needed, and they would do as they were told. In 1911, however, Frederick Taylor introduced **Scientific Management.** The aim of Scientific Management was to find the "one best way" to perform any given task, such as the best way to make pins or the best way to shovel coal. One aspect of finding the best way to do a job was to find the best person for the job. Thus, Taylor stressed the importance of people in organizations.[1]

Taylor was talking mostly about the kinds of jobs for which strength or hand speed were important. Although he did consider the human element, Taylor's views generally are not seen as very humane today. Taylor emphasized the efficiency of workers, not the satisfaction of workers. For instance, he wrote that the kind of person who made a good pig-iron handler was "of the type of the ox." Scientific Management led to simplified jobs, with each worker going through the same few motions time after time—boring, but efficient.

The Hawthorne Studies

Despite the work of Taylor and a few early psychologists, it was not until the 1930s that the importance of the human element was really recognized. Then, in a series of studies at the Hawthorne Plant of the Western Electric Company, researchers tried to determine the best level of lighting, length of workday, and length of rest periods in terms of maximizing worker productivity. What they found was surprising. Among other things, when the level of light in the plant was increased, the level of production went up. But when the lights were then turned down, even to the level of moonlight, productivity kept going up!

It might be expected that the level of work would increase as the lights were brightened; but it would also probably be expected that productivity would decrease as the lights were lowered. What could account for the result? The answer is that workers became more productive because they felt special. They had been singled out for the experiment and wanted to do a good job to show that they were worthy of the attention. This change in behavior because of being singled out for attention is now called the "Hawthorne Effect." In a more general sense, the Hawthorne studies showed that distinctly human factors are as important as pay or working conditions in motivating employees.

MOTIVATION THEORY TODAY

The basic thing we can say about people is that they have needs. A **need** is something that is required. **Satisfaction** is the condition of need fulfillment, such as when a hungry person sits down to eat, or when a person driven by the desire for success finally achieves that goal. **Motivation** is the attempt to satisfy a need. The practice

---

[1] F. W. Taylor, *The Principles of Scientific Management* (New York: Harper and Bros., 1911).

of management is largely concerned with motivating employees to work harder, more efficiently, and more intelligently. We will look at four approaches to motivation and at how each relates to motivating people in the workplace.

Maslow's Need Hierarchy

Abraham Maslow did much of the classic work on motivation theory. Maslow believed that motivation should be examined in terms of five classifications of goals or needs.

1. *Physiological*: the need for food, sleep, water, and sex.
2. *Security*: the need for safety, family stability, economic security, and absence from illness and pain.
3. *Social or affiliation*: the need to belong, to interact with others, to have friends, and to love and be loved.
4. *Esteem*: the need for respect and recognition from others.
5. *Self-actualization*: the need to realize one's potential, to grow, to be creative, and the need for self-accomplishment.[2]

Figure 8-1 ranks these needs in a hierarchy of importance. That is, as we satisfy any of these five needs, they become less important to us and motivate us less. Eating, for example, satisfies the physiological need of hunger and leaves us less interested in food. In the same way, the need for affiliation and friendship is strongest for someone who feels excluded. Once this person makes a few friends, the need to belong becomes less important.

Climbing the Hierarchy. Maslow suggested that we "climb" the hierarchy. That is, we first satisfy our basic physiological needs. Only when we have done so are we motivated by the needs at the next higher level of the hierarchy: the need for safety, security, and freedom from pain. When this group of needs is met, we move on to the next level, and so on.

Variety of Needs. Maslow's system forces us to recognize that people have a variety of needs. How does all this relate to motivation? The answer is that people work for many reasons besides the paycheck which buys them food and shelter.

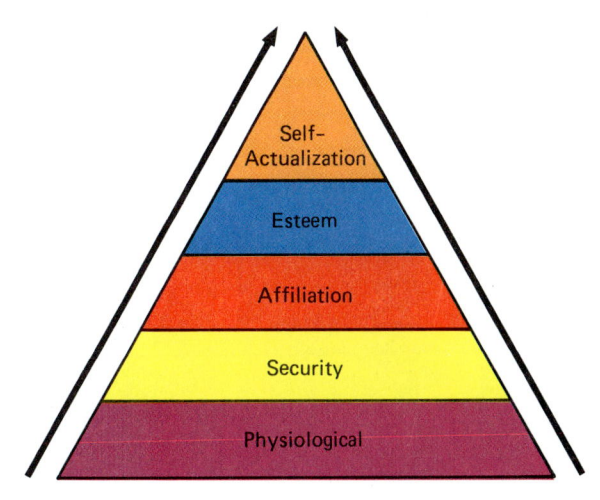

[2]A.H. Maslow, "A Theory of Human Motivation," *Psychological Review*, Vol. 50 (1943), pp. 370-396.

People work so that they can be with others, so that they can gain respect, and so that they can realize their potential. Management must consider these needs when it designs reward systems for employees.

Maslow's need hierarchy has been widely accepted but it still does not seem to be quite correct. For instance, at the top of the hierarchy, satisfaction generally does not lead to a decrease in motivation. Instead, people who are able to self-actualize become *more* motivated to take on self-actualizing activities. Also, the climb up the hierarchy is unpredictable; once we've satisfied needs at the lowest levels, needs at *any* other level may become most important to us.

Need for Achievement

Another way to look at motivation was offered by David McClelland. McClelland focused on three needs: the need for power over others, the need to belong (like Maslow's social needs), and the need for achievement.[3] The last of these—the need for achievement—has received the most attention.

The High Achiever. People with a strong need for achievement want to do well no matter which goal they pursue. They also desire personal responsibility and want quick feedback about how well

---

[3]D. C. McClelland, "Business Drive and National Achievement," *Harvard Business Review*, Vol. 40 (1962), pp. 99-112.

Figure 8-1

Maslow's Need Hierarchy

they have done at a given task. Some jobs, such as those in sales, are best for people with a strong need for achievement. The need for high achievement, however, is not desirable in all work situations. It has been found that Nobel Prize winners, who conduct research over many years and receive very slow feedback, have only an average need for achievement.

Developing Need for Achievement. McClelland argued that need for achievement can be developed in people by getting them to believe that they can change and by helping them to set personal goals. This process also includes learning to "speak the language of achievement." By this we mean that people can be taught to think, talk, and act, as if they in fact were achievement oriented.

In practice, McClelland has been successful in developing the need for achievement. For example, after he conducted a training session in India, the achievement activity of trainees nearly doubled. Achievement activity meant starting a new business or sharply increasing company profits. One trainee, in fact, raised enough money to put up the tallest building in Bombay—the Everest Apartments.

Learning Theory

According to learning theory, the consequences of an act determine whether or not the act will be repeated. Rewarded behavior is repeated; punished behavior is not. This is called the **law of effect**. To illustrate, if we give a child a piece of candy every time we want the child to stop crying, we are actually increasing the chances that the child will cry again. What we're doing is rewarding the child for crying.

Rewarding Poor Behavior. It is interesting to think about some of the other ways that we reward poor behavior.[4] For example, a primary goal of orphanages is to place children in good homes. But since the number of children in the orphanage determines the size of the budget, the size of the staff, and the director's prestige, the orphanage is actually rewarded for *not* placing children in homes. Thus, undesired behavior is rewarded, and the orphanage is less likely to try to find homes for its children.

Managing People. What can learning theory tell us about managing people on the job? First, it tells us that we should reward behavior that we want to occur, not behavior we do not want to occur. If, for some reason, we find that we have been rewarding poor behavior, we should stop doing so. Once that behavior is no longer rewarded, it will gradually stop occurring. The disappearance of a behavior is called **extinction**.

---

[4]S. Kerr, "On the Folly of Rewarding A, While Hoping for B," *Academy of Management Journal*, Vol. 18 (1975), pp. 769-783.

What needs can you identify in these photos? How are those needs being met?

Many people see learning theory as frightening and unethical. The proponents of learning theory believe that managers are always manipulating behavior anyway, whether they are aware of it or not. The trick is to do it right. You can reward whatever you want—quantity of output, creativity, or service to society. The point is, reward what you want and not what you don't want. Unfortunately, it is sometimes necessary to punish on-the-job behavior that we want stopped. Punishment, however, should probably be used only as a last resort.

Expectancy Theory

A final theory of motivation, **expectancy theory**, focuses on employees' desires and expectations. According to expectancy theory, motivating employees to perform well on the job depends on at least three things. First, the rewards given to employees should be what they want. If they don't want them, why should they try to earn them? Second, employees must be made to believe that better performance leads to rewards. If not, why do better? And third, they must believe that trying harder results in improved performance. If it doesn't, why try harder?

Clear-cut as these guides may seem, they are often forgotten. Managers sometimes assume that they know what employees want, or they may give everyone the same rewards no matter how well they do. Failure to reward properly can result in lack of employee motivation.

REWARDING EMPLOYEES

Employee satisfaction is important; after all, people spend one third or more of their adult lives at work. To keep people satisfied, management must understand not only motivation, but also which types of rewards work best.

Classes of Rewards

While no job can give us everything we want, every job should meet at least some of our needs. Basically, there are two types of rewards: extrinsic rewards and intrinsic rewards. **Extrinsic rewards** refer to pay raises, promotions, and other symbols of recognition. They are rewards given to the employee by someone else—usually by someone in management. **Intrinsic rewards** relate to the job itself and the pleasure and sense of accomplishment that it gives the employee.

Until fairly recently, most business firms and management theorists considered only extrinsic rewards—wages and salary, in particular—in the design of jobs and compensation programs. The reason may have been that employers held what is called a **Theory X** set of assumptions. According to Theory X, people are lazy and self-indulgent, require constant supervision, and work only because they get paid. Employers who accept Theory X as the best explanation of employee motivation tend to watch their workers closely, to treat them as inferior, and to pay little attention to job satisfaction. Intrinsic rewards are of little or no concern to managers following Theory X. As an example of Theory X, consider the case of the J. P. Stevens Company. At one time, J. P. Stevens, a textile manufacturer, paid low wages, employed company spies and watchdogs, and even locked employees into their factory rooms.

The alternative to Theory X is **Theory Y**, which views workers as responsible, as liking work, and as wanting intrinsic rewards. Under Theory Y, jobs are designed to be more interesting and workers are allowed more freedom in the performance of their jobs. Hewlett-Packard is an example of Theory Y management in practice. At Hewlett-Packard, a major computer manufacturer, employees are encouraged to make a wide

CONTROVERSIAL ISSUES

Financial Reward—the Best Way to Motivate People to Work!

For years, people have known that reward encourages employees to work harder. Often it was assumed that people work hardest when the reward was extra money. Today, however, companies are questioning whether financial rewards are the best way to motivate employees.

Pro

Yes, money always is the best motivator. Consider the position of the company as a whole. Say you are a supervisor who directs a hundred employees, whose rewards you administer. Now suppose you want to give as rewards free tickets to a musical and, at Christmas, a free weekend at the beach. Unfortunately, some of your employees won't like musicals and others won't like the beach. The rewards will be useless motivators for those individuals. Suppose instead that you use pats on the back and citations on the bulletin board as rewards for superior employees. This time, there will likely be workers who don't care about pats and citations, but who would like something more concrete.

Since you need to give a reward that is uniform among all employees, and you want to please everyone, you do best to give a reward that employees can convert into their favorite form if they aren't happy with cash in hand.

Also, it is wise to reward to an extra degree the worker who did a bit better than other employees. When you give money, you can give amounts tailored to the motivation or output of that particular worker.

Finally, financial rewards can be written off on taxes. Your tax bill is less and your workers are more motivated. The value to the company is much greater. You don't have to worry about rewarding somebody with a promotion that they can't quite handle or rewarding somebody with a holiday they will only use to moonlight to earn extra money.

Give your employees financial rewards. Cash is always the best way to motivate people to work.

Con

No, money isn't the best way to motivate workers. Many employees want things that a cash bonus can't supply.

Above all, today, employees want respect, position, and esteem in an organization. Many modern organizations are designed with the important goal in mind of rewarding employees by the positions they hold and the authority they wield. Rewards must constantly encourage employees to perform better. A cash reward will do that for a short time, but employees who have been promoted know their promotion was based on performance, and will strive constantly to improve their performance.

Recognition motivates many workers, and recognition can come in many forms. Simply citing the performance of workers in the company newsletter can yield big benefits to the company in the form of even greater productivity by employees. Most people like to know their work has not gone unnoticed.

Finally, money ceases to mean as much to people as they are paid more. In a recent study of sales personnel, the better paid sales people were less motivated by higher commissions and bonuses and better motivated by more recognition of their work and more promotions. Financial rewards are certainly nice, but many times other kinds of rewards can be far more valuable and far more motivating.

range of decisions and to shoulder a considerable amount of responsibility. H-P employees also have input in research decisions. Later in this chapter we'll consider how jobs can be designed to provide these intrinsic rewards.[5]

Although the distinction between extrinsic rewards and intrinsic rewards is valuable, perhaps a more useful distinction is that between financial and nonfinancial rewards. After all, when managers design compensation programs, they usually think in these terms.

Financial Rewards. Several studies have shown that financial rewards are the key influence in choice of jobs and in requests for transfers to other jobs. There are many reasons why money is desirable. One reason is that people get pleasure out of the act of making money. The main reason, however, is that money enables people to get the other things they want—that is, money can help satisfy needs at *all* levels in Maslow's need hierarchy which we discussed earlier. Figure 8-2 shows how money can satisfy these needs.

Nonfinancial Rewards. Nonfinancial rewards are rewards given to an employee for doing a good job. Just as the name says, they do not involve money. An example of a nonfinancial reward is **status pay**, such as a new office or travel opportunities. These status symbols show how important a person is within the organization. Consider the case of two bank executives, each with the title of vice-president. One works in a small, windowless office and the other works in a large, paneled suite. Which vice-president is more important in the eyes of the bank?

We should not conclude from this, however, that only top executives care about status. Many people who work in factories view the kinds of clothing they're allowed to wear on the job or access to the dining room as important rewards.

A second type of nonfinancial incentive is **privilege pay**, which is the amount of input an employee has in a management decision. Many employees want to be involved in decision making. Frequently, giving employees this sense of involvement costs the firm almost nothing and makes the employees feel important in the organization. One reason that Japanese automobile companies have been so successful is that workers are encouraged to make recommendations to management as to how cars can be produced better and more cheaply. Workers feel that they are part of the team and not just cogs in a machine.

Giving Out Rewards

Rewards, if given properly, can improve job performance. There are at least four rules for administering rewards. First, tie rewards directly to the behavior that you want repeated. If you want high quality, reward high quality. If you want creativity, reward creativity. Giving people weekly or monthly paychecks rewards them only for showing up for work. Motivating the work force may require something more, whether it be

---

[5] D. McGregor, *The Human Side of Enterprise* (New York: McGraw-Hill, 1960).

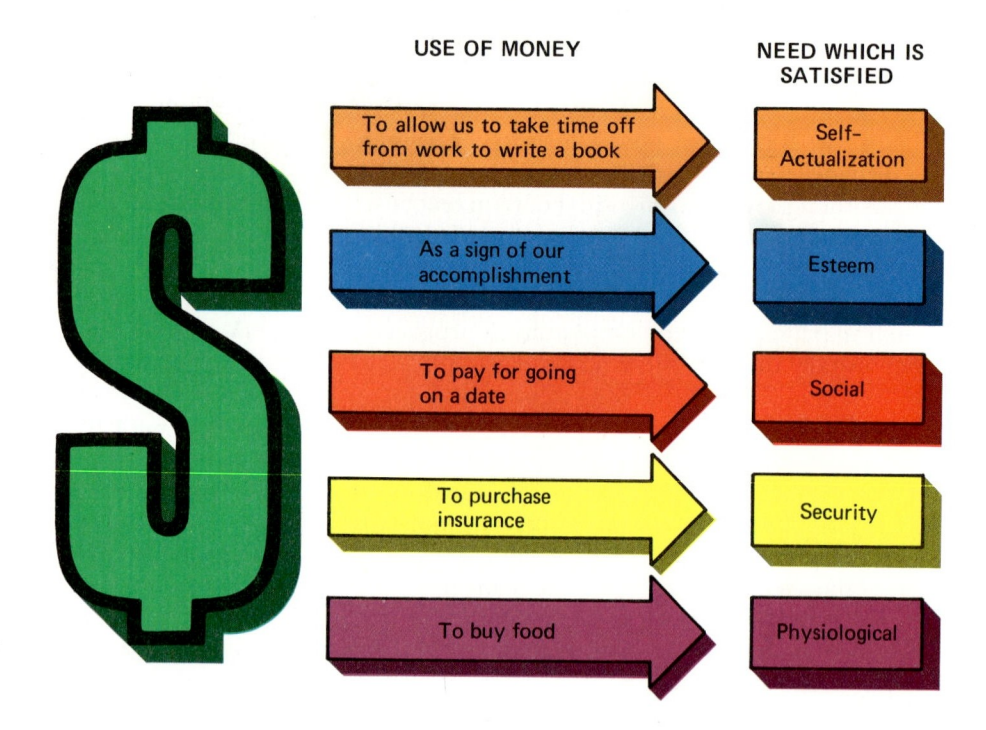

Figure 8-2

How Money Can Satisfy Our Needs

USE OF MONEY	NEED WHICH IS SATISFIED
To allow us to take time off from work to write a book	Self-Actualization
As a sign of our accomplishment	Esteem
To pay for going on a date	Social
To purchase insurance	Security
To buy food	Physiological

extra pay, status, or public praise. Second, let employees know which rewards are available and how they can go about obtaining them. Third, reward desired behavior as soon as it occurs. Rewarding a person in June for a job well done in January does not reinforce the behavior. And fourth, reward people only for what they themselves have done. Plant-wide bonuses for high production levels are fine, but since overall profits are beyond the control of individual employees, such rewards don't do much to increase motivation.

Job Dissatisfaction

Now that we've looked at various approaches to rewarding employees, we're ready to ask ourselves, "What is the real cost of unhappy employees?" It is not always easy to account for the cost associated with job dissatisfaction. The cost to the unhappy employee is almost impossible to measure. The cost of job dissatisfaction for the firm often includes employee illnesses and poorly made products.

Stress. Dissatisfying jobs cause **stress**, a feeling of strain or pressure. Research suggests that job stress is linked not only to mental problems, but also to ulcers and heart disease. Estimates place the cost of stress on executives alone in this country at between $10 billion and $20 billion each year.[6] In 1978, the National Institute of Occupational Safety and Health (NIOSH) ranked 130 jobs on the basis of stress. Ten of the most stressful and ten of the least stressful jobs are shown in Table 8-1.

What do the jobs on each list have in common? Although it is difficult to answer this question exactly, it appears that all the jobs on the "most stressful" list involve either direct and constant supervision or a high degree of risk and responsibility. The jobs on the "least stressful" list involve freedom from direct supervision and a slower work pace.

Partly because of the impact of stress, companies are thinking more about the "wellness" of their employees. That is, they are just as concerned with keeping their employees healthy as they are with taking care of them after they are ill. The Sentry Insurance Company, at its Stevens Point, Wisconsin, headquarters, has a "quiet room" where employees can go to relax. The company has an exercise room open to all employees.

---

[6]J. W. Greenwood, "Management Stressors," *Reducing Occupational Stress* (Cincinnati: NIOSH Research Report, 1978).

Table 8-1

The Most Stressful and Least Stressful Jobs

Most Stressful Jobs	Least Stressful Jobs
Manual Laborer	Clothing Sewer
Secretary	Stockroom Worker
Inspector	Craftsman
Waitress-Waiter	Maid
Clinical Lab Technician	Heavy-Equipment Operator
Farm Owner	Farm Laborer
Miner	Childcare Worker
House Painter	Packer, Wrapper in Shipping
Manager Administrator	College or University Professor
Foreman	Personnel, Labor Relations

Source: U.S. Department of Health, Education, and Welfare, National Institute for Occupational Safety and Health, *Occupational Stress* (1978).

Inferior Products. Employee job dissatisfaction can also show up in poorly made products. Dissatisfied workers stay away from work more often, quit jobs more often, criticize the company, go on strike, do poor work, and so on. Any of these can affect product quality and can cost the firm a large amount of money.

An illustration of these costs is what is called a "Monday car." Many workers at U.S. automobile assembly plants are very unhappy with their jobs. They see themselves as little more than machines. Consequently, many of them do not come to work on Mondays. To keep the assembly line moving, automobile manufacturers have "swing" employees who move from job to job on the assembly line as they are needed. However, since they often cannot do the job as well as the regular employee, the quality of work suffers. As a result, a Monday car often comes off the assembly line. These cars are referred to by their eventual owners as "lemons."

HOW CAN MANAGEMENT MOTIVATE EMPLOYEES?

A few years ago, Chicago author Studs Terkel wrote a book called *Working: People Talk About What They Do All Day and How They Feel About What They Do*. The book consists of a series of interviews with people from all walks of life. What emerged from the book was a sense of the brutality and emptiness of most work today. Terkel began his book by saying,

> This book, being about work, is, by its very nature, about violence—to the spirit as well as to the body. It is about ulcers as well as accidents, about shouting matches as well as fistfights, about nervous breakdowns as well as kicking the dog around. It is, above all (or beneath all) about daily humiliations. To survive the day is triumph enough for the walking wounded among the great many of us.[7]

This is certainly a depressing view about the nature of work in the United States. Still, as we know, many jobs are exciting and satisfying.

Whether a job is enjoyable or frustrating, as well as whether an employee is motivated or not, depends largely on management. We have already looked at the issue of rewards and how they can improve job performance. We now look at three other ways to build morale in a business: job enrichment, flextime, and management by objectives.

---

[7] S. Terkel, *Working* (New York: Pantheon Books, 1972).

Some jobs are more stressful than others.

Profile—
Hewlett-Packard

Hewlett-Packard is a huge computer and semiconductor manufacturer. HP employs 68,000 people, obtains less than one percent of its total capital from long-term debt, and has a large amount of cash and high ratios of short-term assets to short-term obligations. Hewlett-Packard was the first company to introduce a 32-bit microprocessor in a personal computer and was the first company to offer a really professional laboratory computer. The company, which has a wide range of computerized test instruments and equipment, comes out every year with new products that even IBM doesn't try to imitate. Hewlett-Packard's HP-75C is the ultimate microcomputer; its HP 41CV is the ultimate hand calculator; and its HP-10 series is a line of pocket calculators unmatched by competition.

But how does HP do it? As in most other companies, success comes above all from the effective motivation of employees. HP works at this problem in many different ways. For example, managers are chosen on the basis of their ability to excite and rouse their workers. Right from the start, founders Bill Hewlett and Dave Packard believed that the only way to find long-term success was to so stimulate their employees that success was inevitable. Years ago HP did away with time clocks and introduced flexible work hours. Everyone is addressed on a first-name basis. HP employees quickly understand that their company is not a "hire and fire" company (the kind of company that hires workers when needed and fires them when the pace slows down again).

A prime example of HP's concern with motivating employees is its "open stock policy." All electronics, mechanical equipment, and components from storerooms are available to all employees. Employees may take them home, play with them, build projects on their own time, experiment with their own pet projects, and so on. *This* is the kind of motivation that breeds innovation.

How does HP manage to keep at least some control over all this freedom? A phrase coined to describe HP's management approach is "management by wandering around." HP managers do not stay at their desks; they walk into work areas, research labs, and assembly lines to talk with people, check on how they are performing, and find out what problems they are having. This kind of personal attention means a lot to most workers, and it means that every worker is motivated to perform well in order to merit the attention of top management.

Many other techniques are used to motivate employees and to stimulate innovation and productivity. Couches and blackboards are scattered throughout HP buildings so that people can stop in the halls, sketch out an idea, talk about business with people they might not otherwise meet or talk with, and spread awareness of problems or new ideas. When quality control problems arise, individuals are never singled out; everyone shares the blame. Individuals do receive high praise, though, when improvements in quality control occur. Thus, employees are always supported and praised face-to-face, and they are criticized only as part of a group; this spares feelings and encourages improvement in performance.

Because of HP's effectiveness in motivating its employees, analysts foresee 20 percent annual growth in earnings for the next several years. Insiders (management and employees) are more than willing to own their company's stock; more than one third of all of HP's stock is owned by insiders. Clearly, motivation has been very successful at Hewlett-Packard.

Job Enrichment

Earlier, we said that the emphasis of Scientific Management on the "one best way" to do a job resulted in extremely simplified work tasks. An assembly or manufacturing process was broken down into parts, and each worker was given only a small part of the overall work. The worker performed this part over and over again. Assembly line jobs in an automobile plant are an example of these routine, simplified jobs. The idea behind such jobs is that workers have less trouble learning their jobs, do not waste time moving from one part of the job to another, and can easily be replaced if necessary.

Scientific Management did lead to some remarkable productivity gains during the early part of this century in such jobs as metal cutting, pin making, and bricklaying. For instance, by application of the principles of Scientific Management, it was possible in one case to increase the number of bricks laid per worker-hour from 120 to 350. But more recently, as Figure 8-3 shows, people have argued that simplified, routine jobs lead to boredom, dissatisfaction, and other bad outcomes.

In an enriched job, on the other hand, individual employees do a large part of the overall job rather than just a small piece of it. They are also given responsibility to see that the job is done correctly. As a result, enriched jobs give employees the chance to feel they are doing important work. It has been found that people with enriched jobs generally are more satisfied with

Figure 8-3

Turning Boring Work into Interesting Work

Bored people build bad cars. That's why we're doing away with the assembly line.

Working on an assembly line is monotonous. And boring. And after a while, some people begin not to care about their jobs anymore. So the quality of the product often suffers.

That's why, at Saab, we're replacing the assembly line with assembly teams. Groups of just three or four people who are responsible for a particular assembly process from start to finish.

Each team makes its own decisions about who does what and when. And each team member can even do the entire assembly singlehandedly. The result: people are more involved. They care more. So there's less absenteeism, less turnover. And we have more experienced people on the job.

We're building our new 2-liter engines this way. And the doors to our Saab 99. And we're planning to use this same system to build other parts of our car as well.

It's a slower, more costly system, but we realize that the best machines and materials in the world don't mean a thing, if the person building the car doesn't care.

Saab. It's what a car should be.

There are more than 300 Saab dealers nationwide. For the name and address of the one nearest you call 800-243-6000 toll free. In Connecticut, call 1-800-882-6500. Saab 99 L. 2-door, $3,595. 4-door, $3,695. P.O.E. Transportation, state and local taxes, optional equipment, dealer preparation charges, if any, additional.

their work, show less absenteeism and turnover, and produce higher quality work than those with simplified jobs.

Generally speaking, the more highly trained the work force is, the more responsibility management can give to its employees. As an example, many salespeople are simply given a list of possible customers as well as instructions about what to say during the sales call. If the sales force were well trained, however, the job of selling could be enriched by allowing salespersons to determine sales objectives and selling strategies for themselves, to decide which customers deserve extra attention, and to schedule their sales calls for the day.

Flextime

Another way jobs can be changed is through flextime. **Flextime** requires employees to work a certain number of hours during a core work period in the middle of the day, but the employees are free to decide when they want to come to work and when they want to leave. Under flextime, one employee may decide to arrive at work at six o'clock in the morning and leave at three o'clock in the afternoon; another might arrive at ten o'clock in the morning and leave at seven.

Many employees like the idea of flextime because it reduces the stress of getting to work when everyone else does, because it lets employees work when they feel best, and because it gives them a sense of freedom. Flextime has proven particularly useful for young families, for it enables parents to spend more time with their children.

One company which has been a pioneer of flextime is Control Data Corp. (CDC). CDC managers realize that their employees will work better if they can schedule work according to the availability of child care, bus or train times, and the work schedules of other family members. Flextime has solved this problem and has kept motivation and productivity consistently high.

Management By Objectives

Management By Objectives (MBO) may be a useful tool for improving motivation. MBO is based on the theory that people perform best and are most satisfied when they know which goals they are to pursue and when they participate in the process of selecting those goals.

Setting Objectives. The MBO process, as outlined in Figure 8-4, begins by identifying general areas of responsibility that are important to the firm. Once this has been done, the employee and employer get together and agree upon specific objectives that the employee will meet during some future period of time. For example, a key responsibility area in sales management might be sales volume, and the objective might be to increase sales by 35 percent over the next six months. Other responsibility areas and objectives are shown in Table 8-2.

FROM THE FILE

Larry is a production manager at an airplane assembly plant. One day it occurred to Larry that one of his employees, Chuck, was often absent on Mondays and Fridays. Chuck had always seemed a bit unstable but he did good work when he showed up. Larry finally confronted Chuck with the fact that he was apparently the victim of highly selective illnesses—Friday fevers and Monday malaises. Chuck said, "Look, what do you want? I work hard, but I need some time off now and then to recharge. I don't live just to work. I can make enough in three or four days a week to get along fine. Why shouldn't I take long weekends now and then?" Larry was so puzzled by this attitude that he just shook his head and walked away. But he knew that he had to do something.

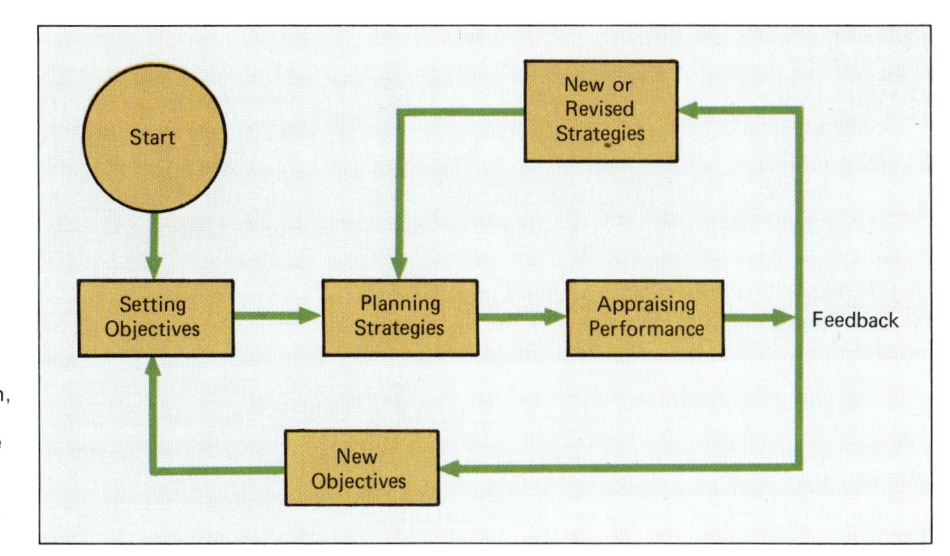

Figure 8-4

The Process of Managing by Objectives

Source: Donald W. Jackson, Jr. and Ramon J. Aldag, "Managing the Sales Force by Objectives," *MSU Business Topics* (Spring, 1974), p. 54. Reprinted by permission of the publisher.

Planning Strategies. Once the manager and employee have agreed upon specific objectives, they develop a strategy together for meeting these objectives. The manager and the employee make a good team: The manager has more general experience with the product and the industry, and the employee knows the details of the job.

Appraising Performance. The manager and the employee then meet periodically to review how the employee has done relative to the agreed-upon objectives. If there is a problem, they discuss why objectives have not been met.

Setting New Strategies or Objectives. The final step is either to set new goals for the next time period or to develop new strategies to meet the previously agreed-upon goals. The entire procedure then begins anew.

Evaluation of MBO. Management By Objectives is a difficult approach to implement. Moreover, it does not always work. Objectives must be specific. Fuzzy goals, such as "Do your best" or even "Get more sales," simply frustrate people. MBO has also been faulted for encouraging people to focus only on goals that can be easily expressed in numbers (such as the number of units produced in a week or the average number of sales calls made per day) and to ignore goals that are hard to measure (such as quality of products or creativity).

On the other hand, MBO does encourage planning and goal setting, and it lets employees know how they are doing on the job. Second, it allows employees to participate in setting goals, which is good for morale and motivation. And it

Table 8-2

Possible Objectives in an MBO Program

Responsibility Areas	Possible Objectives
Sales Volume	Increase sales volume by 35 percent.
Number of Calls Per Day	Increase the number of calls per day to four.
Average Order Size	Increase average order size to $100 by eliminating a certain type of account.
Expenses and Expense Ratios	Reduce cost per call to $30, reduce cost per order to $60, reduce the ratio of selling expense to net sales to 20 percent.
New Accounts	Generate ten new accounts per year.

Source: Adapted from Donald W. Jackson, Jr. and Ramon J. Aldag, "Managing the Sales Force by Objectives," *MSU Business Topics* (Spring, 1974), p. 55. Adapted by permission of the publisher, Division of Research, Graduate School of Business Administration, Michigan State University.

guarantees that deviations in performance from goals will be spotted before it is too late to do anything about them.

IBM provides an example of MBO in action. A salesperson at IBM formulates a planned quota; a repair technician has a specified number of service calls each day; and a warehouse manager understands precisely what inventory standards are expected. IBM employees know that by meeting objectives they are rewarded with raises and promotions. As a result, they are ready to cooperate with management, and managers can confidently predict the output of each area under their authority.

SUMMARY POINTS

1. The aim of scientific management, an early approach to job motivation, was to find the "one best way" to perform any given task.
2. The lesson of the Hawthorne studies was that distinctly human factors are as important in motivating employees as are pay and working conditions.
3. Maslow identified five sets of needs as a basis for human motivation: physiological, security, social or affiliation, esteem, and self-actualization.
4. McClelland looked at motivation in terms of the need for power, the need to belong, and the need for achievement.
5. According to learning theory, the consequences of an act determine whether or not the act will be repeated.
6. Unrewarded behavior eventually stops occurring. This is a process known as extinction.
7. Under expectancy theory, rewards should be consistent with employee desires and expectations.
8. Job satisfaction depends on motivation and a proper system of rewards.
9. Rewards can be either extrinsic or intrinsic. The first refers to pay raises, promotions, and other symbols of recognition; the second refers to the job itself and the pleasure and sense of accomplishment that it gives the employee.
10. According to Theory X, people are lazy and self-indulgent and should be closely supervised on the job.
11. Theory Y views workers as responsible, as basically liking work, and as wanting interesting jobs and intrinsic rewards.
12. Job enrichment involves giving employees a greater degree of authority and more responsibility in deciding how particular tasks should be done.
13. Under a program of flextime, employees are free to decide when to come to work and when to leave for home. They still work a full day but are allowed to vary arrival and departure.
14. Management By Objectives refers to the process of employees and management jointly setting work objectives.

KEY TERMS AND CONCEPTS

productivity
scientific management
satisfaction
motivation
need hierarchy
need for achievement
learning theory
law of effect
extinction
expectancy theory
extrinsic rewards
intrinsic rewards
Theory X
Theory Y
financial rewards
nonfinancial rewards
status pay
privilege pay
stress
job enrichment
flextime
Management By Objectives

REVIEW QUESTIONS

1. Describe scientific management.
2. What did the Hawthorne studies show?
3. Into which of Maslow's need categories does hunger fall? Friendship? Self-worth?
4. What is learning theory?
5. What is the difference between intrinsic and extrinsic rewards? Give two examples of each type of reward.

6. What are some rules for giving out rewards?
7. What are some costs of worker dissatisfaction?
8. Cite some advantages of enriched jobs.
9. What is Management By Objectives? How is it related to goal setting?
10. Describe the process of managing by objectives.

DISCUSSION QUESTIONS

1. Discuss how satisfaction relates to motivation.
2. What are some of the characteristics of people with a strong need for achievement?
3. Of the four theories of motivation presented in this chapter, which do you think offers the best explanation of human behavior in organizations?
4. Is it ever desirable to try to increase conflict in organizations? Why or why not?
5. If you ran a company, would you be a Theory X manager or a Theory Y manager? Explain.

CASE 8-1

Banquet Foods Corporation*

Banquet Foods Corporation was owned by RCA Corp. In September, 1979, RCA decided to sell Banquet, hoping to make a profit on the sale. At the time, Banquet was in sound financial shape and its products were selling well. RCA decided to ask between $150 and $175 million for the company.

Also in 1979, however, there was an oversupply of chickens, as well as reports of cancer-causing agents used on chickens, depressed beef prices, and an upturn in the economy. As people could afford to spend more on food, they turned away from less expensive chicken to buy more of other meats, especially beef, which had become cheaper to buy. Half of Banquet's sales were meals featuring chicken, so Banquet's profits dropped to barely $10 million on about $400 million in sales in 1979. Such low profits could not justify the $175 million price tag.

Finally, ConAgra, a company involved in the chicken business, decided that the demand for chicken would revive and realized that Banquet could be had at a bargain price. ConAgra paid less than $55 million for 80 percent of the company. This was less than half of RCA's asking price.

Because RCA chose to go public with its sale attempts, instead of discreetly using an investment banker to arrange the deal, Banquet's problems were laid out for everyone to see. In the meantime, Banquet's employees were at work every day, knowing that their company was on the auction block. They soon saw that possible buyers didn't think the company was worth what its owners thought it was worth. Employee output had to drop substantially as the demand for chicken decreased.

The marketing staff was told not to use volume price cuts, limited-time sales, or other techniques commonly used to acquire new customers and improve demand. Sales personnel had to fight to convince their buyers that Banquet was not going under. RCA refused to invest additional money in Banquet, which meant that in a poor sales year, many employees went without their expected bonuses or raises. Competitors began spreading rumors that Banquet was going bankrupt and began trying to hire away Banquet's top management personnel. At no time, however, was Banquet in any financial difficulty, nor was its dominant position in the chicken market threatened.

*Source: *Business Week* (March 23, 1981), p. 104; *The Wall Street Journal* (February 8, 1982), p. 29.

1. Briefly summarize the kinds of motivation problems you would expect to find at Banquet among the different groups of employees mentioned in the case.

2. How would scientific management have coped with Banquet's motivation problems? Would scientific management have been a success? Why or why not?
3. What were the sources of job dissatisfaction for Banquet employees?
4. Was Management By Objectives being used properly? What was wrong with Banquet's MBO policy?

CASE 8-2

Control Data Corp. (CDC)

Control Data Corp. (CDC) is a computer company that competes with firms such as IBM and Hewlett-Packard. CDC decided that the company should build plants in economically deprived areas to provide jobs for residents in those areas. The company built a plant in a poor neighborhood of Minneapolis, but found that the workers it hired were burdened with continued worries about financial and health problems, day care for their children, and personal pressures. Although they now had jobs, they were still living in slums. These things deprived them of motivation to work well on the job.

Control Data decided to implement a program called "Fair Break." Employees were given on-the-job training to improve their performance and motivate them to be more reliable on the job. Round-the-clock advisory hotlines were established to counsel employees and their families on finances, health, and personal problems. Special training programs were developed for handicapped and severely disadvantaged community residents. CDC provided car pooling, fitness courses and sports facilities, computer courses on financial planning, cooperative food purchase programs to cut food costs, and programs for obtaining educational loans. CDC also instituted a flexible hours program, whereby employees had to work the same number of hours each day, but could choose the hours they wanted to work. New employee-management arbitration programs were implemented, along with programs to develop greater job security during economic downturns.

Analysts at CDC had realized that their employees lacked motivation, which led to low productivity and high employee turnover. In some companies, these problems might have been attributed to problems within the company. CDC analysts, however, recognized that their own problems stemmed from troubles outside the business. Their response was to expand the sphere of influence of the company into the homes of their employees. CDC hoped to motivate these employees to greater productivity and stability by helping them at home.

1. Why do you think CDC had trouble with productivity and employee turnover? How do you think the programs implemented by CDC motivated employees to perform better on the job?
2. Program by program, describe the benefits CDC would realize from Fair Break. Consider both long- and short-term effects of each program. Describe additional programs you think should be included in Fair Break.
3. If you were a financial planner at CDC, would you plan on funding Fair Break for a period of three years or for the life of the plant? What information might you want to help you decide?
4. If the plant had been built in a middle-class neighborhood in Minneapolis and had employed middle-class workers, how might you change Fair Break?

Human Resources Management

9

After studying this chapter, you should be able to:

- Discuss the four basic stages of staffing.
- Describe three approaches to training and development, as well as the trade-off between recruiting, selection, and placement on the one hand, and training and development on the other.
- Discuss why performance appraisal is important to the firm and how the firm goes about measuring employee performance.
- Describe how job worth, labor market conditions, pay systems, and employee performance determine levels of employee compensation.

From the local delicatessen to the largest New York banking firm, business enterprises are made up of people. The efficiency with which work is organized, people are motivated, and individual employees are assigned to jobs largely determines how well the firm does. This is as true of a work gang on an offshore drilling platform as it is of a group of engineers designing advanced aerospace systems in a high-technology firm. And so we say that human resources management is one of the most important functions of the firm.

This is not to say that a ready supply of low-cost investment funds is of little concern to the firm. Nor is it to say that a supply of affordable raw materials for production is not important. But without a qualified and motivated work force, how would good decisions be made, where would the great new product ideas come from, and how could assembly machines be run efficiently?

In this chapter we consider human resources management. We begin by looking at the problem of staffing, that is, at how firms go about recruiting, hiring, and finding job slots for new employees.

STAFFING THE FIRM

Staffing is a vital part of personnel management. It involves bringing new people into the organization and then making sure that they serve as valuable additions to the work force. The aim of staffing is to match, or align, the abilities of the job candidate with the needs of the firm. Figure 9-1 shows how staffing can make for either a good fit or a bad fit between employees and positions. Staffing consists of four basic stages: recruiting, placement, selection, and training and development.

We can best see this matching process occurring when the new employee enters the firm or when the requirements of the job change. Figure

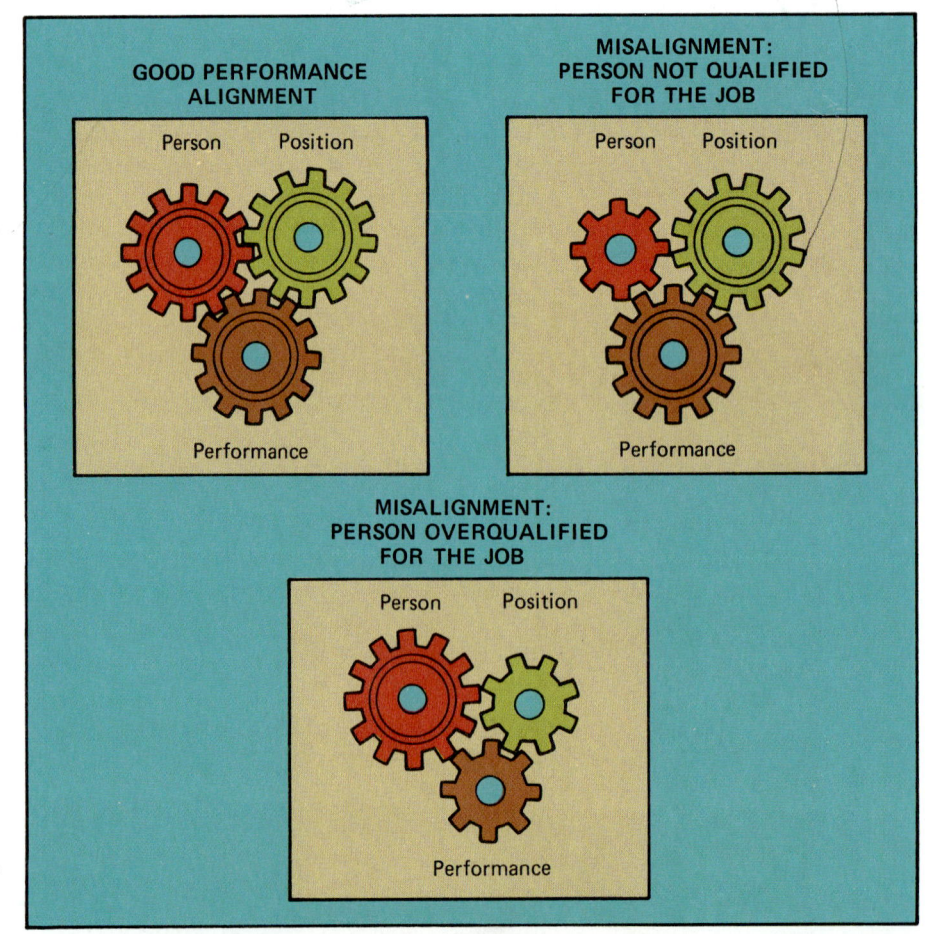

Figure 9-1

Matching Employees and Positions

Source: "Performance Alignment: The Fine Art of the Perfect Fit," by Robert P. Delamontagne and James B. Wietzul, copyright February 1980. Reprinted with the permission of *Personnel Journal*, Costa Mesa, California; all rights reserved.

A good fit between an employee and a job produces high performance. A bad fit — — because the employee is either underqualified or overqualified — — produces low performance.

9-2 illustrates the balancing act necessary between recruiting, selection, and placement on the one side and training and development on the other.

In its personnel practices, should a firm tip the balance to one side or the other? More specifically, should a firm hire people who are ready to step into their jobs now, or should it instead "groom" them through training programs?

Careful selection and placement certainly have their advantages. The new employees can begin work immediately, showing results today rather than in six months at the conclusion of a training program. SEDCO and other offshore drilling companies like to hire undersea welders who are already competent and can do their jobs safely. Acquiring these skills takes years of experience, which SEDCO wants to bypass. Individuals are hired because they already have proven skills; the firm does not have to gamble that they will learn them properly. Brokerage companies such as Bache offer high bonuses to brokers who come from other companies. These brokers already have the needed skills and are of proven ability; Bache doesn't worry about hiring a dozen brokers and having only three or four work out.

Training and development also have advantages. For one thing, people can be hired at lower rates of pay if they come to the firm untrained. Also, the training and development can be tailored exactly to the company's needs. Westinghouse, for example, hires students with degrees in advertising, but the company completely retrains them in a training institute. Ford, Bell Telephone, and even McDonald's have similar training programs for employees who need special skills that cannot be obtained anywhere else. In addition, people trained by a firm often feel loyal to it. Sales and service personnel trained by

Figure 9-2

Balancing the Staffing Mix

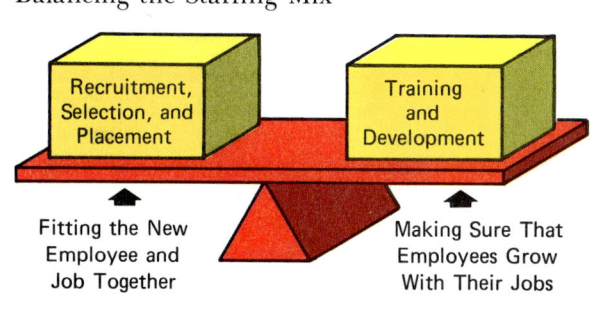

Some positions do not lend themselves to on-the-job training.

IBM feel strong loyalty to their company; they are renowned for their dedication to IBM's interests.

Recruiting

The first step in staffing is to put together a group of job applicants from which to choose. This step is called **recruiting**. No matter how employees are later selected, trained, and motivated, it is important to start out with a good group of job applicants. The greater the number of applicants and the better their qualifications, the more likely the firm will build a solid personnel base.

Sources of Applicants. Job applicants can be found in many ways. We'll look at six sources of applicants. These sources differ in terms of ease of use, cost, and the quality of applicants obtained.

Newspaper Advertisements. The simplest and best-known way to publicize a job opening is through newspaper and magazine advertisements. Although they often bring in many applicants, such advertisements do not function as a screening device. That is, the ads may attract many job seekers, but only a few of them may be qualified for the position advertised.

Referrals. Current and past employees sometimes refer their friends and relatives to the firm. Because these employees usually understand the firm's personnel needs, referrals can be a very good source of job applicants. When companies in the computer industry need new executives, they routinely ask current employees for referrals. The assumption is that their employees will know the best people in the industry.

Private Employment Agencies. These firms are in the business of matching job seekers with suitable jobs. They charge a fee for their services, sometimes to the job seeker and sometimes to the hiring firm. In effect, when a company contracts with an employment agency, it is turning over the task of recruiting and screening applicants to someone else. Many private employment agencies specialize in finding people to fill top management positions.

Public Employment Agencies. Most cities have an office of the state employment agency whose role is to find jobs for unemployed people and to keep track of people receiving unemployment compensation. Some of these agencies also offer training programs.

Educational Institutions. Universities, colleges, junior colleges, vocational schools, and high schools may all be good sources of job applicants. For jobs in great supply, companies may send recruiters to campuses for the purpose of finding and interviewing job applicants.

Labor Unions. For blue-collar and some professional jobs, labor unions are often a good source of applicants. Some unions have hiring halls where employers and job seekers are brought together. Builders and contractors sometimes hire trade construction workers in this way. Union halls, in this respect, function as centralized labor exchanges, where buyers (employers) and sellers (job seekers) jointly determine the allocation of job seekers to specific job slots.

Realistic Job Preview. Most companies present favorable pictures of themselves and their job openings in order to attract job applicants. Partly as a result, many new employees are dissatisfied when they learn the "truth" about the company, and some even quit after a short time there. To avoid this, some companies now use realistic job previews. The aim of the **realistic job preview** is to give the recruit an accurate picture of what the job and company are like. For example, films of people on the job and uncensored comments of current employees may be used to acquaint the new employee with the day-to-day reality of the job. Exxon prints brochures describing the kinds of jobs available for people with varying educational backgrounds, the kinds of promotion and salary opportunities available, and in which parts of the world each individual might be located. Because of its highly developed preview, Exxon has one of the lowest employee turnover rates in the petroleum industry.

Selection and Hiring

The role of recruiting is to locate job candidates; the role of **selection** and **hiring** is to evaluate each candidate and to pick the best one for the position available. Some business firms use informal selection procedures, such as reviewing application blanks and resumes. Others ask their job candidates to take a battery of personality and ability tests. Still others have assessment centers where selecting and hiring new employees almost becomes a science. Let's look at some of the ways in which firms determine whether job candidate qualifications are in line with the requirements of the job opening.

Application Blanks. The first source of information about a potential employee is the application blank. It provides the hiring firm with information about educational background, work experience, and outside interests. Much of this information is especially useful for applicant screening purposes. For example, an applicant for a position as a computer analyst should have had courses in data processing. The application blank would tell the employer right away whether the applicant had the needed training.

However, there are at least two problems with application blanks as sources of information about potential employees. First, the information provided by the applicant may not be relevant to performance on the job. Second, there are legal restrictions as to what can and cannot be asked on an application blank. Figure 9-3 is a partial listing of questions considered to be unfair by the Washington State Human Rights Commission. Clearly,

> Any inquiry that implies a preference for persons under 40 years of age.
>
> Whether applicant is a citizen. Any inquiry into citizenship which would tend to divulge applicant's lineage, ancestry, national origin, descent, or birthplace.
>
> All inquiries relating to arrests.
>
> Inquiries which would divulge convictions which do not reasonably relate to fitness to perform the particular job or relate to convictions for which the date of conviction or prison release was more than seven years before the date of application.
>
> Specific inquiries concerning spouse, spouse's employment or salary, children, child care arrangements, or dependents.
>
> Any inquiries concerning handicaps, height, or weight which do not relate to job requirements.
>
> Whether the applicant is married, single, divorced, engaged, widowed, etc.
>
> Type or condition of military discharge.
>
> Request that applicant submit a photograph.
>
> Sex.
>
> Any inquiry concerning race or color of skin, hair, eyes, etc.
>
> All questions as to pregnancy, and medical history concerning pregnancy and related matters.
>
> Any inquiry concerning religious denomination, affiliations, holidays observed, etc.
>
> Requirements that applicant list all organizations, clubs, societies, and lodges to which applicant belongs.
>
> Inquiry into original name where it has been changed by court order or marriage.

Figure 9-3

Some Unfair Preemployment Inquiries

many of the questions routinely asked on application blanks are violations of state or federal law.

References. References are another popular selection tool. They are written by previous employers, co-workers, or acquaintances. The evidence, however, suggests that references are generally of little value in the employee selection process. The people asked to provide references sometimes do not really know much about the person requesting the reference. At other times, they are not frank because they do not want to say anything bad about the person—especially in writing. As a result, references are generally biased in the applicant's favor.

Interviews. Interviewing involves asking the job candidate a series of questions. In what is called a structured interview, the questions are precise and are asked in a fixed order. In unstructured interviews, there is a looser interchange between the interviewer and the job candidate.

Interviews are very popular and widely used. More than 90 percent of all people hired for industrial positions are interviewed at least once. There are many reasons for the popularity of interviews. For one, it is easier to ask someone a series of questions than to develop a test such as an ability test. For another, interviewing makes the selection process more personal and gives the interviewer an overall idea as to whether the applicant is right for the job.

Despite the popularity of interviews, however, it has been shown that a successful interview does not always mean that the recruit performs well on the job. Interviewers sometimes show many biases, disagree with one another over which recruits are likely to do best, and ignore much of the information available about recruits.

Testing. Testing is a relatively objective way to determine how well a person may do on the job. Many human resources experts and personnel managers believe that testing is the single best selection tool. Tests yield more information about a person than does a completed application blank, and they have less bias than do interviews.

Personnel managers use many types of tests today. The value of a test is based on its **validity**, that is, whether it measures what it sets out to measure. Even tests generally believed to be valid are not always right. This is why we said that tests are a *relatively* objective way to evaluate candidate qualifications. Let's examine four different types of tests.

Ability tests measure whether the applicant is able to perform the tasks required in the job. Mental ability tests assess memory, problem-solving speed, verbal comprehension, ability to deal with numbers, and so on. Examples of some items from mental ability tests are given in Figure 9-4.

Mechanical ability tests measure spatial relations—the ability to see how parts fit together into a whole. Candidates for dental school are often given a block of soap and a knife and asked to carve a tooth or other readily identifiable shape. The idea is that a candidate who can create a tooth in the correct proportions will be able to perform well when operating in a patient's mouth. Psychomotor ability tests assess reaction time and finger dexterity. They are given to people applying for jobs involving physical, rather than mental, tasks. Psychomotor tests are routinely applied to draftees for professional football teams.

Personality tests measure the strengths or weaknesses of personality characteristics that might be important on the job. Job applicants are asked to describe themselves in terms of traits or behavior. The Ghiselli Self Description Inventory, for example, lists 64 pairs of adjectives. Applicants are asked to pick the trait in each pair that best or least describes themselves.

— capable   — defensive   — weak
— discrete   — touchy   — selfish

On the basis of responses to such pairs, scores on personality dimensions—initiative, decisiveness, self-assurance—are obtained.

Interest tests measure a person's likes and dislikes for various activities. One popular interest test is the Kuder Vocational Preference Record, where the person is given many sets of

Extensive testing may aid the selection process for some jobs.

Chapter 9 • Human Resources Management 161

> *Verbal comprehension:* to understand the meaning of words and their relations to each other; to comprehend readily and accurately what is read; measured by test items such as:
>
> Which one of the following words means most nearly the same as *effusive*?
> 1. evasive
> 2. affluent
> 3. gushing
> 4. realistic
> 5. lethargic
>
> *Word fluency:* to be fluent in naming or making words, such as making smaller words from the letters in a large one or playing anagrams; measured by test items such as:
>
> Using the letters in the word *Minneapolis*, write as many four-letter words as you can in the next two minutes.
>
> _____
> _____
> _____
> _____
>
> *Number aptitude:* to be speedy and accurate in making simple arithmetic calculations; measured by test items such as:
>
> Carry out the following calculations:
> 346   8732   422 × 32 = ____
> +722   −4843   3630 ÷ 5 = ____
>
> *Perceptual speed:* to perceive visual details quickly and accurately; measured by test items such as:
>
> Make a check mark in front of each pair below in which the numbers are identical.
> 1. 367773 ____ 367713
> 2. 471352 ____ 471352
> 3. 581688 ____ 581688
> 4. 324579 ____ 334579
> 5. 875989 ____ 876898

Figure 9-4

Mental Ability Test Items

Source: From *Personnel Selection and Placement*, by M.D. Dunnette. Copyright © 1966 by Wadsworth Publishing Company, Inc. Reprinted by permission of the publisher, Brooks/Cole Publishing Company, Monterey, California.

three activities and told to pick his or her favorite. A typical set is:

    ____ play baseball
    ____ work a puzzle
    ____ watch a movie

Responses to such items result in scores on ten interest categories, such as literary, outdoor, and mechanical.

Work sample tests measure how well applicants perform selected job tasks. These tasks might include typing speed for typists or judgment tests for police officers.

Although testing works well, it is not without problems. Valid tests are expensive to develop. Also, some jobs, such as those of top management, are hard to describe, and the abilities and interests required may be all but impossible to predict on the basis of test results.

There is also the danger that tests can be faked. William H. Whyte wrote about "How to Cheat on Personality Tests" in his 1957 book, *The Organization Man*. He suggested that companies want conservative people who are neither very soft nor very dominant. Accordingly, test takers were advised in his book to check these kinds of responses:

(√)   I like things pretty much the way they are.
(√)   I never worry much about anything.

CONTROVERSIAL ISSUES

Theory Z is a variation on two company styles called Theory A and Theory J. Theory A, the traditional American style, stresses rapid promotion, allows hiring of employees for all levels outside the company, allows rapid turnover, and generally pits employees against each other in a competitive atmosphere. Theory J, on the other hand, is the traditional Japanese style: Workers who come to a company are expected to work for that company for the rest of their lives. In Theory Z, companies do hire and fire, but only at low levels in the organization. Companies stress the stability of their work force and obtain higher productivity by offering greater job security and more appealing personal working conditions. Will Theory Z work in America?

Theory Z: Will It Work in American Business?

Pro

Generally, employees today are most concerned about job security and personality problems with their employers. Most managers cite excessive employee turnover as their major problem. Few companies have kept employee turnover low by traditional American methods. For the vast majority of companies—particularly large manufacturing firms—employee turnover costs millions.

Because U.S. society places less and less value on sustained family ties, employees feel adrift and insecure. Any company that can create feelings of attachment—feelings that the company represents a family to the employee—will have loyal and stable workers. Theory Z is designed specifically for this purpose.

In particular, Theory Z emphasizes giving individuals as much responsibility as they can handle. It encourages and makes possible the use of looser organizational structure, which is more comfortable to workers and is more flexible and adaptable in a rapidly changing environment.

Overall, Theory Z is a good idea for modern American business.

Con

You have to take Theory Z with a grain of salt. First, recognize that Theory J was forced upon Japanese companies. Due to strong family ties, Japanese workers do not move often. Further, they expect family-like conditions in the workplace.

In America, people move often. Therefore, no matter how much of a Theory Z framework a company offers, employees will still want to move, making the point of Theory Z quite useless. And what about cases where both husband and wife work? What if one wishes to move, but the other does not? Theory Z just complicates this problem.

Another problem that American companies face that the Japanese have largely avoided is labor unions. Unions are not likely to support Theory Z, since Theory Z advocates slower promotions, high stability of employment, and promotion largely from within. The need for labor unions would decrease dramatically. Naturally, unions would fight such a movement.

Also recognize that in Japan, many highly successful companies use a straight Theory A style and have done very well with it. By the same token, many American companies are famous for their successes with Theory A. Therefore, there is no equating Japanese success with the use of Theory J (or Theory Z).

Last, Japan has had success with Theory J through a long and continuous growth period. America, however, faces recurring periods of economic instability. While companies and employees both will be relatively satisfied with their situations during good economic times, it is during recessions that ideas like Theory J or Theory Z are really tested. Companies like Ford, GM, U.S. Steel, and Motorola have had to lay off workers during recessions because they couldn't afford to keep paying them; under Theory Z, these companies wouldn't be able to lay workers off. How could companies survive financially under such conditions?

No, Theory Z isn't feasible. To use Theory Z means a commitment for over a generation of employees; the evidence doesn't justify that commitment.

(√) I loved my father and my mother, but my father a little bit more.
(√) I love my spouse and children, but I don't let them get in the way of company work.

Assessment Centers. Instead of using just an interview or a test, many large companies approach the employee selection process more systematically. They use a variety of procedures combined in the form of an assessment center. These centers have psychologists and other experts on human behavior as well as tests, interviews, group discussions, and other approaches.

One such approach is **role playing**, where job recruits pretend they are, for instance, marketing managers or first-line supervisors in a real decision situation. Another approach to discovering how recruits hold up under fire is the **in basket**. The recruit is given a basket piled high with memos, phone messages, letters, and other things to be done. Each person's performance is evaluated in terms of how the tasks are sequenced, how promptly they are completed, whether the most important ones in the pile are finished, and how good the proposed problem solutions are.

Assessment centers, on the average, cost about $100,000 to maintain each year. But they may be worth the cost to the large firms which use them, such as AT&T, IBM, and General Electric. Virtually every study of assessment centers has shown them to make better predictions of employee performance than other approaches to selection.

Placement

Placement means fitting people and jobs together. It includes everything from helping new employees feel at home in the firm to promoting them to positions of greater pay and responsibility to demoting them to less desirable positions when necessary.

Orientation. **Orientation** involves introducing new employees to their jobs and to the company. It is their first "inside" look at the company, and it can make an important impression. If properly done, job orientation reduces employee uncertainties, makes company policies and expectations clear, and provides a good idea of what the firm, plant, and co-workers are like. Often, both the personnel department and the new employee's supervisor are involved in the orientation efforts. Figure 9-5 shows the characteristics of successful orientation programs, as well as some of the precautions a company should observe, as recommended by Walter St. John, a director of the National-American Wholesale Grocers' Association.

Promotion. The most pleasant job move is the promotion. A **promotion** is a move up, generally to a new title, more responsibility, and better benefits.

Promotions are handled carefully because they usually mean moving a person into a position of greater potential impact on the firm. Legal restrictions also complicate the promotion process. Additionally, the fact that the promoted individual did well at the old job is no guarantee that that person will do well at the new, higher level job. Jobs at different levels in the firm may require vastly different skills and interests. All too often, a good salesperson or engineer becomes a poor manager.

This tendency is called the Peter Principle. The **Peter Principle** asserts that good workers are continually promoted to positions of greater authority. Eventually, they reach their "level of incompetence" and will not be promoted again.

It is important to fit the person to the job.

Figure 9-5

Orientation Program Characteristics and Cautions

> **Ten Characteristics of Successful Orientation Programs**
>
> Ten results characterize an effective orientation program. If your orientation program has been successful, the results should be:
>
> 1. Feeling of security in the new employee.
> 2. Opportunity to meet top-level management, supervisory staff and fellow workers.
> 3. Basic understanding of the company: history, products, organization, and services to workers.
> 4. Knowledge of help available to get the job done.
> 5. Information on supplies and equipment available and how to secure them.
> 6. Familiarization with basic job duties and responsibilities, how the job relates to other jobs, and supervisors' performance standards and expectations.
> 7. Clear understanding of terms of employment and working conditions.
> 8. Information on opportunities for on-the-job training and advancement.
> 9. Understanding of community and customers served.
> 10. Understanding of company policy, rules, regulations, traditions, and ways of doing things.
>
> **Ten Cautions to Observe**
>
> 1. Be sure to tailor your orientation topics and procedures to fit your company.
> 2. Don't rely strictly on managers and supervisors to plan the orientation program—do include a cross-section of employees.
> 3. Avoid overwhelming employees with too much information too fast.
> 4. Anticipate employees' potential problems and needs for information—be proactive as well as reactive.
> 5. Use a check list system for topics to be discussed by the personnel department and supervisory crew to assure all pertinent topics are covered.
> 6. Share the most important information both in writing and verbally—don't rely solely on the written word.
> 7. Be certain to show how the employee's job is related to other jobs and how his or her duties affect the final results.
> 8. Spell out clearly job expectations, work responsibilities, goals, performance standards and criteria, and acceptable conduct at work, with a liberal amount of time for questions and discussion.
> 9. When selecting a "buddy" to assist the supervisor's orientation, be sure he or she is an effective, well-informed worker with positive attitudes toward work, the job, the department and the company.
> 10. Include the spouse at one session to secure family understanding of and commitment to the job and company.

Source: "The Complete Employee Orientation Program," by Walter D. St. John, copyright May 1980. Reprinted with the permission of *Personnel Journal*, Costa Mesa, California; all rights reserved.

Carried to its extreme, the Peter Principle says that employees are ultimately promoted to positions for which they are not qualified. Most practicing managers can point to examples of the Peter Principle at work in their firms.

Promotions can also cause problems for the people promoted. Many employees are happier in their current jobs than they would be if promoted to positions requiring greater responsibility, new skills, and geographic moves.

Demotion. A movement down in title, responsibility, or benefits—called **demotion**—is rare in organizations. Demotions are stressful for employees, of course, and they are likely to be resisted by unions. Still, especially during economic recessions, employees may have to make the choice between demotion or unemployment. Some companies have experimented with demoting employees temporarily so that they can relate better to their subordinates. Also, some employees ask for their old, lower level jobs back if they are unhappy with their promotions.

TRAINING AND DEVELOPMENT

The training of employees and the development of their careers and expertise has many advantages for the firm, not the least of which is helping the firm meet its immediate human resource needs. Over the long run, however, it ensures that the firm's employees are ready to meet future challenges. A wide range of approaches to training and development have been devised, some with notable success.

Determining Training Needs

Training needs may arise for many reasons. In some situations, specific skills may be required which are not readily available, such as computer programming, accounting, and mechanical skills. New employees also need to find out who the shop steward is, who has the ear of management, and which parking spaces are reserved for the president of the company. All are important parts of training.

Other training efforts are in anticipation of future personnel needs or are designed to promote career development among employees. Sometimes training takes the form of counseling employees on how to handle stress, overcome dependence on alcohol or other drugs, or to manage their time. It may also be necessary for firms to set up special training programs for women, minorities, and the handicapped in order to meet affirmative action goals. For example, the Gates Rubber Company in Denver instituted an employee assistance program in December of 1974, providing help for alcoholism and other personal problems. The company credits the program for reduced employee turnover and absenteeism.

Approaches to Training

The two general aims of training are to teach specific skills, such as operating fiberglass-molding equipment and to improve organizational processes, such as communications among widely scattered plants and warehouses of the same company. There are many ways to conduct training programs. Let's take a look at three of the more popular ones.

Group Discussion. Under this technique, trainees meet to discuss a specific problem, share knowledge, and seek solutions. A trainer states the problem and tries to keep the group on track. Discussion groups are popular and seem to result in discovery of a variety of solutions to specific managerial, financial, or personnel problems.

Case Studies. Case studies involve the presentation of a large amount of information about a business problem, such as how to finance expansion of a new plant for manufacturing prefabricated houses. Trainees are asked to analyze the material and present recommendations. This may both enhance their knowledge about specific matters and improve their decision-making skills.

Case studies are commonly used in management development programs which universities and some companies devise to retrain company executives. Such studies are particularly useful because they can be presented in a classroom and their benefits then transferred to real work situations.

Profile—
E. Pendleton James

When business people speak of human resource management, they soon bring up the notion of "headhunters," individuals or companies whose job it is to hire competent and otherwise appropriate individuals to fill employment slots in a company. The ultimate headhunter is E. Pendleton James, personnel headhunter for the White House.

James was director of his own executive search firm in California from 1976 until 1981. He also spent two years on Nixon's White House personnel staff. When Ronald Reagan became a leading Presidential contender, James was invited to develop staffing programs that Reagan could implement, were he elected to the White House in 1980. James devised programs and procedures that followed Reagan's progress step by step from the Republican nomination to the election and the transition to the presidency, and finally through the inauguration itself. At each stage, he specified the key jobs that needed to be filled and the kinds of people needed to fill them.

Since the start of Mr. Reagan's term in office, James has become the man in charge of all recruitment and hiring in the executive branch of government. As Assistant to the President for Presidential Personnel, James and his operation are responsible for Cabinet and sub-Cabinet appointments in all departments and agencies, as well as appointments to regulatory agencies, boards, commissions, and ambassadorships.

James' job hasn't been an easy one. Congress, during the Carter Administration, responded to a kind of post-Watergate hysteria by passing a series of laws that many have considered to be poorly conceived, controversial, and even contradictory. These ethics-in-government laws require exhaustive financial disclosures, elaborate security checks, and research of past relationships that might in any way impinge upon the jobs the appointees will be asked to perform. Furthermore, under the Freedom of Information Act, these disclosures become public knowledge; consequently, people willing to work for the government must also be willing to have their entire financial history and business relationships exposed to public view. The Carter Administration also sharply limited pay raises to government employees in highly responsible positions, in part a reflection of the decreased esteem in which they were held by Americans after Nixon's resignation. A "turnaround law" was even imposed, which forbade former government employees from taking a job that would substantially involve functions they had performed while in government service.

It is small wonder that James can't hire the kind of people he wants. His headhunting has to be the most diligent and yet the most disappointing. The more competent and experienced an individual may be, the more unwilling he or she may be to bear the extreme brunt of current federal hiring laws. At the same time, James is bombarded from every direction with complaints or requests. In every administration there is a struggle to gain control of the appointments process. Presidents Johnson and Nixon both lost the authority of the process to their Cabinet officers. This is not happening to this administration.

James doesn't intend to stay with President Reagan for the duration of his term in office. He will return to the private sector in executive search. In the time he has spent so far at his White House task, however, he has amply demonstrated the skills a headhunter can employ to manage human resources to the benefit of an organization.

On-the-Job Training. As the name says, **on-the-job training** is conducted while employees perform job-related tasks; they are not taken out of the office or plant and put in a classroom. Not surprisingly, on-the-job training is the most direct approach to training and development; it offers the employer the quickest return in terms of improved performance. Such training is also conducted in anticipation of future job requirements. For example, many large companies rotate their managers through a variety of positions in order to broaden their knowledge of the company.

APPRAISING PERFORMANCE

Up to this point in the chapter, we have looked at some of the issues involved in recruiting job applicants, selecting the best ones from among them, placing them in the organization, and improving their skills through training and development programs. The question should now arise as to how their subsequent performance in the company is evaluated. The answer is **performance appraisal**, which is the measurement of employee performance. Before we look at some of the techniques for performance appraisal, let's ask ourselves why performance should be appraised in the first place.

Why Appraise Performance?

There are many reasons to measure how well employees are performing. First, many administrative decisions, such as those dealing with promotions, salary increases, and layoffs, depend on performance appraisals. Second, if employees are to do their jobs better in the future, they need to know how well they have done them in the past. Then they can make adjustments in their work patterns. Finally, performance appraisal is necessary as a check on new policies and programs. For example, if a new pay system has been implemented, it would be useful to see whether it has had an effect on employee motivation.

Types of Performance Measures

There are at least three major ways by which performance may be appraised. Appraisal can focus on employee traits, behavior, or accomplishments.

Trait Approaches. Under these approaches, a manager or performance appraiser rates an employee on such traits as friendliness, efficiency, and obedience to commands. Presumably, these traits are related to performance. One such approach asks the appraiser to check the word or phrase (such as "outstanding," "average," or "poor") that best describes how an employee rates on each trait.

These trait approaches are very popular, but they suffer from the number of problems. For instance, words such as "superior" and "average" may mean different things to different people. The people appraising performance are sometimes biased in their ratings. They may also feel uncomfortable giving a co-worker a low score on efficiency, decisiveness, or supervisory ability, especially if their ratings will be shown to the person being rated.

Behavioral Approaches. This type of approach involves the recording of specific employee actions. With the "Critical Incidents Method," for example, the performance appraiser keeps a list of all the things that the employee did which were especially good or bad. A newer and somewhat related approach, the "Behaviorally Anchored Rating Scale," presents a list of possible employee actions, ranging from very desirable to very undesirable. The rater checks the action on the scale that the employee would be most likely to engage in. By focusing on specific actions, this approach is an improvement upon the earlier trait approaches. However, behavioral approaches sometimes give employees the feeling that the rater is always looking over their shoulders.

Outcome Approaches. Rather than considering traits or actions, some appraisal techniques rate what the employee is supposed to accomplish on the job. One of these approaches, Management By Objectives, was discussed in the last chapter. As noted there, this approach is time consuming and may cause people to focus only on objectives that can be easily expressed in numbers. It does, however, get directly at the things that the company cares most about.

COMPENSATING EMPLOYEES

The salary or wages paid to employees, as well as other job benefits, depend in part on how well the employees perform on the job. Other factors influencing employee compensation are the relative worth of each job within the firm, labor market conditions and prevailing wage rates, and the type of pay system used. Let's take a closer look at these determinants of employee compensation.

Job Analysis

The systematic study of a job to determine its characteristics is called **job analysis**. How is the information gathered for a job analysis? One common method is to observe workers on the job, noting which tasks they perform, the order in which the tasks are performed, and the time it takes to perform each one. Another method is to interview employees about the nature of their work. Sometimes employees are asked to supply the needed information by filling out written questionnaires. The value of this information, however gathered, is that it allows the job description to be written.

Job Description

A **job description** is a short summary of the basic tasks making up a job. A job description usually includes the title of the job, work activities and procedures, work conditions, and hours and wages. An example of a job description is shown in Figure 9-6.

Job descriptions serve a number of important functions. First, they clarify organizational structure by specifying who is to perform each task; they also minimize job overlap, wherein two people are assigned the same task. Second, job descriptions can be used to introduce new employees to their jobs. In this way, they are given a good idea of what to expect on the job before they actually start work.

Other uses of job descriptions are also worth noting. For example, they are important in developing job specifications, performance standards, and the criteria for job evaluations. A **job specification** is a summary of the qualifications needed in a worker for a specific job. A job specification is especially useful in recruiting job applicants and making hiring decisions. **Performance standards** define the goals to be achieved by a worker over a specified period of time. The purpose of a **job evaluation** is to determine the relative worth of a job in the firm.

The more important the job, the higher the level of pay. The job analysis and the job description provide the information needed for the job evaluation. The result of the job evaluation process is a rank ordering or rating of job importance which, of course, is useful in setting wage and salary scales.

Now let's look at Figure 9-7 on page 170 to see where each of these factors fits into the process of setting employee wage and salary rates. Can you see the logic so far behind the pattern of influences on employee compensation levels?

Labor Market Conditions

Supply and demand cause the wages for some jobs to be higher than the wages for others, even though the jobs may be of similar difficulty, responsibility, and so on. The level of wages is also influenced by the competitive wage in the local area. For example, machine shops in the same town will all tend to pay the same wage, especially if a union contract is in effect. Because of this tendency, some companies conduct surveys of local wage rates to make sure that their own are in line.

As Table 9-1 on page 170 shows, there is quite a bit of variability in average hourly wage rates for the same job in different parts of the country. On average, the hourly wage rate for tool and die makers in Dayton, Ohio, is $4.58 more than that for the same job in Portland, Maine. For janitorial workers in manufacturing, the wage differential between Dayton and Dallas-Fort Worth is $4.26. Notice that office workers (secretaries, payroll clerks, computer operators) in Los Angeles and Long Beach are paid more than in Dayton, but factory and warehouse workers (tool and die makers, forklift operators, shipping packers, janitors) are paid less.

Pay Systems

Even after the value of a job is determined (and the local and regional wage differences are taken into consideration), one person may be paid more for the same job than another person. We can identify at least five other factors that account for wage differentials.

Seniority. Seniority refers to the number of years spent with the company. The more years of ser-

Figure 9-6

A Job Description

> **TITLE OF POSITION: Specialist, Employment**
>
> *Basic Purpose*
>   To recruit, interview, and select candidates for employment, ensuring timely replacement, effective orientation, and accomplishment of the plant's affirmative action goals.
>
> *Duties and Responsibilities*
>   1. Recruits and interviews hourly and salaried candidates. Selects all hourly candidates in unskilled and semiskilled job categories; recommends candidates and schedules interviews with department supervisors for skilled and salaried vacancies.
>   2. Plans hourly interview, preemployment physical and orientation schedules to ensure that manpower needs can be met.
>   3. Develops effective recruitment sources to expedite filling employment vacancies and meeting Affirmative Action Program goals.
>   4. Conducts candidates' reference checks to include employment records, character, and safety habits.
>   5. Maintains hourly hire ledger, application log, and hourly employment application files.
>   6. Conducts orientation sessions with new hourly hires to familiarize them with working rules and benefits; also completes the necessary paperwork.
>   7. Prepares periodic reports on applicant flow; provides data on hiring or rejection of minority, handicapped, and Vietnam-era veteran applicants.
>
> *Organizational Relationships*
>   This position reports to the Supervisor, Employment and EEO. Frequent contact with various levels of management within the organization on employment and affirmative action matters.
>
> *Position Specifications*
>   Bachelor's Degree in Business Administration or related field or equivalent plus minimum of one year experience in a comparable position. Must be able to communicate effectively, both orally and in writing.

Source: Reprinted, by permission of the publisher, from JOB DESCRIPTIONS IN MANUFACTURING INDUSTRIES by John D. Ulery, pp. 40-41 © 1981 by AMACOM, a division of American Management Associations, New York. All rights reserved.

vice, the greater the level of pay. Wage or salary increases are automatic rewards for duration of service. The idea is that seniority reflects loyalty to the company as well as experience.

Individual Performance. How much individual employees are paid is also based on how well they do on the job. Under a **piece-rate system** of compensation, total wages paid are tied directly to output. For example, a worker in a toy factory may get one dollar for every puppet produced. Obviously, the more efficient the worker, the bigger the paycheck. Piece-rate systems are often justified because they encourage employee motivation.

Group Performance. Workers performing similar or related tasks are sometimes organized into work groups. In such situations, pay scales are often tied to group performance. How much each person takes home, therefore, is based on how well the group as a whole does. Because wages for one worker are determined by the efforts of others, group members have an incentive to push slow workers to do better. Again, we

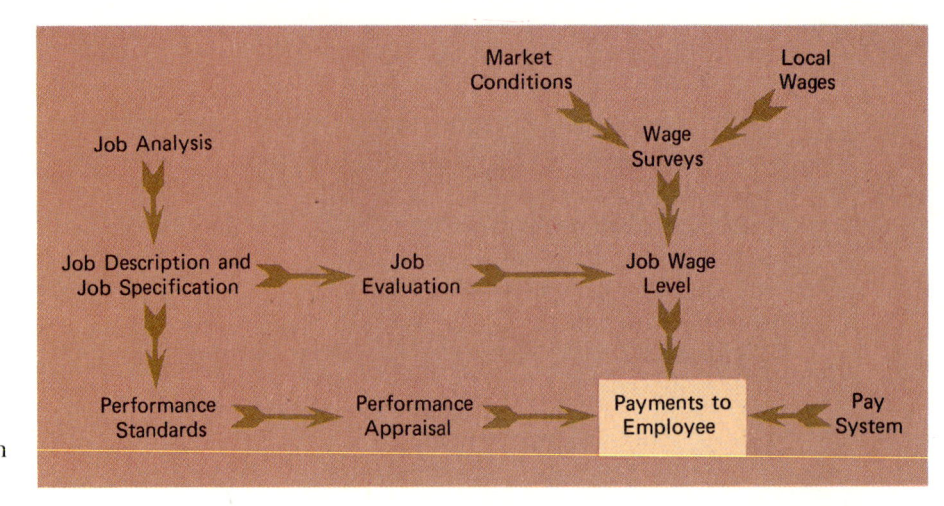

Figure 9-7

The Wage Determination Process

see that compensation systems and job motivation are related.

Plant-Wide Productivity. Employee rates of pay can be based on how well the entire organization does. If the company has a good year, each worker receives a bonus. One popular plan of this type is the **Scanlon Plan**, under which groups of employees suggest to management how productivity might be improved. Then, at regular intervals, such as once a year, the productivity of the organization is evaluated. If productivity is up, each worker is rewarded with a bonus. Some Japanese companies have adopted an interesting variation of this plan; they have annual picnics at which new ideas, inventions, and improvements devised by their employees are exhibited and demonstrated by the company president.

Profit-Sharing Plans. Many companies today feature **profit-sharing plans**. The idea is simple: If company profits increase, employees are given a bonus, in the form of either a cash payment or company stock. What is the difference between the Scanlon Plan, or other group incentive programs, and profit sharing? Under the first, bonus payments are tied to productivity standards; under the second, they are tied to profit.

Lincoln Electric, a major manufacturer of welding equipment, has a highly successful profit-sharing plan which makes employees interested in improving profitability. Lincoln Electric has an impressive record of growing through recessions, coming up with innovations that maintain its lead in the welding industry, and continually increasing its profitability and earnings.

One problem with profit-sharing plans, as well as with tying bonuses to plant productivity, is that employees are not rewarded on the basis of individual performance. Research evidence

Table 9-1

Average Hourly Wage Rates for Selected Jobs by City

Job	Portland, Maine	Dayton, Ohio	Dallas/ Fort Worth	Los Angeles/ Long Beach
Secretaries	$6.32	$ 7.14	$ 7.36	$ 8.23
Payroll Clerks	5.58	6.18	6.56	7.41
Computer Operators	6.33	7.22	7.01	7.94
Tool & Die Makers	8.39	12.97	11.09	11.82
Forklift Operators	5.93	9.40	8.26	8.07
Shipping Packers	5.15	9.55	5.46	5.98
Janitors, Manufacturing	5.85	8.88	4.62	6.05

All wage quotations for December 1981, except for those for Los Angeles and Long Beach, which are for October 1981.
Source: U.S. Department of Labor, Bureau of Labor Statistics, *Area Wage Surveys* (1982).

FROM THE FILE

Tina recognized that her company, a brokerage and diversified financial services house, would have to hire and promote more women if it were to meet its affirmative action goals. In fact, she estimated that to make satisfactory progress toward the goals, she would virtually have to stop hiring men for the next few years and slash promotions of male employees by about 50 percent. She assumed that this would cause many complaints, if not resignations or other actions. She wondered whether she should try to meet the goals and, if so, how she should communicate them to current employees.

---

clearly shows that the more closely rewards are tied to individual performance, the more strongly the employee will be motivated. Also, employees do not like to be penalized for things outside of their control, such as low company productivity or profit. As a result, plant-wide productivity plans and profit-sharing plans may make employees "feel good" about the company, but they probably do not have much impact on performance.

SUMMARY POINTS

1. The aim of the four-stage staffing process is to match the abilities and interests of the job candidate or employee with the changing needs of the firm.
2. The four stages of the staffing process are recruiting, selection and hiring, placement, and training and development.
3. Six popular sources of job applicants are newspaper and magazine advertisements, referrals, private employment agencies, public employment agencies, educational institutions, and labor unions.
4. The selection and hiring of new employees is based on information provided by application blanks, references, interviews, testing, and assessment centers.
5. Placement involves fitting people and jobs, promoting them to positions of more responsibility, or demoting them to positions of less responsibility.
6. The two basic goals of training and development are to help the firm meet its immediate human resource needs and to prepare employees to meet future job challenges.
7. Performance appraisal methods can generally be classified as trait approaches, behavioral approaches, or outcome approaches.
8. The wages or salary paid to employees depends on their performance on the job, the relative worth of jobs, labor market conditions, and various attributes of the pay system used.
9. Job analysis refers to the study of the essential characteristics of a job and job description to the systematic listing of the tasks making up a job.
10. Five pay system factors that can account for wage differentials are seniority, individual performance, group performance, plant-wide productivity, and profit-sharing plans.

KEY TERMS AND CONCEPTS

staffing
recruiting
realistic job preview
selection
hiring
interviewing
validity
ability tests
personality tests
interest tests
work sample tests
assessment centers
role playing
in basket
placement
orientation
promotion
Peter Principle
demotion
on-the-job training
performance appraisal
job analysis

job description seniority
job specification piece-rate system
performance standards Scanlon Plan
job evaluation profit-sharing plans

REVIEW QUESTIONS

1. What is the basic goal of staffing?
2. In what sense do recruiting, selection, and placement differ from training and development?
3. Name the six primary sources of job applicants.
4. What is the aim of the realistic job preview?
5. In the selection and hiring process, how does a personality test differ from an interest test?
6. Explain how the Peter Principle works. Give an example.
7. What are the two basic aims of training?
8. What are some of the reasons why it is necessary to appraise employee performance?
9. Name some of the problems with trait approaches to employee performance appraisal.
10. What is a job description? What is it used for?

DISCUSSION QUESTIONS

1. Under what conditions might letters of reference be useful in the selection and hiring process?
2. What role should psychological testing play in the selection and hiring process? Is there a danger with these tests? If yes, in what ways could they be misused?
3. What are some of the situations in which a demotion in rank or responsibility would be preferable to firing an employee?
4. Based on your experience in the classroom, write a job description for a college teacher.
5. How important should seniority be in determining the wage paid to an employee? Does tying pay to years of service punish some workers unfairly?

CASE 9-1

Smith Pipe and Supply, Inc.*

George Smith spent most of his life working with oil field pipe companies. These companies sold and serviced pipe and related equipment used in oil-drilling operations on oil fields. With the rapid growth of the oil production industry during the 1970s, these companies also grew very rapidly and became wealthy.

Smith started to work with little formal education because he needed to support his family. By 1976, he was relatively secure, but somewhat dissatisfied with his job. He wanted control of a company, so he created Smith Pipe and Supply, Inc. In its first five years, his company pushed annual sales to $57 million and employed 135 people.

Oil field operations, for the most part, require skills learned on the job. Several oil field supply companies have found that hiring college graduates does not work. The graduates don't really know the oil field and they often don't get along well with oil field managers or meet the managers' needs.

The skills needed for the salespeople for oil field supply companies are quite diverse. For example, salespeople have to understand and appreciate the oil field workers themselves. They have to understand the time and cost pressures facing oil field managers. They have to understand how oil field operations work. They also have to be good at communicating with workers in the field as well as their supervisors and office staff at company headquarters.

*Source: PBS, "In Black America," 8–14 February 1982.

Finally, salespeople have to be able to apply basic mathematics and basic business principles in order to carry out business efficiently.

Finding a well-qualified oil field supply salesperson was very difficult for George Smith. They were in great demand. Many different oil field supply companies were trying to lure salespeople from other companies in exchange for higher pay or privileges. Smith Pipe and Supply was unusual because its owner was black and preferred to see blacks hired for as many positions in the company as possible. This preference made hiring salespeople even more difficult. Nonetheless, Smith found many superb black salespeople, and the company became one of the best in the oil field supply industry. Most of the salespeople at Smith Pipe and Supply were very happy with their company.

1. When looking for new employees for sales positions, how much emphasis should Smith Pipe and Supply place on recruitment, selection, and placement, and how much on training and development. Why?
2. What are the advantages Smith would find in training people for his sales positions, rather than in hiring at a premium people with a record of success at other companies?
3. Where could Smith Pipe and Supply look for potential salespeople?
4. Write a possible employment test for potential salespeople at Smith Pipe and Supply.

CASE 9-2

Gala Cosmetics, Inc.

Gala Cosmetics is a small chain of retail stores selling very expensive and prestigious brands of perfumes and cosmetics in wealthy areas of New York City, Atlanta, Houston, and Aspen. Gala stores are very richly appointed with heavy marble, cut glass doors, and plush carpeting. They are located in exclusive shopping malls or on exclusive streets. The cosmetics sold in these stores range from about $15 per item to nearly $1,000, with most items selling for $75 to $300. The majority of Gala's customers are affluent white couples.

To match the appearances of the stores, the salespeople are expected to dress well. Most wear at least some expensive jewelry, and all wear expensive gowns or suits. While no dress code is specified, no employee has ever sought to challenge the silent agreement that nice clothes will be worn.

Three women answered an advertisement for a new salesperson at Gala Cosmetics' new store in Washington, D.C. All three were interviewed by the store manager from New York City. The interviews were informal: A few basic questions were asked and then the store manager discussed job skills and qualifications with the job candidates.

Deborah Holmes was a recent graduate of Loyola University. Deborah was 23 years old, from a lower-to-middle-class background, and was black.

Sally Devereaux was 34 years old and recently divorced from a wealthy husband. Her state did not allow alimony payments, so she had to find a job immediately. She had not worked while she was married, but she had finished a master's degree in education and once had a teaching certificate which qualified her to teach in high schools. She had two children, aged two and eight, and she received the family home in the divorce settlement. Sally had been caught shoplifting two years before; she had received probation in exchange for repaying the store and agreeing to see a psychologist. She had shoplifted not out of monetary need, but because it was a "thrill."

Elizabeth Feldmann was 39 years old. She was single and quite well off financially, thanks to an inheritance from some relatives. Elizabeth was articulate and had a degree from her community college, but she was nearly a hundred pounds overweight. She was Jewish, but she did not demand time off from work to observe Jewish holidays.

The following topics were included during the interviews:

1. Do you think you are old enough to sell to our customers, who are mostly older women?
2. Do you have any criminal record? Would you allow us to perform a polygraph (lie detector) test on you?
3. What is your marital status? Do you have children? Will you have to leave work or schedule your work to take care of them?
4. How much formal education do you have?
5. What sales experience do you have? What experience do you have with cosmetics?

Deborah observed that her interview lasted only ten minutes, while Sally's lasted nearly an hour. Sally was asked in detail about her shoplifting conviction. Elizabeth had worn a Star of David around her neck, and the interviewer had commented on it as a piece of jewelry and on her Jewish faith (neither comment was derogatory). The interviewer also said that she doubted whether a woman as overweight as Elizabeth could sell cosmetics effectively—that the salespeople needed to be beautiful themselves if they were to sell beauty products.

Sally was hired for the job. Both Deborah and Elizabeth were told they would not be suitable for future job openings at Gala. Deborah and Elizabeth agreed that they were discriminated against because of Deborah's race and Elizabeth's faith and weight.

1. Of the five topics covered in the questioning, which were legal and which were not? How would you have reacted had you heard any of them, were you interviewing with Gala?
2. Of the comments directed specifically at any of the three women, which were legal and which were not? Why?
3. Write a series of basic interview questions that Gala could use that would avoid any risk of a discrimination lawsuit.

Labor-Management Relations

10

After studying this chapter, you should be able to:

- Describe the role of labor unions in today's economy and explain how labor unions are structured.
- Explain the process by which unions are organized.
- Identify the key issues in collective bargaining and in contract negotiation.
- Discuss three procedures for settling labor-management disputes.
- Analyze the sources of negotiating strength for labor and for management.
- Discuss three new developments in labor-management relations and the future of organized labor.

The 1980s got off to a bad start. The 1981 baseball season was split in half by a players' strike. A year later pro football players walked off the job. Dinah Shore stopped doing advertisements for a textile firm whose blatant violations of worker rights inspired the Oscar-winning movie *Norma Rae*. President Reagan fired more than 11,000 striking air traffic controllers.

What did major league baseball, professional football, Dinah Shore, and the not-so-friendly skies have in common? They were all victims of breakdowns in labor-management relations. How labor and management settle their differences largely determines whether their relationship is productive or whether it ends in hostility, strikes, or employee firings and plant closings. This chapter examines how labor and management deal with each other in order to achieve their individual and joint goals.

LABOR UNIONS

A union is a collection of people or organizations joined together for a common purpose. A **labor union** is an organization made up of workers who have united to achieve their goals. Labor unions work to ensure that their members get a fair "price" for their services, safe working conditions, more interesting work, and job security. By forming unions, workers can bargain more effectively than if each worker dealt with management separately. Some types of union security are summarized in Figure 10-1.

Role in Today's Economy

The labor union plays an important role in our economy. Most of this country's basic industries—steel, automobiles, rubber, glass, machinery, mining—are heavily unionized. Union membership in the United States rose

Union Security Clauses*	Description
Simple-Recognition Shop	The employer recognizes the union as the sole bargaining agent for all employees in the bargaining unit.
Agency Shop	Employees are not required to join the union but they are required to pay a fee to the union to help support it.
Maintenance-of-Membership Shop	Employees who voluntarily join the union must remain members in good standing. During an "escape" period, they may drop their membership before it becomes effective.
Union Shop	The employer may hire anyone, whether or not they are members of the union. New employees must then join the union in order to stay employed.
Closed Shop	Only current members of the union may be considered for employment. Closed shops are generally illegal.

Figure 10-1

Forms of Union Security

*In 1980, about 69 percent of all contracts between labor and management provided for union shops, 17 percent for simple recognition shops, 8 percent for agency shops, and 4 percent for maintenance-of-membership shops.

dramatically from under 4 million in 1930 to over 14 million in 1950. By 1980, membership was over 22 million. While this was up over 40 percent from 1950, membership as a percent of the labor force actually declined over that period. We'll examine labor unions from the perspective of their impact on workers and their impact on management.

Impact on Workers. Labor unions affect workers in many ways. Successful bargaining results in economic security and fair treatment for union members. Unions give workers a sense of belonging and a feeling of being in control. They also provide a formal channel through which workers' grievances can be aired. But not all employees want to be in a union. Many believe that their companies are already doing the best they can for workers and that a union would only tie the hands of management. The employees of Lincoln Electric have agreed for years that they do not need a union; they earn more money under the firm's profit-sharing plan than they would if they were unionized. Moreover, the company provides a good measure of job security; it has not laid off an employee since 1951.

Impact on Management. It is safe to say that most companies in the United States would rather not be unionized. The presence of a unionized work force generally weakens management's control over how work is staffed and organized, how performance is appraised, and how wages are set. For example, some municipal bus drivers' unions are very strong. These unions can almost dictate route schedules, numbers of buses per route, and hours of operation. They also set the standards by which management evaluates drivers and establishes wage rates and seniority systems.

The presence of a labor union can often create a power struggle between labor and management. Such a struggle has the potential to harm the company economically through strikes and other means. A vote by workers to join a union may even be perceived by management as a "slap in the face."

Still, the picture is not completely one-sided. In the long run, the presence of a union, by helping to meet employee needs, may lead to a stronger, more satisfied, more highly skilled work force. A union can also serve as a communication channel, providing a way for management to learn of employee concerns. Moreover, some unions may take over responsibility for disciplining employees, one of the more unpleasant functions of management.

Labor Union Structure

There are three major levels of labor organizations. They are the national union, local unions, and union federations. Let's look at each of them now.

National Unions. Most unions in this country are organized on a national basis. The biggest national union is the Teamsters Union, with almost 1.9 million members, followed by the United Automobile Workers with over 1.3 million members. The ten largest labor unions are listed in Table 10-1.

Most union power rests at the national level. By law, the leaders of national unions must be elected at least every five years. These elections are usually held during national labor conventions.

The structure of a national union can be as complex as the structure of a corporation. Figure 10-2 presents an organization chart for another important union, the United Steelworkers of America (USW). The figure shows that the USW

Table 10-1

Ten Largest U.S. Labor Unions in Terms of Total Membership

Union	Members (Thousands)
Teamsters	1,891
Automobile Workers	1,357
Food and Commercial	1,300
Steelworkers	1,238
State, County & Municipal Employees	1,098
Electrical	1,041
Carpenters	832
Machinists	745
Service Employees	650
Laborers	608

Source: U.S. Department of Labor, Bureau of Labor Statistics, 1980.

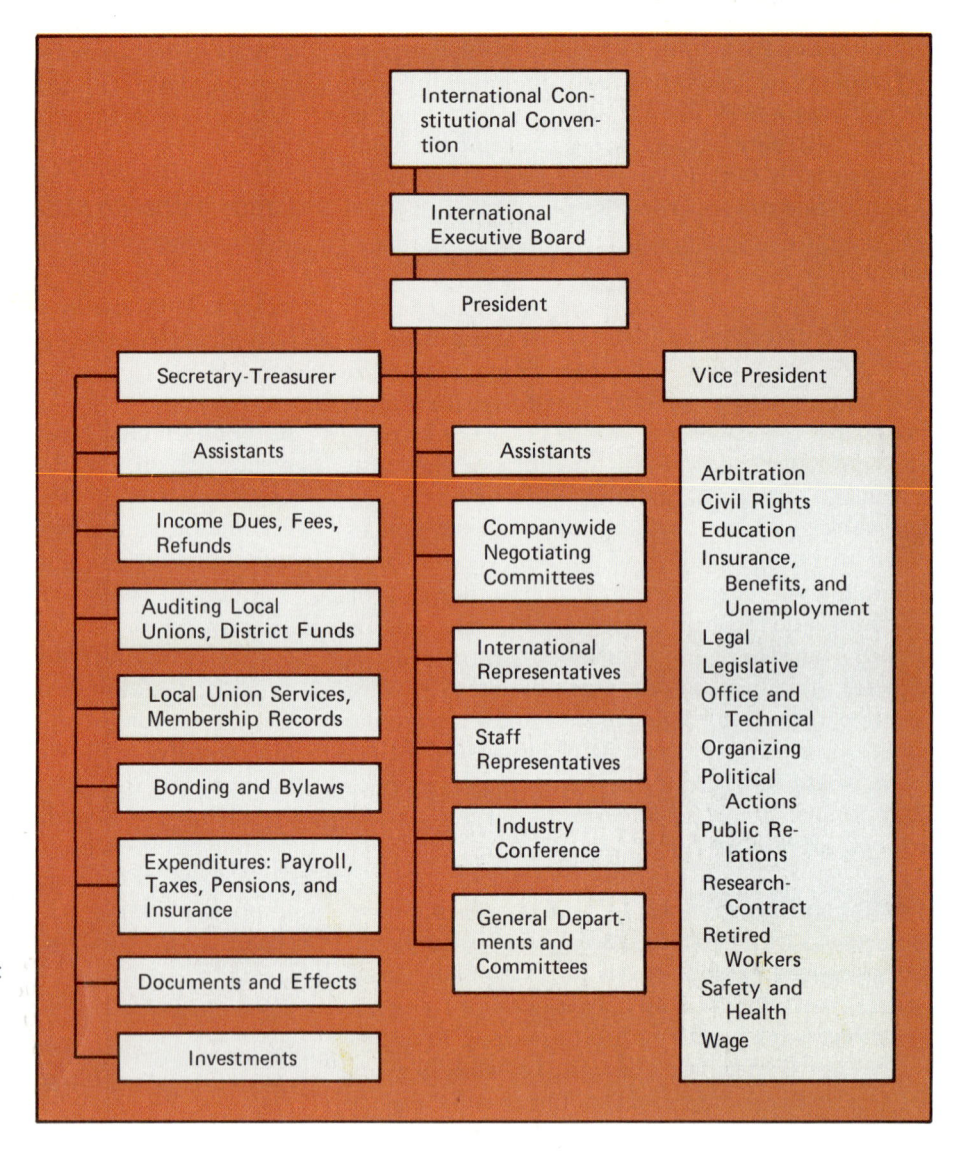

Figure 10-2

Structure of the Steelworkers' Union

Source: Adapted from *How the Union Serves*, Pamphlet no. PR 225 (Pittsburgh, Pennsylvania: United Steelworkers of America, 1975). Changes made in structure in 1976 are not reflected in this chart.

```
                    International Con-
                    stitutional Conven-
                          tion
                            |
                    International
                    Executive Board
                            |
                        President
                            |
        ┌───────────────────┼───────────────────┐
   Secretary-Treasurer                     Vice President
        |                   |                   |
    Assistants          Assistants         Arbitration
        |                   |              Civil Rights
  Income Dues, Fees,   Companywide         Education
     Refunds           Negotiating         Insurance,
        |              Committees            Benefits, and
  Auditing Local           |                  Unemployment
  Unions, District Funds International       Legal
        |              Representatives      Legislative
  Local Union Services,    |                Office and
  Membership Records    Staff                 Technical
        |              Representatives      Organizing
  Bonding and Bylaws       |                Political
        |               Industry              Actions
  Expenditures: Payroll, Conference         Public Re-
  Taxes, Pensions, and    |                   lations
     Insurance         General Depart-      Research-
        |              ments and              Contract
  Documents and Effects Committees          Retired
        |                                     Workers
     Investments                            Safety and
                                              Health
                                            Wage
```

has units to handle membership records, pensions, dues, investments, and negotiations. In addition, departments and committees deal with such matters as civil rights, education, organizing, contract research, and safety and health.

What does a national union do for its members? Consider the United Mine Workers (UMW). To help local UMW affiliates, UMW representatives periodically visit small independent mines to encourage miners to sign up with the union, and they monitor large mining operations to be sure that the union holds its strength there. To help individual members, the UMW maintains a pension fund for mine workers, as well as health programs, special disability programs, and extensive welfare programs for the families of miners killed at work. It spends millions of dollars each year researching black lung and other occupational hazards of mining. When a mine disaster occurs or when economic conditions shut down a mine, the UMW comes into town and provides emergency loans, unemployment compensation, special counseling, and other help for miners and their families. Meanwhile, the UMW conducts economic research to improve its bargaining position in Congress and with mining companies. There are at least six functions which national unions perform for their members and local affiliates.

- Unionize workers.
- Manage pension funds and other benefit programs for members.

CONTROVERSIAL ISSUES

Robots today can be designed to perform virtually any job in the industrial workplace that a human worker can do. And they can do it more efficiently, at lower cost, and with less potential danger to humans than the traditional manual labor force. But, do these robots put workers out of work? Are they really good for labor?

Pro

Thankfully, the evidence so far is that robots improve the lot of the factory worker. Most of the evidence comes from automobile assembly lines in Scandinavia and Japan. Consider, for example, the shops where new automobiles are painted. Once Japanese factories required three workers to paint a car. They had to sand down rough spots on the surface, remove any dents or bumps, and then paint the body. Several Japanese factories introduced robots that were equipped with computer programming capable of interpreting video signals. These robots were able to scan the body of a car, identify rough spots or dents, direct robot arms that corrected the faults, and then spray paint the car. They performed their job much better than the three workers originally assigned had done.

What happened to those people? The companies retrained them in basic computer programming, quality control techniques, and skills for adjusting, repairing, and directing robots. They were then sent back into their own shops as operators of the robots. Having painted the same cars for years, they were supremely competent to run the robots in the best way possible. They were paid more money because their robots were more cost-efficient, making more money available for salaries. They had been taught skills that made them more versatile within the factory organization and that gave them initial preparation for promotion into managerial ranks. And they seem to enjoy their work today much more than their manual labor of the past.

Robots Are Good for Labor.

In America, robots are used extensively in semiconductor chip factories. Robots now produce the chips, while the people formerly employed to solder connections under microscopes are employed to run quality control procedures and to reprogram robots as different chip runs are ordered. The use of robots has increased quality standards so that chips can be used in more applications, which ultimately means more workers hired.

Robots do help labor. They take over dangerous or dull jobs, perform them better than humans ever could, and the laborers they replace are often given higher positions that pay better.

Con

No, robots are *not* good for labor. Suppose, for example, that you tried to entirely automate the auto plants of General Motors. You would be looking not just at cases where robots could outperform humans so well that humans could be reassigned jobs for more money, but at cases where robots simply performed better so that the company chose to use them instead of human employees. Soon the auto companies would not be able to relocate all their employees displaced by robots, and a massive glut of auto workers would occur. These people based their lives on acquiring skills in a specialized business; their skills are not readily transferable to other industries.

In Japan, most companies would not fire employees because robots had replaced them, but in America, cost efficiencies would readily support such firings. American management does not have the sense of loyalty to its employees that Japanese management does. And even if companies decided to retrain and advance all displaced workers, how many workers are prepared to relearn a trade? Japanese employees are encouraged to move up through the ranks and ascend to upper management. American industrial workers have less latitude, so they value their present jobs more and restrict their education to topics concerning their immediate jobs. Do you really think you can retrain a thousand auto assembly line workers in computer methods and quality control analysis so they can become robot managers? And what about unions' reactions to robotization? Certainly unions will not support a work force of robots. American companies are looking at the bottom line when they look at robots. They won't protect the American worker.

- Conduct economic and social research as an input in collective bargaining.
- Give financial aid and emergency assistance to member locals.
- Lobby legislatures for labor's point of view and economic interests.
- Negotiate contracts with management that serve as a model to other unions.

Local Unions. Local unions are usually affiliated with a national labor organization. UAW Local 72 is the name of the local affiliate of the United Auto Workers in Kenosha, Wisconsin, site of one of American Motors Corporation's assembly plants.

Local unions represent workers in a particular geographic area. They may be organized along craft lines (such as plumbers or electricians), industry lines (such as steelworkers), or both. Locals may represent a single plant, all plants in a geographic area, or several smaller companies in an area. Most workers have direct contact with their local rather than with the national organization.

Some unions are organized by craft.

The members of a local are represented in a plant by **union stewards**. The responsibilities of stewards include interpreting the contracts between labor and management for members of the local, acting as spokespersons for employees in disputes with management, and working out acceptable solutions to these disputes. Union stewards at the Ford Motor Company are assigned to each assembly line or manufacturing department. They monitor safety standards, report contract violations or complaints both to Ford and to their unions, and act as mediators between Ford managers and union representatives.

Union Federations. Most national unions in the United States have joined federations. The largest of these, the American Federation of Labor-Congress of Industrial Organizations (AFL-CIO), has about 14 million members. AFL-CIO member unions include the Federation of State, County, and Municipal Employees, the United Steelworkers of America, and the Ladies' Garment Workers. Labor federations engage in several important activities, such as organizing nonunion workers, resolving disputes between member unions, lobbying the U.S. Congress and state legislatures for prolabor legislation, and publicizing the activities of member unions.

WHEN IT'S TIME TO ORGANIZE

There are two basic ways that workers organize into unions. Dissatisfied workers may decide on their own to join a union, or professional union organizers may come into a plant to convince workers that a union would advance their interests. In either situation, several steps are usually followed. Let's look at these steps now.

Organizing Campaign

At the start of the organizing process, some workers will favor the idea of joining a union. These workers try to persuade others to sign authorization cards. **Authorization cards** designate the union as the workers' bargaining agent. The organizing campaign continues until the majority of employees have signed up. When the union believes that it has a majority, it may ask the employer for official recognition. If the employer

Labor Law

Early in this century, labor-management relations were generally unregulated. With the coming of the Great Depression, however, the Congress passed laws which encouraged collective bargaining and which tried to bring about a better balance between management and labor. The major provisions of some of these acts follow.

NORRIS-LaGUARDIA ACT (1932). Until the early 1930s, employers could go to court to prevent organizing, bargaining, and striking activities. They could also force workers to sign "yellow-dog contracts"—a promise that they would not join a union if hired by the company. The Norris-LaGuardia Act outlawed these contracts and prohibited the courts from standing in the way of lawful union activities. The act strengthened the position of unions but did not deal with the rights of individual workers.

WAGNER ACT (1935). The Wagner Act, formally known as the National Labor Relations Act, recognized the right of employees to engage in union activities, to organize, and to bargain collectively without interference from employers. The act stipulates that when a majority of employees in a given work unit wants union representation, the employer must bargain collectively regarding wages, hours, and terms of employment. The act also established the National Labor Relations Board, which is responsible for conducting representation elections and for investigating charges of unfair labor practices.

TAFT-HARTLEY ACT (1947). The Taft-Hartley Act, also known as the Labor-Management Relations Act, restricted the power of unions, which, some people felt, had been given an unfair advantage in the bargaining relationship by passage of the Wagner Act. Passed over President Truman's veto, the Taft-Hartley Act attempted to provide balance. Specifically, it said that employees were free to refrain from, as well as to engage in, union activities; it recognized that both unions and employers are capable of unfair labor practices; it established the Federal Mediation and Conciliation Service to provide help in negotiations when both parties request it; it outlawed the closed shop; and it gave the President the authority to halt a strike for 80 days if the strike posed a threat to the national security. The act also allowed states to pass "right-to-work" laws. These laws prevent unions from negotiating labor contracts which make union membership mandatory.

LANDRUM-GRIFFIN ACT (1959). The Landrum-Griffin Act was passed to combat corruption. Under the terms of the act, also called the Labor-Management Reporting and Disclosure Act, unions and management must provide the government with a variety of information concerning their activities. Unions must report their constitution and by-laws, administrative policies, and financial dealings. Employers must report any expenditures designed to prevent employees from organizing. The act also provided a Bill of Rights of Union Members, under which every union member has the right to nominate candidates for union office, vote in union elections, attend union meetings, examine union accounts and records, and seek relief in court if deprived of these rights.

CIVIL SERVICE REFORM ACT, TITLE VII (1978). Executive Order 10988, issued by President Kennedy in 1961, established the right of government employees to be represented by labor organizations and to enter into agreements concerning working conditions. However, these employees were not given the right to strike, to demand that unsettled grievances go to arbitration, or to make demands concerning job security or economic matters.

The Civil Service Reform Act of 1978 replaced Executive Order 10988 and clarified the relationship between federal employee unions and the government. It set up a Federal Labor Relations Authority as an independent body to monitor labor-management relations in this area and required binding arbitration of unresolved grievances. Government workers still do not have the right to strike, however.

---

refuses, the union can then petition the National Labor Relations Board (NLRB) for an election.

This organizing process is often the hardest part of introducing a union. There were two stumbling blocks to unionizing the textile firm of J.P. Stevens. The first was persuading a majority of employees to sign up; the second was getting the company to recognize the union. Similarly, banks still fight vigorously against any attempts to enroll employees in unions.

Determining the Bargaining Unit

After the NLRB receives a petition, it conducts a hearing to determine the appropriate bargaining unit. The **bargaining unit** is the group of employees which the union will represent if it receives a majority of votes. Since some employees are likely to want the union more than others, how the bargaining unit is defined—that is, who is included in the unit—often affects the outcome of the election. Therefore, both union and management argue for units that improve their chances of winning. To determine the most appropriate bargaining unit, the NLRB considers worker demands, the geographical distribution of workers, the similarity of interests among workers, and how other bargaining units are defined in the industry.

Representation Election Campaign

Both labor and management work hard to win employees over to their sides. Union people argue that workers will be treated more fairly under a union and that they will have better benefits and more power. Management argues that workers can do just as well without a union and that union dues will cost more than the union will return in benefits.

If the union wins the election, it becomes the exclusive representative of all employees in the bargaining unit, including those who do not belong to the union. If it loses, it can try again for recognition in a year.

COLLECTIVE BARGAINING

Collective bargaining is the name for the process whereby representatives of labor and management formulate an agreement governing pay scales and terms of work. The negotiations leading to a labor contract are often time-consuming, difficult, and heated. A contract between a large union and an industry such as automobiles or steel is of considerable economic consequence and involves thousands of workers and billions of dollars in wages.

Key Issues

Collective bargaining focuses on issues that are important to management, workers, and any unions that may be involved. Let's look at several of the key issues.

Union Security and Management Rights. The union and management are each concerned with preserving and strengthening their relative positions. The union generally wants some form of security (see Figure 10-1) and may demand a checkoff. With a **checkoff**, the worker's union dues are deducted directly from the paycheck. A **management-rights clause** lists the areas of operation in which management may take actions without having to obtain permission from the union.

Compensation. Wages are almost always a major concern in collective bargaining. For instance, wage rates, determination of pay grades, incentive systems, and pay for particular jobs are all vital matters here. Generally, a union tries to get the same pay for its members as other workers in similar jobs.

Because of the impact of inflation on real purchasing power, many unions have pushed for **cost-of-living adjustments** (**COLAs**). Under a COLA, wages are adjusted during the life of the contract in relation to changes in the consumer price index. As an example, if inflation went up by 10 percent, wages would automatically increase by the same percentage. More than one half of all large unions now have cost-of-living adjustments in their contracts.

Fringe Benefits. This is another important issue to both labor and management. **Fringe benefits** are any benefits received by employees in addition to their regular pay. They include such things as paid vacations, sick leaves, welfare programs, and health and life insurance. The cost of fringe benefits is increasing much more rapidly than wages. One fringe benefit that unions have been stressing recently is the pension. Pension funds certainly are not small: The Teamsters' fund currently is valued at $3.5 billion.

Job Security. In the early 1980s, there was a sharp increase in the number of agreements calling for employee givebacks. **Givebacks** are reductions in wages and benefits, or delays in receiving increases granted earlier. Because of the hard economic times, employees are willing to make such sacrifices in return for more job security. At the Lordstown, Ohio, plant of General Motors, workers are now stressing security over other issues. If the choice is between concessions or jobs, many workers choose concessions.

Hours of Work. This issue refers to the length of the workday, the length of the workweek, and the

Profile—
Douglas A. Fraser

In the midst of Chrysler Corporation's financial crisis in the late 1970s, the company's management realized that the survival of the company lay in the hands of labor, and thus in the hands of the United Auto Workers (UAW), the union that stands behind virtually all auto assembly line workers in America. In June of 1980, the board of directors of Chrysler Corporation voted into a seat on the board the president of the UAW, Douglas A. Fraser.

Fraser was born in Glasgow, Scotland, but grew up in Detroit during the Great Depression. With his father out of work, Fraser scrounged for coal in the winters and took odd jobs in the summers. He left high school before being graduated and began working and organizing labor unions. Before he was 25, he had risen to presidency of his local union.

The man who preceded Fraser as local president, Dick Leonard, went on to become vice president of the United Auto Workers, which was founded in 1936 and was just finding its footing in the American auto industry. Fraser became a close ally of Leonard and at his side survived the early civil war in the UAW. Leonard, impressed by Fraser's work, urged him to leave his local and become an officer at the UAW. In 1950, Fraser was a leader of a 104-day strike against Chrysler. He attracted the attention of the union leadership and began to move up rapidly in the UAW, finally becoming president of the union in 1977.

The UAW won the seat on the Chrysler board during negotiations in 1979. The management scarcely expected Fraser's vigorous response to his election. Immediately after joining the board, he proposed sweeping plans to examine the effects of Chrysler plant closings on workers and the communities in which they lived. Thus began a new era of management-labor interaction.

Fraser gained the union's right to examine Chrysler's financial records to ensure that members' pay cuts were truly justified. Fraser revived the concept of profit-sharing and conceived a bold new involvement of labor in management policy. Today, workers at Chrysler have the right to insist that a portion of their pension fund be placed in "socially desirable" investments, such as non-profit nursing homes, nursery schools, health maintenance organizations, or similar institutions in communities where there are large concentrations of UAW members. In addition, the union may submit annually to the trustees of the pension fund a list of up to ten companies which should be denied investments because they practice racial discrimination in South Africa. Management and labor have agreed to a policy of "equality of sacrifice," which states that labor and management will share equally in hardships that result from Chrysler's restructuring.

Chrysler was rescued from the brink of bankruptcy only by extraordinary action, a key component of which was federal legislation that required worker concessions if the company was to receive government loan guarantees. Fraser's role in a time of crisis in the auto industry has been particularly difficult. After three years of very distasteful wage and benefit concessions, the UAW workers at Chrysler demanded wage hikes to compensate for high inflation and massive layoffs and plant closings. Fraser, along with the UAW leadership at Chrysler, realized that large pay increases were impossible. But they managed to gain a reinstatement of cost-of-living protection and other gains which started the Chrysler workers back toward parity with workers at Ford and General Motors. While Fraser believes strongly in labor-management reform and radical new employee participation in companies, he also understands the need for intelligent restraint, both by Chrysler management and by his union.

Fraser has been successful, however. Rank-and-file union workers like Fraser's presence on the board and want more UAW representatives on the Chrysler board of directors. Chrysler is equally happy: "He's ethical and fair minded, and at the same time it's clear he has the interests of his membership at heart." Lee Iacocca, chairman of the board, has asked Fraser to remain on Chrysler's board even after Fraser passes retirement age and resigns his union leadership.

It is clear that the auto companies and the auto workers' union must work together with mutual interests at heart. Douglas Fraser has been a bold luminary in this effort, and he will be remembered as one of the great figures of union leadership.

nature of work shifts. How employees are compensated for extra work—such as time and a half for overtime—is also an important negotiating issue. Some unions are pressing now to strip management of the right to make workers accept overtime assignments even when they do not want them.

Safety and Health. With rising costs of health care and growing concern about environmental dangers, unions have begun to place greater emphasis on contract provisions dealing with employee health and safety. A major oil workers' strike occurred in 1980 because employers refused to cover the full cost of medical insurance. In other industries, special contract provisions cover safety equipment, health safeguards, and training programs on safety.

Quality of Work Life. Until recently, unions pushed for "hard" gains, such as wage increases. Job enrichment and democracy in the workplace were thought to have little meaning to the average worker. Today, however, evidence that quality of work life (QWL) has a major impact on employee health, satisfaction, and behavior is so strong that some unions are paying closer attention to it. Major QWL programs at General Motors and elsewhere have had promising results.

The Give-and-Take of a Contract

The negotiation of a labor contract is a give-and-take process. Both parties get something and give up something in return. Figure 10-3 summarizes the contract signed in 1982 between the United Auto Workers and General Motors. It was approved by a majority of only 52 percent of voting GM employees. Seventy-three percent of Ford employees approved a similar contract.

Figure 10-3

The Give-and-Take of a Contract

HERMAN

"If you don't think you can make it into work tomorrow, give me a call."

Source: Copyright, 1982, Universal Press Syndicate. Reprinted with permission. All rights reserved.

Contract at a glance

Here's a brief look at the major provisions of the 29-month contract with General Motors Corp. approved Friday by the United Auto Workers. The contract, affecting 470,000 active and laid-off workers, will take effect Monday.

The union:
- Gives up nine paid days off a year.
- Gives up annual pay increase of 3%.
- Defers cost-of-living pay increases for three quarters of a year. These increases are restored in the final three quarters of the contract.
- Accepts subscale wages and benefits for newly hired employees.
- Agrees to economic penalties for chronic absenteeism.
- Agrees to negotiate at local level to eliminate restrictive work rules.

The company:
- Agrees to profit sharing.
- Establishes a prepaid legal-services plan for workers.
- Reopens four plants scheduled to close and agrees to a two-year moratorium on plant closings as a result of shifts to outside suppliers.
- Guarantees 50% or more of pay until retirement for laid-off workers with 15 years' seniority (10 years' seniority if plant is closed permanently).
- Increases employee discount for purchase of new GM cars.
- Increases tuition benefits for laid-off workers.

Source: *The Milwaukee Journal* (April 11, 1982).

Prenegotiation

Unions and management engage in months of preparation before bargaining begins. The union gathers information about other contract settlements, inflation rates, and worker demands. Management tries to anticipate what the union will ask for. It also assesses its own needs, how much it can afford to give up, how various settlements would affect its competitive situation, and so on. If a contract currently exists, union and management may use it as a starting point. Each then tries to improve its position and to clarify areas of confusion or controversy.

Negotiation

Negotiations usually begin with a presentation by the union of a list of demands. For bargaining purposes, management may also write up a list of its own. Through the process of bargaining, the sides come closer and closer together. Various demands of each side are dropped, revised, or traded off. At some point in the process, the union may call for a strike vote as a show of member support.

The negotiating atmosphere may range from genuine cooperation to outright hostility. Each side attempts to win the "game." Some examples of negotiating behavior are presented in Figure 10-4.

Typically, bargaining continues until the last minute, just before the existing contract expires. Both sides want to show their supporters that they have done everything possible to have their demands met. Once a tentative agreement is reached, it must generally be agreed to by union members and by a management body, such as a board of directors. If a mutually agreeable settlement cannot be reached, some other means may be needed to resolve the dispute.

SETTLING DISPUTES

Attempts by the union and management to work out an agreement may reach a dead end, either before or after the start of a strike. In such cases, mediation or arbitration may be necessary.

Figure 10-4

Negotiating Behaviors

Deemphasizing Differences

"Who won?" was the question as the two parties proceeded to the next room for the formal announcement and picture taking (after the completion of the 1955 Ford Motor-UAW negotiations). "We both won," Reuther (union leader) replied. "We are extremely happy to announce that we have arrived at an agreement... Both the Company and the Union have worked very hard and very sincerely at the bargaining table."
Source: B.M. Selekman, S.K. Selekman, and S.H. Fuller, *Problems in Labor Relations* (2d ed.; New York: McGraw-Hill, 1958), pp. 428-429.

Complimenting Opponent's Behavior

Management negotiator during bargaining: "I might inquire as to the job-evaluation committee. I want to say that you people have gone along in pretty fine style there. It is new to you and the reason you are doing well is because you have an open mind."
Source: A. Douglas, *Industrial Peacemaking* (New York: Columbia University Press, 1962), p. 331.

Punishing Opponent's Behavior

A union delegate to management: "We have been very reasonable this year; if the company does not take advantage of it, *things will be different*. It appears to me that the company is not sincere; General Motors has settled, John Deere has settled, and yet the company has done nothing."
Source: R.E. Walton and R.B. McKersie, *A Behavioral Theory of Labor Negotiations* (New York: McGraw-Hill, 1965), p. 254.

Separating Negotiators from Their Behaviors

Management negotiator during bargaining: "I have found that your union representatives, even when they were angry and sore and mean—and they get that way just the way we get that way, because we are all human—even their worst moments, they were all men whose word could be trusted."
Source: Selekman, Selekman, and Fuller, p. 550.

Source: R.E. Walton and R.B. McKersie, *A Behavioral Theory of Labor Negotiations* (New York: McGraw-Hill, 1965). Reproduced with permission.

Mediation

Mediation is a process wherein an experienced and knowledgeable neutral person, the mediator, assists the union and management in reaching an agreement. State agencies or the Federal Mediation and Conciliation Service provide these mediators if requested. The mediator clarifies each side's position, suggests possible compromises, and tries to bring the sides together. However, mediators only make recommendations; neither management nor labor has to accept the recommendations.

Arbitration

Some disputes between labor and management cannot be resolved through mediation. In such cases, arbitration may be necessary. **Arbitration** is the process wherein an arbitrator (again, an experienced neutral person) listens to the arguments of labor and management, weighs the merits of each argument, and then makes a binding judgment. Since most managers and labor leaders do not want to risk a third party's judgment on crucial contract issues, arbitration is rarely used to resolve collective bargaining stalemates.

Strike Outcomes

Most strikes do end with an agreement between labor and management. In recent years, over 80 percent of all strikes ended either with all issues resolved or with a procedure set up to handle any remaining differences. It is rare that strikes end with the employer going out of business. It is also rare that a strike is "broken"—that is, the workers go back to work without their demands being met.

Contract Administration

After a contract has been signed by labor and management, the process of **contract administration** begins. This means that the contract has to be interpreted and followed on a daily basis. Contracts usually list a set of steps to be followed when disputes over contract provisions arise. These steps make up the **grievance procedure**.

Labor and management usually try to avoid strikes.

A grievance procedure may be needed when, for example, an employee disagrees with a supervisor over the interpretation of the contract as to which duties the employee is to perform. If the employee and the supervisor cannot work out a solution themselves, the disagreement becomes a formal grievance, and the employee contacts the shop steward. The steward tries to work things out with the supervisor. If that fails, the steward can put the grievance in writing and submit it to management.

Then, representatives of the union's grievance committee and management's grievance committee meet to settle the matter. If the results of this meeting are unsatisfactory, a grievance committee made up of union and management representatives discusses the issue. The last step, if all others fail, is that the grievance goes to arbitration and is settled by an independent third party.

SOURCES OF NEGOTIATING STRENGTH

Labor and management both approach the negotiating table with certain weapons, or sources of strength, at their disposal. The function of these sources is to give labor or management leverage during the negotiating process.

Labor

Labor can use its financial and political power to help achieve its goals. Strikes, pickets, and boycotts are the sources of labor's financial strength. Labor's sheer numbers provide political clout.

Strike. The ultimate source of labor's strength is the **strike**. By stopping work, employees hope to pressure management to agree to their demands. Each day that workers are off the job, the firm loses money. At some point, the cost of meeting worker demands becomes less than the cost of letting the strike go on.

Of course, a problem with striking is that strikers pay a price, too—mostly in terms of lost wages. You may remember the 1981 strike of the Screen Actors Guild, a union representing actors. Striking union members lost payments for movies and television shows that they might have made had they not been on strike. In addition, many of the actors' shows were canceled or rescheduled. This permanently affected the incomes of the production companies as well as the incomes of the actors involved.

As shown in Figure 10-5, the number of work stoppages has dropped in recent years. The percentage of time lost to stoppages has also dropped.

Picket. Union members often **picket** when striking. Picketing workers march back and forth in front of the entrances to the workplace, carrying signs listing their grievances and demands. The idea is to make the views of the union known, to generate sympathy for the strike, and to persuade nonstrikers not to cross the line. Many nonstriking union members show their support for the union by refusing to cross the picket line. As a result, a small striking union may get enough support to cause major problems for a company or an industry.

Britain's economy has suffered for years from the strong support that small independent unions can stir among the British people. Striking British transport workers are often joined by workers from other transportation industries; consequently, nearly all passenger and commercial transportation across England comes to a stop.

Boycott. Under a **boycott**, union members and other people who agree with the union's goals refuse to purchase or handle the company's goods or services. The result can be tremendous financial pressures on a company. A **primary boycott** occurs when a union tells its members not to patronize a business involved in a dispute with labor. When the union goes even further and tries to persuade other parties, such as suppliers and customers, to stop dealing with the company, it is called a **secondary boycott**. Secondary boycotts are generally prohibited by law. This does not apply to the United Farm Workers, however, who have used the secondary boycott to restrict the sale of grapes, lettuce, and wine of growers from whom the union was trying to gain recognition.

Political Influence. Many unions can use the size of their memberships as a potent political weapon. For instance, they can endorse and provide financial support to "prolabor" candidates for political office. Even though all unions may not support the same candidates, they form an important voting bloc. Interestingly, Ronald Reagan was the first union member to be elected President of the United States—he is a former president of the Screen Actors Guild.

Figure 10-5

Major Work Stoppages

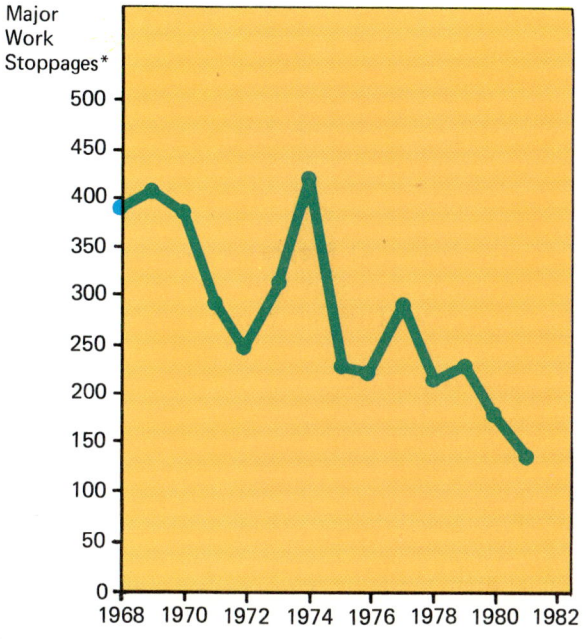

*Work stoppages include all known strikes or lockouts involving 1,000 or more workers and lasting a full shift or longer.

Source: U.S. Department of Labor, Bureau of Labor Statistics, Bulletin 2092.

Management

Management also has a variety of resources that it can draw upon to protect its interests. Let's look at those that are most commonly used.

Lockout. A **lockout** occurs when a company shuts down its operations, thereby preventing union members from working. Sometimes, when a union strikes against one employer, other firms lock out their employees to show solidarity and to weaken the union's position. In other cases, a company may lock out its workers before they strike, thus controlling the timing of the work stoppage. Because of "bad press," however, lockouts are rarely used.

Injunction. An **injunction** is a court order saying that employees must return to work or face a penalty. At one time, injunctions were frequently issued to stop any strike that might interfere with business. Recently, court injunctions have been used by local governments to stop illegal strikes by public employees. The President can issue an injunction to halt strikes if the strikes are believed to be harmful to the public interest. For example, in 1981 President Reagan invoked a no-strike law (applicable to federal employees) to order the 15,000 members of the Professional Air Traffic Controllers Association (PATCO) to go back to work. PATCO argued that the government's contract offer did not include a big enough pay increase. Moreover, PATCO said, the contract did not provide for early retirement and a shorter work week—both critical issues in an industry characterized by tremendous job stress. The union went out on strike anyway, disobeying the President's order. His response, as mentioned earlier, was to fire all striking workers.

"Business As Usual." Firms can sometimes carry on "business as usual" during a strike. One way is by having managers take over strikers' duties. Another is by hiring "strikebreakers," who are workers willing to cross the picket line. This can cause considerable bitterness. Strikebreakers are referred to as "scabs" by striking employees and their sympathizers. On the other hand, keeping a plant in operation by whatever means does minimize loss of revenue. Management may even gain a better understanding of workers' jobs. And contract terms after a strike are generally more favorable to management when operations continue than when the union is able to force a plant shutdown.

Agreements and Organizations. Just as some unions have banded together for their mutual benefit, some companies have formed associations to help one another in the event of a strike. For instance, if one company is struck, others may provide financial and other support to help it hold on against the union. The National Association of Manufacturers is one national organization that helps companies in their mutual struggle against unions.

To illustrate, many newspapers share printing facilities, computer equipment, and even delivery trucks when one newspaper is crippled by a strike. Newspaper management places high priority on continuing operation and only rarely will it stop publication. Similarly, the Shipowners' Mutual Strike Insurance Association helps shipping companies continue operation during strikes.

Employee Relations Programs. Some companies prevent labor problems by not having unions in the first place. They do this by making unions

FROM THE FILE

Tony knew that the employees at the company's glassworks plant were preparing to go out on strike, but he didn't know when. Until they did, things were up in the air. He couldn't confidently schedule production. He didn't want to purchase materials and build up inventories that might gather expensive dust. He couldn't give customers a firm delivery date for the plant's products. All things considered, he thought a lockout might be his best option. But what, he asked himself, did he stand to lose by a lockout?

unnecessary. One company that has been successful with this approach is DuPont. By stressing employee well-being and keeping wages competitive, DuPont for more than eight years has successfully held off attempts by the steelworkers union to win a company-wide union election.

NEW DEVELOPMENTS IN LABOR-MANAGEMENT RELATIONS

In this section of the chapter, we'll look at three rather varied topics: employee purchases of companies, ombudsmen, and robots in the workplace. Then we'll examine the future of organized labor in this country.

Employee Purchase of Companies

Perhaps the easiest way for workers to understand the concerns and views of management is for them to actually become owners of the firm. There are now more than 250 companies in the United States that are employee-owned. While some employee-owned firms have been very successful, others have had problems.

In July of 1980, members of a Waterloo, Iowa, meatpackers' union agreed to buy a majority share in Rath Packing Co., by putting part of their wages into company stock. The company was saved from bankruptcy. Productivity immediately increased at the plant, and absenteeism and tardiness fell. Workers soon became dissatisfied, however, believing that they were not getting a real say in management even though they owned the company.

Ombudsmen

Some companies attempt to forestall unionization of their work force, or at least to keep the work force satisfied, by employing an **ombudsman**, whose job is to check out and resolve employee complaints. Ombudsmen are now found in corporations, government, and educational organizations. General Electric and Xerox have both used them successfully. When employees have complaints in organizations such as these, they go to the ombudsman, who operates in an atmosphere of confidentiality so that employee identity is protected. The ombudsman then presents the complaint to management. Ombudsmen help ensure that employees are treated fairly; they also give management another way to diagnose problems in the work force.

Robots

Labor leaders have long feared automation—the replacement of humans by machines. They argued that machines would take jobs from people. To cushion the impact of automation, labor leaders have called for shorter work weeks, more holidays and vacation time, and earlier retirement.

Automation, once an impersonal and faceless threat, now often has a face, hands, and perhaps even a voice and a name. Companies today are purchasing robots and installing them on production lines. At its Lordstown, Ohio, plant, GM has 26 advanced Unimate robots that apply 450 welds to every car that comes off the line. The robots are efficient, accurate, tireless, and seldom complain. The Unimates have "super seniority"—they stay in the plant during layoffs and shutdowns and are back at work as soon as they are needed. A Unimate costs $45,000 and pays for itself in less than 15 months by replacing two $28,000-a-year welders.

The Future of Organized Labor

The percentage of the U.S. work force in labor unions is declining. It is now under 20 percent, down from more than 25 percent in 1953. This decline is largely due to the inability of unions to win as many representation elections as they did in the past. What are some of the causes of this trend? What can organized labor do about it?

Challenges for Labor. Many factors have contributed to labor's current problems. Some of them are discussed below.

- The work force is changing. Unions have had their best success in organizing blue-collar workers, but white-collar workers now account for two thirds of the work force. The work force is also becoming better educated: High school diplomas are held by less than 50 percent of workers 65 or over but by 90 percent of those workers between the ages of 20 and 24.

- Labor costs are increasing sharply. Some of our trade problems are blamed on high labor costs. Nonunion wages are usually lower than union wages.
- Some younger workers show a high level of political involvement. They do not see unions placing as much emphasis on social and political issues as they would like.
- Companies are taking steps to make work more satisfying and stimulating. When those steps are successful, employees do not see a need for unions.
- Public support for unions is waning. Many people point to what they think are unreasonable wage demands as a major cause of inflation.

Prospects for Union Response. If organized labor is to respond to these challenges successfully, it must turn them into opportunities. For example, although white-collar employees have traditionally resisted unionization, they form a huge potential source of members, if approached the right way. In fact, an increasing number of professionals and other white-collar workers—including teachers, nurses, and government employees—are joining unions to fight inflation and to gain greater control over their work lives.

In addition, organized labor may need to rethink its contract demands. For instance, even though economic factors and job security are still crucial issues for most employees, job challenge, responsibility, and the quality of work life are also important issues. If unions assess their strengths and weaknesses and adopt flexible recruitment and bargaining strategies, they may ultimately grow stronger as a result of these challenges.

Unions face new problems and opportunities because of changes in the workplace.

SUMMARY POINTS

1. A labor union is an organization of workers who have united to achieve their common goals. By so doing, they hope to increase their bargaining power with management.
2. Over the years, labor unions have strived to win higher wages, greater economic security, and fairer treatment from management.
3. Management generally resists the formation of unions because unions weaken management's control over how work is staffed and organized, how performance is appraised, and how wages are set.
4. The three main levels of labor organization are the national union, local unions, and union federations.
5. Union organizing involves several steps—the signing of authorization cards by workers, petitioning the National Labor Relations Board for an election, determining the bargaining unit, and holding a representation election.
6. Collective bargaining is the name for the negotiations leading to a work contract between labor and management.
7. Some important collective bargaining issues are union security and management rights, compensation, fringe benefits, job security, hours of work, safety and health, and the quality of work life.
8. When negotiations between labor and management reach a stalemate, the parties involved often turn to mediation or arbitration to find the solution.
9. Contract administration refers to the day-by-day process of interpreting a work contract after it has been signed by labor and management.
10. The sources of negotiating strength for labor are strikes, pickets, boycotts, and political influence.
11. The sources of negotiating strength for management are lockouts, court injunctions,

strikebreakers, trade associations, and employee relations programs.
12. Three new developments in labor-management relations are employee purchase of companies, the increasing use of ombudsmen, and the use of robots instead of humans on production lines.

KEY TERMS AND CONCEPTS

labor union
union stewards
authorization card
bargaining unit
collective bargaining
checkoff
management-rights clause
COLA
fringe benefits
givebacks
mediation

arbitration
contract administration
grievance procedure
strike
picket
boycott
primary boycott
secondary boycott
lockout
injunction
ombudsman

REVIEW QUESTIONS

1. What are the goals of labor unions with respect to their members?
2. What does the national union organization do for its members?
3. What is a union steward? What does this person do?
4. Explain why the definition of the bargaining unit is important to both labor and management.
5. How does a cost-of-living adjustment in a labor contract work?
6. Why are workers sometimes willing to sign labor contracts calling for employee givebacks?
7. How does mediation differ from arbitration?
8. Explain the difference between a strike and a boycott.
9. Describe the major sources of management's strength in contract negotiation.
10. What are some of the reasons for organized labor's recent decline in membership?

DISCUSSION QUESTIONS

1. Management generally resists unionization of its facilities. How might the presence of a union actually benefit the firm?
2. In your opinion, has organized labor become too strong? Have its wage demands in the auto industry, for example, where line workers earn as much as $20 an hour, become excessive? If so, what can management do about it?
3. Both labor and management come to the negotiating table with certain advantages, or sources of strength. Which party, in your opinion, is usually in a better position?
4. What are some of the long-term consequences of the replacement of human workers on production lines by machines and robots? Is this development good for the labor force?
5. Do you think that in the years ahead organized labor will become a greater or less important force in our society? Why?

CASE 10-1

General Motors Work Rules

Automobile companies today—and General Motors in particular—face a major expense in union-sponsored work rules. These rules are specifications describing exactly what each employee is allowed to do. An electrician, for example, may rewire an electric socket, but may not take the screw out of the cover plate—a millwright must do that part of the work. When both welding and milling are required on an engine block, a union welder and a union millwright are involved. Each does part of the job while the other waits. GM claims that the jobs could be combined because the welder and the millwright are competent in each other's skills.

GM claims that it pays billions of dollars every year in excess labor costs because of unnecessary work rules. The United Auto Workers (UAW) admits that eliminating rules that the union itself considers to be "inefficient" would increase productivity by about 10 percent. This would reduce the cost advantage of the Japanese auto makers by about 25 percent.

The problem for the UAW is two-fold. First, UAW leaders fear that they will be forced into granting additional concessions. For example, in Defiance, Ohio, foundry workers at a GM plant are given three minutes to wash up before lunch. GM management wants to eliminate this time. Without the three minutes, workers either will not wash up or will have to take part of their lunch time to do so. The UAW doesn't want to budge on this problem, although it would be willing to talk about other rules.

Second, UAW membership has dropped by one third since 1979. This is a result of prolonged layoffs, salary concessions by workers, and generally a weakened control by the UAW over auto company factories. Union leaders are afraid that if productivity is increased, more auto workers will disappear from the factories and from union rolls. The financial future of the UAW could be weakened.

General Motors persuaded the UAW to start negotiations about relaxing work rules, even though their labor contract had two more years to run. By agreement, local labor and management bargainers would try to make individual deals. If they failed, UAW's General Motors department and GM's management would step in to help. Final decision-making authority would remain with the local labor and management bargainers. If all this failed, GM and the UAW agreed to keep the current work rules until the contract ran out in two years. At that point, top UAW and GM management would try to draw up a contract which the union locals would accept.

1. How is the role of the labor union changing in its dealings today with General Motors?
2. How are mediation and arbitration being used to settle disagreements in this situation?
3. What are labor's and management's strengths in this situation? Which side do you think will win? Is a "win" for either side really a "win" for anybody in the long run?

CASE 10-2

Louisville, Kentucky

Louisville, Kentucky, has been called "the strike capital of the world." The accompanying table shows how many days have been lost per worker by strikes in a recent ten year period in different cities:

City	Days Lost Per Worker
Louisville	9.56
St. Louis	8.13
Pittsburgh	7.42
Dayton	7.02
Memphis	5.84
Philadelphia	5.82

San Francisco	5.53
Birmingham	5.51
Indianapolis	5.04
Detroit	4.78
Cincinnati	4.56

Source: U.S. Bureau of Labor Statistics

All eleven cities listed had more days of work lost due to strikes than the national average of 4.39 days per worker per year. But obviously, Louisville did significantly worse than the rest. Many companies now refuse to build in Louisville, and many companies with factories already in Louisville are closing them or are planning to close them. Louisville's unemployment is high and the city has no other way to employ laid-off industrial workers.

Who is to blame? Management claims that unions are too greedy and strike for too much money. Unions claim that management is too tightfisted. Some people in Louisville claim that the numbers are high only because the workers involved in walkouts at three factories (General Electric, Ford, and International Harvester) represent such a large proportion of Louisville's labor force. Other people claim that unions negotiated labor contracts so liberal that employees could—and did—walk off their jobs over issues as minor as dress codes and job assignments. Researchers at the University of Louisville think that employees are accustomed to a Southern tradition of management devotion to its employees, while the companies that have built factories in Louisville have had Northern standards which stress holding employees at a distance and bargaining for every cent of wages and every extra hour of work.

1. What role do you think unions have played in creating the current economic conditions in Louisville?
2. What is labor's strength in Louisville? management's strength?
3. How have collective bargaining and the handling of disputes been successful or unsuccessful in Louisville?
4. What is the future of unions in Louisville?

11

Production Management

After studying this chapter, you should be able to:

- Describe how production management differs in the short run and the long run.
- Discuss three production transformation processes as well as some of the attributes of the modern manufacturing facility.
- Identify the fundamental steps in materials purchasing and the fundamental elements of inventory control.
- Explain the production planning and control process.
- Define quality control and discuss how statistical quality control works.
- Describe three basic maintenance policies.

The modern production facility is generally large and complex. Vast amounts of raw materials are used to produce a great variety of industrial and consumer goods. To keep the wheels of industry turning, new manufacturing plants must be built and equipped, raw materials ordered and stored, production plans designed and implemented, and output quality checked. These and the many other tasks needed to run the production facility of today are the responsibility of **production management**.

Large manufacturing complexes play an important role in our economy. Consider the fact that the 50 largest U.S. manufacturers together account for about 24 percent of the total value added by manufacturing. The 200 largest companies account for 44 percent. **Value added is the sales dollar value of output minus the cost of all the raw materials and semifinished inputs bought from other manufacturers.** Some value is added to a product at each stage in a production process.

THE MANAGEMENT TASK IN PRODUCTION

Economists make a distinction between the short run and the long run. In the short run, the basic production plant and equipment cannot be changed in size or design; in the long run, they can. That is to say, the production capacity of the plant is fixed in the short run but variable in the long run.

Let's clarify this distinction with an example from the publishing industry. Suppose a textbook publisher faces a printing deadline on one of its new books. The printing presses are already working at full speed. Management could solve this problem by employing an overtime shift to handle the extra work, but it would not install a new press to accommodate just one book. In the short run, therefore, labor costs increase but plant capacity remains the same. However, if the company intends to publish many books over the next five years, the solution is to increase the size of the plant and the number of its presses.

The production manager's task in the short run is to use existing facilities in the best way possible—through proper maintenance, inventory control, and production scheduling. In particular, the production manager can:

- Vary the amount or type of inputs such as by purchasing fewer materials.
- Use the production facility more effectively through multishift operations, overtime, or improved work methods.
- Temporarily add capacity by hiring another company to do part of the work (this is called subcontracting).

Over the long run, the production manager's job is to search for ways to improve existing facilities and to modify or expand them as needed. Inland Steel Company, the nation's seventh largest steel producer, recently completed a $1 billion plant expansion and modernization program. The purpose of the program was to lower production costs and to improve product quality, thereby hoping to boost its share of the steel market.

MODERN MANUFACTURING

Let's now consider a few of the basic manufacturing processes as well as some of the characteristics of the modern manufacturing facility. In doing so, we can get an idea of just how complex the production manager's job is.

Transformation Processes

As shown in Figure 11-1, **production refers to the transformation, or change, of material and energy inputs into outputs desired by consumers.** Most people probably envision a production process as an assembly line, along which automobiles or radios move from one work station

Figure 11-1

The Transformation Process

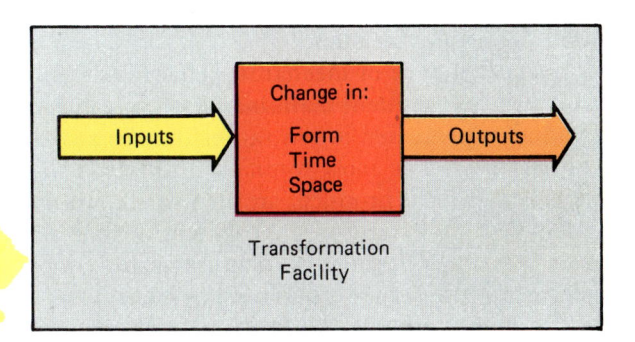

to the next. But the assembly line is only a special case of production processes involving a **form transformation**. Whenever raw and semifinished materials are processed and converted into finished products, production involves a transformation in form.

In a **synthetic transformation** process, basic parts, components, or chemicals are combined to form a finished product. The production of appliances from steel, plastic, and other inputs is an example of a synthetic transformation in form. In an **analytic transformation** process, a basic material is broken down into one or more final products. Examples include the refining of iron ore or crude oil and the milling of logs into lumber, plywood, composite board, and other building materials.

Production inputs can also be transformed in time and in space—**temporal transformation** and **spatial transformation**, respectively. Storage is an example of a temporal transformation. Rental warehouse space is the product, and it is purchased for a period of time. A transportation service, such as commercial air travel or package shipment via Federal Express, is an example of a spatial transformation. Here, the transformation process involves the movement of people or packages from one place to another. As we can see from this discussion, the output of a production or transformation process can be either a good or a service.

Mechanization

Since the Industrial Revolution of the 18th and 19th centuries, machine operations have increasingly replaced handwork in the production of goods—that is, we have mechanized. Mechanization is probably most characteristic of **continuous manufacturing** processes, which produce a flow of goods at a predetermined rate. These processes are typical of chemical plants and large food-processing facilities.

Another type of mechanized manufacturing process is **intermittent manufacturing**, in which a product is processed in lots rather than in a continuous flow. The most common example is the **job shop**, where products are manufactured or assembled to a customer's purchase order or specification. Intermittent manufacturing does not permit the high level of mechanization found in continuous processes.

Which type of transformation has taken place here?

Computers and Mathematical Models

Computer technology plays an important role in the modern manufacturing plant. **Automation** refers to the substitution of machine tools for human laborers in production processes. Computers are used increasingly to direct and control these machines. General Electric has already spent more than $1 billion automating its manufacturing plants which make such varied products as dishwashers, jet engines, locomotives, and toaster ovens. The company expects to have 1,000 computer-controlled robots at work in the plants in the near future. We'll talk more about the role of computers in Chapter 22.

The complexity of production management makes it suitable for the application of mathematical models. Several of these models are discussed later in the chapter. **Management science**, or **operations research** as it is also called, is concerned with the development and application of these models to business problems.

MATERIALS PURCHASING AND INVENTORY CONTROL

Purchasing is the link between the firm and its suppliers. It concerns decisions about which supplies to buy, when, from whom, and for how much. Inventories act as a cushion between the firm and its environment. The challenge of inventory control is to balance the various costs involved to achieve the lowest total cost. Let's examine materials purchasing first, and then we'll take a close look at inventory control.

Materials Purchasing

Most people in production management would argue that purchasing and materials handling have a big impact on company profits. For instance, it has been estimated that moving materials from one place to another, say, from a pipe company to a plumbing supply house, accounts for 20 to 50 percent of all production costs. The total amount of money spent on supplies and raw materials in any given year exceeds the gross national product, and 50 percent of the sales dollar of most big firms is spent on purchasing. Clearly, even a small savings in the purchasing budget can be very important.

Understanding the purchasing cycle is the key to understanding materials purchasing. The purchasing cycle begins with a decision to buy materials for production and ends when the materials are accepted by the department requesting the order. There are six steps in the cycle:

- *Requisitions*. Personnel from the various production units turn in purchase requisitions to the purchasing agent or buyer. These requisitions indicate the type and number of items needed.
- *Value Analysis.* The purchasing agent conducts a systematic appraisal of the purchase requisition. The idea is to find the lowest cost way to satisfy the request. Questions asked by management at this stage are: Do the requested items include too many unnecessary features? Can packaging or shipping requirements be reduced? How available are these items in the forms needed?
- *Supplier Selection*. A list of approved suppliers is developed. The list rates suppliers on the basis of price, quality, reliability, and services. The purchasing agent then obtains quotes on prices and delivery times.
- *Order Placement*. A formal purchase order is completed. The purchase order describes the goods requested, unit prices, quantities desired, shipping instruction, and so on. The purchasing agent can often obtain quantity discounts by ordering large amounts of requested materials at one time. Buying more than is needed right away is called **forward buying**.
- *Order Monitoring*. The purchasing agent regularly checks important orders to make sure they are on schedule. Communicating with the supplier is crucial at this stage.
- *Order Delivery*. A receiving clerk checks the delivered goods against a copy of the purchase order. If the shipment is correct, the purchase is recorded and payment is made.

Inventory Control

Most firms keep plenty of inventory on hand. In this way, they are protected from such threats to their supply lines as a strike by the employees of a supplier. Ample inventories of finished goods also enable firms to meet a sudden surge of customer demand. And so we say that inventories cushion against both supply-side and demand-side shocks. Holding inventories is expensive, however, and this forces the production manager to evaluate the benefits of large inventories against the costs. This trade-off is pictured in

CONTROVERSIAL ISSUES

Quality control circles are small groups of relatively autonomous workers from a single industrial division of a company. They volunteer to meet a couple of times a month after work and are paid to discuss quality control and productivity problems. Should U.S. industries employ the same techniques?

Pro

Yes. Japanese industry has shown capabilities never dreamed of by those who reconstructed Japan's economy after the war. Japanese output is the most cost-effective, the most productive, and of the highest quality found anywhere in the world.

The Japanese worker-level participation is usual; those companies which do not have this participation are often among the relatively few firms which are not successful. At the same time, industry polls in the United States have shown that lack of quality is the single greatest criticism of American industry. Product recalls are common. Even the space program experiences delays and disappointments because of mechanical failures.

The Japanese have found that the more intelligent and the more educated its quality control circle members are, the more productive they are. By that standard, U.S. quality control circles should be fantastic. Why aren't U.S. firms using their human resources more wisely?

America Should Get on the Stick and Use Japanese Quality Control Methods.

For quality control circles to be effective, management has to trust the members and give them the important data they need as well as the authority to implement their ideas. U.S. industry is beginning to relinquish some of its traditional rights and is sharing financial data, profits, and product improvements with its employees. As a result, employees' interest in their companies is increasing. The time is ripe for workers to suggest and implement quality control circles. Quality circles work in Japanese industry. U.S. firms should try them too.

Con

No. Japanese quality control circles don't always work in Japan. We cannot expect them to work in the United States.

First, management in U.S. firms will *not* relinquish control over production. Management does not trust employees; after all, American executives are college-educated for the most part and usually enter business at a high level. Japanese executives are promoted up through the work force, so they have far more respect for worker capabilities.

Second, Japanese quality control circles give rewards only to the circle, not to individuals. In Japan, this is fine since workers still regard the company as a kind of family. In the United States, individuals expect to be rewarded personally, not as part of a group. That's why the use of technical quality control experts has always worked in the past and will always work in the future.

Third, U.S. industry is looking for—and needs—short-term answers just to survive. Quality control circles may work well, at least in Japan, but they are long-run solutions, and would not help U.S. industry now. Many plans in Japan took years to develop.

Finally, many people confuse Japanese quality control methods with actual Japanese output. The Japanese have new factories (all built since the war) and few unions with senior employees hanging on. They have rebuilt with the best technology in the world. They didn't have to compensate for outdated factories already in operation. In addition, Japan has been able to build its industry without the drain of supporting a large military establishment such as the United States maintains. Japan knows better than to credit its economic miracles to quality control circles. U.S. industry should realize that it needs more than just quality controls to be competitive with Japan. It has major rebuilding to do. So put our energies into more productive channels for now.

Figure 11-2, along with other typical production management trade-offs.

Inventory Costs. Three types of costs must be considered for proper inventory control: holding costs, ordering costs, and stockout costs. **Holding costs** refer to the expense of storing, or holding, the inventory in the firm's warehouse or on its stock shelves. Examples of such costs are warehouse rental and utility bills. **Ordering costs** are the expenses involved in placing an order. These are mostly paperwork and management time. **Stockout costs** result when the firm runs out of inventory. The dollar value of lost production time or the value of a lost sale and the possible decline in customer goodwill are examples of stockout costs.

As an example, holding costs for a Toyota retail dealership include the interest on loans required to purchase an order of cars from the factory and the cost of showroom space, and the cost of accessories (such as radios and tape decks) which are mounted in the cars and cannot be sold separately. Ordering costs include the cost of paperwork, customs fees, arranging shipping to the dealer's lot, taxes and title fees, and so on. If the dealership is out of a model, stockout costs include the profits lost when customers give up on a Toyota and buy a Honda instead. The long-term costs of stockout include the failure of those customers to return to the Toyota dealer when they buy another car. Also, repeated reports of stockouts may spread to other potential customers.

Reorder Point and Reorder Quantity. The total of the three inventory costs depends on the size of inventories at the **reorder point** (when an order is placed) and the **reorder quantity** (size of the order). Figure 11-3 shows how inventory levels may vary over time, the reorder point, and reorder quantity. If demand is known and steady from one day to the next, the reorder point is chosen so that new supplies are delivered just as the last product moves off the shelf. In the figure, average daily demand is ten units, and the time from order placement to delivery, called **lead time**, is three days. The firm reorders when the level of inventory drops to 10 × 3 = 30 units, and the reorder quantity is 80 units.

It is usually best to build some slack into an inventory control system. For example, it might be safer to reorder when inventory levels drop to 40 units rather than 30.

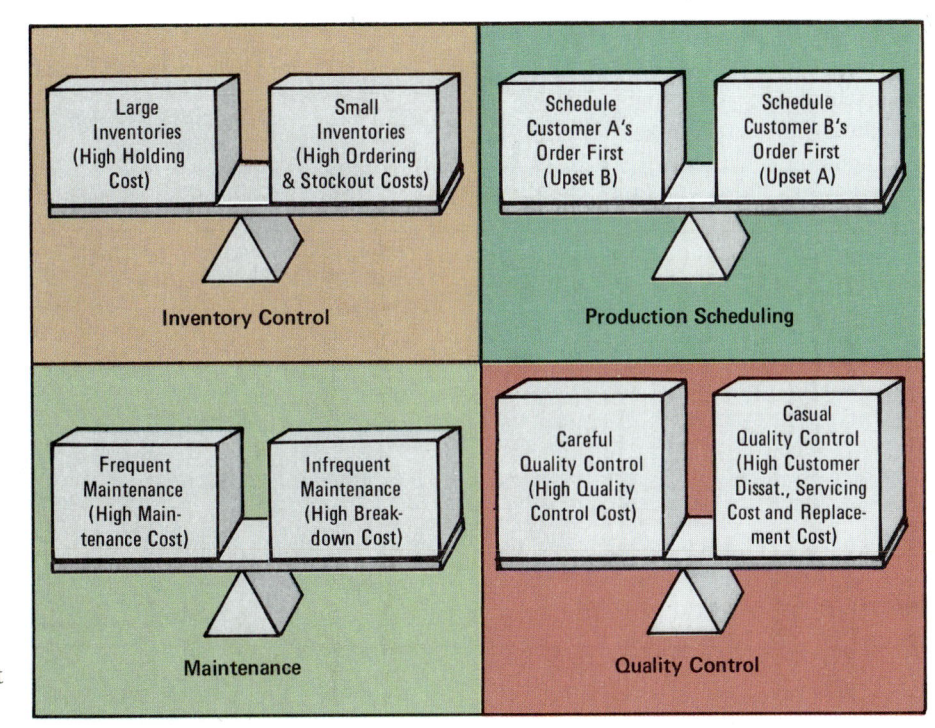

Figure 11-2

Production Management Trade-offs

Figure 11-3

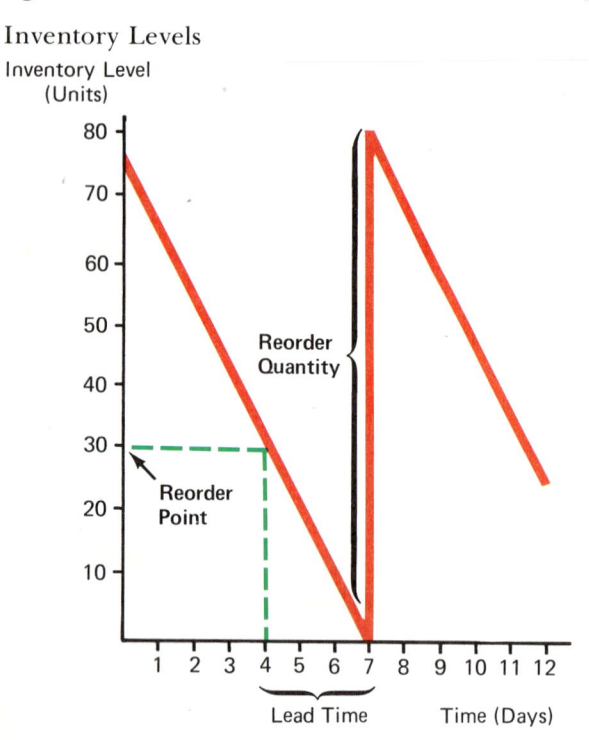

Inventory Levels

(graph showing inventory level in units over time in days, with labels for Reorder Quantity, Reorder Point, and Lead Time)

Economic Order Quantity. The choice of the best reorder quantity requires a balancing of the various inventory costs. If the reorder quantity is large, average inventories will be high, so holding costs will be high. If the reorder quantity is small, the number of separate orders will be high, so total ordering costs will also be high. If demand is not known with certainty, which is almost always the case, small inventories may result in disappointed customers. Here, a small reorder quantity may lead to high stockout costs. Holding costs, on the one hand, versus ordering and stockout costs on the other, determine the least-cost reorder quantity, or the **Economic Order Quantity (EOQ)**.

A Safeway store, which holds inventories of perishable goods, must determine an accurate EOQ for each of its products. Accuracy is especially important since profit margins are extremely small in the grocery trade and are quickly eaten up if inventories are too large and produce spoils, or if inventories are too small and customers are lost to other stores. The EOQ will be different for fresh lettuce than for canned soups or dried beans.

Keeping Track of Inventories. Many companies today keep a running count of their inventory levels. This is called a **perpetual inventory**. Under such an inventory system, the firm knows exactly how much inventory it has at any moment. Both additions to inventory and draw downs are immediately noted on the inventory records. This continuous method of accounting for inventory is maintained on a transaction-by-transaction basis. Computers are often used for this.

Under a **periodic inventory** system the firm does not keep a continuous count of inventory. Rather, at the end of each accounting period—six months or a year—the firm takes a physical count of the inventory. These periodic counts are often used as a check on the accuracy of a perpetual inventory system.

New Developments in Inventory Control. Two recent developments have changed the nature of inventory control. **Kanban**, a Japanese term that roughly translates to "just in time," is a method of inventory control whereby the firm maintains very small inventories. Suppliers deliver parts and other materials to an assembly line "just in time" for use. The cost savings of reduced storage under a precision Kanban approach can be substantial. General Motors is estimated to spend $3 billion annually to maintain its inventories valued at $9 billion. With kanban, analysts believe General Motors could cut this cost to about $1 billion.

"Who forgot to order the cabbage?"

Profile—
George Lucas

In the movie business, everything from stages and cameras to actor contracts, movie theaters, and promotional offices traditionally belongs to the big studios. So there was great concern throughout the industry when George Lucas, the creator of "Star Wars," "The Empire Strikes Back," and "Raiders of the Lost Ark" who also produced superb special effects in other successful movies, decided to break away from Hollywood protocol and form his own business.

Lucas grew up in Modesto, California, determined to be a race car driver. When he narrowly escaped death in a car crash, he decided the arts were more his style. The simplest art form, he decided, was film, so he persuaded a friend who was a famous cinematographer to help him get into the University of Southern California. In 1968, he produced and directed a science fiction movie short entitled "THX 1138." From it, he won a Warner Brothers scholarship, which brought him onto the film stage of "Finian's Rainbow," which was being directed by Francis Ford Coppola. Lucas and Coppola became close friends, and Coppola taught Lucas the importance of writing his own screenplays. Lucas then wrote and filmed a feature-length version of "THX 1138." In 1971 Lucas formed Lucasfilm Ltd. and subsequently wrote an original script for "American Graffiti." Lucas based the story on his own youth in Modesto, and he enlisted Coppola's help in selling the film. "American Graffiti" was a huge success, in great part due to Lucas' sense of vision. Lucas was on his way.

Lucas discovered, however, that he had no control over the film. The studio tried to recut it. "American Graffiti" was released without the stereophonic sound for which it had been specially written. Coppola and Lucas were unable to enter the studio because of a strike by the Screen Writers Guild, of which they were members, so they watched helplessly as the studio nearly ruined the film.

Lucas started writing "Star Wars" in 1972, and spent the next two years writing the original screenplay. He suspected then that there might be a market for Star Wars t-shirts, records, models, dolls, and countless other kinds of merchandise. He did no market research. When he sold the distribution rights for the movie to 20th Century Fox, he kept control of these merchandising rights.

When the film was released, the returns to Lucasfilm were phenomenal. In one month, $260,000 worth of Star Wars bubble gum was sold. George Lucas finally had the money he needed to make his company privately owned and completely independent of the big studios. Lucas owns the rights to sequels of "Star Wars" and has complete control over "The Empire Strikes Back," "Return of the Jedi," and succeeding Star Wars films.

Lucas used his own company to finance "The Empire Strikes Back" and "Raiders of the Lost Ark," so that all profits went to Lucasfilm. When his technicians and special effects company aren't engaged in producing films for him, Lucas sells their services to other producers. The effects of Steven Spielberg's smash hits "E.T." and "Poltergeist" were produced on the stages of Industrial Light & Magic, Lucas' special effects company.

To date, "Star Wars" has returned more than $230 million to 20th Century Fox, of which Lucasfilm received 40 percent—after advertising costs and a 30 percent distributing fee were subtracted. Sales of Star Wars merchandise totaled in excess of $200 million, of which Lucasfilm received over $20 million. When "The Empire Strikes Back" was released, it also become a blockbuster, and in anticipation of further profits accruing from "Return of the Jedi," Lucas' marketing division prepared an extensive promotional campaign long before filming of the movie was finished.

George Lucas epitomizes the entrepreneur. He started his own company to avoid the restrictions of the studios for which he could have worked. With a product that he hoped would sell, Lucas used the free enterprise system and the notion of private ownership to sculpt an empire of his own.

Ford and Chrysler have recognized savings of hundreds of millions of dollars by applying kanban techniques.

Materials requirement planning (MRP) is another new inventory control technique. When component parts are assembled into products, such as automobiles, they are not used independently of one another; instead, they are needed at exact times in the production cycle. They have to be ordered to fit into that cycle. MRP relies on computer programs to coordinate information about customer orders, the amount of various materials on hand, and the sequencing of production operations. A master schedule which helps guarantee that the right materials are available at the right time in the production cycle is then formulated.

PRODUCTION PLANNING AND CONTROL

Production planning and control is concerned with the ordering and monitoring of work-in-process. It includes control of the flow of materials, people, and machines. The aim is to use these resources in the most efficient way possible.

The Planning and Control Process

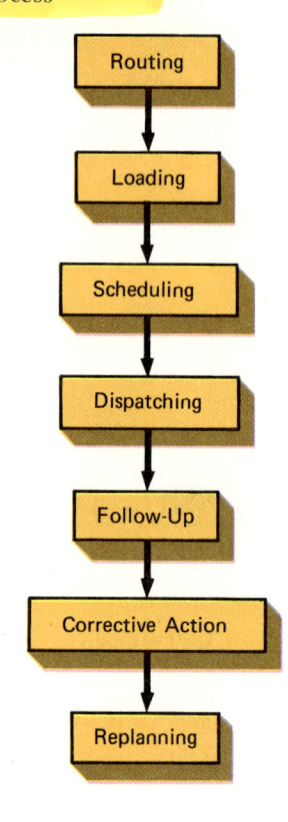

Effective planning and control involves seven basic steps or actions, as shown in Figure 11-4. Let's take a close look at each of these steps.

Routing. The movement of a mechanical part or other piece of work from one operation to the next traces out a route. **Routing** is the process of determining these work flows. In the case of an assembly line, the routing of work is built into the design of the plant itself. Volvo, for example, is famous for the efficiency of its automobile assembly lines. Even the Japanese automakers have inspected Volvo plants closely before building their own factories.

Loading. **Loading** refers to the process of determining how long it takes to perform a particular operation at a machine or work station and then adding that amount of time to the time for work already scheduled there. The result is a "load chart" showing how much each machine or work station will be used. Because of setup time, maintenance, and other factors, most machine tools cannot be used for more than seven hours of an eight-hour shift.

General Electric faces heavy production schedules for its Hotpoint air-conditioner assembly plants just before the summer starts. The company prefers to schedule its maintenance around this busy period so that it can load its plant as fully as possible. When the assembly line has to be set up for a new product, maintenance work is often done at night so it does not interfere with normal shift operations.

Scheduling. The planning and control function of **scheduling** refers to the process of determining *when* an operation is to be performed at a machine or work station. At McLouth Steel, foundries sometimes have to be booked weeks or months in advance for an operation that may take only a few hours. If the facilities are not available on time, an expensive batch of iron can be lost.

Figure 11-4

Steps in the Planning and Control Process

Routing → Loading → Scheduling → Dispatching → Follow-Up → Corrective Action → Replanning

Chapter 11 • Production Management 203

FROM THE FILE

> Karen was overwhelmed by the job she had been given. The job was to coordinate the move of her company's fruit and vegetable canning plant to a new location. The relocation would take months, at least, and a tremendous amount of coordination of effort. Some equipment, supplies, and workers would have to be moved before others. Karen could tell everyone to begin moving immediately, but she knew that wasn't necessary. In fact, it would be wasteful. She wondered what she should do. Was there a way to plan the move systematically?

Dispatching. After the routing, loading, and scheduling functions are performed, the start of each operation on the shop floor is authorized through **dispatching**, or the preparing and issuing of work orders. For example, if four machine operations are required, work orders for each operation would be prepared and issued at this point.

Follow-Up. Another function of production planning and control is keeping track of work completed and any time lags or delays that may have occurred. This is called **follow-up**. Some jobs will run behind schedule and others will always run ahead. With effective follow-up procedures, the time savings from jobs running ahead of schedule can be used to bring lagging jobs back on schedule.

Corrective Action. We might think that a well-managed plant would have everything running on schedule. In fact, though, a plant that does not encounter production delays sometimes is probably not being used efficiently. Because delays have to be expected in a well-run plant, management should be ready to deal with them. It may take such **corrective action** as scheduling overtime or shifting work to other machines.

The United States Postal Service, for example, usually operates at maximum capacity. When delays are encountered, post office managers schedule overtime or send part of their volume to post offices with additional automation, where sorting and delivery can be completed more efficiently.

Replanning. In response to changing market conditions, manufacturing methods, or labor force availability, new plans may sometimes be needed. The development of new routing, loading, and scheduling is called **replanning**. In the semiconductor industry, production managers have to develop new production schedules for new products weekly or monthly.

Planning and Control Procedures

Production managers have several analytical tools available to help them with production planning and control. We'll study two such tools now.

Schedule Charts. One simple way to keep track of work-in-process is with the schedule chart. The **schedule chart** shows when each of a series of job orders is to be performed at each machine, work station, or department. One such schedule chart, known as a **Gantt chart**, is shown in Figure 11-5. According to this figure, the production manager has scheduled several job orders on each of three lathes over a six-week period. Notice that lathe #1 is frequently idle and that the production manager has anticipated maintenance time and delays on lathes #2 and #3. Also, job order #16 is ahead of schedule. With scheduling charts, production managers are able to monitor the flow of materials through a production process or the flow of work through a job shop. And the production manager always knows the status of work performed in relation to work scheduled.

PERT and the Critical Path. Many times, a production manager has a major project to finish by a contract deadline. The project is made up of many separate activities or steps, each of which

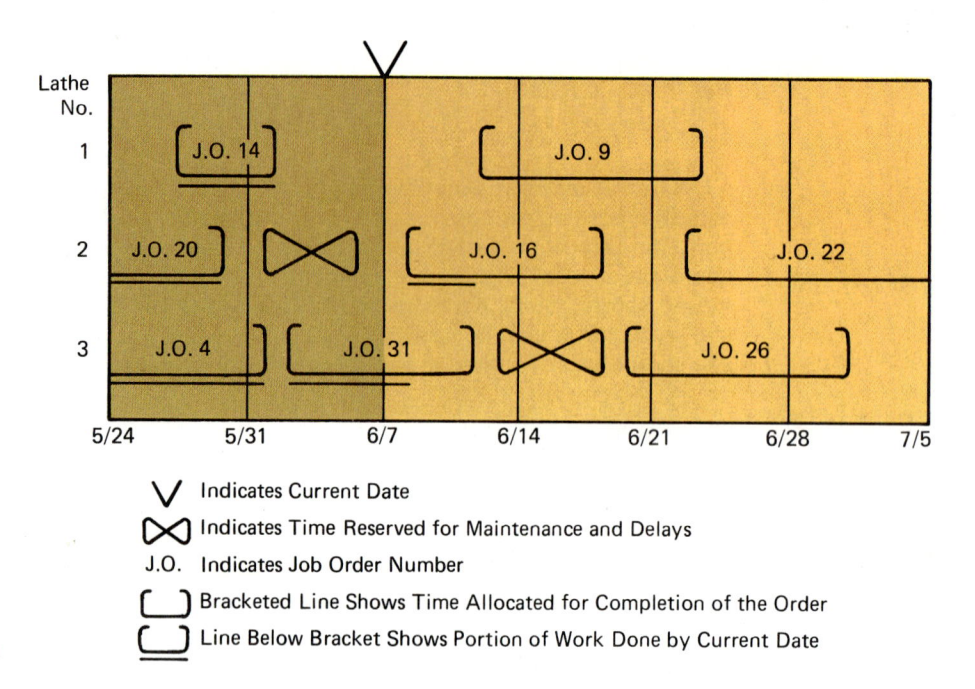

Figure 11-5

A Gantt Chart

requires a certain amount of time for completion. Usually, one activity cannot be started until another is completed. This activity, in turn, is followed by still others. The problem is to coordinate all these activities. Most projects, from the company picnics to the construction of an offshore oil drilling platform, fit this description. Some projects can involve many thousands of separate activities.

The production manager who is faced with such a project often develops a **Project Evaluation and Review Technique (PERT) chart**. An example of a PERT chart is shown in Figure 11-6. It depicts each activity involved in the completion of a project, the sequencing of these activities, and the time allotted for each activity.

Whenever possible, it is desirable to carry out several activities at the same time ("in parallel") rather than one after another ("in series"). In Figure 11-6, activities B and C can be performed at the same time because the start of one does not depend on the completion of the other. However, activity A must be completed before B and C can be begun. Thus, activity A and activities B and C must be performed "in series." In a marketing research project, for example, the choice of research goals necessarily precedes the writing of the survey questionnaire and the selection of data analysis methods.

The aim of a PERT network is to minimize project delays through effective scheduling of project activities. Such scheduling depends on the identification of the **critical path**. This is the sequence of in-series activities requiring the longest time for completion. In Figure 11-6, the sequence of activities along the critical path is such that the project cannot be completed in fewer than ten weeks. Activities B and C are "in parallel," but activity B is along the critical path because that path (ABDFG) takes the most time to complete. Activity C is on a path (ACEG) which takes only seven weeks to complete. So, activity C could be delayed as much as three weeks (10 − 7) without slowing project completion. Because activity C can be delayed somewhat without slowing down the project, it is not on the critical path.

It should be apparent by now that the completion of a project on time depends on the careful management and control of activities along the critical path. When necessary, the production manager can divert resources from noncritical activities to critical activities to get them done sooner. Also, the production manager can look for other opportunities to schedule activities in parallel which are now in series.

QUALITY CONTROL

Not too long ago, the term "Made in Japan," was synonymous with cheap products and inferior construction. It was usually written on the

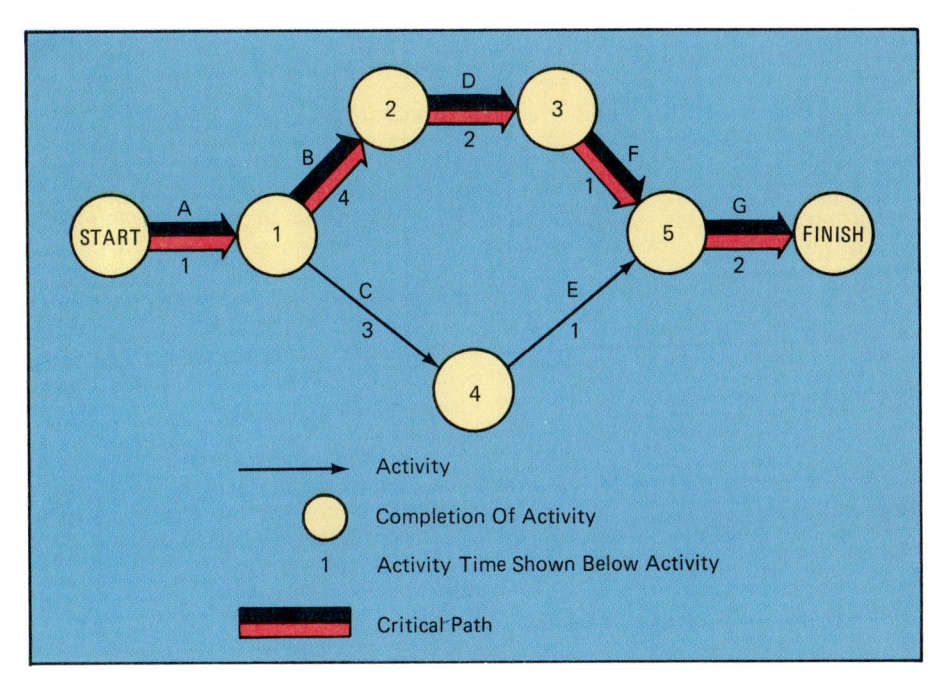

Figure 11-6

A PERT Chart

bottom of products found in discount bins. Now, however, consumers speak with pride about their Japanese autos, cameras, televisions, stereo systems, watches, and porcelain dinnerware. More often than not, it is U.S. products that are thought to be of inferior quality.

Many companies in this country have responded to the problem of declining product quality by setting up quality improvement programs for employees. For instance, "zero-defects" programs use a combination of posters, slogans, pep talks, and praise to encourage employees to work more carefully. **Quality circles** use a committee of workers that analyzes and solves problems relating to quality. Quality circles provide a form of participative management by letting workers make important inputs to key decisions. One company reported a 60 percent drop in product defects and a 10 to 20 percent jump in product quality as a result of a quality circle program.

Inspection

We can define **quality control** as the process of setting manufacturing standards and measuring products against these standards. **Inspection** refers to the second part of this definition: It involves comparing products against the standards, approving those that meet them, and rejecting those that do not. Inspection serves as a check on the quality of incoming material and finished goods.

Many advanced techniques, including ultrasonic and magnetic tests, X-rays, computerized scanners, and television cameras, are used for inspection. But some judgments, such as whether a wine tastes "bad" or a flaw is "serious enough" to cause rejection, cannot be made so objectively.

Statistical Quality Control

Statistical quality control was first applied in the Bell Telephone Laboratories in the early 1920s. W. Edwards Deming introduced statistical quality control concepts to Japan in 1950 and is widely credited with turning around product quality there in just a few years. The assumption behind **statistical quality control** is that most quality problems, perhaps as many as 85 percent, are the result of flaws in manufacturing systems, not of errors by production workers.

Random Variation or Out of Control. The goal is to determine whether something has gone wrong with the manufacturing system. Statistical quality control relies on the laws of probability to do this. By checking a sample of the output of a process and applying the right statistics, it is possible to tell whether the system is "out of control."

Plant Location Decisions

For most companies, the decision of where to locate a new plant, or to relocate an old plant, is a critical one. The location of a manufacturing facility with respect to raw materials, a skilled labor force, or customer markets can mean the difference between success or failure. Firms compete with one another by keeping transportation, labor, and distribution costs low. Imagine a lumber mill located on the high plains of Kansas. Or a bioengineering firm without a nearby supply of college graduates. Or a sod farm located far away from its customers. All of these firms would be at a severe competitive disadvantage.

The accompanying list suggests some important factors in plant location decisions. As the list shows, both cost and noncost factors are considered in these decisions. Most business costs have risen sharply in the past decade. Labor costs and taxes have each risen by 100 percent between 1970 and 1980. Transportation, construction, and utility costs have increased by more than 200 percent.

In times of economic slump, states and localities work hard to attract desirable industries. In the late 1970s, the number of states granting tax breaks to attract firms almost doubled. In addition, Ireland, Puerto Rico, and Canada are actively vying for new plants. Federal minimum wage laws and other nationwide standards may make plant location outside the United States more attractive in years to come.

Factors in Plant Location Decision		
Factors	Industry Where This Might Be Especially Important	Recent Developments
Cost Factors		
Labor Costs	Automotive	Labor costs are up, but minimum wage laws and nationwide competition for skilled labor have evened them out across the country.
Transportation Costs	Cement	These have gone up very rapidly since 1975. Trucking rates more than doubled and rail rates went up about four-fold.
Construction Costs	Warehousing	These have doubled since 1975. They still vary substantially across the country.
Utility Costs	Steel	Energy resources are quickly being used up. Costs are skyrocketing and will continue to be a major consideration.
Taxes	Oil	Many states and territories (particularly Puerto Rico) are now giving industries substantial tax breaks.
Noncost Factors		
Environmental Conditions	Paper	New laws and social pressure have had great impact on many companies. Industry has spent tremendous amounts on air pollution and waste disposal equipment.
Living Conditions	Various	Many employees are no longer willing to just go where the company tells them. Quality of life in the community is becoming more important.
Availability of Resources	Canning	Industry use of water will more than triple by the year 2000. Supplies are low in Los Angeles, Denver, and Chicago. The Gulf Coast from Texas to Alabama suffers from a shortage of groundwater.
Availability of Skilled Labor	Genetic Engineering	The labor force will decline in numbers by 1990, creating new labor shortages.

Without quality control, many products would be unsatisfactory.

To illustrate, suppose that our plant produces a machine part for oil well pumps. The part is designed to be 6" in diameter, but we know from experience that it is sometimes slightly more than or less than 6" for individual parts. Now suppose we pull one of the finished parts off the assembly line and find its diameter to be 6.01". Is this deviation of .01" simply a random, unimportant variation? Or is the deviation a sign that the production process is out of control, therefore requiring adjustment?

The Control Chart. To answer this question, we need to look at the past outputs of our production process and determine their average characteristics (such as the average diameter of 6") and the typical variation around these averages. We also need to know the probability that various deviations may have occurred by chance alone. These probabilities are provided by statistical analysis of the type considered in the Appendix in Part 6.

For example, it might be known that a part with a 6.01" diameter occurs ten times in a hundred by chance alone. Thus, our sampled part with the 6.01" diameter does not concern us very much because the deviation is very likely due to chance. But suppose the diameter of the sampled part was 6.03" and the probability of this occurring by chance was known to be only one in ten thousand. What then? In this case, we can be fairly sure that the production process is out of control and that more defective parts will be produced.

A control chart is usually used in conjunction with statistical control. A control chart for our example is shown in Figure 11-7. The chart shows the average diameter as well as an upper control limit and a lower control limit. If a part has a diameter greater than the upper control limit or smaller than the lower control limit—in this case, 6.02" and 5.98", respectively—the production system is somehow flawed. If the diameter is within that range, then the system is operating satisfactorily. These control limits might be measurements (such as the diameter in our example), frequencies (such as the number of bad light bulbs in a sample), or number of defects per unit (such as the number of flaws on a piece of glass).

Monitoring the Quality of Supplies

Quality control problems in production are often the result of poor quality inputs. Some companies have strong programs for ensuring the quality of incoming production materials and

Figure 11-7

A Control Chart

X (6.03")

———————— 6.02" Upper Control Limit

These values are so far from the average level that they probably were not caused by random fluctuations. We should check the system.

X (6.01")   These values would be expected to occur by chance. We don't have to check the system.

———————— 6.00" Average Value

X (5.99")

———————— 5.98" Lower Control Limit

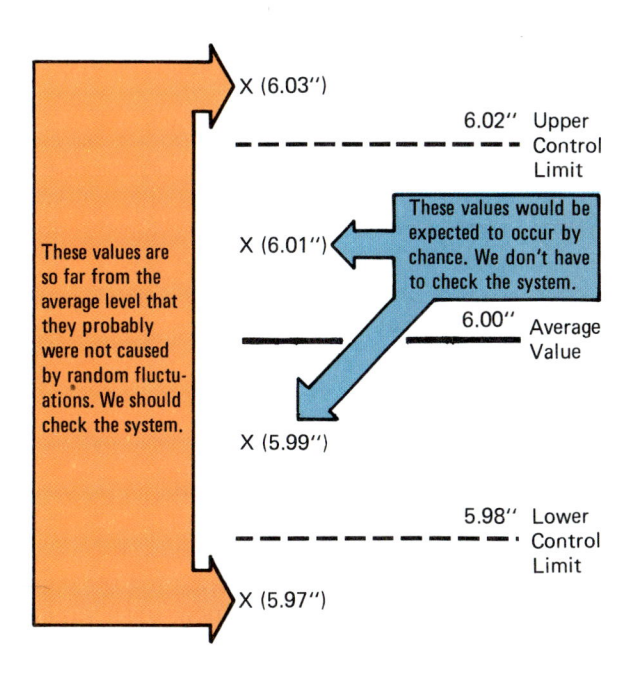

X (5.97")

"Hello? Beasts of the Field? This is Lou, over in Birds of the Air. Anything funny going on at your end?"

Source: Drawing by Ziegler; © 1974 The New Yorker Magazine, Inc.

supplies. Xerox has a four-point program to assist suppliers. From the beginning of its new product development process, Xerox involves its suppliers in writing specifications for production materials and components. Xerox makes sure that its suppliers understand these specifications before supply orders are placed. It also operates a hotline for suppliers who have any last-minute questions. Finally, Xerox uses statistical quality control on its suppliers' manufacturing systems, and it uses a team approach for a check on the packing and handling of materials. Marked quality improvements have been attributed to Xerox's program.

MAINTENANCE POLICIES

A breakdown in a large piece of production machinery can be extremely expensive in terms of lost production time and repair costs. Keeping production equipment in good repair is a big job: More than $14 billion a year is spent on maintenance alone by companies in the United States. Maintenance can take one of three forms.

- Corrective maintenance—fixing a machine that is not working properly.
- Preventive maintenance—designing, inspecting, and servicing machinery so that breakdowns are less likely to occur.
- Predictive maintenance—employing monitoring instruments to estimate when machine failure is most likely to occur.

Preventive maintenance is usually less costly than corrective maintenance and so is preferred by most production managers. Predictive maintenance is especially appropriate for complex, highly automated production processes.

Management should answer several questions concerning maintenance. For instance, how much maintenance is needed? Can computers and statistical methods be of help? Should an in-house maintenance staff be used or should outside people be brought in? Would preventive or predictive maintenance be less expensive?

Most maintenance policies are just good common sense. For instance, it is usually best to try to schedule maintenance for periods when things are slow. If much maintenance is needed during peak periods, thought should be given to contracting out some work. And, there is usually a "best" time to replace or service equipment. If done too soon, money is wasted; if done too late, repair may be costly or impossible.

SUMMARY POINTS

1. Production management is an important and complex task. The production manager must be concerned with both the short-run and long-run effectiveness of the production facility.
2. Transformation processes may produce outputs by changing inputs in form, place, or time. The modern manufacturing facility performs a form transformation. It is characterized by specialization, mechanization, and heavy reliance on computers and mathematical models.
3. About half of the sales dollar of most large firms is spent on purchasing. The steps of the purchasing cycle try to ensure that needed materials are acquired for the best possible prices.
4. Inventories serve as cushions between the firm and its environment. The decisions of when and how much to order depend on a balancing of various costs. Such tools as Economic Order Quantity (EOQ) help guide managers in making these decisions.
5. Production management involves many trade-offs. Inventory control, production scheduling, quality control, and maintenance all require careful juggling of various costs and competing interests.
6. Production planning and control coordinates work-in-process to see that materials, people, and machines are used in the best way possible. This requires determination of routes for parts, loading and scheduling or operations on machines, and subsequent control. Schedule charts and project planning methods help with production planning and control.
7. Inspection, quality control programs, and statistical quality control are useful in maintaining quality.
8. Maintenance may be corrective, preventive, or predictive in nature.

KEY TERMS AND CONCEPTS

production management
value added
production
form transformation
synthetic transformation
analytic transformation
temporal transformation
spatial transformation
continuous manufacturing
intermittent manufacturing
job shop
automation
management science
operations research
value analysis
forward buying
holding costs
ordering costs
stockout costs
reorder point
reorder quantity
lead time

Economic Order Quantity
perpetual inventory
periodic inventory
kanban
materials requirement planning
routing
loading
scheduling
dispatching
follow-up
corrective action
replanning
schedule chart
Gantt chart
PERT
critical path
quality circles
quality control
inspection
statistical quality control
control chart

REVIEW QUESTIONS

1. What is the production manager's task in the short run? in the long run?
2. Describe three types of transformation processes.
3. List and describe the steps in the purchasing cycle.
4. Describe four key trade-offs in production management.
5. What are the three costs associated with inventory control?
6. List the seven steps in the production planning and control process.
7. Discuss two analytical tools for production planning and control.
8. Explain how a control chart is used.
9. What are the three forms of maintenance?

DISCUSSION QUESTIONS

1. Give two examples of companies using:
   a. Synthetic transformation processes.
   b. Analytic transformation processes.
   c. Temporal transformation processes.
   d. Spatial transformation processes.
2. Consider the characteristics of the modern production facility. How do you think those characteristics affect efficiency? worker satisfaction? flexibility?
3. Which of the factors in the plant location decision do you think will become more important in the future? less important? Why?
4. Can you describe a product for which stockout costs might be especially important? unimportant?
5. Do you feel the quality of products made in the U.S. is lower than that of those made in Japan? in South America? in Germany? Do you feel quality differences are due more to statistical quality control, worker motivation, or other factors?

CASE 11-1

Lubella Furniture Company

Lubella Furniture Company is a small, high-quality furniture manufacturing plant located in northern Virginia. Lubella produces a wide line of stylish modern home furniture. This furniture is very solidly built with much more wood than is usually included in commercial furniture. It also features unusual metal fittings that allow the furniture to be taken apart for easy moving or shipping, all without the use of tools. For example, a sofa splits down into a back, a bottom, two sides, and cushions. The entire sofa can fit into a Volkswagen Rabbit—an advertising claim the manufacturers are quite proud of.

The manufacturers originally thought of the metal latch design as a way to promote "portable" furniture for people who move often and want the convenience of furniture that can be dismantled and transported easily. However, as production began, the company realized another very significant advantage of the design. Lubella found that on a very small assembly line, it could produce a large number of sofa sides, then a large number of sofa backs, then a large number of cushions, and so on. There was no need to work with one complete sofa at a time, so assembly-line techniques became much more efficient. It also became much easier to inventory the parts needed to assemble furniture than to inventory whole sofas, chairs, and loveseats. In fact, the manufacturers soon made minor design changes so that all their furniture used the same sides and cushions. Only the backs and bottoms were different. They designed the arms so that the metal latch fittings could be screwed onto either side of the arm. This way, only one arm assembly had to be created for all sofas, love seats, and chairs. Fittings could even be mounted on both sides of an arm to create an extended sofa or to attach end tables and other furniture—all of which used the same fittings.

Lubella found a very good response among the retail furniture stores that marketed its products. Lubella was an extremely small operation, with very limited funds and equipment. The company was always waiting for enough sales to come in so it could expand and develop a larger production line.

1. When Lubella performed value analysis, what criteria besides cost were being considered? Which criteria were most important?
2. Is forward buying a good idea for Lubella? Why or why not? What kinds of discounts might Lubella be able to enjoy from its suppliers?
3. Compare the different kinds of inventory costs Lubella has to face. Which are the most significant to Lubella?
4. How does the design of Lubella's product make materials requirement planning easy or difficult?

CASE 11-2

Williams Greenhouses

Ellen Williams has for five years run a small greenhouse selling plants wholesale to retail plant dealers. She built the greenhouse on the outskirts of St. Louis, Missouri. Her business has prospered until she now has more orders for plants than she has room for in her greenhouse. She either must expand her greenhouse or move elsewhere.

Ellen delivers plants to greenhouses early in the spring. She specializes in unusual ferns and other semitropical house plants which are highly temperature sensitive. Retail plant dealers in most of the country buy only in the spring when they feel sure that a late freeze won't kill the contents of their greenhouses or cost so much in utility bills to destroy their profits. Ellen, of course, faces the same kinds of problems. The small pots of plants are easily shipped; she usually loads a van with several thousand plants and delivers them to retailers throughout the Midwest and South a few weeks before Easter each year.

Ellen spoke to a business consultant at her bank about expanding or moving her operation. He pointed out that she could obtain a long-term lease on some land, build a greenhouse, and purchase the necessary heating equipment; he is prepared to extend her the financing necessary, although he admits that interest rates are still rather high. He also pointed out that St. Louis is in a central location for shipping plants around the country; good highways run out of St. Louis in all directions (since she delivers plants herself, she does not have to worry about trucking costs). With high unemployment in St. Louis, Ellen can get plenty of inexpensive help.

Ellen also spoke to a retailer who carries a large variety of plants grown by a wholesaler in Edinburg, Texas. The retailer referred her to the wholesaler for more information. The wholesaler pointed out the following advantages of moving to Edinburg: Because winters are very mild, utility costs are very low; there is plenty of rural land available, and it can be purchased (which has many tax advantages); there is no income tax in Texas; there are plenty of people looking for work in Edinburg who would be willing to work for low wages; Edinburg has good access to major north- and east-bound interstate highways, so shipping to retailers is fairly simple. The only problem with Edinburg, according to this wholesaler, is the 400- to 700-mile drive to get out of the state—it is a BIG state! But the plant business is booming in Texas, and Ellen might be able to make all her sales within Texas.

1. Having heard the advantages and disadvantages of St. Louis and Edinburg, where should Ellen locate her expanded greenhouse? Why?
2. Ellen was assuming that she would continue to deliver her plants herself. (She enjoyed this part of the greenhouse business the most.) If her operation

expanded, and she had to remain at the greenhouse and have a shipping company send her plants, how might her choice change? Would Edinburg be more or less favorable? What about St. Louis?
3. What other factors should Ellen take into consideration in moving to Edinburg?

Inventory Control

Your inputs to this program include the annual storage cost per unit, the cost to place an order, the units of demand per year, and the number of days it takes to receive an order. The program computes the amount that should be ordered to minimize total costs (reorder quantity) as well as the inventory level at which an order should be placed (reorder point). It then gives you the option to perform another analysis.

Here's the Program

```
10 PRINT
20 PRINT "********INVENTORY CONTROL ANALYSIS********"
30 PRINT
40 INPUT "ANNUAL STORAGE COST PER UNIT..$";CS
50 INPUT "COST PER ORDER.................$";CO
60 INPUT "UNITS OF DEMAND PER YEAR.......";D
70 INPUT "DAYS UNTIL ORDER IS RECEIVED...";TR
80 Q=SQR(2*CO*D/CS)
90 Q=INT(Q*100+.5)/100
100 PRINT
110 PRINT "********INVENTORY CONTROL RESULTS********"
120 PRINT
130 PRINT "ANNUAL STORAGE COST PER UNIT...$";CS
140 PRINT "COST PER ORDER.................$";CO
150 PRINT "UNITS OF DEMAND PER YEAR.......";D
160 PRINT "DAYS UNTIL ORDER IS RECEIVED....";TR
170 PRINT "REORDER QUANTITY (UNITS).........";Q
180 R=TR*D/365
190 R=INT(R*100+.5)/100
200 PRINT "REORDER POINT (UNITS)............";R
210 PRINT
220 PRINT "---------------------------------------------"
230 PRINT
240 INPUT "ANOTHER ANALYSIS? (1=YES;2=NO)";X
250 IF X=1 THEN GOTO 10
260 END
```

Here's Sample Output

Two sets of output are provided. All inputs are summarized in the output. Try some other runs using your own figures.

```
********INVENTORY CONTROL RESULTS********
    ANNUAL STORAGE COST PER UNIT...$ 10
    COST PER ORDER..................$ 100
    UNITS OF DEMAND PER YEAR........ 12500
    DAYS UNTIL ORDER IS RECEIVED.... 5
    REORDER QUANTITY (UNITS)........ 500
    REORDER POINT (UNITS)........... 171.23

    ----------------------------------------

********INVENTORY CONTROL RESULTS********
    ANNUAL STORAGE COST PER UNIT...$ 10
    COST PER ORDER..................$ 100
    UNITS OF DEMAND PER YEAR........ 8000
    DAYS UNTIL ORDER IS RECEIVED.... 5
    REORDER QUANTITY (UNITS)........ 400
    REORDER POINT (UNITS)........... 109.59

    ----------------------------------------
```

Questions

1. Will the optimal reorder quantity go up, go down, or remain unchanged if:
   a) Annual storage costs per unit increase? Why?
   b) Stockout costs per unit increase? Why?
   c) The number of days to receive an order increases? Why?
2. What is the relationship between the reorder quantity and the average inventory level?
3. In the second sample run, the number of days to receive an order was 5 and the optimal reorder point was about 110 units. What would be the approximate optimal reorder point if the number of days to receive an order were 10?

Marketing Management

4

12

Marketing: The Strategic Input

After studying this chapter, you should be able to:

- Explain the functions of marketing in society.
- Identify the four marketing mix variables and discuss how business managers use them to sell the firm's products.
- Discuss the marketing concept.
- Explain the importance of market segmentation, how it's done, and what it tells the firm.
- Explain how marketing research tells the firm about market conditions.

"Nothing happens until a sale is made"—an old saying but one with more than just a grain of truth to it. A business can make the right investment, production, and management decisions, but if it does not have the right product available for the market at the right time and place, then all its other efforts have been wasted. Even though marketing may not be any more important than the other business functions, the success of the enterprise is determined in the marketplace.

People sometimes complain of not being able to "see the forest for the trees." What they are saying is that they are too close to a situation to see it clearly. Phrased a different way, they need to "see the big picture." So it is with marketing. You will have a better understanding of how marketing works for a firm if you first recognize marketing's role in society. We will first look at macromarketing—the forest—and then at micromarketing—the trees.

MACROMARKETING—THE FOREST

The purpose of marketing is to create time and place utility for the buyer. What do we mean by time and place utility? Utility is a general measure of the extent to which a product or service satisfies a consumer need. It is created when the characteristics of a product match the needs of the buyer. **Time utility**, therefore, is a measure of whether the product is available *when* the buyer wants it. **Place utility** is a measure of whether the product is available *where* the customer wants it. All our purchases are attempts to maximize time and place utility.

Time and place utility are created by marketing. For example, think of fresh bread at the bakery. The product itself creates utility—bread is nutritious, it tastes and smells good, and purchasing it is easier than baking it yourself. But what if you could buy bread only on Mondays at a bakery located 30 miles from your house? Now, imagine that the same bakery sold its bread through several nearby supermarkets, and they were open seven days a week. Doesn't this second situation, in which the product is more actively marketed, bring an added convenience to you, the buyer? This added benefit or convenience is time and place utility.

The creation of time and place utility is responsible for about one half of the cost of consumer products. If a product costs $1.00, then raw materials, labor, and overhead account for $.55, and moving the product from the factory to the final consumer accounts for $.45. This is not to say that marketing simply inflates the price of products. We have already seen that marketing adds value to products in the form of time and place utility. The extra $.45 in our example is a measure of that added value.

The cost of marketing products and services can be reduced through gains in efficiency. There are three major ways that marketing makes more efficient the sale of goods and services in society. They are the information, inventory, and exchange functions. Together, these three functions comprise **macromarketing**, the study of how goods and services are distributed from buyers to sellers. Macromarketing concerns the economy as a whole. Let's take a closer look at the three functions of macromarketing.

Information Function

An effective marketing system acts as an information network linking together producers and consumers. Information flows from producers to consumers in a continuous, back-and-forth pattern. This information is important if producers are to meet the changing needs of consumers in a cost-efficient manner, and if consumers are to maximize the utility of their purchases.

The automobile industry is an example of how this information function works. Automobile manufacturers look to the market to see which features, options, and economy ratings people want in a new car. Manufacturers analyze the

Goods and services must be available when and where customers want them.

safety and mileage standards required by the government. They also check with their suppliers to find the lowest cost combination of glass, steel, rubber, and other production inputs. The buying public examines model prices, dealer information, and such automobile magazines as *Road and Track* in order to get the best buy. The more timely and accurate the information flowing through the network, the more efficient the market. Figure 12-1 illustrates the information flows in the automobile market. Note that some of the communication flows are two-way while others are one-way.

Inventory Function

Merchandise does not move in an even stream from producers to consumers. Both supply and demand change over time, sometimes surging ahead and other times dropping off. The ups and downs of the production cycle are not always matched with the ups and downs of the consumption cycle. The task of equating supply and demand falls on the marketing system, specifically, on the inventory function.

Inventories are built up when production is strong and demand is slack. Inventories are drawn down when production is weak and demand is brisk. If the entire United States wheat crop were put on the market immediately after the autumn harvest, the price of wheat would fall so low that most farmers would be wiped out. The problem for the wheat farmer is that demand is fairly constant over the year, but production tends to peak in certain months. As a result, much of the wheat crop is stored for several months and is only gradually released to the market. This keeps supply and demand in line and makes the price of wheat fairly stable. The trade-off for the farmer is between the increase in price that results from temporarily withholding wheat from the market and the added cost involved in warehousing it. In this example, these storage costs are more than offset by the higher market price.

Exchange Function

The marketing system also centralizes the exchange of goods and services. This increases distribution efficiency for society and creates time and place utility for individual buyers. Consider an economy consisting of five businesses. Each business produces an extra amount of a product and trades that surplus for some of the products made by the other businesses. Figure 12-2A shows that ten separate exchanges are required if our miniature economy has no central market. Figure 12-2B shows that only five exchanges are needed when centralized exchange is introduced. In the same way, think of how trading is centralized in the stock, bond, or gold markets. Think how much easier it is for us to shop when products from many manufacturers are brought together in a large shopping center.

MICROMARKETING—THE TREES

While macromarketing is the study of how goods and services are moved from producers to

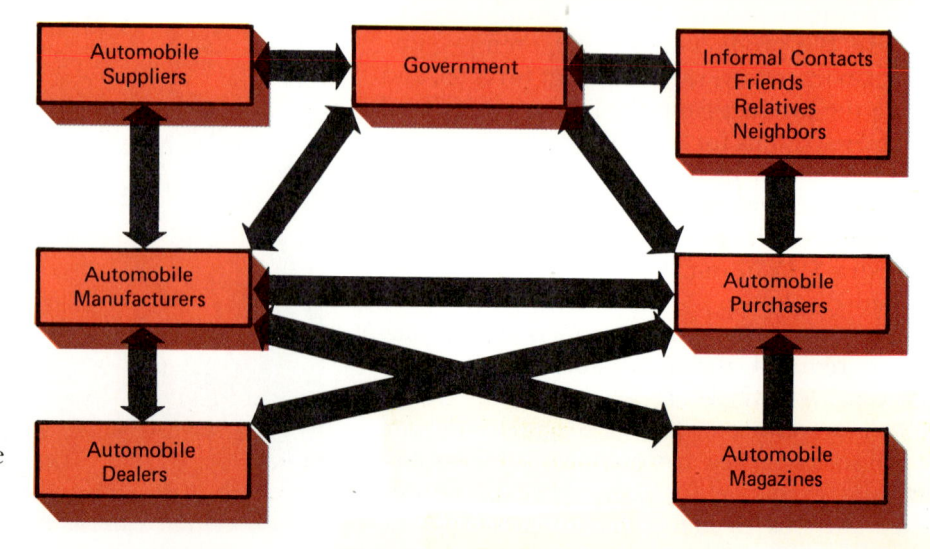

Figure 12-1

The Automobile Information Network

Figure 12-2

Exchanges in Decentralized and Centralized Markets

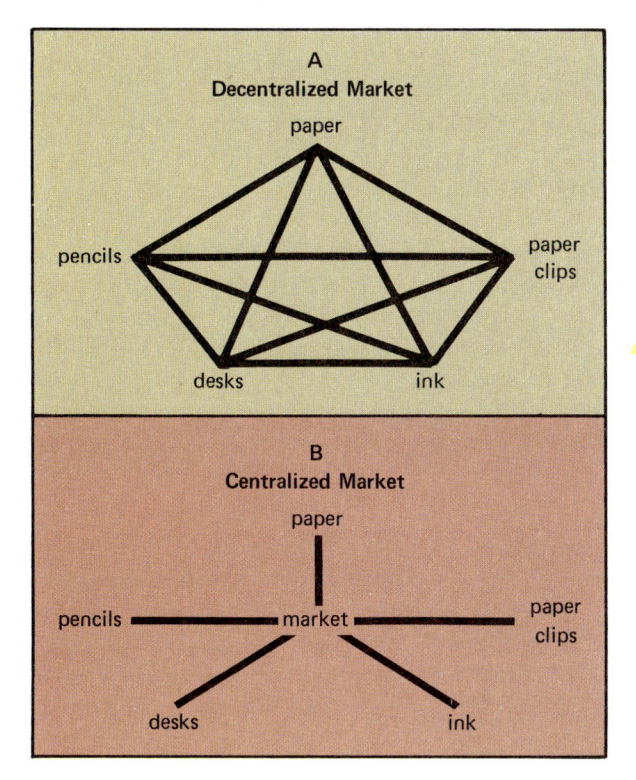

consumers micromarketing focuses on the individual firm and the decisions its managers must make in a competitive world. In other words, micromarketing represents the trees in the forest. **Micromarketing** is the process of planning and carrying out a product development, distribution, pricing, and communications strategy that enables the firm to earn a profit.

Four Key Elements of the Marketing Mix

Marketing decisions involve four key elements—product, distribution, price, and communication. These elements combined make up the **marketing mix**. Every marketing strategy involves decisions about which products to make available to the marketplace, where to sell them, how much to charge for them, and what to tell the public about them. Weakness in any decision area could mean the failure of a product or low profits for the firm.

The marketing mix for each product is different. Note the product, distribution, price, and communication decisions and the way they are combined in the marketing mix for automobile batteries and for men's shaving cream. Figure 12-3 illustrates that the marketing mix for batteries is much different from the marketing mix for men's shaving cream. Let's take a closer look at the elements of the marketing mix.

Product. The product element is concerned with developing a product that people are willing to buy. The product must satisfy a customer need; otherwise, people won't want it. Specific product decisions concern size, color, brand name, packaging, and product options. But the marketing manager is concerned about more than just physical features. A product is made up of all the factors a customer considers in making a purchase. For example, how is the product to be serviced? What about installation? Should the product carry a warranty? If so, what kind of warranty? What kind of reputation will the product have?

Distribution. The distribution element of the marketing mix refers to where the product is sold, how it is delivered, and by whom. Distribution decisions involve manufacturers, retailers, and a variety of intermediaries, or wholesalers. The group of marketing institutions which links together the manufacturer and the consumer is called the **channel of distribution**. Wholesalers and retailers are examples of such institutions.

The right distribution decisions create time and place utility for the buyer, which means more profit for the seller. Marketing managers need to answer many questions when constructing a channel of distribution: Who should sell the product? Should the manufacturer own the distribution network, or should a wholesaler be used? How much inventory should be kept at the retail level and at the wholesale level? What types of stores should sell the product?

Price. How much to charge for a product is one of the most important decisions facing managers. Pricing decisions involve more than the number on the price tag. They also involve discounts, markups, and delivery terms. We will look at these factors in Chapter 15.

The pricing decision can be simple if the product is similar to other ones on the market. Here, the firm sets the selling price roughly equal to the market prices of competing products. But, if the product has features that make it different

Figure 12-3

The Marketing Mix for Automobile Batteries and Men's Shaving Cream

	Automobile Batteries	Men's Shaving Cream
Product	Short-, Medium-, and Long-lived Batteries	Regular, Mentholated, etc. Shaving Cream
Distribution	New Car Manufacturers; Replacement Battery Market—Gasoline Stations, Sears, Montgomery Ward	Drugstores, Supermarkets, Discount Stores
Price	$20.00-$120.00	$0.59-$1.85
Communications	Direct Sales to Automobile Manufacturers; Primarily Newspapers for Replacement Market	Primarily Television and Magazines; Store Displays

from competing products, or if it is an entirely new product, then the decision is much more difficult. Should the product be priced to earn immediate profits or long-term profits? Should price be based on demand or on cost factors? Would a higher price or a lower price earn greater total profits? Do buyers believe price is a direct indication of product quality? How should one model of the product be priced in relation to a slightly different model?

Communications. Even a great product cannot sell itself. People must be told about the product before they can buy it. Some businesses promote their products through personal selling, that is, through direct face-to-face interaction between a salesperson and the customer. Avon sells its cosmetic products this way. Most makers of consumer products, however, rely on advertising to reach their markets. They may supplement their advertising with point-of-purchase displays, free samples, and coupons.

Whatever the methods used, the firm must communicate with the public. Otherwise its products will grow old on the shelf. This is just as true of service organizations as it is of product manufacturers. Airlines tell the public about new routes, changing ticket prices, and the comfort of their flights. Even the United Way advertises to convey its service messages to the public. Some of the questions that businesses and nonprofit organizations ask themselves are: Should we advertise directly to the final consumer? Or should we direct our advertisements at wholesalers? How much should we spend on advertising? Should we give away free samples? How should we pay salespeople? How should we select new salespeople? What about plant tours and other publicity devices?

Marketing Mix Interaction

Just as managers must work together as a team if the firm is to operate efficiently, so must the elements of the marketing mix work together. A decision with respect to one element has an impact on decisions for the others. Figure 12-4 depicts this interaction.

Figure 12-4

Interaction of Marketing Variables

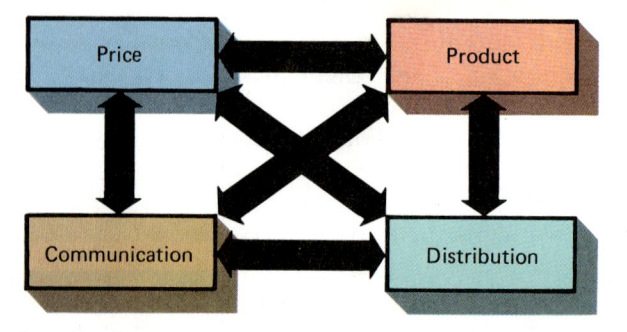

CONTROVERSIAL ISSUES

The Marketing Concept! Is It a Hoax?

The marketing concept began as a philosophy to replace the sell-at-any-cost, unpleasant and demanding sales and marketing approaches used by most companies. But isn't the marketing concept just a cover-up for the same old methods of selling?

Pro

Yes, in fact, if we look around at today's advertising, we can't help laughing at the marketing concept. If marketing efforts are really aimed at satisfying customer needs, how can we justify plastering our countryside with billboards, cheapening our streets with neon lights, and filling our magazines and television shows with ads which are often offensive?

Marketing research is hardly ever really looking for what the consumer wants. That's another hoax of the marketing concept. Marketing research is used to find how much of a product a company can sell and where the company can sell it. Most companies already have the product and want only to anticipate profits.

Consider, for example, how the American auto industry responded to fuel shortages. Ideally, according to the marketing concept, the auto companies would have examined changing American demands and retooled their factories to produce small fuel-efficient cars. Instead, they decided to sell existing models, and they used aggressive advertising to downplay the length and severity of the oil crisis and to extol the other features of their cars.

The Japanese automakers, however, when faced with the same problem, rebuilt and reinvested to improve their product as demand changed. They were successful because they met the needs of car buyers everywhere. But why didn't U.S. auto manufacturers try to implement the marketing concept?

The reason is obvious. American companies won't use the marketing concept. It is a hoax—a nice way to cover the fact that American companies are interested in selling what they already have, ignoring the demands of consumers. They seem to think that advertising will eventually buy anyone's purchasing power.

Con

Sure, companies have failed to fully implement the marketing concept. But that isn't the fault of the philosophy. The marketing concept was created as an ideal that companies should aspire to, and not as a way to describe what already existed.

Let's consider a company that implemented the marketing concept properly. Sony had been getting letters for years, demanding that companies make small portable tape recorders with decent earphones.

Sony devoted millions of dollars to researching what precisely the consuming public *wanted*. Sony discovered that people liked the idea of a tape recorder they could carry around, even while jogging. That meant that the recorder had to be moisture resistant and sturdy enough to avoid inevitable drops and pounding. Sony also discovered that people liked the idea of a device similar to the portable tape recorder, but which used FM radio signals instead of tapes as a source of music.

The result was the Sony Walkman—a well-made tape recorder that is durable, gives extremely good sound reproduction, and uses very comfortable earphones. The FM radio version features all the same characteristics. Sony's price was high at first—up to $350—but the company planned from the beginning to lower the price quickly so it would be affordable for all users.

Sony remained receptive to changes in consumer demand. People wanted two headphone jacks on a single Walkman, so two people could listen to the same tape. Other people wanted a Walkman that could both play and record—the original Walkman recorder could not record. Still others wanted both FM and tape capability in a single unit. Sony used marketing research—properly, according to the marketing concept—to determine what different groups of people wanted.

Sony responded with new Walkman models, all priced to meet the pocketbooks of the intended consumers and all with the features desired by those consumers. Improvements and changes were made immediately, buyers got a quality product, and Sony made plenty of money.

Sony proved the marketing concept works. The philosophy is a good one when used properly.

Promotion is an important element in the marketing mix. Do you know what company promotes pineapple?

Many products fail in the marketplace because the firm does not coordinate its marketing mix decisions. A California-based consumer products firm introduced a food blender to the New York market during Christmas. The product had several advantages over competing products and was roughly 25 percent less expensive. The firm advertised the product heavily, and New York stores ran out almost immediately; the manufacturer simply did not have a distribution system that could meet the large number of orders. Consequently, most of the promotional dollars were wasted, and many interested customers were turned away.

This type of mistake could have been avoided if the manufacturer had considered the interactions among the marketing mix elements. The firm should have reviewed some combination of higher price and less promotion in order to control demand until its distribution system was improved.

THE MARKETING CONCEPT

The **marketing concept** is a contemporary philosophy of business. It says that marketing is a customer-oriented activity. The objective of the firm, and of the marketing department, is to develop products that satisfy customer needs, not just to produce high-quality goods and services.

Schlitz and the Marketing Concept

A well-known American company that got into trouble because it lost track of the market is the Schlitz Brewing Company. Schlitz was the second largest selling beer in the country for many years. In 1977, though, Schlitz altered the brewing process and produced what many industry experts believed to be an inferior beer. Unfortunately for Schlitz, the beer-drinking public agreed with the experts, and consumption of Schlitz in 1980 fell to nearly 25 percent below the 1978 level.[1]

Schlitz made the mistake of focusing more on its product costs than on the market. It disregarded the marketing concept when it overlooked the potential consumer reaction to the new brewing formula in the increasingly competitive, taste-conscious beer market. Why do you suppose Schlitz tampered with a successful product?

Schlitz has now returned to the "classic" Schlitz formula. Also, much of Schlitz's 1980-1982 advertising stressed the fact that its new president, Frank Sellinger, is an expert brewmaster committed to making a high-quality beer. Al-

---

[1] Christy Marshall, "Turnaround Plans: New Products, Flagship Brand are Keys to Schlitz Salvation," *Advertising Age* (January 14, 1980), pp. 3, 72, and Jacques Neher, "Taste: That's Key to Schlitz Drive," *Advertising Age*, Vol. 51, No. 18, pp. 2, 90.

though Schlitz's new management may be able to return the company to its traditional place in the market, it is clear that the company lost money because of its decision to change the brewing process.

Substitutes and Profits

The marketing concept is based on two important principles. An understanding of them can save a firm from the kind of problem that Schlitz encountered.

Belief in Competitive Substitutes. A firm which practices the marketing concept realizes that even its most profitable product will someday be obsolete. It monitors the changing needs of its customers so that it may be the one to bring out the new item that replaces the original. Success, however, makes many firms complacent, and they stay with the same old products year after year. They may be surprised when their products are no longer wanted by the buying public.

A classic example of complacency in the face of rapid market change can be found in the railroad locomotive industry. Steam-powered locomotives, most of them made by the American Locomotive Company, once pulled all of this country's trains. When diesel locomotives were introduced by General Motors and General Electric, the railroads converted to diesel power. Because the American Locomotive Company did not foresee the impact of these diesel engines, the last steam locomotive produced by the company was sent directly to the Smithsonian Institution as an "antique." Figure 12-5 lists other products that became obsolete overnight. Do you remember any of these "old products"?

Concern with Profit, Not Sales. Business firms must make a profit if they are to continue serving the needs of the market. A firm must make enough money to pay all its expenses and to provide income for its investors. According to the marketing concept, the task of marketing is to increase profits, not simply to increase sales. The entry of General Electric into the booming computer market shows why sales do not always mean profits.

A few years ago, General Electric ventured into the computer business, competing directly against IBM, Control Data, and Honeywell. Looking to the future, GE made a detailed study of the market and decided that it did not have a good chance to earn a profit because of the intense competition in the industry. It then sold its computer division to Honeywell.

MARKET SEGMENTATION

Most businesses do not attempt to sell their products to every person or firm in the United States. Instead, they pick out smaller markets within the overall market and direct their selling efforts at these **target segments**. The process of identifying these segments and modifying the product or the firms' selling strategies to match the characteristics of each segment is known as **market segmentation**.

Volkswagen—USA

For many years, the Volkswagen "Beetle" was the best selling imported car in the United States. Volkswagen's strategy was simple: sell as many of the same basic automobile as possible to the price-conscious, small-car market. This market segment was made up primarily of young, college-educated people who were short on cash and long on affection for the economical "bug." What they wanted was what they got: a rear-

Figure 12-5

Examples of Obsolete Products and Their Replacements

Market	Old Product	New Product
Cities	Trolley Cars	Buses
Education and Engineering	Slide Rules	Slide-Rule Calculators
Accounting	Adding Machines	Printing Calculators
Data Processing	Punch Card Systems	Computers
Private Homes	Wood Stoves for Cooking	Electric Stoves for Cooking

engine, air-cooled, four-passenger, easy-to-maintain automobile.

In the early 1970s, the economy car market in the United States changed dramatically. Japanese automobile manufacturers—Datsun, Toyota, Mazda, Subaru, and Honda—flooded the U.S. car market with small cars in every shape, color, style, and design. These producers took the small car market, previously dominated by Volkswagen, and broke it up into many smaller market segments. Economy-minded customers no longer had to purchase a two-door, rear-engine car when what they really wanted was a four-door station wagon. As a result of this competition, Volkswagen began to diversify and introduced a series of new cars—Rabbit, Dasher, Scirocco, and then Jetta, Quanta—to meet the needs of individual market segments.

Two Approaches to Market Segmentation

There is no single "best" way to segment markets; a segmentation approach that works for one market will not always work for another. The business executive should study a variety of courses before deciding which is appropriate for the situation at hand. Two of the easiest methods of segmenting markets are **demographic segmentation** and **geographic segmentation**.

Demographic Segmentation. The most widely used segmentation variables are demographic, such as income, ethnic background, and age.

Income. Family income is often very useful in segmenting markets. The German statistician Ernst Engel first noticed that as family income increases, the percentage spent on clothing and transportation increases, the percentage of income spent on food decreases, and the percentage spent on housing remains constant. The producers of expensive cars, homes, and vacations, then, aim their marketing campaigns at high-income families. More recent research has shown that income is a useful segmentation tool for such items as cosmetics, detergents, paper towels, beer, frozen foods, furniture, and women's and men's clothing.[2]

For example, even though income is not evenly distributed throughout society, high-income families are quite easy to identify. As Figure 12-6 on page 226 shows, high-income families, when compared with the population as a whole, have the following characteristics: the head of the family is between 45 and 64 years of

---

[2] James H. Myers, Roger R. Stanton, and Arne F. Haug, "Correlates of Buying Behavior: Social Class vs. Income," *Journal of Marketing* (October, 1971), p. 12; James H. Myers and John F. Mount, "More on Social Class vs. Income as Correlates of Buying Behavior," *Journal of Marketing* (April, 1973), p. 73.

Most firms segment their markets. How many bases for segmentation can you identify in these photos?

age, went to college, works as a professional or manager, and lives in the suburbs.

Ethnic Background. A second set of demographic variables useful for segmenting markets includes nationality, religion, and race. For example, research has shown that Hispanic-Americans, even though they come from many different countries, usually prefer brand-name products.[3] In the same manner, religion influences some aspects of market behavior. Jewish people are the major buyers of Kosher foods; Mormons do not buy tobacco or liquor; Christian Scientists do not visit doctors or use medicine. Using race as a predictor of some market behavior, researchers found that black people, on a per capita basis, consume about half the amount of coffee as do white people.[4]

Age. Many marketing managers find that segmenting markets by age works well for their products. Families with infants are the primary market for baby foods. People over 65 years of age are the principal users of medical services and prescription drugs. But other aspects of age are not quite so obvious. Firms that sell products to teenagers must study teenagers' ever-changing social attitudes in order to decide which products are in demand. One way to do this is to determine what influence current popular entertainers have on the teenage market.

It is also important for the marketing manager to define both the percentage and the geographic distribution of the age group of interest. In other words, how big is the target age group and where do its members live? Figure 12-7 on page 227 shows that the number of children under the age of five will increase as a percentage of the population until 1990 and then decrease through year 2000. This type of population change will have a major impact on manufacturers of baby food, diapers, toys, and children's breakfast cereals.

Geographic Segmentation. Another relatively easy way to segment markets is geographically—or by region. The demand for many products varies from one section of the country to another and results from historical and cultural distinctions. For example, consumption of Mexican food is highest in southern California, Arizona, New Mexico, and Texas. Note that this is a difference based on geography alone and not on population as discussed earlier.

Changes in climate may also account for variations in demand. Residents of Michigan, Wisconsin, and Minnesota will not purchase the same

---

[3]"Spanish Speaking are $20 Billion U.S. Market," *Advertising Age* (November 21, 1973), p. 56.

[4]Del I. Hawkins, Kenneth A. Coney, and Roger J. Best, *Consumer Behavior: Implications for Marketing Strategy* (Dallas: Business Publications, Inc., 1980), p. 131.

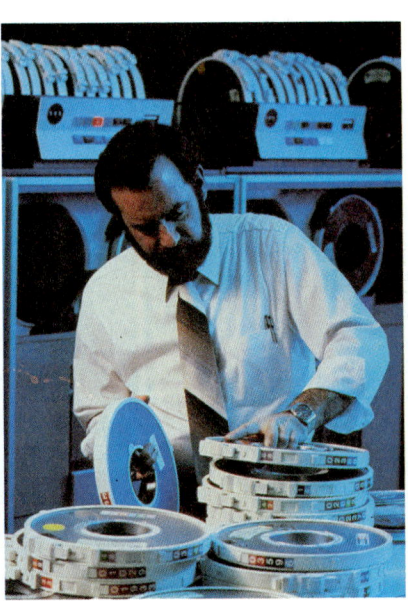

Figure 12-6

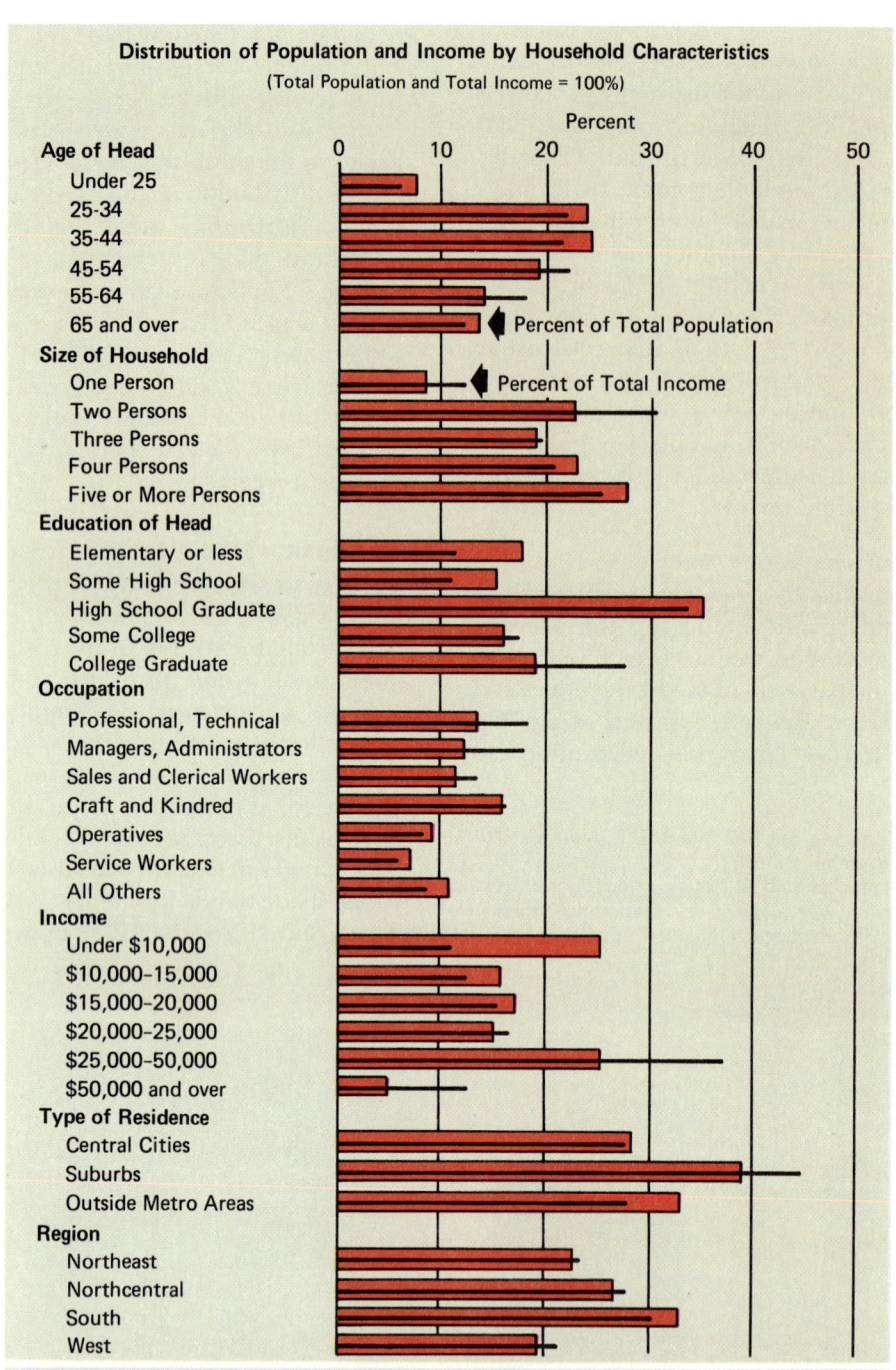

Distribution of Population and Income by Household Characteristics
(Total Population and Total Income = 100%)

Age of Head	
Under 25	
25-34	
35-44	
45-54	
55-64	◄ Percent of Total Population
65 and over	
Size of Household	
One Person	◄ Percent of Total Income
Two Persons	
Three Persons	
Four Persons	
Five or More Persons	
Education of Head	
Elementary or less	
Some High School	
High School Graduate	
Some College	
College Graduate	
Occupation	
Professional, Technical	
Managers, Administrators	
Sales and Clerical Workers	
Craft and Kindred	
Operatives	
Service Workers	
All Others	
Income	
Under $10,000	
$10,000–15,000	
$15,000–20,000	
$20,000–25,000	
$25,000–50,000	
$50,000 and over	
Type of Residence	
Central Cities	
Suburbs	
Outside Metro Areas	
Region	
Northeast	
Northcentral	
South	
West	

The bars in this graph represent the distribution of the population according to household characteristics. Thermometer lines denote the proportion of total income accounted for by each household group. Where the thermometer extends beyond the bar, the per capita income of a particular household group is higher than the all-country average. Conversely, where the thermometer is shorter than the bar, per capita income is below average. (For example, households in the 55-64 age class hold some 13.7% of all persons, but account for 17.4% of total personal income. Thus the per capita income here is some 27% above average—17.4% divided by 13.7%.)

SOURCE: Fabian Linden, "Per Capita-ism," *Across the Board*, June 1980, p. 67.

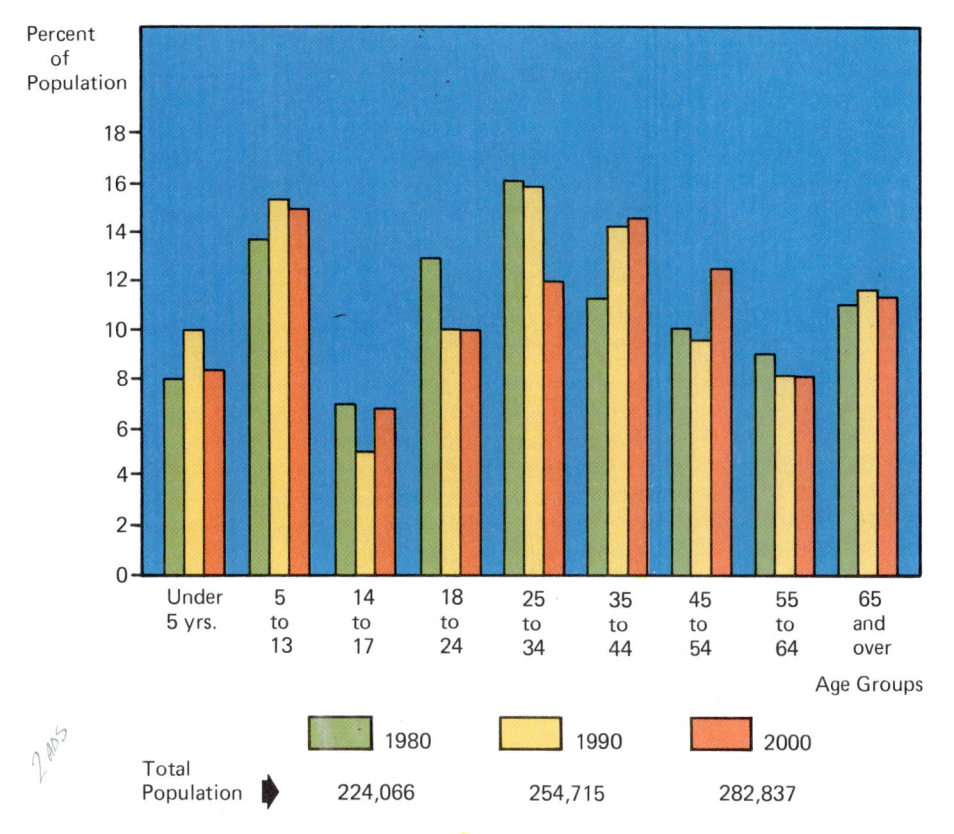

Figure 12-7

Age Distribution of U.S. Population, 1980-2000

Source: U.S. Department of Commerce, Bureau of the Census Projection of the Population of the United States, 1977-2050, Series P-25, No. 704 (July, 1979), p. 10.

| Total Population | 1980: 224,066 | 1990: 254,715 | 2000: 282,837 |

winter clothing as do people in Florida and Georgia. A national retailer such as Sears must take these demand differences into consideration so that its merchandise may be properly matched to the needs and preferences of its customers.

Market segmentation is an example of the marketing concept in action. It recognizes the existence of market groups which have different sets of product or service needs. Firms use segmentation strategy to aim their marketing programs at those groups that will benefit most from product or service offerings.

Implementing the marketing concept through a strategy of segmentation requires an investment in marketing research. Without the information that such research provides, firms would not know which products are in demand or how to group customers into market segments.

MARKETING RESEARCH

The American Marketing Association defines **marketing research** as "the systematic gathering, recording, and analyzing of data about problems relating to the marketing of goods and services."[5] Marketing research acts as a kind of intelligence unit for the firm, identifying and solving market-related problems, spotting new product opportunities, tracking the changing composition of the market, and monitoring the legal, social, and consumer environment. The right marketing mix decisions depend on accurate research.

This part of the chapter discusses the uses and limitations of marketing research. The actual methods of collecting information for marketing research studies will be discussed in the appendix to Part 6.

What Does Marketing Research Tell the Firm?

Business firms do marketing research when they have a question that is too important to be answered by guessing alone. Often they conduct research in order to estimate the sales of their products and to study alternative advertising and

---

[5]"Report of the Definitions Committee of the American Marketing Association" (Chicago: American Marketing Association, 1961).

Profile—
Lore Harp

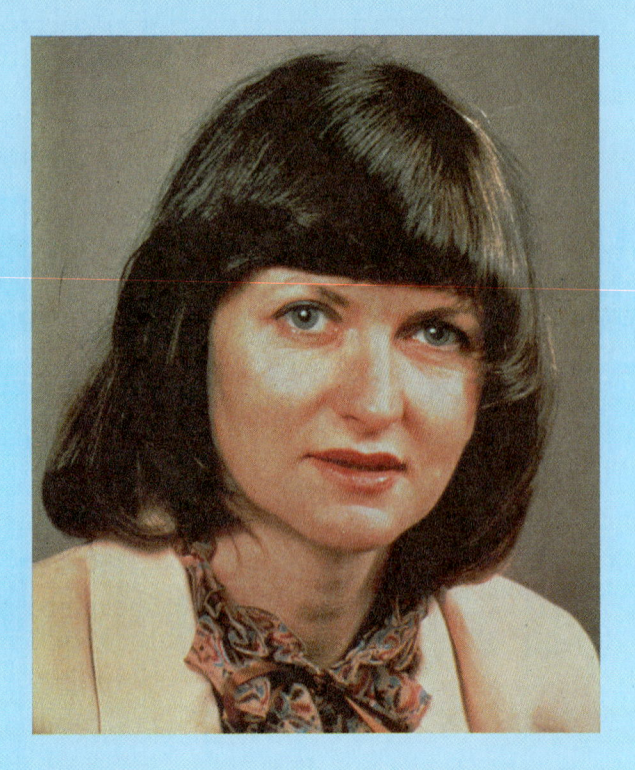

In 1976 Lore Harp and her friend Carole Ely were housewives looking for a good cause for which to work. They had no business training, no specialized technical skills, and no ideas in mind. Harp's husband, Bob, a scientist at Hughes Research Laboratories, supplied the idea—computers—and Harp and Ely supplied the rest. Today their company, Vector Graphic, Inc., is the acknowledged leader in its field.

Here's how the company got its start: Bob Harp was in the practice of tinkering with electronic equipment on weekends; in the process, he had designed a computer memory board, a system of computer circuitry that plugs into a computer to increase its memory capability. He thought it would sell, and he suggested that his wife and her friend take over the marketing of the product while he handled its production. Bob Harp was paid a royalty for the design of the board. He joined the new company full-time in 1977.

The three spent about $6,000 on the materials needed to assemble the memory boards. The Harps' dining room was turned over to test equipment for the boards; styrofoam packing was stored in a shower downstairs; and the rest of the house was soon occupied with various aspects of production and marketing.

Their efforts were soon rewarded. When the three partners knew they had a winner, they decided to take the plunge—to assemble entire computers, specializing in desk-top microcomputers. Soon there was no room left in their house, so they moved to a large office and manufacturing facility. Today Vector Graphic, Inc., employs about 400 people and occupies 120,000 square feet of office and production space.

At today's prices, the company's stock is worth around $55 million. Vector Graphic's sales jumped from $404,000 in 1977 (the year of the memory board only) to $36 million in 1983 (with a line of eight microcomputer models). Already, more than 30,000 Vector Graphic microcomputers have been sold.

With only a computer circuit designed by Bob Harp, why did Vector Graphic, Inc., do so well? The answer is marketing, that is, service and support. Many of the early microcomputer manufacturers sold their products through catalogues and mail-order houses. Lore Harp and her partners understood that distribution was as important as price or product, and that a good distribution network was essential if consumers were to be supplied with needed information about the company's products. Accordingly, Vector Graphic sells through a network of established value-added retail dealers.

The partners also realized that reliable service was essential, and so, in addition to requiring servicing from their dealers, they contracted with TRW, a giant electronics and aerospace company, to supply service through TRW's service facilities around the country. Above all, they understood the importance of the marketing concept: Consumers wanted microcomputers with a certain combination of price, features, reliability, and availability. Vector Graphic, Inc., targeted its efforts precisely at that need, and the company never went wrong.

Benefit Segmentation

Another popular form of segmentation is **benefit segmentation**. Instead of segmenting a market on the basis of income, ethnic background, age, or geographic location, practitioners of benefit segmentation look to the attributes, or "benefits," that people seek in a product. For example, a product may have two benefits: style and low cost. Consumers favoring style as the primary benefit make up one segment; consumers favoring low cost make up the other. Although people would like to get as many benefits as possible from a product, certain benefits are usually given much greater weight in purchase decisions.

Once these key product benefits have been identified, the next step is to compare each benefit segment with the rest of the market. Do the segments have unique demographic characteristics, consumption patterns, or media habits? Answers to such questions provide many clues about how to reach each segment and about which advertising appeals might prove effective.

The market for toothpaste provides a good illustration of how benefit segmentation works. This market can be segmented in terms of four product benefits: flavor and product appearance, brightness of teeth, decay prevention, and price. As the accompanying table indicates, four variables describe each segment. People concerned with the brightness of their teeth tend to be young, usually in their teens. Many people in this segment also are smokers worried about cigarette stains. Generally more "sociable" than people in other segments, they often buy such products as Gleem or Ultra Brite. If we were to introduce a new product to the "brightness" market, our advertising should stress the "social success" that users of our brand can expect. The media selected should be appropriate for teens and young people. Can you conduct this type of market analysis for the other three benefit segments?

Principal Benefit Sought	Demographic Strengths	Special Behavioral Characteristics	Personality Characteristics	Brands Disproportionately Favored
Flavor, product appearance	Children	Users of Spearmint-flavored toothpaste	High self-involvement	Colgate, Stripe
Brightness of teeth	Teens, young people	Smokers	High sociability	Gleem, Ultra Brite
Decay prevention	Large families	Heavy users	High hypochondriasis	Crest
Price	Men	Heavy users	High autonomy	Brands on sale

selling strategies. Although these activities are closely related to each other, it is best to look at them separately.

Evaluates Sales Potential. A market can be defined as the total number of units of a product sold in a given period of time such as one year. How big is the market for a particular product? A market can range in size from the multi-billion-dollar market for automobiles in the United States to the quite small market for advanced physics textbooks.

Information on the size and growth rate of a market is essential in the decision to develop a new product. Firms like to enter fast-growing markets. In 1974, total worldwide sales of digital watches stood at 700,000 but were expected to climb to 53,000,000 by 1980. This was all Texas Instruments and National Semiconductor needed to hear before they introduced digital watches of their own.

How many units of its product can the firm hope to sell? Forecasts based on research of company sales, especially short-range forecasts, tell the firm how much raw material it should order and how many units it should produce. A firm's sales forecast is usually made on the basis of a marketing plan; the greater the level of marketing effort involved in the plan, the higher the expected sales level.

Evaluates Promotional Strategies. How do people respond to different advertising messages? Are they more likely to remember one

FROM THE FILE

Jessica's publishing venture was in trouble. Her company published *Fleet Feet*, a monthly magazine for joggers. The magazine, sold nationwide, was not selling very well. The magazine contained articles of interest to runners and was sold at $3.00 a copy through running stores and supermarkets. The company's sales agents talked to the store owners each month when they brought the new month's issue. One store owner complained that the marketing mix for the magazine was poor. Another said that the company did not know enough about its market. And people in the subscription sales department were even talking about market segmentation. Jessica wondered what to do.

---

message rather than another? An advertiser may test the effectiveness of different messages by showing a group of people five trial television commercials of its product. The advertiser will pick the best commercial based on the response of the sample group.

Limitations of Marketing Research

The bottom line of marketing research is a concern with tomorrow. Research findings serve as inputs to business decisions which change the future courses of the firm. Some business executives do not believe in the value of marketing research because the predictions are occasionally wrong. We can think of at least two reasons why this cynicism is not justified.

First, marketing research is concerned with the behavior of people in the market. It aims to forecast future behavior based on current behavior. But even powerful research tools allow us to understand only a small part of human behavior since people are very complex and often change their minds.

Second, the firm's economic, legal, and social environment changes all the time. A prediction based on one set of assumptions about the future may turn out to be wrong if any single assumption is incorrect. Imagine a five-year forecast of the number of new housing starts in the United States based on a 10 percent mortgage interest rate. Now, let's assume that the government, in an attempt to slow down inflation, adopted a tight credit policy. The result is that the mortgage rate climbs to 16 percent, and many fewer families can buy a house. Thus, a forecast based on the 10 percent interest rate would overstate the actual number of housing starts at the 16 percent rate.

We must remember that the purpose of marketing research is to reduce the risk of making a bad decision. Although it is not possible to eliminate this risk completely, the more timely, accurate, and relevant the information provided by the marketing research staff, the better the resulting business decisions.

SUMMARY POINTS

1. Marketing creates time and place utility. Time utility is a measure of whether the product is available *when* the buyer wants it; place utility is a measure of whether the product is available *where* the customer wants it.
2. An effective marketing system acts as an information network linking producers and consumers.
3. Equating supply and demand is the job of the inventory function.
4. The marketing system centralizes the exchange of goods and services, which increases the distribution efficiency of society.
5. The marketing mix is made up of four key variables: the product offered to the market, the price charged for the product, the way the product is distributed to the buyer, and the promotional tools for informing buyers about the product.
6. The marketing concept says that the firm should focus on the needs of buyers. Two important principles behind the marketing concept are a belief in competitive substitutes and the need to generate profitable sales.

7. Market segmentation involves dividing the overall market into many smaller markets. The firm then provides products or develops promotional strategies to match the needs of individual market segments.
8. There is no single "best" way to segment markets. Two widely used segmentation techniques are demographic segmentation and geographic segmentation.
9. Two common marketing research tasks are estimating sales potential and evaluating alternative advertising and promotional strategies.
10. Marketing research studies are never perfect because they are concerned with the behavior of people in the marketplace and because the firm's economic, legal, and social environment changes over time.

KEY TERMS AND CONCEPTS

time utility
place utility
macromarketing
information function
inventory function
exchange function
micromarketing
marketing mix

channel of distribution
marketing concept
target segments
market segmentation
demographic segmentation
geographic segmentation
marketing research
market

REVIEW QUESTIONS

1. Is it true that marketing creates time and place utility? Explain.
2. Explain what is meant by macromarketing. What are the three key functions of macromarketing?
3. How many exchanges are required if an economy consisting of four businesses has no central market place?
4. How does micromarketing differ from macromarketing?
5. What are the four key elements in the marketing mix?
6. Define the marketing concept.
7. Why is there no single "best" way to segment markets?
8. Discuss the major uses of marketing research.
9. Describe the major limitations of marketing research.

DISCUSSION QUESTIONS

1. What do we mean by the old saying that "Nothing happens until a sale is made"?
2. Is the marketing mix the same for all products? Explain.
3. Why is it important to coordinate the firm's marketing mix? Give an example of how you would coordinate the marketing mix for inexpensive hand-held business calculators.
4. Give an example of a company with a market orientation and one without such an orientation. Which one do you think will be the most profitable in the long run? Why?
5. Should a firm be concerned more with profits or with sales?

CASE 12-1

Budweiser*

The U.S. beer market has long been one of the most fiercely competitive markets in America. Every year, hundreds of small local breweries try to survive as the giants wage their wars against one another. The two largest competitors in the last few years have been Budweiser, produced by Anheuser-Busch, and Miller, produced by Miller Brewing Company.

Budweiser and Miller locked horns recently in a battle brought on by several unusual developments in the industry. Coors beer tried national distribution. Many analysts now believe that Coors was in great demand when supply was short and the beer enjoyed a certain mystique; once Coors was readily available in most of the country, the mystique vanished, and the product was judged solely by taste and price in comparison to other beers. At about the same time, new management at the Joseph Schlitz Brewing Company decided to change its brewing process, and produced a poor-tasting beer that the public wouldn't buy; its market share plummeted. At the same time, hundreds of imported beers were finding favor among American beer drinkers.

Budweiser and Miller realized that with the sliding fortunes of Coors and Schlitz, there was significant new market share to be captured. And they had to act fast, or imported beers would dominate. Miller's strategy initially won out, and Miller High Life beer increased its sales by nearly 30 percent a year for several years. It finally knocked Budweiser out of first place. Miller achieved this feat by acquiring nearly 70 percent of all television sports broadcast advertising, the best way to advertise to the most common beer drinker—the young adult male.

Budweiser market analysts realized what Miller had done, and they started a similar campaign of their own. Budweiser found in particular that it had lost most to Miller among young people and minorities. Budweiser began sponsoring the world land speed record attempt, car races, balloon races, hydroplane boat races, tractor pulls, and similar events. Budweiser identified segments of the beer-drinking market a bit better than Miller did, found the kinds of advertising that appealed to the important segments, and spent its advertising money there.

The results were impressive. Starting in 1978, when the new marketing strategy began, Budweiser increased its volume by 13.1 percent a year, and in three years acquired a 20.6 percent market share, compared to Miller's 12.2 percent share. Once again, Bud was the "king of beers."

Budweiser's extensive market segmentation has continued to pay off. Realizing the appeal of light beers, Bud launched Budweiser Light, a low-calorie beer that has made substantial inroads on Miller Lite and other low-calorie beers.

1. Why did Budweiser choose to use market segmentation to correct its marketing program?
2. Why did Budweiser marketers segment the market on the basis of age, sex, and race? Should they have considered occupations, location in the country, educational level, income, or personal involvement in sports? If they had used these bases for segmentation instead, what results might you have expected?
3. To improve sales of a light beer, would massive sports sponsorship still be the best approach? Why or why not? How would you try to segment the light beer market, and how would you use your results to determine how best to sell light beer?

*Source: *DUNS* (February, 1982), p. 83; *The Wall Street Journal* (September 7, 1982), p. 14.

CASE 12-2

Marshall Field & Company

For decades, Marshall Field & Company (MF) was the most prestigious and exclusive department store in Chicago. Recently, however, MF has been adversely affected by several trends. The population of the downtown Chicago area has decreased as more people have moved to distant suburbs and chosen to shop near their homes. At the same time, several out-of-town department store chains such as Saks Fifth Avenue, Neiman Marcus, and I. Magnin, have opened branches in central Chicago, and other department stores are planning branches. MF had to find a way to compete successfully.

Marketing specialists at MF identified two possible paths they could follow. First, MF could diversify into different kinds of products, becoming the super-department store that characterized Foley's, Bloomingdale's, and Carson Pirie Scott. Second, MF could stick to fashionable clothing—the market it knew best—and move out of town for some of its business. Traditionally, MF's most reputable and most profitable departments were its clothing departments for men and women.

The marketing specialists carefully examined MF's management, salespeople, and buyers. They felt that MF would risk losing its prestigious reputation if it went into different kinds of merchandise. They also felt that MF did not have the expertise already on hand to branch out successfully into other products.

The marketing specialists recommended that MF conduct a geographic segmentation study in an attempt to find new geographic markets in which to operate. Management agreed, and the study was carried out, with very encouraging results. The name of MF was well-known throughout the country, but MF goods were scarce or unavailable in most areas. In particular, MF goods were in demand in cities on both coasts and up and down the midwest strip of the United States.

MF began acquiring new outlets in these areas in 1978. It did so at first by purchasing department store chains that it could renovate and rename. It acquired a large store chain in California as West-Coast headquarters and ten department stores in Oregon and Washington State. The next year it bought a 23-store chain in Florida and the Carolinas. To build up its anticipated Midwest market, MF purchased a 6-store chain in Columbus, Ohio. To serve the Texas market, MF budgeted to build four large department stores.

Says MF's president, "Our premise has been to lessen our concentration in the Midwest and expand into areas where there will be more growth. We could have looked at some nonretail areas, but I felt that first and foremost we were retailers, and that our strategy would be better served expanding in something we already knew."

1. Explain how MF's marketing specialists used the elements of the marketing mix to analyze marketing plans relating to expansion or diversification.
2. Distinguish the results the marketing specialists obtained from demographic segmentation and geographic segmentation. What kind of errors could MF have made had only one kind of segmentation been conducted?
3. What kind of information did marketing research give MF? What kinds of techniques might market researchers have used?

13

Product Management

After studying this chapter, you should be able to:

- Understand how products are classified as either consumer products or industrial products.
- Identify a five-stage model of the product life cycle.
- Discuss the importance of branding and the features of a good brand name.
- Analyze the new product development process.
- Explain what makes a product successful.

A few years ago, marketing people had relatively little to do with product development. Everyone knew that engineers designed products and that marketers sold them. But this has changed for firms that have adopted the marketing concept. Now, marketers work together with design people to develop products that are closely matched to the needs of the market. The new goal is to make products that are easy to sell. We'll begin our discussion of product management by looking at how marketers classify their products.

Chapter 13 • Product Management

PRODUCT CLASSIFICATION

Different kinds of products are marketed in different ways. How products are classified can tell us a lot about how they are marketed. Product classification recognizes that people buy a product for various reasons. This is why we said in Chapter 12 that a product is more than just the sum of its physical attributes; a product description also involves consideration of servicing, warranties, and delivery terms as well as the equally important image attributes of prestige, reputation, and perceived quality. In a product description, buyer perceptions are just as important as the manufacturer's specifications.

The most basic product distinction is between consumer products and industrial products. These two types of products are not marketed in the same way. Because we're more familiar with consumer products, let's begin our discussion with them.

Consumer Products

Consumer products are goods produced for sale to individuals and families for personal consumption. They, in turn, are classified as either convenience goods, shopping goods, or specialty goods. Figure 13-1 lists the differences among them in terms of shopping time, profitability, and marketing technique.

Convenience Goods. **Convenience goods** are purchased frequently, immediately, and with little shopping effort. The cost of making price and quality comparisons is much greater than the benefits resulting from such comparisons. Some examples of convenience goods are milk, magazines, soap, and cigarettes. Can you think of others?

The key to marketing convenience goods successfully is location. Most people buy consumer goods at the nearest store. This is why Southland Corporation has more than 9,000 neighborhood 7-Eleven stores. Southland's strategy is to make it as convenient as possible for people to shop at one of their outlets.

Convenience goods are sold primarily by mass advertising, not by personal attention and sales technique. When people buy milk or cigarettes, they usually don't ask the clerk which

Even convenience goods usually acquire a definite image.

brand is best. They realize that the salesclerk's job is to take their money, not to give them advice on such products.

Convenience retailers must keep in mind that other nearby stores sell the same products. Pricing is about the only way for such retailers to contrast their merchandise with that of the competition across the street or down the block. People tend to be price conscious when they shop for convenience goods. If the price of aspirin, potato chips, or masking tape is too high, the store may lose business to a nearby competitor. Accordingly, the profit margin on convenience goods is quite small. **Profit margin** is the difference between a product's cost and its selling price.

Shopping Goods. In the case of **shopping goods**, the buyer actively considers price, quality, style, and value before making a purchase decision. The buyer believes that the benefits of an intelligent purchase decision are worth the extra shopping effort. Examples of shopping goods are refrigerators, microwave ovens, vacuum cleaners, and stereo equipment.

Selling shopping goods successfully depends on retail advertising: The retailer must tell the public which brands it carries. Salespeople should be able to explain the advantages and disadvantages of the various brands carried. Since customers rely on this information, it is essential

Figure 13-1

Characteristics of Convenience, Shopping, and Specialty Goods

Characteristics	Convenience Goods	Shopping Goods	Specialty Goods
Searching Time	Milk, Candy Bars Low, First Available Product is Purchased	Refrigerators, Vacuum Cleaners Significant; Customer Analyzes Characteristics of Several Brands	Expensive China and Jewelry Customer Looks for a Particular Brand
Per Unit Profit	Low	Moderate	High
Distribution	Many Retailers	Several Retailers	Few Retailers
Sales Techniques	Mass Advertising	Mass Advertising and Personal Selling	Highly Trained Sales Force

for the retailer of shopping goods to have a good sales staff.

Shopping goods are usually marketed through a combination of the manufacturer's advertising and the salesperson's efforts. A manufacturer runs expensive national advertising campaigns on television or in magazines to tell people why they should purchase its products. Curtis Mathes, for instance, advertises its televisions as more expensive than most others, but "darn well worth it." The advertisement in Figure 13-2 lists some of the desirable features of a Pontiac TransAm.

As a percentage of selling price, the profit on shopping goods is usually much higher than it is on convenience goods. The retailer needs a higher profit margin in order to cover the costs of more expensive sales staffs, store fixtures, and advertising budgets required to sell shopping goods.

Specialty Goods. **Specialty goods** are goods for which shoppers are willing to make a "special" shopping effort. Whether a product is a specialty good or not depends upon whether shoppers know which brand they would buy before actually feeling the need to purchase the product. If the next suit you intend to buy is a Calvin Klein suit—even though you have no intention of buying a suit now—then a suit by Calvin Klein is a specialty good for you. Specialty goods command brand loyalty. Is there any product that is a specialty good for you?

It is important for manufacturers of specialty goods to select retailers that will present their products properly. Specialty goods are promoted on the bases of product quality, reliability, and image. Thus, the image of the retailer should be consistent with the image of the product.

Profit margins are quite high for specialty goods because competition among retailers tends to be limited; relatively few stores in a given community sell the same specialty goods. In addition, people who can afford expensive specialty goods are usually more concerned about buying the "right" product than about price.

Industrial Products

Industrial products are goods and services which are sold to private business firms or public agencies, and which are later used in the production of their goods and services. The buyers of these goods are not final consumers, but professional purchasing agents. The market for industrial goods includes utility companies, manufacturing firms, contractors, mining firms, wholesalers, and retailers as well as local, state and federal governments. Examples of industrial goods are iron ore, petrochemical products, cleaning fluids, machine tools, and computers for office use.

Chapter 13 • Product Management 237

Figure 13-2

What makes the selling of industrial goods unique? First, most industrial goods are sold by salespeople who call on buyers in their places of business. Second, mass advertising is generally limited to trade journals such as *Hardware Age* or *Mining Record*. These journals are read by people in specific industries. Third, the markets for industrial goods are more concentrated than the markets for consumer goods. There are about 230 million people and 75 million households in the United States, but only 14 million businesses. Organizations within an industry tend to cluster in certain parts of the country. The automobile industry is centered in Detroit; the apparel industry, in New York City and South Carolina. Finally, purchase decisions are often made by teams or committees, not by individuals. According to a study of more than one hundred industrial firms, nearly 80 percent of the purchase decisions involved three or more people.[1]

PRODUCT LIFE CYCLE

The **product life cycle** is another important concept in marketing. It is based on the idea that products pass through several stages from the time they are introduced to the market to the time they disappear. We will analyze a five-stage model of the product life cycle and then look at what the model has to say about how products should be marketed.

---

[1]Albert W. Frey, *Marketing Handbook* (2nd ed.; New York: The Ronald Press Co., 1965), Section 27, p. 18.

Stages in the Product Life Cycle

Research has shown that most products move through five separate stages (see Figure 13-3). First, the product is introduced to the market and sales increase slowly. Sales begin to pick up during the second stage as more people discover the product. In the third stage, competition stiffens and product sales increase at a slower rate than before. Sales in the fourth stage rise and fall with the health of the economy. The fifth stage arrives when people begin to switch to new products. Eventually, the product is taken off the market. Figure 13-4 shows the current stage of the life cycle for several consumer products.

Market Development. After getting the product out to the market, the marketer's primary task is to keep it alive. Many times, design and promotional changes are in order. It's a trial-and-error process: Production and design engineers work on product quality, and the marketing staff checks public reaction to the product and modifies the selling and promotion strategy as needed. The price of the product is usually high during the market development stage. But most products, even successful ones, lose money at first because of high production and marketing costs.

Rapid Growth. Product sales increase quickly during the **rapid growth** stage as the product catches on in the market. Other firms introduce competing products of their own, but industry supply still falls short of product demand. New products can begin to generate substantial profits during this stage, however, with proper cost control. The establishment of a strong distribution network that will support the product during the rest of its life is an important concern.

Turbulence. Industry supply eventually catches up with market demand. It is during the **turbulence stage** of the product life cycle that competition heats up within the industry. Firms slash prices, offer more product options, cut delivery time, and redesign packaging—all in an attempt to increase their share of the profit pie. The intense competition drives the weaker firms out of the industry. For a firm and its product to survive, the firm needs a well-developed dealer structure and, again, an effective cost control program. Profits tend to be quite high at the beginning of the turbulence stage but then decline thereafter.

Maturity. The fourth stage may last a long time. The weaker firms—those unable to set up a good distribution system—have left the market, and only the strongest remain. Very few firms enter the market now because of the large amount of capital required and because the other firms have a head start.

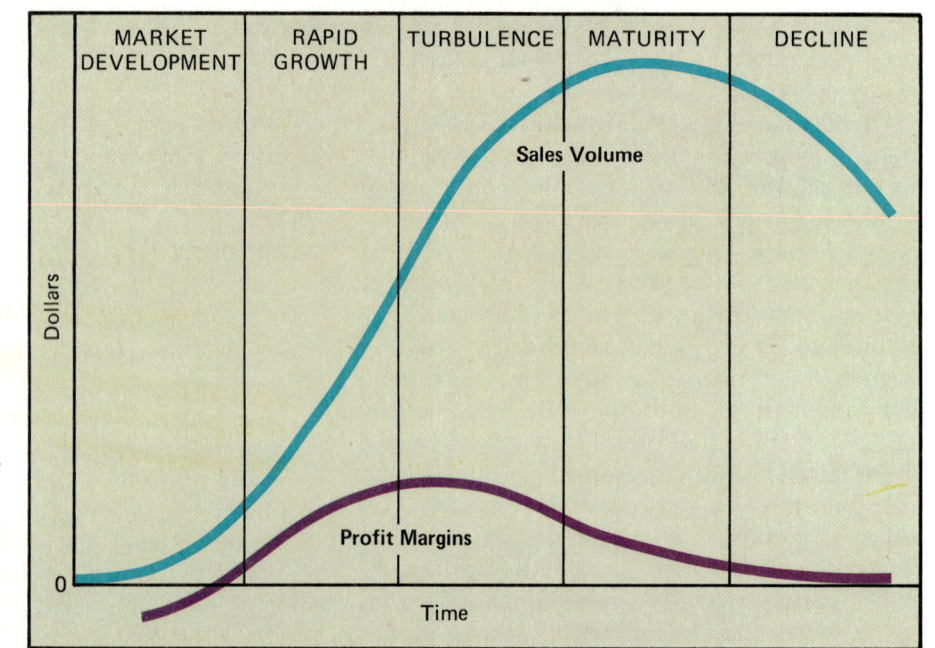

Figure 13-3

The Product Life Cycle

Source: Rolando Polli and Victor Cook, "Validity of the Product Life Cycle," *Journal of Business* (October, 1969), p. 386. © 1969 by The University of Chicago Press. All rights reserved.

Figure 13-4

Life Cycles of Various Products

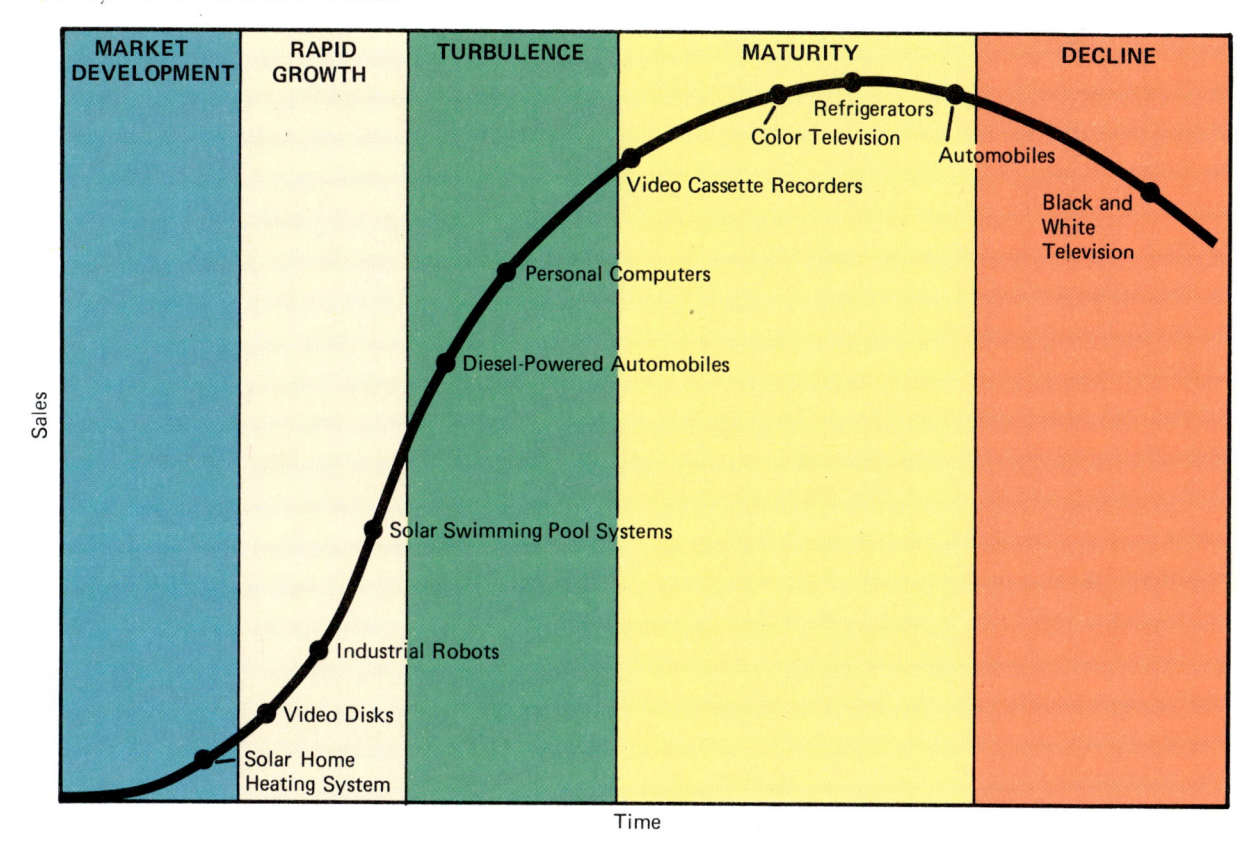

MARKET DEVELOPMENT | **RAPID GROWTH** | **TURBULENCE** | **MATURITY** | **DECLINE**

- Refrigerators
- Color Television
- Automobiles
- Video Cassette Recorders
- Black and White Television
- Personal Computers
- Diesel-Powered Automobiles
- Solar Swimming Pool Systems
- Industrial Robots
- Video Disks
- Solar Home Heating System

Sales / Time

The basic goal of the firm during the **maturity stage** is to hold on to market share—or to maintain its current percentage of industry sales of the product. A great year for a "mature" product is a one- or two-percent gain in market share. Profits can still be made during this stage if the economy is strong and the product is selling well. A sales slump, whether induced by a recession or a change in consumer tastes, can wipe out profits entirely.

The automobile is clearly in the maturity stage of its life cycle. Throughout the 1970s, Ford was one of the most profitable companies in the nation. Yet the auto giant lost a billion dollars in 1981, when Ford sales dropped 12.1 percent below the 1979 level.

Decline. By the time a product enters the **decline stage**, its glamour days are over. Demand for the product has lessened, producing only enough sales to keep a few firms in business. Can you think of a product in the decline stage?

A firm with a product in the decline stage should invest only enough money to keep the production line running. It does not make sense to buy new high-speed production equipment for a product that may soon disappear from the market. The firm should also try to make as much cash as possible on the product, that is, keep it on the market for as long as demand for it exists. The goal here is to maximize short-run profits.

Product Life Cycle—A Powerful Tool

Now we're in a position to examine the product life cycle's usefulness for management. Let's look at three ways that business managers use the life cycle idea.

Forecasting Sales. One area in which the product life cycle is applied is product sales forecasting. When General Electric introduced electric toothbrushes to the market, sales skyrocketed. An inexperienced forecaster might have assumed that this high rate of sales growth would continue indefinitely. Company planners, however, knew that competition would increase and that demand would weaken in the product's maturity stage. This would cause sales to peak and then to decline.

Introducing New Products. The product life cycle says that the profits for a product are a function of how long it has been on the market. High profits are not typical of the maturity stage. When a product enters this stage, therefore, the firm should have another product ready for the market. This new product then keeps the firm in business as it moves into the profitable stages of its life cycle.

Hand-held calculators are an example of how new products can be successfully introduced one after another. The first calculators were equipped with only addition, subtraction, multiplication, and division functions. By the time these products came to the maturity stage, their manufacturers had introduced more sophisticated models with percentile, square root, and other complex functions. Many hand-held calculators today are programmable and offer such options as "canned" software and attachments for printing output.

Managing Products. The product life cycle is also useful as a guide in product management. The way a product is marketed changes as it moves through its life cycle. In the market development stage it is important for advertising to stress product advantages. The early advertisements for Sony's home video system talked about the uses and benefits of this new product, rather than about the Sony name itself. Its later advertisements, which were run after video systems had become common and people had become familiar with them, focused on why consumers should prefer a Sony system to those of its competitors.

We'll talk further in Chapter 16 about the relationship between advertising and the product life cycle. Now let's turn to branding.

BRANDING

A **brand** is any name, symbol, or design which identifies the firm and its products. Chevrolet, Adidas, the Izod alligator, and the Purina checkerboard are all either brand names, symbols, or designs. A brand that has been granted legal protection so that it cannot be used by anyone else is called a **trademark**. In this section we'll consider the objectives of branding and the characteristics of a good brand name.

Why Branding?

A brand name identifies the seller and establishes a limited form of "control" over the buyer. Control means that the buyer learns to associate a particular brand name with a particular need or a particular class of products. Consider the case of photocopiers. When most people think of photocopiers, they think of Xerox: "Would you Xerox this for me, please?" In the same way, the brand name "Campbell's" is synonymous with soup. Consumers will pay more for the product if they are familiar with the brand name. Or at least they will tend to select the product with little or no comparative shopping. Two more specific objectives of branding are to generate repeat sales and to make it easier for the firm to introduce new products.

Repeat Sales. If Jane liked her first Schwinn bicycle, she may buy another one—that's what we mean by repeat sales. Branding fosters repeat sales; satisfied customers seek the company's products for repurchase. Think about it: If you were happy with your last purchase of Del Monte canned peaches, wouldn't you look for them again the next time you're in the supermarket?

Branding is also important in word-of-mouth advertising. Satisfied customers are a seller's best friends. They tell other people about the product and their good experiences with it. Word-of-mouth promotion works best for shopping and specialty goods such as televisions, refrigerators, and automobiles.

New Product Sales. A firm with a well-established brand name often has an easy time introducing new products. Consumers and industrial buyers alike believe that a firm with a reputation for quality products will continue to offer such products in the future. For example, when the Gillette Razor Company was preparing its "Cricket" lighter for market introduction, some of Gillette's managers wondered whether the company's name and reputation would help the product in the marketplace. Since Gillette had no experience selling lighters, some argued that the Gillette name should not appear on the package. They

CONTROVERSIAL ISSUES

Firms that manufacture a variety of products have two ways to handle product management. They can use the traditional system of managers in functional areas such as production, marketing, and finance, or they can use product managers who integrate all the different managerial roles related to a given product and are responsible for the success of that one product. Should all companies consider using product managers?

Pro

Yes, every manager knows that the traditional management system has never worked properly. There is an awkward transition of authority when a finished product is transferred from the production manager responsible for it to the sales manager who will handle it next. Sometimes companies feel so uncomfortable with this arrangement that they insert an intermediate manager to handle the transition. A product manager performs all these duties while moving a product from initial conceptualization to the shelf in a neighborhood store.

Product managers become especially important when a company manufactures products that require different kinds of production, marketing, research, or sales. You can't expect a general sales manager to appreciate and implement the various kinds of sales approaches that different kinds of plastics at DuPont might require, or

Product Managers Are Important for Good Product Management.

that different vehicles made by Ford—automobiles, trucks, semi-trailers, special dock-loading trucks, tractors, and so on—might require. It's asking too much of that one person to have such skills. But it's quite natural to expect an individual who is a specialist in a given product to know what that product needs.

The situation becomes even more complex in highly diversified companies such as United Technologies, TransAmerica, or General Electric. It is impossible to imagine that a company could assign a sales manager or a production manager to the sales or production of every kind of product from helicopters to hospital diagnostic supplies. It only makes sense to have a specialist—a product manager—handle each different kind of product.

Con

No, product managers aren't a good idea. First, they duplicate the same training and skills for every product the company makes. A firm that makes 50 or 60 products would have 50 or 60 product managers, all with similar training and skills.

Second, product managers are naturally very possessive about their products. Consequently, if you asked a general sales manager which product should be dropped from the company's product line, you would probably receive an objective answer. Product managers are likely to be more subjective, however, for they will defend their product to the end.

When a product fails, someone is likely to get the blame. Product managers are tailor-made for this role. It's a common story that when a product fails, it's the product manager who is first to go. In the long run, this problem results in an erosion of any sense of responsibility in the organization, and soon nobody worries if a product fails, and nobody wants to be a product manager.

Last, it takes a very special kind of person to be a product manager. Not only is *all* the responsibility for a product laid on that one person's shoulders, but that person must also be extraordinarily competent in order to grasp problems relating to a diversity of different areas. A good product manager is a rare individual, and you aren't likely to find many people to fill that role. So, while some product managers are successful, they are the exception. Generally, the use of product managers means inefficient management.

feared that if Cricket failed, the sales of other Gillette products would suffer, too. Others disagreed, arguing that the Gillette name "presold" the lighter. Top management decided to put the Gillette name on the package, and for whatever reason, Cricket has been a success.

Family Brands vs. Individual Brands

When most or all of a firm's products bear the same brand name, they are said to be sold under a family brand. An example is the Heinz 57 Variety brand name, which is carried on many Heinz products. We just saw that a brand name makes new product introduction easier. It also stimulates the sales of other products in the firm's line. Why then do some firms sell each of their products under a different brand name? We can cite two reasons: to protect existing products and to stimulate internal competition.

Protect Existing Products. Shoppers sometimes perceive two or more of a firm's products as almost the same, even though they have different technical characteristics and vary considerably in price and quality. In such situations, the firm usually makes an effort to differentiate its products from one another—especially when introducing a new, inexpensive product to the market. The concern is to prevent the new product from jeopardizing sales of an older, more expensive product.

The Bulova Watch Company is an example of a company that was careful not to let a new product take sales away from an older product. Bulova has a well-established reputation for making high-quality watches. When Bulova introduced an inexpensive watch to the market, it sold the new watch under the name Caravelle rather than under the family brand name. Bulova's managers were concerned that the public would not see any differences between the expensive and the inexpensive watches if both were named Bulova. As a result, buyers might "trade down" from the expensive to the inexpensive (and less profitable) watches.

Stimulate Internal Competition. A second reason why a firm might adopt an individual branding strategy is to stimulate competition within the organization. In the highly competitive laundry soap business, successful manufacturers offer a variety of products to the market. Each product stands alone in the market and competes against the products of other firms as well as against the other soaps produced by the same company and sold under a different name. Procter & Gamble produces such well-known laundry soaps as Tide, Cheer, and Bold.

What Makes a Brand Name Good?

Choosing the right brand name involves a combination of creativity, market research, and good luck. However, there are four rules of thumb which can be helpful.

1. The name should be short, easy to spell, and easy to understand. Examples: Jell-O, Wisk.
2. The name should be right for the product and should emphasize its major attributes. Examples: Swingline stapler, Kool-Aid, Right Guard.
3. The name should be distinctive. Examples: Exxon, Zest.
4. The name should be easy to remember. Examples: Betty Crocker, Uncle Ben's, Log Cabin.

Two problems commonly occur when selecting a brand name. First, the name chosen may have already been used by another company. When Budweiser introduced Natural Lite beer, the Miller Brewing Company sued Budweiser, saying that Miller had trademarked the term "lite." The courts ruled that Miller did not have exclusive rights to the word "lite," but only to "Miller Lite."

A second problem is top management indecision. Many years ago, Ford was attempting to name a new car. The company wanted a name that fit the car's image and "personality." Not wanting to pick the wrong name, Ford tested two thousand different names for the car on people in New York, Chicago, and Ann Arbor. The people were asked to state what the sample names brought to mind. One of the names, "Edsel" (the name of Henry Ford II's father), was associated with "pretzel," "diesel," and "hard sell." Despite these negative associations, the company used Edsel.[2] The rest is history: The car was a fiasco

---

[2] Robert F. Hartley, *Marketing Mistakes* (2nd ed.; Columbus, Oh.: Grid Publishing Co., 1981), pp. 118-119.

Did its name cause its failure?

and the name Edsel is now a classic example of an American business failure.

NEW PRODUCT DEVELOPMENT

The introduction of new products to the market is essential for the survival and financial success of most businesses. Today's profits come from products currently on the market. Tomorrow's profits come from products currently on the drawing boards.

When firms run into financial problems, they sometimes reduce the number of people working on new product ideas. In the early 1980s, Chrysler laid off many of its engineers. This move may have been necessary because of the firm's financial crisis, but it made it harder for the company to develop new cars in the future.

What's "New" About a New Product?

A **new product** is one that performs an entirely new function for the buyer. Since relatively few new products are able to do this, we should extend the definition to include products that represent a significant improvement over existing products. When the cathode-ray tube (CRT) computer display terminal became available, for example, it did not perform a new function. Line printers had been displaying computer output for more than 20 years. Yet the CRT was "new" because it represented a significant improvement over older technologies and products. Now information could be retrieved instantly from the computer in large, easy-to-read letters.

The two columns of Figure 13-5 list several new-product attributes. The first column shows attributes that make it *easier* for the seller to market a new product; the second shows attributes that make it *harder* to market a new product. New products that do have a lower price than those already on the market and that are perceived to be more dependable are relatively easy to sell. Complex products, featuring what the public perceives to be unimportant benefits, are harder to sell.

Honda recognizes that buyer perception is behind the success of a new product. The advertising for its Prelude stresses the sporty appearance of the car, its good gasoline mileage, and the many standard luxury features. The slogan in the advertisement is, "Honda—we make it simple."

Figure 13-5

Ways in Which a Product Is New

Attributes Making It Easier for the Seller	Attributes Making It More Difficult for the Seller
• Lower price. • Greater convenience in use. • More dependable performance. • Easier to purchase in terms of time, place, or credit. • Positive conspicuous consumption. • Positive new appearance. • New markets.	• More complex methods of use. • Unfamiliar patterns of use. • Unfamiliar benefits. • Unimportant benefits. • High risk of costly errors. • Negative new appearance.

Source: Adapted from Chester R. Wasson, "What is 'New' About a New Product," *Journal of Marketing* (July, 1960), p. 54.

Profile—
Walter L. Ross

Walter Ross first studied political science thinking he might want to go into politics. Soon, however, he realized "politics has limited access to money and power. I'm a capitalist at heart and my temperament is better suited to the business world." He went on to earn a master's degree in business. He then went to work for Union Carbide, the large Connecticut chemical company. Ross discovered that working in a large company meant that he had control of only a very small part of the business, and he wanted to run the whole firm.

The word went out to friends that he wanted to buy a company. After about three years, in 1981, he discovered that Rubbermaid, Inc. had an automotive products subsidiary that it wanted to sell. An executive at a large investment banking house told Ross about the company, and Ross went after it. He borrowed $5 million and personally assumed responsibility for about $1 million more worth of liabilities owned by the auto products subsidiary. This company was perfect for what Ross wanted, and Rossmark Specialty Products, Inc. came into being.

Rubbermaid had dropped its auto products subsidiary because it found that its major product line consisted mostly of kitchen and houseware products—dishpans, garbage cans, silverware trays, and so on. Its auto products line consisted mostly of rubber floor mats for cars, which Rubbermaid decided couldn't be sold with the same business practices and marketing tactics used for the rest of its products. Ross, however, realized that there were product management techniques ideally suited to rubber floor mats for cars.

Ross commissioned a market research study which showed that color, fit, and durability were the three major features customers looked for in a floor mat. Rossmark responded by manufacturing a wide range of vinyl and carpet floor mats, offered in a variety of styles, shapes, materials, colors, and prices. Ross also expanded his product line into other plastic automotive accessories such as portable coolers, litter bags, snack trays, and soft drink can holders.

The real secret to Ross's plan lay in his understanding of the automobile accessory market. When the economy is healthy, people can afford to buy new cars or to spend more money on repainting or reupholstering older cars. When the economy is poor, however, people can't afford these extravagances, so they try to improve their cars by simpler means. One such way is with new floor mats, seat covers, and other inexpensive products designed to dress up the appearance of an older car.

Ross appealed to this market by selling a wide line of products and distributing them efficiently to attain high sales volume at low cost. His success was inevitable, given his efficient company management and his flair for product management. He realized that auto products sold to two kinds of buyers: original equipment manufacturers, such as Ford or GM; and a secondary market composed of automobile owners. Having already addressed the market of car owners, Ross approached the auto companies for contracts to manufacture original equipment floor mats for installation in brand-new automobiles. He has been equally successful with the auto companies.

Product management, for Ross, is basically a matter of fashion. Even car mats are sold on the basis of fashion, he claims, and not because they are essential to the safe operation of a car. They help to make one's car look more *fashionable*. Ross uses market research extensively and keeps a close line on his own operations, his competition, and the market in order to identify the particular mats that are in demand. With a smaller company, Ross has found that he can change his product line far more rapidly than Rubbermaid ever could, and that product management becomes much more effective. Ross has proven the value of product management and has shown how it can turn a company around and make its product line successful.

Why Introduce New Products?

Business firms introduce new products primarily in order to show profits year after year—however, there's more to the strategy of new product introduction than that. We'll now look at three more reasons why there are so many new products on the market.

Achieving Sales Growth Objectives. Business firms like to see their sales grow at a rate of 10 to 30 percent annually. Sometimes it is easier to meet these ambitious growth objectives by introducing new products than by selling more of the firm's old products. One group of marketing executives has said that more than 80 percent of their yearly sales growth is expected to come from new products.[3]

Meeting Competition. A move by a competitor (or an *anticipated* move by a competitor) often causes a firm to introduce a new product. General Motors introduced its new J-car in 1981 to compete with the many foreign economy models. While it can be argued that General Motors should have been the leader in the small car market rather than a follower, it can also be argued that GM would have made an even bigger mistake by staying out of the market altogether.

Completing a Product Line. The third reason for introducing new products is to complete a product line. A well-known desk manufacturer in South Carolina recently added a set of small tables to its stock of office products. The company did so not because it hoped to make a great deal of money on this product, but because it wanted to round out its merchandise. Many members of the company's sales force had complained of losing customers who wanted to buy a complete set of desks, credenzas, and tables at one time.

Developing New Products

Firms that introduce successful new products usually aren't just lucky; they have a system. Any new product development system should have three features. First, it should encourage as many new product ideas as possible. Second, it should allow company analysts to screen new product ideas quickly and inexpensively. Third, it should be rigorous so that only the best ideas are used.

Figure 13-6 depicts a six-stage model of the new-product development process. Each stage will be discussed briefly.

Stage 1: Idea Generation. New product ideas from all sources are collected in the first stage. Management should encourage as many new product ideas as possible. Some businesses, such as DuPont, Westinghouse, General Electric, and IBM, have large, well-funded basic research departments. But even though these departments have been responsible for such revolutionary new products as nylon and computer chips, most new product ideas come from customers, salespeople, and competitors.

Stage 2: Product Evaluation. The purpose of this stage is to eliminate new product ideas that are not consistent with the firm's long-term objectives. Two of the factors usually considered when a firm evaluates a new product idea are expected sales volume and the compatibility of the new idea with the firm's current marketing and production procedures.

To illustrate, a large manufacturer of industrial cleaning compounds developed a new product for cleaning bathrooms. Top management

A new product must meet a need.

---
[3] Philip R. McDonald and Joseph O. Eastback, Jr., "Top Management Involvement with New Products," *Business Horizons* (December, 1971), p. 24.

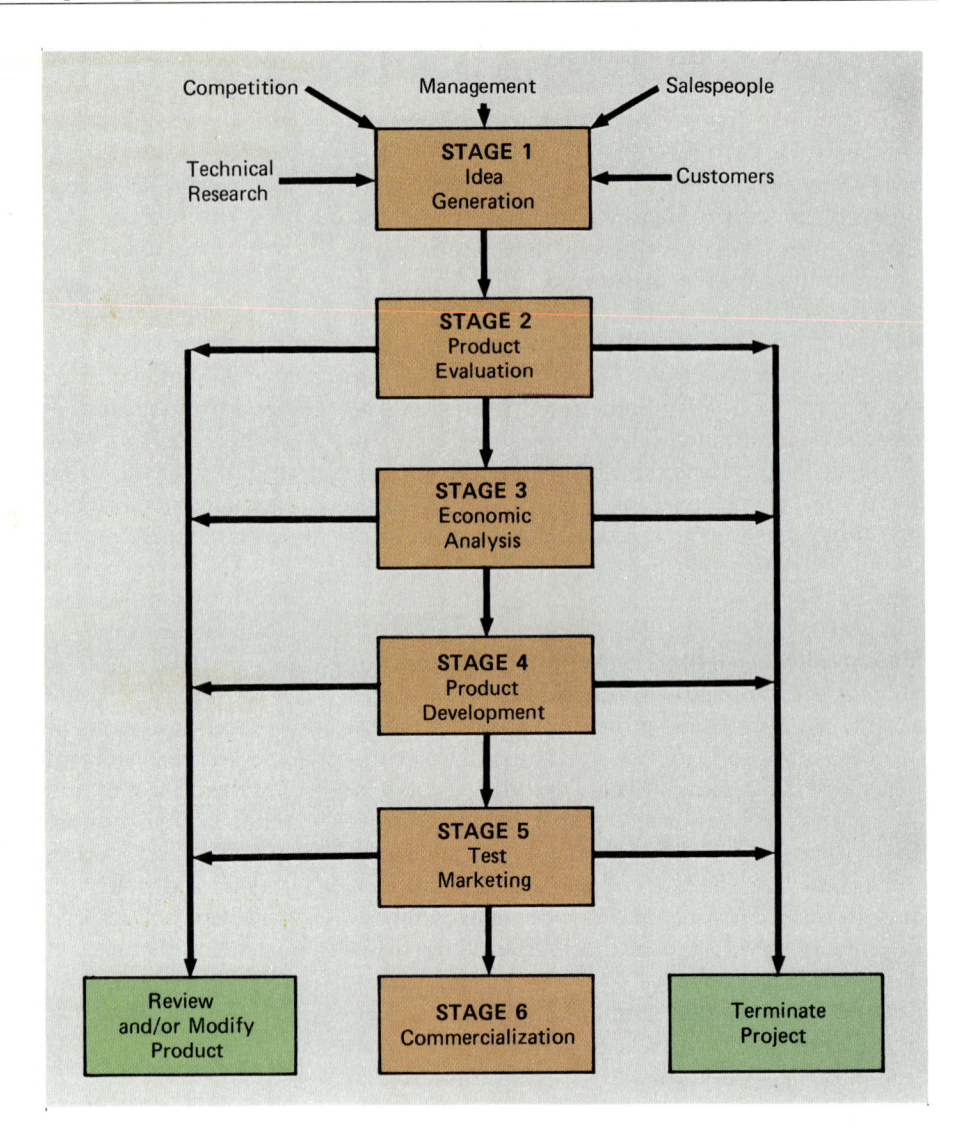

Figure 13-6

New Product Development Process

saw that the product could be highly profitable in the consumer market. The firm decided, however, to sell the formula to a consumer products firm. There was no question that the new product had a strong sales potential and that the firm could easily produce it. What was at issue was the ability of the firm, primarily a maker of industrial products, to market the new product successfully at the consumer level. The firm avoided a potentially disastrous mistake by considering this and other criteria.

Stage 3: Economic Analysis. The likely profitability of the product is estimated during the third stage. In so doing, it is sometimes necessary for a firm to make guesses about production costs and sales revenue. These guesses are based on careful analysis, but they are still guesses. The firm's cost accountants make the production costs estimates. The market research staff is the usual source of the sales estimates.

Stage 4: Product Development. At the product development stage, the product becomes more than just an idea. The firm's production design engineers develop a prototype of the product. A **prototype** is a physical model or a first, custom-made version of the product. It enables the firm to see what the product will look like and whether it can be produced at an acceptably low cost. It also gives the marketing research people something to show prospective customers.

Stage 5: Test Marketing. In Stage 5, the marketing research staff evaluates the product.

This group of people is concerned with several questions. How many consumers or businesses are likely to buy the product? How much will they pay for it? What product features do they like best? What forms of promotion will be most effective? How many units of the product can be sold in the first year?

Stage 6: Commercialization. The last step in the new product development process is making the product available to the market. The firm begins this stage by designing its promotional strategy in light of what was learned during the test-marketing stage.

It is also necessary to decide how to distribute the product. Many firms with the ability to distribute a product nationwide prefer to "roll" the product out to the market. This means that the product is first sold in one part of the country only. As the firm learns more about the product and which selling strategies work best, it then introduces the product to other parts of the country until, eventually, it is sold from coast to coast.

WHAT MAKES A PRODUCT SUCCESSFUL?

The failure rate of new products in the United States is astonishing. One study found that up to 20 percent of new industrial products and 40 percent of consumer products are unsuccessful in the marketplace.[4] These percentages are particularly surprising when we realize that a failure is defined as a product that is pulled off the market. Many other products are left on the market even though they do not earn much money for the company.

Why do so many new products fail? Some of the reasons are shown in Figure 13-7. Let's look at what one study found to be the two most important reasons why some products succeed and some don't.[5]

Significant Price or Performance Advantage

Seventy-four percent of all successful new consumer products, the study reports, offered the public better performance in comparison with competing products. It is interesting to note that price was not a critical factor when the product was perceived to be superior. It seems that people are willing to pay higher prices for better products.

Significant Differences from Other Products

New products that are different from other products have a greater chance of success than those that are mirror images of them. However,

---

[4]David S. Hopkins and Earl L. Bailey, "New Product Pressures," *The Conference Board Record* (June, 1971), p. 20.

[5]J. Hugh Davidson, "Why Most New Consumer Brands Fail," *Harvard Business Review* (March-April, 1976), pp. 119-120.

FROM THE FILE

Hector is chief executive officer for the Galvanic Television Corporation, maker of a popular line of televisions and video cassette recorders. Although these two products have not been selling well lately, Hector believes that the popularity of video games and microcomputers—which often use televisions for the video display—can only help his company's sales. One day, the chief marketing researcher for the company asked an interesting question: If Hector expected video games and microcomputers to be so popular, why didn't Galvanic come out with its own line to go with its televisions? Besides being big sellers, these new products might also stimulate sagging television sales. But how would the company go about developing video games and microcomputers and introducing them to the market?

Figure 13-7

Four Principal Causes of Failure of New Products

Cause of Failure	Percentage of Companies Citing*
Inadequate market analysis	45
Product problems or defects	29
Lack of effective marketing effort	25
Higher costs than anticipated	19

*Percentages total to more than 100 because some companies reported multiple causes of failure.

Source: David S. Hopkins and Earl L. Bailey, "New Product Pressures," *The Conference Board Record* (June, 1971), p. 20.

---

we can qualify this statement in two ways. First, product distinctions or improvements must be readily visible to the buyer. Highly technical differences which only experts understand may not contribute to success at all. Second, these differences must not be so great that buyers feel uncomfortable purchasing the product. For example, what if you invented a new typewriter with an entirely different keyboard arrangement? Instead of the letters "q," "a," and "z" being at the left of each row of keys, they're someplace else. Would people feel comfortable with this machine? Would they be willing to learn the new keyboard arrangement? Do the benefits of the changes justify this effort? Would customers buy the typewriter? Many new products have failed because management failed to answer these questions.

SUMMARY POINTS

1. Consumer products are classified as either convenience goods, shopping goods, or specialty goods.
2. Industrial products are used to produce other goods and services; they are purchased by professional purchasing agents.
3. Most successful products move through five separate stages in their life cycle: market development, rapid growth, turbulence, maturity, and decline.
4. The product life cycle concept is useful in forecasting demand, in deciding when to introduce a new product, and in modifying advertising strategy as the product moves through its life cycle.
5. Brand names help bring about repeat sales and facilitate new product introduction.
6. A good brand name should be short, easy to spell, right for the product, distinctive, and easy to remember.
7. A new product is one that performs a new function for the buyer or provides a significant improvement over other products.
8. Firms introduce new products to help them achieve sales growth objectives, meet competition, or complete a product line.
9. The six stages of the new product development process are idea generation, product evaluation, economic analysis, product development, test marketing, and commercialization.
10. Successful products usually perform better than unsuccessful products and feature several highly visible improvements.

KEY TERMS AND CONCEPTS

consumer products
convenience goods
profit margin
shopping goods
specialty goods
industrial products
product life cycle
market development stage
rapid growth stage
turbulence stage
maturity stage
decline stage

brand
trademark
family brand
new product
idea generation
product evaluation
economic analysis
product development
prototype
test marketing
commercialization

REVIEW QUESTIONS

1. What is the key to the marketing of convenience goods?
2. What role does advertising play in selling shopping goods?
3. In what ways does the selling of industrial goods differ from the selling of consumer goods?
4. During the market development stage of the product life cycle, what can the firm do to move its product into the rapid growth stage?
5. Generally speaking, how profitable are products during the maturity stage of the product life cycle?
6. Discuss the role of the product life cycle in the introduction of new products.
7. Why do firms place brand names on their products?
8. Which product attributes make it easier to sell a new product? Which attributes make it harder?
9. Describe the six-stage model for developing new products.
10. Why do some products fail and others succeed?

DISCUSSION QUESTIONS

1. What is meant when we say that a product is more than just the sum of its physical attributes?
2. When did you last purchase a specialty good? Why was the product a specialty good for you? Would it necessarily be a specialty good for other people?
3. Explain why the product life cycle is so important to most business people.
4. Do all products go through the same stages in the product life cycle? Explain.
5. Give an example of a new product that you purchased recently and discuss what's "new" about it.
6. Why do you think there are so many new products in the personal computer market?

CASE 13-1

Firestone Tires

Firestone Tire & Rubber Co. has experienced the situation of its product reaching the maturity stage in its life cycle. When the OPEC oil embargo escalated oil prices and decreased driving, tire sales dropped over four-fold. Drivers were trying to economize by replacing tires less often, by using retreads (thereby avoiding purchase of new tires), and by driving less. Classified ads even began offering used tires for sale. Many people sold their spare tires when money became even scarcer.

At the same time, the radial tire was coming into its own. The early radials designed by Michelin had been perfected, eliminating blowout problems and premature or uneven wear. Automobiles were being designed with suspension systems to optimize steering and control with radial tires, and stronger rims to withstand the greater stresses imposed by radials. Amid extensive government studies and tire manufacturer advertising boasting the superior gas mileage offered by radials, drivers who were replacing tires on their cars were replacing them with radials, not with bias-ply tires. Luxury cars began arriving equipped with radials, first as an option and then as standard equipment. Within a few years, almost all cars were equipped with radials. The rapid influx of Japanese and other foreign imported cars brought new popularity to the small metric-sized tires, since these cars drove far better with radials than with bias-ply tires.

Firestone realized that its overall market—automobile tires—was starting to decline: After all, tires were lasting longer, car sales were down, and driving was down. The submarket of radial tires, however, was due for rapid growth. After a major promotional campaign, Firestone gained a large portion of the radial market with its Firestone 500 radial. Unfortunately, the 500 turned out to be a highly dangerous and failure-prone tire which cost the company millions of dollars in lawsuits and replacement tires.

Firestone created the Firestone 721 radial, and then the Firestone 721 Metric, trying to recapture the market share it had lost with its 500 failure. Firestone had a chance to take a dominant share of the radial market with the 500, but the company today has to compete on more or less equal footing with several established radial manufacturers. Whether Firestone will ever recover its original market share is still unclear.

1. Do you think it makes a difference if a company enters the growth stage of a product (such as radial tires) early in the growth stage or late (as Firestone is now doing)? Why?
2. Why do you think Firestone marketing managers had to segment the automobile tire market before they established Firestone's line of new automobile tires?
3. In what stage of its product life cycle is the radial tire today? In what stage is the nonradial bias-ply tire? From these two conclusions, can you determine the stage in which car tires are found overall? Why or why not?

CASE 13-2

Atari

When home video games were first introduced, everyone expected them to sell. But no one expected them to sell as well as they have. Marketing plans revolved around early saturation of the market, with a fast drop-off in sales. Some companies even thought that they were too expensive to sell in huge numbers; they would sell at high prices to a few people, just like expensive cameras or expensive stereo equipment. Wrong! By 1982, home video games were a $2 billion a year business.

On top of the boom was Atari, which sold $740 million worth of video games in 1981. Atari's first game machine was very popular, well-priced and versatile. The game cartridges—really nothing more than a plug-in pack containing the few basic electronic circuits necessary to program the game machine for the new game—could be purchased for a small amount. And they were designed to fit only into Atari game machines.

Atari owns nearly two thirds of the market in game cartridges and more than two thirds of the game machines on the market. With that kind of lead, Atari has been able to purchase the great majority of the successful electronic games, the most famous of which is Pac-Man. Atari routinely introduces new and even better games.

At the same time that the video game craze hit America, personal computers were coming into vogue. In fact, many game manufacturers who disbelieved the popularity of video games thought that computers would soon take over the market and people would buy game programs for personal computers. The market proved them wrong, however.

Personal computers soon came to be marketed on the bases of price and good memory. But these features were not compatible with the extensive circuitry needed to produce good visual effects, color, and sophisticated game control demanded by new game cartridges. As a result, computers did not take over the market. In fact, Atari launched a new sophisticated game machine that included a computer keyboard so the machine could be used like a simple computer for around-the-home duties. Atari's sales continued to grow.

Atari foresees considerable product growth in the near future. Marketing consultants estimate that half the homes in America will have home video games by 1985. In Europe, the video game market will be expanding so fast during the same period that no one knows just where it will stop. Atari is spending vast amounts each year to ensure that its games and game machines stay the leaders in the video game market.

1. Is the home video game a consumer or an industrial good? Is it a convenience, shopping, or specialty good? What information helps you define the video game's product class?
2. In what stage of the product life cycle is the video game? How can its position in the product life cycle be used by Atari?
3. Every Atari game cartridge and game machine features the Atari name prominently displayed on its package. Why does Atari take branding so seriously? What does Atari gain by using its name so prominently? What are the advantages of the name Atari?
4. Describe briefly how the method of introducing new products was followed for video games. Why was the video game, and Atari's video game in particular, so popular?

14

Channels of Distribution

After studying this chapter, you should be able to:

- Describe a channel of distribution and explain how channels function in our economy.
- Describe the role of wholesaling and the various types of wholesalers.
- Identify six types of retail outlets.
- Explain physical distribution's role in the marketing process.

    A channel of distribution and a river are somewhat alike. Each begins at a source, which for a channel of distribution we shall call the manufacturer, and each flows along until it reaches either the sea or the great industrial and consumer markets. Each encounters obstacles along the way and attempts to overcome them in the most efficient manner possible. Water flows around granite bedrock and cuts its way through softer sedimentary stone; goods and services, ideally, flow around warehousing bottlenecks and follow a course involving the least transportation cost and the greatest delivery efficiency.

Chapter 14 • Channels of Distribution 253

This chapter examines channels of distribution—what they are, what they do, and how they do it. We look at the role of wholesalers and retailers in the channel. We then explore some topics relating to transportation, inventory management, and warehousing.

CHANNELS OF DISTRIBUTION

The image of a channel of distribution as a river may seem a bit contrived, but it does emphasize the idea of a *flow* of goods and services. Not surprisingly, marketing channels are also frequently referred to as "conduits" and "pipelines." Let's now look at a more exact definition of the channel of distribution.

Distribution Channel Defined

A **distribution channel** is an organized network of individuals and businesses (called intermediaries) through which goods and services flow from producers to end users. These individuals and firms include such channel members as wholesalers, retailers, and other intermediaries. It is through distribution that goods and services are made available to buyers at the right place and at the right time.

Channel distribution management is dynamic. Consumer tastes and preferences change rapidly, and new selling and transportation opportunities present themselves almost every day. Phonograph records were once sold in hi-fi stores exclusively; now they're sold in supermarkets and drugstores too. A change in the distribution pattern of a product can create sweeping changes in the commercial landscape: Think of how supermarkets have almost replaced neighborhood, individually owned grocery stores. Or how fast-food restaurants have just about replaced meals at home for an entire generation.

What Kinds of Channels Are There?

Figure 14-1 shows channels of distribution for consumer and industrial products. The distribution channels for consumer products usually feature both a wholesaler and a retailer. That is, the manufacturer sells its products to a wholesaler (sometimes through an agent) who then sells the products to retailers. Some manufacturers of consumer products, however, sell directly to retailers, and a few even sell directly to final consumers. Singer Corporation owns many of its retail establishments. Avon and Fuller Brush have well-established sales forces that call on customers in their homes.

Channels of distribution for industrial goods often have only one intermediary between the manufacturer and the user. Figure 14-1B shows

Figure 14-1

Channels of Distribution for Consumer and Industrial Goods

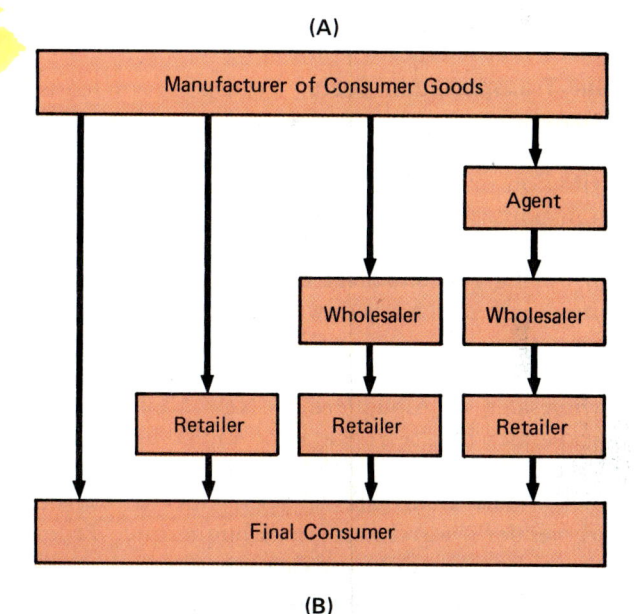

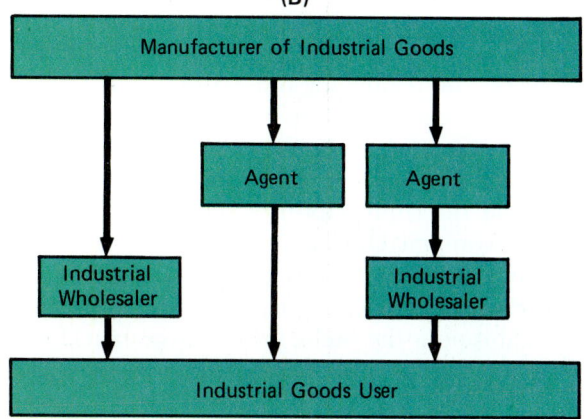

(A)

Manufacturer of Consumer Goods → Agent → Wholesaler → Retailer → Final Consumer

Manufacturer of Consumer Goods → Wholesaler → Retailer → Final Consumer

Manufacturer of Consumer Goods → Retailer → Final Consumer

Manufacturer of Consumer Goods → Final Consumer

(B)

Manufacturer of Industrial Goods → Agent → Industrial Wholesaler → Industrial Goods User

Manufacturer of Industrial Goods → Agent → Industrial Goods User

Manufacturer of Industrial Goods → Industrial Wholesaler → Industrial Goods User

Manufacturer of Industrial Goods → Industrial Goods User

industrial wholesalers and agents providing the sole link between a manufacturer of industrial goods and its buyers.

Functions of the Channel

Are intermediaries really needed in the channel of distribution? Would products be cheaper if there were no wholesalers? Do channel members make money for themselves at the expense of an unwary public? Before answering these questions, let's look at what intermediaries actually do in the channel.

Contact Potential Customers. The most important function of a channel of distribution is to link producers and customers. This is done through product messages that flow from the manufacturer to the customer. Every time you see Advent speakers displayed in a stereo store, you are in "contact" with the manufacturer.

Cut Transportation Costs. Transportation costs are a major element of total marketing costs. The presence of intermediaries in the channel of distribution provides an opportunity for significant transportation cost reductions. Retailers and wholesalers minimize overall transportation costs by buying goods in large quantities and breaking these bulk purchases down into smaller amounts for resale.

Suppose there is an electrical supply wholesaler in Albuquerque, New Mexico. The wholesaler buys a truckload of 45,000 light bulbs from a General Electric plant in Louisville, Kentucky. The bulbs are shipped directly to the wholesaler's warehouse in Albuquerque. From here, they are distributed to retailers who sell them to people around the Southwest. Now imagine this option: Every time people in the Southwest want a light bulb, they call the GE plant on the telephone and order a half dozen. GE then sends each order via parcel post or United States Mail. Think of how this example illustrates the amount of transportation cost savings and the contribution of such savings to national economic efficiency.

Which of these two alternatives involves the lower transportation costs? Obviously, the first one. Shipping the bulbs in one large truckload, warehousing the shipment in Albuquerque, and then selling the bulbs in smaller quantities to retailers makes much more sense economically. These transportation cost savings mean lower prices and greater convenience for consumers.

Stimulate Demand. Wholesalers and retailers work with manufacturers to encourage people to buy the manufacturer's products. This is because the success of retailers and wholesalers depends on the success of the products they carry. Gillette's wholesalers employ more than 22,000 salespeople to call on retailers and to promote Gillette products.

Figure 14-2 shows that wholesalers also run product advertisements in magazines directed at retailers. The purpose of these ads is to convince retailers to stock the advertised product. Similarly, retailers spend a great deal of money advertising locally. All of these promotional efforts, whether launched by the manufacturer, wholesaler, or retailer, serve to stimulate demand for the manufacturer's products.

Maintain Inventory. The success of a manufacturer depends largely on its ability to deliver products rapidly to buyers. Manufacturers like to see their products inventoried close to the buyer—that is, at wholesalers' warehouses around the country and in retail stores themselves. In this way, the product is available *where* and *when* the buyer wants it.

Relay Market Information. The last important function of wholesalers and retailers is that of relaying market information to the manufacturer. Product information—advertisements, sales promotions, product demonstrations—flow through the distribution channel from the manufacturer to retailers and consumers.

Information about changing consumer tastes and preferences and about what people like and do not like about the manufacturer's products moves up the channel from consumers to retailers to wholesalers to manufacturers. These information flows are shown in Figure 14-3.

Channel Intermediaries: Who Needs Them?

We are now ready to ask who needs channel intermediaries. The answer: both consumers and

Chapter 14 • Channels of Distribution   255

Figure 14-2

An Advertisement Directed at Retailers

Figure 14-3

Information Flows in the Channel of Distribution

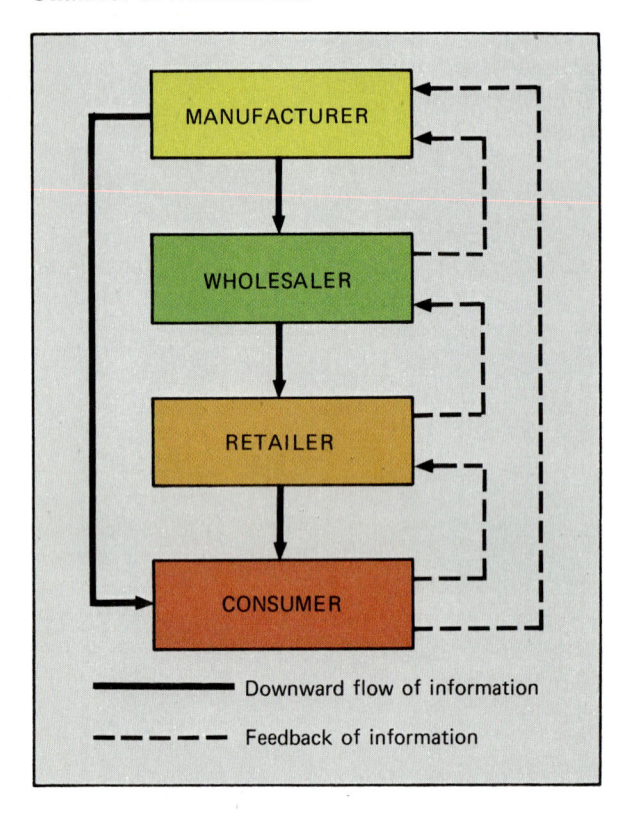

manufacturers do. We as consumers need intermediaries if we want our material needs served efficiently—that is, if we want the right products available at the right place and at the right time. Manufacturers need intermediaries for at least two reasons. First, most businesses cannot afford to own the entire channel of distribution themselves. General Motors, for example, has more than 17,000 independent dealers in the United States. The average dealership is worth about $3.5 million. Thus, GM would have to pay nearly $60 billion dollars to buy all its dealers. Even the world's largest carmaker does not have that much cash. Second, some manufacturers know a great deal about production but very little about wholesaling and retailing. Therefore, most manufacturers let intermediaries distribute their products for them.

Even if a manufacturer elected to "eliminate the intermediary (middleman) and pass the savings on to you," someone would still have to perform the intermediary functions. If not a wholesaler or retailer, then that someone would be the manufacturer or even the consumer. It is only reasonable that the manufacturer would then charge its customers for performing at least some of these functions.

WHOLESALING

For some people, buying at wholesale simply means paying significantly less than the regular list price for a product. But this use of the term "wholesale" doesn't shed much light on the role of wholesalers in a distribution channel and wholesalers' contribution to economic efficiency. We shall define a **wholesaler**, then, as any firm that helps a manufacturer sell its products to other businesses, usually retailers, for eventual resale to final consumers. Wholesalers are intermediaries in the channel of distribution; they do not themselves deal with final consumers.

How Big Is the Wholesaling Industry?

Wholesalers are certainly an important part of our economy. Wholesale sales in 1980 amounted to more than $1.2 trillion while retail sales barely exceeded $1 trillion. This is because products are often wholesaled several times en route from manufacturer to retailers and final consumers. There are a great many wholesale firms in the United States. There were about 382,800 in 1980, employing nearly 4.4 million people. Total inventory of wholesale firms is valued at more than $82 billion.[1]

Are All Wholesalers the Same?

Wholesalers are successful only if they are able to serve the needs of their customers. Since customer needs differ, wholesalers differ in the type and scale of their operations.

Most wholesalers have always offered product delivery services for their customers, but today many of them also perform some or all of the channel functions discussed earlier—contacting, transportation cost savings, demand stimulation, inventory maintenance, and market information. Let's look at the four major kinds of wholesalers and the services they offer.

---

[1] U. S. Bureau of the Census, *Census of Wholesale Trade* (Washington, D.C.: U. S. Government Printing Office, 1980).

CONTROVERSIAL ISSUES

In the past 20 years or so, door-to-door salespeople have almost disappeared from American society. The only survivors are occasional roofing contractors, lawn cutters, or painters. Has America gotten rid of a method of distribution that was really very good?

Pro

Yes, door-to-door is a great way to sell products. Consider Tronics Marketing Corporation, a company that sells computers both door-to-door and through small gatherings such as those used by Tupperware and Amway. After its first year of operation, Tronics had 10,000 salespeople throughout the country and revenues of over $3 million. Its success has encouraged the formation of other door-to-door computer sales companies.

Tronics finds that it has a great edge over the large computer stores. A salesperson can see exactly what a customer wants and can tailor demonstrations and explanations to the customer better than can be done in a store. Also, through the use of demographic data the salesperson can better identify potential customers who can afford to buy home computers. Less time is spent talking to people who could not buy a computer even if they wanted one.

Door-to-door selling has even been used to sell automobiles. Automobile dealers face high costs in keeping a showroom and a large supply of vehicles on a display lot. These facilities and supplies are maintained for the potential customer who elects to walk through the door and look at a new car. By selling door-to-door, the dealer avoids the expense of a showroom, and the customer makes a purchase decision in familiar and comfortable surroundings. Additionally, door-to-door selling is an effective way to encourage people to think about buying a new car. As a result, automotive companies who do not choose to sell door-to-door have to advertise heavily to encourage potential customers to come to their dealerships. As the costs of selling a product become higher and higher, door-to-door sales should be a channel of distribution that more companies consider.

Companies Should Sell More Products Door-to-Door.

Con

No, door-to-door selling is not an effective means of selling. The reason we don't see many door-to-door salespeople today is that homeowners don't like them. Many door-to-door salespeople tend to be abrasive, pushy, and pesty. Many towns have outlawed door-to-door selling and many condominiums and apartment complexes prohibit it.

Furthermore, commercial advertising is already pushy enough in making people buy things. Imagine how a parent would feel if a door-to-door salesperson allowed the children to play with several expensive toys and then handed the parent a bill for the toys.

Finally, it's one thing to buy a piece of Tupperware or a box of Amway detergent from a door-to-door salesperson, but people buying a personal computer or a car want to know that computer software, auto service facilities, and other such services back up the sale. Most people want to see what they're getting for their money. The problem would be even worse if a large auto dealer from Los Angeles sent salespeople to Ames, Iowa, to sell cars door-to-door. The prices might be quite good, but delays in delivery, lack of service and follow-up care, and other problems would make this kind of arrangement quite unsatisfactory.

No, door-to-door sales is not recommended. American businesses knew what they were doing when they decided to end the practice.

Full-Service Merchant Wholesalers. As Table 14-1 shows, full-service merchant wholesalers offer a broad range of services to their customers and suppliers. These wholesalers take title to and possession of the products they sell. In taking title, they actually own the merchandise from the time they get it from the manufacturer to the time they resell it to the retail buyer. The wholesalers' operating margin, therefore, is the difference between the amount they pay for a product and the amount they sell it for. They also make contact with potential buyers of the product, generate transportation efficiencies through volume purchasing, and stimulate demand for the manufacturer's products. More than 80 percent of U.S. wholesalers are full-service merchant wholesalers.

In addition, full-service merchant wholesalers provide market information to their customers about what types of products final consumers are buying and about how these products can best be advertised and sold. They also relay information back to manufacturers about how customers like the products. This information helps manufacturers modify their products so that more people will want to buy them. Finally, these wholesalers often finance the purchases of their customers and provide the customers with general managerial advice.

Limited-Service Merchant Wholesalers. Limited-service merchant wholesalers also take title to and possession of their merchandise. Although they perform the functions of contacting and transportation, they usually have only a small sales force to call on customers. They rarely provide market information to their suppliers or credit and managerial services to their customers.

Manufacturer-Owned Wholesalers. We've already talked about why many manufacturers prefer to let other people handle the wholesaling function for them. But some manufacturers still act as their own wholesalers. Why? First, it may be less expensive than using an independent wholesaler. Second, a reliable, efficient wholesaler sometimes cannot be found to sell the manufacturer's products. Third, the manufacturer may want to retain full control over the selling of its products.

Merchandise Agents. Unlike full-service and limited-service merchant wholesalers, merchandise agents do not buy merchandise (that is, they do not take title) and hold it for resale. Instead,

Table 14-1

Functions of Various Types of Wholesalers

Function	Full-Service Merchant Wholesaler	Limited-Service Merchant Wholesaler	Manufacturer-Owned Wholesaler	Merchandise Agents
Takes Title	x	x	x	
Transportation Efficiency	x	x	x	
Contacting	x	x	x	x
Demand Stimulation	x	Limited	x	x
Inventory Maintenance	x	x	x	
Marketing Information	x		x	x
Credit Assistance	x		x	
Managerial Assistance	x		x	Limited

Profile — George Weissman

George Weissman, chairman of the board at Philip Morris, began his career working for a newspaper. After serving in World War II as a Naval officer, he took a job promoting movies for Sam Goldwyn, the famous movie producer. His experience and the reputation he earned won him a job at Benjamin Sonnenberg, a classy New York publicist and consultant to Philip Morris, a producer of cigarettes, beverages, and other products. Weissman became the account executive for Philip Morris, and four years later left Sonnenberg to join Philip Morris.

In 14 years, George Weissman jumped from a public relations executive to president of Philip Morris. He entered the company during a reorganizational period in which new marketing concepts were first being tried by American corporations. He was responsible for introducing Marlboro cigarettes and then for converting Parliament cigarettes from a luxury product to a mass-purchased brand. In 1957, his success with cigarettes earned Weissman a vice presidency and, in 1966, he became president after creating Philip Morris International, an international marketing and distribution branch of Philip Morris.

Today, Philip Morris specializes in products that are, in Weissman's words, "high-volume, relatively low-cost products that are basic to any store—supermarket or convenience store—that wants to build volume and profit on a square-foot basis. Also, they're all what I call pleasurable products. They're among the last things you would give up in a recession." In particular, Weissman has stressed high-quality products which enjoy a good reputation for that quality: Marlboro cigarettes, Miller beer, and 7-Up soft drinks are just a few examples. They are all products that Philip Morris distributes through every supermarket, grocery store, convenience store, vending machine, gas station, and at virtually every cash register in the country.

The distribution problems are immense. One major problem that Philip Morris faces is the marketplace to which it distributes its products. Beer, for example, is sold by independent distributors who negotiate prices with the breweries by one-on-one dealing. In the inflationary economy of the past 15 years, Weissman realized that such dealing was not feasible—it cut profit margins to a point where companies couldn't survive. Similarly, profit margins among cigarettes are fairly low, so discounting prices can be disastrous for the manufacturer. When competitors began discounting their cigarettes to edge in on Philip Morris' brands, Weissman simply told distributors that he would keep his prices up and keep the distributors' profit margins up if they would keep his cigarettes selling. Naturally, the distributors liked this approach and the price wars failed. In every market, with every product, Weissman has been a magician who can create the perfect price and the perfect appeal for a product to assure successful distribution.

In particular, Philip Morris has created a niche for itself at convenience stores. About 40 percent of convenience store sales involve cigarettes, beer, and soft drinks. In each of those categories, Weissman works to maintain a powerful share. Consequently, the convenience store managers know that Philip Morris is essential to their own success, and they protect and promote Philip Morris brands. Weissman never lets them down. He knows that his company sells its customers an image as it sells a product. People buy Marlboros, Miller Lite, or 7-Up because those purchases are statements about the purchaser. Weissman realizes that his major duty is to maintain the reputation and image that makes people buy those products. As long as he does this, Philip Morris sales are assured.

they are paid a fee for bringing buyer and seller together, much like real estate agents are paid a commission by home sellers for helping them find buyers.

Merchandise agents normally have a great deal of knowledge about the marketplace. They share this information with both the buyer and the seller. Merchandise agents are common in a variety of industries, including textiles, industrial machinery, chemicals, and canned foods.

RETAILING

We often think of retailing as a very simple business: **Retailers buy products, mark them up 20 to 50 percent**, and sell them over the counter to customers. But there is much more to retailing than this.

Large retail stores, such as Sears, Montgomery Ward, and J.C. Penney, are sophisticated professionally managed firms that use the most modern business techniques to generate

Merchandise agents bring buyers and sellers of products together.

profits for their stockholders. The managers of these firms devote a great deal of time and money to analyzing their markets, to studying social and cultural trends, and to designing advertising and promotion strategies.

One of the most exciting things about retailing is the many career opportunities it provides. Perhaps you would like to work for yourself. If so, take note of the fact that 85 percent of all retail stores in the United States are individually owned. Or you may want to work for a very large business. If so, look at Table 14-2 which shows that the largest retailers sell more than $160 billion worth of goods annually and employ more than 2 million people.

What Kinds of Retail Stores Are There?

Think of the different retail stores found in your city or hometown, or in a nearby shopping mall. Although they sell many goods, the stores themselves can be classified into just six categories, including supermarkets, convenience stores, specialty stores, department stores, discount stores, and hypermarkets.

Supermarkets. **Supermarkets are the primary sellers of food products in the United States.** The managers of supermarkets know that location is an important consideration. Most people won't drive past one supermarket just to go to another. It is also important that supermarkets offer competitive prices and high-quality meat and produce. Nationally known goods, such as Birds Eye frozen corn, offer few opportunities for supermarket managers to make their stores seem better than others.

A minor revolution is currently underway in supermarket merchandising. This revolution concerns the marketing of "generic" products. **Generic products are nonbranded and nonadvertised products.** They are usually lower in quality than name brand items, and their packaging, as shown in Figure 14-4, does no more than describe the contents. Many consumers like generic products because they sell for about 30 percent less than nationally branded products and about 15 percent less than store brands. The most successful generic products have been bleach, cooking oil, and paper towels, but many people believe that soon 30 to 40 percent of all supermarket products will be generic.

Table 14-2

Twenty Largest Retailing Companies Ranked By Sales

Rank 1981	Company	Sales ($000)	Net Income ($000)	Net Income as a Percentage of Sales	Number of Employees
1	Sears Roebuck (Chicago)	27,357,400	650,100	2.4	337,400
2	Safeway Stores (Oakland)	16,580,318	114,556	0.7	157,411
3	K Mart (Troy, Mich.)	16,527,012	220,251	1.3	280,000
4	J.C. Penney (New York)	11,860,169	386,809	3.3	187,000
5	Kroger (Cincinnati)	11,266,520	128,045	1.1	127,271
6	F.W. Woolworth (New York)	7,223,241	81,870	1.1	139,800
7	Lucky Stores (Dublin, Calif.)	7,201,404	95,452	1.3	66,000
8	American Stores (Salt Lake City)	7,096,590	64,552	0.9	64,000
9	Federated Department Stores (Cincinnati)	7,067,673	258,508	3.7	120,800
10	Great Atlantic & Pacific Tea (Montvale, N.J.)	6,989,529	(48,049)	—	60,000
11	Winn-Dixie Stores (Jacksonville)	6,200,167	95,395	1.5	63,000
12	Montgomery Ward (Chicago)	5,742,491	(124,120)	—	95,900
13	Southland (Dallas)	5,693,636	94,191	1.7	49,600
14	Jewel Companies (Chicago)	5,107,614	101,670	2.0	36,922
15	Household Merchandising (Des Plaines, Ill.)	5,079,932	53,262	1.0	59,900
16	Dayton Hudson (Minneapolis)	4,942,859	173,420	3.5	70,000
17	Grand Union (Elmwood Park, N.J.)	3,626,231	34,327	0.9	36,000
18	Albertson's (Boise)	3,480,570	48,478	1.4	30,300
19	May Department Stores (St. Louis)	3,413,204	126,203	3.7	68,000
20	Supermarkets General (Woodbridge, N.J.)	2,999,379	30,256	1.0	30,000

Source: FORTUNE (July 12, 1982), pp. 140-141. "© 1982 Time Inc. All rights reserved."

Convenience Stores. **Convenience stores** are actually minisupermarkets. They carry many of the same food and nonfood items which are sold in supermarkets but offer a limited selection in terms of brands and package sizes. Convenience stores, such as 7-Eleven or Stop-N-Go, do not usually have a meat or fresh produce department.

Since convenience store prices are typically higher than supermarket prices, we should ask why people shop at them. You can probably answer this from your own experience. First, shoppers tolerate the higher prices because their convenience store purchases are quite small (averaging less than $2.50). Second, shoppers are willing to pay a little extra for the convenience of being able to make purchases quickly and easily—no lines at checkout counters, no parking problems. And third, convenience stores, as the name says, are conveniently located at busy intersections or near residential neighborhoods. This cuts down on consumer travel time to and from the store. In effect, the convenience store retailer charges the consumer a premium for this time savings.

Specialty Stores. **Specialty stores** meet the needs of a particular market segment. They usually sell only one type of product, such as clothing, jewelry, or furniture. Although many smaller specialty stores are owned and managed by one person, most of the larger ones are members of a chain. A **chain** is a group of stores owned by one individual or firm.

The successful specialty store is able to compete against larger stores by spotting new trends in the marketplace and by making the right inventory adjustments quickly. Large department stores, which have much more money available for buying merchandise, are sometimes slow to react to market changes because of inflexible bureaucratic procedures.

Department Stores. **Department stores** sell a wide assortment of merchandise, ranging from women's dresses to kitchen appliances. Before World War II, traditional downtown department stores, such as Sanger-Harris in Dallas, Dayton's in Minneapolis, and Macy's in New York, dominated the retail markets. But these stores lost

Figure 14-4

Generic Products

their markets as people moved to the suburbs. Sears and Montgomery Ward, which are themselves department stores, were among the first to build in the suburbs. The older, more established downtown stores eventually realized the impact of this population move and also began locating branch stores in fast-growing suburban areas. Today, more than 80 percent of most department stores' sales are from suburban branch stores.

Discount Stores. During the last 30 years, the term **discount store** has meant several things. When discount stores first appeared on the retail scene in the early 1950s, they sold primarily name-brand products at low prices. Popular items included jewelry, luggage, electrical appliances, and silver-plated items. One reason why they could afford to feature such low prices was that they did not offer delivery or credit services to the buyer. This cut costs.

In the early 1960s, however, a dramatic change occurred in the discount world: Kresge's, K-Mart, Jupiter, Korvette, Arlans, Stop & Shop, Shopper's Fair, Gibson's, and other such stores began to sell little-known brands at low prices.

Today, the merchandise lines of discount stores are limited to the most popular items and colors. Other characteristics include self-service, long operating hours, Sunday business hours, inexpensive interior features, and ample parking.

Hypermarkets. **Hypermarkets** are a type of large discount store that developed in Germany. Hypermarkets sell grocery products as well as most of the other products sold in discount stores. Like other discount stores, hypermarkets specialize in low-priced merchandise that sells very quickly.

It is still too early to tell whether hypermarkets will play a major role in retailing in the United States. We do know that discount stores have become larger and carry a wider variety of products than before. Whether in this country it is possible to sell everything from apple sauce to washing machines under one roof remains to be seen.

Market Coverage

Market coverage refers to how readily available a product is to consumers, that is, whether the product is sold through most retail outlets or through only a few. At issue here is how far consumers can be expected to travel to buy the

"I think we may be just the store for you, sir!"

Source: Drawing by Gahan Wilson; © 1980 The New Yorker Magazine, Inc.

FROM THE FILE

> Three years ago, Sherry started Rosebud Creations, Inc. The company produces very lifelike and beautiful roses carved from wood. Each wooden rose is sold in a little box with a vase. The roses are low-priced, and the company's advertising presents them as a superior alternative to real roses from a florist. Moreover, they look just as nice and don't wilt. Currently, Rosebud products are sold in a few department stores, but Sherry knows that she needs to develop a better retailing system. At a staff meeting one day, she posed the question: In what kind of retail stores should we try to place our wooden roses?

product—around the corner or to the other side of town. Let's look at three levels of market coverage: intensive, exclusive, and selective.

Intensive. When a product is made available through as many stores as possible, **intensive distribution** is being used. This approach to retailing is based on the idea that sales of a product are greatest when it is sold nearly everywhere. Intensive distribution usually means that the manufacturer or wholesaler of the product must have a large sales force to stay in touch with each retail store. Examples of products sold intensively are candy, milk, and cigarettes. These are primarily convenience goods. Do you remember the characteristics of convenience goods discussed in Chapter 13?

Exclusive. If a product is made available through one or only a few stores in a geographic market, **exclusive distribution** is being used. Exclusive distribution is the opposite of intensive distribution. Exclusive distribution involves lower costs because the manufacturer needs only a few salespeople to service the smaller number of stores carrying the product. Two products often sold exclusively are expensive watches and fine china. These are specialty goods.

Selective. Selective distribution falls in between intensive distribution and exclusive distribution. **Selective distribution** involves selling products through several—but certainly not all—retailers in a market. Shopping goods, such as television sets, refrigerators, and furniture, are examples of such products.

What Determines the Level of Market Coverage?

The answer to the question of which distribution strategy is right for a product depends on where shoppers expect to find the product. If consumers expect to see it at nearby stores, then it should be sold intensively. We know, for example, that consumers expect to be able to buy milk at convenient, nearby locations. Most people will not drive great distances for a particular brand of homogenized milk. In contrast, people expect expensive watches to be sold in fine jewelry stores by experienced salespeople. Smart watch manufacturers do not display their watches next to the soft drink cooler at the local convenience store.

PHYSICAL DISTRIBUTION

We now need to examine how products are actually moved from the manufacturer to the final buyer. This activity is called **physical distribution**. How should products be transported to the buyer? Which transportation mode—truck, rail, airline—is the least costly? What about the trade-off between delivery speed and cost? Should the firm own or rent its warehouses? How much inventory should be maintained? These are just a few of the many challenging questions that physical distribution managers must attempt to answer.

We begin our discussion of physical distribution by examining its relationship to marketing. We then look at the total cost approach and at alternative transportation carriers.

Scrambled Merchandising

Not long ago, grocery stores and supermarkets in the United States sold only food or food-related products. More recently, these stores adopted **scrambled merchandising**—the practice of selling unrelated products in one store. Supermarkets now sell such nonfood items as motor oil, diapers, pots and pans, cosmetics, books and magazines, and toys.

To see why supermarkets have begun scrambling their merchandise, we need to look at their profit margins. As the following table shows, many major supermarkets make only a little more than one penny (before tax) on each dollar of sales. Total return on investment for supermarket shareholders averaged only 14 percent before taxes in 1981. Both the low profit on sales and the low return on investment are direct results of the fact that the **gross margin** (defined as selling price minus direct purchase cost) on food items is only 18 to 22 percent. On the other hand, the gross margin on many nonfood items ranges as high as 40 percent. Stocking these nonfood items gives supermarket managers an opportunity to earn more money.

Other types of retail stores with shrinking profit margins can be expected to "scramble" their merchandise assortment in the future in an effort to push profit margins up.

PROFITABILITY OF SIX LARGE SUPERMARKETS

Store	Percentage Return on Investment	Net Income as a Percent of Sales
Safeway Stores	10.3	0.7
Kroger	15.9	1.1
Great Atlantic & Pacific (A&P)	(loss)	(loss)
Jewel Companies	18.3	2.0
Supermarkets General	18.1	1.0
Giant Food	15.1	1.2

SOURCE: FORTUNE (July 12, 1982), pp. 140-141. "© 1982 Time Inc. All rights reserved."

Physical Distribution and Marketing

An efficient physical distribution system makes it easier for the firm to sell its products. How? By reducing product delivery time and by making the order cycle more consistent.

Reducing Product Delivery Time. Most people want to buy high-quality products at fair prices. The same is true of business firms, whether they buy coal for the production of power or televisions for resale to the consumer. Equally important, firms like to have their purchases delivered quickly.

To see the importance of physical distribution, picture yourself as the purchasing agent for the Amerex Climate Control Company. Your job is to choose a supplier of galvanized metal sheeting for the fabrication of heating and cooling ventilation ducts, one of your company's top-selling products. You've narrowed your choices to two suppliers. One of them promises three-day delivery on all shipments; the other offers no better than two-week delivery. All else equal, which supplier would you pick? Obviously, the one offering better delivery terms.

It is not hard to see that in a competitive marketplace, the supplier with an efficient physical distribution system wins more new customers and sells more of its products.

Improving Order Cycle Consistency. The **order cycle** is the length of time between the placing of a purchase order and the delivery of the merchandise to the buyer. Order cycle consistency refers to whether ordered products are regularly delivered when they are supposed to be delivered. A promise by a supplier of three-day delivery means three-day delivery, not ten-day delivery or even five-day delivery.

Returning to the Amerex example, let's assume that your fabrication plant has limited room for storing sheet metal. In fact, you have enough warehouse space for only three days' worth of production. To keep the production line running you need to receive a new shipment of metal sheeting at least every three days. If the shipment is even a day late, you have to shut down the production line and send the work force home at full pay until the sheeting arrives. In this instance, consistent three-day delivery means the difference between operating the plant and closing it down temporarily. If its supplier cannot promise consistent delivery, then Amerex should buy from someone else.

What, therefore, is the precise connection between physical distribution and marketing? The connection is quick delivery and order cycle consistency. These are two of a supplying firm's most effective sales tools. Especially when competing products are essentially alike, the supplier with the best distribution system usually has the greatest sales and, more important, the greatest profits.

Total Cost Approach

The goal of physical distribution is to create time and place utility by delivering products at the right place and at the right time. The basis for making physical distribution decisions is the total cost approach. What this approach, or principle, says is that any decision about one cost element in a distribution system should be considered in terms of its effect on other cost elements in the system. The idea is to minimize *total system* cost, or to maximize *total system* efficiency—not just to focus on one particular element.

To understand how the total cost approach works, we need to think about the trade-off between transportation costs and warehousing costs. A manufacturer of precision scientific testing equipment could choose to locate several warehouses around the country. Out of its single manufacturing plant, the firm periodically sends a truckload of its products to each warehouse. The managers of these warehouses then fill their customers' orders. Alternatively, the firm could do without the network of warehouses and, instead, fill each order individually from plant headquarters. Customer orders would be sent to the shipping room, where the equipment would be crated, delivered to the loading dock, driven to the airport, and sent to the buyer via air freight.

The trade-off in this example is between a system that minimizes transportation costs (the first alternative) and one that minimizes warehousing costs (the second alternative). Which system involves the least cost without sacrificing customer service? Probably a combination of the two, in which a concern for each cost element is balanced with a concern for total system cost.

How Are Products Transported?

The five major modes of transporting merchandise and materials are airlines, trucks, railroads, pipelines, and waterways. Railroads still handle a greater percentage of intercity freight in the United States than any other type of carrier. Their share of the freight market, however, has declined steadily since 1930, while the shares of airlines, pipelines, and trucks have all increased. The percentage of the market for inland waterways has remained surprisingly stable. Let's take a brief look at each type of carrier.

Airlines. Air transport specializes in the movement of high-value, lightweight, perishable products, such as flowers and medicines. As Table 14-3 indicates, air freight is much more expensive than any other way of transporting merchandise.

With the development of the jumbo jets, such as the Boeing 747, airlines have begun to haul bulk cargo. United Airlines has its "Soft-Touch" container service. The container is a sealed box holding up to 10,000 pounds in 457 cubic feet. Soft Touch is now used by computer companies as an alternative to truck transportation.

Trucks. Next to air freight, truck shipment is the most expensive form of transportation. Trucks, however, tend to compete more directly with railroads than with airlines. The major advantages of

Table 14-3

Freight Transportation Costs

Mode	Price (Cents/Ton Mile)
Air	42.68
Truck	6.53
Rail	2.78
Pipe	0.84
Water	0.25

Source: U. S. Bureau of the Census *Statistical Abstract of the United States, 1981* (Washington D.C.: U. S. Government Printing Office, 1981), pp. 612-613.

truck transportation are door-to-door service, frequency, convenience, and flexibility of service.

The major disadvantage of highway shipment, at least compared to rail, is cost—6.53 cents versus 2.78 cents per ton mile. Also, some products are too large to be sent by truck. Although the soaring cost of diesel fuel has driven up the cost of truck transport over the past decade, the nation's highways will continue to serve as major freight arteries through the 1980s and 1990s.

Railroads. Railroads are used primarily for shipping products over very long distances, especially products that do not need to arrive at their destination quickly. Twenty-five years ago, trains carried a wide variety of products, but today they haul mostly heavy manufactured goods and raw materials.

More recently, railroads have tried to regain lost markets by developing special cars for hauling complete truck trailers ("piggy back") as well as automobile-carrying freight cars ("stack-back" and "vert-a-pac"). The railroads have also developed special rapid "run-through" freight trains that reduce product delivery time significantly. If railroads are able to repair their rail beds and upgrade their equipment, they should continue to be a major force in the long-haul shipment business.

Pipelines. Pipelines are used for moving products such as crude oil. While the product moves slowly, 3 to 4 miles per hour, it moves all of the time. Transportation via pipelines is also very dependable—they are almost completely automated and, as a result, are not affected by labor problems or the weather.

Railroads still compete as long-distance carriers.

Inland Waterways. Shipment on inland waterways is one of the oldest ways of moving freight. Although inexpensive, it does have two disadvantages. First, inland waterways are affected by the weather. The Great Lakes are shut down for up to four months each year because of ice. Similarly, major floods render navigation impossible on some rivers in the spring. Second, water transportation is very slow. Whereas trains average 25 miles per hour, barge traffic moves at 6 to 9 miles per hour.

SUMMARY POINTS

1. A channel of distribution is an organized network of individuals and business firms through which goods and services flow from producers to consumers.
2. Most channels of distribution for consumer goods have both a wholesaler and a retailer. Most distribution channels for industrial goods have only a wholesaler or an agent serving as a link between buyer and seller.
3. The key channel functions are contacting potential customers, cutting transport costs, stimulating product demand, maintaining inventory, and relaying market information.
4. Four common types of wholesalers are full-service merchant wholesalers, limited-service merchant wholesalers, manufacturer-owned wholesalers, and merchandise agents.
5. Most manufacturing firms rely on independent wholesalers to distribute their products because of the expense involved and because wholesalers know more about distribution.
6. Six types of retail institutions are supermarkets, convenience stores, specialty stores, department stores, discount stores, and hypermarkets.

7. Market coverage refers to the relative availability of a product to the consumer—specifically, to the number of outlets serving a given geographic market.
8. Where consumers expect to find a product determines whether it is marketed through intensive, selective, or exclusive channels of distribution.
9. Two benefits of an efficient physical distribution system are reduced product delivery time and improved order cycle consistency.
10. The total cost approach to physical distribution says that a decision concerning any one element must be viewed in terms of how it affects the cost and efficiency of the entire distribution system.
11. The five major modes of transporting merchandise domestically are airlines, trucks, railroads, pipelines, and waterways.

KEY TERMS AND CONCEPTS

distribution channel
channel intermediaries
wholesalers
full-service merchant wholesalers
limited-service merchant wholesalers
manufacturer-owned wholesalers
merchandise agents
retailers
supermarkets
generic products
convenience stores
chain
specialty stores
department stores
discount store
hypermarkets
market coverage
intensive distribution
exclusive distribution
selective distribution
physical distribution
order cycle
scrambled merchandising
gross margin

REVIEW QUESTIONS

1. What is dynamic about a channel of distribution?
2. Why do most manufacturers use independent wholesalers and retailers?
3. How does a wholesaler differ from a retailer?
4. How is a full-service merchant wholesaler different from a limited-service merchant wholesaler?
5. Explain the role that merchandise agents play in distributing products.
6. How have department stores reacted to the movement of consumers from the downtown areas to the suburbs?
7. Describe the differences between intensive, exclusive, and selective distribution.
8. What is the relationship between physical distribution and marketing?

DISCUSSION QUESTIONS

1. Would products be cheaper if there were no wholesalers or retailers? Explain.
2. Will convenience stores continue to increase their sales during the 1985-1990 time period? Why or why not?
3. Why have supermarkets adopted scrambled merchandising? Do you believe supermarkets will continue to use scrambled merchandising during the next ten years?
4. Do you think that the total cost approach to physical distribution will be more or less important in the future than it is today?
5. Will airlines be able to significantly increase their share of the freight market in the future? Why or why not?

CASE 14-1

John Deere

John Deere, a farm implements company, produces tractors, harrows, and other kinds of farm machinery. Deere sells its implements through local distributors who normally carry only John Deere products. These distributors think very highly of John Deere for several reasons. John Deere provides distributors with low-rate financing which keeps the cost of maintaining an inventory of expensive and slow-selling equipment to a minimum. This also makes it easier for distributors to offer low-cost financing plans to farmers who must usually buy on credit.

John Deere has very good buy-back policies. That is, if harvests are poor one year, farmers won't have much money the next year to buy new machinery. Because the distributor can't afford to keep a big inventory, John Deere buys the surplus equipment and either stores it itself or redistributes it to other parts of the country where harvests are better or where farmers are better off. In addition, if Deere produces a new product, such as an improved tractor, it buys back the old tractors still in distributors' inventories or it waits to announce the new tractor until all old tractors have been sold. This keeps distributors from acquiring unsalable old models that they finally have to dispose of at a loss.

Farmers demand reliability and rapid repair service. John Deere supplies distributors with large parts inventories and skilled repair staffs. Distributors face less expense to maintain service departments, and farmers are very pleased with the rapid and professional repairs they get. This makes them more inclined to buy John Deere products when they need new equipment. Farmers and distributors also favor John Deere because the company doesn't change its product line frequently. That means that a five-year-old harrow is still the same model being sold today, so its owner can sell it for more on the used-equipment market. The distributor can conduct a better business in used equipment, and everyone has fewer worries about unavailability of parts for older models.

In the inflation of the late 70s and early 80s, farmers have suffered severely, and purchases of farm machinery have decreased dramatically. Since farm equipment is made to last for many years, and repairs and overhauls are generally quite simple, a farmer facing a few bad years will repair old equipment rather than buying new. Moveover, Japanese companies have realized that American farmers will buy Japanese farm equipment—which is often of superb quality—so American farm implements manufacturers face new foreign competition.

1. Why does John Deere make such a great effort to please its distributors?
2. Why do you think that John Deere doesn't sell directly to farmers? Why doesn't it open its own distributorships, owned by the company?
3. Why has spending so much money and time on its distributors actually improved John Deere's own financial position?
4. If Deere's products changed substantially from year to year, would its current policies with distributors have to change? What might Deere offer instead, should products change substantially each year? (Remember that in the face of new Japanese imports, this is not an unlikely possibility.)
5. Why would you, as a farmer, buy from a John Deere distributor rather than from a distributor of another implement brand?

CASE 14-2

Revco

Revco is a chain of 1,600 drugstores, whose sales exceed $1.3 billion annually. Revco is widely recognized for its innovative approaches to handling its distribution system.

Computers help Revco organize the entire store so as to minimize the personnel needed to run it, to minimize wasted employee time, and to minimize any other unnecessary expenses. Revco also has used computers to determine the best arrangement of products on every shelf.

Research showed that a customer walking down the aisle tends to look most often just below eye level on the right side of the aisle. This seems logical since most shoppers are right handed and use their right hands to reach for products. Therefore, Revco positions its private label products on the right side, just below eye level. Revco's private label products are packed in bottles similar to those of major name brand products; for instance, their generic dandruff shampoo is packaged in a bottle that looks like the Head and Shoulders bottle. This makes customers a little more willing to accept the private brand. Revco makes much more profit on its private-label brands—about 40 percent of the retail price—and prefers that customers buy private-label brands rather than name brands.

Revco found that buyers have some unexpected buying habits. To illustrate, most women shop for cosmetics by brand rather than by type. This means that if all mascaras were grouped together, all nail polishes were grouped together, and so on, a woman would be likely to buy one cosmetic item and, not seeing more products of the same brand right in front of her, would move on. Revco grouped all brand products (such as Revlon and Max Factor) together. Such product grouping encourages impulse purchases.

Revco offered senior citizens a 10 percent discount and profited tremendously from it. Senior citizens buy about three times as many prescriptions per year as younger people, and they more readily develop store loyalties. Revco's sales improved enough to make the discount very profitable to the stores.

Weekly discount sales are frowned upon at Revco because they require greater advertising, bookkeeping, and produce more confusion at the checkout stands. Since many drugstore shoppers come into a store to buy only the products on sale, the company doesn't really profit from them. Revco uses "everyday discount prices" to create more customer loyalty and to streamline operations.

1. Why do you think efficient distribution is so critical to the drugstore market?
2. What are the advantages in selling a "private-label" brand, and what does Revco do to maximize those sales? Why are consumers hesitant about buying "private-label" brands, and what does Revco do to minimize their fears?
3. Do you think that Revco groups all products by brand, as it does cosmetics? If yes, do you think that this might be a mistake?
4. Would you offer the senior citizen discount if you sold dress clothing? televisions? automobiles? Why or why not?

15

Pricing

After studying this chapter, you should be able to:

- Analyze the role that price plays in our economic system.
- Identify the three most common pricing objectives.
- Analyze the two basic approaches to setting price.
- Discuss alternative pricing policies.

In early 1983 one of the major U.S. airlines offered a special round-trip excursion fare of $198 on its long-distance flights. Many competing carriers soon announced similar price reductions. In an attempt to sell more automobiles, both manufacturers and dealers have offered cash rebates to new car buyers. With interest rates so high, some car sellers have even arranged for a discount off the interest rate charged on new car loans. Pricing decisions such as these are among a firm's most critical in today's business environment. The selling price of a product influences the public's image of the product, who buys it and how often, and how much profit the firm earns on the product.

THE MEANING OF PRICE

The **price** of a product is what the seller feels a buyer is willing to pay for it. Most prices are fixed by the seller, but for some products, the price is negotiated between the buyer and the seller. This section of the chapter looks at fixed vs. negotiated prices and at the role of price in our economic system.

Fixed vs. Negotiated Price

Most consumer products are sold at a fixed price—namely, the figure on the price tag. The price of the good may be reduced during a sale; nonetheless, the designated price is the price you pay. There is little, if any, bargaining between buyer and seller.

When buying a gallon of milk, for example, you usually don't corner the supermarket manager and start negotiating the price. If the price is too high, you don't buy it.

In contrast, there are a number of products for which price can be negotiated. You very likely will negotiate with the seller when you buy a new car. Depending on the make of the car, the time of the year, and competition in the market, you may be able to buy the car for considerably less than the price shown on the window sticker. The more you know about the product, the better your negotiating position. The least you must know in the case of an automobile is how much the dealer paid for it. You can obtain this information by looking in *Edmund's New Car Price Buying Guide.*

The Role of Price in Our Economy

The price mechanism serves many important functions in our economy. It enables consumers to compare value, it stimulates production and demand, and it allocates scarce goods and resources among competing buyers. Let's take a closer look at each of these functions.

Comparison. The price of a product allows the buyer to estimate its value, or worth, relative to other products. A pineapple may be worth two oranges, three guavas, and one and a half papayas, but it is more convenient to express

In some economies, bargaining between buyer and seller is commonplace.

value in terms of dollars and cents. That way, all goods have a common measure of value. A higher price is generally equated with greater product quality. Which camera is of higher quality? Probably the more expensive one.

Stimulation. Price also performs a **stimulation function**. In this sense, price acts as a signal which tells producers whether they should produce more goods, and consumers whether they should buy more goods. All else equal, a price increase, by increasing sales revenue and profits, stimulates production. A price decrease, by extending the consumer's purchasing power, encourages greater expenditures on goods and services. That is, it stimulates demand.

Rationing. Finally, the pricing mechanism is said to ration scarce goods and resources. Imagine a society in which there is no scarcity. All goods are infinitely abundant and, therefore, free. Money, in effect, grows on trees, as does everything else. Since all goods are freely available, they have no real value, and people take as much as they want.

Now imagine a society in which all goods are scarce to one degree or another. Each good has value and, therefore, a price. The buyer who wants a good must purchase it. Buyers with limited amounts of money compete for scarce goods. This is what we mean by rationing. Who purchases each particular good is determined by the price of the good, the income of the buyer, and the expected utility of the purchase.

PRICING OBJECTIVES

According to theory, business firms in an economy such as ours select a price for each good so as to maximize profits from the sale of that good. We say that the rational business person is a profit maximizer. However, in reality, business firms have other pricing objectives besides maximizing profits. It may be that they lack the information needed to make profit-maximizing decisions. Or that their goal in making pricing decisions is somewhat less ambitious—satisfactory profits rather than maximum profits. Some of the more common of these pricing objectives are pricing to achieve a specified return on investment, pricing to obtain a target market share, and pricing to meet or match the competition. Research has shown that most large firms have one primary pricing objective. Figure 15-1 shows the pricing objectives of ten large firms.

Achieving a Target Return on Investment

Target-return-on-investment pricing refers to the practice of setting price to achieve a specified, or target, yield on investment. For example, if a company has a $1,000,000 investment in productive assets and wants a 10 percent before-tax return, the product should be priced to earn expected profits of $100,000 (.10 × $1,000,000).

Achieving Target Market Share

Many firms price their products with the goal of achieving a target share of the overall market. Such a goal might be 15 percent of all transistor sales in the United States in the upcoming business year. Typically, a price reduction leads to an increase in market share, and a price hike leads to a decrease in market share. Do you know why?

A target-market-share objective is sometimes stated in terms of a market-share maximum. Most firms consistently strive to increase market share, but others attempt to limit it. These firms are concerned about possible antitrust violations and prosecution by the federal government. Excessively large market share is usually viewed as a restraint of trade. Thus, a firm may raise its prices in order to reduce sales and to hold market share constant. Whether a particular share is "too large" depends on the nature of the industry involved and a variety of facts specific to that industry.

Meeting or Matching the Competition

Some firms do not have a specific pricing policy of their own; they let other firms make their pricing decisions for them. The firm raises or lowers its prices in response to the actions of its competitors. DuPont, for example, has a policy of adopting the market price on products for which it is not the industry leader.

Figure 15-1

Pricing Objectives of Ten Large Firms

Source: Robert Lanzillotti, "Pricing Objectives in Large Companies," *Marketing Classics*, Ben M. Ennis and Keith K. Cox, eds. (Boston: Allyn and Bacon, 1977), pp. 413-434.

Company	Principal Pricing Objectives
Alcoa	20% ROI; higher on new products
American Can	Maintenance of market share
A&P	Increasing market share
DuPont	Target ROI—no specific figure provided
General Electric	20% ROI after taxes
General Motors	20% on investment (after taxes)
Goodyear	"Meeting competitors"
Gulf	Follow price of most important marketer in each area
International Harvester	10% ROI after taxes
Johns-Manville	ROI greater than last 15 years' average
Kroger	Maintaining market share
Sears Roebuck	Increasing market share
U.S. Steel	8% ROI after taxes

SETTING PRICE

Now that we've studied the meaning of price, the role of price in an economy, and some common pricing objectives, we are ready to look at how firms go about setting the prices of their products. There are two basic approaches to setting price: cost pricing and demand pricing.

Cost Pricing

It stands to reason that firms consider product-related costs in making their pricing decisions. The selling price must be greater than the cost of production if the firm hopes to make a profit. Under this approach, production or purchase cost is the starting point in making pricing decisions.

Markup Pricing. **Markup pricing**, or **cost-plus pricing**, is the practice of establishing price by adding a predetermined percentage to the cost of manufacturing or purchasing the product. The **markup** is the amount in dollars added to production or purchase cost. The cost plus the markup equals the selling price.

Markup pricing, because it makes sense and is easy to understand, is used by many retail firms, especially those that sell a variety of products. The markup percentage varies from one type of good to another. In a grocery store, the markup on canned food might be 15 percent; on meat, 25 percent; and on frozen foods, 30 percent. The two things which determine the markup percentage for products are the level of competition and the level of risk associated with selling the products.

Markup is normally stated as a percentage of selling price, but it can also be stated as a percentage of cost. Assume that a furniture store paid $300 for a sofa and added a $100 markup to purchase cost. The sofa sells for $400. As Figure 15-2 indicates, the markup is 25 percent if defined in terms of selling price but 33.33 percent if defined in terms of purchase cost. Ideally, the markup percentage, however defined, should reflect both the demand for the product and the cost of stocking and maintaining it.

Break-Even Analysis. A second approach to cost pricing, **break-even analysis**, shows how alternative prices affect the firm's profit position. Before we see how break-even analysis works, we need to define two terms: variable costs and fixed costs.

Variable costs, as the name indicates, vary with the level of production or sales of the product. As production or sales go up, total variable costs go up. An example of a variable cost is the cost of the cotton-polyester fabric used in the manufacture of sport shirts. As more shirts are produced, the total cost of the material used increases. If production is stopped completely, variable costs will drop to zero.

Fixed costs are costs that do not vary with the level of production or sales. If our shirt manufacturer stops making shirts, it will still have to pay its fire insurance premiums and the salaries of its executives. These are fixed costs. Figure 15-3 lists other examples of costs that are usually classified as variable and fixed.

Figure 15-2

Markup Calculation

	Percentage of Selling Price	Percentage of Cost
Retailer's Cost	$300.00	$300.00
Markup	100.00	100.00
Price	400.00	400.00
Percent Markup =	$\dfrac{\text{Dollar Markup}}{\text{Selling Price}}$ $\dfrac{100}{400} = 25\%$	$\dfrac{\text{Dollar Markup}}{\text{Cost}}$ $\dfrac{100}{300} = 33.33\%$

Figure 15-3

Examples of Fixed and Variable Costs

Fixed Costs	Variable Costs
Management's Salaries	Heating Expenses
Trade Association Dues	Labor Costs
Building Security	Raw Materials
Depreciation on Plant and Equipment	Shipping Expenses
Property Taxes	Electricity to Run Machines

Now that we've looked at the difference between variable and fixed costs, we're ready to discuss break-even analysis and to examine its usefulness in pricing decisions. The **break-even point** is the volume of sales in units at which total revenue exactly equals total cost. When sales of any product are greater than the break-even point, the product begins to earn a profit. When sales are less than the break-even point, the product loses money. The break-even point is calculated using this formula:

$$\text{Break-Even Point in Units} = \frac{\text{Total Fixed Costs}}{\text{Unit Selling Price} - \text{Unit Variable Cost}}$$

Consider the case of a product with an $80 selling price, variable costs of $30 per unit, and fixed costs of $10,000. The break-even point for this product is 200 units, calculated as follows:

$$\frac{\$10,000}{\$80-\$30} = 200 \text{ Units}$$

Viewing this relationship another way, if the firm sold 200 units at a margin of $50 per unit (Selling Price − Variable Costs Per Unit), it would generate $10,000 in revenues. This is just enough to cover the product's fixed costs. The break-even point can be calculated for any price level by substituting that price (say, $75 or $90) in the formula.

The break-even relationships are shown in Figure 15-4. The fixed-cost curve is horizontal, indicating that fixed costs do not change with the level of production. Variable costs are added to the fixed costs and increase as the level of production increases. The total-cost curve is the sum of total variable costs and total fixed costs. Finally, the total-revenue curve is the price per unit multiplied by number of units sold. The higher the price, the steeper the angle of the revenue curve. The total-revenue curve intersects the total-cost line at the break-even point—in this case, at 200 units and at total revenue of $16,000 ($80 × 200 units). What happens to the break-even point if the price is lowered to $70?

Break-even analysis is a good tool for examining the relationship between costs and revenue. *Note, however, that break-even analysis does not determine a product's price.* Rather, it enables the pricing executive to determine the effect of a price change on the number of units the firm must sell in order to break even. The higher the price, the lower the break-even point; the lower the price, the higher the break-even point. It is also useful for evaluating the impact of a change in fixed or variable costs.

The biggest problem with break-even analysis is that it is based strictly on costs. That is, after conducting a break-even analysis, we know how many units it will take to break even, but we do not know whether consumers will buy the good at the price used to calculate the break-even point. This can be determined only after studying the market for our product or service. A second problem is that break-even analysis assumes that fixed costs are constant no matter how many units are produced. Although this may be true for some products, it is not true for all products.

Demand Pricing

The second basic approach to making price decisions is demand pricing. The price of a product should reflect the level of demand for it. Products in great demand tend to be more expensive; products for which demand is weak tend to be less expensive. We'll look at the demand curve as an introduction to demand pricing. We'll then turn to two demand pricing techniques: prestige pricing and differential pricing.

What are some of the variable and fixed costs associated with refining oil?

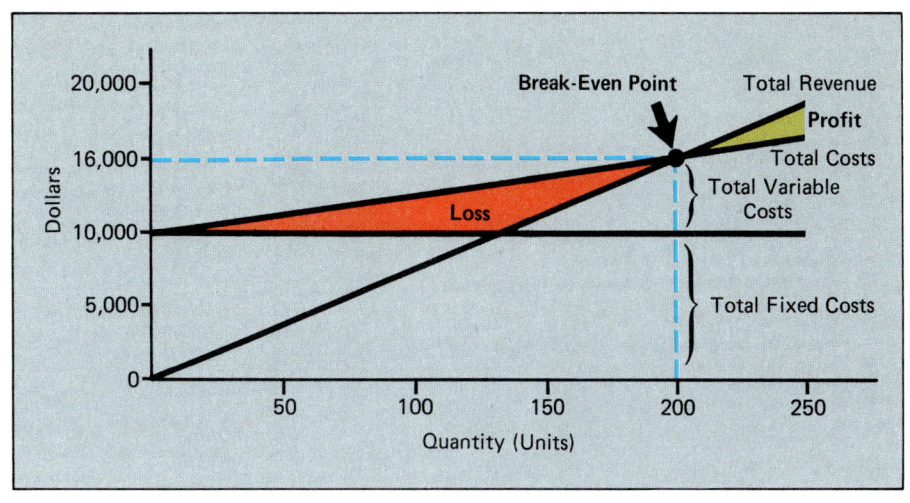

Figure 15-4

Break-Even Analysis

At the break-even point, total sales revenue (200 × $80 = $16,000) equals fixed cost ($10,000) plus variable costs (200 × $30 = $6,000). At sales greater than 200 units, the firm earns a profit of $50 on each unit sold. At sales of fewer than 200 units, the firm incurs a loss.

The Demand Curve. The **demand curve** is the fundamental tool of economic analysis. It shows the relationship between the price of a product and the amount of the product that is sold. The demand curve for most products slopes downward, that is, as the price of a product decreases, more of the product is demanded and sold. Figure 15-5 shows a typical demand curve.

Figure 15-5

The Demand Curve

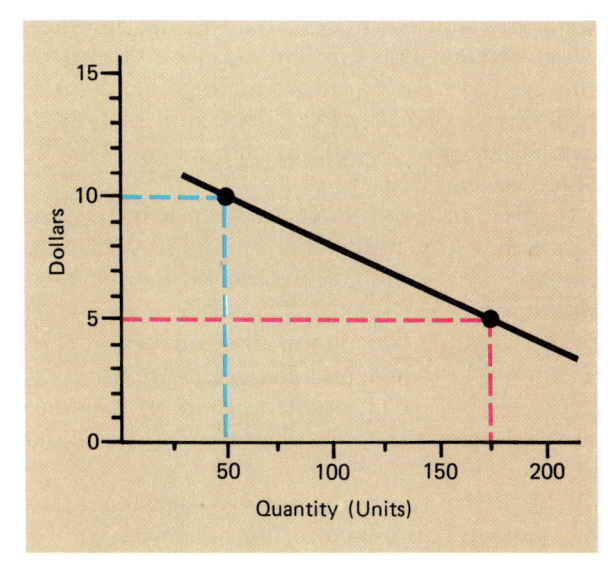

At a price of $10, the firm sells 50 units of the product. At a price of $5, the firm sells 175 units. Thus, quantity sold varies inversely with the price.

The demand for home heating fuel provides an excellent illustration of how heavy consumption is associated with low price and reduced consumption is associated with high price. Several years ago, home heating oil cost only $.20 a gallon. Many people at that time installed oil heating units and heated their houses to 78° or higher during the winter. Fuel was cheap, so why not be comfortable? In recent years, however, the price of heating oil has risen to more than $1.60 per gallon, causing people to cut back on their consumption of oil. They have turned their thermostats down to 62° to 65°, insulated their homes, and even changed to alternative heating systems, such as electrical heat pumps, solar energy, and woodburning stoves.

Prestige Pricing. Although the demand curve for most goods is downward sloping, there are goods for which the demand curve first slopes upward and then bends backward. As the prices of such products increase, people are willing to buy more of them but only up to a certain price. Thereafter, the volume of their purchases decreases as price increases. A backward-bending demand curve is shown in Figure 15-6.

Prestige pricing is practiced within the upward-sloping part of the demand curve. People associate quality with the price of a good and purchase more of that good as its price increases. The association between quality, higher price, and desirability of purchase is why this tactic is called **prestige pricing**. Prestige pricing

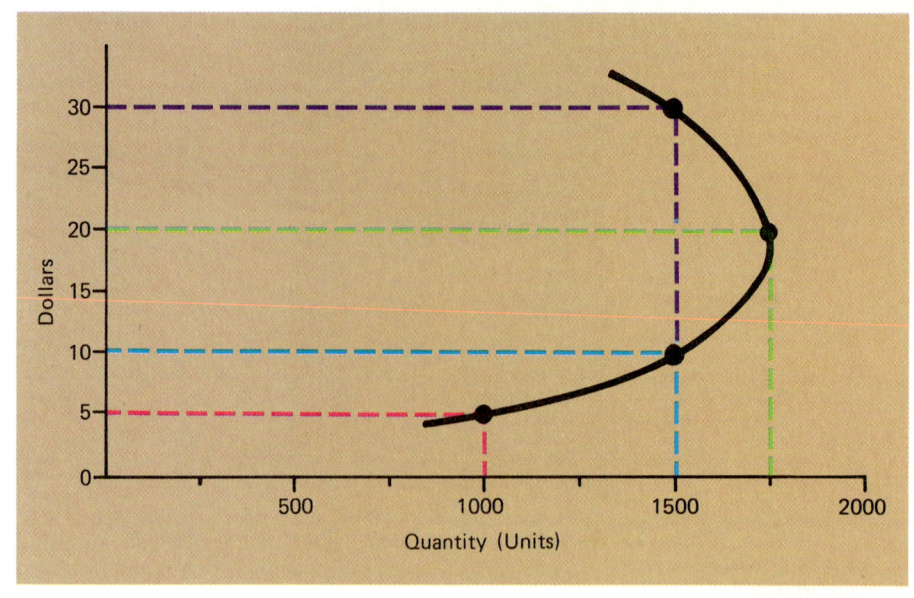

Figure 15-6

The Backward-Bending Demand Curve Associated with Prestige Pricing

At a price of $5, the firm sells 1,000 units of the product; at a price of $10, it sells 1,500 units; and at a price of $20, 1,750 units. The demand curve slopes upward during this part of its length. At prices greater than $20 the demand curve bends backward as increasingly higher prices are associated with reduced purchases. At a price of $30, only 1,500 units of the product are sold. During this backward-bending part of the curve, the relationship between price and quantity sold is negative.

works for some goods; the manufacturers or sellers of these goods increase total sales revenue and profits by raising their prices—that is, up to the prices at which sales start to decline.

For prestige pricing to work, two conditions must be met. First, there must be large differences in quality among the products of the particular type considered. Second, most consumers must not be able to judge these differences for themselves. Wine is an example of a product meeting both these conditions: In terms of quality, Chateau Rothschild's finest is a far cry from ordinary table wine, but many people could not tell the difference without the label on the bottle. The lesson in this is that winemakers should not charge too low a price for their better wines. People might associate the budget price with poor quality and not buy the wine at all.

Differential Pricing. A second demand-pricing technique is **differential pricing**. It is used when the market for a product is made up of several distinct segments. (Market segmentation was discussed in Chapter 12.) The product is sold at a higher price to people willing to pay more for it. That's one segment. It is sold at a lower price to people who value it less. That's another segment.

The important point here is that the difference in price is not a result of difference in cost. It is a result only of a difference in demand.

Differential pricing is normally based on time or location. In terms of time, the demand for a product frequently varies with the season of the year or the time of day. Resort hotels in Florida, for example, charge higher rates in the winter, when demand is greatest, than in the summer, when demand falls off. The telephone company charges different rates for long distance calls depending on the day of the week and the time of day. Table 15-1 illustrates the system used by Southwestern Bell.

Location-based differential pricing is also commonly practiced. Theater tickets are an example. A seat close to the stage is more expensive than one in the back. The difference in ticket price is again a function of demand, not of cost. The more heavily demanded tickets are more expensive. The cost of installation and maintenance of the seats is the same regardless of their location.

As we have seen, the firm can use either a cost or a demand approach for setting price. We will now look at the pricing policies that guide many of the pricing decisions made by business managers.

Choose your seat, but be ready to pay the price.

PRICING POLICIES

Pricing policies provide the framework for making consistent, realistic pricing decisions. Although policies are always hard to develop, the firm with a good set of pricing policies will make better pricing decisions than a firm without such policies. Unfortunately, there is no perfect set of pricing policies that works all of the time. The policies must be tailored to the needs of each firm. Let's look at four of the most important aspects of pricing policy: price discounts, price lining, new product pricing, and geographic pricing.

Price Discounts

Most products have a **list price**. This is the publicly stated price for which the firm or store expects to sell each of its products. It is called a list price because many manufacturers publish a list of prices for their products in a book or folder which is given to their customers. Resellers, however, whether wholesalers or retailers, often charge less than the manufacturer's suggested list price. In such cases, the difference between the list price and the selling price is referred to as the **discount**. Discounts are usually based on the quantity purchased, the season of the year, the firm's sales objectives, or the terms of payment.

Quantity Discounts. Most firms offer discounts on large orders. **Quantity discounts** encourage customers to purchase a larger order than they otherwise might. Quantity discounts not only help sell more products but also reduce the cost of making a sale. One large order of 100 units requires much less paperwork than 10 orders of 10 units each. Also, a large order does not take much more of a salesperson's time than does a small order.

Seasonal Discounts. A price reduction is called a **seasonal discount** when it is based on the time of year. The sales of many firms vary dramatically

Table 15-1

An Example of Differential Pricing

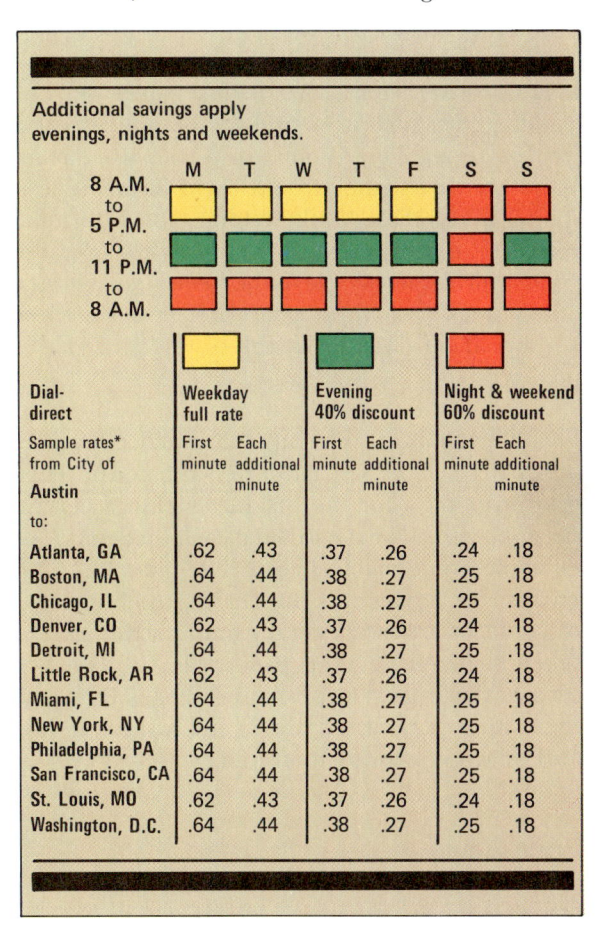

Dial-direct Sample rates* from City of Austin to:	Weekday full rate First minute	Weekday full rate Each additional minute	Evening 40% discount First minute	Evening 40% discount Each additional minute	Night & weekend 60% discount First minute	Night & weekend 60% discount Each additional minute
Atlanta, GA	.62	.43	.37	.26	.24	.18
Boston, MA	.64	.44	.38	.27	.25	.18
Chicago, IL	.64	.44	.38	.27	.25	.18
Denver, CO	.62	.43	.37	.26	.24	.18
Detroit, MI	.64	.44	.38	.27	.25	.18
Little Rock, AR	.62	.43	.37	.26	.24	.18
Miami, FL	.64	.44	.38	.27	.25	.18
New York, NY	.64	.44	.38	.27	.25	.18
Philadelphia, PA	.64	.44	.38	.27	.25	.18
San Francisco, CA	.64	.44	.38	.27	.25	.18
St. Louis, MO	.62	.43	.37	.26	.24	.18
Washington, D.C.	.64	.44	.38	.27	.25	.18

Source: *Greater Austin Telephone Directory*, © Southwestern Bell Telephone Company, 1982. Reprinted with permission.

from one month to the next. A retailer of swimming suits will sell 80 percent of its suits in May and June. Beginning in late July and August, the retailer offers shoppers a seasonal discount in order to sell off the remaining suits in stock. Alternatively, the retailer could hold the line on price, sell a few swim suits, and inventory the rest until the next year. The problem with this approach is that the retailer is forced to pay inventory costs on the leftover stock until the following May. Moreover, styles may change, and people may not want last year's styles.

Promotional Discounts. There are two types of promotional discounts: markdowns and loss leaders. A **markdown** is a discount designed to encourage customers to buy a product that they would not otherwise want at that time. Markdowns are common in the clothing industry. If a retailer purchases a new style of women's suit and the public does not like it, the retailer will "mark down" the suit in order to sell more of it.

A **loss leader** is a product that is sold below cost in order to stimulate the sales of other products. Grocery stores frequently advertise loss leader items, such as a package of hotdog buns for 15¢ or a gallon of milk for $1.60. Store managers know that they would be in big trouble if shoppers purchased only hotdog buns and milk. However, it is hoped that the low prices on these goods will attract people to the store who will then buy a week's worth of groceries. It is on these additional purchases that the store will make its profits.

Cash Discounts. It is a common practice in many industries for the seller to offer a discount when the buyer pays for the product within a certain period of time. This is called a **cash discount**. For example, some invoices read "2/10, net 30." This means that payment is due in 30 days but that a discount of 2 percent on the amount due can be taken if the entire bill is paid within 10 days. An invoice that reads "net 30 days" means that payment for a purchase is due in full within 30 days and that no discount is offered.

Price Lining

Most products are priced within certain price ranges. This practice is known as **price lining**. A men's clothing store appealing to the college market might carry three lines or grades of suits—$110, $150, and $180. A suit manufacturer who wants to sell to this store must be sure that its products can be sold by the store within one of these three price ranges.

A policy of price lining narrows the decision-making process for the customer. The customer first decides how much to spend and then looks at suits within that price range only. Price lining also permits the retailer to carry less inventory. Rather than stocking suits at all prices, the retailer need carry suits in only three price lines.

New Product Pricing

The pricing of new products is more difficult than the pricing of old products. For an old product, the seller generally selects a price that is close to the price charged by other sellers of the product. A new product competes with no other product. The seller may set its price through skimming or penetration strategy.

Price Skimming. Price skimming refers to the strategy of pricing a new product at an artificially high price. By an "artificially" high price we mean a price that the firm will not be able to hold as other sellers move into the market with products of their own. A strategy of price skimming works best when there are many buyers willing to pay a high price, or a "premium," to be among the first owners of the product. The demand curve in Figure 15-7 on page 281 shows the relationship between price and quantity sold for a new product under a strategy of price skimming.

Price skimming segments the market according to how much people are willing to pay for the product. At first, the seller sets a high price for a product and sells it to those people willing to pay that price. As the firm meets this demand and as competitors move into the market, the seller successively lowers the original price.

Price skimming by automobile dealers occurred when Datsun introduced its Turbo ZX. The car carried a list price of $17,250. Initially, some dealers sold the car at a premium of up to $5,000, that is, at a price of about $22,250. Within six months of the car's introduction, however, there were many Turbo ZX's available, and it was

CONTROVERSIAL ISSUES

Many supermarkets re-mark the prices on items already stocked on shelves to allow for increases in wholesale costs on these items. A few supermarket chains tried to stop this practice after consumer groups protested loudly, but most of these stores returned to re-marking prices as the clamor died down. Should grocery stores re-mark prices?

Pro

Supermarket chains should *not* re-mark prices once merchandise is stocked on the shelves. All they are doing is increasing their profits. By re-marking items, they increase the inflation rate, making the whole situation worse.

Supermarket chains are profitable because of their ability to buy and warehouse large amounts of inventory. If they choose to operate this way, they should bear the burden of keeping their prices constant. People would not protest as much if smaller stocks were carried on the shelves of a supermarket and were marked at a higher cost only when replaced. This way isn't pleasant, but it is acceptable. What is so unfair is when a grocery store has to get that extra 2¢ on each of a dozen cans of tomato sauce. Was it worth 24¢ to pay a clerk to re-mark the cans, to correct entries in inventory records, and to inform and remind cashiers of the new price?

After all, the re-marked merchandise hasn't been on the shelf *that* long. For the time that it *has* been on the shelf, inflation has been eating away at the shopper's buying dollar. Isn't the supermarket just being greedy by tacking the additional price increase on products?

Grocery Stores Should Not Re-mark Prices on Shelved Merchandise.

The supermarket should be able to absorb the cost of inflation on its stocked merchandise. After all, Safeway sales totaled $16,580,300,000 in 1981. That's more than the increase in the Federal deficit for that year; that's over $16 *billion*! And there are 21 supermarket chains that in 1981 had sales of over $1 billion. Surely they could spare us the price increases on those cans already on the shelves.

Con

Supermarkets must re-mark the prices of items already on the shelves. Sure, Safeway makes a lot of sales each year. But it also has very high costs which require that it re-mark prices. The secret to a supermarket chain is not only that it can buy and warehouse large inventories, but also that it can operate *very* close to a zero-profit line. In 1981, for example, the 49 largest supermarket chains reported the following breakdown for each dollar of sales:

- 31¢ went to the farmer or producer
- 31¢ was paid to employees
- 5¢ was paid for transportation of goods
- 8¢ was paid for packaging
- 4¢ was paid for electricity
- 17¢ was paid for miscellaneous expenses such as leasing costs and equipment replacement

Only 4¢ was saved out of every dollar for gross profit *before taxes*. That's only a 4 percent return on sales—a level of profitability that would drive most other companies bankrupt. A supermarket's survival on such a low profit margin depends on extreme efficiency. If it loses only 1¢ on each dollar of sales because it doesn't re-mark prices, it loses a *quarter* of its profits.

Furthermore, take a look at the future. Supermarket chains expect costs of doing business to increase significantly, while retail prices will rise only moderately. To keep the overall increase in prices as low as possible, supermarkets *do* have to re-mark goods already on their shelves. Consumers may not like seeing all those price stickers, but they are necessary. Grocery stores can't afford to pay someone to peel off all the old labels.

So let's not gripe about price re-marking. The supermarkets are just trying to keep your grocery bill down.

Profile—
Southwest Airlines

When pricing practices come to mind, some companies always stand out. There are companies, such as Polaroid, that are known for price skimming, or Volkswagen, known for penetration pricing. But one of the most phenomenal success stories is that of Southwest Airlines.

On-time service, high-frequency flights from convenient close-in airports at a fair fare—all in a fun-to-fly atmosphere—that's the spirit of Southwest Airlines, and Southwest has been spreading that spirit to the traveling public since June, 1971, first as a carrier serving only Texas and, since 1979, as a Civil Aeronautics Board carrier with the addition of interstate flights.

This new flair for flying was born in 1967 when a group of Texans decided there was a definite need for commuter jet service within Texas. But the journey from idea to sky in 1971 was one burdened with a 3½-year legal safari through the courthouse that saw Southwest's right to serve Texans defended all the way to the United States Supreme Court. The way was cleared for the start of service by the Texas airline in December of 1970.

Launched against heavy competition, Southwest operated in its first full month with a three-plane fleet of Boeing 737s and 200 employees. It carred 15,458 passengers with a 14 percent load factor (the percentage of seats sold). It served three cities—Dallas, Houston, and San Antonio. Today Southwest is a national airline operating in 8 states serving 21 cities.

During its 11 years of service, Southwest has introduced a number of innovations to the air travel marketplace. Many of these innovations have centered on pricing policies. For example, in October of 1972, the company inaugurated a two-tier pricing system, giving a further price break to evening and weekend travelers. Southwest is believed to be the first commercial carrier to do so. Southwest also introduced its discount ticket books in 1972. Today passengers traveling with discount ticket books enjoy discounts of over 8 percent on a book of 12 one-way tickets. Generally Southwest fares are the lowest non-restricted fares in the marketplace. This attention to fares has developed a new kind of traveler; often persons who never flew before are deserting their automobiles for air transportation— via Southwest—that is more economical and pleasurable.

Southwest has also refined some existing procedures. For example, Southwest tickets are easy to obtain. They are issued from a cash register quick ticketing machine. It's not fancy, just functional, allowing Southwest to assist many passengers in a short period of time.

In 1979, Southwest began using automatic credit card ticketing machines to avoid congestion at its ticket counters. In ten seconds the machines automatically issue a one-way or round-trip ticket. Southwest tickets are also available through most travel agencies.

Cost advantages are crucial to any successful pricing program, and Southwest has had many. By using a small number of planes, the company has kept servicing costs down. By serving relatively few airports, Southwest has minimized the costs of maintaining airport employees and offices and of paying rental on hangar and terminal space.

How successful has Southwest been? Growth in stock investment has been dramatic—a $1,000 investment in Southwest Airlines in 1971 would have purchased 91 shares of common stock at $11. As of year end 1982, this investment would represent 960 shares, including stock splits of 5-for-4 in 1977; 3-for-2 in 1978, 1979, and 1980; 5-for-4 in 1981; and a 2-for-1 split in 1982. The company has paid cash dividends for 26 consecutive quarters since starting to declare dividends on its common stock in August of 1976.

During 1982, Southwest carried 7.9 million passengers, a steep climb from the 108,544 it carried between commencement of operations on June 18, 1971, and the end of that year. The total number of passengers boarded between 1971 and year end 1982 was 36 million. The airline's 1982 revenues were $331 million and net income was $34 million.

Southwest Airlines obviously has a winning formula for success. According to the firm's president, "We're proud of our people; their spirit, dedication, and caring are the real bonus for our passengers, combined with low fares and frequent service."

Figure 15-7

Price Skimming

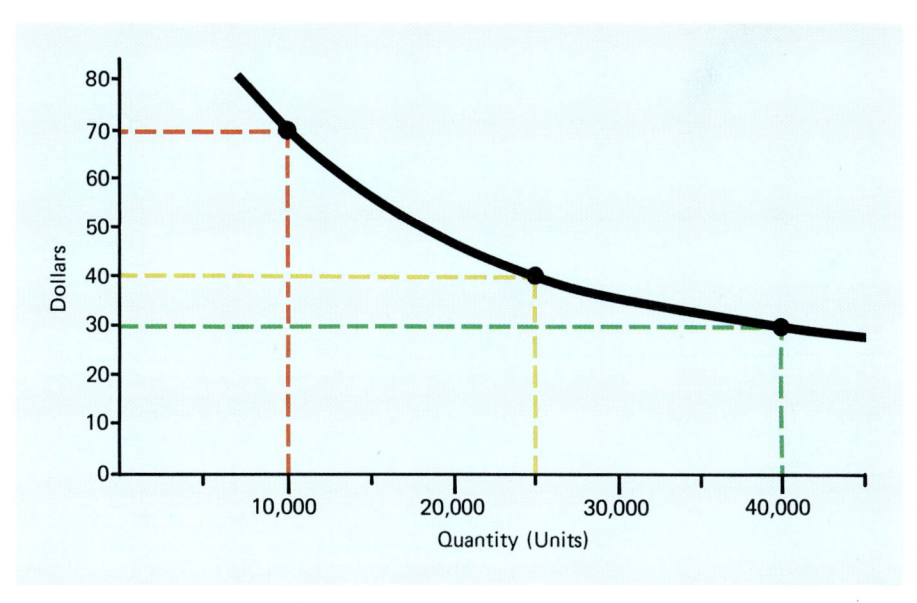

At an initially high price of $70, the firm expects to sell 10,000 units. If it were to reduce its price to, say, $40, it could sell an additional 15,000 units. Thus, the curve in the graph is nothing more than a demand curve.

In order to maximize profits, the firm introduces its product at the high price of $70. This is before competitors enter the market. Sales volume at this price is 10,000 units. The firm gradually lowers the price, thereby attracting those buyers not willing to pay the $70 price. Eventually, after competitors have introduced products of their own, the price of the good stabilizes at $30.

no longer possible to charge a premium above the suggested retail price.

Penetration Pricing. Penetration pricing, the opposite of skimming, is the practice of introducing a product to the market at a low price. This strategy works best when customers are very price conscious. For instance, a new laundry soap, even with "blue and green chips," is not the kind of product for which people will pay a premium. Manufacturers therefore introduce such products at a low price that will attract many buyers. Figure 15-8 shows how penetration pricing works.

Evaluation of New Product Pricing. It is impossible to generalize and say which strategy is the best. In fact, some multiproduct firms use both strategies. The best strategy depends on the situation at hand. Price skimming, for example, allows the firm to segment its market and to recover its investment quickly. This is especially important to a new company that may not have much cash. The major problem with price skimming is that the initial high price tends to attract potential competitors who want to cash in on the early profits themselves.

Penetration pricing has two major advantages. First, profits are small in the beginning because of the low price. Small profits are not desirable in and of themselves, but they do tend to discourage competitors from entering the market, and that is desirable. As we said before, large profits attract competitors. Small profits do not.

The second advantage relates to the first. A penetration policy often results in greatly increased sales because the low price attracts many buyers. Heavy sales mean large production runs. At some point, the firm begins to benefit from economies of scale; that is, as the volume of production increases, the per unit cost of production goes down. Thus, at a constant selling price, unit profit increases as unit product cost decreases.

To show how economies of scale lower production costs, imagine a company that produces plastic, reusable champagne glasses for outdoor cocktail parties. The firm chose a strategy of penetration pricing and produced 20,000 units per month at a unit cost of $.06. At a production run of 3,000 units, the unit cost might have been $0.14. The large production run of 20,000 units made the champagne glasses much more profitable.

Figure 15-8

Penetration Pricing

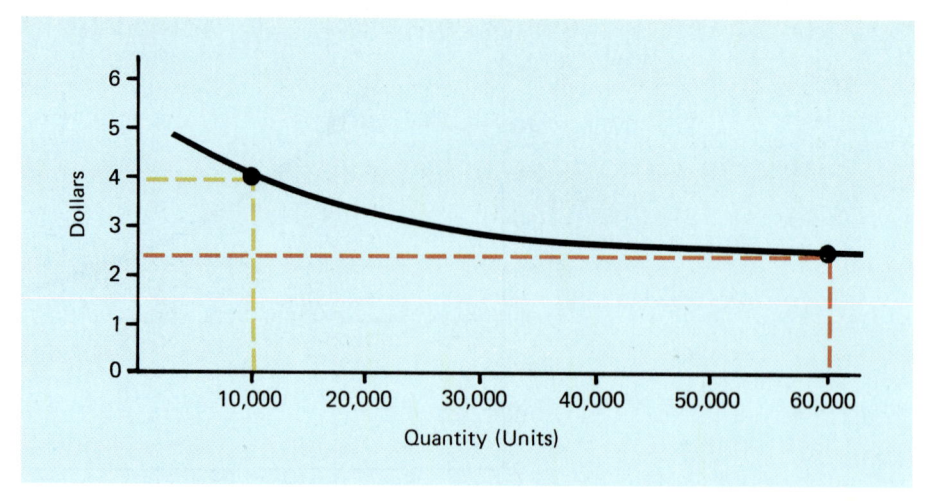

In the case of laundry soap, a price of $4.00 per box results in sales of 10,000 boxes. But if the price were reduced to $2.50, sales would rise to 60,000 boxes.

With such a demand curve, the amount sold is extremely sensitive to price. As a result, the firm should try to keep the price of the product low. Specifically, it should adopt a penetration strategy. In that way, it should be able to sell many units of the product and to keep competitors out of the market.

Geographic Pricing

A final pricing policy issue to consider is that of delivery cost. After a sale has been made, who pays the cost of shipping the product to the buyer? Do the buyers pay, or do the sellers pay? It all depends on the geographic pricing policy of the selling firms. The policy, or set of procedures, is called "geographic" because the buyers are assumed to be located at some distance from the sellers' places of business. Also, the products are assumed to be too big for the buyers to carry them home in their pockets. The product consequently is shipped by a suitable transportation carrier. We'll look at four approaches for allocating transportation costs: FOB-factory, FOB-destination, uniform-delivered, and zone-delivered pricing.

FOB-Factory Pricing. FOB is a common term in transportation. It means "free on board." Usually, the price is stated as "FOB-factory." The seller is responsible for loading the product aboard a transportation carrier, but the buyer is responsible for paying all transportation charges after the merchandise leaves the seller's place of business. In short, FOB-factory means that the buyer pays shipping costs.

There is one big problem with FOB-factory pricing. The further the buyer is from the seller's place of business, the more the buyer pays for the product. Remember: The buyer's total cost equals selling price plus transportation costs. As a result, it is often difficult for the seller to market its products to customers located closer to another supplier of the product.

FOB-Destination Pricing. Under FOB-destination pricing, the seller pays all transportation costs. This type of geographic pricing policy is appropriate for products with relatively low transportation costs. A wholesaler of expensive diamonds probably would not bill its retail buyers for shipping costs. It seems unlikely that a firm selling a product that may cost more than $10,000 would worry about a $30.00 transportation fee.

Uniform-Delivered Pricing. Under uniform-delivered pricing, the seller charges its customers the same delivered price regardless of where the customers are located or how much it costs to ship the merchandise. Every buyer pays the same price for the product. The selling price in this situation equals the regular selling price plus an amount equal to average shipping cost.

Uniform-delivered pricing is used most often when transportation costs are small in relation to selling price. In addition, some businesses, such as furniture stores, operate on the assumption that "free" delivery improves their competitive position.

Setting Prices According to the Markup Method

Markups are typically stated in terms of selling price. The accompanying illustration shows how a markup chain is calculated. Notice how the product, a table lamp, moves down a distribution system from the manufacturer to a wholesaler and then to the retailer. The markup chain follows the same path. At each stage in the chain, the selling price of the lamp increases as markups are added to the purchase cost.

DIRECT AND INDIRECT COST. The cost figure used in marking up a product—that is, in setting its selling price—is the direct cost of producing or acquiring it. In the case of our markup chain, this is the $40 production cost for the manufacturer, the $60 purchase cost for the wholesaler, and the $80 purchase cost for the retailer. We know that this cost plus the dollar markup equals selling price. The markup in dollars at each stage must be big enough to cover all the indirect costs associated with the production, acquisition, and sale of the lamp. Indirect costs include the rent on buildings, insurance and utility costs, telephone bills, and salaries. Also, the dollar markup must allow for a profit on each unit sold. For example, the retailer buys the lamp from the wholesaler for $80. The retailer's accountant has estimated per unit indirect cost at $60. The retailer selects a selling price of $160, marking up the product $80. This leaves a per unit profit of $80 − $60 = $20. Remember: profit equals selling price minus the sum of indirect cost and direct cost.

CALCULATING THE MARKUP PERCENTAGE. To calculate the markup percentage, we need to know the direct cost of the product and the selling price. For the lamp manufacturer, the purchase cost is $40 and its selling price is $60. The dollar markup is $60 − $40 = $20. When expressed as a percentage of selling price, the markup percentage always equals the dollar markup divided by the selling price. The markup percentage for the manufacturer is $20 ÷ $60 = 33 percent.

SETTING PRICE WITH THE MARKUP PERCENTAGE. Now we're ready to use a markup percentage to set selling price. If the customary practice in the wholesaling industry were to mark up products 25 percent, then we could easily calculate the selling price. The wholesaler buys the product for $60. If the markup percentage is to be 25 percent, then the direct cost to the wholesaler must equal 75 percent of its selling price. This is because cost plus markup always equals selling price. The wholesale price of the lamp, therefore, is set using the following formula:

$$.75x = \$60$$
$$x = \$60/.75$$
$$x = \$80 = \text{Selling Price}$$

The wholesaler buys the lamp for $60 and, knowing that the appropriate markup percentage is 25 percent, computes the selling price of $80. The retailer would follow the same steps in setting the retail selling price.

MARKUP CHAIN FOR A TABLE LAMP

Manufacturer:	$	%
Cost	40	67
Markup	20	33
Selling Price	60	100
Wholesaler:	**$**	**%**
Cost	60	75
Markup	20	25
Selling Price	80	100
Retailer:	**$**	**%**
Cost	80	50
Markup	80	50
Selling Price	160	100

Zone-Delivered Pricing. Zone-delivered pricing is a modification of uniform-delivered pricing. The seller assigns each customer to a geographic zone and charges the customers within each zone the same delivered price for the good. Each customer within the zone pays the average cost of shipping the product to buyers in that zone.

Let's assume the following system for a department store in Cincinnati, Ohio. All people living within 20 miles of downtown Cincinnati would belong to the primary market, which is called Zone 1. People living outside a 20-mile radius would be assigned to other zones. The store delivers merchandise free to all its Zone 1 customers, but charges a transportation fee equal to 2 percent of the product's selling price for people living in Zone 2, 4 percent for people living in Zone 3, and 6 percent for those living in Zone 4. For the seller the nice thing about zone-delivered pricing is that customers living outside the seller's primary trading area pay the cost of delivering their purchases to them.

FROM THE FILE

Andres' idea was to produce a knit sport shirt, similar to the many stylish shirts in vogue on campus. Embroidered on each shirt in silver, red, or gold thread would be a small duck. If an alligator and a polo player could become popular, why not a duck? Andres had located an apparel company to manufacture an initial production run of 30,000 shirts at low cost. A team of student sales representatives would sell the shirts at college campuses across the country. Andres had one big decision still in front of him: Should the shirts be priced according to a skimming or a penetration pricing strategy?

SUMMARY POINTS

1. Most products are sold at a fixed price, with little, if any, bargaining between buyer and seller.
2. Price has three important roles in the economy: it allows consumers to compare the value of products, it stimulates production and demand, and it rations scarce resources.
3. Under target-return pricing, the firm sets price so as to achieve a specified yield on investment.
4. Under target-market-share pricing, the firm sets price so as to win a certain percentage of sales within the overall market.
5. The pricing strategy of some firms is to meet or match the competitors' prices.
6. The two cost-oriented pricing techniques are markup pricing and break-even pricing.
7. Prestige pricing and differential pricing are demand-oriented pricing techniques.
8. The four common types of price discounts are quantity discounts, seasonal discounts, promotional discounts, and cash discounts.
9. The practice of pricing products within certain traditional ranges is known as price lining.
10. Two ways of pricing a new product are price skimming and penetration pricing. The first involves an artificially high price; the second, a low price.
11. Under FOB-factory pricing, the buyer pays all transportation costs. Under FOB-destination pricing, the seller pays all transportation costs. Under uniform-delivered pricing, the seller charges all of its customers the same delivered price. Zone-delivered pricing is a modification of uniform-delivered pricing, whereby all buyers in the same zone pay the same price.

KEY TERMS AND CONCEPTS

price
fixed price
negotiated price
target return on investment
target market share
meeting or matching competition
cost pricing
markup pricing
cost-plus pricing
markup
break-even analysis
variable costs
fixed costs
break-even point

demand pricing
demand curve
prestige pricing
differential pricing
list price
discount
quantity discount
seasonal discount
promotional discount
markdown
loss leader
cash discount
price lining
price skimming

penetration pricing
FOB-factory pricing
FOB-destination pricing
uniform-delivered pricing
zone-delivered pricing

REVIEW QUESTIONS

1. Explain the role that price plays in our economy.
2. How does price encourage firms to produce more products?
3. Outline the differences between target-return-on-investment pricing and target-market-share pricing.
4. Define break-even point. What is the formula for calculating the break-even point?
5. What is the major problem associated with using break-even analysis to set the price of a product?
6. Why does the demand curve for most products slope downward?
7. Explain why firms offer seasonal discounts.
8. How does a markdown differ from a loss leader?
9. What does "3/20, net 30" mean?
10. What is meant by FOB-destination pricing? When would a firm use this pricing approach?

DISCUSSION QUESTIONS

1. Why are most prices fixed in our economy?
2. Why do so many firms use markup pricing? How should a business set its markup on a particular product?
3. Why does prestige pricing work for some products and not for others? Should you use prestige pricing to sell automobile tires?
4. Does General Motors use price lines to sell their products? Has General Motors' attitude toward price lining changed in recent years?
5. When should a business use penetration pricing to introduce a new product? Should penetration or skimming pricing be used to introduce a new light beer?

CASE 15-1

Paper Plates

Nearly $2.5 billion worth of paper plates are sold each year. Two thirds of these plates are sold to fast-food restaurants, sports arenas, concession stands, and institutions such as schools or hospitals, which choose their plates almost exclusively on the basis of price. The remaining one third, sold in supermarkets to individual consumers, are also purchased mostly on the basis of price.

Plain paper plates sell for about a penny apiece and yield only very small profits for their manufacturers—sometimes less than one one-hundredth of a cent per plate. Other negative features of the old white paper plates are that they are ugly, they transmit heat rapidly (so your hand burns or your food gets cold), and they are flimsy. Since fast-food restaurants are obligated to replace spilled food and clean up the mess when paper plates collapse, the restaurants finally demanded better plates.

The paper plate manufacturers tried two approaches. First, they manufactured plates from a fairly rigid porous plastic foam. These plates insulated quite well, could be molded into any desired shape, didn't soften when food was placed on them, and they could be made to be reasonably attractive. These plates cost more to make, however, so profit did not really increase. Second, they produced plates pressed from paper pulp; these plates were two to four times as thick as the old plates and were somewhat rigid. Profits still didn't improve.

Then a marketer realized that the same plates could be decorated. Plates with designs were salable at a much higher price and, because the decoration cost very little, at a much higher profit.

Measuring profit on a basis of wholesale profit per foot of grocery shelf space, one foot of fully loaded shelf gave $.69 to $1.37 profit on traditional white paper plates, $.88 to $3.76 profit on pressed pulp or plastic foam undecorated dishes, but $5.10 to $6.80 profit on the same plates after decoration.

1. What kinds of pricing strategies do you think are being employed here?
2. Why do you think paper plate buyers are so sensitive to price? What do you think would have happened with plain white paper plates had manufacturers simply raised prices to increase profits? Why? Do you think the same thing will happen if prices are raised on the decorated plates?
3. How would you, as a new competitor, use pricing to enter this market?

CASE 15-2

Wham-O

In 1948, Richard Knerr and Arthur "Spud" Melin started a toy company. Since their first product was a slingshot, they decided to call the company "Wham-O." For ten years, the firm introduced several inexpensive and gimmicky toys. In 1956, however, Wham-O struck gold when it bought the rights to a product now known as the Frisbee.

The Frisbee sold by the millions. Knerr and Melin had realized that times were ripe for a mass-produced, low-cost toy that everyone could afford. The Frisbee was perfect. Wham-O had also seen some potential in an Australian twirling ring and began marketing it as the Hula Hoop. In one six-month period, over 80 million Hula Hoops were sold.

Wham-O had discovered that while some toys were made to be priced expensively, there were also toys that *everyone* would buy, given the right price. And the people at Wham-O were superb marketers. They knew that Americans were looking for low-priced toys, so they flooded the country with their creations. They also knew that, as the markets for Hula Hoops and Frisbees matured, there would be additional sales to be had if Wham-O offered more expensive versions of the same toys. These toys could be sold for more money (and more profit) to people who *wanted* expensive toys. As a result, competition Frisbees, fluorescent night-use Frisbees, miniature Frisbees, magnum Frisbees, and dozens of other specialty Frisbees appeared on the market. Wham-O made millions, and Frisbees are still selling well.

Wham-O knew it had a successful pricing formula that almost guaranteed success in the toy business. Today, Wham-O produces only ten products, and none of these products costs over $20. Wham-O's products, like the company itself, are durable, simple, and universally appealing.

Many of the other toy companies have spent millions of dollars in research and development to bring out electronic games and other similar high-priced products. While electronic games have sold extremely well, they have been expensive in a recession-prone economy. Consequently, sales are dependent on the economy. Wham-O, on the other hand, just keeps selling and selling.

1. What kind of pricing strategies does Wham-O use to sell its products?
2. What has Wham-O done to minimize its costs? Compare Wham-O's products to electronic games in terms of their intended markets and their cost structures.
3. In an unstable economy, why do you think that Wham-O's pricing strategies are more profitable and/or less risky than those of the electronic games manufacturers?

16

Promotion

After studying this chapter, you should be able to:

- Describe how a firm develops its communication strategy.
- Discuss some of the objectives of advertising, the types of advertising, as well as the problems involved in measuring advertising effectiveness.
- Discuss career opportunities in selling, the roles and responsibilities of salespeople, and the six-stage sales process.
- Explain how sales promotions contribute to a firm's marketing strategy.

    A business must communicate with its markets. How else are people to know about its products, services, and way of doing business? Between a firm and its markets flows a continuous stream of communication: advertising, personal selling, and sales promotions. You've probably heard the old saying: "Build a better mousetrap and the world will beat a path to your door." In truth, the saying should read: "Build a better mousetrap and promote it properly, and the world *might* beat a path to your door." Let's begin our discussion of product promotion by looking at how firms develop their communication strategies.

DEVELOPING A COMMUNICATION STRATEGY

Firms communicate with their markets in different ways. Many firms spend a great deal of money on advertising. Procter and Gamble, for example, spent $521 million in 1981 on television advertising alone. Procter and Gamble's total advertising budget in that year, which included newspapers, magazines and television, exceeded $650 million. In contrast, Amway Products, believing that face-to-face communications is the best way to sell its products, spends very little on advertising.

Even though business firms may have very different communication strategies, they all go through the same basic three-stage process in developing these strategies. This process is shown in Figure 16-1.

Product Analysis

In the first stage, the firm considers the type of product it is selling, the price charged, and the way the product is distributed. Many products have been poorly promoted because pricing and distribution issues were not considered during the planning of the promotional strategy.

Positioning Analysis

The second stage involves a decision as to how the product should be positioned relative to other products. **Positioning** refers to the use of advertising to establish in the mind of the consumer an association between the product advertised and an already popular product or type of product. For example, 7-Up called itself the "UnCola." In its advertisements, 7-Up was "positioned" as an alternative to the many popular cola drinks. Avis was known for a long time as the company that "tried harder" because of being second behind Hertz in the car rental market. Note how the company has positioned itself favorably in relation to the market leader. B.F. Goodrich is the company *without* the blimp. Through this clever bit of positioning, Goodrich takes advantage of the immense popularity of the Goodyear blimp. In effect, the blimp benefits Goodrich almost as much as it benefits Goodyear.

Communication Program Analysis

In the third stage of communication strategy development, the firm gets down to the specifics of its advertising, personal selling, and sales promotion programs. Questions to be answered in-

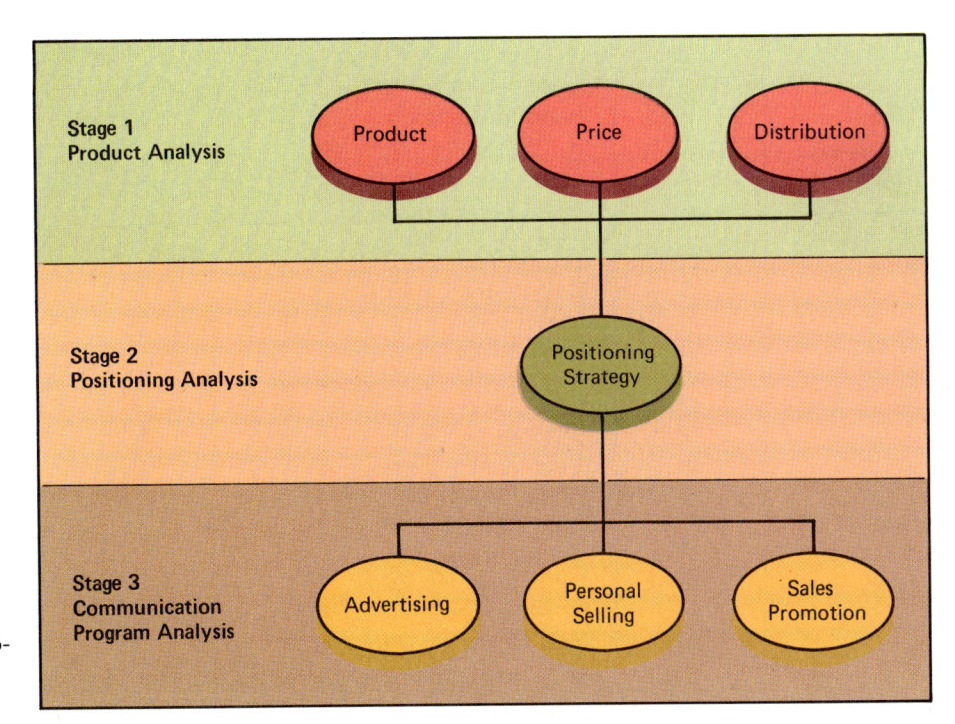

Figure 16-1

The Process of Developing Communication Strategies

clude: Which combination of advertising, personal selling, and sales strategy is best? Would television or radio be more effective? How about billboard advertising? How often should company salespeople call on customers? Should the firm consider in-store displays to attract attention to its product? Would product demonstrations help sell the product? How should the firm decide whether the promotional strategy is working?

Let's take a closer look at the three basic ways—advertising, personal selling, and sales promotion—through which a business firm communicates with its markets.

ADVERTISING

Advertising is defined as "any paid form of nonpersonal presentation and promotion of ideas, goods, and services."[1] The purpose of advertising is to tell the public about the firm and its products, and to persuade potential buyers that the firm's products are better than those of its competitors. Stated another way, the purpose of advertising is to stimulate demand. It does this by showing how the product can meet a consumer need or by providing information about the product.

Who Advertises?

Most business people believe that good advertising increases both sales and profits. Table 16-1 shows the amount of money spent on adver-

---
[1] Ralph S. Alexander and the Committee on Definitions, *Marketing Definitions* (Chicago: American Marketing Association, 1963).

Table 16-1

Leading National Advertisers, 1981

Rank	Company	Advertising $ Millions
1	Procter & Gamble	$671.8
2	Sears, Roebuck & Co.	544.1
3	General Foods Corp.	456.8
4	Philip Morris Inc.	433.0
5	General Motors Corp.	401.0
6	K Mart Corp.	349.6
7	Nabisco Brands	341.0
8	R.J. Reynolds Industries	321.3
9	American Telephone & Telegraph Co.	297.0
10	Mobil Corp.	293.1
11	Ford Motor Co.	286.7
12	Warner-Lambert Co.	270.4
13	Colgate-Palmolive Co.	260.0
14	PepsiCo Inc.	260.0
15	McDonald's Corp.	230.2
16	American Home Products Corp.	209.0
17	RCA Corp.	208.8
18	J.C. Penney Co.	208.6
19	General Mills Corp.	207.3
20	Bristol-Myers Co.	200.0
21	B.A.T. Industries PLC	199.3
22	Coca-Cola Co.	197.9
23	Johnson & Johnson	195.0
24	Chrysler Corp.	193.0
25	Ralston Purina Co.	193.0

Source: Adapted from a table appearing in Marion Elmquist, "100 Leaders Spend 14% More in 1981," *Advertising Age,* Vol. 53, No. 38 (September 9, 1982), p. 1.

CONTROVERSIAL ISSUES

Why do people have to be bombarded with advertising that adds to the cost of the item being advertised? Does advertising justify its existence or is it a "con job," or an unethical way to sell a product?

Advertising Is an Unethical Way to Sell a Product.

Pro

Yes, advertising is unethical. Let's discuss one kind of advertising, known as "subliminal advertising." This is a method theaters used to increase sales of food and drink at their concession stands in the 1950s, until Congress outlawed the practice. In one case, a theater flashed a split-second image of a steaming hot hamburger during the middle of a love scene. Before the scene had ended, the concession stand was crowded with moviegoers asking for hamburgers. Some moviegoers even asked for dressings on the hamburgers that they later admitted they didn't like—dressings that were portrayed on the hamburger flashed on the screen.

Such ads create their effect at an unconscious level in your mind, so you can't reject them the way you would any other kind of ad. They are commercial brainwashing. Some alcoholic beverage ads in magazines and newspapers use subtle photographic retouching to create sexual images that enhance the appeal of the product. Not everyone recognizes these images, and often people can't recognize the images when they are pointed out and described to them. But the images *do* sell more alcohol, and consumers don't have any choice in the matter.

Have you ever wondered why everyone drinking a particular soft drink on television is smiling, dancing, and partying with friends? Does the advertiser's product really make you happier and more sociable? Probably not. Advertising makes you buy products for the wrong reasons. And that's unethical.

Con

No, advertising is not unethical. First, much advertising is very informative. Automobile advertisements give information on gas mileage and prices. Stereo equipment ads usually give specifications about technical features of the product. As it becomes increasingly more expensive in gas and time to shop for a purchase, ads become more valuable by describing what stores have to offer.

Advertising helps buyers discriminate between two products that are almost identical; otherwise, there could be a monopoly for every product at a given quality level, and free enterprise would be almost impossible. In that sense, advertising is crucial to a free enterprise system.

In our complex world, a producer needs to have a way to announce new products. Manufacturers cannot wait for word-of-mouth to get news of a new product circulated. New products *must* have advertising, and new products are the bread-and-butter of a competitive free enterprise economy.

And what about subliminal advertisements? They have been the victim of incredible hype; scientific research has demonstrated that many people are unaffected by them. Many more people never recognized the ads.

No, advertising is not unethical. It is the way businesses distinguish between similar products, it is how new products are announced, and it can actually increase the efficiency with which a purchase of a product satisfies a given emotional or physical need.

Profile—
Lee A. Iacocca

The board of directors of Chrysler Corporation elected Lee A. Iacocca as chairman of the board of directors and chief executive officer of the corporation in September of 1979. He had been president and chief operating officer and a board member since November 2, 1978. Before coming to Chrysler, Iacocca spent 32 years with the Ford Motor Company, rising from management trainee to president and chief operating officer.

Through the 1940s and 1950s, Iacocca campaigned for new car designs tailored to changing American tastes. In the early 1960s, Iacocca turned his attention to the small car market and gave Ford an enormous head start with the Falcon, the Mustang, and the Pinto. He became famous for his ability to pick the right car for the right time.

During his eight years as president of Ford, Iacocca continued to push for small, fuel-efficient front-wheel-drive cars. He anticipated a new kind of market with consumers seeking energy-efficient cars. For his trouble, he was dismissed by Henry Ford II in November, 1978. Iacocca joined Chrysler the day after he left Ford.

In 1979, Chrysler was expected to lose more than $1 billion and to go bankrupt. Iacocca went to work immediately to save the company. He put his credibility on the line by agreeing to do commercials for Chrysler. He organized his troops to put pressure on Washington to guarantee loans so that Chrysler could continue to convert to front-wheel-drive cars. After an enormous legislative battle, the Loan Guarantee Act passed both houses of Congress by large bipartisan majorities. However, the act required Chrysler to raise $2.5 billion of its own before any loans would be guaranteed. Iacocca determined that the only way he could succeed was by spreading the burden equally over all groups involved. Hence, "equality of sacrifice" was born along with the "new Chrysler Corporation."

Labor made concessions amounting to $1 billion. Banks took 15 to 30 cents on the dollar on loan paybacks. Stockholders gave up dividends. Suppliers delayed their billings and bought debentures. White-collar workers took pay cuts. Only then did the government agree to guarantee $1.2 billion in loans.

All through the crisis, Chrysler engineers, stylists, and designers continued to work on the four-phase front-wheel-drive program. The Omnis and Horizons—the first phase—won Car of the Year. The K Cars—Aries and Reliants—became the best selling cars in Chrysler's history. The next phase, the LeBaron and Dodge 400, proved that a front-wheel-drive car could have size and comfort. Finally, the fourth phase, the E-series, was introduced in 1982 to generally good reviews.

Aside from the front-wheel-drive program, Chrysler continued to innovate and seek out market niches. It brought back the convertible, expecting to sell no more than 5,000 units. By late summer of 1982, 20,000 units had been sold. Chrysler also announced a historic 5-year, 50,000-mile warranty program. Nor surprisingly, Chrysler's profitability, market share, and stock price all increased.

But Chrysler is not Lee Iacocca's only labor of love. He was appointed chairman of the Commission to Restore the Statue of Liberty and Ellis Island. He is also active in a wide range of charitable and civic organizations. He is a member of the Joslin Diabetes Foundation, the board of governors of the Bob Hope International Heart Research Institute, and numerous other civic and professional organizations.

Iacocca earned a bachelor of science degree from Lehigh University in 1945 and a master's degree in mechanical engineering from Princeton University in 1946. He has since received several honorary doctorate degrees from colleges and universities, and he is an honorary trustee of Lehigh University.

In many ways, Iacocca embodies the free enterprise dream: the child of immigrants who becomes the leader of a large company because of inventive genius, persistence, and hard work. And then, like countless others, becomes committed to repaying the system that provided that opportunity.

tising in 1982 by 25 of the biggest U.S. advertisers. Besides commercial firms, many nonprofit organizations are advertising these days. The Sierra Club promotes conservation practices; the American Cancer Society discourages smoking; the United Way encourages donations. In addition, advertising is used to promote political candidates. It was but a few years ago that only people running for national office regularly bought television and radio time. Today, it is common for a candidate for city council in a large city to spend well over $100,000 on political advertising in a single campaign.

Advertising Objectives

The ultimate objective of most advertising is to sell more products. In practice, however, most advertising campaigns have more immediate objectives. Meeting these objectives, it is thought, will result in the achievement of the ultimate objective. Let's look at three of these other objectives.

Increase Frequency of Product Use. Some advertisements encourage people to use the advertised product more often. Greater frequency of use naturally implies greater frequency of purchase. One marketing executive for a popular brand of toothpaste has said, "If we could just get people to brush three times a day, our sales would increase almost 33 percent and the American public would be much better off." Figure 16-2 shows an advertisement with this type of objective.

Introduce Complementary Products. Another common advertising objective is to introduce a new product to a product line. Marketing managers know that if their firm has a good reputation for a particular type of product, it will be easier for them to add a new product to their line. In such cases it is hoped that the firm's reputation for quality will carry over to the new product. Figure 16-3 shows an advertisement for a new product in a product line.

Enhance Corporate Image. Other advertisements talk about the advertiser itself, rather than about a particular product or product line. The purpose of these ads is to enhance corporate image. This is called **institutional advertising**. As an example, General Electric's current advertising theme is, "We bring good things to life." What is the purpose of these ads? Certainly not just to sell more light bulbs, washing machines, or nuclear reactors. Rather, it is to stress GE's contribution to society and to technological advancement. The hope is that a favorable image will help the company sell more products. Figure 16-4 on page 295 shows another example of institutional advertising.

Types of Advertising

Not all advertising is the same. It can be directed to members of the channel of distribution, to industrial buyers, or to the general public. Advertising aimed at the general public can be sponsored by local retailers or by manufacturers. These types of advertising differ greatly in their objectives and format. Let's look at each of them.

Trade Advertising. The purpose of **trade advertising** is to communicate with members of the channel of distribution, including wholesalers and retailers. Manufacturers run advertisements in trade papers and magazines in order to convince wholesalers and retailers to carry their products. Examples of such publications include *Hardware Retailer*, *Supermarket News*, and *Advertising Age*. The advertisement in Figure 16-5 on page 296 is a typical trade advertisement.

Trade advertising is much more informative and detailed than the advertising that consumers encounter in popular magazines and newspapers. Trade advertisements describe the product offered, make suggestions as to how it can be properly displayed, and point out reasons why the wholesaler or retailer should carry the product. Trade advertising frequently includes a mention of sales contests and sales training courses.

Industrial Advertising. As we discussed in Chapter 13, many firms sell industrial goods—machinery, tools, parts, and fabrication equipment—to other firms, which then use these goods in the manufacture of their products. The makers of industrial goods also advertise to reach their markets. This type of advertising, known as **industrial advertising**, tells customers how they can use the advertised product to make their businesses more profitable.

294   Part 4 • Marketing Management

Figure 16-2
Frequency of Use Advertisement

Figure 16-3
New Product in Product Line Advertisement

Chapter 16 • Promotion 295

Figure 16-4

Institutional Advertisement

What do you see when you look at a tree?

It depends on your perspective. You might see a source of jobs.

You might see a source of lumber, plywood, paper, packaging—"need" products as opposed to "want" products.

You might see an ideal base for a growth business, a natural resource that, managed properly, renews itself perpetually.

You might see a splendid example of Nature's artistry.

When we look at a tree, we see all these things, and more. We see our life's blood. Much of what we do depends on trees. So we take care of ours.

We strive to manage them in a way that reconciles your perspectives and ours, so they'll provide jobs, products, profits and splendor forever.

If we succeed, everybody wins. You the worker, consumer, investor and citizen. And we the employees and shareholders of Boise Cascade.

Reason enough to try, don't you think?

Boise Cascade Corporation
A company worth looking at.

Figure 16-5

Trade Advertisement

It is the job of industrial buyers to understand the technical characteristics of the products they buy. An effective industrial advertisement, therefore, must be informative above all else. It acts as a "stand-in" for a sales representative, and answers the kinds of technical questions that an industrial buyer would ask a sales representative if one were present. Emotional appeals, as often used in consumer advertising, are generally not used in industrial ads. Figure 16-6 shows an industrial advertisement.

Retail Advertising. Retail advertising is performed by retail stores. The aim of retail advertising is to encourage people to buy consumer products at the sponsor's retail outlets.

Some retailers advertise both locally and nationally. J.C. Penney and Sears advertise products through national television and magazines as well as through local newspapers. The idea behind national retail advertising is to tell the public that the national retailer is a good company to do business with. Its aim is to make shoppers, wherever they live, more loyal to the retailer and its products. In contrast, local retail advertising is directed at shoppers in a particular retail market; its aim is to make a sale at a specific store. As a result, local advertising stresses the styles, prices, and types of products carried at that store along with the image that the store would like to convey to the public. Figure 16-7 on page 298 is an example of a local retail advertisement.

National Advertising. This last type of advertising is very familiar to everyone. National advertising is paid for by manufacturers and directed at consumers. The purpose of such advertising is to tell consumers about a product and its advantages, a change in product features, or about new uses for an old product. In this way, manufacturers attempt to draw customers into any and all retail establishments to buy their products.

Some of the best examples of national advertising by manufacturers can be found on prime time television. Many of the commercials seen on evening television are paid for by such manufacturers of nationally distributed products as Procter and Gamble, Bristol-Myers, General Motors, General Electric, and General Mills.

Advertising and the Product Life Cycle

In Chapter 13 we discussed the product life cycle. We identified five stages in the life of a product—market development, rapid growth, turbulence, maturity, and decline—and talked briefly about how advertising changes over the life of a product. We used the Sony home video system as an example. Now we are ready to discuss in greater detail the relationship between the product life cycle and advertising message and objectives.

Figure 16-8 on page 299 shows the product life cycle curve and the three stages in the life of an advertising campaign. Notice the correlation between the five product life cycle stages and the three advertising stages. In short, as a product moves through its life cycle, it requires three distinct stages of advertising. These stages differ in their messages and in their objectives, as we'll now see. The stages make up what we shall call the **advertising spiral**.[2]

[2] This section adapted from Otto Kleppner, *Advertising Procedure* (Englewood Cliffs, N.J.: Prentice-Hall, Inc., 1979), pp. 41-48.

Figure 16-6
Industrial Advertisement

Figure 16-7

Local Retail Advertisement

Figure 16-8

Advertising and the Product Life Cycle

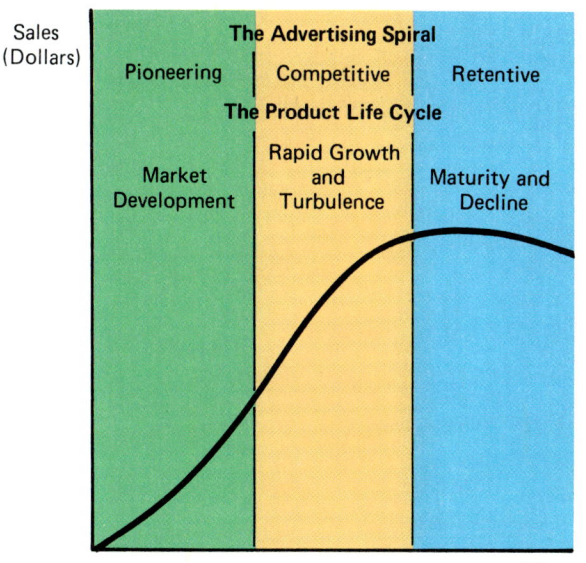

Pioneering Stage. The **pioneering stage** in the advertising spiral corresponds to the market development stage of the product life cycle. Here, the advertiser introduces the product to the public. This generating of interest in a product—or causing people to recognize a need for it—is called **primary demand stimulation**.

A classic example of primary demand stimulation can be found in RCA's advertisements introducing color television to the American public in the 1950s. RCA's pioneer advertising stated:

> See the World Series Baseball in Living Color... Rarely in the lifetime can you share a thrill like this... You can see baseball's greatest spectacle come alive in your own home in color... You'll sense a new on-the-spot realism in every picture of the crowd, the players, the action... Made by RCA—the most trusted name in electronics.

Note how this ad emphasized the benefits of color television in general, with only minor mention of the RCA name. The purpose of the ads was to sell people on the "idea" of color television. The problem of selling the RCA brand name was left for later advertisements.

Competitive Stage. The **competitive stage** corresponds to the rapid growth and turbulence stages of the product life cycle. By this time, the need for the product is well established in the minds of buyers. People no longer ask, "Should I buy the product?" Instead, they ask, "Which brand should I buy?"

Many of the products we buy are in the competitive stage of the advertising spiral. Examples are cigarettes, soap, and watches. Competitive advertising stresses the unique features of the product, especially the features most desired by buyers and supposedly absent in competing products. These are the competitive advertising themes for several products:

- You deserve National attention. (National Car Rental)
- People trust Seiko more than any other watch. (Seiko Watch Company)
- The more you care about color, the more you need Kodacolor II film. (Kodak)
- A whole carton of Carlton has less tar than a single pack of Kent, Winston Lights, Marlboro, Salem, Kool Milds, or Newport. (Carlton Cigarettes)

The idea behind each of these slogans is that the advertised brand is better than other brands. Figure 16-9 shows another example of a competitive advertisement.

Retentive Stage. The **retentive stage** of the advertising spiral corresponds to the maturity and decline stages of the product life cycle. By now the product is used by many people, so the aim of advertising in this stage is to foster brand loyalty. That is, the firm, through its advertising, attempts to hold on to as many current customers as possible.

Typically, the firm relies on name advertising during the retentive stage of the advertising spiral. The goal of **name advertising** is to put the name of the product (or the company's trademark) in front of as many people as possible. Think of the familiar red and white signs that encourage you to drink Coca-Cola. Why does Coke advertise? To increase brand awareness can't be the reason because everyone has already heard of Coke. Coca-Cola advertises in order to keep the name of the product in front of you. This makes you just a little more likely to reach for a Coke the next time you're thirsty. The makers of Pepsi-Cola, Dr. Pepper, 7-Up, and Royal Crown Cola also advertise their products heavily for the same reason. All of these soft-drink makers are fighting for market share in the intensely competitive soft-drink industry. Thus, another objective of name advertising is to take market

Figure 16-9

Competitive Advertisement

share away from competitors. Figure 16-10 shows a good example of name advertising.

Measuring Advertising Effectiveness

It is always difficult for a firm to determine whether its advertising program has been effective. As we have seen, advertisements may have very different objectives. If a clothing store advertises a spring clearance sale and attracts no more than the usual number of shoppers, then it's probably safe to say that the advertisements were not effective. Other situations are not so clear cut. For example, what if a business introduced a new product to the market, and it failed miserably despite a huge advertising campaign? Should we conclude that the ads themselves were the problem or that it was the product itself, the timing of its introduction to the market, the choice of a distribution strategy, or the media chosen for the ads?

Although the measurement of advertising effectiveness can become quite complex, there are at least two ways to approach it: reach and frequency.

Reach. **Reach** is a measure of how many people actually saw or heard the advertisement in a given medium. But reach in itself may not mean much. What if very few of the people who see the ad are interested or are qualified buyers? A few years ago, the University of Texas advertised a new type of Masters in Business Administration (M.B.A.) program. The program, designed for business executives, was advertised in local newspapers and in the southwest edition of *The Wall Street Journal*. Of the 475 applicants to the program, more than 300 read about it in local papers; only 75 read about it in the *Journal*. The other 100 heard about the program from other sources. Of the 300 who read the local newspaper, however, only 10 were qualified applicants, whereas 62 of the 75 who read *The Wall Street Journal* were qualified. The *Journal* was a much more effective medium even though the local paper's advertisements had greater reach.

Frequency. Another important concept is **frequency**, which is the number of times a person is exposed to an advertisement. Advertisers know that the more often people see or hear an advertisement, the more likely they are to remember it. Therefore, an ad with greater "frequency" has a better chance to achieve its objective.

Wrap-Up

As we have seen, advertising alone is not responsible for the success of a product. If the price of a product is too high or if it obviously is not as good as one made by a competitor, then the product probably will not sell very well. Most advertising experts now believe that advertising should be evaluated in terms of reach and frequency.

For example, a successful ad may be one that is seen an average of 2.5 times each by 25,000 viewers in the local television broadcast market. Or an ad that results in a 30 percent increase in product awareness. Or one that is remembered by half of the people who see it. The assumption in this last case is that people who remember an advertisement and who have a positive attitude toward the product will buy it.

PERSONAL SELLING

As we said at the start of Chapter 12, "Nothing happens until a sale is made." At least that's what many salespeople tell their friends in production and accounting. What they are saying is that making a sale is the single most important thing a business does. Without a sale, what good were the long hours spent by the firm's production engineers in designing an efficient manufac-

Figure 16-10
Name Advertisement

turing process? Or the efforts of the finance people in raising money for a plant expansion? Or the work of the advertising staff in developing an ad campaign for the firm's products?

Let's begin our discussion of personal selling by looking at opportunities in selling. Then we will talk about what salespeople do and how the sales process works.

Opportunities in Selling

Personal selling involves direct face-to-face encounters between salespeople and potential buyers. Many men and women in business work as salespeople. They sell everything from used cars to satellite dish antennas. Their goal is to make money for themselves and their company by enabling their customers to get what they need at a price they can afford. There are a variety of career opportunities in selling as well as career rewards.

Career Opportunities. In many firms, the people working in the marketing department began their careers with the sales force. This is not so much an accident as it is a matter of policy. Why do firms want their marketing staff to have sales experience? The answer is simple: Sales experience gives these people an understanding of the unique problems faced by salespeople. The people who design the marketing strategy must understand exactly how the products are sold. It doesn't make much sense for managers in the marketing department never to have seen a customer. In the same way, it is absolutely necessary for anyone seeking a position as sales manager to have had sales experience.

Financial Rewards. Salespeople can earn a good living for themselves and their families. Table 16-2 shows compensation figures for sales trainees, salespersons, senior salespersons, and sales supervisors for the period of 1976 to 1982. The average income for salespeople has increased significantly. The average income for a senior salesperson climbed from $22,768 in 1976 to $36,000 in 1982. This is a 58.1 percent increase.

A large number of salespeople are paid on a commission basis. That is, their pay is tied to how much they sell. It is not unusual for salespeople on commission to make much more money than their sales managers. Such people frequently turn down jobs in marketing or sales management because they can't afford the cut in pay.

Freedom from Direct Control. A career in selling can provide independence for people who do not like to be closely supervised in their work. Many successful salespeople operate almost as if they were independent business people. They plan their day's work and decide for themselves how to approach each customer.

Salespeople: Roles and Responsibilities

The most important function of the salesperson, of course, is to sell the firm's products. We'll look more closely at this particular function when we get to the end of this section. Now we'll examine four other roles of the salesperson.

Credit Reviewer. Most products sold to businesses are sold on credit. Regardless of how soon pay-

Table 16-2

Average Total Compensation for People in Sales Positions

	1976	1978	1980	1982	Percentage Change 1976-1982
Sales Trainee	$12,588	$15,217	$17,523	$22,350	77.6
Salesperson	17,592	20,252	23,974	29,087	65.3
Senior Salesperson	22,768	26,530	29,948	36,000	58.1
Sales Supervisor	26,143	31,575	36,764	43,400	66.0

Source: Adapted from *Sales & Marketing Management* (February 21, 1983), p. 72.

ments are to be made, the salesperson's job is to determine whether the buyer is qualified, that is, whether the buyer can afford to make the purchase and pay the bill. In the case of a small company, the salesperson may have to look at the company's financial statements and obtain a letter of recommendation from the company's bank.

Team Manager. Often, products are sold not by one person but by a team of people in the company. For example, an electric utility in the market for a new steam turbine needs a great deal of highly technical advice. Most members of a turbine manufacturer's sales force, even if trained as electrical engineers, would not be up-to-date on the precise specifications of the newest steam turbines. As a result, they would ask technical experts from their company to talk to the electric utility's technical experts. In this situation, the salesperson decides who from his or her company would be the most helpful and when that person should visit the customer.

External Consultant. The salesperson also acts as an advisor, or external consultant. Customers rely on the advice of a salesperson as to which products are best for them. In short, the buyer has a problem—which product to buy—and the salesperson has a solution. National Chemsearch, for instance, sells high quality cleaning supplies to other businesses. The salesperson for National Chemsearch calls on the purchasing agent at the buying firm and on the person who actually uses the cleaning materials. National Chemsearch believes that it is important for its salespeople to explain to the user how its products can best be utilized.

Glad Handler. The last role is that of glad handler. This means listening to the customer's problems, some of which are personal and some of which are business oriented. A salesperson also takes customers out to lunch. Why? To talk business and to build and maintain a good personal relationship.

Selling the Firm's Products

The sales process is pictured as a circle in Figure 16-11. The circular nature of the sales process means that the last stage leads back to the first. Let's take a quick look at the six stages of the sales process.

Stage 1: Prospecting. The salesperson begins the sales process by locating new customers, that is, by prospecting. Sometimes, new customers are found by making cold calls. The salesperson walks into a business and tries to sell the product without having called on the business before and without knowing much about the business. Cold calls are not usually very successful.

At other times, current customers recommend new customers. Here, the salesperson's job is to follow up the recommendations. Finally,

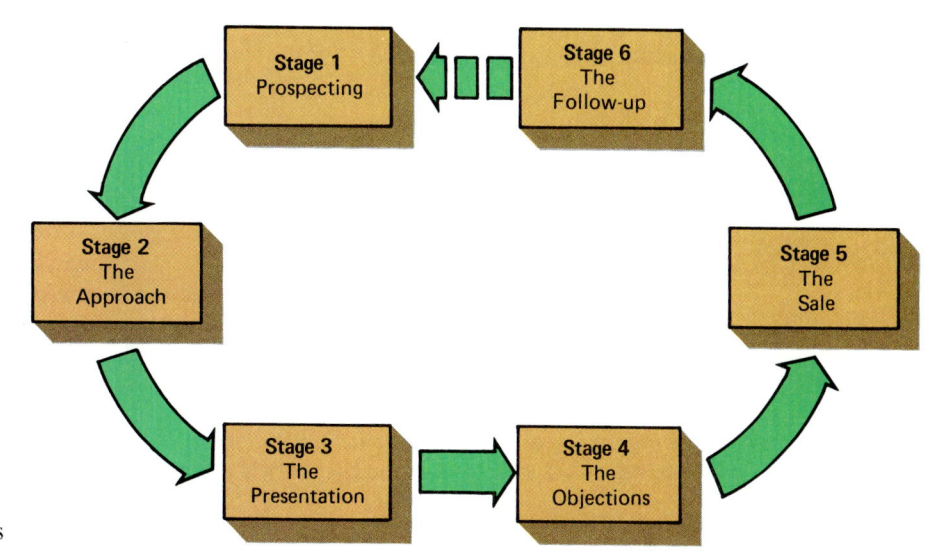

Figure 16-11

The Sales Process

prospective customers may be people with whom the salesperson has done business before.

Stage 2: The Approach. During the second stage, the salesperson decides how best to approach the prospective customer. The salesperson will need to find out what kind of products the customer needs, and determine who actually makes the purchase decision. If the salesperson has a good personal relationship with someone inside the buying firm, this information is not hard to obtain.

Stage 3: The Presentation. At this stage, the salesperson presents the firm's product to the customer. The presentation may include several charts, graphs, or even slides. If possible, it is a good idea to demonstrate the product too. If a picture is worth a thousand words, then a well-planned demonstration is worth ten thousand words.

Stage 4: The Questions and Objections. Very few sales are made without the customer asking questions or raising objections. These are usually nothing more than an attempt to learn more about the product. The salesperson with a good product and with a good understanding of it has no reason to fear these questions and objections.

Stage 5: The Sale. If the salesperson answers the customer's questions well, then the customer will very likely buy the product. Unfortunately, some customers have a difficult time making a decision. The salesperson, therefore, attempts to make it as easy as possible for the customer to say yes. The salesperson does this by asking such questions as: "Who should I see about filling out the order?" "Do you want to purchase one or two months' supply?" "Would you like to pay for the product in 30 days or 45 days?"

Stage 6: The Follow-Up. The last stage in Figure 16-11 is follow-up. This is the stage where the salesperson, after the sale has been made, pays a return visit to the customer. The idea is to see whether the buyer is happy with the product. If there are any problems with the product, the salesperson can help solve them.

Now notice in Figure 16-11 the dotted line between the follow-up stage and the prospecting stage. This line closes the circle and means that if the salesperson takes good care of the customer after the sale, it will be much easier to do business with the customer in the future. This is why the sales process is pictured as a circle.

SALES PROMOTION

Sales promotions are another way for the firm to communicate with potential customers. Examples of **sales promotion** are point-of-purchase displays, free samples, coupons, gifts, and product demonstrations. Before looking at each type of sales promotion, let's discuss sales promotion objectives.

Why Sales Promotion?

Sales promotion is essential for most businesses. It is impossible to know exactly how much money is spent each year on sales promotion in

---

FROM THE FILE

Suzanne is marketing director for Creative Products, Inc., which manufactures and sells a variety of pens, pencils, shoelaces, balloons, and dishes stamped with an inscription of the buyer's choosing. All of the company's products are inexpensive: A gross of custom-stamped pencils, for example, retails for $15.95, or only about $.11 apiece. Creative Products, Inc., has promoted its merchandise through a small catalog, using a mailing list supplied by another company. With postage rates increasing almost every year, Suzanne has been asked to come up with a list of alternative ways to market the company's merchandise line. Can you help her?

the United States. However, in 1982 there were as many as 100 billion coupons in circulation in the United States. And coupons are only one sales promotion tool. In general, sales promotions have four objectives: (1) to get people to buy a product that they have not bought before, (2) to encourage people who use a product to use it more often, (3) to suggest new uses for a product, and (4) to give a product a good image.[3] Figure 16-12 shows a sales promotion ad. Of the objectives just listed, which do you think characterize this promotional device?

Sales Promotion Tools

Now we are ready to look at some specific sales promotion tools. We'll examine five of them. When was the last time you saw each one?

Point-of-Purchase Displays. Point-of-purchase displays direct the attention of the buyer to the product. They are placed at the point of purchase, that is, in the store. Almost any product can benefit from these displays. However, they are vital for products sold in supermarkets where customers are expected to find products for themselves.

An excellent example of a point-of-purchase display is the L'eggs "boutique." The clever display rack has certainly contributed a great deal to the success of L'eggs panty hose.

Samples. Manufacturers and retailers give away free samples in order to get people to try a new product, especially food or household items. For samples to be an effective promotional device, they must be given to as many people as possible. They, therefore, are a very expensive way to promote a new product. Finally, samples are useful only if the product sampled is truly superior to competing products.

Coupons. A coupon is a piece of paper entitling its holder to a discount on a particular product. Most coupons are printed in the Thursday edition of local newspapers. They also are sometimes sent to people's homes.

Generally speaking, coupons are a good way to get people to switch from one brand to another. Most people do not feel much loyalty to any particular brand of product, especially if it is a convenience item. As a result, if they have a

---

[3] John Young, Scott Paper Company, as quoted in Eugene S. Mahani, "Premium 'Tie Breakers' Stand Out in Marketplace Glut," *Advertising Age* (May 3, 1976), p. 39.

Figure 16-12

Sales Promotion Advertisement

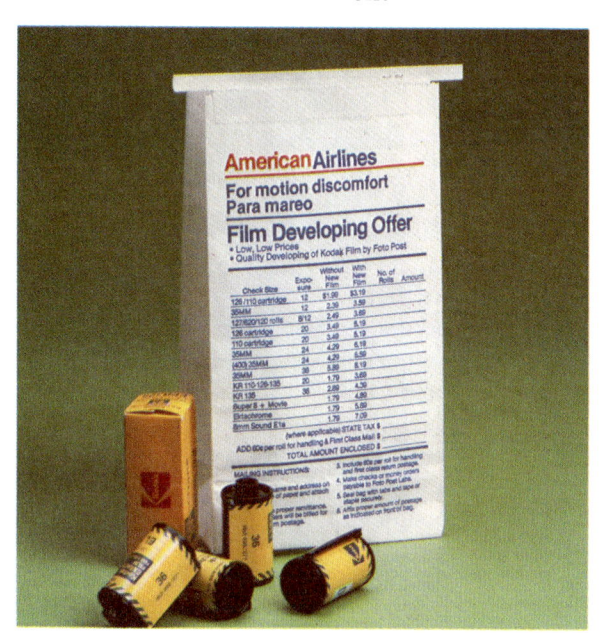

chance to buy a new laundry soap at 10 to 15 cents off, many of them will do so.

Gifts. Makers of candies, laundry soaps, food, and other consumer products often use gifts to build customer loyalty for their products. Sometimes, the gift is presented to the customer at the time of purchase. For example, Gillette gave away disposable razors to people buying a large can of Foamy shaving cream. This helped sell shaving cream and, at the same time, introduced customers to the disposable razors.

Product Demonstrations. Demonstrations help sell a great many products. Many of us have been called on in our homes by vacuum cleaner salespeople, who offer not only to vacuum all the floors but also to shampoo the living room rug and to bathe the dog—all with the same machine. Sewing machines, microwave ovens, dishwashers, and new types of food products are frequently demonstrated in stores. The key to a successful demonstration is getting the customer involved with the product. This is why automobile salespeople always want you to test drive their cars.

SUMMARY POINTS

1. The three stages of communication strategy development are product analysis, positioning analysis, and communication program analysis.
2. The purpose of advertising is to increase sales or profits by showing how a product can satisfy a consumer need or by providing information about the product.
3. Three specific advertising objectives are to increase the frequency of product use, to introduce new products to the product line, and to enhance corporate image.
4. Differing in their objectives and format, the four types of advertising are trade advertising, industrial advertising, retail advertising, and national advertising.
5. The advertising spiral shows how the advertising for a product changes as it moves through its product life cycle. The pioneering, competitive, and retentive stages of the advertising spiral correspond to the five product life cycle stages.
6. The idea behind name advertising is to put the brand name of the product in front of as many potential buyers as possible.
7. Two measures of effectiveness are the number of people exposed to the ads (reach) and the average number of exposures per person (frequency).
8. Besides selling the firm's products, many salespeople today also act as credit reviewers, team managers, external consultants, and glad handlers.
9. We can picture the sales process as a circle consisting of six stages: prospecting, the approach, the presentation, questions and objections, the sale, and the follow-up.
10. Like advertising, the objectives of sales promotions are to increase product purchase and use, to suggest new uses for an old product, and to enhance product image.
11. Five types of sales promotions are point-of-purchase displays, free samples, coupons, gifts, and product demonstrations.

KEY TERMS AND CONCEPTS

communication strategy
positioning
advertising
advertising objectives
trade advertising
industrial advertising
retail advertising
national advertising
advertising spiral
pioneering stage
primary demand stimulation
competitive stage
retentive stage

name advertising
reach
frequency
personal selling
commission
cold calls
sales promotions
point-of-purchase displays
samples
coupons
gifts
product demonstration

REVIEW QUESTIONS

1. What is meant by "positioning"?
2. Outline the differences between industrial and retail advertising.
3. Describe the uses of primary demand stimulation. When is it important for advertisers to engage in primary demand stimulation?
4. How do advertisements differ between the pioneering stage and the competitive stage of the advertising spiral?
5. What is the difference between the advertising concepts of reach and frequency?
6. Why is it important for people in the marketing department to have some selling experience?
7. List the six stages of the sales process. Why is this process pictured as a circle? What is the importance of the follow-up stage?
8. Why do business firms engage in sales promotions?
9. When are free samples most effective as promotional devices?

DISCUSSION QUESTIONS

1. Describe the communication strategy development process for a heavy duty farm tractor.
2. What is the relationship between the product life cycle and the advertising spiral? Show how the five stages of the first correspond to the three stages of the second.
3. What are some of the problems involved in using changes in product sales as a measure of advertising effectiveness?
4. If you were a salesperson would you rather be paid on a straight commission or straight salary?
5. Which types of sales promotions would be most appropriate for introducing a new deodorant to the consumer market?

CASE 16-1

Mendel's Book Stores

Americans spend an average of $28 a year on books—far less than they spend on either movies or phonograph records. And at $3 to $5 apiece for paperback novels (much more for bestsellers and hardcovers), this is not a lot of books. Even so, the book market is currently growing rapidly, and many companies are jumping into the chain bookstore market.

At one point, Mendel's Book Stores, a large nationwide bookstore chain, was considering ways to increase sales. Mendel's wanted to boost its sales early so it could expand its chain as fast as possible to keep ahead of the competition.

Since sales prices on books are usually forbidden by contracts signed with publishers, Mendel's was considering a sweepstakes in which customers would receive a coupon with each purchase. Rubbing off the opaque film over the coupon, customers might find a promise of a free paperback, a gift certificate, trips, or even a grand prize of a sports car whose trunk and back seat were filled with books.

Mendel's employed two marketing consultants to advise on whether to go ahead with this promotion. One consultant told Mendel's not to use it: "In the short run, sweepstakes are pretty effective. But in the long run, people value your promotion more than your product. A bookstore needs to develop store loyalty and needs to develop long-term reading behavior to keep book purchases up in the long run."

The second consultant was for the sweepstakes: "It appeals to greed. Every book buyer will think of winning that car. It doesn't even matter if buyers don't read the books. As long as you get people used to spending more money on books than on records or movies, you've achieved your goal—to build reading as a cheaper and more interesting alternative to movies, records, electronic games, and so on."

Mendel's management was not at all sure what it should do.

1. What is the goal of any promotion? What should be Mendel's goal, regardless of the promotion method used?
2. Do you think the book market, given the information above, is a good market in which to use a sweepstakes? What kinds of problems do you think might arise?
3. Why do you think the use of sale prices on paperback best sellers and other popular books is frowned on by book publishers (and disliked by retailers as well)?
4. Evaluate the opinions of the two consultants. Neither one is entirely correct. Explain how each is wrong and how you would improve each argument.

CASE 16-2

Prince Tennis Rackets

The market for expensive tennis rackets is an extremely competitive one. Millions of dollars are spent in promotion of new racket models. Tennis stars are hired to promote each manufacturer's racket, and every gimmick or technological advance is employed to gain a greater share of the market.

Into this chaos stepped Howard Head, the inventor of the Prince racket. It's hard to miss Prince rackets—that's part of Head's sales strategy—since they're 50 percent larger than traditional tennis rackets.

Head entered the racket market at a time when the tennis industry was going into a sharp decline. Head introduced a racket which rebounded a tennis ball properly from a much larger area of the strings. Tennis players discovered that it helped them play better. In two years, Prince rackets jumped from claiming 8.5 percent of the racket market to 30.7 percent.

Head needed, but couldn't get, the established professionals to promote his rackets. These professionals were used to standard-sized rackets and weren't about to relearn their tennis games for a sponsor's sake. Consequently, Head had to look elsewhere for promoters. Realizing that the tennis racket market was in a slump, he reasoned that he had to sell new rackets to current players. And some of the best role models for these current players were the up-and-coming teenage professionals, especially on the women's circuit. They were new enough at the game to be willing to switch to an unorthodox racket design. He put Prince rackets in the hands of several of the new young tennis stars and achieved remarkable success. Head also realized that the tennis players he needed to sell to were going to buy the new rackets only if they were moving up from lower-quality rackets. As a result, he made his oversized rackets of the very best materials and priced them very dearly (some over $500). His odd promotional strategy worked.

Today, Prince rackets are seen throughout the professional circuit and are used by amateur players everywhere. Head has also designed rackets for other companies. Using strict enforcement of his patents on oversized rackets, however, he has developed a near-monopoly in the oversized racket market. Prince will be a powerful force in the racket industry for years to come.

1. Do you think Head should have pursued the established professional players further to get them to promote his rackets?
2. In which stage of its product life cycle is the standard-sized tennis racket? In which stage is the Prince oversized racket? How does this affect Prince's promotional strategies?
3. Why do you think Prince enforces its patents so stringently? What would have happened to Prince's promotional strategy had the Prince design been used by other manufacturers?
4. Would Prince rackets be a good candidate for a discount pricing promotional offer? Would they be a good candidate for a promotion featuring special professional tennis instruction clinics?
5. What kinds of other promotions would you suggest for Prince rackets?

Break-Even Analysis

This program performs a break-even analysis. You input the variable cost per unit, total fixed costs, and selling price. The program next computes the break-even point and the total costs at the break-even point. It then gives you the option to change the selling price or to perform an entire new analysis.

Here's the Program

```
 10 PRINT
 20 PRINT "***********BREAK-EVEN ANALYSIS***********"
 30 PRINT
 40 INPUT "VARIABLE COST PER UNIT..$";CV
 50 INPUT "TOTAL FIXED COSTS.......$";CF
 60 INPUT "SELLING PRICE...........$";P
 70 X = CF / (P - CV)
 80 X = INT (X * 100 + .51) / 100
 90 PRINT
100 PRINT "******************************************"
110 PRINT
120 PRINT "VARIABLE COST PER UNIT..........$";CV
130 PRINT "TOTAL FIXED COSTS...............$";CF
140 PRINT "SELLING PRICE...................$";P
150 PRINT "BREAK-EVEN POINT (UNITS).........";X
160 TC = CF + X * CV
170 TC = INT (TC * 100 + .51) / 100
180 PRINT "TOTAL COST AT BREAK-EVEN........$";TC
190 PRINT
200 PRINT "******************************************"
210 PRINT
220 PRINT "DO YOU WANT TO CHANGE THE"
230 INPUT "SELLING PRICE? (1=YES;2=NO) ";Z
240 IF Z = 1 THEN GOTO 60
250 PRINT "DO YOU WANT TO DO ANOTHER"
260 INPUT "BREAK-EVEN ANALYSIS? (1=YES;2=NO) ";Y
270 IF Y = 1 THEN GOTO 10
280 END
```

Here's Sample Output

Two sets of output of the break-even analysis program are provided. All inputs are summarized in the output. In the first run, the break-even point is 125 units and the total cost at the break-even point is $3,000. In the second run, the break-even point is 100 units and total cost at break-even is $2,500.

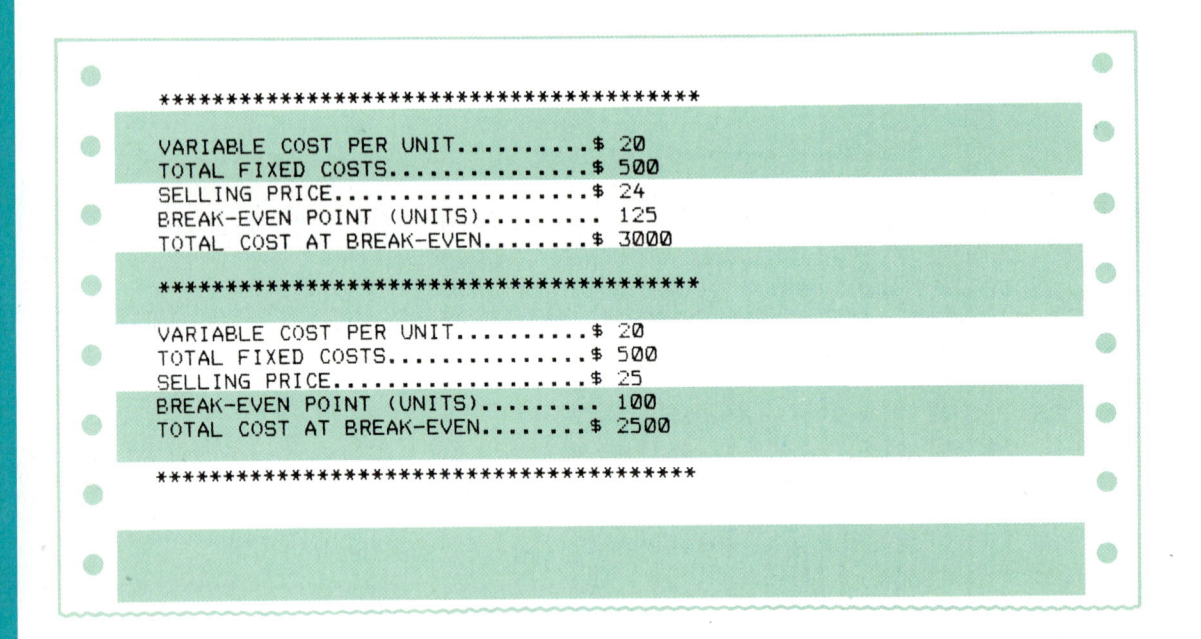

```
******************************************
VARIABLE COST PER UNIT..........$ 20
TOTAL FIXED COSTS...............$ 500
SELLING PRICE...................$ 24
BREAK-EVEN POINT (UNITS).........  125
TOTAL COST AT BREAK-EVEN........$ 3000
******************************************
VARIABLE COST PER UNIT..........$ 20
TOTAL FIXED COSTS...............$ 500
SELLING PRICE...................$ 25
BREAK-EVEN POINT (UNITS).........  100
TOTAL COST AT BREAK-EVEN........$ 2500
******************************************
```

Questions

1. If the variable cost per unit and the selling price each increase by the same amount, what will be the impact on the break-even point?
2. At the break-even point, can fixed costs ever be greater than total revenues? Why or why not?
3. Does the break-even analysis indicate what selling price should be set? Explain.

5
Financial Management

17

Short-Term Financing – The Banking System

After studying this chapter, you should be able to:

- Explain why firms need to borrow short-term money.
- Discuss the five major sources of short-term money.
- Describe the commercial banking system, including how banks create money, types of accounts, as well as three other financial institutions.
- Discuss the structure of the Federal Reserve System and how it controls the size of the nation's money supply.

Nearly all business firms borrow money at one time or another. They do so because the timing of the flow of sales revenue into the firm does not always coincide with the timing of expenses and other cash obligations. Business firms borrow money today in anticipation of making money tomorrow. This chapter examines why businesses borrow money for short periods of time and where they obtain this money. We also take a brief look at commercial banking and at the Federal Reserve System.

Chapter 17 • Short-Term Financing—The Banking System

WHY BORROW SHORT TERM?

Short term refers to a period of one year or less. **Short-term financing**, therefore, refers to debts with a maturity date of one year or less. Some examples of short-term debt are outstanding bank loans payable within 12 months, money owed to suppliers for goods purchased on credit, and income tax liabilities incurred but not yet paid. Long term, on the other hand, refers to a period of several years or more. In finance, **long-term debt** is usually taken to mean debt with a maturity date of ten years or more. The time between the short term and the long term is often called the middle term.

Timing of Work and Cash Flows

Business firms borrow money for one primary reason: They do not have enough cash on hand to pay for the production and sale of their products. In a large firm, short-term financing can involve day-to-day decisions. The job of a **financial manager** is to make sure that the firm has enough cash to meet obligations and to obtain this cash from the least costly sources.

To understand how short-term financing works, we need to consider the timing of work and cash flows. Figure 17-1 illustrates these flows for a manufacturer of Christmas cards. As with most other businesses, there are certain times in the year when this company needs more cash than it receives.

Work Flow. During the first two or three months of the year, the company's artists design the Christmas cards that will appear in stores that December. In March, the company starts producing cards and inventorying them in its stockroom. Retailers begin placing their orders in June, but the cards are not shipped until September.

Cash Flow. Not until November and December does the company see any cash for its production run that year. And yet the company incurred production, inventory, insurance, and other costs throughout the year which had to be paid. In order to meet these obligations, the Christmas card manufacturer borrows short term from a local bank. The cash received at the end of the year from retailers is then used to pay back the loan.

Firms Seldom Borrowing Short Term

Some firms rarely, if ever, need to borrow short-term money. These firms can be one of two types. The first is a business with stable sales

Figure 17-1

Business Activities and Short-Term Money Needs for a Christmas Card Manufacturer

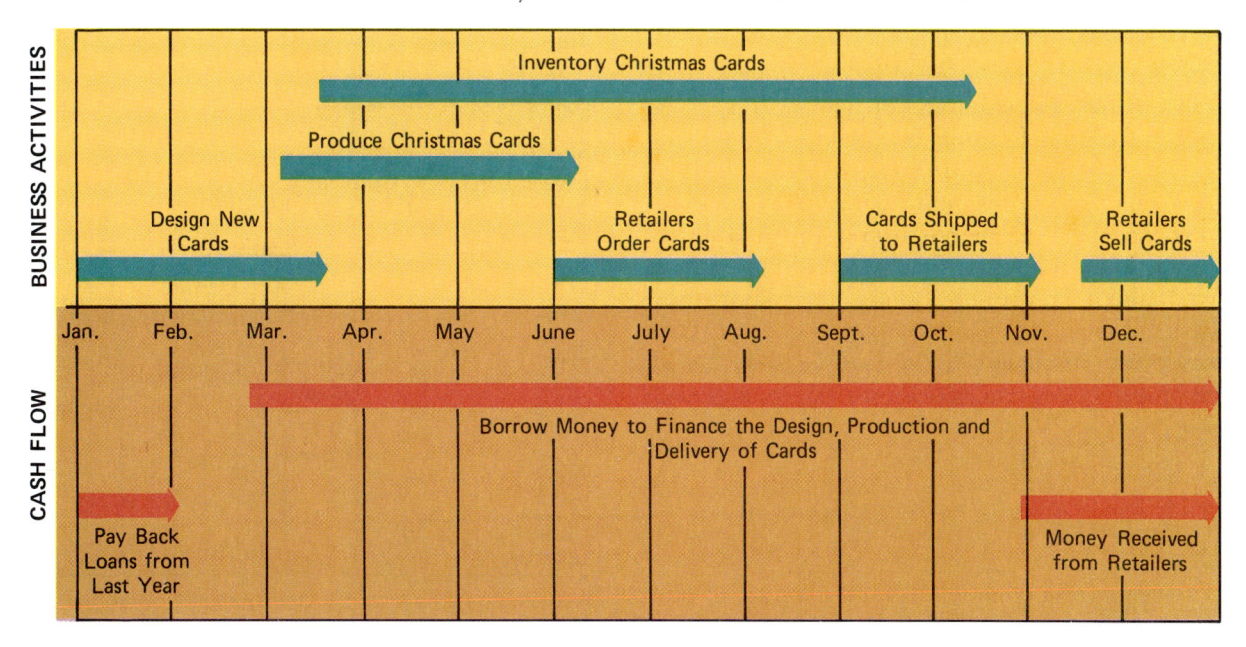

Many retailers increase short-term borrowing at certain times of year.

throughout the year. An example is a supermarket chain. Food sales are typically constant from one month to the next, and so supermarkets do not need to build up inventories in one period in order to sell them off in the next.

Another type of business rarely borrowing short term is one that is extremely cash rich. Such businesses finance operations out of their own profit streams. Few firms are this lucky. About one third of the total debt of the nation's top 500 corporations is short term.

SOURCES OF SHORT-TERM FUNDS

Business firms in need of short-term funds can obtain them from any of five sources: trade credit, unsecured bank borrowing, commercial paper, secured borrowing from banks and other financial institutions, and factoring accounts receivable. Short-term borrowing is certainly an important part of the financial pictures of most companies. Figure 17-2 shows total short-term debt for five large U.S. companies in 1981. Let's begin our discussion by looking at trade credit, the most widespread source of short-term financing.

Trade Credit

When one company buys a product or service from another, it pays for the purchase either with cash at the time of delivery or with credit. Most suppliers offer trade credit to their business customers. **Trade credit** means that the supplier finances the purchase by giving the buyer 30 days or more to pay. In effect, the buyer obtains financing from the supplier rather than from a bank.

Even a small manufacturer of gift housewares, such as coffee mugs and kitchen aprons, would have several sources of trade credit. The production of kitchen aprons, for example, involves the purchase of raw materials and services from fabric brokers, contract sewing companies, and offset and silkscreen printers. Each of these suppliers is a potential source of credit.

Types of Trade Credit. There are three basic types of trade credit. Most merchandise purchases are financed through **open book credit**, or on **open account**, as it is also called. Under this informal credit arrangement, a buyer makes purchases and pays for them later. An invoice usually accompanies the shipment of goods to the buyer. The invoice specifies which products were purchased, how many, at what price, and when the buyer is expected to pay the seller. This type of credit purchase is "open" in the sense that the buyer is not required to sign a written repayment agreement in advance of each purchase. Open-account buying is one big reason for the smooth flow of business transactions in our economy.

The **promissory note** is another form of trade credit. A promissory note is a signed "promise to pay." The note indicates in writing the amount of money owed by the buyer and the re-

Figure 17-2

Short-Term Obligations for Five Large U.S. Companies

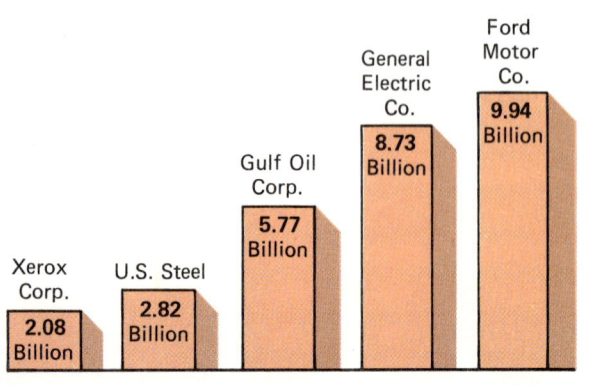

Xerox Corp.: 2.08 Billion
U.S. Steel: 2.82 Billion
Gulf Oil Corp.: 5.77 Billion
General Electric Co.: 8.73 Billion
Ford Motor Co.: 9.94 Billion

Source: Standard & Poor's *Corporation Records*. All figures as of December 31, 1982.

CONTROVERSIAL ISSUES

Variable-Rate Mortgages! Great for Consumers.

Traditionally, the loan industry in America has relied on long-term, fixed-interest-rate mortgages to finance private home purchases. In recent years, however, mushrooming inflation and rapid unpredictable ups and downs in the economy and in the interest rates charged to banks and savings and loans have wiped out profits lenders would have realized from millions of house loans. Furthermore, lenders are uncertain as to the interest rate that should be charged now to make loans profitable in the future. Variable-rate mortgages (VRMs) help to solve this problem. They allow federally chartered savings and loans institutions to increase or decrease the interest rates on loans no more than ½ percent per year, and no more than 2.5 percent for a 30-year loan. Rate increases are optional for lenders, but decreases are obligatory under similar standards. Are VRMs really better for the consumer?

Pro

Yes, variable-rate mortgages serve the consumer better than fixed-rate mortgages do. Certainly, if inflation rates were stable, everyone would prefer fixed rates, just to be sure in advance what one would be paying to amortize a loan.

The government has always tried to set a ceiling on interest rates to keep banks from overcharging. However, when interest rates change so rapidly, the government cannot respond quickly enough to counter these changes with new interest ceilings. Variable-rate mortgages mean that the government has a little breathing room when interest rates change: VRMs allow the rate to change automatically. This also means that the government doesn't have to set largely arbitrary interest rates. Naturally, banks and savings and loans will not want to lend money if they expect to lose on the loan. VRMs help to assure a better chance of a profit on a loan, and hence make loans possible in an unstable loan market. Such loans may cost more, but at least they are available.

Since regulations mandate that interest rates on VRMS have to fall as economic indicators fall, home purchasers need not feel that they must wait to buy a house. The interest rate on their loans will fall if the economy does. So, VRMs more closely relate home-owning costs and benefits to overall economic conditions than do fixed-rate mortgages.

Finally, remember that fixed-payment mortgages will still be available to those willing to pay the high interest rates that lenders will have to charge to earn a profit. Those still wanting that kind of mortgage can have one.

Con

No, VRMs can be harmful. During periods of economic instability, many people may find themselves out of work. If they are exposed to unstable mortgage payments at the same time, surely they are being treated unfairly. Defaults and foreclosures are likely to be far more common under these conditions.

A major problem with variable-rate mortgages is the difficulty of negative amortization. That is, when a monthly payment no longer covers the interest charge, the remainder of the interest charge is added to the principal (the value actually borrowed less whatever has been repaid). Given today's VRM policies, the balance of a loan (not the interest rate) can increase by as much as 10 percent a year. As a result, the mortgaged value of the property can rise above any reasonable price the house is worth. In urban areas, if negative amortization increases the mortgage value of a house above its real worth, the house could be abandoned since the owner will never break even—much less make a profit. And the threat of this may cause banks to deny mortgages to many high-risk urban neighborhoods.

Furthermore, VRMs cause people to continue to expect high inflation. They encourage home purchases, because people believe they have more buying power than they really do. Thus, VRMs can hurt our attempts to correct contemporary inflationary problems.

Last, many people are unable to understand basic fixed-rate mortgages. They often have little understanding of how much they actually will pay to own the home. Is it reasonable to expect that they will have any better understanding of VRMs? Probably not.

Variable rates do not belong in consumer mortgages. They are inflationary, risky, and unfair.

payment date. It is drawn up by the buyer in advance of the purchase. Promissory notes are a popular way of obtaining credit in the fur and jewelry businesses.

A third type of trade credit is the **trade acceptance**. This credit instrument is similar to a promissory note except that it is the seller, rather than the buyer, who draws up a trade acceptance. The customer indicates acceptance of the credit agreement by signing it. Trade acceptances are often used by manufacturers when shipping merchandise to customers with doubtful or unknown credit standings.

Terms of Trade. The conditions given by the seller to the buyer when it offers short-term financing are called **terms of trade**. The **net period** is the length of time for which the seller has extended credit. The Hi-Tone Paint Company sells its heat-resistant latex paint to retail customers for $6 a gallon. The terms of trade may be net 30 days, 2/10, n/30, or 3/20, n/60. Do you remember how to compute payments with such terms? If not, review Chapter 15.

From the customer's perspective, it makes sense to take a discount and pay a bill early. Also, by paying the bill on the last day of the discount period, rather than on the first or the second, the buyer obtains as much cost-free credit as possible without losing the benefit of the cash discount. If unable to take the discount, the buyer should wait until the end of the net period to pay the bill—for example, on the 30th day rather than earlier when the terms of trade are "2/10, net 30." Why? In order to use interest-free credit for as long as possible. This practice is referred to as stretching accounts payable. **Accounts payable**, as discussed in Chapter 21, are short-term obligations, namely, bills that are due within one year.

Trade credit is an important source of short-term funds for most firms. It is "free" in that the firm is not required to pay a finance charge. Even if the firm has extra cash around, why should it pay for its purchases before the seller wants the money? The danger of trade credit is that the firm may overextend itself by taking too much.

Unsecured Bank Loans

Commercial banks are the second most important source of short-term business funds. The real business of most banks is lending money to commercial borrowers, such as retail stores, manufacturers, service companies, and construction firms. Total bank lending in this country exceeded $225 billion by year-end 1981.[1]

Types of Bank Lending. The three forms of bank loans that we will examine are lines of credit, revolving credit, and special transaction accounts. A **line of credit** is an agreement between a bank and a borrower specifying how much the bank is willing to lend the borrower over a certain period of time. For example, a bank might establish a $500,000 line of credit over a 12-month period for one of its customers. The quoted interest rate might be 15 percent. At any time during the year, the customer can automatically obtain funds from the bank so long as the total amount borrowed does not exceed $500,000.

The advantage to the borrower of a line of credit is the ease of periodically obtaining funds. The bank, however, is under no obligation to

---

[1] "The Perilous Hunt for Financing," *Business Week* (March 1, 1982), p. 44.

Pepper . . . and Salt
THE WALL STREET JOURNAL

"My goodness, man, you don't need a loan granted, you need three wishes granted."

Source: From *The Wall Street Journal*, Permission—Cartoon Features Syndicate.

lend up to the maximum amount. If the bank runs low on money or if the borrower's credit rating deteriorates, the bank may refuse a request for another loan. It may also reduce the customer's line of credit.

A **revolving credit agreement** is similar to a bank line of credit. Again, a credit limit is specified. However, under a revolving credit agreement, the bank is obligated to extend funds up to the credit limit. Revolving credit agreements are typically negotiated for periods of twelve months to three years. Some banks charge a fee for a revolving line of credit, normally ½ to 1 percent of the value of the credit agreement.

As we said, the maturity of most "revolvers," as they are called by bankers, is three years or less. Big borrowers can sometimes work out other arrangements: TRW Inc., a diversified manufacturer of electronics devices, car and truck components, and products for energy exploration and production, recently negotiated an eight-year, $500 million revolving credit agreement with 22 of its lenders. Loans of this size usually involve the participation of many banks so that the risk of default for any one of them is minimized.

When a borrower needs money for a specific purpose, such as to finance a seasonal variation in inventory, a capital equipment purchase, or a construction project, it may approach the bank for a **transaction loan**. To illustrate, a builder may need to borrow $100,000 for the construction of a house. When the house is sold, the loan is repaid. The bank considers each loan request from the builder on a case-by-case basis. A transaction loan is called a **note payable** on the borrower's books. Although banking is changing rapidly these days, most banks do not like to make such loans for periods of time longer than five to ten years.

Interest Rates. Banks make money by charging interest on their loans. **Interest rate** is the price paid for the use of money over a stated period of time. Assuming an annual interest rate of 10 percent, the total cost of borrowing $200,000 for a year would be $20,000. From the perspective of a firm in need of short-term funds, the big difference between a bank loan and trade credit is that the firm pays interest on the bank loan but not on trade credit.

The minimum interest rate that a bank charges its best customers is called the **prime rate**.

The prime rate is usually set by one or more of the nation's largest banks. This rate goes up or down as the cost of money to the bank itself goes up or down. For example, Citibank adjusts its prime lending rate to keep it 1½ percentage points above the rate that it must pay on a 90-day negotiable certificate of deposit (CD). A **negotiable certificate of deposit** is a bank savings account held by a corporation or person in an amount usually in excess of $100,000. The rates paid on negotiable CDs are themselves variable. Thus, as Citibank increases the interest rate on CDs in order to attract depositors, it adjusts its prime lending rate upward. The goal is to keep the spread between its cost of obtaining funds and the prime rate relatively constant.

As shown in Figure 17-3, the prime rate did not change very much during the 1950s and 1960s. From 1961 to 1965, the prime rate stayed at an annual average of 4.5 percent. The cost of borrowing money was very low then. Since 1965 the interest rate has gone up and down with some regularity. In 1977, the interest rate began a steady upward movement, eventually skyrocketing to 18.9 percent in 1981. In at least six months of that year, the prime rate stood at more than 20 percent.

Rising interest rates on short-term money have a major impact on the cost of borrowed funds. The Royal Night Music Company bor-

Figure 17-3

Short-Term Interest Rates, 1950-1982

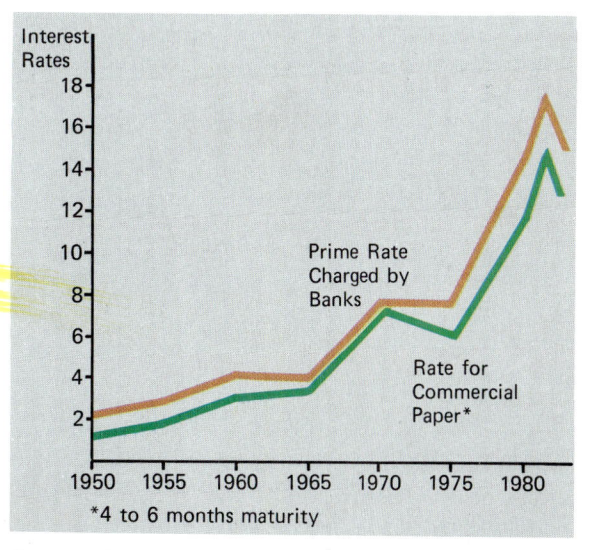

Source: *Economic Report of the President* (February, 1982), p. 310.

rowed $100,000 from its banker in 1977, paying a 9 percent rate of interest, or two points over prime. Total interest charges for the year were $9,000. Four years later, when the prime rate jumped to nearly 20 percent, the annual cost to the company of borrowing $100,000 soared to $22,000, again assuming a lending rate two points over prime. In just four years, the cost of borrowed funds more than doubled.

Commercial Paper

Commercial paper refers to unsecured, short-term promissory notes issued by large corporations (usually industrial firms, bank holding companies, or public utilities). In recent years, state and municipal governments have also begun to issue commercial paper. Only the largest and most credit-worthy firms—such as DuPont, with $173 million in paper outstanding at year-end 1981—are able to sell commercial paper. The number of issuers is currently about 1,200. As shown in Figure 17-4, the total amount outstanding has risen from $33.4 billion in 1970 to $171.9 billion in 1982. Most of this increase occurred during the late 1970s and early 1980s, when depressed stock prices and high interest rates made long-term financing less attractive.[2]

---

[2] Evelyn M. Harley, "The Commercial Paper Market Since the Mid-Seventies," *Federal Reserve Bulletin*, Vol. 68 (June, 1982), pp. 327-334.

Commercial paper is purchased by money market funds, life insurance companies, pension funds, bank trust departments, and other large investors. Most paper matures in 30 to 90 days, with a maximum maturity of 270 days. It is usually sold in blocks of $100,000.

Discount on Commercial Paper. Strictly speaking, commercial paper is noninterest-bearing. That is to say, it is sold at a discount below par and matures at par. Suppose that Mobil Oil issued $10 million in commercial paper. Through a commercial-paper dealer, such as Merrill Lynch Money Markets, Inc., several investors purchase the paper for $9.8 million. This is the amount that Mobil receives. In 60 days, when the paper matures, Mobil buys it back at par for $10 million. Thus, Mobil has the use of $9.8 million for 60 days at a total cost of $200,000. This $200,000 is the discount. Figure 17-3 shows the interest rate on commercial paper for the period 1950-1982. Note how the commercial paper rate is always lower than the prime rate.

Uses of Commercial Paper. An issue of commercial paper is a substitute for a bank loan. The purpose of commercial paper is to cover immediate cash needs. Many firms use commercial paper to finance inventory buildup for seasonal sales. Others "roll-over" commercial paper to obtain a continual source of funds. That is, when one issue of paper matures, the firm sells another to pay for the maturing issue.

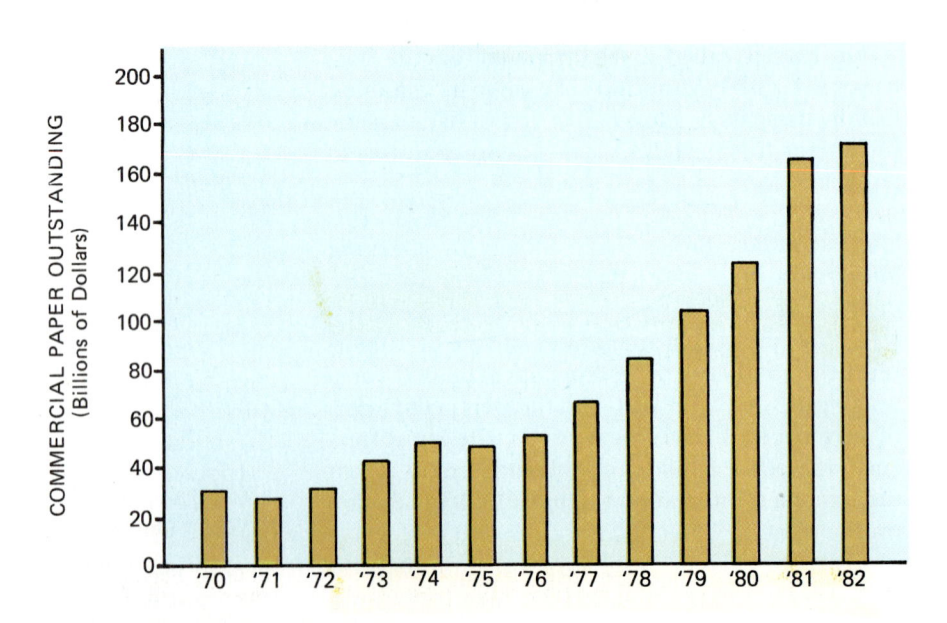

Figure 17-4

Commercial Paper Outstanding, 1970-1982

Source: *Federal Reserve Bulletin* (June, 1982), p. 329; (July, 1982), p. A25; (January, 1983), p. A26.

Profile—
Louise Q. Lawson

Chicago was once a town where no black person could ever hope to get a bank loan, for either personal or business purposes. In 1935, Illinois Federal Savings, a savings and loan company providing service especially to blacks in the Chicago area, was opened. It was started by a small group of young black business people with an initial investment of $7,000, and it grew steadily during the next few years. Louise Q. Lawson joined Illinois Federal Savings in 1945.

A native of Mississippi, Lawson earned a business degree from a small college in her home state. She was tough and persistent, and because of these qualities she was hired by Illinois Federal Savings. She quickly mastered the savings and loan business and rapidly moved through the ranks of Illinois Federal. In 1957, she became assistant secretary. In 1965, she became executive secretary and then managing officer. Finally, in 1975, she became president and chief executive officer.

Lawson faced challenges throughout her advancement through the company. She often felt at a disadvantage when seeking a promotion simply because she was a woman. The only reason she received promotions, she now recalls, was because no man knew the business as well as she did. When she finally became president and chief executive officer, Lawson says, it was only because a man couldn't be found for the job and she wouldn't train one.

In 1976, Illinois Federal merged with another savings and loan to become Illinois Service Federal. In 1981, it took over another savings and loan, becoming the only black-owned savings and loan in Chicago. Oddly enough, the company does so well under Lawson's control because of the very forces that made her advancement to the head of the company so difficult—namely, its conservatism. She states, "Basically, the reason we're still here and doing well is because we're more conservative than most. We have to be careful because we operate in a limited market. We've tried to be of service to our local community, but not to the point where we would go overboard."

Lawson has had to address many of the unique problems a black savings and loan faces today. Black savers often believe that their money is safer in a white-owned bank, so they put their savings elsewhere and come to Illinois Service Federal only when they can't get loans anywhere else. And those who do save at Illinois Service Federal do not keep as much savings as do savers at most white-owned banks. In addition, withdrawals from savings are more frequent, so operating costs for Illinois Service Federal are much higher than those for similar institutions. Many of its loans are also for low-yield mortgages on small homes, which are subject to high rates of default. Lawson has been instrumental in getting Illinois Service Federal past these problems and onto more stable ground.

Lawson was appointed by President Carter to the Task Force on Minority Enterprise and was offered the job of executive vice president of the Government National Mortgage Association. She has also served as president of the American Savings and Loan League. Obviously, she is respected by people outside her own company.

Lawson is very vocal about providing jobs for blacks, but she also demands competence: She climbed to the top because she was *good*, and she demands the same of her employees. According to Lawson, "Moving up is something you just have to think about. I tell our employees they have a unique opportunity. The one thing you don't have to deal with here is color. That's a major plus. If you are working here, you should want to be what I am."

Secured Borrowing

Trade credit, bank lines of credit, revolving credit agreements, and commercial paper are all examples of unsecured loans. That is, the firm borrows money on the basis of its good name only; it does not put up property or other valuable assets as collateral. Transaction loans from commercial banks, on the other hand, can be either secured or unsecured, depending upon the credit standing of the borrower, the amount of money advanced, and the purpose of the loan. A **secured loan** requires that the borrower pledge some form of asset as payment for the loan in case the borrower cannot repay the loan. Let's look at some of the assets that are frequently pledged as security for short-term loans.

Accounts Receivable. The open-book accounts owed to a firm by its creditors are called **accounts receivable**. Most businesses expect their receivables to be paid within 30 days. As individual accounts are paid off, the firm makes more credit sales and acquires new receivables. As a result, the total value of outstanding receivables may be constant over time, although it generally grows as the firm's sales revenue increases.

Using accounts receivable as security, or collateral, for short-term loans is called **pledging**. Here's how pledging works: The borrowing firm gives the lender a list of its current receivables. The lender then decides which of the receivables it will accept as collateral. As these receivables come due, the cash received as payment is forwarded to the lender until the loan plus interest is repaid. The firm is still liable for the entire value of the loan should one or more of its customers default on its debt.

Commercial banks regularly make accounts receivable loans. Other types of financial institutions, such as General Motors Acceptance Corporation, General Electric Credit Corporation, and Transamerica Financial Corporation, are also involved in this type of lending.

Inventory Financing. Inventories are second in importance to accounts receivable as collateral for short-term loans. We should first identify three different types of inventory:

- Raw Materials Inventory—basic inputs a manufacturer uses to produce other goods. For example: sheet steel for the production of Chevrolet auto bodies.
- Goods-in-Process Inventory—products or inputs that have already undergone some stages in a manufacturing process. For example: sheet steel shaped into fenders, hoods, and other Chevrolet body parts.
- Finished Goods Inventory—products that have undergone all stages in a manufacturing process. For example: new Chevrolets waiting in a GM lot for shipment to dealers.

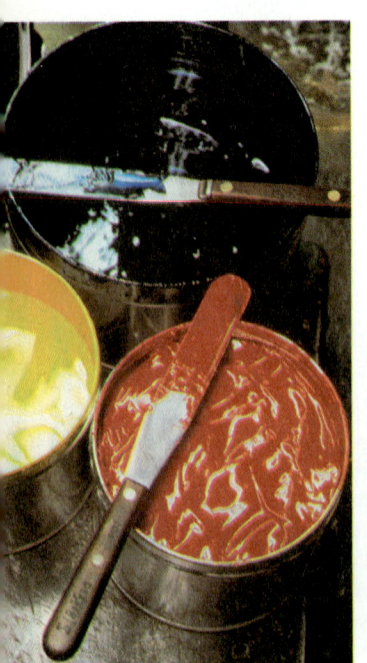

Inventories—important collateral for secured loans.

These distinctions are important because the lender needs to know the nature of the inventory involved before it decides whether to accept it as collateral. Most lenders will lend against raw materials and finished goods inventories only.

When the DeLorean Motor Car Company went bankrupt in 1982, a market still existed for the completed DMC cars. Some of the raw materials, such as stainless steel and special plastics, also had resale value. But the half-finished Deloreans had little value as collateral (who would buy one?).

In assigning a dollar value to collateralized inventory, most banks first determine the original cost of the inventory and then lend up to 65 to 75 percent of that amount. The borrower repays the loan no later than when the inventory is sold as a finished product.

Other Assets. Other widely used forms of security for short-term loans are stocks and bonds and such moveable property as automobiles, trucks, and production equipment. Whatever is held as security on a loan must have resale value. When pledging automobiles and trucks, the borrower usually signs over their certificates of title. The borrower is thereby prevented from selling the pledged property until the loan is repaid. In the event of default, the lender takes possession of the property.

Factoring Accounts Receivable

Pledging accounts receivable means using them as collateral on short-term loans. In contrast, **factoring accounts receivable** involves selling them to a financial institution, called a **factor**. Business firms factor their accounts receivable to obtain cash immediately; financial institutions buy them in order to make money. Typically, factors are paid a fee of 1 to 3 percent for their services. A retail department store selling $10,000 in receivables would net $9,700 if the factor fee were 3 percent. It is also a common practice for factors to charge interest on the funds advanced. As a result, factoring receivables is an expensive way for a firm to obtain short-term funds.

Here's how factoring works: A firm makes a credit sale (net 30 days) to a customer. It then sells the receivable to the factor for an amount less than the face value of the receivable, say, for 3 percent less, as mentioned above. The customer is directed to pay its bill directly to the factor. The value of factoring to the firm is that it obtains its money from credit sales immediately. Factoring was once used only by firms with major cash problems. Today, however, firms in the sporting goods, automotive accessories, plastics, building materials, and communications equipment industries regularly factor their receivables.

COMMERCIAL BANKING

Banks generally act as financial intermediaries in channeling money from savers to investors—that is, from the people and organizations who deposit money in banks to those who borrow it to finance consumer purchases or business expansion. We use the term "commercial banks" to distinguish them from mutual savings banks, which will be discussed later in the chapter, and from investment banks, which will be discussed in Chapter 19. Commercial banks are unique in the financial community in that they are able to create money.

The Banking System Today

At the end of 1982, there were 14,787 domestically chartered commercial banks in the United States. Roughly two thirds of these are state banks and the remainder national banks. **State banks** receive their operating charter from the state in which they are located; **national banks** receive theirs from the federal government. Although fewer in number, national banks held 55 percent of all commercial bank deposits in 1981. The deposits in nearly all U.S. banks are insured by the Federal Deposit Insurance Corporation (FDIC), which was established in 1934 to protect depositors from bank failure. Over the years, the FDIC has provided the financial system with critically needed stability. Bank failures still occur—42 in 1982 alone—but thanks to the FDIC no depositors lost money.

Table 17-1 lists the 20 largest U.S. commercial banks, ranked according to asset size. The assets of a bank consist of its loans and investments. The largest bank is BankAmerica, headquartered in San Francisco, with total assets of more than $120 billion. Most of the other big

Table 17-1

Twenty Largest U.S. Commercial Banks Ranked According to Total Assets

Rank	Bank	Assets $ mil.	Deposits $ mil.	Loans $ mil.
1	BankAmerica (San Francisco)	121,158	94,369	73,662
2	Citicorp (New York)	119,232	72,125	79,595
3	Chase Manhattan (New York)	77,839	55,300	51,331
4	Manufacturers Hanover (New York)	59,109	42,462	40,661
5	Morgan (J.P.) (New York)	53,522	36,024	28,830
6	Continental Illinois (Chicago)	46,972	29,594	32,876
7	Chemical New York (New York)	44,917	29,430	29,175
8	First Interstate Bancorp (Los Angeles)	36,982	27,407	21,777
9	Bankers Trust New York	34,213	23,345	19,109
10	First Chicago	33,562	25,555	20,568
11	Security Pacific (Los Angeles)	32,999	23,446	22,939
12	Wells Fargo (San Francisco)	23,219	16,854	17,970
13	Crocker National (San Francisco)	22,494	16,495	14,380
14	Marine Midland Banks (Buffalo)	18,682	14,096	10,987
15	Mellon National (Pittsburgh)	18,448	11,838	10,108
16	Irving Bank (New York)	18,227	14,006	10,102
17	InterFirst (Dallas)	17,318	12,559	10,017
18	First National Boston	16,809	11,020	9,551
19	Northwest Bancorp. (Minneapolis)	15,141	11,386	8,874
20	First Bank System (Minneapolis)	14,911	11,023	8,067

Source: Reprinted from the April 12, 1982, issue of *Business Week* by special permission, © 1982 by McGraw-Hill, Inc., New York, NY 10020. All rights reserved.

banks are located in New York City, the financial center of the United States. Citicorp, the second largest bank in terms of assets, is the nation's leading bank lender, with nearly $80 billion of loans outstanding at year-end 1981.

Money

Money, which can be defined as that which is generally accepted as payment for goods and services, is the lifeblood of an economy. Even a basic understanding of money will take us a long way toward comprehending how our financial system works. Most of us spend a good deal of our lives chasing after money. We talk about it nearly every day, and we work hard for it. But have you ever considered what actually makes money valuable? Let's explore this question by considering the functions of money.

Functions of Money. Money's primary function is to serve as a **medium of exchange**. Anything that is accepted as a medium of exchange—whether coins, paper currency, IOU's, or even shells and pretty stones—can be called money.

Money also serves as a **standard of value**. We routinely compare the value of objects by how much each is worth in dollars: A $10,000 car is more valuable than a $5,000 motorcycle. Money also acts as a **store of value**. Accumulated cash can be "stored" in a cookie jar or bank until needed for future purchases. As a store of value, money is a measure of savings. Through investment, this accumulated wealth can be stored in the form of land, steel ingots, gold bullion, famous works of art, or corporate stocks and bonds. When kept as cash, wealth is said to be **liquid** because it can readily be used in exchange for needed goods and services.

What gives money its magic, therefore, is that it is generally accepted throughout the economy as a medium of exchange, a standard of value, and a store of value. The paper on which a dollar bill is printed is not worth much more than a few square inches of newsprint. A dollar is valuable because it is believed to be valuable. If people lost confidence in our currency, it would no longer

Chapter 17 • Short-Term Financing—The Banking System   323

perform its three functions and would become worthless.

The Money Supply. In the United States, money consists of total currency in circulation (paper money and coins) and checking account balances at commercial banks. Less than 25 percent of the nation's money supply is in the form of circulating currency. Growth in the money supply for the period 1974-1982 is shown in Figure 17-5. The amount of money now in circulation is about $480 billion.

How Banks Create Money. Another question relating to money is, "How do banks create money?" To answer this question, we first need to talk about demand deposits. A **demand deposit** is a checking account at a commercial bank. Demand deposits are part of the money supply because they can be withdrawn "on demand" and converted immediately into currency at the option of the holder of the account. As we can see from Figure 17-5, demand deposit balances are the leading component of the nation's money supply. A **check** is a piece of paper legally authorizing the bank to withdraw the specified amount of money from the account and to pay it to the person or organization to whom the check is written.

Banks create money when they make loans. In making a loan, a bank does not take cash out of its vault and hand it over to the borrower; rather,

Money—a medium of exchange.

it credits the borrower's checking account for the amount of the loan. The borrower, then, may write checks on the account. Figure 17-6 on page 325 illustrates this process of money creation.

In Step 1, Ms. Appel deposits $3,000 in the First State Bank, joining thousands of others in her city who hold checking and savings accounts there. The First State Bank then lends $3,000 to Mr. Smith for a new car. It does this by crediting

FROM THE FILE

Ivan is the owner and manager of Ivan's Flowerpot World. More than 80 percent of its output consists of relatively expensive flowerpots and planters. During the spring and summer seasons, people buy these pots as fast as they are manufactured, but sales fall off dramatically during autumn and winter. The sale of other kinds of pottery does not make up for the decline in flowerpot sales during the off-season.

To deal with the seasonal nature of sales in his business, Ivan decided to buy a truckload of clay, hire an assistant, and make flowerpots and planters during the winter. In this way, he would have plenty of inventory on hand when customer demand picked up in the spring. Ivan's banker told him that a line of credit with the bank was out of the question. However, Ivan did have a lot of equipment and would soon—with financing—have a large inventory of finished pots. What kind of financing could Ivan get?

Figure 17-5

Money Supply Movements*, 1974-1982

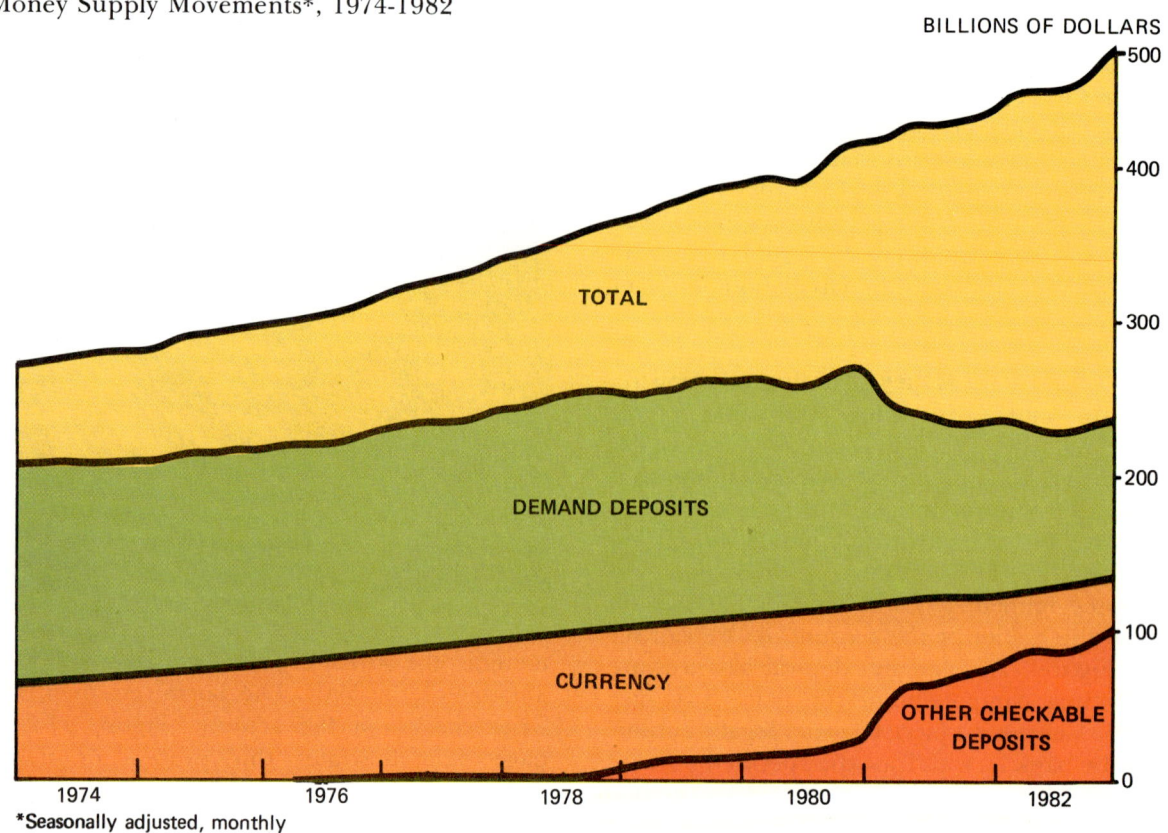

[Figure: Stacked area chart showing money supply in billions of dollars from 1974 to 1982, with layers for Currency, Demand Deposits, Other Checkable Deposits, and Total, rising from about 275 to 500 billion dollars.]

*Seasonally adjusted, monthly

Source: *Federal Reserve Chart Book* (November, 1982), p. 4.

Mr. Smith's account for $3,000. At this point, the bank has created $3,000 in demand deposits (minus what must be held as reserves, which we'll discuss a little later).

The process of money creation continues through Step 6. By now, Mr. Smith has bought his new car from Mr. Trustworthy, who deposits the $3,000 payment in the Second State Bank. This bank then lends $3,000 to Ms. Smart to buy a new personal computer. Her bank does this by placing $3,000 in her account. Once again, the banking system has created money. Because so much of our money supply is in the form of demand deposits, the lending activity of commercial banks has an important effect on the economic health of the country.

Types of Accounts

Commercial banks offer a variety of deposit accounts to the public. Let's take a brief look at five of them now.

Checking Accounts. Most of us probably hold checking accounts. Checking accounts do not pay interest on the money in the accounts and are offered only by commercial banks. In terms of total dollar amount, the vast majority of business transactions in this country involve payment by check rather than by cash.

Passbook Accounts. A passbook account is the basic type of savings account. For years, these accounts have paid an interest rate of 5¼ percent. The money in a passbook account can be withdrawn at any time without an interest penalty. Because of the many accounts now paying higher rates of interest, total balances in these accounts may begin to decline.

NOW Accounts. To the holder, a NOW account (negotiable order of withdrawal) can be viewed as either a checking account that pays interest or as a savings account on which checks can be written, since it combines some features of both. Technically, however, a NOW account is not considered

Figure 17-6

How Banks Create Money

Step 1: Ms. Appel deposits $3,000 in the First State Bank.

Step 2: First State Bank lends Mr. Smith $3,000 for a used car.

Step 3: Mr. Smith buys a used car from Mr. Trustworthy for $3,000.

Step 4: Mr. Trustworthy deposits check for $3,000 in the Second State Bank.

Step 5: The Second State Bank lends Ms. Smart $3,000 to buy a new microcomputer.

Step 6: Ms. Smart buys a $3,000 microcomputer from Computerland.

a demand deposit. Since their nationwide introduction in 1980, total balances in NOW accounts have skyrocketed to more than $80 billion, as shown in Figure 17-7. NOW accounts currently pay 5¼ percent, but this interest rate ceiling will be lifted by 1986. An **interest rate ceiling** is the maximum amount by law that a financial institution may pay on an account of a given type. NOW accounts are available to individuals, sole proprietorships, and nonprofit organizations only.

Time Deposits. Time deposits are also called certificates of deposit (CDs). By opening a time deposit, the individual or organization agrees to leave funds on deposit with the bank for a specified minimum period of time. The longer the period of time, the higher the rate of interest paid. This is done to encourage deposits of longer maturity. Today, the interest rate on most time deposits is tied to U.S. government security and money market rates.

Money Market Accounts. A relatively new account on the financial scene is the money market account. These accounts, requiring a $2,500 minimum deposit, have no interest rate ceiling or fixed maturity. Moreover, deposits in these accounts are federally insured, which makes them especially attractive. As of January, 1983, total balances in these accounts stood at more than $115 billion.[3] They allow for up to six third-party transfers a month. On the new "super NOW" accounts, introduced in early 1983, an unlimited number of checks may be written. Offering an ideal combination of features—market rates of interest, unlimited checking, and federal backing—these "super NOW" accounts may cause a substantial movement of funds out of interest-free checking accounts and small-size time deposits.

Other Financial Institutions

Commercial banks are not the only institutions that play an important role in our financial

---

[3] *Wall Street Journal* (February 15, 1983), p. 27.

Figure 17-7

Growth of NOW Accounts, 1976-1982

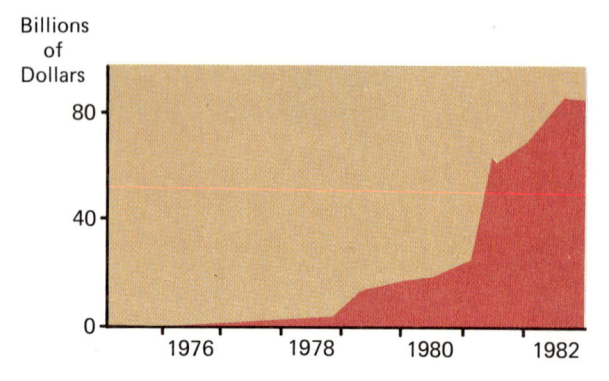

Source: *Federal Reserve Bulletin* (June, 1982), p. 395.

system. Three other depository institutions include savings and loan associations, mutual savings banks, and credit unions. Do you have a savings account at any of them?

Savings and Loan Associations. Savings and loan associations (S&Ls) are thrift institutions that accept time deposits from individual savers and businesses and that make primarily home mortgage loans. Historically, their interest rates on time deposits were allowed by law to be slightly higher than those offered by commercial banks. These higher rates enabled them to attract deposits, which were then used to finance home construction. Mortgage loans accounted for more than 75 percent of all S&L loans and investments in 1982.

In the last few years, the traditional distinctions between commercial banks and S&Ls have begun to blur. Starting in 1978, both types of institutions were authorized by the federal government to issue deposit accounts with interest rate ceilings tied to the prevailing rate on U.S. government securities. The Depository Institutions Deregulation and Monetary Control Act of 1980 gave thrift institutions the authority to offer NOW accounts. And in 1982, the Garn-St. Germain Depository Institutions Act enabled them to offer their own money market deposit accounts.

One effect of deregulating the financial community has been a radical change in the composition of deposits at savings and loan associations. In 1978, fixed-ceiling deposits, such as passbook accounts paying 5½ percent, accounted for 75 percent of all thrift institution liabilities. By June, 1982, the percentage had fallen to 22. During these same four years, the percentage share of time deposits paying market rates of interest increased from 9 percent to 53 percent. Money market certificates alone accounted for more than half of these deposits in 1982.[4] These changes in deposit levels brought about by financial deregulation and rapidly fluctuating interest rates pose major challenges to the managers of thrift institutions in the years ahead.

Mutual Savings Banks. Mutual savings banks are similar to savings and loan associations. Their deposits consist mostly of small savings accounts. These deposits totaled about $160 billion in 1982. Most of these funds are invested in real estate mortgages. The majority of the nation's 500 savings banks are located in the northeastern states.

Mutual savings banks have also recently experienced a dramatic shift in funds out of fixed-ceiling accounts and into higher yield accounts paying market rates of interest. These market rate deposits now make up more than half of savings banks' total liabilities. Fixed-ceiling deposits, including passbook accounts, NOW accounts, and time certificates of deposit, are down significantly.

Credit Unions. Credit unions are another type of savings institution. Functioning as cooperatives, they are owned by their member depositors rather than by stockholders. To borrow from a credit union, one must become a member. Membership is usually limited to people with something in common. For example, membership in the University Federal Credit Union in Austin, Texas, is limited to employees of the University of Texas. Credit union membership is also popular among military and state government employees. The employees of such companies as IBM have also formed credit unions. In terms of total number of establishments, credit unions are the fastest growing financial institutions in the country. There are 22,000 credit unions, with total deposits quickly approaching the $100 billion mark.

---

[4] Michael J. Moran, "Thrift Institutions in Recent Years," *Federal Reserve Bulletin*, Vol. 68 (December 1982), p. 728.

Credit unions specialize in making short-term loans for automobiles, furniture, and other consumer items. They offer a variety of savings plans, such as Individual Retirement Accounts (IRAs) and certificates of deposit. Since 1980, credit unions have been allowed to offer **share draft accounts**, which function like the NOW accounts offered by banks and S&Ls.

FEDERAL RESERVE SYSTEM

The Federal Reserve System, more commonly called the Fed, operates as the central bank of the United States. The Fed was established in 1913 to provide a source of short-term funds to banks, and to add stability to the nation's banking system. In effect, the Fed operates as a bank for bankers. Although owned and managed by its member banks, of which there are now more than 5,500, the Federal Reserve is operated in accordance with the public interest. Interestingly, the United States was one of the last major countries to set up a central bank. Let's examine the structure of the Fed as well as some of its more important functions.

Structure of the Fed

The activities of the Federal Reserve System are coordinated and directed by a seven-member Board of Governors, who are appointed by the president and confirmed by the Senate. Each member of the board serves a 14-year term. Because of this feature, political pressure on the policy decisions of board members is minimized.

Geographically, the Federal Reserve System is made up of 12 districts, each with its own Federal Reserve District Bank. The 12 districts and the locations of the Fed's branch banks are shown in Figure 17-8. The Board of Governors of the Federal Reserve is located in Washington, D.C.

Controlling the Money Supply

The primary activity of the Federal Reserve System is controlling the rate of growth in the nation's money supply. The goal of the Fed's monetary policy is to promote economic growth while holding down inflation.

The rate of growth in the supply of money has a direct effect on credit availability and interest rates. The more money flowing through the economy, the lower the rate of interest on borrowed funds, and the greater the rate of economic expansion. Unfortunately, when the economy grows too fast, prices start going up, too. Figure 17-9 on page 329 lists the Fed's three major policy tools and how each affects the money supply, interest rates, and economic growth.

Reserve Requirements. As we just saw, commercial banks create money when they make loans. The Federal Reserve, through its reserve requirements, controls the rate at which a bank can create money. **Reserves** are the percentage of total demand and time deposits that a bank must hold as cash in its vault or as deposits in the regional Federal Reserve bank. That is to say, a bank cannot lend all of its depositors' money. Reserve requirements change periodically in response to the health of the economy and the goals of the Fed's monetary policy. In early 1983, banks were required to maintain reserves equal to 12 percent of their demand deposits in cash. A bank with $200 million in demand deposits, therefore, would be required to hold $2.4 million as reserves. In this way, the bank has cash on hand to meet withdrawals.

To see the impact of the reserve requirement on the money supply, look at Figure 17-6 again. When Ms. Appel deposited her $3,000 in the First State Bank, the bank could not, in fact, make $3,000 in new loans and thus add $3,000 to the money supply. Instead, it had to keep $360 ($3,000 × 0.12) on hand because the reserve requirement was 12 percent at that time. As a result, the bank could create only $2,640.

Now suppose the Board of Governors of the Federal Reserve decided that the economy was growing too fast, with an unwanted rise in prices. To slow the rate of inflation, the Fed might raise the reserve requirement to 13 percent. Ms. Appel's bank could now create only $2,610. By slowing the rate of money creation, the Fed makes credit less available. Interest rates begin to rise as borrowers compete for loanable funds. The result is that investment in new factories, housing projects, and office buildings begins to decline, thereby slowing the rate of economic expansion and the general rise in prices.

Figure 17-8

The Federal Reserve System
Boundaries of Federal Reserve Districts and Their Branch Territories

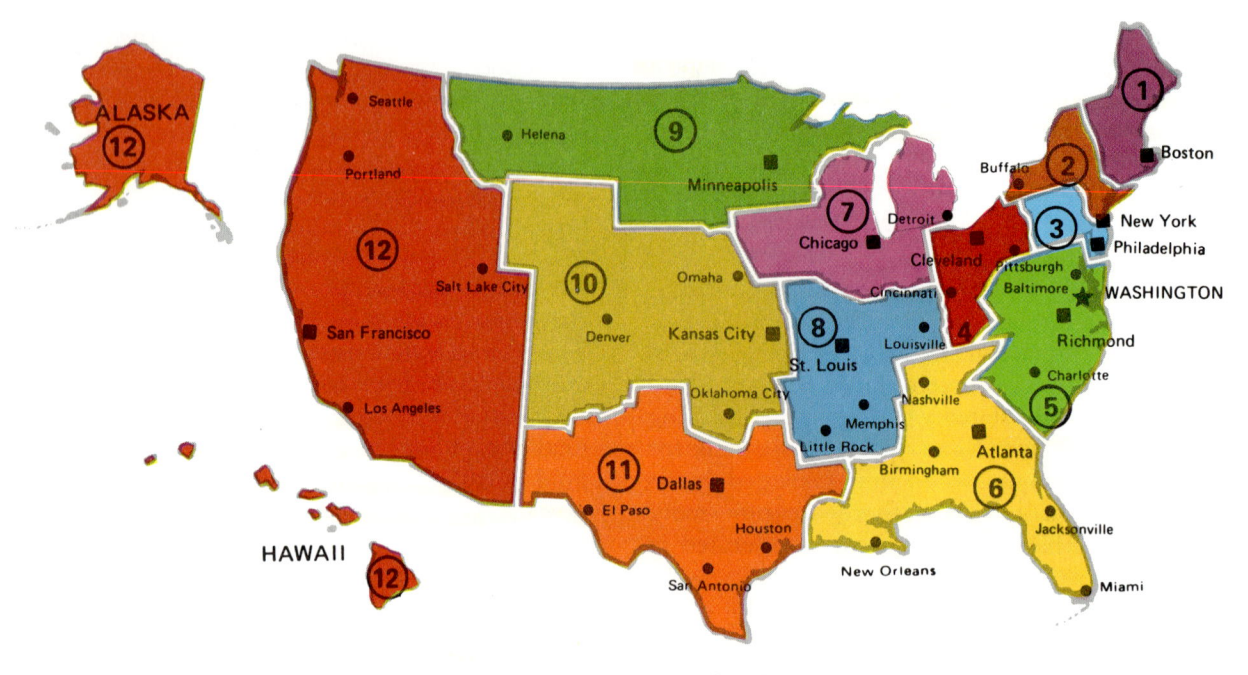

= BOUNDARIES OF FEDERAL RESERVE DISTRICTS

★ BOARD OF GOVERNORS OF THE FEDERAL RESERVE SYSTEM

• CITY WHERE A BRANCH OF FEDERAL RESERVE BANK IS LOCATED

LEGEND

■ CITY WHERE FEDERAL RESERVE BANK IS LOCATED

③ FEDERAL RESERVE DISTRICT NUMBER. THIS NUMBER APPEARS ON THE CURRENCY ISSUED BY THE FEDERAL RESERVE BANK IN THE DISTRICT.

Source: *Federal Reserve Bulletin* (January, 1983), p. A88.

In the example, the $30 difference in the amount of money created when the reserve requirement was raised to 13 percent may not seem like much. But when all deposits in all banks across the country are considered, the impact can be substantial. For this reason, the reserve requirement is the Fed's most powerful weapon for controlling the money supply.

Open Market Operations. A second and more common way of controlling the money supply is through open market operations, that is, through the buying and selling of U.S. government securities on the open market. This trading is done through specialized dealers in New York.

Figure 17-10 shows how open market operations work. Suppose the Fed wanted to inject more money into the economy. To do this, the Federal Reserve Bank of New York, under the direction of the Federal Open Market Committee, might purchase $100 million in short-term treasury notes from a dealer in these securities. The bank writes a cashier's check for the amount, and the dealer hands over the securities and deposits the check in a commercial bank. This exchange of money for government securities adds more money to the economy because the Fed itself created $100 million and because the dealer's bank now has $100 million (minus the reserve requirement) more in loanable funds on

Figure 17-9

How the Federal Reserve Controls the Economy

Federal Reserve Action	Impact on Money Supply	Impact on Interest Rates	Impact on the Economy
Reserve Requirements			
Lower Reserve Requirements	Increase Money Supply	Reduce Interest Rates	Foster Economic Growth
Raise Reserve Requirements	Decrease Money Supply	Increase Interest Rates	Discourage Economic Growth
Open Market Operations			
Buy Securities from the Public	Increase Money Supply	Reduce Interest Rates	Foster Economic Growth
Sell Securities to the Banks	Decrease Money Supply	Increase Interest Rates	Discourage Economic Growth
Discount Rate			
Lower the Discount Rate	Increase Money Supply	Reduce Interest Rates	Foster Economic Growth
Increase the Discount Rate	Decrease Money Supply	Increase Interest Rates	Discourage Economic Growth

deposit. Figure 17-10 also shows how the Fed reduces the money supply by selling off government securities from its holdings of such securities.

Discount Rate. From time to time, commercial banks borrow short-term money from their regional Federal Reserve Bank to meet the reserve requirement or to cover other cash obligations. The **discount rate** is the name for the interest rate charged on these loans. Only member banks may borrow from the Federal Reserve at the discount rate.

A lowering of the discount rate stimulates growth in the rate of money creation and in the rate of economic expansion. Funds borrowed from the Fed and on deposit in the commercial bank's account with the regional Federal Reserve bank act just as the bank's other deposits do—they increase the amount of money available for

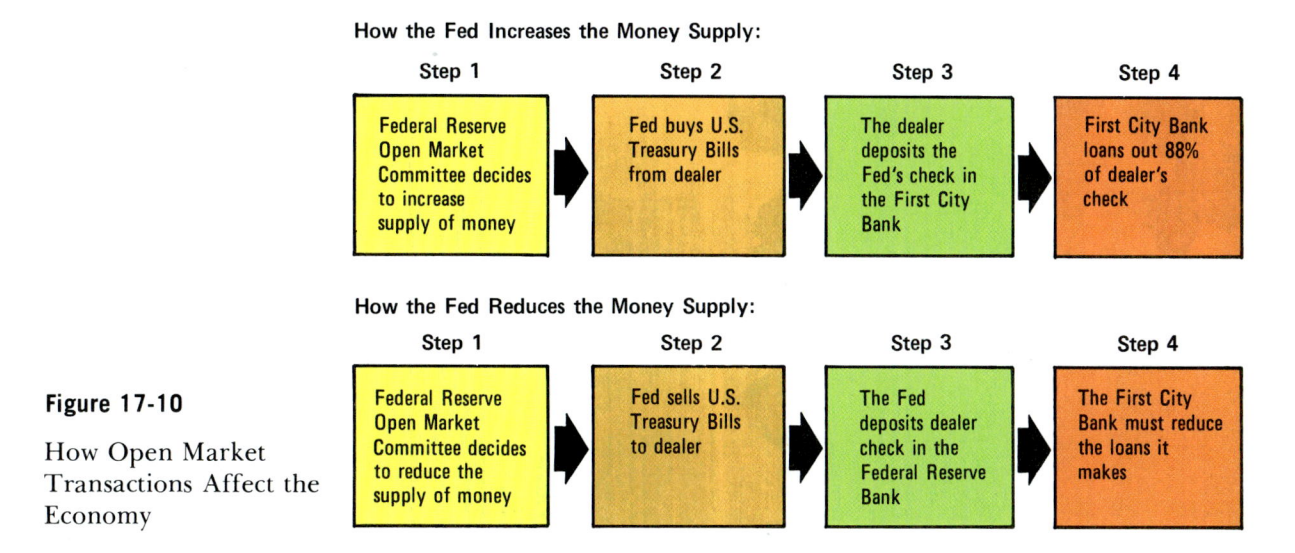

How the Fed Increases the Money Supply:

Step 1	Step 2	Step 3	Step 4
Federal Reserve Open Market Committee decides to increase supply of money	Fed buys U.S. Treasury Bills from dealer	The dealer deposits the Fed's check in the First City Bank	First City Bank loans out 88% of dealer's check

How the Fed Reduces the Money Supply:

Step 1	Step 2	Step 3	Step 4
Federal Reserve Open Market Committee decides to reduce the supply of money	Fed sells U.S. Treasury Bills to dealer	The Fed deposits dealer check in the Federal Reserve Bank	The First City Bank must reduce the loans it makes

Figure 17-10

How Open Market Transactions Affect the Economy

lending. A reduction in the discount rate, therefore, encourages bank lending. The subsequent decline in interest rates throughout the financial sector promotes economic growth. By similar reasoning, raising the discount rate discourages such growth.

Check Clearing

Have you ever wondered what happens to a check after it is deposited in a bank? Suppose that Nick and his sister Annie have checking accounts at the same bank in Baltimore. Nick writes a check to Annie for $60. In this situation, the processing of the check is simple. The bank subtracts $60 from the balance in Nick's account and adds $60 to Annie's account.

The processing of a check is much more complicated, however, when the bank at which the check is drawn and the bank at which it is deposited are in different cities. The Fed plays a major role in clearing intercity checks to ensure that the nation's banking system works efficiently. Each year, it processes billions of checks.

Figure 17-11 details the path of a check drawn on an account in a Chicago bank and written to a merchant in San Francisco. Two Federal Reserve banks as well as Mr. Longley's bank in Chicago and the merchant's bank in San Francisco are involved in the transaction. The Fed is normally able to process a check such as this one in fewer than ten working days—quite an accomplishment when you realize how many checks it processes each day.

Figure 17-11

How a Check Travels Through the Federal Reserve System for Intercity Collection

1. Harold Longley, a resident of Chicago, Illinois, buys a present for his son while on business in San Francisco, California. He pays for the purchase with a check drawn on his Chicago bank.

2. The merchant in San Francisco from whom Mr. Longley bought the present deposits the check in her account at a local bank.

3. Her bank in San Francisco deposits Mr. Longley's check in the Federal Reserve bank in San Francisco.

4. The Federal Reserve bank in San Francisco sends Mr. Longley's check to the Federal Reserve bank in Chicago for collection.

5. The Federal Reserve bank in Chicago sends the check to Mr. Longley's bank in Chicago.

6. The bank in Chicago subtracts the amount of the check from the balance in Mr. Longley's checking account.

7. Mr. Longley receives the cancelled check from his bank at the end of the month.

SUMMARY POINTS

1. Short-term financing refers to debts with a maturity of one year or less.
2. Business firms borrow short-term because the timing of cash flows rarely coincides with the timing of work flows.
3. The most widespread source of short-term financing is trade credit, through which the purchase of the good or service is financed by the seller for 30 days or more.
4. A promissory note is a written "promise to pay" indicating the amount of money owed by the buyer and the repayment date.
5. A trade acceptance is a trade agreement drawn up by the seller of the good or service.
6. Three common forms of bank lending are lines of credit, revolving credit agreements, and transaction loans.
7. The interest rate is the price paid for the use of money over a stated period of time. The prime rate is the minimum interest rate charged by banks to their best and most credit-worthy customers.
8. Commercial paper is unsecured, short-term promissory notes issued by large corporations for 270 days or less. The buyers of commercial paper include money market funds, life insurance companies, pension funds, and bank trust departments.
9. Among the assets that may be pledged as collateral for short-term loans are accounts receivable, raw materials inventory, finished goods inventory, stocks and bonds, and moveable property.
10. Commercial banks are at the heart of our financial system. Besides serving as an important source of short-term funds, they act as intermediaries in channeling money from the people and organizations who deposit it in banks to those who borrow it to finance consumer purchases and business expansion.
11. Money serves as a medium of exchange, a standard of value, and a store of value. The nation's money supply consists of circulating currency and checking account balances.
12. Commercial banks create money when they make loans, that is, when they credit borrowers' checking accounts for the loan amount.
13. Five types of deposits at commercial banks are checking accounts, passbook accounts, NOW accounts, time deposits, and money market accounts.
14. Three other important financial institutions are savings and loan associations, mutual savings banks, and credit unions.
15. The Federal Reserve System acts as the central bank of the United States—a bank for bankers. A seven-member Board of Governors directs the activities of the Federal Reserve.
16. The Federal Reserve System controls the rate of growth of the nation's money supply through three primary tools of monetary policy: reserve requirements, open market operations, and the discount rate.

KEY TERMS AND CONCEPTS

short-term financing
long-term debt
financial manager
trade credit
open book credit
open account
promissory note
trade acceptance
terms of trade
net period
accounts payable
line of credit
revolving credit agreement
transaction loan
note payable
interest rate
prime rate

negotiable certificate of deposit
commercial paper
accounts receivable
pledging
inventory financing
factoring accounts receivable
factor
commercial bank
state banks
national banks
money
medium of exchange
standard of value
store of value
liquid
money supply
demand deposit

check
checking accounts
passbook accounts
NOW accounts
interest rate ceiling
time deposits
money market accounts
savings and loan associations

mutual savings banks
credit unions
share draft accounts
Federal Reserve System
reserve requirements
reserves
open market operations
discount rate

REVIEW QUESTIONS

1. Why do business firms need to borrow short term from banks and other sources?
2. What is the difference between a promissory note and a trade acceptance?
3. What is the difference between a line of credit and a revolving credit agreement?
4. How does a transaction loan differ from a bank line of credit?
5. Suppose a $20 million issue of commercial paper, maturing in 180 days, netted $19 million for the issuer. How much does the issuer pay for use of the borrowed funds?
6. Compare how pledging accounts receivable and factoring accounts receivable work as sources of short-term credit.
7. Identify three important functions of money. Why is money valuable?
8. What is the difference between a NOW account and a standard passbook savings account?
9. What are the distinguishing features of a savings and loan association, a mutual savings bank, and a credit union? How do all three differ from a commercial bank?
10. Suppose the Federal Reserve makes a large purchase of government securities on the open market. Does this add to or subtract from the money supply?

DISCUSSION QUESTIONS

1. How might too great a reliance on short-term credit endanger the competitive health of a firm?
2. With an example show how rising interest rates affect the cost of borrowed money.
3. Discuss how commercial banks create money.
4. In your opinion, how will NOW accounts and the new "super NOW" accounts affect our definition of the money supply?
5. How might the Board of Governors of the Federal Reserve System move the economy out of a recession? Present your answer in terms of all three of the Fed's monetary policy tools.

CASE 17-1

Nike, Inc.

Nike, Inc., sells a wide range of athletic shoes and clothing throughout the world. Nike was created in 1968 and by 1980 had overtaken Adidas as the largest athletic shoes and clothing seller in the United States. Nike has grown extremely fast and has used short-term financing quite heavily to develop its current position.

Nike's earnings are somewhat seasonal, but not excessively so. The table gives quarterly sales (in millions of dollars). Note that sales are growing rapidly, so the increase in sales from Winter to Summer is largely due to overall growth.

Year	Winter	Spring	Summer	Fall
1979	—	—	55.6	54.8
1980	66.7	92.7	103.0	110.0
1981	109.9	134.8	176.6	145.1
1982	166.8	205.1	210.0	200.0

Also note that sales do not drop so severely that seasonality of Nike sales is enough of a reason to justify massive use of short-term financing.

Nike uses short-term financing to start massive new operations; it then either uses profits to pay off the debt, or it issues new stock and uses the proceeds of that stock issue to pay off the debt. Nike has maintained for the past few years a very low level of long-term debt (at least as compared with the shoe industry as a whole or the athletic products industry as a whole).

More recently, Nike has been trying to expand its sales into Europe and Japan. To do so, it first obtained substantial short-term financing. By June of 1982, Nike had outstanding short-term borrowing from banks of $112,673,000 and from Nissho Iwai American Corp., of an additional $52,406,000. Nike also had about $10,234,000 of unused credit remaining at banks and $57,594,000 unused credit remaining with Nissho Iwai. Then in September, 1982, Nike signed a $140 million revolving credit agreement with six banks, giving it short-term use of bank funds to finance its overseas expansions. To pay off this debt, Nike registered a new stock offering that hopefully will generate $60 million to $90 million that will be used to repay this more recent short-term debt.

How has the use of short-term financing altered Nike's financial position? In 1979, Nike's ratio of long-term debt to total capitalization was 27.9 percent (27.9 percent of Nike's total funds came from long-term debt). By 1980, this had dropped to 9.4 percent, and by 1981 it had dropped to 6.4 percent.

1. Why might Nike prefer to use short-term financing rather than long-term debt to fund its operations? (Hint: Look at the table of quarterly sales revenues.)
2. What is the advantage of a revolving credit agreement over an informal line of credit when a company operates its financing the way Nike does?
3. If Nike had to obtain a large sum of money for similar operations today, what factors would it consider in deciding to use short-term financing?

CASE 17-2

Grinberg Telecommunications Systems, Inc.

Grinberg Telecommunications Systems, Inc., was founded in 1976 to produce high-quality telephone and radio systems suitable for transmitting data to and from large computers. Grinberg found immediate demand for its products. Its products were very expensive and often were custom-designed for buyers. Grinberg's sales revenues soared, and the company sold an issue of common stock to finance a larger research and manufacturing center and to make more cash available.

Grinberg continued to need more financing. The company had been started by a group of brilliant young electrical engineers and physicists who knew little about financing a business. They depended on their accountant, who explained what they needed, what alternatives they had, and sent them to a major commercial banker.

Grinberg charged from $210,000 to $14,000,000 to produce a basic communications system. The fee was negotiated with the customer. One third was paid down (in advance) on the work, and the remainder was held in escrow (in an account under the control of the bank so neither the customer nor Grinberg would withdraw it until the job was done). Grinberg, however, found that one third of the price usually didn't cover the costs. More money was needed before the job was completed. Grinberg's owners pointed out to the banker that the down payment was usually enough to pay for all but approximately the last six months' worth of expenses. Of course, all expenses were covered once the customer picked up the equipment and paid the remaining amount. The banker was favorably impressed by the fact that the money was being held in escrow and that Grinberg had a reputation for completing jobs successfully and on time. Although Grinberg could obtain long-term credit or other kinds of financing, the banker suggested that a stable line of credit would be just the thing to supply money when it was needed.

1. What kind of line of credit would be suitable for Grinberg? What kind would not? Why?
2. Did the banker overlook a kind of short-term financing that might be better than a line of credit? If so, what are its advantages and disadvantages?
3. As Grinberg continues to grow, can it expect to keep itself financially stable with short-term financing? Where would short-term financing begin to be unacceptable?

Long-Term Financing – The Capital Markets

After studying this chapter, you should be able to:

- List the sources and uses of long-term funds.
- Define retained earnings and discuss the trade-off between retaining earnings and paying dividends.
- Describe the various types of bonds, some of their special features, and the relationship between risk and return.
- Discuss the essential features of common stock and the ways in which the purchase of common stock can benefit investors.
- Explain how preferred stock combines some of the features of bonds and common stock.
- Discuss the advantages and disadvantages of each source of long-term financing.

All business firms, big or small, require financing in order to purchase needed assets. Our concern in this chapter is with long-term financing. By **long-term financing** we mean money contributed by the owners of the business or money from lenders who do not expect repayment within ten years. Long-term money is often referred to as **capital**.

18

The mammoth Rockwell International Corp., with sales of about $7.8 billion in 1982, relies on a mix of long-term money—including debt, stock, and retained earnings—to fund its business. Total long-term debt for the company stood at $272.8 million in March of 1982. The annual interest payment on this debt was $28.1 million. The total numbers of issued shares of common and preferred stock were 75,976,376 and 837,673, respectively. Over the years, Rockwell has also consistently reinvested a share of its after-tax earnings.

USES AND SOURCES OF LONG-TERM FUNDS

One of the basic principles of finance is that long-lived assets are purchased with long-term funds. Long-lived assets are called **fixed assets**, and they include land, plant, and equipment. An appliance manufacturer acquires a 35-acre tract of land on the edge of town for construction of a factory. Land is the 35-acre tract; plant, the factory building; and equipment, the metal-stamping machinery, forklift trucks, and other long-lived items used in production. Land, plant, and equipment are the *uses* of long-term money.

What about the *sources* of long-term financing? How does a firm fund an expansion program? In this chapter, we will discuss four sources of long-term financing: retained earnings, bonds, common stock, and preferred stock. Most big firms are not able to fund growth through profits alone, so they must look elsewhere for the needed cash. They have two basic choices: obtain the cash through borrowing or through the sale of ownership shares. Borrowed funds are called **debt capital**, and funds provided by owners are called **equity capital**. Bonds are an example of debt capital; retained earnings, common stock, and preferred stock are examples of equity capital.

Business firms use long-term money, but who supplies it? The firm itself supplies some of the money in the form of profits, but the people and organizations who buy bonds and stocks supply most of it. As buyers of these debt and equity securities, they are called **investors**. Figure 18-1 shows the relationship between the sources and uses of long-term financing, and how money flows from investors to business enterprises in need of capital. Let's begin our discussion of the four sources of long-term financing by looking at retained earnings.

RETAINED EARNINGS

The first source of long-term financing for a corporation is the excess of revenues over costs after all expenses and taxes have been accounted for. This excess amount or surplus is called profit. Successful firms can use their accumulated profits to fund long-term expansion programs. An operating surplus also makes it easier for a firm to raise money in the capital markets, that is, to sell stocks or bonds. This is because investors perceive profitable firms as being less risky and therefore good investments.

What Are Retained Earnings?

This first source of capital is retained earnings. We can define **retained earnings** as the amount of money left at year-end after all expenses, interest payments, taxes, and dividends

How are long-term funds being used by this manufacturer?

Figure 18-1

Sources and Uses of Long-Term Money

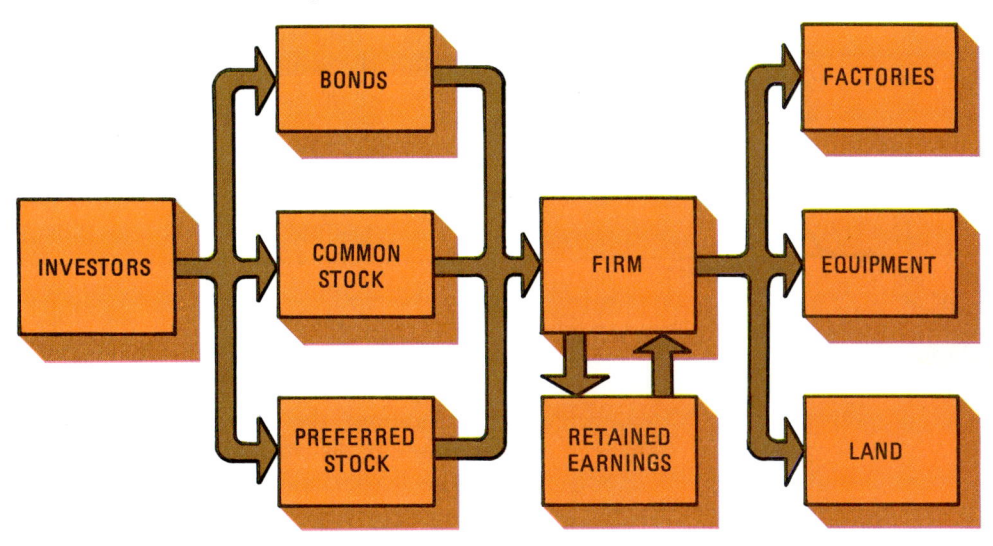

have been paid. It is the amount of money available to "plow back" into the business. How important are retained earnings as a source of capital? In 1982, total profits of all U.S. corporations were approximately $160 billion. Of this total, nearly $60 billion was paid out to stockholders as cash dividends. The remainder, about $100 billion, was available for new investments by the corporations. For many smaller companies, retained earnings are just about the only source of capital.

Perspective of the Firm

Should a successful firm retain its earnings or pay them out to shareholders? The decision rule is that a business firm should pay cash dividends only when it cannot find a better use for the money. According to this rule, the firm examines investment opportunities at the end of the fiscal year. If it finds a productive use for its surplus, such as a new assembly plant in a fast-growing part of the country, it retains the surplus, plowing it into the proposed investment. Otherwise, it distributes the surplus as dividends.

For many years, Teledyne, a California-based conglomerate, had a policy of investing all of its operating profit. From 1974 to 1981, in fact, the company did not pay out a single penny in dividends. During this time its annual profits increased from $31 million to $412 million, while the price of its stock went from $6 to $174.

Perspective of the Investor

In practice, dividend policies are as much a function of stockholder expectations as they are of investment prospects. If the main concern of investors is capital gains, not cash dividends, then investors neither expect nor want dividends. Teledyne stockholders, for example, are clearly more interested in the value of their stock than in yearly dividend income. Not all investors and not all companies are the same, however. AT&T shareholders look for dividend income. As Figure 18-2 shows, AT&T has paid out nearly 80 percent of its after-tax profits in dividends each year since the early 1970s. Many of the stockholders in AT&T are older people who rely on their cash dividends as a source of income. Nonpayment of these dividends by AT&T might weaken investor confidence.

BONDS

The second source of long-term financing is bonds. A **bond** is a contract between the bond's issuer and the bond's buyers. The purchase price of the bond represents a loan to the issuing firm. In return for this loan, the issuer promises to make regular interest payments to the buyers of the bond—individuals, pension funds, or other corporate investors—in specified amounts. The issuer also promises to repay the principal at a

Figure 18-2

AT&T Profits and Dividends, 1970-1982

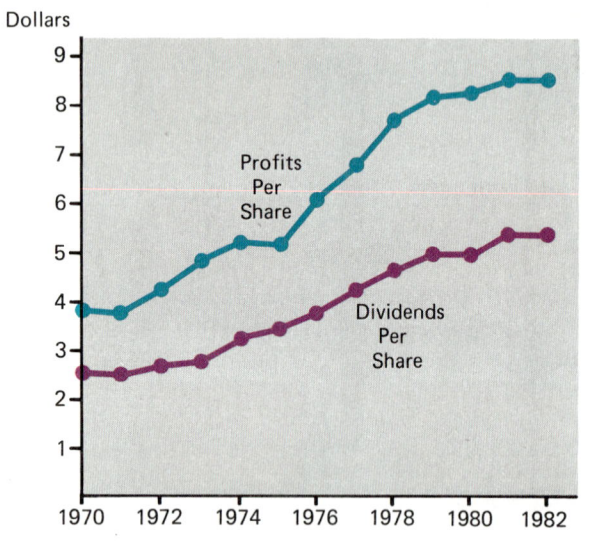

Source: *Value Line Investment Survey* (December 31, 1982).

stated maturity date. The terms of the lending agreement are set forth in the **bond indenture**. A bondholder is a creditor rather than an owner of the issuing firm. In short, a bond indicates a debt. Bonds are usually sold in units of $1,000, $10,000, or $100,000. Figure 18-3 shows what a bond certificate looks like.

Bond Classification

Bonds can be classified in many ways. For example, they can be classified on the basis of the underlying security, the type of issuing organization, or the degree of risk involved. For our purpose, we shall classify bonds into five basic types.

Debentures. A bond that does not include a pledge of specified assets as a guarantee of repayment is called a **debenture**. The holder of a debenture relies on the good name and overall earning power of the issuing firm as the guarantee that the bonds will be paid at their maturity date. Accordingly, only well-established companies issue debenture bonds. In early 1982, Enserch Corporation issued $100 million in debentures paying 16.375 percent interest. The maturity date of the bonds is the year 2007.

Subordinated Debentures. Subordinated debentures are also unsecured bonds. How do they differ from the debentures just discussed? The difference concerns the order in which claims against the issuing firm's assets are honored in the event of the firm's default. Specifically, the claims of the holders of subordinated debentures are secondary, or "subordinated," to the claims of the holders of other debenture issues.

An example will help make this point clear. Suppose the Infinity Corp., a maker of long-lasting automobile parts, sells an issue of debentures and then an issue of subordinated debentures. Unfortunately, the firm fails a few years later and is forced out of business. To meet its obligations, the firm's assets are sold off and the proceeds distributed to the firm's bondholders. The holders of the regular debentures will receive payment first. Only after these creditors are paid in full do the holders of subordinated debentures receive any repayment on the amount of principal outstanding. Because of this feature, subordinated debentures involve more risk than

Figure 18-3

Bond Certificate

CONTROVERSIAL ISSUES

The concept of a market for the purchase and sale of corporate stocks has been around for hundreds of years. Only since the Industrial Revolution, however, have corporations needed funds for expansion so badly that they placed great emphasis on a stock market as a potential source of funds. But do they really find the funds they need in the stock market, or is it just a marketplace for speculators?

The Stock Market—Speculation or a Source of Funds?

Pro

The stock market is no more than a marketplace for speculators. Nearly every stock bought or sold on the market already belongs to a stockholder, so the sale means nothing to the corporation itself. Not a penny of additional investment accrues to the company. Only rarely is new stock offered by companies, and then it is priced lower because it has to compete in a market with preexisting stock offered for sale by stockholders.

Furthermore, new stocks suffer from extensive reporting and legal constraints, which can be so expensive that stock offerings are prohibitive for small companies or in small amounts for larger companies. In the end, companies considering stock offerings often have to make financial decisions that are not in their own best interest but are only in the interest of buyers in the stock market.

And because of the speculative nature of the stock market, even a highly stable stock's value can change dramatically with the mood of investors. Consequently, the perceived worth of the company can vary tremendously, which can then make bond offerings harder to sell and commercial bank loans harder to obtain.

Last, a company never knows what it will receive for its stock on the market. For those small companies which sell their stock directly to investors, the stock acquires whatever price the investors are willing to pay. Often, the stock isn't valued highly enough to make the offering worthwhile. When larger companies sell stock offerings, they sell them through investment bankers who take a substantial cut of the proceeds as fees. Thus, a company receives only part of the money paid by investors for ownership of the stock.

The stock market isn't a good source of funds for corporations. It is a speculative game, nothing more.

Con

It's ridiculous to say that the stock market is totally speculative. It does many things for corporations. For example, the average company offering stock does not have the resources to sell any kind of securities—stocks, bonds, or whatever—directly to investors. The stock market, however, brings buyers and sellers together.

Second, the market supplies information. While that may sound trivial, it's crucial to realize that the stock market actually prices stock very accurately. To price stocks properly, it both uses and generates all kinds of information. Just as in any market, investors can make much better purchases if they have accurate information with which to work.

Third, a corporation may get more for its stock than the face or par value on the stock. This means that the company receives more investment in exchange for the same amount of voting rights or dividend rights conferred by the sale. This means that before-the-sale stockholders become richer without losing as much voting power or as much of the company's returns. Obviously, the stock market appeals to those stockholders.

Fourth, there are countless variations on common and preferred stocks up for sale on the stock exchanges. Thus, a company can offer precisely the kind of investment opportunity that best suits its needs and the investment goals of investors.

Of course, the stock market *is* speculative, but the market does give companies a valid way of obtaining funds without having to repay them on a fixed date. The market should be taken seriously. It does a lot for American corporations and investors alike.

Profile —
Felix G. Rohatyn

One of the most powerful customers in capital markets is the American city. Open a *Wall Street Journal* almost every day and you will find advertisements for long-term financing programs offered by cities or by utility companies, hospital systems, or transportation systems within those cities.

New York City is no stranger to capital markets. Strained financially for years, the Big Apple closed out the 1970s fighting to avoid bankruptcy. Its streets were cracked and full of potholes. Its hospitals were broken down and poorly equipped. It couldn't clear its garbage in the summer or its snowfall in the winter. Crime was out of control. New York City residents had to pay income taxes not only to the federal government, but to New York State and to New York City as well. Sales taxes were the highest in the country and the city had tried to tax almost everything in one way or another.

Into this financial disaster came Felix G. Rohatyn. In May of 1975, New York Governor Carey asked him to join a committee investigating the city's financial problems. Carey decided to create the Municipal Assistance Corporation, a company dedicated to managing the resurrection of New York City. A decade later, the Municipal Assistance Corporation has done its job. New York City's financial health is much improved. Its bridges are still weak and dangerous, its police are still underpaid, and its taxes are still too high; but New York City bonds are being purchased with confidence again and the city's creditors are being paid off without problems. Felix Rohatyn had become the "guardian angel" of the big city.

Rohatyn was born in 1928 in Vienna, the son of a brewer. The Rohatyn family later moved to France, and Felix finally came to New York in 1940. After completing his education at Middlebury College in Vermont, Rohatyn took a job at Lazard Frères, a major New York investment banking company. Surrounded by legendary financiers such as Andre Meyer, Harold S. Geneen, David Sarnoff, and Charles Revson, Rohatyn received the highest quality education in the workings of capital markets.

Consequently, when New York asked him to mastermind the Municipal Assistance Corporation, Rohatyn was already experienced in the intricacies of capital market manipulations. He had handled the sale of Avis Corporation and the Hartford Fire Insurance Company to IT&T and the mergers of Kinney and Warner Brothers; he had acquired a fine reputation for immaculate capital market operations. He also had a reputation for believing in the importance of strong financial control in public government and economy. Rohatyn didn't believe in simple free-market solutions to problems; he felt that federal legislation wasn't enough to solve capitalism's problems. Said one economist, Rohatyn "is an extraordinarily enlightened capitalist who knows that the messy American economy requires occasional intervention." Rohatyn himself said, "A democratic capitalistic society in a stagnating phase has to have bargaining structures because the sacrifices that have to be made have to be bargained out."

Today, with New York City's future more secure, Rohatyn has gone on to new projects. He is arranging new short-term notes offered by the Municipal Assistance Corporation itself, rather than by the city. He is also helping other troubled cities such as Cleveland and Detroit. He hopes for new super-organizations, such as a Reconstruction Finance Corporation, that would revive America's economy by arbitrating bargaining between labor, capital, and government. He sees the need for a Common-Market-like organization among large and troubled American cities. Certain that what is now being done just isn't working, Rohatyn is fighting fiercely for improvements in the way capital markets help American cities. With his experience and record, one naturally expects Rohatyn to succeed.

other unsecured bonds; they also typically pay more interest.

Mortgage Bonds. Unlike a debenture, a **mortgage bond** is secured with a fixed asset—building, equipment, or land—named in the bond agreement. In the event the issuer of a mortgage bond cannot repay the loan, the holders of the bond are entitled to the secured property. This pledge of assets as a guarantee of repayment makes mortgage bonds less risky to investors.

Figure 18-4 shows how a mortgage bond issued for $50 million was announced in *The Wall Street Journal* on July 9, 1982. The issuer of the bond is the Dallas Power & Light Company. Notice that the bond pays a 16 percent interest rate and that the maturity is 30 years. The companies listed on the bottom of the announcement are investment bankers. These companies helped market the bond issue to the public. The role of investment bankers in the issuing of new securities will be discussed in the next chapter.

Income Bonds. An **income bond** is a bond on which the issuing firm is required to pay interest only when the firm earns enough money to do so.

Figure 18-4

An Announcement for a New Mortgage Bond Issue

This announcement is not an offer to sell or a solicitation of an offer to buy any of these securities. The offering is made only by the Prospectus.

NEW ISSUE   July 9, 1982

$50,000,000
DALLAS POWER & LIGHT COMPANY

FIRST MORTGAGE BONDS, 16% SERIES DUE JULY 1, 2012

PRICE 100%
plus accrued interest from July 1, 1982

Copies of the Prospectus may be obtained in any State in which this announcement is circulated only from such of the Underwriters as are qualified to act as dealers in securities in such State.

Blyth Eastman Paine Webber
Incorporated

Goldman, Sachs & Co.

Dean Witter Reynolds Inc.

The First Boston Corporation	Merrill Lynch White Weld Capital Markets Group	Salomon Brothers Inc
	Merrill Lynch, Pierce, Fenner & Smith Incorporated	
Bache Halsey Stuart Shields	Bear, Stearns & Co.	Dillon, Read & Co. Inc.
Incorporated		
Donaldson, Lufkin & Jenrette	Drexel Burnham Lambert	E. F. Hutton & Company Inc.
Securities Corporation	Incorporated	
Kidder, Peabody & Co.	Lazard Frères & Co.	Lehman Brothers Kuhn Loeb
Incorporated		Incorporated
L. F. Rothschild, Unterberg, Towbin		Shearson/American Express Inc.
Smith Barney, Harris Upham & Co.	Warburg Paribas Becker	Wertheim & Co., Inc.
Incorporated	A. G. Becker	
Advest, Inc.	J. C. Bradford & Co.	Alex. Brown & Sons
Butcher & Singer Inc.	Janney Montgomery Scott Inc.	Ladenburg, Thalmann & Co. Inc.
Legg Mason Wood Walker	Moseley, Hallgarten, Estabrook & Weeden Inc.	Oppenheimer & Co., Inc.
Incorporated		
Robinson-Humphrey/American Express Inc.	Rothschild Inc.	Thomson McKinnon Securities Inc.
Tucker, Anthony & R. L. Day, Inc.	Wheat, First Securities, Inc.	Sanford C. Bernstein & Co., Inc.
First Albany Corporation		Interstate Securities Corporation

Source: Dallas Power & Light Company.

Leverage

We can think of **leverage** as the amount of risk a company assumes in order to increase its earnings for stockholders. There are two kinds of leverage. **Operating leverage** is the use of high fixed costs to make the total cost of *production* lower. A company uses operating leverage when it buys a factory full of very expensive robots to replace workers. The robots represent a fixed cost and increase the company's risk because they still have to be paid for even if sales are poor. **Financial leverage** is the use of high levels of debt to make the total cost of *financing* lower. It is financial leverage that we are most interested in here.

Consider the two companies shown in the accompanying table. Both are worth the same amount—$25,000,000—and both want to invest $10,000,000 for one year in a real estate project. At the end of the year, they will sell their investments to repay the loan principal and the interest. Both expect to make the same dollar profit on the project. The difference is that High Leverage, Inc., wants to borrow money to pay for the entire project, while Low Leverage, Inc., wants to borrow only 20 percent of the total sum and pay for the rest with company profits that would otherwise have been paid to stockholders.

After paying off the principal of the loan, High Leverage, Inc., has $2,000,000 in gross profits if the year is profitable, and $500,000 if not. It then must pay $1,000,000 in interest expenses (payable regardless of the economic conditions). In a good year, High Leverage, Inc., earns $1,000,000. In a bad year, it will lose $500,000.

After paying off the principal of the loan, Low Leverage, Inc., has the same gross profits but must pay only $200,000 in interest expenses. In a good year, Low Leverage, Inc., earns $1,800,000. In a bad year, it still earns $300,000.

It might seem that Low Leverage, Inc., has the best deal, since it earns more profit no matter what the economy does. But remember that High Leverage, Inc., has invested *none* of its own money in the project, while Low Leverage, Inc., has invested $8,000,000, as shown on the last line of the table. If Low Leverage, Inc., always invests this way, it will be limited in its investments to the total amount of cash it has on hand, and thus its stockholders will receive only limited dividends. High Leverage, Inc., in contrast, is willing to borrow extensively, so it can acquire for investment much more money than it has on hand. This means it can earn more profits for its stockholders.

Obviously, High Leverage, Inc., also faces greater losses if sales are poor—that is the riskiness of leverage. Companies have to choose the degree of financial leverage that suits the desires of their stockholders. Also, many banks limit the amount of debt that their corporate borrowers can acquire, thus limiting the degree of leverage these companies can use.

The difference between these two companies is the key to leverage: With higher leverage, the rate of return increases in a good year, but the risk of losing more increases if the year's profits are bad. With lower leverage, there is a lower rate of return, but there is less risk of incurring a loss.

If it does not earn enough money to pay the interest, none is paid until the next year. The issuers of other types of bonds are required to pay the interest charges whether they have the money or not.

To see how this interest payment feature of an income bond works, let's look at the Pantech Power Valve Company. Suppose that the annual interest charges on this company's income bonds are $75,000. Because of bad management and a "soft" market for power valves, Pantech has only $25,000 available for interest repayment. Under the terms of a debenture or mortgage bond, the company would be in default of its bond agreement, but under an income bond, it pays the $25,000 to the bondholders. The $50,000 due is carried forward to the next year. Total interest charges in that year would then be $50,000 + $75,000, or $125,000.

Income bonds involve quite a bit of risk for the investors. The main reason is that the annual interest payments are not fixed but can vary over time. This uncertainty adds to investment risk. Income bonds are usually issued during the reorganization of an unsuccessful company.

Industrial Development Bonds. All the bonds considered so far have been corporate bonds. Industrial development bonds are issued by state and local governments under the auspices of an industrial development agency. The purpose of these bonds is to raise money for an industrial project that will benefit the local economy.

To illustrate, local government in an economically depressed area may decide that it would be in the public interest to attract more industry to the area. It may issue a series of industrial development bonds, making the funds avail-

HOW LEVERAGE WORKS

	High Leverage, Inc.	Low Leverage, Inc.
Stockholder investment in company	$25,000,000	$25,000,000
Dollar cost of proposed project	10,000,000	10,000,000
Financing method:		
Loan	10,000,000	2,000,000
Interest on loan (at 10%/year)	1,000,000	200,000
Cash drawn from stockholder investment	0	8,000,000

At the end of one year, with *good profits* of $2,000,000 reported before interest, net profit after interest expense is:

Gross profit (after paying principal; before interest)	2,000,000	2,000,000
less interest paid	1,000,000	200,000
Net profit on investment	$ 1,000,000	$ 1,800,000

At the end of one year, with *poor profits* of $500,000 reported before interest, net profit after interest expense is:

Gross profit (after paying principal; before interest)	500,000	500,000
less interest paid	1,000,000	200,000
Net profit on investment	$ 500,000 (LOSS)	$ 300,000
Company investment of its own funds in the project	0	$ 8,000,000

---

able to a large manufacturing company for the construction of a factory. Since these bonds are issued by a municipality, the interest income earned on them is tax free to the holders. Tax-free bonds always feature a lower interest rate than taxable corporate bonds.

Repayment and Retirement of Bonds

Besides the underlying security, a number of other bond features are of interest to investors. All the features discussed next concern the timing and method of bond retirement.

Callable Bonds. Some bonds may be retired before the maturity date stated on the indenture agreement. Such bonds are said to be **callable** at the option of the issuer. The **call price** is the price at which the issuer buys back the bond. Why would a firm want to "call" a bond issue? One reason is to take advantage of lower interest rates. Suppose the Alpha Centauri Company, a leading producer of costume jewelry and synthetic stardust, sells an issue of bonds paying 14 percent. Several years later, the interest rate on bonds of the same quality drops to 10 percent. Alpha Centauri could call the issue and then float a second issue paying the lower rate of interest. Most new bond issues have a call provision.

Convertible Bonds. A **convertible bond** is a bond that can be "converted" into shares of stock at the option of the bondholder. The convertibility feature makes these bonds very attractive to investors. Initially, as the holder of a bond, the investor has the security of a guaranteed return. If the firm's stock increases in value, the investor can exercise the convertibility option and thereby, as an owner, share in the profits of the firm. A substantial stock price increase usually triggers conversion.

Sinking Funds. A **sinking fund** is a savings account at a financial institution into which the bond issuer periodically makes cash payments. These cash payments build up over time and accumulate interest. They are timed so that, at the bond's maturity date, there is exactly enough money available to redeem the bond in full. A sinking-fund provision protects both the corporation and the investor by providing a schedule for repayment of principal. Sinking-fund payments are seldom made until the issue is at least five years old.

Risk and Return

The people and organizations that buy bond issues look at two basic factors in evaluating them: risk and return. There is a trade-off between the safety of the bondholder's investment and the interest rate offered on the bond. We can define **risk** as the probability that the issuing firm will not be able to meet its periodic repayment obligation over the life of the bond. Therefore, a riskier bond issue, in which there is some doubt about the issuing firm's long-term earnings prospects, usually pays a higher rate of interest. Alternatively, investors can purchase a nearly risk-free bond, but they must sacrifice a few percentage points of interest to do so. The **return** on a bond is easily checked by looking at the stated rate of interest on the bond certificate itself. But how does the investor determine the riskiness of a bond issue? Several experts have already done this for most publicly traded bonds.

Published Bond Ratings. Two organizations that publish bond ratings are Standard & Poor's Corporation (S&P) and Moody's Investors Service, Inc. Their rating systems are explained in Figure 18-5.

S&P uses ten categories from AAA, which indicates that a company is extremely strong, to D, which indicates that a company is in default on its interest or principal payments. The range of Moody's ratings is from Aaa to C. A bond rated AAA (S&P) or Aaa (Moody's) is considered to be the safest investment next to U.S. government securities. The bonds of only the strongest companies carry this rating. A sampling of companies with AAA bonds is shown in Figure 18-6 on page 346. Bonds rated AA or Aa by the rating services are also very safe investments. A few of these bonds are shown in the table, too.

Medium-grade bonds are usually rated BBB (S&P) or Baa (Moody's). They are felt to be somewhat speculative, but the issuing companies have little trouble paying them off under normal economic conditions. Bonds rated B or lower are quite speculative and expose the bondholder to considerable risk. If the issuing firm has no trouble meeting the interest payment schedule, the bondholders stand to make a good return on their investment since these bonds pay more interest than bonds with higher ratings.

The average interest rates paid on three-month U.S. Treasury securities and on corporate bonds rated Aaa and Baa are shown in Figure 18-7 on page 346. The first thing to notice is that the interest rate on both government and corporate bonds increased steadily from 1960 to 1981. This upward trend in interest rates parallels the upward movement in prices throughout the economy. Also, the interest rate on the riskier Baa bonds is consistently higher than the rate on the safer Aaa bonds. In 1960, for example, the rate on Aaa bonds was 4.4 percent and on Baa bonds, 5.2 percent. By 1982, these rates had climbed to 13.5 percent and 15.7 percent, respectively.

Importance of Bond Rating. A good bond rating is very important to a firm. It means that the firm's interest charges will be low. Remember, bonds with a higher rating carry a lower rate of interest. Also, an improvement in rating can have a big effect on the size of the market for a bond. Many institutional investors, such as pension and retirement funds, are prohibited from buying bonds with a BB (S&P) rating or lower. A favorable change in rating, then, can open up a whole new segment of the market.

COMMON STOCK

Holders of common stock are the owners of the corporation. By purchasing a share of stock, an investor is buying a "share" of the ownership pie. Thus, common stock is an equity security.

Figure 18-5

Standard & Poor's and Moody's Bond Ratings

Standard & Poor's	Moody's	Description
AAA	Aaa	Highest rating; capacity to repay interest and principal is very secure.
AA	Aa	High quality; differ from highest rated bonds only to a small degree.
A	A	Upper medium grade; interest and principal payments may be in jeopardy when a deep long economic recession occurs.
BBB	Baa	Medium grade; adequate capacity to pay interest and principal in normal economic periods.
BB	Ba	Quite risky; modest capacity for interest and principal payments.
B	B	Poor investment, highly speculative; assurance of interest and principal payments over a long period are quite small.
CCC	Caa	Poor standing, may be in default; purchased for speculative purposes only.
CC	Ca	Highly speculative, often in default.
C	C	Very poor prospects for ever being a good investment.
D	—	Default; relatively little chance this bond will ever be repaid.

Source: *Standard & Poor's Register* (New York: Standard & Poor's Corporation, 1983); *Moody's Handbook* (New York: Moody's Investors Services, Winter, 1982-1983).

The total number of shares held by all investors represents the total ownership of the corporation. At the time of purchase of a stock, the investor receives a **stock certificate** which signifies ownership of a share of the company. An example of a stock certificate is shown in Figure 18-8 on page 347.

Characteristics of Common Stock

Business firms sell common stock for the same reason they issue bonds: to finance long-term expansion projects. Stocks differ from bonds in several important respects. Let's look at common stock from the perspective of liability, maturity, and the voting and income rights of shareholders.

Limited Liability. One of the most important characteristics of common stock is that it carries limited liability. **Limited liability** means that the stockholders cannot be sued by the corporation's creditors for recovery of the creditors' claims. If the corporation declares bankruptcy, the loss to stockholders is limited to the value of their

Figure 18-6

Examples of Highly Rated Corporate Bonds*

Triple A Bonds (AAA S&P; Aaa Moody's)	
Procter & Gamble	IBM
Tennessee Valley Authority	Gulf Oil
	Exxon
Texas Commerce Bancshares	Manufacturers Hanover
Minnesota Mining & Mfg. (3M)	Dallas Power & Light
General Electric	

Double A Bonds (AA S&P; Aa Moody's)	
Consolidated Edison	DuPont
Southern Railway	Nabisco Brands
R.J. Reynolds	Wells Fargo
Kimberly-Clark	Xerox
Arkansas-Louisiana Gas	General Foods

*February, 1983
Source: *Standard & Poor's Register* (New York: Standard & Poor's Corporation, 1983); *Moody's Handbook* (New York: Moody's Investors Service, Inc., Winter, 1982-1983).

shares; individually or jointly, they are not liable for the corporation's debts.

Maturity. Another characteristic of common stocks is that they never mature. Nor are they callable at the option of the issuing corporation. Stocks are held in perpetuity unless the investor can find another buyer. This feature makes the secondary market especially important to stockholders. We'll talk about the secondary market in the next chapter.

Voting Rights. The common stockholders of a corporation elect the board of directors, who in turn choose the firm's Chief Executive Officer. Even though stockholders are the owners of the corporation, they in no way act as its managers. Stockholders have only indirect control through their choices of board members.

Holders of common stock sometimes are asked to approve certain actions proposed by the board. They may be asked to vote on the board's choice of a certified public accountant (CPA) to audit the firm's financial records, or to approve the acquisition of another company through an exchange of stock.

In each of these instances, the stockholder may cast one vote for each share of stock held. A stockholder with 5,000 shares has 5,000 votes. Stockholders who cannot vote in person are given a chance to vote by **proxy**. When stockholders sign proxy statements, they give the managers of the corporation the right to vote their shares for them. If stockholders are pleased with the way the company is performing, they willingly give management their voting rights.

Income Rights. As the owners of the company, common stockholders are entitled to receive a share of its after-tax earnings. When distributed to shareholders, these earnings are called **dividends**. There is no legal requirement that a corporation pay dividends; the decision to do so is made by its board of directors. Whether dividends are paid depends on the earnings record of the firm, its need for capital, and the expectations

Figure 18-7

Bond Interest Rates, 1960-1982

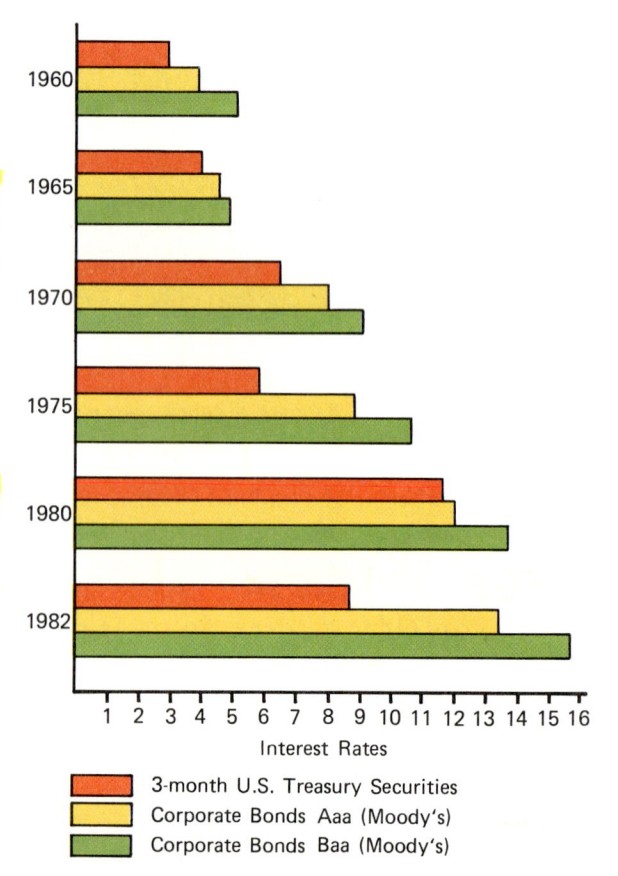

Source: U.S. Department of the Treasury; Moody's Investors Service, Inc.

Figure 18-8

Stock Certificate

of shareholders. The best indication that a firm is likely to pay dividends is whether it has paid them consistently in the past.

A firm that pays dividends consistently can also stop paying them. In 1982, the Manville Corporation trimmed its quarterly dividend from $0.48 a share to $0.20. This was the first reduction since 1940. In the next payout period, the company skipped the dividend entirely. The reason was the growing number of asbestos-related damage claims against the company. The company wanted to build up its cash reserves in the event of unfavorable court rulings.

Authorized and Issued Shares

As discussed in Chapter 4, corporate charters are granted through state agencies. The charter specifies the total number of shares of common stock that a corporation may sell to the public. These are called **authorized shares**. All shares held by the public are called **issued shares**, or **outstanding shares**. The number of issued shares can never be greater than the number of authorized shares. From time to time, corporations buy back some of their issued shares of common stock. These repurchased shares are called **treasury stock**. Treasury stock is given to employees as part of their compensation program. Many managers receive such stock bonuses when their firms are very successful.

Par Value. Par value is the face value of a common stock. It is the value printed on the stock certificate. Some stocks are sold on a par value basis, but many others today are not. In any case, new stock issues always sell for more than par, so the concept of par value is no longer of much practical significance.

Market Value. The most important concept of value for common stocks is **market value**, which is defined as the current selling price of a stock. Stock prices are listed every business day in *The Wall Street Journal* and in the financial sections of most daily newspapers. Why not pick a stock, and follow its market value daily in your local newspaper?

Generally speaking, supply and demand determine the selling price of a stock. Identifying the many factors that influence investors' willingness to buy or sell is one of the most interesting areas of study in finance. Indeed, stock price changes can be dramatic. In 1979, a share of Tandy Corp., operator of Radio Shack stores, sold for as little as $2.62; by late 1981, the price of a share had zoomed to $39.25. But the news from the stock market is not always good. In December of 1979, the stock of Kirby Exploration Company struck black gold at $52 a share. Thirty-one months later, in July of 1982, the well was running dry—Kirby was selling for only $7.50 a share. Table 18-1 shows the high and low selling prices for the stocks of nine large U.S. corporations over the period 1971-1982.

Some stock market values change daily.

Stock Dividends

Good news to an investor can come in several ways: a big stock price gain, a large quarterly dividend check, or a stock dividend. In the case of a **stock dividend**, the investor receives additional shares of stock rather than cash. A 10 percent stock dividend involves the distribution of one additional share for every ten shares held. The investor with a hundred shares would receive ten more shares. The Energy Minerals Corporation declared a 10 percent stock dividend in September, 1981.

Stock Splits. Under a **stock split**, one or more new shares are distributed to stockholders for every share held. A "two-for-one" split is probably the most common example. Here, the investor with 500 shares receives an additional 500 shares. Put another way, 500 old shares have become 1,000 new shares—hence, a two-for-one split. By splitting its shares in this way, the issuing corporation doubles the total number of its shares outstanding. The Intel Corp., a leading designer and manufacturer of semiconductors for computer systems, announced a two-for-one split in late 1980.

Figure 18-9 shows how a two-for-one split works. Note that each investor owns the same percentage of the company after the split as before. Note also that the market price of the stock has been cut in half.

The Reason for Stock Splits. Stocks are most actively bought and sold when their prices fall within a certain range. This is typically $30 to $90 a share. When the price is too high, many investors buy fewer shares. The Indivisible Diamond Company might split its stock two-for-one when the price reaches $100 a share, bringing it down to a more attractive $50 a share.

Vigorous trading has two important benefits to the firm. First, it brings more investors into the market. Most large companies like to have many shareholders. The more shares outstanding, the less likely someone is to obtain a controlling interest in the company.

Second, at the new lower price, the value of

Table 18-1

High and Low Stock Prices for Nine Large U.S. Corporations, 1971-1982

Company	Price Range, Jan. 1, 1971 to Dec. 31, 1982	Last Price Bid Year-End 1982
Eastman Kodak	151-3/4—41-1/8	65-1/4
Pan American World Airways	20-1/4— 1-1/4	4
E.I. du Pont de Nemours	67-7/8—28-1/8	40
E.F. Hutton	48-7/8— 1-5/8	40
IBM	98 —37-5/8	98
Playboy Enterprises	32-3/4— 2	7-3/4
Prime Computer	49-1/4— 1/8	42
Revco Drug Stores	47-3/4— 3-3/4	38-7/8
Southwest Airlines	31-7/8— 1/4	30

Note: Price range gives highest ask and lowest bid prices for the period indicated. The last price bid is for the closing market day of 1982, December 31, 1982.

Source: *Standard and Poor's Stock Guide* (January, 1983 and February, 1983 issues).

Figure 18-9

A Two-for-One Stock Split

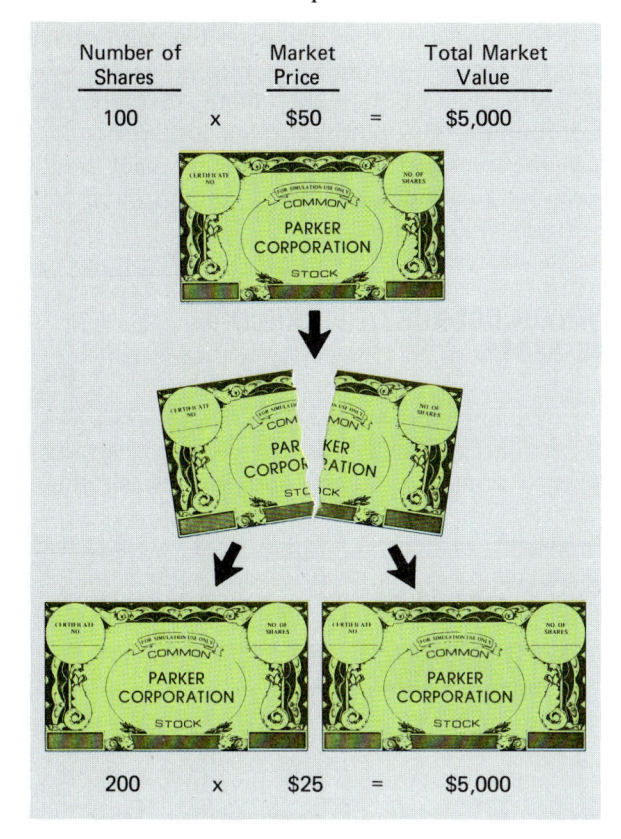

Number of Shares		Market Price		Total Market Value
100	x	$50	=	$5,000
200	x	$25	=	$5,000

the stock often begins a steady climb. This certainly is not a sure bet, but when it happens, the total worth of the corporation increases. This makes top management happy. It also makes investors happy because the value of their investments increases, too. Why does the price of the stock go up? Because stock splits are usually perceived as indications of the financial strength and growth prospects of the company.

PREFERRED STOCK

Preferred stock represents a cross between the two other types of long-term financing which we have discussed—corporate bonds and common stock. Preferred stock, compared to retained earnings, bonds, and common stock, accounts for a much smaller percentage of new corporate financing. In 1981, there was almost $3 billion worth of new preferred stock sold in the United States. This compares with $45 billion in bonds and $18 billion in common stock.

A Hybrid Security

Preferred stock has some of the features of a bond and some of a common stock. Like a bond, preferred stock carries a fixed income payment or dividend. But the dividend represents a distribution of corporate profit, not payment of interest on debt. Consequently, nonpayment of this dividend does not mean default, just as nonpayment of common stock dividends does not mean default. If dividends are not paid to preferred stockholders in a given year, they cannot be paid to common stockholders either.

Ownership of preferred stock, like ownership of common stock, represents ownership of the issuing corporation. Because it is an equity security, preferred stock does not have a maturity date. In the event of liquidation of the firm, the claims of preferred stockholders come before those of common stockholders—but after those of bondholders

Special Provisions

Most preferred stock issues sold today are both cumulative and participating. Both provisions make these securities more marketable.

Cumulative. As we said, a corporation is not required to pay a preferred stock dividend in any particular year. However, if the stock issue is **cumulative preferred**, dividends not paid in one year are carried forward to the next year. The corporation cannot pay a dividend to its common stockholders until it pays all past and current dividends due to its preferred stockholders. Suppose the Eleusis Pharmaceuticals Company has an issue of cumulative preferred stock paying $3.50 annually as its fixed dividend. Three years pass before the company can afford to pay a dividend. In the fourth year, it must pay $14 per share of preferred stock (4 years × $3.50 a share) before it can pay *any* dividends on common stock.

Participating. Through a **participating** feature, preferred stockholders can share along with common stockholders in the corporation's operating profits. Typically, this feature works as follows: When the per share dividend on common stock is equal to the per share dividend on preferred, any additional income to be distributed is divided equally between the two on a per share basis.

Let's assume that in the fourth year, Eleusis Pharmaceuticals pays the dividends due its preferred stockholders. The next year is a banner year for the company; profits soar and there is much income to be distributed among the company's owners. The preferred stockholders are paid their $3.50 a share, and the holders of common are paid an equal amount, but there is still income to be distributed. These additional funds are distributed evenly between the two types of securities on a per share basis. The total dividend payments per share might be $4.50 for preferred and $4.50 for common. Note that each share of preferred receives the same extra amount as each share of common.

Central Louisiana Electric Company, Inc., recently issued 800,000 shares of cumulative preferred stock. As shown in Figure 18-10, the stock pays an annual per share dividend of $4.18. The selling price is $27.50 a share. The percentage return for the investor, therefore, is $4.18 ÷ $27.50, or 15.2 percent. Note that the announcement says nothing about a maturity date for the security. You'll remember that bonds carry maturity dates but that common and preferred stocks do not.

WHICH SOURCE OF FINANCING IS BEST?

We have just looked at four sources of long-term funding for a business: retained earnings, bonds, common stock, and preferred stock.

Figure 18-10

An Announcement for a New Issue of Preferred Stock

Source: Central Louisiana Electric Company, Inc.

This announcement is under no circumstances to be construed as an offer to sell or as a solicitation of an offer to buy any of these securities. The offering is made only by the Prospectus.

NEW ISSUE   August 5, 1982

CLECO

800,000 Shares

Central Louisiana Electric Company, Inc.

$4.18 Cumulative Preferred Stock, Series of 1982
Par Value $25 Per Share

Price $27.50 Per Share

Copies of the Prospectus may be obtained in any State in which this announcement is circulated from only such of the undersigned or other dealers or brokers as may lawfully offer these securities in such State.

Merrill Lynch White Weld Capital Markets Group   Blyth Eastman Paine Webber
Merrill Lynch, Pierce, Fenner & Smith Incorporated   Incorporated

Bache Halsey Stuart Shields   The First Boston Corporation   Bear, Stearns & Co.   Goldman, Sachs & Co.
Incorporated

E. F. Hutton & Company Inc.   Kidder, Peabody & Co.   Lehman Brothers Kuhn Loeb
Incorporated   Incorporated

L. F. Rothschild, Unterberg, Towbin   Salomon Brothers Inc   Shearson/American Express Inc.

Smith Barney, Harris Upham & Co.   Wertheim & Co., Inc.   Dean Witter Reynolds Inc.
Incorporated

Alex. Brown & Sons   A. G. Edwards & Sons, Inc.   Rauscher Pierce Refsnes, Inc.   Thomson McKinnon Securities Inc.

Robert W. Baird & Co.   William Blair & Company   Blunt Ellis & Loewi   J. C. Bradford & Co.   Butcher & Singer Inc.
Incorporated   Incorporated

Dain Bosworth   First of Michigan Corporation   Howard, Weil, Labouisse, Friedrichs   Janney Montgomery Scott Inc.
Incorporated   Incorporated

Ladenburg, Thalmann & Co. Inc.   McDonald & Company   Moseley, Hallgarten, Estabrook & Weeden Inc.

Piper, Jaffray & Hopwood   Prescott, Ball & Turben   Rotan Mosle Inc.
Incorporated

Tucker, Anthony & R. L. Day, Inc.   Wheat, First Securities, Inc.

Which source is best? What are the pros and cons of each? Is there a single best mix of long-term funding sources? Although there are no easy answers to these questions, let's look at some of the main issues involved.

Sources of Funds: Pros and Cons

For many smaller businesses, the option of issuing bonds, common stock, or preferred stock is impossible. They cannot offer the investor a proven record of stability because they are too small. Such companies rely on retained earnings to fund growth. Moreover, proprietorships and partnerships are prohibited by law from issuing common or preferred stock. Only corporations can do so.

Retained Earnings. The big advantage of retained earnings as a way to fund growth is that they are safe. If sales and profits decline, the firm does not need to worry about interest or sinking-fund payments, as it would have to with bonds. Reinvesting retained earnings is also much less costly than raising money in the stock market.

As a source of funds, however, retained earnings are not without problems. First, they may not be sufficient for the firm to take advantage of all good investment opportunities. Second, a policy of relying on retained earnings may conflict with the dividend expectations of investors. A dollar retained and reinvested is one less dollar paid out in dividends. To the extent that investors expect hefty quarterly dividends, the firm may have to look toward the capital markets for long-term money.

Bonds. Bonds have at least three advantages as a source of funds. First, they are less expensive than equity securities. Bond payments are treated as a business expense and, therefore, are paid with before-tax dollars. Also, issuing bonds does not involve a loss of control, as does the selling of common or preferred stock. The firm borrows money rather than trading ownership for money. Finally, issuing bonds allows the firm to increase its rate of return on equity. This is known as leverage as discussed earlier.

Bonds are not perfect, however. The major problem with them is the risk from the firm's point of view. If the firm cannot make the bond interest payments, it can be taken over by its creditors.

Common Stock. The advantage of issuing common stock is that it does not add to financial risk. Payment of dividends is voluntary, whereas payment of interest charges is mandatory. At least in this respect, common stock has one big advantage over bonds. But common stock can be expensive to the firm. One reason is because dividends are paid out of profits, and profits are calculated after payment of taxes. Unlike bond interest payments which are tax deductible, dividend payments are not. Also, depending on conditions in the stock market and the confidence of investors, the firm may have to sell many shares of stock in order to raise the needed amount of money. The more shares issued, the more the price of the stock falls, and the more control sacrificed by the original stockholders.

Preferred Stock. Our last source of long-term money is preferred stock. Like the buyers of bonds, preferred stockholders do not share in the control of the business; the holders of preferred shares cannot vote on major issues unless the firm is in real trouble financially. This leaves more control in the hands of the original common stockholders. And issuing preferred stock, like issuing common stock, does not add more risk to the the firm. However, preferred stock can be expensive because dividends are paid with after-tax dollars.

Capital Structure

Most large companies, like Rockwell International, do not rely on one source of long-term financing but rather on a mix of all four. **Capital structure** is the term used to describe a company's financing mix. Most commonly, it describes the amount of debt capital (bonds) in relation to total equity capital (retained earnings, common stock, and preferred stock).

The right capital structure for a firm depends on many factors. Among them are the type of industry in which the firm operates, the nature of the assets purchased, the prevailing interest rate on debt, and the firm's earnings record. Table 18-2 shows the long-term financing mix for ten U.S. companies. Each company is from a different industry.

Table 18-2

Long-Term Financing for Ten Large U.S. Companies
($Millions)

	Common Stock	Preferred Stock	Bonds	Retained Earnings
Boeing Co.	$ 832.6	$ 0.0	$ 327.0	$ 1,826.8
Bell Telephone Co. of PA.	1,584.9	0.0	1,596.9	664.8
Singer Co.	166.1	25.3	307.3	216.8
Safeway Stores, Inc.	106.9	0.0	1,137.6	1,003.8
General Motors	508.0	263.6	3,801.1	15,340.0
General Mills	196.6	0.0	348.6	955.4
Frontier Airlines	4.4	0.0	99.4	103.3
Hughes Tool Company	55.1	0.0	410.2	610.2
Hewlett-Packard Co.	481.0	0.0	26.0	1,439.0
General Electric	579.0	0.0	1,059.0	8,088.0

Source: 1981 Annual Reports.

FROM THE FILE

Micaela is a financial vice-president for the Terra Nova Publishing Company. Founded 35 years ago, the company publishes religious books such as hymnals and prayer books. Twice before, the company issued mortgage bonds and reliably made all its interest and principal payments. The company's board of directors wanted to issue another series of bonds to finance a new printing facility. Because publishing houses had been especially hard hit by the recession, however, the company's bond rating was to be lowered by Standard & Poor's from AA to A. Since many religious organizations and retirement funds bought its bonds in the past (and were sensitive to a lowered bond rating), Terra Nova's board members were very upset.

Micaela agreed with them that the issuing of common stock would result in a dilution of control for the company's current owners. The market for preferred stock was not too strong either. Micaela hoped to recommend a solution to the long-term financing bind. If you were in her position, what would you recommend?

SUMMARY POINTS

1. Long-term funds are used for the purchase of land, plant, and equipment. Long-term funds are supplied through the reinvestment of retained earnings or the sale of bonds, common stock, or preferred stock.
2. Borrowed funds are called debt capital. The funds originally or subsequently provided by the firm's owners are called equity capital.
3. Retained earnings refer to the amount of money

left at year-end after all expenses, interest payments, taxes, and dividends have been paid.
4. Whether to reinvest earnings or to pay them out as dividends depends on the availability of profitable investment opportunities as well as the dividend expectations of investors.
5. By purchasing a bond, an investor is lending money to the issuing corporation in return for regular interest payments. A bond, therefore, is a debt security.
6. Five types of bonds are debentures, subordinated debentures, mortgage bonds, income bonds, and industrial development bonds.
7. Callable bonds may be retired by the issuing company before their stated maturity date. The call price is the price at which the issuer buys back the bonds.
8. A bond with a convertibility provision can be exchanged for shares of common stock at the option of the bondholder.
9. A sinking-fund provision requires the bond issuer to deposit specified dollar amounts in a savings account to ensure that money is available for bond redemption at the issue's maturity date.
10. Risk is the probability that the bond issuer will not be able to make the periodic interest payments over the life of the bond. The riskier a bond, the greater the percentage return offered to investors.
11. Common stock is an equity security that represents ownership in a corporation.
12. Four characteristics of common stock are limited liability, no maturity date, the right of shareholders to vote on certain issues, and the right of shareholders to a percentage of the corporation's profits.
13. Authorized shares refers to the total number of shares that a corporation can offer without changing its charter. Issued shares refers to the total number held by the public.
14. The market value of a share of stock is determined by supply and demand.
15. Stock investors earn money when the price of a stock changes favorably or when the issuing corporation pays a cash or stock dividend.
16. Under a stock split, additional shares are distributed to stockholders, but the total value of shares held does not change.
17. Preferred stock has the fixed-income payment feature of a bond but the equity ownership feature of a common stock. Most preferred stocks sold today are cumulative and participating.
18. Capital structure refers to a company's mix of long-term financing—specifically, the amount of debt capital in relation to the amount of equity capital.

KEY TERMS AND CONCEPTS

long-term financing
capital
fixed assets
debt capital
equity capital
investors
retained earnings
bond
bond indenture
debenture
subordinated debentures
mortgage bond
income bond
industrial development bonds
callable
call price
convertible bond
sinking fund
risk
return
bond ratings
common stock

stock certificate
limited liability
maturity
voting rights
proxy
income rights
dividends
authorized shares
issued shares
outstanding shares
treasury stock
par value
market value
stock dividend
stock split
preferred stock
cumulative preferred
participating
capital structure
leverage
operating leverage
financial leverage

REVIEW QUESTIONS

1. What are the four major sources of long-term funds?
2. Define retained earnings.
3. How are retained earnings used as a source of capital?
4. How are debentures, mortgage bonds, and income bonds different from each other?
5. Why is a convertible bond attractive to many investors?
6. What is a sinking fund?
7. What is meant by limited liability as it pertains to common stock?
8. What voting rights do common stockholders have?
9. What is the difference between authorized shares and issued shares of common stock?
10. How do most corporations use treasury stock?
11. Explain the differences between preferred stock and common stock.
12. What is meant by cumulative and participating preferred stock?

DISCUSSION QUESTIONS

1. As an investor in a corporation, how much of a cash dividend would you like the company to pay?
2. How can local governments use industrial development bonds to attract new industry? Should local governments be able to issue industrial development bonds for this purpose?
3. Why do people often purchase medium-grade bonds rather than high-grade bonds? Which would you purchase?
4. Why does a stock split frequently help push up the price of a firm's stock?
5. What type of long-term financing do you feel is best for most businesses?

CASE 18-1

Trammell Crow Co.

Trammell Crow began his company by renovating grain warehouses and selling them at fantastic profit as general warehouse space. Trammell Crow Co., soon moved on to larger building projects. In Atlanta, the company built Peachtree Center, and in San Francisco, the Embarcadero Center. These are among the largest and best known shopping centers in the United States.

But Crow hails from Dallas, and it is there that his most impressive high-finance operations are conducted. Dallas has become a major center of wholesale merchandising and sales. The majority of all catalogs in America are produced there—Sears and Montgomery Ward, for example, both have their catalogs produced in Dallas and buy much of their retail goods from wholesalers displaying in Dallas. This isn't to say that all these goods are produced in Dallas, but they are marketed there. And those marketing operations needed space.

Crow discovered that a trade mart was the perfect solution to everyone's problems. It offered plentiful space that rented for half the cost of office building floor space. And for the developer, trade marts cost less than half of what office space costs to produce. Furthermore, trade marts are virtually recession-proof: Even in poor economic times, manufacturers need to display their goods to improve sales.

Crow built the Dallas Market Center which offers 900,000 square feet of display space to wholesalers. Costing over $500 million, it became the hub of a wide variety of other construction projects. Crow broke ground for a 542-room hotel to serve wholesalers and buyers, and he added a large video and film area for producing advertisements right at the Market Center. Wholesalers could stay at a luxury hotel along with their buyers, use plentiful display space for their wares, and then offer nearby facilities to produce all kinds of promotional material. Trammell Crow Co. is also building shopping facilities featuring restaurants, spas, office space, warehouse space, and elegant stores to complement the Market Center. Crow spent $630 million on the Center and budgeted another $2 billion in new construction.

To finance construction, Crow went to the insurance companies. They liked the idea of profitable and recession-proof investments like his trade mart, and they gave Crow low interest rates on long-term debt in exchange for equity ownership in his company. Equitable, Metropolitan, and other insurance companies now own 44 percent of Trammell Crow Co. But Crow also owes banks less than 3 percent of his total $1.6 billion debt, and his company owns $2.7 billion in total assets.

1. Why are investors essential to the kind of long-term financing that Trammel Crow needed?
2. Why were retained earnings a good way to build up the company before it got into large shopping center projects?
3. Why were retained earnings a poor way to finance the massive investments Crow wanted to make when he began producing large shopping and trade centers?
4. Why was debt arranged with insurance companies that received equity ownership better for Trammell Crow Co., than issuing bonds?

CASE 18-2

Genentech

Genentech was one of the first major companies to look into the possibilities of genetic engineering. It was formed by a pioneer in genetic engineering, Herbert Boyer, with a partner who provided initial capital. In the beginning, Genentech asked venture capitalists to buy ownership in the company—that is, to provide financing. Venture capitalists trade money for the chance of owning a company that will one day be valuable. Genentech also obtained financing by contracting with drug and chemical companies to perform genetic engineering research.

After a few years, Genentech realized that it needed more laboratory space, more personnel, and much more financing. Several different kinds of long-term financing were examined. In evaluating each kind of financing, the following information was important.

- Genetic engineering was not expected to become financially profitable for several years—some people thought five years, others thought twenty or thirty. At the time, not a single economically feasible product had been manufactured by genetic engineering. Thus, investment in Genentech would be a highly speculative and risky venture.
- Several other companies had also started up, conducting research in genetic engineering and competing with Genentech for contracts from large corporations. Above all, these firms were competing with Genentech to produce and patent genetically engineered products.
- Boyer, his partner Swanson, and their major venture capitalist backer, Lubrizol Enterprises, did not want to forfeit their ownership and control of the company—at least not in the near future. They had long-range goals in mind and did not want to give up control to stockholders who would force Genentech to go into productive operations rather than expand its research base properly.
- Genentech needed a substantial amount of financing—more than it could hope to get from a bank or other similar lender. It also needed to hold onto the money for a longer period of time than most lenders would tolerate.

- Genentech had no real credit rating. Furthermore, it was clear that many genetic engineering companies were very poorly financed and very likely to fail, so any rating Genentech could obtain initially would not be very good.

1. What were the financing alternatives open to Genentech?
2. Why were bonds favorable or unfavorable as a financing method for Genentech?
3. Why was common stock favorable or unfavorable as a financing method for Genentech?
4. Would Genentech have wanted to use preferred stock? Why or why not?
5. Which source of financing was ultimately the best for Genentech? Why?

The Securities Markets

19

After studying this chapter, you should be able to:

- Explain how the primary market serves as a source of new capital and why trading on the secondary market makes the primary market more effective.
- Identify the six objectives of a personal investment program.
- Name the major national and regional stock exchanges.
- Describe how stocks are bought and sold, paying special attention to the role of the stockbroker, the various types of buy and sell orders, and transaction costs.
- Discuss the risks involved in speculative trading on the securities markets.
- Explain how mutual funds work and why people invest in them.
- Identify four frequently quoted stock market indicators.

The Dow Jones Industrial Average finished at 911.93 today, up 8.85 points in another day of slow trading. The total volume of trading on the New York

Stock Exchange was only 40,700,000 shares. Volume on the Midwest Exchange was 2,784,500 shares. Two of the most actively traded stocks were Cities Service and AT&T, which closed at $55, down $0.25 from the day before. High technology and defense issues headed up the list of stocks showing strong price gains. Bond prices did not change much as concern over the massive borrowing needs of the government continued to mount. The per share value of the leading mutual funds was generally up.

This sampling of a financial report is typical of what we hear on the nightly news. More detailed financial information is reported every business day in *The Wall Street Journal*. Much of this information concerns trading activity on the securities markets, where buyers and sellers jointly determine the prices of common stock, corporate bonds, stock options, mutual fund shares, and other securities. Let's look at securities markets from the perspective of both the firm and the investor.

PERSPECTIVE OF THE FIRM

The securities markets perform two essential functions for the business firm. First, they provide a ready way for firms to raise money for industrial expansion. Second, they provide a central place where outstanding shares of the firm's stock can be traded.

New Issues

As stated in the last chapter, business firms raise long-term money by retaining earnings, selling common or preferred stock, or issuing bonds. When a firm uses the securities markets as a source of new capital, it is said to be using the **primary market**.

Investment Banks as Underwriters. **Investment banks** help firms raise needed capital in the securities markets by underwriting the sale of new stock or bond issues. By underwriting we mean that the investment banker agrees to buy all of the stock or bond shares that remain unsold after a certain period of time. The banker, of course, anticipates that the shares will eventually be sold.

Since a stock offering can be for as much as $300 million or more, investment banks often form partnerships when underwriting new issues. In this way they spread the loss if the security does not sell for as much as anticipated. Twenty investment banks participated in the 1982 sale of 1,350,000 shares of common stock for Godfather's Pizza, Inc. The list of investment banks included E.F. Hutton, Bache Halsey Stuart Shields, Salomon Brothers, and Dean Witter Reynolds, Inc.

Other Investment Bank Services. Investment banks perform other services, too. They help the issuing firm register the stock or bond sale with the federal government. They also market some of the shares to large investors, such as pension funds and insurance companies, as well as to smaller investors through their brokerage offices around the country. The fee charged by investment banks is usually about 1 to 3 percent of the total value of the security.

Outstanding Issues

The main reason why people are willing to buy *new* securities is that the securities can eventually be resold to other investors. All trading that takes place between investors is referred to as the **secondary market**. Secondary trading is not itself a source of new capital for a firm; it refers to transactions between investors, not between a firm and an investor. If you bought 100 shares of Westinghouse stock through your broker, you would be buying stock that someone else previously owned. Accordingly, your payment would go to the previous owner, not to the company that issued the stock. Active trading in the outstanding shares of a firm's stock makes it that much easier for the firm to issue new shares in the future.

Secondary trading in the securities markets is also important to the firm because its new stock and bond offerings are priced in relation to its currently traded securities. Investment bankers generally advise that new stock offerings be priced at least 5 percent below their current market price; and new bond offerings, 3 percent below their current price.

PERSPECTIVE OF THE INVESTOR

Most of the 32 million people who own shares in U.S. corporations are not looking to make a "killing" in the market. Rather, their aim is to make a reasonable return on their investments. This is as true of stock investors as it is of bond investors. Other buyers of securities try to maximize short-term gain. These people, called **speculators**, are willing to accept greater risk if it means a potentially greater profit.

Let's look at the six objectives of a personal investment program. Although their order of importance depends on the particular investor, the first is of great importance to all investors.[1]

Safety of Principal

All investors are concerned about the safety of their investments. The price of a stock or bond sometimes falls below the amount paid for it, but there is always the hope that the price will bounce back.

There are two basic ways to safeguard investment principal: careful analysis and diversification. Most smart investors examine various financial, managerial, and marketing characteristics of each company in which they are considering buying stock. They want to know how strong a company is and what its prospects are. They look at the general health of the industry in which the firm operates. In this way, they avoid investing in risky companies or in industries without much growth potential. What industries would you consider "growth industries" right now?

Smart investors also use **diversification** to

---

[1] George A. Christy and John C. Clendenin, *Introduction to Investments* (New York: McGraw-Hill, 1978), pp. 4-5.

Wall Street—home of the New York Stock Exchange.

protect their investments—that is, they don't buy too much of any one stock or bond. Instead, they buy a variety of stocks and bonds in many different companies representing many different industries. Thus, if the price of one stock falls, the investor has not lost all of his or her money.

Liquidity

Most investors like to have some assets that they can quickly turn into cash—cash that might be used for a family emergency or to take advantage of an unusual investment opportunity. One of the big advantages of stocks and bonds as an investment is that they are liquid. That is, they can be converted to cash quickly, especially if they are regularly traded in one of the big securities markets. Normally, it takes only about five business days for the seller to receive the money from the sale of a security.

Stability of Income

Some investors buy stocks or bonds because they pay high dividends. Many retired people, for example, supplement their social security and retirement income with dividends. If dividends are a large part of the investor's income, then stability of dividend payment over time can be a paramount investment objective. This type of investor looks to such companies as IBM, Wisconsin Electric, and General Electric. These companies have long histories of paying dividends regularly. Figure 19-1 shows the dividend payments of IBM for 1970 to 1982.

Maintenance of Purchasing Power

Investors are concerned about inflation. They know that when prices go up 10 percent a year, the value of their investment must also increase by at least 10 percent if they are to stay even in terms of real purchasing power.

Many investment specialists believe that in the long run the rate of stock price increase is greater than the rate of inflation. Unfortunately, inflation has devastated the stock market in recent years. From January 1972 until January 1982, the value of all stocks traded on the New York Stock Exchange went up 23 percent, while the consumer price index (the popularly accepted indicator of price activity) increased 142 percent.

Appreciation in Value

People buy stocks and bonds not only for safety of principal, quick access to funds, stability of purchasing power, and maintenance of income, but also because they hope the price of the security will rise. The stock and bond markets are highly irregular; the price of the average security fluctuates by as much as 20 percent a year. By purchasing the right stock at the right time and by selling it at the right time, the investor can make a very good return indeed.

Freedom from Care

Speculators spend a great deal of time watching their investments. They read *The Wall Street Journal* every morning and visit their stockbroker several times a week. Many investors, however, buy stocks or bonds and then forget about them. The last thing they want is constant worry over whether they should sell their shares and buy something else.

The less hassle an investor is willing to tolerate, the better the grade of stock or bond that should be purchased. But even with high-grade ("blue chip") stocks it is sometimes necessary to sell the stock and buy something else. For many years the automobile companies were a growth business—the stock of Ford, General Motors, and Chrysler all performed very well. Today, however, their industry is no longer a growth industry, and the price of their common stock reflects this. Figure 19-2 shows the stock prices for Ford, General Motors, and Chrysler from 1970 through 1982. Do you know the price for any of these stocks now? Why don't you look them up?

THE STOCK EXCHANGES

Ownership shares in corporations are bought and sold through stock exchanges. The New

Figure 19-1

Dividends per Share of IBM, 1970-1982

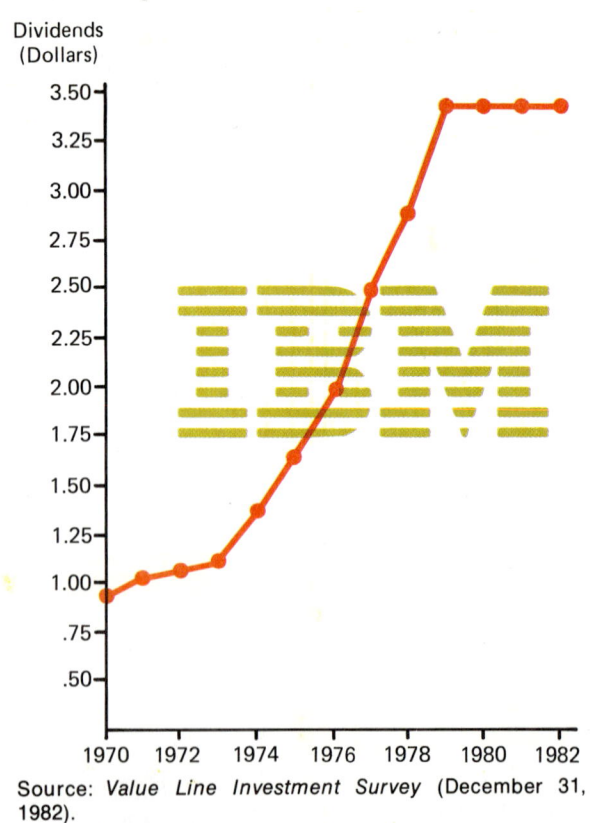

Source: *Value Line Investment Survey* (December 31, 1982).

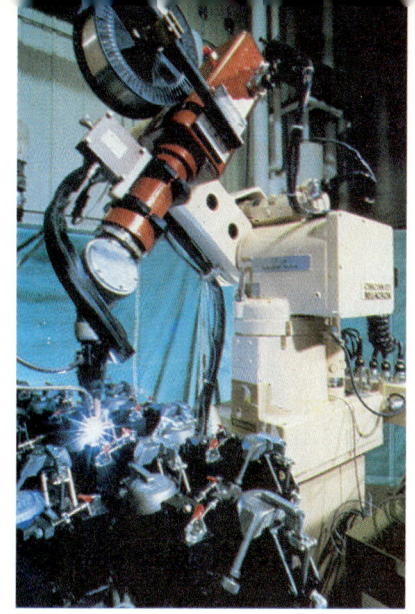

Liquidity? Income? Appreciation? Choose stocks carefully to achieve your goal.

York Stock Exchange and the American Stock Exchange are the two national exchanges. Several regional exchanges and the over-the-counter market also play a vital role in our economy.

New York Stock Exchange

The New York Stock Exchange (NYSE), founded in 1792 only a few blocks from its current location on Wall Street, is an association of 1,366 members. Its purpose is to help its members buy and sell stock for their customers. To accomplish this, NYSE provides a building for conducting stock transactions, modern communications equipment for reporting these transactions, and a set of regulations governing all transactions.

Only stocks listed on the exchange can be traded there. There are nearly 1,600 companies listed on the New York Stock Exchange today. They are generally the older, bigger companies. To be considered for listing, a company must have at least one million shares of stock outstanding. Although in 1981 the New York Stock Exchange traded the stocks of less than one quarter of 1 percent of the nation's corporations, the value of all stock traded was more than $476 billion. This is shown in Table 19-1.

Figure 19-3 shows the daily trading volume on the New York Stock Exchange for a period of three months in 1982. Note that during most of the June-August period roughly 45 million shares were traded daily. However, beginning on August 15, 1982, the daily trading volume jumped considerably. On August 25, for example, a record 138 million shares were traded. The big reason for the increase in trading activity was the expectation of declining interest rates.

Figure 19-2

Stock Prices for Ford, General Motors, and Chrysler, 1970-1982

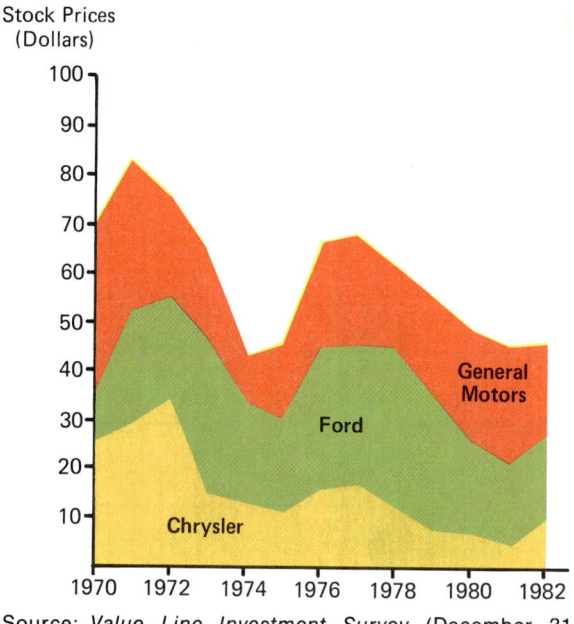

Source: *Value Line Investment Survey* (December 31, 1982).

American Stock Exchange

The American Stock Exchange (AMEX) is like the New York Stock Exchange, except that the companies listed there are not nearly as large

361

Table 19-1

Value of Securities Traded on Leading United States Stock Exchanges, 1981

	Total Value of Stocks
National Exchanges	
New York	$476,841,096,000
American	39,482,544,000
Regional Exchanges	
Midwest	28,011,360,000
Pacific	14,288,340,000
Philadelphia	11,053,740,000
Boston	2,718,588,000

Source: Adapted from *SEC Monthly Statistical Review* (Washington: U.S. Government Printing Office).

or as powerful as those listed on NYSE. They are generally small- to medium-size businesses with some potential for growth. Each of the 900 companies listed on AMEX has at least 400,000 shares of stock outstanding. Also, to be considered for listing, a company must show a pretax income of $750,000 or more for the preceding year.

Many companies try to move from the American Stock Exchange to the New York Stock Exchange in the belief that being on the "big board" attracts more attention. Many large companies, however, are listed on the AMEX, including Alcoa, Arrow, the *New York Times*, and Ozark Airlines. In 1981, the total volume of AMEX trading in common stock was nearly $40 billion.

Regional Exchanges

There are several regional stock exchanges in the United States. These exchanges serve as trading places for the stocks and bonds of local companies. Table 19-1 shows that the volume of trading on the top four regional exchanges is not as great as the volume on either of the two national exchanges.

The federal government recently has encouraged the regional stock exchanges to deal in the stock of nationally owned corporations. But regional exchanges usually trade the stock of these corporations only when there are enough stockholders in their locale to make a market for the stock. Currently, General Electric, Exxon, and Gulf are traded on five regional exchanges; General Motors and IBM are traded on six.

Over-the-Counter Market

The term **over-the-counter (OTC) market** is misleading: There is no counter and there is no market in the sense of one place where traders come together to buy and sell stock. It is a way of trading stocks rather than a central place for trading them.

The over-the-counter market was originally a complex network of brokers who communicated with one another by telephone. Today, the OTC market has an automated computer service called NASDAQ (the National Association of Securities Dealers Automated Quotations). This service col-

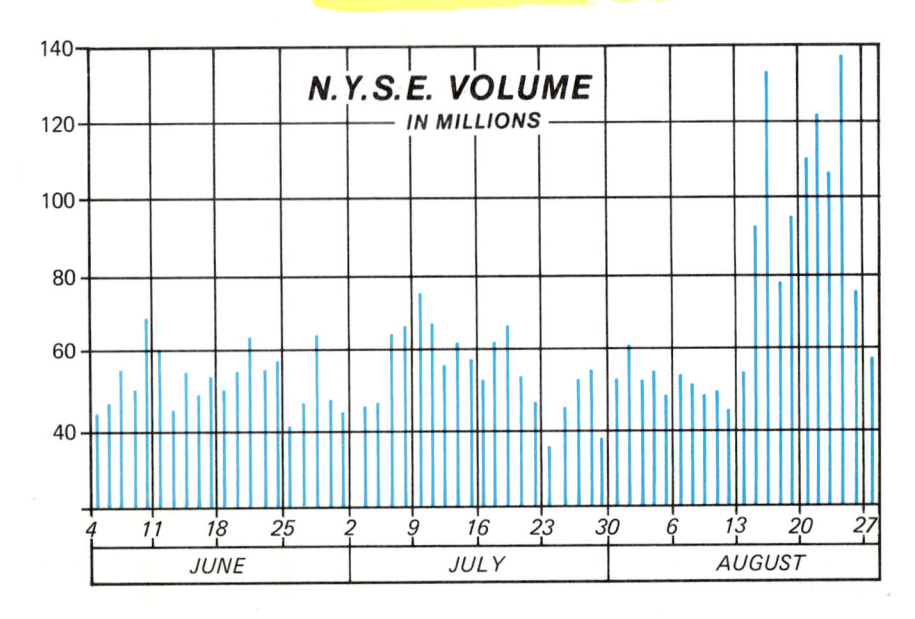

Figure 19-3

Daily Trading Volume of New York Stock Exchange

Source: Reprinted by permission of *The Wall Street Journal*, © Dow Jones & Company, Inc., 1982. All Rights Reserved.

The cash floor and futures board of the Minneapolis Grain Exchange.

lects, stores, and displays on computer terminals in bankers' offices the prices of about 2,500 of the most actively traded OTC stocks. All other OTC stocks are still sold the old way.

Approximately 30,000 stocks are periodically traded on the OTC market. Remember, this compares to fewer than 2,000 companies traded on the New York Stock market and fewer than 1,000 on the American Exchange. There are no requirements as to how big a company must be before its stock can be traded on the over-the-counter market. As a result, most OTC firms are quite small.[2]

HOW STOCKS ARE BOUGHT AND SOLD

The way in which stocks and bonds are sold is quite fascinating. Just as with any other good or service, there must be a buyer, a seller, and an agreed upon selling price. Stocks and bonds are different from other goods and services in that prices in the stock exchange are not "fixed" by the seller, and both buyer and seller operate through brokers.

Post Trading and Price Setting

Most stock exchanges use a **post trading** system; that is, each stock traded on the exchange is assigned to a "post," or trading area. Any broker with an order to buy or sell walks over to that area and attempts to make a trade for the stock.

Prices in the secondary market are determined in a "double-auction" manner: Buyers and sellers converge at the trading area and bid on a particular stock. For example, at 2:30 on Wednesday afternoon, suppose five people want to buy Delta Airlines stock and ten want to sell it. Unless at least one buyer and one seller agree upon a price, there won't be a sale. It is important to remember that a stock exchange does not buy and sell stock itself, nor does it even set the price of stocks. It is merely a place for people to come together to buy and sell. What determines the selling price of a stock is the strength of demand for it in relation to the extent of supply. In other words, selling price depends on how much buyers are willing to pay and how much sellers are willing to accept. Figure 19-4 explains how to read stock price quotations in *The Wall Street Journal*.

Role of the Stockbroker

As Figure 19-5 shows, the process of buying or selling a stock begins with a visit to a **stockbroker** who wires the investor's buy or sell instructions to a commission broker on the floor of an exchange. In a minute we'll discuss what we mean by "instructions." The **commission broker** is the one who walks over to the trading area and buys or sells the stock for the stockbroker's customer. The commission broker often works for the same company as the stockbroker.

Besides relaying messages to commission brokers, many stockbrokers perform other services for their customers. They make available expensive financial periodicals and reporting services, such as *Value Line Investment Survey*. Some brokerage firms have research departments that study the stock market and selected companies, and share the results with the brokers' customers. Some firms have a trading room where traders can watch reports from the stock market.

Type of Order

We mentioned earlier that the stockbroker wires the investor's instructions to a commission broker who works on the floor of the exchange. These instructions specify the name of the stock

---

[2]Sid Mittra and Chris Gassen, *Investment Analysis and Portfolio Management* (New York: Harcourt Brace Jovanovich, 1981), pp. 56-57.

Figure 19-4

Explanation of a Stock Quotation
As Reported Daily in *The Wall Street Journal*

52 Weeks High	52 Weeks Low	Stock	Div.	Yd. %	P-E Ratio	Sales 100s	High	Low	Close	Net Chg.
27	15 3/4	RCA	.90	3.8	12	2498	23 3/4	22 7/8	23 5/8	+7/8
(1)	(2)	(3)	(4)	(5)	(6)	(7)	(8)	(9)	(10)	(11)

(1) The highest price paid for RCA common stock in the past year.
(2) The lowest price paid for RCA common stock in the past year.
(3) An abbreviation for the name of the company.
(4) The annual dividend per share.
(5) The current annual yield, computed by dividing the dividend by the closing price.
(6) The price-earnings ratio, computed by dividing the current price of a share by the annual earnings per share.
(7) The number of shares sold for the day reported, expressed in lots of 100.
(8) The highest selling price for the day.
(9) The lowest selling price for the day.
(10) The closing price per share for the day.
(11) The change from the closing price of the previous day.

---

to be traded, the number of shares to be traded, and the type of order—that is, how the stock is to be traded. The three different types of stock orders are market order, limit order, and stop order.

Market Order. Under a market order, the most common type of stock order, the commission broker has the authority to buy or sell the stock at the best possible price. If the stock involved is traded actively, the investor knows that the selling or purchase price of the stock will be roughly the same as it was when the stock was last traded. Market orders can usually be carried out in fewer than five minutes.

Limit Order. A limit order "limits" the action that the commission broker can take. Specifically, the customer tells the commission broker that the stock in question is to be purchased at a certain price, or lower, or sold at a certain price, or higher. For example, an investor, believing that Westinghouse is a good buy at $25, issues a limit order to purchase 200 shares of Westinghouse at $25 or below. This type of order prohibits the broker from paying more than $25 for the stock.

Stop Order. A stop order is an instruction to protect a stock price gain or to minimize a price loss. Suppose that two months ago, you purchased stock in Hilton at $48 a share. The price of the stock has since risen to $62 a share. Believing that the price will go even higher, you decide to hold on to it for a while. At the same time, however, you're concerned about a possible price decline. Since you want to make at least some profit on your Hilton stock purchase, you place a stop order on the stock at $55. This means that you have told your broker to issue a sell order to the commission agent if the price of Hilton falls to

Figure 19-5

How Stocks Are Bought and Sold

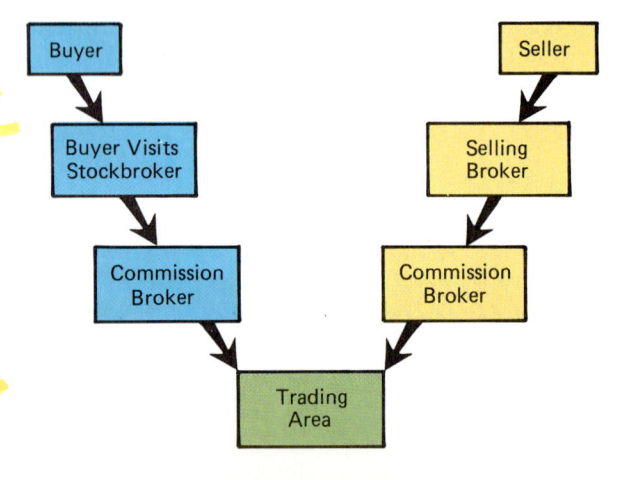

CONTROVERSIAL ISSUES

In recent years, the United States has faced many of the same economic problems present before the onset of the Great Depression. Many people wonder whether history will repeat itself. Will it?

Pro

In 1979, America's longest peacetime expansionary period in history ended. Since 1979, economic conditions have deteriorated seriously. The jobless rate has skyrocketed, while industrial production and real GNP have both decreased.

The signs indicate that a depression, not just a recession, may be possible. William McChesney Martin, for example, chairman of the Federal Reserve under Presidents Truman through Nixon, comments, "Too many people have become overextended." He sees "a somewhat greater chance of a depression today, [although still] only one or two in ten."

Charles P. Kindleberger, an MIT economist, has stated concern that America no longer worries about the effect of its economic policies on other countries. The currencies of all the Western countries are so interdependent that American inflation is reflected in inflation throughout the world. World inflation then returns to our shores to further destabilize the American economy.

Harvard's John Kenneth Galbraith foresees conditions for another depression in the Reagan administration curtailments of social-welfare spending. Galbraith feels that Reagan has eliminated many of the social supports, the so-called "safety net," that have averted severe recessions or even depressions in past years.

America doesn't have the economic stability to withstand economic downturns without plunging into a true depression, and recent policies have removed many of the restraints that would have prevented a depression as severe as that of the 1930s. Yes, America *could* have another Great Depression.

America Could Have Another Depression and Stock Market Collapse.

Con

No one can seriously believe that the American political and economic system will allow another calamity such as befell it in 1929, when the stock market crashed. Everywhere you look, the government has taken measures to protect us. Let's consider the factors that make a new depression impossible.

First, America's economy has changed completely since 1929. At that time, two thirds of all working Americans were employed in production jobs. These jobs were very sensitive to inventory cutbacks and decreases in demand; layoffs and business failures were common. Today, only half that many Americans still work in production jobs; over two thirds of the work force is employed in the service sector, where employment survives recessions, and inventories are of little concern. To illustrate, one researcher points out that if Americans were still employed as they were in 1929, we would have over 20 percent unemployment.

Second, in 1929, the federal government collected virtually no statistics describing the course of the American economy. Today, the government collects tremendous amounts of information and spends large sums of money on economic forecasting. This is so policymakers can anticipate economic changes and correct unfavorable ones most efficiently.

Third, the federal government now has agencies such as the Federal Deposit Insurance Corporation, which insures bank deposits, and the Securities and Exchange Commission, which regulates the stock market. These and other agencies protect the investments of Americans so the massive failures that occurred in 1929 will not be repeated. Furthermore, programs such as unemployment compensation and farm-price supports exist now to help those who do suffer from a recessionary downturn.

Last, in 1929, the federal government was reluctant to spend money to spur the economy upwards, and it actually decreased the amount of money available to the economy by 30 percent. Today, more sophisticated concepts of economics will prevent such careless action.

Actually, conditions prohibiting a depression have improved. For example, since 1979, the FDIC insurance limit has been raised on accounts from $40,000 to $100,000, the inflation rate has dropped, and the percentage of the work force employed in the service sector has risen. No, a new depression is not possible.

Profile— Ralph Wright

Ralph Wright was born the son of a Newark, New Jersey, automobile assembly plant worker. When he graduated from high school, Ralph needed a job. On the recommendation of his future brother-in-law, he went to the New York Stock Exchange to look for a position.

When most people think about the Stock Exchange, they see only the brokers rushing about the floor of the Exchange; they often fail to realize that there are hundreds of people that back up the trading on the floor. Wright knows these people, because he moved up to the specialist position from the very bottom of the ladder. He started as a carrier, then became a page, a tube clerk, and finally an Exchange reporter. As a reporter, he accompanied a specialist around the floor, recording the specialist's purchases and sales.

Specialists employed by Carl H. Pforzheimer & Co., one of the oldest firms trading on the floor, recognized Wright's skills and asked him to join their company. He started as a clerk again and after three years had worked his way to senior clerk. In 1981 when he was clerk for a specialist who had been trading in Standard Oil (Indiana) stock, Wright's diligence in fulfilling his duties during a dramatic rise in Standard Oil's stock brought him to the attention of the managing partners of the firm. As a result, Wright became the first black specialist on the floor of the New York Stock Exchange, at the age of 30.

As a specialist, Wright is responsible for overseeing all transactions relating to seven major stocks listed on the Exchange. Specialist firms, like Pforzheimer, authorize their traders to buy and sell stock of their client companies (such as Standard Oil) using Pforzheimer's capital in order to maintain orderly markets. When brokers give "limit" orders (orders to buy or sell stock when prices decline below a set limit), the specialist makes commissions on these purchases or sales. Wright records orders in a book he keeps for each stock. His records must be in meticulous order and perfectly accurate at every moment.

Pforzheimer hopes to make a profit on its own positions, which—in the case of the seven companies—are managed by Wright. When he isn't committed to buying stock for "limit" orders, he can make purchases for his company with credit extended by Pforzheimer. Often he will buy and then resell the stock on the same day, or even within the same hour, if prices change dramatically. He might also buy stock at times just to expand his volume of sales and fulfill his specialist function.

Specialists are not chosen right out of business schools. They spend years in lower positions learning the ropes of trading on the floor and contributing to their firm's success. The main determinant that promotes a clerk to specialist is the ability to make money. Ralph Wright has demonstrated that ability.

$55. You're protected against a severe price decline because the commission broker automatically sells the stock when it hits $55. The problem with a stop order is that the stock price might slide to $55 once during the day and bounce back to $58 by the close of afternoon trading. Without the stop order in this case, you would have been ahead $3 a share.

Round Lots and Odd Lots

Stock trading is typically conducted in **round lots** of 100—100 shares, 200 shares, 300 shares, and so on. These round-lot transactions are handled by commission brokers. Round-lot purchases are often out of reach for the typical investor. On Tuesday, February 16, 1983, it would have cost $3,100 to buy a round lot of 100 shares of Warner Communications stock. Not many small investors could afford that much and still make an attempt to diversify their holdings.

Odd lots, on the other hand, refer to transactions involving fewer than 100 shares. The problem with odd-lot transactions, such as nine shares of Motorola, is that it is not always possible to find someone who wants to buy or sell exactly nine shares.

To trade odd lots effectively, stock exchanges employ the services of odd-lot brokers. These brokers combine several odd lots to make a round lot which can then be sold all at once. Most stockbrokers charge an extra fee for handling odd-lot transactions.

Trading Specialists

Another important person in the making of a market for securities is the specialist. The job of the specialist is to stay at one trading area and to watch all trading in a particular stock. Specialists perform two vital functions. First, they assist commission brokers trying to sell a large number of stocks. Second, they maintain an "orderly and fair" market for their particular stock by buying and selling it on a regular basis. If a commission broker wants to buy a stock at $41 but sellers won't take anything less than $42, the specialist will offer to buy or sell stock at a price between $41 and $42. Although specialists cannot prevent all short-term fluctuations in stock prices, they do minimize such fluctuations.

Transaction Costs

Securities transactions are not without cost to investors. A few years ago, there was little mystery as to the cost of buying or selling securities; a well publicized fee schedule prevailed throughout the brokerage industry. All that changed in 1975 when the Securities and Exchange Commission (SEC) ruled that investors had the right to negotiate these transactions costs with their stockbrokers. The Securities and Exchange Commission is a powerful federal agency that regulates the sale of securities in the United States.

Many informed people in the industry thought that this ruling would bring down the established brokerage houses and encourage cutthroat price competition. However, it is now clear that the SEC's pricing decision did not cause panic in the stock market; nor did it destroy Merrill Lynch or any of the other big brokerage houses. Merrill Lynch and its competitors adjusted to the new market rules.

Full-Service Brokers. Earlier in this chapter, we pointed out that stockbrokers not only buy and sell stocks but also provide research and other services to their customers. This type of stockbroker is referred to as a full-service broker. Merrill Lynch, Pierce, Fenner & Smith is the largest full-service firm in the brokerage industry.

Discount Brokers. One outcome of the SEC ruling was the development of the so-called discount brokerage houses. The fees that these firms charge their customers are 30 to 70 percent lower than the fees that the full-service brokers charge. Not surprisingly, therefore, discount stockbrokers do not usually offer research services to their customers. Most of them also do not maintain local offices. Buy and sell orders are executed over the telephone via a toll free long-distance number, and the stock is distributed through the mail.

Cost Comparison. Table 19-2 shows how much it would cost to sell 50, 100, 300, and 1,000 shares of IBM common stock through two full-service brokers and one discount broker. Indeed, the discount broker is much cheaper, but you must remember that it does not assist the seller in any way. Some customers of discount brokers

Table 19-2

Cost Comparisons Between Two Full Service and One Discount Brokerage Firms*

Number of Shares of IBM Stock**	Full Service — Merrill Lynch, Pierce, Fenner & Smith	Full Service — Dean Witter Reynolds	Discount Broker — Charles Schwab
50	$74.05	$55.19	$45.00
100	92.00	92.00	45.00
300	276.00	276.00	120.00
1,000	688.07	688.80	225.00

*Costs quoted in Spring, 1982.
**The IBM stock was assumed to be selling at $70 per share.

have complained that their orders have not been transacted as swiftly as they would have been with a full-service broker.[3]

SPECULATIVE TRADING TACTICS

Most investors buy securities and hold them more or less permanently. Others are interested in turning a profit within a few months, weeks, or even hours. Speculative trading, as it is called, is quite risky: Speculators stand to make a great deal of money very quickly or to lose a great deal just as quickly. Speculators use different trading tactics depending on whether they believe stock prices are heading up or down. Three of the most popular trading tactics are discussed now.

Selling Short

We usually can't sell something until we have first bought it. But with a short sale the investor first sells the stock and then buys it! Selling short is an ingenious tactic because it gives the investor a chance to make money when stock prices are falling. Investors normally make money when their stocks increase in value.

To sell short, the investor borrows the stock from the broker, and then sells it. The proceeds from the sale are held by the broker as collateral on the borrowed stock. On instruction from the investor, the broker later buys the stock back. The broker keeps the stock, and the investor keeps the difference between the high selling price and the low purchase price.

Investors sell short only when they think that the price of a particular stock will fall. Suppose Superior Oil is currently selling for $35 a share. An investor believes that the price will slide to $25 in the near future. The investor borrows 100 shares from a broker and sells them at the current price of $35 in the hope of buying the shares in a few weeks for only $25. The difference between the selling price, $35 a share, and the purchase price, $25, is the investor's profit.

But what if the investor is wrong and the price of Superior Oil goes up instead of down? Then the investor loses money. Can you explain why?

Buying on the Margin

When **buying on the margin**, the investor finances part of a stock purchase with borrowed money. Currently, investors may borrow up to 50 percent of the purchase price. Margin requirements are set by the Board of Governors of the Federal Reserve.

Table 19-3 shows how margin trading works. The investor in the figure, Fred Fearless, wants to buy 100 shares of Upjohn at $50 a share. Fred can either put up the $5,000 himself ($50 × 100 shares) or borrow up to $2,500 from his stockbroker. Suppose that Upjohn goes to $60 in a year. If Fred had put up all the money himself, he would have made a return of $1,000 ($6,000 − $5,000), or 20 percent ($\frac{\$6,000 - \$5,000}{\$5,000}$). But if

---

[3]"A Big Setback for Discount Brokers," *Business Week* (August 18, 1980), pp. 94-95.

FROM THE FILE

Jean-Claude had just inherited $10,000 and wanted to invest in the stock market. The market had been shifting a lot lately, and he didn't know which stocks to buy. A broker suggested that he sell PPG Industries short. The broker reasoned that PPG—a major producer of glass, paints, and plastics used in construction and in the manufacture of automobiles—was likely to be hurt by the slack economy, and thus its stock price would drop substantially. Jean-Claude still was not sure. He wondered about the pros and cons of selling short.

he had invested $2,500 of his own money and borrowed the other $2,500 from his broker, paying a total of $250 in interest charges on this borrowed money, the return on his investment of $2,500 would have been $750 ($1,000 − $250), or 30 percent ($\frac{\$1,000 - \$250}{\$2,500}$). Conversely, as Table 19-3 shows, if the price of the stock had fallen to $40, Fred's loss would have been 20 percent on the full cash transaction and 50 percent on the margin transaction. It's not hard to see why margin trading is both exciting and risky.

Trading on the Options Market

Another speculative tactic is trading on the options market. An **option** gives its holder the right to buy or sell a specified stock at the current market price for a certain period of time. Speculators trade options much as they trade stocks. A **call** is an option to buy, say, Honeywell at $70 a share anytime within the next nine months. Using the same example, a **put** is an option to sell Honeywell at $70 anytime in the next nine months. The option itself may cost only a few dol-

Table 19-3

Impact of Buying Stock on Margin in Good Times and Bad Times

	Initial Cash Purchase	Initial Margin Purchase	Cash Purchase One Year Later Good Times	Cash Purchase One Year Later Bad Times	Margin Purchase One Year Later Good Times	Margin Purchase One Year Later Bad Times
Selling Price	$50	$50	$60	$40	$60	$40
Number of Shares	100	100	100	100	100	100
Total Value of Investment	$5,000	$5,000	$6,000	$4,000	$6,000	$4,000
Investor's Cash	$5,000	$2,500	$5,000	$5,000	$2,500	$2,500
Borrowed Cash	None	$2,500	None	None	$2,500	$2,500
Interest Charges			None	None	$250*	$250*
Net Profit (Loss)			$1,000	$(1,000)	$750	$(1,250)
% Return on Investment			$\frac{1,000}{5,000} = 20\%$	$\frac{(1,000)}{5,000} = (20\%)$	$\frac{750}{2,500} = 30\%$	$\frac{(1,250)}{2,500} = (50\%)$

*Interest charge in the example is 10% of $2,500, or $250.

lars, so don't confuse the purchase of an option with the purchase of a stock. Today, the Chicago Board Options Exchange is the only exchange trading exclusively in stock options, although the American, Philadelphia, and Pacific stock exchanges also handle them.

How can a speculator make money playing the options market? To answer this question, let's return to our Honeywell example. Suppose Honeywell is currently selling for $70 a share. Our speculator in this case, Ina Intrepid, buys 100 options at $2.35 an option; that is, she acquires the right to buy 100 shares of Honeywell at $70 until the options expire. If the price of Honeywell stock climbs to $85 within the option period, she has made a profit: By exercising her options, she can buy stock for $70 that is currently selling for $85. Also, the options themselves have value. This is the difference between the 100 shares at $70 and the 100 shares at $85. Instead of exercising the options, she could sell them to another speculator. But if the price of Honeywell, rather than climbing, were to sink to $55, her $235 in options ($2.35 × 100 options) would be worthless.

MUTUAL FUNDS: A NEW WAY TO SHOP WALL STREET

At the close of trading on Thursday, February 18, 1983, the net per share value of the New England Life Growth Fund stood at $21.19, up $.03 from the day before. Intercapital's Natural Resources Fund was down $.05 to $7.78 a share. National Securities' Bond Fund was up $.01; the Chancellor Group's Charter Fund was down $.05.

All of these are mutual funds. By the end of this section, you will know what mutual funds are, why people invest in them, and how one fund differs from another.

The Mystery of Mutual Funds

The first mutual funds were formed in the mid-1920s, but they did not become very popular until the late 1970s. Figure 19-6 shows the total value of all assets (stocks, bonds, and cash) held by mutual funds as well as the yearly sales of mutual funds from 1971-1980.

Here's how a mutual fund works. Suppose you have 19 good friends, each of whom, plus yourself, has $1,000 to invest. You could pool your money and buy $20,000 worth of stock in a variety of companies. Many small investors thus have become one bigger investor. If the value of your stock purchases climbed to $25,000, each person's share of the "fund" would be $25,000 ÷ 20, or $1,250. That means a gain of $1,250 − $1,000, or $250.

Now suppose that you and your 19 friends decide to restrict membership in the fund to yourselves. In so doing, you are creating what is called a **closed-end trust**. If you decide to admit new investors into the investment pool at its current per share value, you are creating an **open-end trust**, more commonly called a mutual fund. If each new investor then pays $1,250 to join the fund, the value of a share will not be diluted, and overall there will be more money available to invest.

Reasons for the Popularity of Mutual Funds

As the above illustration suggests, many people do not invest in the stock market because, by themselves, they cannot diversify their stock holdings sufficiently. A few thousand dollars is not enough money to achieve a reasonable degree of diversification. Moreover, they may want a greater amount of professional advice than they can get from a stockbroker. When the small investor is looking for diversification and professional advice, a mutual fund is generally the answer.

Types of Mutual Funds

Not all mutual funds are the same. We can identify at least five different types of mutual funds: load, no-load, stock, bond, and money market funds.[4]

Load and No-Load Funds. Managers of mutual funds are paid an annual operating fee by the members of the fund. The usual annual charge is is .75 to 1.0 percent of the total value of the fund. In addition, a load fund involves the payment of a sales commission at the time the stocks comprising the fund are purchased; a no-load fund does

---

[4]Louis Engel, *How to Buy Stocks* (Boston: Little, Brown & Co., 1976), pp. 272-273.

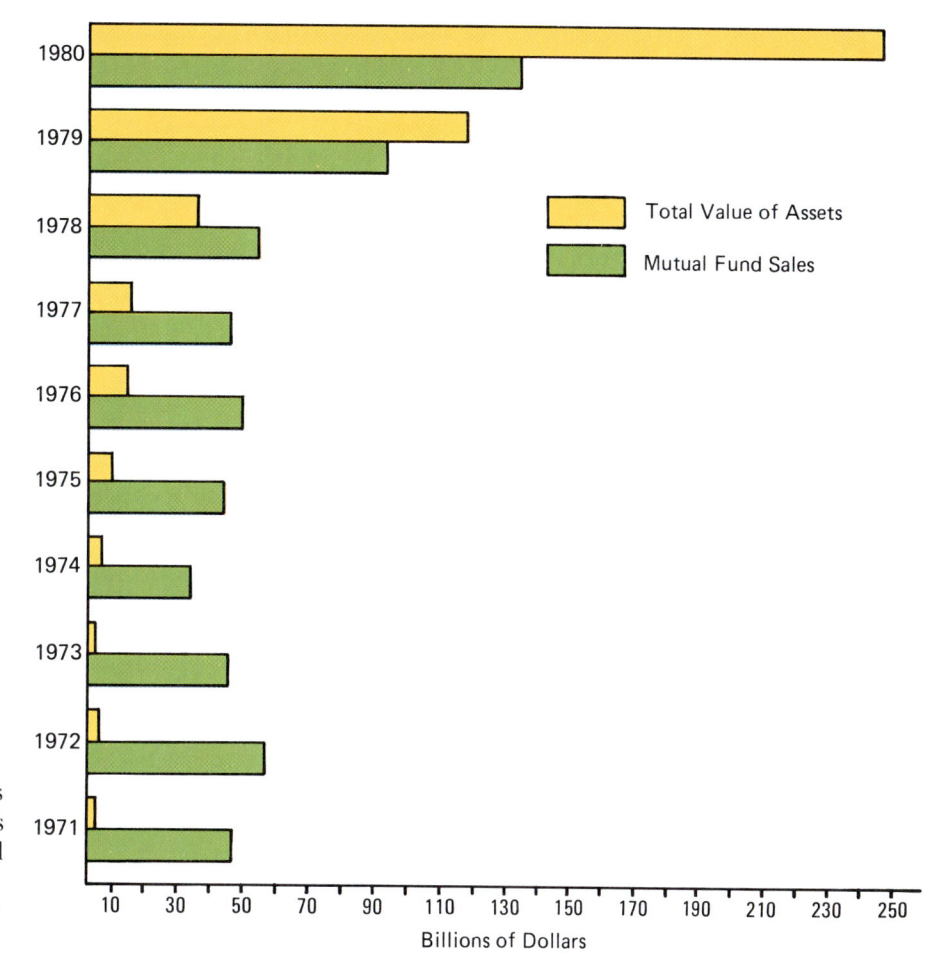

Figure 19-6

Total Value of Assets Held by Mutual Funds and Sales of Mutual Funds, 1971-1980.

Source: U.S. Department of Commerce.

not. Today, nearly 40 percent of all mutual funds are no-load funds.

Bond and Stock Funds. Remember that a mutual fund is a diversified portfolio of investment securities. These securities can be either stocks or bonds. **Bond funds** are characterized by conservative investment policies and a fairly stable rate of return. But even with a bond fund, a profitable investment is not guaranteed.

In contrast to a bond fund, the aim of which is to generate a steady dividend stream, a **stock fund** can have any of several objectives. For example, some stock funds attempt to outperform the market as a whole; they are made up of a variety of high-quality stocks that are expected to do well. Others are made up entirely of stock from companies in the same industry, such as banking or energy production, or of stock from small companies with great short-term growth potential. These are called **specialty funds** and **growth funds**, respectively. And, of course, some funds consist of both stocks and bonds. Smart investors always carefully consider their investment objectives before selecting a fund.

Money Market Funds. **Money market funds** have been one of the brightest new stars in the financial heavens. They are made up of short-term, high-yield government notes ("T-bills"), commercial paper, and negotiable certificates of deposit. Because of their investment policies, money market funds are just about risk free, offering their investors a return only a few percentage points below the prime rate. The prime rate, again, is the rate of interest that the leading banks in the country charge their biggest, most reliable corporate borrowers.

It is not an exaggeration to say that money market funds revolutionized the way small investors save their hard-earned dollars. The total amount invested in these funds went from practically zero in 1975 to more than $180 billion in November of 1981.[5]

How Good Are Mutual Funds?

There is no question that money market funds have given small investors a chance to earn high returns. The real question is whether stock and bond mutual funds have successfully met their objectives. Although most funds do well at one time or another, the evidence is clear that on the average they perform no better than the stock and bond markets as a whole.[6] This is not to say that investing in a mutual fund is a mistake. Remember, one of the important features of a mutual fund is that it gives investors a chance to diversify their holdings.

STOCK MARKET INDICATORS

Most investors follow the fortunes not only of selected stocks of interest but also of the stock market as a whole. They do this so that they can judge the performance of a particular stock against the performance of the market. Let's look at four of the top stock market indicators.

Dow Jones Industrial Average

The Dow Jones Industrial Average is the most widely quoted stock indicator. One feature of evening network newscasts is the quotation of the closing value of the Dow Jones Industrials for the day's trading. The Dow Jones Industrial Average is made up of a cross-section of 30 well-

---

[5]Michael Dotsey, Steven Englander, and John C. Partlan, "Money Market Mutual Funds and Monetary Control," Federal Reserve Bank of New York, *Quarterly Review* (Winter, 1981-82), p. 11.

[6]Michael C. Jensen, "The Performance of Mutual Funds in the Period 1945-64," *Journal of Finance* (May, 1968), pp. 389-416; William Sharpe, "Mutual Fund Performance," *Journal of Business* (January, 1966), pp. 119-138.

How to Read The Wall Street Journal

The circulation of *The Wall Street Journal* is currently more than *two million a day*. The *Journal* is without question the most current and complete daily business news publication in the United States. However, many people who look at the *Journal* daily do not really know how to read it.

THE FIRST PAGE. Begin with the "What's News" feature on page 1. It is the most popular feature in the *Journal*. Column 2 summarizes important U.S. and international business news stories. Column 3, "World-Wide," provides a quick overview of world news.

Column 5 on page 1 presents a "Special Report." The Monday report focuses on the economic scene, while Tuesday's and Wednesday's deal with major issues of labor and taxes. Thursday's "Special Report" focuses on new marketing and production trends, while the Friday report covers news out of Washington. On Friday, particular attention is also paid to economics, politics, foreign policy, and legislation.

Columns 1, 4, and 6 each present a feature story. These stories range from an analysis of Federal Reserve policies to the problems of growing a beautiful lawn in New Zealand.

THE BACK PAGE. On the back page of the first section of the Monday issue, you'll find a column dealing with personal finance. It examines such topics as estate planning, income tax returns, and the purchase of expensive automobiles. On Tuesday through Friday, the back page features a story on an industry abroad.

THE INSIDE BACK PAGE. The inside back page features the "Abreast of the Market" column. On Monday, it presents the opinions of professional money managers on the current investment environment. Tuesday through Friday, the column summarizes trading activity on the major stock exchanges. This part of the paper also shows the Dow Jones Averages.

CHECK THE MARKETS. The inside of the second section lists current bonds, stocks, mutual funds, and option prices. The *Journal* publishes daily the most complete compilation of financial data in the United States.

Source: "How to Read *The Wall Street Journal* Like a Pro," Merrill Lynch, Pierce, Fenner and Smith, Incorporated.

established companies traded on the New York Stock Exchange. Each company is considered to be an industry leader.

Figure 19-7 shows how the Dow Jones is displayed in *The Wall Street Journal*. As the figure shows, the Dow Jones climbed from about 790 on August 13, 1982, to more than 900 two weeks later. This increase took place at a time when interest rates were expected to fall. Many investors believe that falling interest rates are linked to rising corporate profits. The prospect of these profits attracts investors to the stock market. All this added up to a tremendous surge in demand for stocks, an increase in stock prices, and thus an increase in the value of the Dow Jones. By late 1982 and early 1983, the Dow Jones was consistently above the 1,000 mark.

Standard & Poor's 500 Index

Another stock market indicator is Standard & Poor's 500 Index. The S&P Index, covering 500 NYSE companies in 88 industries, is much more broadly based than the Dow Jones. It is made up of 400 industrial companies, 40 public utilities, 20 transportation companies, and 40 financial institutions. As a result, many people believe that Standard & Poor's Index provides a representative measure of market activity.

NYSE Composite Index

The NYSE Composite Index includes all common stocks listed on the New York Stock Ex-

The Dow Jones Averages®

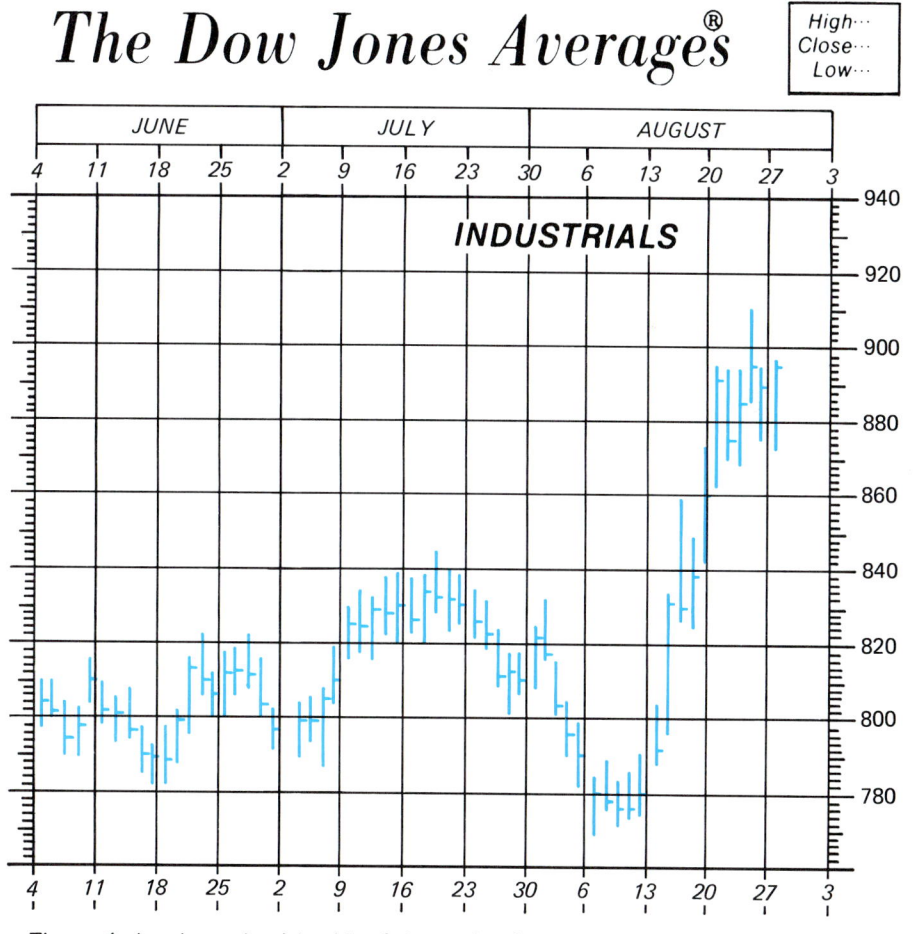

Figure 19-7

The Dow Jones Industrial Average

Source: Reprinted by permission of *The Wall Street Journal*, © Dow Jones & Company, Inc., 1982. All Rights Reserved.

The vertical scale on the right side of the graph refers to the value of the Dow Jones. The horizontal scale refers to time. Each of the little vertical lines across the graph represents the high, low, and closing value of the Dow Jones for that day. To illustrate, on August 27, 1982, the high for the Dow Jones was 896; the low, 873; and the closing value, 893.

Check today's *Wall Street Journal* to see where the Dow Jones stood at the close of trading yesterday.

change. It was developed in 1966 partially because investors did not believe that the Dow Jones reflected market activity. The base value for this index was set at 50, which approximated the average NYSE stock price for 1966. In February of 1983, the index stood at 86. In other words, the average stock on the New York Stock Exchange had risen 36 points, or 72 percent, since the index was first reported.

ASE Market Value Index

The ASE Market Value Index is made up of the stocks listed on the American Stock Exchange. Its base value is 100. Since the index was first reported in 1973, it has fallen to as low as 58 and has risen to as high as 361. The volatility of this index in comparison to the NYSE Composite Index reflects the dramatic stock price changes that occur on the American Stock Exchange.

SUMMARY POINTS

1. When firms use the securities markets as a source of new capital, they are using the primary market.
2. Investment banks underwrite the sale of new stock and bond issues.
3. The term "secondary market" is the name given to security trading among investors.
4. The six objectives of a personal investment program are safety of principal, liquidity, stability of income stream, maintenance of purchasing power, appreciation in stock value, and freedom from care.
5. The two national stock exchanges are the New York Stock Exchange and the American Stock Exchange.
6. The stocks of many smaller companies are traded on the regional stock exchanges or on the over-the-counter market.
7. In a stock exchange, the prices of stocks are determined in a double-auction manner: Buyers and sellers converge at a trading area on the floor of the exchange and bid on the price of the stock of interest.
8. The price of stocks in the secondary market is determined through buyer demand and seller supply.
9. Three different types of stock orders are market order, limit order, and stop order. The commission broker, or sometimes a trading specialist or an odd-lot broker, is the one who carries out the order on the floor of the exchange.
10. Stock trading is typically conducted in round lots of 100. Odd lots refer to transactions involving fewer than 100 shares.
11. Stockbrokers are generally either full-service brokers or discount brokers. The former offer many more services to investors, but they also charge a much higher fee.
12. Three speculative trading tactics are selling short, buying on the margin, and trading on the options market.
13. When investors trade on the margin, they buy stock with money borrowed from their brokers.
14. A stock option gives its holder the right to buy or sell a named stock at its current market price for a certain period of time. An option to buy a stock is a call; an option to sell is a put.
15. A mutual fund is an open-end trust, managed by an investment expert, in which investors pool their money for the purpose of acquiring a variety of stocks, bonds, and other securities.
16. Money market funds are made up of short-term government notes, commercial paper, and negotiable certificates of deposit.
17. Four of the most widely quoted stock market indicators are the Dow Jones Industrial Average, Standard & Poor's 500 Index, the NYSE Composite Index, and the ASE Market Value Index.

KEY TERMS AND CONCEPTS

primary market
investment banks
secondary market
speculators
diversification
liquidity
stock exchange
over-the-counter market
post trading
stockbroker
commission broker

market order
limit order
stop order
round lots
odd lots
full-service brokers
discount brokers
selling short
buying on the margin
option
call

put	bond fund
mutual fund	stock fund
closed-end trust	specialty funds
open-end trust	growth funds
load fund	money market funds
no-load fund	stock market indicators

REVIEW QUESTIONS

1. What is the difference between the primary market and the secondary market regarding common stock?
2. What is the role of investment bankers in the sale of common stock?
3. What is meant by liquidity? What types of investments are the most liquid and the least liquid?
4. What is the role of regional stock exchanges in our economy?
5. What is the over-the-counter market?
6. Explain the difference between a limit order and a stop order.
7. How do investors make money by selling short? Is selling short very risky? Why or why not?
8. Why is buying on the margin so risky?
9. What is the difference between a closed-end trust and an open-end trust?
10. Why do some experts say that the Dow Jones Industrial Average does not represent stock market activity accurately?

DISCUSSION QUESTIONS

1. What are the six objectives of a personal investment program? Which one would be the most important to you?
2. What is the main reason why many investors diversify their holdings? If you had a million dollars and wanted to invest it, would you diversify or not?
3. How important are trading specialists in the buying and selling of stocks? What risks do they take?
4. Would you rather do business with a regular stockbroker or with a discount stockbroker? Explain.
5. How do speculators make money by trading on the options market?
6. What, in your opinion, are the big advantages and disadvantages of mutual fund investments?

CASE 19-1

General Electric

Ordinarily, people assume that the stock of a company that performs well in the marketplace and gives good and reliable returns on stockholders' investments will be valued highly. But that isn't always the case.

Consider General Electric. General Electric has an AAA bond rating (the best). Its earnings exceed $1.6 billion each year, and it pays 44 percent of its profits after taxes as dividends. To keep it healthy in an unstable economy, GE maintains almost $1.5 billion in cash and marketable securities. All these numbers mean that General Electric has been performing very well indeed.

Even more important, GE is huge. It is involved in many industries in the country: railroad locomotives, transistors and integrated circuits, robots, electric cars, equipment for space flights, submarine electronic guidance equipment, and light bulbs. General Electric owns timber land, vast coal and oil reserves, and large pieces of property in most major cities in the United States. All in all, GE owns enough of everything that when one part of the economy falls, some other part is still in good shape and holds up GE's earnings. Through 70 years and two recessions, GE has never failed to improve on its earnings ratio.

Oddly enough, however, people won't buy GE stock. The size that makes GE so stable and so productive in bad times means that GE can't rebound in spectacular fashion when the economy is good. Consequently, too many investors apparently believe that GE is so big that it is only capable of following the trends of the national economy.

Investors should realize, though, that stocks are valued in two ways: on the basis of expected returns and on the basis of risk. GE management has chosen to foster stability (that is, low risk) at the expense of high (if erratic) returns. This stability policy has paid off so well that GE now actually pays better than average returns, and does so with less risk than other companies with similar returns.

Smart investors are realizing that companies like GE, with very stable track records and good earnings, manage to do what an investor tries to do with a number of different stocks—diversify your risk so that you lose a little of your expected return but increase the probability that you will receive those returns on time.

1. What are the features that characterize GE that investors use to determine the value of GE stock?
2. In a high-inflation era with unstable stock markets, such as the late 1970s and early 1980s, what traits do you think investors would (or should) value in a company? How do you think GE has let them down?
3. What was *your* initial impression of GE (before you read this case)? How would you have valued GE stock, based on your feelings?
4. What could GE's management do to increase the price of the firm's stock?

CASE 19-2

Cessna Aircraft Company

Cessna Aircraft Company is a respected and long-established manufacturer of airplanes intended for personal or company use. Although small, these aircraft are still quite expensive—usually over $100,000 apiece. Nonetheless, many individuals and companies have for years purchased Cessna aircraft for ease of transportation.

In the early 1980s, however, several events occurred that placed a severe strain on Cessna Aircraft. The combination of high fuel prices and an economic recession made people unwilling to pay the costs of flying private airplanes, which were often less fuel-efficient than the new commercial jets. Several crashes had cast private air flight in a bad light, and many corporations were forbidding their chief executives to fly private planes. As more companies and individuals stopped flying private planes, a large market in used private aircraft developed, further hampering Cessna's attempts to sell new planes. Finally, airline deregulation lowered air fares on many routes so that commercial air travel was cheaper than flying private planes. The last blow came when airport air controllers staged a strike. When the federal government replaced the striking controllers, airports were forced to limit the air traffic allowed, which curtailed the use of private planes.

By 1981, Cessna was hurting badly. The company was unable to make enough profit to pay dividends to its investors, and at the same time keep enough cash to maintain the health of the company. Cessna therefore decided, on a one-time-only basis, to omit dividends and pay the money back into the company to tide it through the recession.

1. Would failure to pay dividends affect the market price of Cessna's stock? Why or why not?
2. Do you think that an investor would think differently of foregoing dividends if the company was healthy? What part do you think irrational emotional feelings play in valuing a company after a dividend payment is skipped?

3. How would valuation of a company on the basis of its dividend payments differ if you were holding the stock for short-term profits rather than for long-term gains?
4. If you were a mutual fund purchasing Cessna stock for your stock portfolio, would you be prompted to sell this stock after it fails to pay a dividend? Why?

20

Risk Management and Insurance

After studying this chapter, you should be able to:

- Define risk and discuss four risk management techniques.
- Describe the five key principles of insurance.
- Identify the two sources of insurance.
- Discuss property insurance, liability insurance, loss-of-earning-power insurance, employee insurance, and life insurance.

The need for people to protect their homes against fire loss became painfully evident in 1666. In that year, a fire in London destroyed 14,000 buildings and left more than 200,000 people homeless. The first fire insurance company was formed the next year. In the United States, Benjamin Franklin started the first successful fire insurance company in 1752. The company is still in existence. Today, we can buy insurance to protect ourselves against many such calamities.

RISK MANAGEMENT

Risk is defined as the uncertainty of loss. Risk is the possibility that events will not turn out the way that we want them to. We all face risk every day. When Oscar tries to register for a college course, he faces risk: The course might be full and he cannot take it. When Alicia drives to work or school, she faces the risk that another driver will hit her.

Anticipated risk is not a problem. For example, to cover the cost of spoilage, supermarkets charge a little extra for their vegetables. This reduces operating risk by building in some additional profit margin. Unanticipated risk, however, exposes the individual or company to possible financial loss.

As a prelude to our discussion of risk management and insurance, let's identify two basic forms of risk—pure risk and speculative risk.[1] Understanding the difference between the two is important because insurance companies protect against only one of them.

Pure Risk

Pure risk characterizes situations in which the only possible outcomes are loss or no loss. There is no possibility of gain *per se*. When a person buys a house, there is a chance that the house will be destroyed by fire, a burglar will break in and steal the furniture, or a windstorm will blow out all the windows. All of these possibilities are examples of pure risk. There is no way that the homeowner can reasonably gain from any of these misfortunes. Insurance companies are prepared to protect people against this sort of risk.

Speculative Risk

Speculative risk involves both a possibility of loss as well as of gain. It is the risk of either making money or losing it. Gambling is the classic example of speculative risk. Mike bets his friend Sally that the Washington Redskins will beat the Dallas Cowboys in the big football game. The bet is $10 and the odds are even. Mike is risking a loss of $10 in the hope of winning $10.

The introduction of a new product also involves a great deal of speculative risk. The product could either be very popular or a total failure. The entrepreneur accepts the risk because of the possibility of making money.

Insurance companies will not protect people or businesses against speculative risk. When DuPont introduced Corfam, an artificial leather for shoes, many people believed that the product was going to be a big success. The leather industry responded with the slogan: "Naturally you prefer leather; that's why they're trying to imitate it." DuPont also experienced production problems with Corfam, and buyers of Corfam shoes complained that the shoes did not breathe or adjust to the buyers' feet. The result was that Corfam technology failed, and DuPont lost nearly $100 million.[2] Insurance companies do not insure against this type of loss; too many things can go wrong for an insurance company to accept the speculative risk involved with new product introduction.

Managing Pure Risk

The rest of the chapter is concerned exclusively with pure risk, that is, risks that are insurable. There are four ways a person or firm can manage pure risk.

Risk Reduction. One way to manage pure risk is to reduce it. A family concerned about the risk of burglary can take several steps to reduce it before leaving on a trip. The family can stop delivery of newspapers and mail, lock the house securely, ask neighbors to watch the house, and plug several lights into a timer so that they come on at night and give the house a lived-in look.

Self-Insurance. Another way to reduce risk is to put money aside each month to pay for unexpected losses. Instead of buying fire insurance, a business firm could deposit money into a savings account. This would establish a fund to pay for losses in the event of a fire. Although some people and businesses do insure themselves in this manner, it is not a good protection against risk, as we'll soon see.

---

[1] Emmett J. Vaughan and Curtis M. Elliott, *Fundamentals of Risk and Insurance* (2d ed.: Santa Barbara: Wiley Hamilton, 1978), p. 11.

[2] Robert F. Hartley, *Marketing Mistakes* (Columbus, Ohio: Grid Publishing, Inc., 1981), pp. 132-134.

Now that's a "risky" situation.

Current Income. Some people and organizations decide to pay for losses out of current income rather than out of a special account or fund. For example, most states do not insure their office buildings against fire or wind damage. If a fire destroyed a state building, the state legislature would simply appropriate money for a new building. A private firm could replace a truck destroyed in an accident with a new one. This is probably the least satisfactory way to manage pure risk, especially when the potential loss is great.

Insurance. Many people and business firms choose insurance as the way to protect themselves against risk. Even with insurance, however, there is still the risk that fire will destroy the business, or that a firm's delivery truck will slide into a ditch. What the insurance company does do, within the limits of the policy issued, is reimburse the owners for all or part of their losses.

PRINCIPLES OF INSURANCE

The insurance business is based on a set of five principles. Insurance companies have learned that if they follow these principles, they can avoid such major financial problems as losing money for shareholders or not being able to pay off a policyholder in the event of a loss. Let's look at each of these five principles.

Law of Large Numbers

The first principle of insurance is the **law of large numbers**. This law allows insurance companies to predict the probability that a particular loss-causing event will occur. The event could be flood, hurricane, or death. Insurance companies, from statistical or actuarial tables, know roughly how many houses will burn down this year in the United States and how many automobile accidents will occur in a particular city.

Table 20-1 demonstrates the law of large numbers. Insurance companies do not know how long each of us will live, but they do know about how many deaths will occur per 1,000 people in a given year. They also know the life expectancy of people in different age brackets. As the table shows, only 1.74 out of 1,000 people who are 19 years old will die this year. In addition, the average person this age will live 51.28 more years. This type of information allows insurance companies to set rates for life insurance policies in such a way that the companies can make a profit.

Definite and Measurable Risk

Insurance companies protect against measurable losses that result directly from a specific event, such as a collision with another car or the theft of a car from a firm's fleet. Insurance protection does not apply to losses that occur gradually over time, such as the gradual loss in value resulting from the daily operation of a company car.

Insurance companies also need to know when the loss occurred and the extent of loss involved. In the case of an automobile accident, the company must know the time of the accident and the estimated cost of repairing or replacing the damaged vehicle.

Accidental Loss

The loss must be something that may or may not happen. That is, it must be accidental. If an insurance company knows that a house is going to burn down, it will not insure it against fire loss. To do this, it would have to charge a premium large enough to pay for both the house and the cost of administering the insurance program.

Loss Not Subject to Catastrophic Hazard

Insurance companies expect losses to occur, and they expect to pay some money to the people they insure. They do not expect to pay everyone at once. Therefore, they spread risk so that no single disaster forces them to pay all their clients at the same time. Many insurance companies have violated this principle and have paid dearly for doing so. For example, a tornado may destroy all the houses in a five-block area, or a hurricane may wipe out an entire city. If one company insured all the houses in the affected area, it would suffer an extremely large loss. In fact, the company might not have enough money to pay all the loss claims.

Insurable Interests

Finally, buyers of insurance policies must show that they would suffer financial loss from an accident of the type covered by the policy. Let's say Mr. Jones wants to insure Ms. Smith's house against fire, naming himself as the beneficiary of the policy. Mr. Jones would not suffer a loss if Ms. Smith's house burned down, but, in fact, would profit from the insurance policy. He might even be tempted to set Ms. Smith's house on fire to obtain the insurance money. An insurance company would not issue such a policy. The only accidents that are insurable are those that would cause the policyholder a real financial loss.[3]

SOURCES OF INSURANCE

The two basic sources of insurance are the federal government and private insurance companies. We'll begin our discussion by looking at the federal government, the largest source of insurance in the United States.

Federal Government

The federal government provides two basic types of insurance. First, it offers voluntary in-

---

[3]Vaughan and Elliott, p. 151.

Figure 20-1

Mortality Table

Source: Commissioners Standard Ordinary Table, *Life Insurance Fact Book, 1978* (Washington: American Council of Life Insurance, 1978), p. 108.

Age	Deaths Per 1,000	Expectation of Life-Years	Deaths Per 1,000	Expectation of Life-Years	Age
0	7.08	68.30	9.11	22.82	51
1	1.76	67.78	9.96	22.03	52
2	1.52	66.90	10.89	21.25	53
3	1.46	66.00	11.90	20.47	54
4	1.40	65.10	13.00	19.71	55
5	1.35	64.19	14.21	18.97	56
6	1.30	63.27	15.54	18.23	57
7	1.26	62.35	17.00	17.51	58
8	1.23	61.43	18.59	16.81	59
9	1.21	60.51	20.34	16.12	60
10	1.21	59.58	22.24	15.44	61
11	1.23	58.65	24.31	14.78	62
12	1.26	57.72	26.57	14.14	63
13	1.32	56.80	29.04	13.51	64
14	1.39	55.87	31.75	12.90	65
15	1.46	54.95	34.74	12.31	66
16	1.54	54.03	38.04	11.78	67
17	1.62	53.11	41.68	11.17	68
18	1.69	52.19	45.61	10.64	69
19	1.74	51.28	49.79	10.12	70
20	1.79	50.37	54.15	9.63	71
21	1.83	49.46	58.65	9.16	72
22	1.86	48.55	63.26	8.69	73

surance programs to U.S. citizens. These programs provide protection against floods, damage to farm crops from drought or hail, and nuclear accidents. Figure 20-1 outlines several types of voluntary insurance programs offered by the government.

The federal government also provides insurance that many people are required to purchase. The most important example of required insurance is **social security**. Today, social security provides more protection to more people than any other type of insurance. More than 34 million people receive monthly social security benefit checks.

Benefits. When social security was begun, its primary aim was to provide income to retired workers. The amount of money each person received was based on the worker's previous average

Program	Protection
Federal Crop Insurance Corporation (1938)	Protects the farmer's income by reducing losses from natural disasters. Insures 23 commodities from drought, flood, hail, insects, frost, and disease.
Federal Flood Insurance (1968)	Protects homes and small businesses against floods. Protection limited to $35,000 for a single-family home and $10,000 for a business.
Federal Home Mortgage Loan Insurance (1934)	Protects private savings and loans and banks from loss resulting from default on the part of the borrower. The program promotes home ownership by encouraging loans.
Federal Crime Insurance (1970)	Protects businesses and homes against burglary, robbery, and theft other than auto. Available only in states where there is a shortage of crime insurance at affordable rates.
Nuclear Energy Liability Insurance (1957)	Provides liability coverage to power companies for nuclear accidents. Maximum coverage is $560 million with $140 million deductible.
Post Office	Provides protection against the loss of mail. The post office sells loss insurance on registered mail, parcel post, and express mail.
Medical Insurance (Medicare, 1979)	Provides people 65 years of age and older with medical insurance. It covers physicians' services, diagnostic x-ray and laboratory tests, ambulance services, surgical dressing, splints, and rental of medical equipment.

Figure 20-1

Selected Voluntary Federal Insurance Programs

CONTROVERSIAL ISSUES

Legislators have suggested that the federal government create a national health insurance program, funded from taxes and taxpayer contributions, to ensure that everyone is guaranteed protection from extensive medical bills. Is such national health insurance the best choice?

Health Insurance Should Be Nationalized.

Pro

Yes, health insurance should be nationalized. A major risk faced by Americans today is how to cover the costs of massive medical treatments for injury or disease. Medical costs have reached unreasonable levels, and medical insurance has risen to cover those costs. Many people spend more on health insurance than they save for retirement!

We must either lower medical costs themselves or lower the costs of insuring for them. To lower medical costs, the only likely approach would be to nationalize (or socialize) medical care. People disagree as to how efficient this remedy has been in countries where it has been tried. And there would be serious constitutional questions about the legality of socialized medicine. So we are left with reducing the cost of insuring for medical costs.

Health insurance could be handled very efficiently and quite economically by the federal government. Premiums could be taken from paychecks along with Social Security taxes and income taxes. Consistent premiums could be charged across the country, so that older people would not be charged more for insurance than they can afford and so that poor-risk individuals do not have to forego health insurance. National health insurance could be a powerful social-policy tool, since it could be used, for example, to penalize cigarette smoking. It could be used to provide part of the aid required in natural disasters, and could include special insurance clauses for drug or alcohol rehabilitation. The poor and unemployed could be covered by national health insurance, with the government picking up some or all of the costs.

Health insurance taxes would be collected to pay for expenses incurred at the same point in time, while Social Security taxes have to be collected to pay for expenses the government incurs often after many years. In an era of erratic economic changes and rampant inflation, a national health insurance program would never face the prospects of deficits that Social Security now faces. Yes, national health insurance is a good idea.

Con

Nationalized health insurance is potentially dangerous. Of course, health insurance is of vast importance to Americans. But consider the power the government would have over individuals by controlling their health insurance. Government has cut food stamps to the poor, eliminated aid to public schools, and removed countless programs for the poor. What happens to individuals if government slashes national health insurance coverage?

And what happens to the countless people who have spent millions of dollars on private company-directed health insurance programs? Many companies have health insurance programs that have accumulated substantial funds to pay off claims. What happens to these monies, and who gets compensated when the money is returned?

Further, although national health insurance won't face the same dangers from inflation that Social Security does, it still is just as prone to abuse. Consider the scandals surrounding Medicare. Who is to guarantee that a national health insurance program won't be corrupted like most other governmental welfare and social care systems have been? Mismanagement or fraudulent use of funds would require additional tax support of the health insurance program, and then everyone would have to pay more.

Let's keep government out of the health insurance business. It cannot handle what it already has to do, and health insurance is too important to have it botched up the way Social Security has been. In the end, national health insurance will cost more money and might cost us some of our valuable freedoms. Let's keep things the way they are.

monthly earnings. Now, to protect the elderly against inflation, the government increases the size of benefits if annual inflation exceeds a certain percentage. In 1981, the maximum monthly benefit for a single retired worker was $534.70; for a family, $935.70.

The social security program also provides insurance to workers between the ages of 50 and 64 who become disabled. In the case of death, retirement benefits transfer to the surviving spouse. The most significant change in social security was Medicare which began in 1979. As of that date, the social security program began to pay most hospital bills for people 65 years of age or older.

Costs. Social security has become a very expensive program. At first, it was financed by a 1 percent tax on each worker's first $3,000 of annual earnings. The employer paid a matching amount for each employee. The percentage and the base have since been increased many times. As we saw in Chapter 6, the base income increased to $35,700 in 1983. Table 20-2 shows the social security tax rates for 1980-1983 and the estimated rates for 1984-1985.

Private Insurance Companies

Private insurance companies can be either stock companies or mutual companies. Both types offer a variety of insurance.

Stock Companies. Stock insurance companies are organized to provide insurance for policyholders and profit for stockholders. Stock companies operate very much as other private companies do. If profitable, they pay a dividend to their stockholders; if unprofitable, their stockholders bear the loss.

The major difference between stock insurance companies and most other private companies is that the former are highly regulated by state insurance laws and agencies. Each state decides how much money insurance companies operating within their jurisdiction must have available to pay losses. Most states permit stock companies to sell all types of insurance except life and health insurance.

Mutual Companies. Mutual insurance companies are nonprofit corporations owned by the insur-

Table 20-2

Social Security Tax Rates, 1980-1985

Year	Taxable Wage Maximum	Percentage Tax Rate Paid by Both Employer and Employee[1]	Maximum Amount of Tax Due Per Worker, Payable by the Employer and by the Employee
1980	$25,900	6.13	$1,587.67
1981	29,700	6.65	1,975.05
1982	32,400	6.70	2,170.80
1983	35,700	6.70	2,391.90
1984	38,100[2]	7.00	2,667.00
1985	39,600[2]	7.05	2,793.00

[1] Includes Old Age Security Insurance (OASI), Disability Insurance, and Health Insurance.

[2] Estimate subject to Congressional action or automatic increase based on new inflation forecasts.

The taxable wage maximum refers to the maximum amount on which a worker's social security tax obligation is figured. For workers with taxable incomes of $35,700 or more in 1983, the taxable wage maximum times the percentage tax rate equals the amount of tax payable by the employer *and* by the employee. This amount is shown in the last column. For workers earning less than $35,700, the amount of tax due equals taxable income times the percentage tax rate. Tax obligations for other years are figured in the same way.

Source: Social Security Administration, *Social Security Bulletin, Annual Statistical Supplement, 1981* (November, 1982), p. 29.

ance policyholders. There are no stockholders. The policyholders elect a board of directors which manages the company.

When a mutual company has revenue in excess of its costs, it pays a dividend to its policyholders, reduces the costs of insurance premiums, or keeps the money for company expansion. When a mutual company does not have enough money to meet its expenses or to pay losses, the law allows the company to collect an assessment from policyholders to offset company losses.

TYPES OF INSURANCE

Insurance can be classified in many ways. We have divided insurance into five categories: property, liability, loss of earning power, employee, and life. Figure 20-2 describes the protection provided by each type of insurance.

Property Insurance

It would be very risky for a business to operate without adequate property insurance. Some businesses probably could not operate at all. What kinds of property insurance are there?

Fire. The New York Standard Fire Policy of 1943 is now used in nearly all states. It has been widely adopted because it is so easily understood. Before the adoption of this standard, fire insurance policies were written specially for each client. The result was that policies were very complex, often understandable only by legal experts.

A fire policy protects the insured building and its contents against financial loss caused by fire. The more risk underwritten by the fire insurance company, the more expensive the policy. A wooden building without a sprinkler system costs more to insure than a brick building with a sprinkler system.

Fire insurance does not cover losses resulting from fire intentionally started by the owner of the building. Of late, there has been an unfortunate tendency for the owners of failing businesses to "sell the building back to the insurance company"—that is, to burn it down for the insurance money. Insurance experts believe that arson may be responsible for as many as 37 percent of all business-related fires.

The standard fire policy also has three other exclusions. The fire policy does not cover new, potentially risky plant additions if the insurance company has not been previously informed of them. Fire insurance does not protect against losses to a building left vacant for 60 days or more. And it does not protect against a fire caused by explosion or riot.

Extended Coverage. Fire insurance is the basic business property insurance policy. But it is also possible to "extend" a fire insurance policy to protect against other risks. Extended coverage protects a building and its contents against windstorm, hail, explosion, smoke, civil strife, riot resulting from a strike, and damage from aircraft, automobiles, and trucks. The firm's cost of protecting itself against those risks with an extended policy is much less than if a policy for each were purchased individually.

Marine. The two types of marine insurance are ocean marine and inland marine. Ocean marine is the oldest form of insurance, and it protects ship owners against damage to the ship and its cargo. Inland marine insurance has very little to do with ships. Rather, it protects against damage to property being transported by ship, truck, or train. Most moveable property can be protected by inland marine insurance.

What types of losses are covered by marine policies?

Policy	Protects Against
Property	
Fire	Losses to building and contents from fire.
Extended Coverage	Losses to building and contents from nine major risks, including windstorm, hail, and civil commotion.
Marine	Losses to ships and property being moved from one place to another.
Automobile	Damages to people and property from automobile accidents.
Burglary, Robbery and Theft	Losses from crimes involving either employees or nonemployees.
Liability	
Public Liability	Losses relating to the ownership and maintenance of property and the acts of a company's employees.
Product/Service	Damage from products or services purchased by consumers.
Loss of Earning Power	
Business Interruption	Losses from not being able to sell a product because of some extraordinary event.
Extra Expense	The high cost of keeping a business operating after a major accident has occurred.
Rain	Losses resulting from rain.
Employee	
Fidelity Bonds	Losses resulting from dishonest employees.
Workers' Compensation	Accidents to employees or work-related diseases.
Health	Expenses related to the loss of health.
Disability Income	Loss of income resulting from illness, disease, or injury.
Life	
Term Insurance	Losses from premature death.
Whole Life	Losses from premature death, and creates a cash value for the insured.
Endowment Life	Losses from premature death, and creates a retirement fund.
Universal Life	Losses from premature death, and creates a variable rate cash value for the insured.

Figure 20-2

Types of Insurance

Automobile. There are nearly 25 million automobile accidents each year in the United States. These accidents result in 50,000 deaths, 5 million injuries, and $60 billion in losses. There are many types of automobile insurance available.

1. Bodily injury liability: provides money to protect the policyholder against claims from injuries to pedestrians, passengers, or people in other cars. The protection applies to the owner of the car or to anyone else driving the car with the owner's permission.
2. Medical payments insurance: covers medical expenses resulting from an automobile accident injury. This insurance protects the policyholder, family members living at home, and any guest riding in the car.
3. Uninsured motorist coverage: pays the owner of the car and any family member for medical expenses resulting from an accident caused by an uninsured motorist or a hit-and-run driver.
4. Property damage liability: pays the cost of damage, resulting from an auto accident, to other people's property. This coverage applies not only to other cars but also to other property, such as lamp posts, telephone poles, and buildings. Most states require that all drivers carry liability insurance.
5. Collision insurance: pays for damage to the policyholder's car in the event of an accident. Such damage may result from a collision with another car, a collision with a building or house, or from rolling the car over. Collision insurance is normally sold with a deductible of from $100 to $500. This means that the policyholder pays the first $100 to $500 in damages, and the insurance company pays the rest. If the other driver is at fault, then his or her company pays for damages suffered. In this case, the driver not at fault is totally reimbursed for the cost of repairing the car.
6. Comprehensive insurance: covers expenses resulting from the theft of an automobile. It also pays for damages resulting from fire, glass breakage, falling objects, explosion, earthquake, windstorm, flood, and vandalism. Comprehensive insurance is normally sold with a $50 to $250 deductible.[4]
7. No-fault insurance: a new type of automobile insurance which developed in response to the high costs of automobile insurance. Under no-fault insurance, the parties to an accident recover their medical and hospital expenses and any losses in income (resulting from the accident) from their own insurance companies. Medical and related expenses are paid to each person by his or her insurance company regardless of who was at fault. Expensive litigation is therefore avoided. No-fault laws vary from state to state. The states shown in Figure 20-3 have adopted no-fault insurance, while six more have passed some form of limited no-fault automobile insurance.

Burglary, Robbery, and Theft. Crime is a major problem in the United States. It is also a very expensive problem. As Figure 20-4 shows, crime increased to near epidemic levels during the 1970s. **Burglary**, defined as forced entry, increased 43 percent during this period, while **robbery**, defined as the taking of property by force, increased 29.5 percent. Automobile theft was up 8 percent.

---

[4]James R. Marks, *Sharing the Risk* (New York: Insurance Information Institute, 1981), pp. 13-14.

Figure 20-3

No-Fault Automobile Insurance States

Source: *Insurance Facts 1981/1982* (New York: Insurance Information Institute, 1982), pp. 67-68.

(Limited)	Arkansas		Minnesota
	Colorado	(Limited)	New Hampshire
	Connecticut		New Jersey
	Delaware		New York
	Florida		North Dakota
	Georgia	(Limited)	Oregon
	Hawaii		Pennsylvania
	Kansas	(Limited)	South Carolina
	Kentucky	(Limited)	South Dakota
(Limited)	Maryland	(Limited)	Texas
	Massachusetts		Utah
	Michigan	(Limited)	Virginia

Figure 20-4

The Grim Statistics of Crime

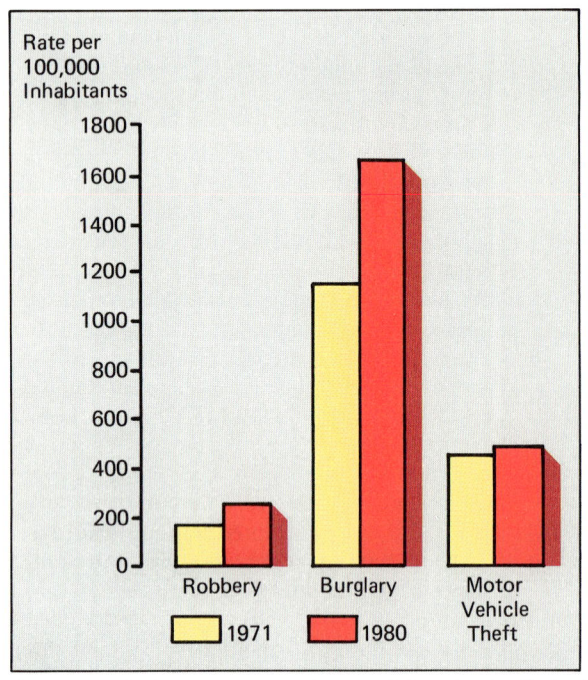

Source: U.S. Department of Justice, *Crime in the United States* (Washington: U.S. Government Printing Office, 1982).

Financial institutions—banks and savings and loan associations—purchase what is called a **banker's blanket bond**. This protects the financial institution from losses resulting from employee fraud or dishonesty as well as from robbery, burglary, and theft. Retail stores and other non-financial institutions purchase different forms of crime insurance, depending on their needs. However, any business dealing with money, securities, or other valuable assets needs adequate insurance against crime.

Liability Insurance

An important risk for all businesses is loss resulting from legal liability for harm to an individual. A business's employees are protected through workers' compensation, which will be discussed later in the chapter. But, a firm also needs to protect itself against damage claims filed by the public. For example, on May 25, 1979, a DC-10 jetliner lost an engine as it took off from Chicago's O'Hare International Airport. The plane crashed, killing 274 people. It may be 1990 before damage suits totaling $100 million are settled. Even for a company the size of McDonnell Douglas, the manufacturer of the DC-10 aircraft, $100 million is a lot of money. Thus, aircraft companies insure themselves against such disasters.

Before we explore the concept of liability further, let's identify two forms of liability—public liability and product, or service, liability. Both can be covered by a comprehensive, general liability insurance policy.

Public Liability. This covers the normal forms of business risk: typically, the ownership and maintenance of property. If a customer in a retail store stumbles on torn carpeting and breaks a leg, the retailer is usually held responsible for the injury. The retailer must pay all medical expenses, and possibly monetary damages to compensate for the "pain and suffering" experienced by the injured person as a result of the fall. Public liability also relates to the conduct of a firm's employees. That is, the firm is responsible for any damage caused by one of its workers.

Product or Service Liability. Until a few years ago, manufacturers were held responsible only for product defects and breaches of warranty. Today, courts hold manufacturers liable for product safety even when the victim contributes to the injury.[5] Not long ago, a manufacturer was sued successfully for $111,000 when one of its products caught on fire. The product was roofing primer. The trouble started when a user of the product heated it over a fire. This "thinning" procedure was not recommended by the manufacturer. The court ruled that the manufacturer was liable for damages suffered by the user because it did not print a warning that the roof primer would release explosive gases when heated.[6]

An individual offering a service is responsible for correctly and properly administering that service. A doctor cannot provide medical services without liability protection. A misdiagnosis could cost hundreds of thousands of dollars in lawsuits. And doctors are not alone in this regard. Other

---
[5]Marks, p. 78.

[6]*Panther Oil & Grease Mfg. Co. v. Segerstrom*, 224 Fed. 2d 216.

Profile—
Robert A. Beck

When people speak of insurance companies, "the Pru"—the Prudential Insurance Company of America—is usually the first name mentioned. The largest insurance company in the world, it insures more than 50 million people through more than 24,000 agents. With $450 billion of life insurance in force and assets of $62.5 billion, the Pru increases its assets by more each year than many other companies might hope to claim throughout their lifetimes.

The chief executive officer of Prudential is Robert A. Beck. Born in 1925 in New York City, Beck became an officer in the famed 82nd Airborne Division during World War II. He was injured during a parachute jump and became the insurance officer for his division, responsible for selling government-sponsored life insurance. His is the story of an insurance agent who made it to the top.

Beck became a full-time agent with the Pru in 1951. He spent the next 20 years in 15 towns selling Prudential life insurance policies, first as an agent, then as agency manager, and finally as a director of agencies in Prudential's South-Central Regional Home Office in Jacksonville, Florida. In 1963, he became an executive general manager at Prudential's headquarters in Newark, New Jersey. In 1965 he became a vice president, then a senior vice president only a year later. In 1974, he became the company's president, and in 1978, chairman of the board and chief executive officer.

Today, Beck is a perfect example of an insurance company chairman. Having made his way up through the ranks, he is highly regarded within Prudential. Beck keeps in close touch with his company and its employees at all times. He does a great deal of his paperwork in his car on the way to and from work. Demand for his time is so great that his appointment schedule is often booked months in advance.

Beck is renowned for his understanding when agents fall into slumps, having suffered an eight-week slump of his own when he couldn't sell a single policy. He knows how devastating such times can be. Consequently, his agents and managers all feel that Beck is solidly behind them and aware of their needs and expectations.

Early in his career, Beck knew that he wanted to be head of Prudential. He had always liked the feeling of being with the best team, whether it was the 82nd Airborne or Prudential, and he believed in both himself and his talent. Through his work, he has helped Prudential become one of the most famous and highly respected insurance companies in the world.

Despite his 16-hour work days, Beck still manages to make time for himself and his family. Beck fishes, scuba dives, plays golf, and is a good bridge player and dancer. In fact, he'll try almost anything. He once tried hang gliding, but when his own company refused to issue him more life insurance and showed him the statistics on hang gliding accidents, he agreed to give up that sport.

As chairman of the Business Roundtable's Task Force on Social Security, Beck became acutely aware of the problems facing the United States as its population of older citizens rises dramatically. Thus, it was a logical decision for Beck to be chosen to serve on the National Commission on Social Security Reform in 1981. As a result of his association with this commission, Beck has emerged as one of the nation's premier spokespersons on the social security system, and is one of its staunchest supporters.

professionals, such as lawyers, accountants, insurance agents, CPAs, and even hairstylists, must carry liability insurance, too. One beauty salon had to pay $15,000 in damages because of injury to a customer's hair when a cold wave was applied incorrectly.[7]

Loss-of-Earning-Power Insurance

Many businesses buy insurance to protect themselves against loss-of-earning power because of some unusual event. An accident may occur which not only destroys the property of a business but also makes it impossible for the business to meet its regular expenses. The most common form of loss-of-earning-power insurance is business-interruption insurance. Let's take a closer look at this type of insurance, as well as extra-expense insurance and rain insurance.

Business-Interruption Insurance. Businesses face many types of risk. One type of risk, as mentioned above, is that uncontrollable events will temporarily disrupt a business's regular operations. The following example shows how business-interruption insurance protects a business.

Imagine a major strike at United States Steel. The strike causes a division of Ford Motor to stop the production of cars—no steel, no cars. In this situation, business-interruption insurance pays all of the Ford division's continuing expenses even though operations have halted. These expenses for Ford might include the cost of fire insurance, plant security, and lineworker layoffs. In addition, business-interruption insurance would pay Ford for the loss of normal profits. These are the profits that Ford would have made if there had not been a steel strike.

Extra-Expense Insurance. Certain businesses cannot afford to shut down when their facilities are destroyed or heavily damaged. Banks, newspapers, public utilities, oil dealers, and dairies must somehow continue to make their services available. Even a short-term shutdown of any one of these businesses would injure the public or mean the loss of most of its customers to a competitor.

Extra-expense insurance makes it possible for a business to meet the needs of the public even after its property has been severely damaged. Extra-expense insurance pays such expenses as the rent on temporary office space and office machines. It pays overtime allowances for employees working long hours to keep the business operating.

Rain Insurance. April showers bring May flowers, but they can also drown a firm's profits, no matter in which month the showers occur. Outdoor rock concerts, for example, depend on good weather for their success. Rain insurance protects the entrepreneur for a short period of time against financial losses resulting from sudden rainstorms. The insurance company does not usually pay the policyholder unless the local branch of the U.S. Weather Bureau verifies that at least one tenth of an inch of rain fell during the time the insurance was in effect.

Employee Insurance

Most business executives believe in the importance of holding employee insurance. This insurance not only protects the health and safety of employees but also protects the firm from dishonest employees.

Fidelity Bonds. Fidelity bonds protect an employer from losses resulting from a dishonest employee. They are particularly important for businesses handling a great deal of cash. The best example is a bank. However, even convenience stores, such as 7-Eleven or Stop-N-Go, purchase fidelity bonds because most of their transactions involve cash.

There are two types of fidelity bonds: individual and blanket. An **individual fidelity bond** protects a business against losses brought about by one or more specified individuals. A **blanket bond** protects the business against losses caused by any of its employees. With blanket bonds, the employee responsible for the theft need not be identified by name. Rather, in order for the business to collect on its policy, it must merely show that the loss suffered resulted from employee theft.

---

[7]*White v. Louis Creative Hair Dressers, Inc.*, 10 CCH Neg. 2d 526.

Workers' Compensation. Workers' compensation insurance protects employees from job-related accidents and disease. Today, all 50 states have workers' compensation laws on the books. Roughly nine out of ten people in the United States are covered by some form of workers' compensation insurance. Although the specific benefits vary from state to state, the following forms of protection are usually provided:

- Medical—payment for hospital, doctor, and other medical expenses.
- Disability—payments of lost income to an injured employee unable to work.
- Rehabilitation—payment of the cost of therapy designed to return the injured worker to the job.
- Survivor benefits—payment to surviving family members in the case of death resulting from a work-related accident or disease.[8]

Health Insurance. Many businesses offer their employees and families free health insurance, or at least an opportunity to buy health insurance at reduced rates. The importance of this benefit is obvious when we consider the rapidly rising costs of medical care and health insurance premiums. Between 1950 and 1970, the cost of health insurance went up 23 times. In 1980, total national health expenditures amounted to 9.4 percent of GNP, up from 4.4 percent in 1950.

A wide variety of health insurance plans are available. These plans cover most or all of the cost of hospitalization, surgical procedures, physician office visits, and diagnostic tests. Dental coverage is not offered on most policies.

[8]Marks, pp. 66-67.

Disability-Income Insurance. Another form of insurance is disability-income insurance. Unfortunately, most people in the United States do not have disability income insurance. Under this form of insurance, the issuing company pays all or part of a person's salary when that person is unable to work because of illness, disease, or injury. These policies offer a great deal of protection to the disabled worker's family. Most disability income plans pay the insured person for a specified number of years only, although lifetime protection can also be obtained.

Life Insurance

Some of the largest companies in the United States sell life insurance. Table 20-3 shows that the 15 largest life insurance companies have more than $2 trillion worth of life insurance in force. In addition, these 15 companies employ almost 300,000 people.

As Figure 20-5 on page 393 shows, the value of the average family's life insurance is about twice as great as its annual disposable income. Thus, if the primary wage earner in the family were to die, the family could live for two years on the insurance money.

Most families cannot afford to buy enough life insurance to protect themselves completely against the loss of income resulting from the death of the primary wage earner. To help provide adequate coverage many firms offer their employees the opportunity to purchase some form of life insurance through group plans. In families where both parties have well-paying jobs, complete protection may be less important.

FROM THE FILE

It had been a real struggle, but about two months ago, Wendell led the employees of Sunny Day Lawn Furniture Company in a successful attempt to unionize the plant. As the new shop steward, Wendell was responsible for negotiating the terms of a company insurance policy that would most appeal to company employees. On the other side of the bargaining table, the management of Sunny Day wanted provisions that would protect the company from losses resulting from the actions of employees or the union. Wendell and the head of the union local decided to visit an insurance consultant. On the way there, they tried to figure out which kind of coverage would be best for Sunny Day's employees.

Table 20-3

The 15 Largest Life Insurance Companies, 1981

Company	Assets	Premium & Annuity Income ($000)	Life Insurance in Force ($000)	Number of Employees
Prudential	$62,498,540	$9,935,180	$456,174,632	62,817
Metropolitan	51,757,845	5,131,318	393,590,726	44,000
Equitable Life Assurance	36,758,160	2,400,771	223,874,676	26,485
Aetna Life	25,158,904	4,440,322	163,873,853	16,690
New York Life	21,041,380	2,637,020	137,456,394	18,755
John Hancock Mutual	19,936,798	2,425,567	145,609,204	20,424
Connecticut General Life	15,103,332	2,810,410	90,809,773	14,909
Travelers	14,803,168	4,399,880	116,498,216	41,234
Northwestern Mutual	12,154,318	1,244,436	70,133,741	6,798
Teachers Insurance & Annuity	11,439,344	1,791,958	9,072,398	1,897
Massachusetts Mutual	10,022,231	1,224,967	55,978,807	10,428
Bankers Life	8,765,096	1,533,098	42,680,898	6,266
Mutual of New York	8,388,961	785,245	42,827,888	8,055
New England Mutual	7,273,819	1,101,205	34,991,635	7,913
Mutual Benefit	6,619,044	1,158,830	46,732,485	5,631
Total	**$311,720,940**	**$43,020,207**	**$2,030,305,326**	**292,302**

Source: FORTUNE (July 12, 1982), pp. 136–137. ©1982 Time Inc. All rights reserved.

Life insurance comes in various forms. Let's look at three of them and at some of the questions you need to ask yourself about buying life insurance.

Term Life. Term insurance is "pure" life insurance. It has no cash value once the policy expires—you do not get money back. In short, you must die to collect. But, depending on your needs, it can be beneficial. Term insurance, for example, provides more insurance per dollar of premium paid than any other type of life insurance. For a person 30 years old, a $100 annual premium buys approximately $19,000 worth of term life insurance for one year. The same amount of money spent on whole life insurance, another type of life insurance, buys less than $7,000 worth of protection.

Most people buy term insurance to protect their families in the event of premature death. The Thompson family consists of a husband John, a wife Sue, and two children. Assume that both parents work. Sue takes out $20,000 of term insurance to help pay for their children's college education in the event she dies. The policy expires when the youngest Thompson child would normally be expected to finish college—assuming that Sue lives past that time. If she died before that time, the children would collect.

Most term insurance policies are **convertible**. That is, the policyholder can switch to another type of coverage without being required to pass a physical examination. The advantage of convertible insurance is that it allows the holder to buy the most protection when the need is greatest and then convert to a more permanent type of life insurance later in life.

Whole Life. Whole life insurance protects the insured person for the person's lifetime. Unlike

Some people find obtaining insurance difficult.

Figure 20-5

Value of Life Insurance and Annual Disposable Income

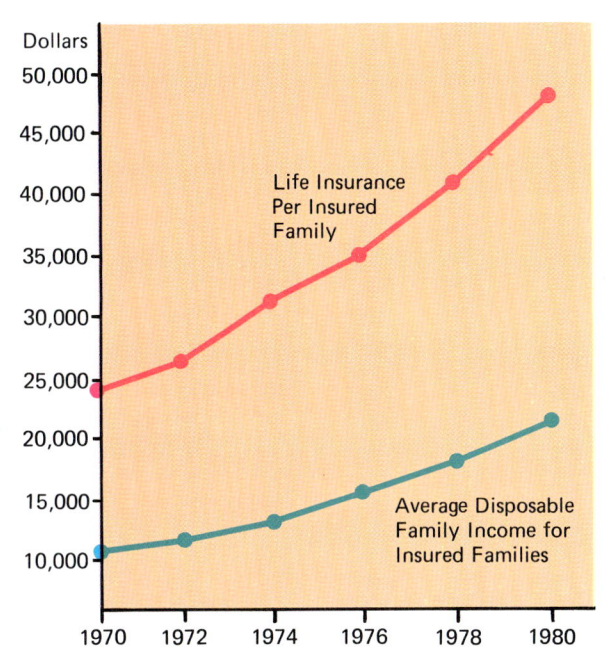

Source: *Life Insurance Fact Book* (Washington: American Council of Life Insurance, 1981).

term insurance, a whole life policy does not automatically expire after a certain number of years.

Whole life insurance comes in two forms. Under ordinary (or straight) life contract insurance, the policyholder pays premiums for life. Under a **limited-life policy**, the policyholder pays higher premiums but only until the policy is paid up. Most limited-life policies are fully paid up in 20 or 30 years.

One advantage of whole life insurance is that it generates a cash value for the insured. Figure 20-6 shows the cash value of both a $10,000 ordinary life insurance policy and a $10,000 limited-life insurance policy. The reason why the limited-life policy generates cash value more quickly is that the premiums paid are greater. For a 30-year-old male, the premiums would be nearly 30 percent higher under the limited-life plan than under the ordinary life plan.

The holder of a whole life insurance policy can collect in one of two ways. For the limited-life plan described in Figure 20-6, the family collects $10,000 in the event of the policyholder's death, or the policyholder can cash in the policy in, for example, 25 years and collect $3,970. The insured person may also borrow against the cash value of the insurance policy. The cost for such borrowing is stated in the policy and is usually quite low.

Endowment Insurance. Endowment insurance is essentially a savings account with some built-in insurance protection. Assume that Tien Chi, age 25, wants to save $200,000 over the next 20 years. Tien could achieve her goal by investing $202.17 at 12 percent interest each month for 20 years. However, if Tien were to die after five years, her spouse would not have the entire $200,000. As an alternative, Tien could buy endowment insurance for roughly another $85 each month for 20 years. This plan guarantees Tien $200,000 at the end of 20 years. If she were to die before the end of 20 years, the insurance company would pay her husband the $200,000. As you can see, endowment insurance acts as a form of guaranteed savings.

Many people buy endowment insurance to obtain an additional source of retirement income. You wouldn't need this type of insurance if you knew you were going to die on the day you retired, or if you were single. You would be better off to invest your money in a bank or savings and loan. However, if you want assurance that your savings goals will be met, endowment insurance may be for you.

Universal Life. Universal life is a new type of insurance. It is designed to give the buyer the protection of term insurance and, at the same time, the opportunity to earn a high yield on funds invested with the insurance company.

Here is how universal life works. The insurance buyer makes a "contribution" to the company. This money is called a contribution rather than a premium because the amount is voluntary. A portion of the contribution is a charge for insurance protection. This is, in reality, term insurance. Next, the company deducts an amount for expenses and profits. The expenses cover the agent's commission and the cost of establishing and maintaining the policy. After all fees have been paid, the insurance company invests the remaining funds at a rate determined by the company. This money is called the policy's cash value.[9]

---

[9]"Universal-life insurance," *Consumer Reports*, Vol. 47, No. 1 (January, 1982), pp. 42-43.

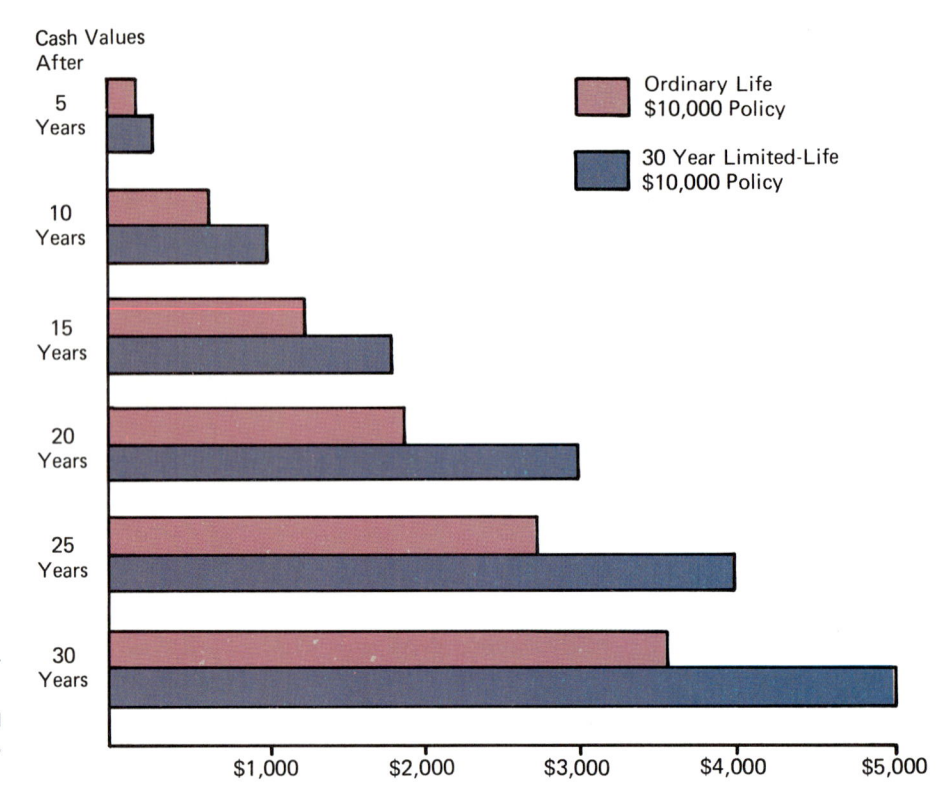

Figure 20-6

Types of Whole Life Insurance

Source: H.O. Copeland and Associates, Austin, Texas, 1982.

There are three major advantages of universal life. First, the contribution is variable. If the policyholder does not want to invest enough money to generate cash value, there is no requirement to do so. Second, the insurance company lists all of the fees so that the policyholder knows exactly how much is going for insurance, expenses, and the buildup of cash value. Third, the cash value part of the policy is invested at a rate that has been averaging almost twice as high as the rate for whole life policies. However, when interest rates go down, the rate paid on the cash value of the policy will also go down. This does not happen with whole life policies.

Evaluation of Life Insurance

Which type of life insurance is best for you? The answer depends on your income and on your needs. If your income is limited but your insurance needs are large, then you should consider term insurance. A term policy offers a great deal of insurance at relatively low cost. On the other hand, if you're interested in a guaranteed retirement income, then, as discussed earlier, an endowment life policy is probably best. For their part, whole life policies have some of the characteristics of both term and endowment plans—they provide a significant amount of protection while creating cash value for the insured.

Finally, universal life insurance is similar to whole life except that there is more flexibility in the payments. In addition, most universal life insurance policies pay a higher return on the money invested with the insurance company than do similar whole life policies. Universal life insurance policies may turn out to be the best type of life insurance for most people. Unfortunately, more time is needed to evaluate how successful such policies will be.

Many business people buy term insurance to protect their families and also participate in regular savings and investment programs for their retirement. They believe that the return on their savings is greater than that afforded by an endowment policy with an insurance company. However, keep in mind that an endowment policy provides both retirement income and insurance protection. Figure 20-7 compares the alternative life insurance programs.

Chapter 20 • Risk Management and Insurance 395

Figure 20-7

Comparisons of Alternative Life Insurance Programs

	Term Insurance	Whole Life — Ordinary Life	Whole Life — Limited Life	Endowment Life	Universal Life
Premium	Lowest available	Higher than term insurance	Higher than ordinary life insurance	Highest available	Higher than term; may vary from one payment period to another
Payment Period	Specified number of years—normally 5, 10, or 15 years	Life of the insured	Specified number of years—normally 20 or 30 years	Specified number of years—normally 20 or 30 years	Specified period
Cash Value	None	Some cash value	More cash value than ordinary life but less than endowment insurance	Largest cash value—equals the value of the policy	Varies with amount "invested" by the insured
Collection Time	Upon the death of the insured	Upon the death of the insured	Upon the death of the insured	Upon the death of the insured or at the time the policy is fully paid for	Upon the death of the insured
Objectives	Protection for a specified period of time; to cover specific and temporary risks	Protection for life; some cash value for insured	Protection for life; some cash value for insured	To create a guaranteed estate; to provide insurance and help finance retirement	Life insurance plus high rate of return

SUMMARY POINTS

1. Pure risk exists when the only possible outcomes are loss or no loss. Insurance companies protect against many types of pure risk.
2. Speculative risk involves the possibility of loss and the possibility of gain. Insurance companies do not protect against speculative risk.
3. The four ways a person or business can manage pure risk are risk reduction, self-insurance, the use of current income, and insurance.
4. Using the law of large numbers, insurance companies can predict the probability that a particular loss will occur.
5. Insurance companies protect against losses that are definite and measurable. Only accidental losses are insurable.
6. Insurance companies spread their risk so that no single disaster forces them to pay all their clients at once.
7. The federal government provides both voluntary and required insurance. Social security is the largest form of required insurance.
8. Stock insurance companies sell insurance to make money for their stockholders. Mutual insurance companies are owned by their policyholders.
9. Fire insurance, the most popular form of property insurance, may be extended to protect against windstorm, hail, explosion, riot, civil strife, smoke, and damage from aircraft and motor vehicles.
10. Ocean marine insurance covers ship owners against damage to the ship and its cargo. Inland marine insurance protects against damage to property being moved by ship, truck, or train.
11. Automobile insurance may protect the policyholder against claims resulting from bodily injury, medical payments, uninsured motorists, property damage, and collisions. With no-fault automobile insurance, the parties to a loss recover from their own insurance companies.
12. Most businesses purchase insurance to protect against burglary, robbery, and theft.
13. Liability insurance protects a business against damage claims by the public. Public liability covers most types of risks, while product or service liability protects the firm against injury to the public from defective products.
14. Business-interruption insurance pays for losses from uncontrollable events that temporarily disrupt a business.
15. Fidelity bonds protect an employer from losses resulting from the actions of dishonest employees. Workers' compensation insurance protects the employee from job-related accidents and diseases. Disability income insurance pays all or a part of a person's income when that person is not able to work because of illness or injury.
16. Term life insurance has no cash value. Whole life insurance generates a cash value which can be used by the insured. Endowment insurance is basically a savings account with built-in insurance protection. Universal life insurance is a new type of policy with flexible cash values.

KEY TERMS AND CONCEPTS

risk
pure risk
speculative risk
risk reduction
self-insurance
insurance
law of large numbers
definite and measurable risk
insurable interests
social security
stock companies
mutual companies
property insurance
extended coverage
marine insurance
bodily injury liability
medical payments insurance
uninsured motorist coverage
property damage liability
collision insurance
comprehensive insurance
no-fault insurance
banker's blanket bond
public liability
product or service liability
loss-of-earning-power insurance
business-interruption insurance
fidelity bonds
individual fidelity bond
blanket bond
workers' compensation
health insurance
life insurance
term life insurance

convertible term insurance
whole life insurance
straight life insurance

limited-life policy
endowment insurance
universal life insurance

REVIEW QUESTIONS

1. Describe the four ways that a person or firm has of dealing with pure risk.
2. What is meant by the law of large numbers?
3. How do insurance companies spread their risk?
4. What is meant by extended coverage insurance policies?
5. Explain the differences between automobile collision insurance and automobile property damage insurance.
6. What risks does public liability insurance cover?
7. Outline the three types of loss-of-earning-power insurance.
8. What is a fidelity bond?
9. What is the primary advantage of whole life insurance compared to term insurance?
10. Why do many people purchase endowment insurance?

DISCUSSION QUESTIONS

1. Why do insurance companies insure against pure risk only?
2. Who does social security cover? Do you want to be covered by social security?
3. Why has no-fault automobile insurance been passed by so many states?
4. Explain the importance of disability income insurance. Would you purchase disability insurance?
5. Do you believe that universal life insurance will replace whole life insurance? Explain.

CASE 20-1

Interminco

Several companies have been formed to search for oil on the continental shelf of the United States. Other firms, such as Sedco, finance and manage the actual construction of huge offshore oil rigs—or floating platforms which are towed to a drilling site, moored, and then serve as the base of operations for large drilling operations. These platforms are highly sophisticated and very expensive. The most expensive ones cost about $250 million to build and more than $1 million a week to rent.

Many companies rent rigs rather than build them. One company which rents oil rigs is International Mining Company, or Interminco. Although traditionally into nickel mining, Interminco decided to go into offshore oil drilling when the price of nickel fell. To do so, it chose to rent six offshore drilling rigs.

Interminco contacted insurance companies to see about adequate insurance coverage for the rigs. Interminco executives remembered that an offshore drilling platform rented to the Mexican government by Sedco had broken down in the Gulf of Mexico, spilling millions of gallons of crude oil into the ocean and polluting over a thousand miles of beach. Legal claims resulting from that pollution were immense. Another rig off Newfoundland, Canada, sank in a storm. Over a hundred workers were drowned and the rig was lost. Lawsuits against the renting company are still in progress, but the families of the dead workers expect to receive over $1 billion before all the suits are settled. Interminco was concerned that its workers be well insured and that the company be well insured against claims should another rig fail.

Interminco would also like insurance against fire, arson, terrorism, delays due to bad weather or mechanical breakdowns, and the possibility that oil is not discovered. Interminco must have special marine insurance to cover the towing of the rig out to its drilling site and insurance against worker injury.

1. What kinds of risk does Interminco face?
2. In what ways could Interminco reduce the risk it faces?
3. What constraints will any insurance company put on Interminco and the property it wants to insure before it will issue a policy?
4. What kinds of insurance does Interminco need to consider purchasing?

CASE 20-2

Safety-Deposit Boxes

For many years, banks have furnished safety-deposit boxes for their regular customers. These boxes, located within the bank's vault and opened only by the customer, provided reasonably secure storage for limited amounts of jewels, papers, and other valuables. Though the contents of the boxes were not insured by the government against loss, some banks did offer insurance policies that protected the contents.

Banks usually offered safety-deposit boxes as loss leaders—they rented for an amount less than what the space actually cost the bank. Consequently, banks were not eager to expand their supply of safety-deposit boxes. However, the boxes encouraged people to become regular customers at the bank.

Demand for the boxes increased dramatically. Rapid increases in burglary and theft rates and rising theft insurance premiums made home storage of valuables riskier. Further, many more people were turning to gold, precious gems, and other similar investments as a hedge against inflation. These investments had to be stored somewhere.

The answer was the private safety-deposit vault. New companies sprang up that purchased a high-security vault and filled it entirely with safety-deposit boxes. Such a vault, with adequate security and room for about 2,000 boxes, cost well over a million dollars. Rental rates for these boxes were high—in some cases, over $1,000 a year. However, with waiting lists stretching up to three years in some cities, there seems plenty of demand to allow growth in this market.

Unfortunately, since there is no regulation by any government agency, many companies put together cheap vaults with poor security. They then overcharge for their services and do not insure against any possible losses. Reputable safety-deposit vault companies look with scorn upon these businesses and fear that the Federal government will step in soon with stringent and costly regulations.

Also, banks may realize the market available in safety-deposit boxes. They may reprice their boxes high enough to justify adding more in their vaults or to justify building additional vaults especially for boxes. The security already available in banks would make additional safety-deposit vaults in banks much cheaper and safer than those offered by the private safety-deposit vault companies.

1. What kind of risk are safety-deposit boxes intended to reduce?
2. How do safety-deposit boxes help to manage risk?
3. What principles of insurance are manifested in the use of safety-deposit boxes?
4. What kind of risk are investors in safety-deposit vault companies taking? How do they manage the risk they face?

Loan Repayment

This program determines the regular payment you must make to pay off a loan, as well as the total payments you would make over the life of the loan. Your inputs include the total purchase price, down payment, length of the loan, interest rate, and number of payments per year. By accepting the option to perform additional analyses, you can see how your payments would change as you alter any of these inputs.

Here's the Program

```
10  PRINT
20  PRINT "**********LOAN PAYMENT PROGRAM**********"
30  PRINT
40  INPUT "TOTAL PRICE....................$";P
50  INPUT "DOWN PAYMENT...................$";D
60  INPUT "LENGTH OF LOAN (YEARS).........";Y
70  INPUT "NOMINAL INTEREST RATE (%)......";I
80  INPUT "NUMBER OF PAYMENTS PER YEAR....";N
90  B=P-D
95  REM ON THE APPLE PLACE A CARET INSTEAD OF [ ON LINE 100
100 R=((I/100)*B/N)/(1-1/((I/100)/N+1)[(N*Y))
110   X=INT(R*100+.5)/100
120 TC=X*N*Y
130   TC=INT(TC*100+.5)/100
140 PRINT
150 PRINT "----------------------------------------"
160 PRINT "NUMBER OF PAYMENTS PER YEAR...";N
170 PRINT "AMOUNT OF LOAN................$";B
180 PRINT "LENGTH OF LOAN (YEARS)........";Y
190 PRINT "NOMINAL INTEREST RATE (%).....";I
200 PRINT
210 PRINT "----------------------------------------"
220 PRINT
230 PRINT "REQUIRED PAYMENT..............$";X
240 PRINT "TOTAL PAYMENTS................$";TC
250 PRINT "----------------------------------------"
260 PRINT
270 INPUT "DO YOU WANT ANOTHER RUN? (1=YES; 2=NO) ";K
280 IF K=1 THEN GOTO 10
290 END
```

Here's Sample Output

Two sets of output of the loan repayment program are provided. Notice that a $2,000 greater down payment resulted in savings of $4,324.80 over the life of the loan.

```
------------------------------------------
NUMBER OF PAYMENTS PER YEAR... 12
AMOUNT OF LOAN................$ 8000
LENGTH OF LOAN (YEARS)........ 10
NOMINAL INTEREST RATE (%)..... 18
------------------------------------------

REQUIRED PAYMENT..............$ 144.15
TOTAL PAYMENTS................$ 17298
------------------------------------------
NUMBER OF PAYMENTS PER YEAR... 12
AMOUNT OF LOAN................$ 6000
LENGTH OF LOAN (YEARS)........ 10
NOMINAL INTEREST RATE (%)..... 18
------------------------------------------

REQUIRED PAYMENT..............$ 108.11
TOTAL PAYMENTS................$ 12973.2
------------------------------------------
```

Questions

1. In the sample runs, why did a $2,000 greater down payment result in savings of more than $4,000 over the life of the loan?
2. Since a larger down payment always results in an even greater saving over the life of a loan, is someone always better off making a larger down payment? Why or why not?
3. If the loan in the sample runs were to be paid off in 15 years instead of 10, how do you think the total payments over the life of the loan would change? Why?

6

Management Control and Information Systems

21

Accounting and Financial Statements

After studying this chapter, you should be able to:

- Discuss the role of the accountant, both public and private, as well as the importance of accounting information.
- Present the basic accounting equation, showing how it is always kept in balance through the double-entry method of bookkeeping.
- Identify each of the major items in a balance sheet.
- Describe how expenses are netted against revenues on the income statement to yield "bottom-line" net income after taxes.
- Explain the inventory valuation problem and how two valuation methods, FIFO and LIFO, address this problem.
- Discuss two ways of interpreting financial statements.

Accounting is one of the most important activities of the firm, and it is also one of the fastest-growing career fields today. Why are accountants in such demand? Because without good financial records, a business would not know how much income tax it owes the government, how much money it can safely borrow, whether it has invested its money wisely, or even whether it has made a profit. In this chapter, we'll look at the accounting process and at how financial statements are interpreted. Let's begin by examining the role of the accountant.

ROLE OF THE ACCOUNTANT

Many people confuse bookkeeping and accounting, or they think that accounting is nothing more than glorified bookkeeping. The two are related, but they are not the same thing. The bookkeeper is responsible for keeping a company's financial records. Much of a bookkeeper's work is clerical. Today, this work is increasingly being done by computer.

The job of the accountant is to design a system for keeping financial records, to prepare financial statements, and to interpret these statements. But an accountant's first job frequently involves some bookkeeping because many senior accounting executives believe that it is important for accountants to understand what bookkeepers do. Bookkeepers are usually supervised by accountants.

Public vs. Private Accounting

There are two types of accounts: public and private. Although their roles in a business differ, they often work closely together.

Public Accounting. Each of the 50 states has laws that provide for the licensing of certified public accountants, or CPAs. The laws require that CPAs have a certain amount of college training and that they pass an examination prepared by the American Institute of Certified Public Accountants.

Many CPAs work as **external auditors**. They are "external" to the firm in that they do not work regularly for the company being audited. As auditors, they review the firm's financial statements to determine whether the statements fairly and accurately report the firm's financial position. Other CPAs provide consulting services to companies on such problems as how to design an accounting system and how to use a computer to keep track of cost and sales data.

Many CPAs work for themselves or as members of locally owned CPA firms. There is also a large number of CPAs who work for one of the "Big Eight" CPA firms shown in Figure 21-1. The Big Eight firms do audits on the nation's largest corporations as well as provide audit services for many small and medium-sized businesses.

Private Accounting. Other accountants work for only one business. They supervise bookkeepers, prepare financial statements, and advise top management as to the financial position of the firm. **Internal auditors**, as they are often called, are responsible for making sure that the firm's accounting procedures are being followed

Figure 21-1

The "Big Eight" Accounting Firms

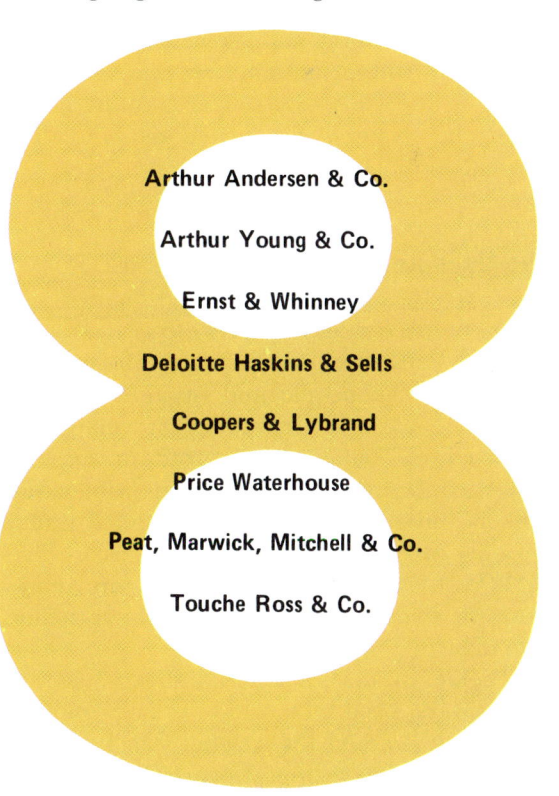

Arthur Andersen & Co.

Arthur Young & Co.

Ernst & Whinney

Deloitte Haskins & Sells

Coopers & Lybrand

Price Waterhouse

Peat, Marwick, Mitchell & Co.

Touche Ross & Co.

Fortunately, modern technology has improved accounting procedures.

properly. The internal auditor often serves as the "eyes and ears" of top management. The Institute of Internal Auditors administers an examination similar to the CPA exam. The accountant who passes the exam is designated as a Certified Internal Auditor, or CIA.

Who Uses Accounting Information?

A complex society such as ours can function efficiently only if reliable financial information is available to the people and organizations that need it. All users of accounting information are interested in "bottom-line" profit or loss, but many people need more detailed information. Bankers and other creditors, for instance, want to know about a firm's financial status before making a loan. As a result, they need information about the firm's assets and long-term and short-term debts.

People in the securities industry, such as stockbrokers, need information to help them determine the amount for which a firm's common stock should be selling. Government agencies need financial information to regulate the firm's business activities. The government is primarily concerned with the firm's tax obligations and the protection of its employees. Labor unions use financial information in negotiations with management for wage increases.

Who else uses accounting information? The owners and stockholders of a business use it to find out whether the business has invested its money wisely and whether it is in a position to raise more capital. Management is concerned with the firm's ability to meet immediate cash needs. Does the business have enough money to pay off its creditors and to purchase needed assets? Figure 21-2 shows some of the questions that the various users of accounting information typically ask.

TWO ACCOUNTING CONCEPTS

To understand how modern accounting works, we must understand the accounting equation and how transactions are recorded in a double-entry bookkeeping system. Following is a discussion of both of these topics.

The Accounting Equation

The properties owned by a business firm are called **assets**, and the rights or claims to these assets are called **equity**. If a firm has $100,000 worth of assets, then it must have $100,000 worth of equity. Hence,

> Assets = Equity
> $100,000 = $100,000

The equity side of the equation is divided into the rights of owners and the rights of creditors. Since the rights of creditors are debts for the firm, we call them **liabilities**. The claims of owners are called **owners' equity**. If our firm owed $25,000 to a bank, we would write the accounting equation as follows:

> Assets = Liabilities + Owners' Equity
> $100,000 = $25,000 + $75,000

Figure 21-2

The Need for Accounting Information

Owners and Stockholders

- Has the firm invested its money wisely?
- Are its profits taxable?
- What is the value of its assets?
- How much long-term debt can it afford?
- How should it raise more money?

Creditors

- How profitable has the firm been historically?
- How much cash does it earn?
- How much long- and short-term debt does it have?
- Have any of its assets been used as collateral?
- Are its assets correctly valued?

Managers

- How much cash does the firm have?
- Which assets need replacing?
- How much debt comes due in the near future?
- How much money do other people or organizations owe the firm?
- Are actual expenses in line with budgeted expenses?

Securities Markets

- How profitable has the firm been during the last five years?
- How many shares of stock does it have outstanding?
- How much long-term debt does it owe?
- What is the value of its assets?

Government

- How has the firm "expensed" its assets?
- How much income tax does it owe?
- How many people work for the firm?
- How much does it pay its employees?
- How many serious job-related accidents have occurred?

Labor

- How stable are the firm's profits?
- How many people were hired recently?
- How many people were laid off recently?
- What is the value of the firm's benefit packages?

We normally place liabilities before owners' equity in the accounting equation. We do this to show that creditors have first rights to assets. That is, if a company were forced out of business, its creditors would be repaid before the owners were given back their investments. It is sometimes useful in this regard to move liabilities to the other side of the accounting equation.

$$\text{Assets} - \text{Liabilities} = \text{Owners' Equity}$$
$$\$100,000 - \$25,000 = \$75,000$$

This shows that owners' equity is a residual amount—in other words, what is left over for distribution among the owners, in the event of liquidation, after all debts have been repaid.

Double-Entry Bookkeeping

Double-entry bookkeeping is based on the accounting equation. Each and every transaction requires two entries in the books. This keeps the accounting equation balanced at all times. Suppose a business borrows $5,000 from the bank to buy a car. The firm's assets increase by $5,000 because it now owns a car valued at $5,000; its liabilities also increase by $5,000 because it owes the bank $5,000 for the car. To illustrate, we'll continue with the example presented in the last section. Before purchase of the car:

$$\text{Assets} = \text{Liabilities} + \text{Owners' Equity}$$
$$\$100,000 = \$25,000 + \$75,000$$

After purchase of the car:

$$\text{Assets} = \text{Liabilities} + \text{Owners' Equity}$$
$$\$105,000 = \$30,000 + \$75,000$$

Note that the accounting equation is still in balance. Both sides of the equation were equally affected by the transaction because both increased by $5,000. Let's now look at how a series of five transactions were recorded by Joel Snyder when he established Snyder's Pizza House and Dance Hall. These five transactions are shown on page 407.

Transaction (A): Establish the Business. To start his business, Joel used $20,000 of his own money to open a bank account in the name of Snyder's Pizza House and Dance Hall. This created $20,000 worth of assets for the firm and, at the same time, $20,000 worth of owners' equity.

Transaction (B): Buy a Building. Joel's next step was to buy a building. The best building available cost $60,000. Fortunately for Joel, the bank was willing to lend him the entire amount. Note that while assets went up by $60,000, liabilities, which represent the debt to the bank, also went up by $60,000.

Transaction (C): Buy Supplies. Joel then bought pizza dough and tomato paste. He spent $2,000 cash on these supplies. All changes occurred on the asset side of the equation. Simply stated, $2,000 cash was converted to $2,000 worth of supplies, leaving the two components of equity unaffected. Note also that the equation is still in balance.

Transaction (D): Record Sales Revenue. After one week, Snyder's Pizza House and Dance Hall was a hit, selling a total of $3,000 worth of pizzas. This revenue is treated as an increase in cash and an increase in owners' equity. Again we see that the equation remains in balance.

Transaction (E): Record Expenses. Joel incurred four expenses while selling his pizzas: He paid $1,200 in wages to servers and to members of the band, $150 in utilities (electricity and water), and $100 in other bills. In addition, he used $750 worth of supplies. These expenses reduced Joel's cash, supplies, and owners' equity accounts. Total assets still equals total equity: The expenses reduced the assets and equity sides of the equation equally.

In summary, Joel's business began with assets and equity both equal to $20,000. It ended up with assets and equity equal to $80,800. It is important to restate two things. First, each transaction required two entries; this is why the accounting system is called double-entry bookkeeping. Second, if the assets do not equal equity, then an error has been made in recording a transaction.

BALANCE SHEET

The **balance sheet** presents a financial "snapshot" of the business at a particular moment in time. It, too, is based on the accounting equation: assets = liabilities + owners' equity. The balance sheet shows the value of a firm's assets as well as the value of its liabilities and owners' equity. The balance sheet is in balance only when assets equal liabilities plus owners' equity.

The balance sheet is used by a firm's creditors in deciding whether to lend more money to the firm. Most firms prepare a balance sheet at the end of each calendar year. This gives the firm and its creditors a picture of its financial position at the same time each year.

Some business firms use a fiscal year approach. Under this approach, the annual accounting period may begin on any day of the year rather than on the first day of January. For example, a fiscal year might begin on July 1 and run through June 30 of the next year. Figure 21-3 presents a calendar year balance sheet for Texas Tile dated December 31, 1983. Texas Tile's balance sheet is in balance because its $927,100 in assets equals its $927,100 in liabilities and owners' equity. Let's look at the major sections of the balance sheet individually.

Assets

There are two basic types of assets: current assets and fixed assets. We can also distinguish between tangible and intangible assets. It is important for a firm's accountants to classify its assets correctly.

Current Assets. **Current assets** are cash and other "liquid" assets that the firm expects to use, sell, or turn into cash within one year. **Cash** is just what you think it is—the money you put in your pocket. Ideally, a business keeps its cash in a safe place, such as in a checking account or in a short-term savings account where it earns interest. Cash would not include money deposited in a two-year time deposit because the firm does not have access to it quickly.

Business firms often sell their products on credit. The amount owed to the firm at any moment in time as a result of these credit sales is listed under the entry called **accounts receivable**. Accountants treat accounts receivable much as

Transaction (A)

	Assets	=	Equity
	Cash	=	Owners' Equity
	$20,000	=	$20,000

Transaction (B)

	Assets			=		Equity	
	Cash	+	Building	=	Liability	+	Owners' Equity
	$20,000						$20,000
		+	$60,000	=	$60,000		
	$20,000	+	$60,000	=	$60,000	+	$20,000
			$80,000	=	$80,000		

Transaction (C)

	Assets		=	Equity	
	Cash + Building + Supplies	=	Liabilities + Owners' Equity
	$20,000 $60,000		$60,000 $20,000
	−$ 2,000 + $2,000		
	$18,000 + $60,000 + $2,000	=	$60,000 + $20,000
	$80,000	=	$80,000

Transaction (D)

	Assets	=	Equity
	Cash + Building + Supplies	=	Liabilities + Owners' Equity
	$18,000 $60,000 $ 2,000		$60,000 $20,000
	+$3,000		+$3,000
	$21,000 + $60,000 + $ 2,000	=	$60,000 + $23,000
	$83,000	=	$83,000

Transaction (E)

		Assets	=	Equity
		Cash + Building + Supplies	=	Liabilities + Owners' Equity
		$21,000 $60,000 $2,000		$60,000 $23,000
	(Wages)	−$1,200		−$1,200
	(Util.)	− $150		−$150
	(Misc.)	− $100		−$100
	(Supp.)		−$750	−$750
		$19,550 + $60,000 + $1,250	=	$60,000 + $20,800
		$80,800	=	$80,800

Figure 21-3

Texas Tile Balance Sheet

TEXAS TILE
Balance Sheet
December 31, 1983

CURRENT ASSETS			
Cash		$ 25,400	
Accounts Receivable	$102,000		
Less Allowance for Bad Debt	6,000	96,000	
Notes Receivable		5,000	
Merchandise Inventory			
Finished Goods	32,000		
Work in Process	45,200		
Raw Materials	21,000	98,200	
Prepaid Expenses		8,500	
TOTAL CURRENT ASSETS			$233,100
FIXED ASSETS			
Land		$220,000	
Building	$335,000		
Less Accumulated Depreciation	87,500	247,500	
Merchandise and Equipment	245,000		
Less Accumulated Depreciation	68,500	176,500	
TOTAL FIXED ASSETS			644,000
INTANGIBLE ASSETS			
Goodwill		$ 26,000	
Patents		24,000	
TOTAL INTANGIBLE ASSETS			50,000
TOTAL ASSETS			$927,100
LIABILITIES AND OWNERS' EQUITY			
Current Liabilities			
Accounts Payable		$ 32,000	
Notes Payable		45,000	
Accrued Expenses		15,500	
Income Tax Payable		10,700	
TOTAL CURRENT LIABILITIES			$103,200
Long-Term Liabilities			
Long-Term Notes Payable		135,700	
Bonds Payable		230,000	
TOTAL LONG-TERM LIABILITIES			365,700
TOTAL LIABILITIES			468,900
Owners' Equity			
Common Stock (7,600 Shares at $25)		190,000	
Preferred Stock (1,000 Shares at $25)		25,000	
Retained Earnings		243,200	
TOTAL OWNERS' EQUITY			458,200
TOTAL LIABILITIES AND OWNERS' EQUITY			$927,100

they do cash; both are current assets. As Figure 21-3 shows, Texas Tile has $102,000 in receivables. It also has $6,000 listed as allowance for bad debts. This indicates that Texas Tile does not believe that it will be able to collect all of its receivables. In effect, Texas Tile is telling the reader of its balance sheet that its accounts receivable are really worth only $96,000.

A **note receivable**, on the other hand, is a signed note in which one person or company promises to pay another person or company a certain amount of money over a designated period of time. Texas Tile has a note receivable of $5,000. The company sold one of its trucks to another company, which promised in writing to pay $5,000 for the truck within six months.

Three types of **merchandise inventory** are also listed on the balance sheet as current assets: finished goods, work in process, and raw materials. As discussed in Chapter 17, **finished goods** are products that are ready for shipment or sale to a buyer. **Work in process** refers to unfinished products; these products still need to move through one or more stages in the manufacturing process. **Raw materials** are the inputs from which the firm makes its products. Packaged clay is a finished good for a clay company, but it would be a raw material for Texas Tile. The value of each component of Texas Tile's merchandise inventory is listed in its balance sheet.

Expenses paid in advance, another current asset, are called **prepaid expenses**. An example of a prepaid expense is automobile and building insurance. Insurance companies require businesses to buy their insurance in advance—normally, six months or one year. Because the firm pays in advance of the period of coverage, this expense is recorded on the balance sheet as a current asset.

Fixed Assets. **Fixed assets** are "long lived" or permanent assets. They are not sold during the ordinary course of operations. Fixed assets include land, buildings and machinery, and equipment. There is no standard for how long an asset must be used in order for it to be called "fixed." Fixed assets, however, must be capable of repeated use, and they are normally expected to last several years.

Note on Texas Tile's balance sheet that its building is listed at $335,000 minus accumulated depreciation of $87,500. **Depreciation** represents the amount of the building's decline in value since its purchase. When depreciation is subtracted from the original value of the building, the balance sheet shows a "net" value of $247,500. The same procedure was also used for merchandise and equipment. Federal tax law regulates the rate at which fixed assets may be depreciated.

Intangible Assets. Patents, licenses, trademarks, and goodwill are all examples of **intangible assets**. All these assets have a common trait—intangibility. That is, none of them is really a physical object.

Goodwill can be a reputation for producing high-quality products. Such a reputation is certainly worth something. Texas Tile enjoys goodwill because its reputation for quality encourages people to buy its products. How can you tell whether a firm has goodwill? The real test is whether the firm earns a return on its assets greater than those of other firms in the industry.

Liabilities and Owners' Equity

This part of the balance sheet shows the amount of money a firm owes its creditors as well as the value of the owners' investment in the business. We'll begin this discussion by looking at current liabilities.

Current Liabilities. A **liability** is a legal obligation requiring payment in the future. **Current liabilities** must be paid within one year. Normally, current liabilities are paid out of current assets. The most common types of current liabilities are accounts payable and notes payable. **Accounts payable** represent purchases for which the firm has not yet paid. Suppose a firm buys computer paper on credit in April and pays for it in June. At the time of the purchase, the cost of the paper is entered under accounts payable; it stays there until the June payment date, at which time the payment is deducted from the cash account. **Notes payable** are like accounts payable except that the firm signs a legal document stating exactly when the amount due is to be paid.

Some services are paid for only *after* they are performed. The amounts owed for such services are listed on the balance sheet as **accrued expenses**. A good example of an accrued expense is the labor provided by employees. You can think

CONTROVERSIAL ISSUES

The United States Needs a Simpler Tax System.

The American taxation system has become incredibly complex and unwieldly. In recent years, homeowners filing even the simple tax returns have been bewildered by tax laws. For corporations, the problem has become mindboggling. America's tax system must be simplified.

Pro

We must have a simplified tax system. There are a number of problems with the current tax system: Taxes have increased dramatically in recent years because of high inflation; the wealthy can often escape paying taxes because of loopholes; interest groups gain tax advantages through contributions to political campaigns; the bulk of the tax burden continues to fall on the middle-class taxpayer; and the system is so complex that individuals and corporations cannot understand it.

When the Internal Revenue Service has been challenged to simplify the tax program, its response has been to change the color of the tax form, to rewrite instructions, or to make more provisions so that taxpayers can delay filing. When Congress has been asked to work out tax problems, it has usually responded either by offering more deductions or by withdrawing deductions it previously had allowed.

What we need *now* is a completely new tax system, a simpler one like the flat-rate income tax proposed by Congress. This tax program will really mean equality for all taxpayers: Every taxpayer pays the same percentage of annual income to the government, with no special deductions or exemptions allowed. The taxpayer saves the cost of expensive bookkeeping and accounting services. Every employer can deduct precisely the amount of withholdings needed, and every taxpayer will know exactly what proportion of income is available for personal consumption. A new simpler tax system *is* better, and we should have it now.

Con

There are many problems with a simple tax system like the flat-rate program. First, it doesn't really save money for poorer taxpayers. The Congressional Budget Office has calculated that in 1984, a taxpayer earning under $30,000 would actually pay *higher* taxes under the flat-rate system. So the flat-rate system actually penalizes the poor and rewards the wealthy through tax benefits. Under the present system, the government has seen to it that poorer taxpayers are treated *more* fairly; now they are being asked to pay more because wealthy taxpayers will be paying less.

Furthermore, consider what these supposedly unfair deductions and exemptions allow under the current tax system. Taxpayers deduct contributions to charities, churches, universities, social service organizations, and welfare organizations from their taxable income. Some people make such contributions because of the tax break they provide. But if all deductions are disallowed, these organizations—crucial to supporting America's ill, old, poor, and young—will find their funds drying up.

If a flat-rate 11.8-percent tax rate were instituted, 62 million taxpayers earning less than $30,000 would have to pay higher taxes. The 18 million wealthy Americans earning more than $30,000 would pay lower taxes. Is Congress really doing the American people a service by saving its wealthy more money? Let's stick with the tax system we have, and try to clean it up from within. Only when Congress finds a tax system that gives poorer people a break and places the greater tax liability on wealthy taxpayers and corporations will it have a tax system that is just.

of employees as earning a small part of their salaries each minute or hour they work. But employees are paid on a weekly or monthly basis. The amount of money that a firm owes its employees for work already performed is listed as an accrued expense on the balance sheet.

The final category of current liabilities listed on Texas Tile's balance sheet is income tax payable. This could be classified as a type of accrued expense. **Income tax payable** refers to the estimated amount of money owed to the government on income already earned.

Long-Term Liabilities. Debts that do not have to be repaid for at least 12 months are called **long-term liabilities**. Typically, they represent borrowings from a bank or insurance company. **Bonds payable** are an obligation to repay long-term bonds.

Owners' Equity. As we discussed earlier, owners' equity refers to the value of the owners' investment in the company. Owners' equity is usually broken into three subaccounts on the balance sheet: common stock, preferred stock, and retained earnings. As we saw in Chapter 18, common stock and preferred stock refer to the amount of money invested in the company by its owners; retained earnings are the cumulative amount of money, after payment of dividends and taxes, that has been left in the business.

It is important to point out once again that the balance sheet for Texas Tile is in balance: Assets equal liabilities plus owners' equity.

INCOME STATEMENT

The balance sheet was described as a "snapshot" of a firm's assets, liabilities, and owners' equity at one moment in time. The **income statement**, on the other hand, records all of a firm's revenues and expenses that have occurred over an interval of time. It shows how much money was made or lost during, say, the last 12 months.

Most income statements are drawn up once each year—at the same time the firm draws up its balance sheet. Texas Tile's income statement is shown in Figure 21-4. Note that it contains several types of income and expenses. The "bottom line" of the income statement shows the firm's operating profit or loss for the year.

Gross Sales

Gross sales refers to income received from the selling of the firm's products or services, including cash sales and sales made on account or charged. To arrive at net sales, all returns and allowances are subtracted from gross sales. **Returns** are products that customers returned to the business and for which they received a full refund. **Allowances** are partial refunds—for example, giving a customer a 20 percent refund because the product purchased was slightly damaged. **Net sales**, therefore, are gross sales minus returns and allowances. Net sales for Texas Tile equals $708,000.

Cost of Goods Sold

The amount of money spent by the seller on the merchandise sold is known as **cost of goods sold**. Retailers and wholesalers use one procedure for calculating cost of goods sold; manufacturers use another.

Firms of all kinds try to increase gross sales.

Figure 21-4

Texas Tile Income Statement

TEXAS TILE
Income Statement
for the Year Ended December 31, 1983

Sales			
Gross Sales	$750,500		
Less Returns and Allowances	42,500		
Net Sales		$708,000	
Cost of Goods Sold		263,400	
GROSS PROFIT			$444,600
Operating Expenses			
Selling Expenses			
Sales Salaries	$ 65,000		
Advertising	12,500		
Sales Insurance	1,350		
Depreciation—Sales Equipment	2,400		
Miscellaneous	1,300		
Total Sales Expenses		$ 82,550	
Administrative Expenses			
Salaries	302,000		
Taxes	8,500		
Depreciation—Office Building and Equip.	9,300		
Insurance	2,000		
Miscellaneous	1,800		
Total Administrative Expenses		323,600	
TOTAL OPERATING EXPENSES			406,150
INCOME FROM OPERATIONS			$38,450
Other Income			
Dividends	$ 4,500		
Interest	2,800	$ 7,300	
Other Expenses			
Loss from Plant Sale		(12,000)	
NET INCOME BEFORE TAXES			33,750
Federal Income Taxes			6,075
NET INCOME AFTER TAXES			$ 27,675

The procedure used by retailers and wholesalers is illustrated in the top half of Figure 21-5. The accountant begins by determining how much inventory the firm had at the beginning of the period—in this case, $150,000 as of January 1, 1983. The dollar value of the inventory purchased during the year ($319,000) is then added to this figure. The sum ($469,000) is the value of the inventory available for sale during the year; it is called **goods available for sale**. The accountant then subtracts the year-end inventory ($125,500) from the goods available for sale to obtain the cost of goods sold during the year ($343,500).

In contrast to a retailer or wholesaler, both of which buy products for resale, a manufacturer makes the products it sells. How does this affect the computation of cost of goods sold for a manufacturer such as Texas Tile? First, the accountant determines the volume of finished goods inventory at the beginning of the year. The next step is to sum the costs of labor, raw materials, and overhead to determine the cost of goods manufactured.

The calculation of the cost of goods sold for Texas Tile, a manufacturer, is shown in the bottom half of Figure 21-5. Note that Texas Tile's accountant added finished goods inventory at the beginning of the year ($30,000) to the cost of goods manufactured ($265,400). This gives the dollar value of manufactured goods available for sale during the year ($295,400). The accountant then subtracted finished goods inventory left at the end of the year ($32,000) to obtain the cost of goods sold ($263,400).

Gross Profit

Gross profit is the difference between net sales and cost of goods sold. It is called gross profit because operating expenses still have not been considered. As shown in its income statement in Figure 21-4, the gross profit of Texas Tile is $444,600.

Operating Expenses

The operating expenses of a business can be classified in a number of ways. However, Texas Tile and most other companies classify them under the two general headings of selling expenses and administrative expenses.

Selling Expenses. As the name implies, **selling expenses** result directly from the firm's sales efforts. They include advertising expenses, insurance on sales force automobiles and office buildings, and salaries of salespeople. The depreciation account would cover the cost of depreciating any physical assets used by salespeople in selling the firm's products. Texas Tile spends $82,550 on sales expenses.

Administrative Expenses. **Administrative expenses** are also called **general overhead** by some accountants. In the case of Texas Tile, they include the salaries of the company president, the president's staff, and the accounting and personnel departments. These are all included under the salaries entry of administrative expenses. The taxes entry brings together all taxes paid by the

Figure 21-5

Calculation of Cost of Goods Sold for Retailers, Wholesalers, and Manufacturers

Retailers and Wholesalers		
Beginning Inventory (January 1, 1983)		$150,000
Inventory Purchased	$345,600	
Less Purchase Discounts	26,600	319,000
Goods Available for Sale		$469,000
Less Ending Inventory (December 31, 1983)		125,500
COST OF GOODS SOLD		$343,500

Texas Tile, Manufacturer	
Beginning Finished Goods (January 1, 1983)	$ 30,000
Cost of Goods Manufactured	265,400
Goods Available for Sale	$295,400
Less Ending Finished Goods Inventory (December 31, 1983)	32,000
COST OF GOODS SOLD	$263,400

How many operating expenses can you identify for Balloons-N-Tunes?

firm except for federal income tax. For most businesses, local property taxes are the most important item under this category. The depreciation entry is used to record the cost of the physical assets, such as office building and equipment, allocated to the firm's main office. The insurance entry includes all the insurance the firm must carry to protect its production assets. Total administrative expenses for Texas Tile are $323,600.

Income from Operations

The accountant next calculates income from operations by subtracting total operating expenses from gross profit. When gross profit is greater than operating expenses, the firm has made at least some operating income. If gross profit is less than operating expenses, then the firm has lost money from operations.

Income from operations is a very important line on the income statement because it tells us whether the firm is making money from its principal business. Texas Tile is making $38,450 from the manufacture and sale of tile. We obtained this figure by subtracting total operating expenses of $406,150 from gross profit of $444,600.

Other Income

Revenue from sources other than the primary activity of the firm is called **other income**. Examples include interest income, dividends, or gains from the sale of physical assets. Texas Tile made $4,500 from dividends and $2,800 in interest income in 1983.

Other Expenses

All expenses that cannot be directly associated with the operations of the firm are called **other expenses**. Texas Tile sold one of its manufacturing plants for a loss. The plant was valued at $102,000, but the best offer was only $90,000, which meant a $12,000 loss on the sale of the plant. Because Texas Tile's primary activity is not the buying and selling of manufacturing plants, the loss from the sale is recorded as an other expense.

Net Income Before Taxes

The totals for other income and other expenses are added together. If this sum is positive, income from operations is increased by this amount to arrive at net income before taxes. If the sum is negative, income from operations is reduced by this amount to arrive at net income before taxes. Since other expenses were greater than other income by $4,700, Texas Tile's net income of $33,750 before taxes is less than its income from operations of $38,450.

Federal Income Taxes

After considering all the firm's expenses and revenues, the accountant estimates the amount owed in federal income taxes. Table 21-1 shows that the more money a business makes, the more taxes it pays. A business making $50,000 a year pays 18.5 percent of this amount to the government. A firm making $10 million a year pays 45.8 percent of its profits to the government as income tax.

Table 21-1

Income and Income Taxes

Yearly Income	Yearly Income Taxes	Yearly Income Taxes as a Percentage of Income*
$ 10,000	$ 1,700	17.0%
25,000	4,250	17.0
30,000	5,250	17.5
50,000	9,250	18.5
75,000	16,750	22.3
100,000	26,750	26.7
200,000	72,750	36.3
500,000	210,750	42.1
1,000,000	440,750	44.1
2,000,000	900,250	45.0
10,000,000	4,580,750	45.8
100,000,000	45,980,750	45.9

*Calculations are based on 1982 federal income tax tables.

Net Income After Taxes

The real bottom line on the income statement is net income after taxes. It is the amount of money the firm made during the year. It is calculated by subtracting federal income taxes from net income before taxes. Net income in 1983 for Texas Tile was $27,675.

INVENTORY VALUATION

As we saw from our discussion of the income statement, the accountant cannot calculate net income without first calculating the cost of goods sold. To calculate this figure, the accountant must determine the value of the firm's ending inventory. Two commonly used methods for valuing inventory are FIFO and LIFO. Before discussing them, let's first take a closer look at the inventory valuation problem.

The Valuation Problem

Additions to inventory and the selling off or using up of inventory occur continually throughout the year. Your local supermarket sells many tubes of toothpaste every day. And at regular intervals, a clerk restocks the toothpaste display.

FROM THE FILE

Frank has been a sole proprietor of a successful bicycle shop in Palo Alto, California, for 12 years. During this time, he has always managed the books himself. He measured the performance of his business by whether he was able to pay the bills on time and by whether any cash was left over with which to reinvest in the business or to pay himself a salary.

Because of an illness, Frank hired an accountant to take over his bookkeeping for three months. The accountant said that Frank could not really measure the performance of his business without a balance sheet and income statement. Frank thought that this was too much work—it was nothing more than a way for the accountant to keep doing business with him. Was Frank right?

Thus, inventory supplies are continuously being both drawn down and replenished.

The problem is one of determining the value of the toothpaste inventory on the day for which the supermarket draws up its balance sheet. Which tubes of toothpaste are left on the shelf: the ones the supermarket purchased last week for $1.20 a tube, or those it bought three weeks ago for $0.95? This problem is not as trivial as it may seem. Large cost changes from one inventory purchase time to another can have a dramatic effect on total inventory valuation. LIFO and FIFO deal with this problem. Obviously, if per unit inventory purchase cost does not vary over the year, then there is no valuation problem. Total value of inventory in this case is the number of units left on the shelf at year-end multiplied by the purchase cost per unit.

With prices changing frequently, just what is the value of current inventory?

FIFO

The **first-in, first-out (FIFO)** method is based on the idea that the first items put in inventory are the first ones taken off the shelf and sold. In other words, current sales revenue is matched against the cost of the first items purchased. As a result, inventory on the shelf at the end of the year is assumed to be made up of the most recently purchased items. Ending inventory, therefore, is valued at the cost of the most recent additions to inventory.

Figure 21-6 shows how FIFO works during a period of rising prices. The firm in this example, as of January 1, had 200 units of inventory on hand. It purchased additional units of inventory on four occasions during the year. On the last day of December, 364 days later, the firm counts 300 units left in inventory. These 300 units, under the FIFO method, would be valued at $3,350. Figure 21-6 shows that the first 100 units are valued at the December 15 unit purchase cost of $11.50. Since only 100 units were purchased then, the other 200 units of ending inventory are valued at the September 19 cost of $11.00, at which time 500 units were purchased. Total inventory value, then, is the sum of $1,150 and $2,200, or $3,350.

LIFO

The other valuation method is **last-in, first-out (LIFO)**. Under the LIFO approach, sales revenue is matched against the cost of the most recently purchased items, and ending inventory is assumed to consist of items purchased first. Thus, the earliest inventory purchase costs determine the value of ending inventory. This is the opposite of FIFO.

Figure 21-6 shows the LIFO calculation of ending inventory value for the same inventory purchase history. Of the 300 units of ending inventory, the first 200 are valued at the January 1 unit cost of $8.00. Two hundred units were purchased at that time for $1,600. The other 100 units are valued at the next earliest unit purchase cost of $9.00. The total LIFO valuation is the sum of $1,600 and $900, or $2,500. Note that LIFO produced a much smaller inventory value than FIFO.

INTERPRETING FINANCIAL STATEMENTS

You should now understand the difference between a balance sheet and an income statement. The next question is how to interpret these statements to gain greater insight into a business firm's financial performance. Has a firm improved its financial position? Is it strong relative to its competition? The answers are in the income statement and balance sheet. The task is to pull

Figure 21-6

Inventory Valuation

Available Inventory			
January 1	Inventory	200 units at $8.00	$1,600
March 1	Purchase	500 units at $9.00	4,500
May 17	Purchase	450 units at $10.00	4,500
September 19	Purchase	500 units at $11.00	5,500
December 15	Purchase	100 units at $11.50	1,150
Available for Sale		1,750 units	$17,250

FIFO Inventory Valuation		
Most recent costs, December 15	100 units at $11.50	$1,150
Next most recent costs, September 19	200 units at $11.00	2,200
TOTAL ENDING INVENTORY	300 units	$3,350

LIFO Inventory Valuation		
Earliest costs, January 1	200 units at $8.00	$1,600
Next earliest costs, March 1	100 units at $9.00	900
TOTAL ENDING INVENTORY	300 units	$2,500

them out. There are two basic ways to do this: comparative analysis and ratio analysis.

Comparative Analysis

One way to evaluate financial statements is to compare, for example, the balance sheet one year with the balance sheet of the previous year. The concern is with changes that have occurred between the two years. These changes indicate whether the company is getting stronger or weaker. The annual reports for many companies show balance sheets and income statements for the current year and for nine preceding years. The reader of these comparative financial statements is thus able to spot performance trends.

Figure 21-7 shows a 1981 and a 1980 balance sheet for the Black and Decker Company. Note how Black and Decker's cash position improved slightly from January 1980 to January 1981, while total current assets declined from $840,884,000 in 1980 to $788,154,000 in 1981. Much of this decrease is a result of the firm's efforts to reduce inventory levels. In terms of liabilities, Black and Decker reduced its short-term borrowing from $92,267,000 to $35,007,000. Its total current liabilities were reduced by more than $100 million. This is very positive from the perspective of Black and Decker's creditors.

Ratio Analysis

A great deal can also be learned about a firm's financial performance by looking at certain financial ratios. These ratios are developed from balance sheet and income statement data. The advantage of ratio analysis is that it allows us to assess the performance of one firm against that of others in the same industry. Comparative analysis, on the other hand, typically involves an evaluation of year-by-year performance for a single firm. The usual procedure for ratio analysis is to look at a firm's financial ratios in relation to industry averages. Let's look at several of these financial ratios using the information in Texas Tile's balance sheet and income statement (see Figures 21-3 and 21-4).

Current Position. Current position analysis tells us whether the firm is able to meet its short-term debt obligations. An important ratio here is the

current ratio, which is calculated by dividing the firm's total current assets by its total current liabilities. Texas Tile's current ratio is:

$$\text{Current Ratio} = \frac{\text{Current Assets}}{\text{Current Liabilities}}$$

$$= \frac{\$233,100}{\$103,200}$$

$$= 2.26$$

This means that Texas Tile has $2.26 in current assets for every dollar of current liabilities.

Is Texas Tile's current ratio of 2.26 acceptable? Would a smart banker make Texas Tile a short-term loan? Unfortunately, there is no simple answer to this question. Of course, 2.26 is better than 1.85, but it is also not as good as 3.15. Many accountants, however, believe that a company with a current ratio of 1.75 or higher is a good risk for a short-term lender.

A second ratio for assessing a firm's current position is the **acid-test** or **quick ratio**. Whereas the current ratio includes all current assets and all current liabilities, the acid-test ratio includes only those current assets that can be quickly converted to cash, but all current liabilities. The numerator of the acid-test ratio includes cash, accounts receivable, and notes receivable, but not merchandise inventory and prepaid expenses. The acid-

Figure 21-7

Comparative Balance Sheet for the Black and Decker Manufacturing Company and Subsidiaries (in Thousands of Dollars)

		1981		1980
ASSETS				
Current Assets				
Cash		$ 58,042		$ 53,752
Short-term Investments at cost, which approximates market value		10,807		17,399
Accounts Receivable	$320,561		$308,211	
Less Allowance for Bad Debt	(8,890)		(10,315)	
Net Accounts Receivable		$ 311,671		$ 297,896
Inventories		390,393		453,925
Prepaid Expenses		17,199		17,912
Total Current Assets		$ 788,154		$ 840,884
Property, Plant and Equipment		337,925		300,787
Other Assets		38,693		41,548
		$1,164,772		$1,183,219
LIABILITIES AND STOCKHOLDERS' EQUITY				
Current Liabilities				
Short-term Borrowings		$ 35,007		$ 92,267
Accounts Payable		79,890		92,914
Accrued Expenses		89,570		95,146
Income Taxes Payable		24,180		48,412
Total Current Liabilities		$ 228,647		$ 328,739
Long-Term Debt		269,032		225,608
Deferred Income Taxes		41,516		39,290
Other Long-Term Liabilities		17,596		15,981
Total Liabilities		$556,791		$609,618
Stockholders' Equity		218,693		217,993
Retained Earnings		389,288		355,608
Total Stockholders' Equity		$ 607,981		$ 573,601
		$1,164,772		$1,183,219

Source: Black and Decker Manufacturing Company Annual Reports.

test ratio is always smaller than the current ratio. Texas Tile's acid-test ratio is shown here:

$$\text{Acid-Test Ratio} = \frac{\text{Cash + Receivables + Marketable Securities}}{\text{Current Liabilities}}$$

$$= \frac{\$25{,}400 + \$96{,}000 + \$5{,}000}{\$103{,}200}$$

$$= \frac{\$126{,}400}{\$103{,}200}$$

$$= 1.22$$

Although several ratios are important in assessing a firm's current position, an acid-test ratio of 1.0 or greater is considered quite good. It means that the firm is "liquid" in that it is able to pay its current liabilities.

Merchandise Inventory. A business firm should have enough inventory to meet the needs of its customers. However, too much inventory ties up money that could be used more productively in other ways. The **inventory-turnover ratio** measures how many times a year the firm sells off, or "turns over," its merchandise inventory. It is computed by dividing cost of goods sold by average inventory. Because monthly inventory data typically are not available to analysts outside the firm, it may be necessary to use the average of the inventory at the beginning of the year and at the end of the year. The inventory-turnover ratio for Texas Tile is based on data from Figures 21-4 and 21-5.

$$\text{Average Inventory} = \frac{\text{Beginning Inventory + Ending Inventory}}{2}$$

$$= \frac{\$30{,}000 + \$32{,}000}{2}$$

$$= \$31{,}000$$

$$\text{Inventory Turnover} = \frac{\text{Cost of Goods Sold}}{\text{Average Inventory}}$$

$$= \frac{\$263{,}400}{\$31{,}000}$$

$$= 8.50$$

Texas Tile turns over its merchandise inventory 8.50 times a year.

Once again, it is hard to define a good inventory turnover ratio. But we do know that the higher the inventory turnover ratio, the less inventory the firm usually has on hand. Although this may indicate efficiency, a high turnover ratio may also mean that the firm is not always able to meet the product needs of its customers because of out-of-stock situations.

Debt to Net Worth. This ratio is calculated by dividing total liabilities by net worth. Net worth, or owners' equity, is simply total assets minus total liabilities. The **debt to net worth ratio** measures the amount of money owed to creditors relative to the equity value of the company. A high debt to net worth ratio indicates that the company has a substantial amount of debt, which means that its interest payments will be large.

The debt to net worth ratio for Texas Tile is calculated in the following manner:

$$\frac{\text{Debt to}}{\text{Net Worth}} = \frac{\text{Total Liabilities}}{\text{Owners' Equity}}$$

$$= \frac{\$468{,}900}{\$458{,}200}$$

$$= \$1.02$$

Texas Tile has borrowed a lot of money, but total debt is still only slightly more than owner's equity. That is, the company has $1.02 in debt for every dollar of owners' equity. As a result, it may still be a good credit risk.

Profitability Analysis. A profitability measure frequently used by investment analysts is **earnings per share** of common stock. In general, the more money a firm makes per share of common stock, the more money people will pay for each

"Oh, That's just our financial report and prospectus."

Source: From THE WALL STREET JOURNAL, Permission-Cartoon Features Syndicate.

share of stock. Earnings per share is calculated by dividing net income after taxes by the number of shares of common stock outstanding. For Texas Tile, it is calculated in this way:

$$\begin{aligned}\frac{\text{Earnings}}{\text{Per Share}} &= \frac{\text{Net Income}}{\text{Shares of Common Stock Outstanding}} \\ &= \frac{\$27{,}675}{7{,}600} \\ &= \$3.64\end{aligned}$$

Another measure of profitability is **return on sales**—that is, the amount of profit generated by each dollar of sales. It is calculated by dividing net income by net sales. From Texas Tile's income statement, the ratio would be as follows:

$$\begin{aligned}\frac{\text{Return}}{\text{on Sales}} &= \frac{\text{Net Income}}{\text{Net Sales}} \\ &= \frac{\$\ 27{,}675}{\$708{,}000} \\ &= .039 \text{ (or 3.9\%)}\end{aligned}$$

How to Read an Annual Report

If profitable stock investments are your objective, take time to read the annual reports of the firms in which you are interested before you invest your money. Here's how to go about obtaining and reading annual reports so that you know how to recognize a good investment prospect.

LOCATING ANNUAL REPORTS. If your school library does not have the report you want on hand, the library may subscribe to an annual report microfiche service. In addition, most libraries and local stockbrokers have the names and addresses of the officers of large corporations. Write the treasurer of the company in which you're considering a stock purchase and request a copy of the firm's annual report.

BEGINNING YOUR ANALYSIS OF THE COMPANY. Turn to the back page of the report. Examine the statement of the certified public accountant. If the firm's financial statements are believed to reflect its true financial position, the accountant will say that the report conforms to "generally accepted accounting principles."

Look carefully at the footnotes to the financial statements. The real story behind a firm's financial strength or weakness often is told in the footnotes. For example, the reason why profits are down may be because of a change from LIFO to FIFO. If so, the firm may not have much of a problem. On the other hand, profits may be up simply because the firm has sold off some of its assets. The footnotes will supply this information.

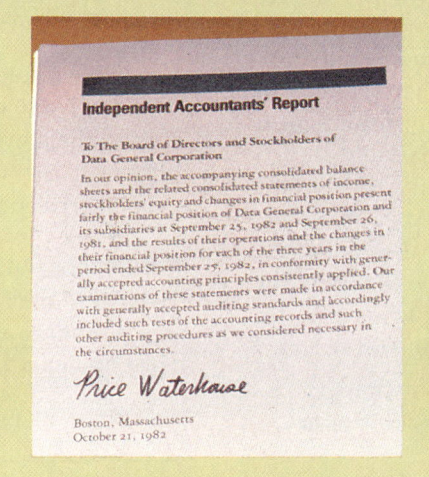

READING THE CHAIRPERSON'S COMMENTS. Turning to the front of the report, you should find the letter from the chairperson of the board. The letter is as much a reflection of the chairperson's personality as it is a statement of the financial well-being of the firm. It usually includes an appraisal of the firm's profitability as well as an explanation of why it made or lost money. If the letter is full of sentences that begin, "Except for..." and "Despite the...," beware!

On the positive side, the letter may also discuss new opportunites for the firm. Ask yourself if management really understands the challenges ahead.

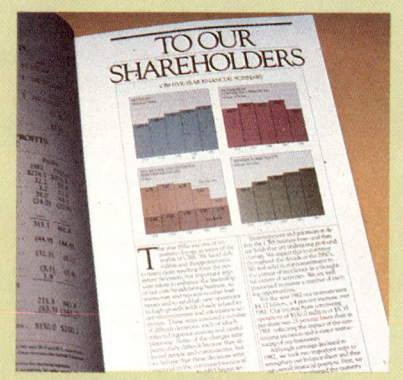

WORKING THROUGH THE FINANCIAL STATEMENTS. In the financial statements, you can see for yourself how the company performed. Make a comparative analysis of the balance sheet. Is working capital growing or shrinking? If it falls too low, the firm may not be able to pay dividends. How about long-term debt? A growing company may need to take on more debt. A firm without growth pros-

Return on sales tends to vary by industry. For example, a jewelry store sells relatively few products; thus, its return on sales needs to be high. A supermarket sells many products in a highly competitive market; its return on sales is low—often less than 5 percent.

A third measure of profitability is rate of **return on equity**. This ratio tells how effective the firm has been in earning money on the invested capital of owners. It is calculated by dividing net income by total owners' equity.

$$\begin{aligned}\text{Return on Owners' Equity} &= \frac{\text{Net Income}}{\text{Owners' Equity}} \\ &= \frac{\$27{,}675}{\$458{,}200} \\ &= .060 \text{ (or 6\%)}\end{aligned}$$

In other words, Texas Tile earned about 4.5 cents on each dollar of owners' equity. Expressed as a percentage, the return on owners' equity was about 6 percent.

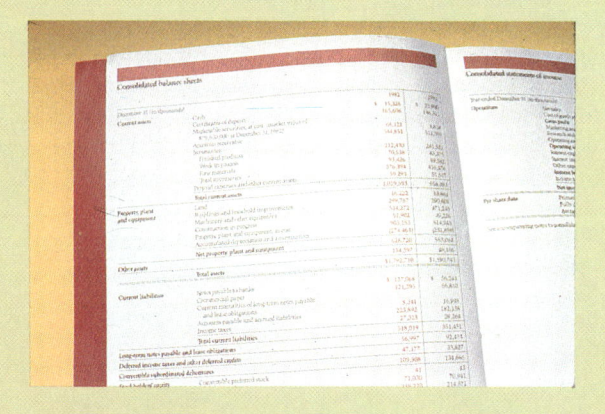

---

pects, however, could choke on the interest charges of additional debt.

Also look at the income statement. Most people care only about net earnings per share. But this figure may fool you. You need to know where the profits came from so that you can tell whether they will keep coming in the future. Have sales increased from year to year? Are sales increasing faster than inflation? If not, sales are declining in real dollars.

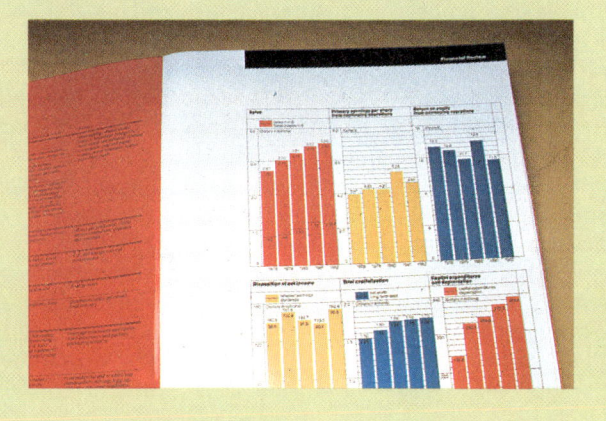

Now you need to conduct a ratio analysis. Calculate the current ratio, acid-test ratio, inventory-turnover ratio, debt to net worth ratio, return on sales, and return on equity. If possible, compare these ratios with those of other leading companies in the industry.

DECIDING WHETHER TO BUY THE STOCK. At this point, you're ready to decide whether or not you should buy the company's stock. What is the stock's current selling price? Is the price in line with your analysis of the company? For example, if the price is down and your analysis indicated that the company's prospects are favorable, then the stock may be a good buy. On the other hand, if the price is high and your analysis uncovered some financial weaknesses, then there is a good chance that the price will fall soon.

KEEPING UP TO DATE. The annual report is an important resource for the investor. However, it comes out only once a year. You should watch your local newspaper, *The Wall Street Journal, Forbes*, and *Business Week* for more timely information.

Source: Adapted from "How to Read an Annual Report," by Jane Bryant Quinn. International Paper Company.

Profile—
Henry Block

In 1955, Richard and Henry Block opened a tax preparation service for individual taxpayers in a downtown storefront in Kansas City. Henry and Richard realized that individual Americans needed somebody who could understand their tax forms and write out their returns quickly and for a reasonably low price. Henry and Richard's service, H & R Block, served that need.

The next year, the Blocks opened two more storefronts in Kansas City, and did even more business. They then tried their idea in New York. H & R Block offices did fabulously in the Big Apple, but the Block brothers didn't like the big town atmosphere. They sold their New York offices for some cash plus 10 percent royalties, and discovered the advantages of franchising.

In following years, H & R Block provided prospective store managers with financial assistance and some training on how to run the business. They put the managers out on their own and expected them to make money. Within a few years, almost every one became successful and the Block name became synonymous with tax return preparers.

In 1972, a tax reform act took about three million Americans off the tax rolls, just when the Blocks were expecting a boost in sales. The company opened 1,200 new offices and nearly lost everything. The brothers had hired an ad agency to develop a massive advertising promotion. The ads were well done, but they didn't appeal to taxpayers. Simultaneously, the Internal Revenue Service was launching an attack on commercial tax-preparation services and urging taxpayers to do their own returns. The IRS opened its own tax-preparation services, newspapers published horror stories about incompetent tax-preparation services, and the IRS commissioner claimed that a fifth grader could fill out a 1040 form.

When it was proven that a fifth grader could *not* fill out a 1040 form, Congress began to study the problem and found that understanding a 1040 required a college education. One reporter took his tax information to several different IRS offices and received different tax bills from each one—exactly the reason behind the IRS's condemnation of commercial preparers.

H & R Block survived the battle. In fact, it was one of few commercial tax-preparation offices that were strong enough to weather the IRS. Other companies tried for several years to get back into the market, but only H & R Block remained profitable.

Henry and Richard Block had done a textbook job of opening a business. First, they found a totally untapped market and entered it so as to discourage any possible competition. Then they developed the market with an eye to operating strictly on a cash basis. Finally, they rewarded their stockholders. The company pays back half of its income each year to stockholders. A stockholder who invested $400 when H & R Block first sold its stock in 1962 has already received over $10,000 in dividends alone; meanwhile, that original stock has split fifteen-fold, making many of the early investors wealthy people. Without large start-up costs, H & R Block has no liabilities, just a lot of owner's equity.

The major problem H & R Block faces is its highly seasonal business: The company does the bulk of its business in the April quarter, its only profitable quarter. To get around this problem, Henry and Richard have started diversifying their interests into public law offices and selling legal services in much the same way they sell tax-preparation services. And they are looking everywhere for services they can provide that can fill out the rest of their year with better and higher earnings.

So far, Henry and Richard have an excellent record. Their stockholders are among the happiest on Wall Street and their management is among the richest in America's service industries. One can't help but expect every new venture to be better than their last.

The rate of return on owners' equity is evaluated in relation to comparable investments. For example, money market funds have paid as much as 15 to 18 percent; high quality corporate bonds, as much as 14 to 15 percent. Before investing in Texas Tile, you would ask yourself how favorably its return compares to these other investment choices, assuming equal risk all around. It would seem that the managers of Texas Tile should do something to increase the company's return on owners' equity.

SUMMARY POINTS

1. Many public accountants or CPAs work as external auditors for their clients. Private accountants prepare financial statements and advise top management about the financial position of the firm.
2. In a complex society, many people, including bankers, creditors, stockbrokers, government workers, labor leaders and the owners and management of businesses need financial information.
3. The accounting equation is Assets = Liabilities + Owners' Equity. It may also be written as Assets − Liabilities = Owners' Equity.
4. Double-entry bookkeeping is based on the accounting equation. Each transaction requires two entries to keep the accounting equation in balance.
5. Assets may be classified as current, fixed, or intangible. Current assets are expected to be sold or used within one year. Fixed assets, such as plant and equipment, are not normally sold during the ordinary operations of a business. Examples of intangible assets are licenses, trademarks, and goodwill.
6. The liabilities and owners' equity part of the balance sheet shows the amount of money owed to creditors and the total value of the owners' investment in the company.
7. Gross sales refers to the revenue received from the sale of a firm's products or services.
8. Cost of goods sold is the amount of money spent to acquire the goods sold by the firm.
9. Gross profit is the difference between net sales and cost of goods sold.
10. Operating expenses are classified as either selling expenses or administrative expenses.
11. Income from operations is determined by subtracting total operating expenses from gross profit.
12. Net income before taxes is calculated by adding other income and other expenses together. This total is then combined with income from operations to yield net income before taxes.
13. Net income after taxes is the amount of money left over after all bills, including federal income taxes, have been paid.
14. The FIFO method of inventory valuation is based on the idea that the first items placed in inventory are the first ones taken out. The LIFO method is based on the idea that the last items placed in inventory are the first ones taken out.
15. One way to evaluate the performance of a company is to compare its financial statements of the current year with those of preceding years. Some useful financial ratios are current ratio, acid-test ratio, inventory-turnover ratio, debt to net worth ratio, earnings per share, return on sales, and return on equity.

KEY TERMS AND CONCEPTS

external auditors
accounting equation
assets
equity
liabilities
owners' equity
double-entry bookkeeping
balance sheet
current assets
cash
accounts receivable
note receivable
merchandise inventory
finished goods
work in process
raw materials
prepaid expenses
fixed assets
depreciation
intangible assets
current liabilities
accounts payable
notes payable
accrued expenses
income tax payable
long-term liabilities
bonds payable
income statement

gross sales
returns
allowances
net sales
cost of goods sold
goods available for sale
gross profit
operating expenses
selling expenses
administrative expenses
general overhead
operating income
other income

other expenses
net income before taxes
net income after taxes
first-in, first-out (FIFO)
last-in, first-out (LIFO)
current ratio
acid-test ratio
quick ratio
inventory-turnover ratio
debt to net worth ratio
earnings per share
return on sales
return on equity

REVIEW QUESTIONS

1. Compare and contrast the duties of the bookkeeper with those of the accountant.
2. How does a CPA differ from an internal auditor?
3. Who are the primary users of accounting information?
4. Assume that a business has $80,000 worth of assets and $30,000 worth of liabilities and that it buys a new microcomputer for $5,000 cash. Show what happens to the accounting equation as a result of the purchase of the computer.
5. When do assets not equal equity in the accounting equation?
6. Describe the different types of current assets.
7. How does the accountant calculate gross profit?
8. A retailer has beginning inventory of $85,000, purchases $176,000 worth of merchandise during the year, and ends up with $90,000 in inventory. What was its cost of goods sold?
9. What does the entry "other income" refer to on the income statement?
10. Define the current ratio and the acid-test ratio. Which is the best ratio for evaluating a firm's financial position?

DISCUSSION QUESTIONS

1. Describe how the accounting equation works.
2. How is the balance sheet used by a firm and its creditors?
3. Why do firms list prepaid expenses on their balance sheets as a current asset?
4. Explain the differences between LIFO and FIFO. Which method of evaluating inventory do you feel most businesses should use?
5. Are there any dangers with using comparative analysis to evaluate financial statements?
6. Select a company of your choice. Carefully examine its financial statements to determine how strong the company is financially.

CASE 21-1

Mississippi Power Company

The Mississippi Power Company (MPC) supplies electric power to a large area in the state of Mississippi. It is characteristic of power utilities in several ways: MPC has extremely high investments in capital assets (power plants, transmission lines, electrical installations, and so on); MPC has no holdings in securities except as short-term investments (which are really only ways to store funds temporarily until they can be reinvested in capital assets); MPC is not allowed by law to invest in securities as noncurrent assets; MPC has the vast majority of its total assets in its plant and equipment and a very large part of its total liabilities in debt. Since MPC finances part of its operation by stock issues, it shows on its balance sheet a large obligation to both common and preferred stockholders.

Several entries on MPC's balance sheet and income statement need clarification. On the balance sheet, "Marketable Securities" are those securities kept

BALANCE SHEET

	1981	1980
ASSETS		
Current Assets		
Cash, Marketable Securities, and Receivables	$ 77,006,000	$109,317,000
Inventory (fuels, supplies, etc.)	58,803,000	72,106,000
Noncurrent Assets		
Power Plant	527,096,000	490,810,000
Miscellaneous	2,090,000	2,973,000
Total Assets	$664,995,000	$675,206,000
LIABILITIES		
Current Liabilities	$ 87,107,000	$108,979,000
Noncurrent Liabilities, Excluding Debt	111,805,000	103,434,000
Total Debt	246,205,000	260,180,000
Owner's Equity and Retained Earnings (1,121,000 common shares, 522,579 preferred shares)	219,878,000	202,613,000

INCOME STATEMENT

	1981	1980
Operating Revenues	$330,549,000	$268,894,000
Revenues from Nonoperating Sources (e.g., interest on investments, rebates, etc.)	1,944,000	1,276,000
Operating Expenses (including taxes)	$279,981,000	$230,249,000
Interest Charges	20,418,000	20,068,000
Net Income	$ 32,094,000	$ 19,853,000
Dividends Paid on Preferred Stock	4,256,000	4,392,000
Net Income After Dividends on Preferred Stock	$ 27,838,000	$ 15,461,000

for short-term investment only; they are very easy to sell and, as stated earlier, constitute a storage for funds. "Noncurrent Liabilities, Excluding Debt" refers to obligations to the cities that MPC serves, power supplies that MPC has already been paid to deliver but that have not yet been supplied, and similar liabilities.

On the income statement, "Operating Revenues" is the same as "Sales Revenue" or "Gross Income." "Operating Expenses" is essentially the same as "Cost of Goods Sold."

Despite some unusual account titles, "Total Assets" for each year will equal "Total Liabilities" for that year. Note that, in accordance with Internal Revenue Service regulations, the cost of interest is deducted from income prior to taxation. MPC's income statement doesn't list "Interest Charges" until after the cost of taxes is listed, but don't let that mislead you. Note also that dividends on preferred stock are deducted after taxes are paid—again in accordance with IRS regulations.

1. Calculate the current ratio, acid-test ratio, debt to net worth ratio, earnings per share ratio, return on sales ratio, and return on equity ratio. Compare these values with those determined in the text for Texas Tile and with the acceptable values (where given) in the text for each ratio.
2. Would you expect a power company or other utility to show unusually high or unusually low ratios? Remember that utilities are considered very secure and stable investment opportunities.
3. Why wouldn't you calculate inventory turnover for Mississippi Power Company? Do you think it really tells you much in this case? Why or why not?
4. Do you think that comparative analysis would be of more or less use, compared to ratio analysis, when comparing electric utilities with each other or with nonutility companies?

CASE 21-2

Texaco

On January 1, 1979, Texaco Oil Company shifted its accounting system to LIFO, so that its financial reports for 1979 first showed the effects of the change. Texaco, like most of the large oil companies, was reporting incredibly high profits and naturally did not want to pay hundreds of millions of dollars in taxes to the government when these dollars could be saved. In its financial report for 1979, Texaco cited a net income of $1,759,069,000. Had Texaco not switched to LIFO, its income would have been $732,200,000 higher. LIFO saved Texaco almost $300 million in 1979—or over a dollar of taxes per share of common stock.

One problem with LIFO is that it works well only in an inflationary and growing economy. LIFO produces a "cushion" of long-standing inventory that remains on the books at a very old and very low price. Unless the company has to sell off its inventory, that cushion stays in place forever. However, if a company has to lower its inventory, it will have to sell part of this "cushion" and report its "Cost of Goods Sold" at a very old and low value. This drives taxable income up dramatically.

In 1980, Texaco was hurting from a glut of oil inventories in the United States. It had to lower its inventories, producing an increase in taxable income of $98,900,000. This increase in income was *not* due to increased sales, but only to the failure of LIFO to cope with recessionary conditions. Thus, in 1980, Texaco had to pay almost $46 million extra in taxes because it chose to value its inventory by LIFO. In 1981, Texaco again had to cut its inventories—this time by 16 percent. While the increased income reported meant that Texaco showed a profit for 1981, the company actually lost money in 1981 (if one ignored the effect of LIFO). In fact, Texaco lost very badly since it had to pay a huge tax penalty for its use of LIFO.

The federal government doesn't allow companies to switch back and forth between LIFO and FIFO as conditions change. Texaco was stuck with LIFO, at least until January 1984.

1. Is LIFO a better valuation than FIFO in the oil business?
2. If the oil glut had not occurred, do you think Texaco would have continued to show reduced income for 1980 and 1981 as it did in 1979? Why or why not?
3. Do you think that LIFO valuation produces misleading financial reports? Why?
4. Would you, as a common stockholder, want to see Texaco's 1980 and 1981 reported income trend continue? Why or why not?

22

Information Management and Computers

After studying this chapter, you should be able to:

- Describe a Management Information System and discuss how it can be designed.
- Explain what a computer is and why it is used.
- Describe the major pieces of computer hardware.
- Describe the major types of computer software.
- Discuss how computers are applied in business.
- Explain how computers can be used to improve decision making.
- Discuss some of the issues or problems raised by the use of computers.

Time magazine's "Man of the Year" for 1982 was not a man, woman or child. The contributions of any individual, *Time* concluded, were small in comparison to the contributions of the computer—*Time's* choice for 1982's "greatest influence for good or evil."

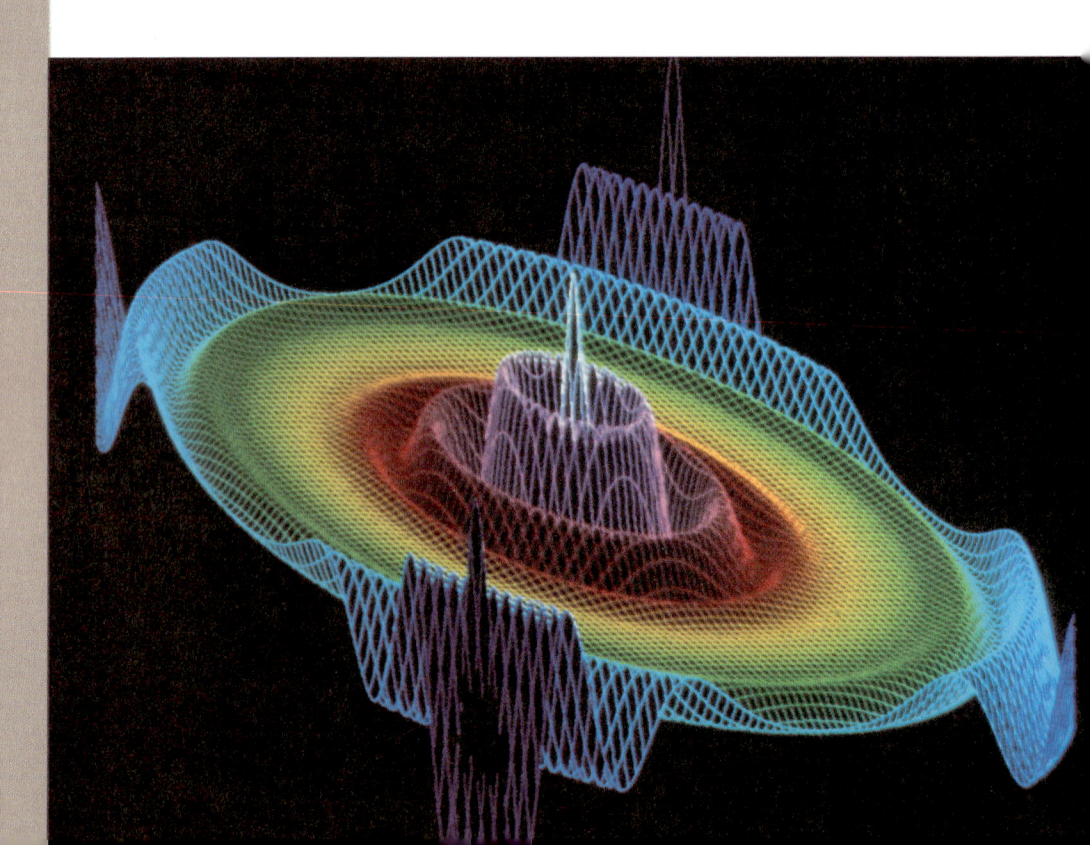

In 1890, 46 percent of the population of the United States was involved in agriculture and 4 percent in information services. By 1979, the percentages had reversed, with 4 percent of the population in agriculture and 46 percent in the information business.[1] This is the age of information. It is an age made possible, in part, by the computer. In this chapter, we examine information management and the role of the computer in business.

INFORMATION AND MANAGEMENT

Six hundred million pages of computer printout. Two hundred thirty-four million photocopies. Seventy-six million letters. These are the *daily* output of U.S. offices.[2] And these figures don't even include managers' phone calls, meetings, or day-to-day observations. Information is the lifeblood of organizations. Flows of information allow organizations to function, to coordinate their parts, and to respond to new challenges. Clearly, managing information is an important and difficult task.

Information Defined

The dictionary defines **information** as "knowledge communicated or received concerning a particular fact or circumstance." Information, therefore, is not just facts and figures and charts and maps. Rather, it is *knowledge* that is passed along in order to enlighten or to inform. Many, if not most, of the figures, calls, and data that managers receive are not really information. Rather than informing, they overwhelm. Still, the problem is not just one of cutting down on paperwork, phone calls, and the like. Much of the information managers need simply does not reach them, or it comes too early or too late.

Management Information Systems

It has been said that "The organizations that will excel in the 1980s will be those that manage information as a major resource."[3] Information is clearly valuable to the firm, and not just because it costs money to collect, process, store, transmit, and display. Of prime importance for management purposes is the fact that information handling systems can be designed to deliver information sooner or later, of higher or lower quality, in the form of text or numbers or images.

To organize and exploit information more effectively, many firms are developing Management Information Systems (MIS). As shown in Figure 22-1, a **Management Information System** is an integrated system of information flows designed to enhance decision-making effectiveness. Good management information is accurate, timely, complete, relevant in form and content, and available when needed.

Components of an MIS. Figure 22-2 on page 431 presents the design of a Management Information System. The figure shows that the MIS is made up of components, activities, and information flows. The components of the MIS are managers, their information requirements, data sources, the data bank, information, and decisions. The activities are the determination of requirements for data, and the subsequent collection, organization, transformation, and analysis of data.

The **demand flow** of information occurs when managers indicate that they need information to make a decision. If the information is currently available in the firm's files or computer, it may need only be retrieved or accessed to be useful. If it is not available, it will need to be collected from any of several data sources, whether within or outside the firm. The **supply flow** of information refers to the appropriate routing of information to the manager.

Design of the MIS[4]. To design an MIS, it is necessary to set objectives, to identify constraints, to determine information needs and sources, and to

---

[1] M.U. Porat, "The Information Economy" (Unpublished thesis, Stanford University). As reported in the *Wall Street Journal* (February 23, 1981), p. 1.

[2] *Data Management* (November, 1981), p. 43.

[3] J. Diebold, "Foreword to the Diebold Group Special Report, IRM: New Directions in Management," *Infosystems*, (October, 1979), p. 41.

[4] This section is based on Robert G. Murdick, Joel E. Ross, INTRODUCTION TO MANAGEMENT INFORMATION SYSTEMS, © 1977, pp. 8, 147, 149. Reprinted by permission of Prentice-Hall, Inc., Englewood Cliffs, New Jersey.

There are many ways to communicate needed information.

put the system together. Managers will be more effective decision makers to the extent that:

- They get early warning signals of trouble ahead.
- They get information to assist in decision making.
- The system automatically makes certain decisions that don't require managerial input.
- Routine clerical operations are automated.
-

Specific objectives should be set to help accomplish these purposes. Figure 22-3 shows how these purposes tie in with MIS objectives and related company objectives. Figure 22-4 presents MIS objectives for some specific functions of the organization, such as purchasing and project control. The figures are on page 432.

Constraints on MIS design may be externally or internally imposed. External constraints may

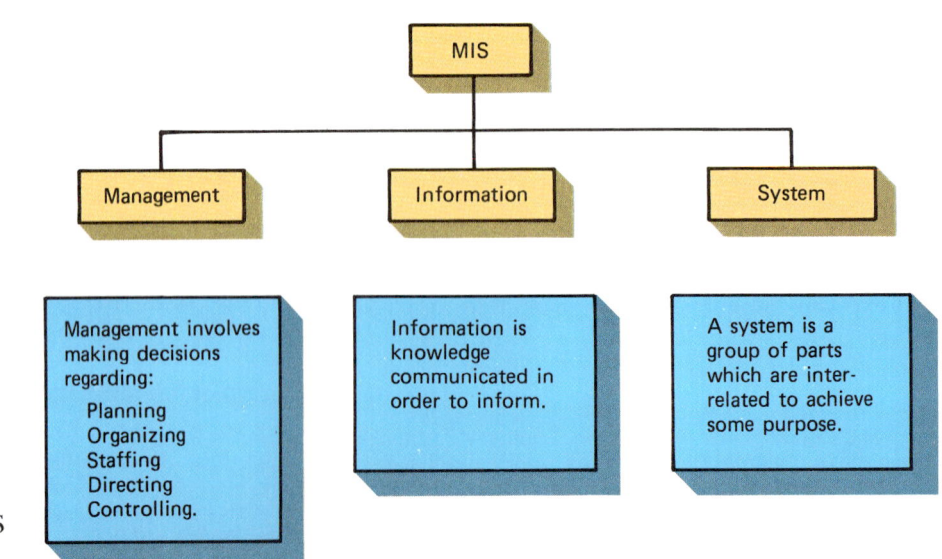

Figure 22-1

The Basic Meaning of a MIS
Source: Murdick and Ross, p. 8.

MIS
— Management
— Information
— System

Management involves making decisions regarding:
　Planning
　Organizing
　Staffing
　Directing
　Controlling.

Information is knowledge communicated in order to inform.

A system is a group of parts which are interrelated to achieve some purpose.

Figure 22-2

The Management Information System

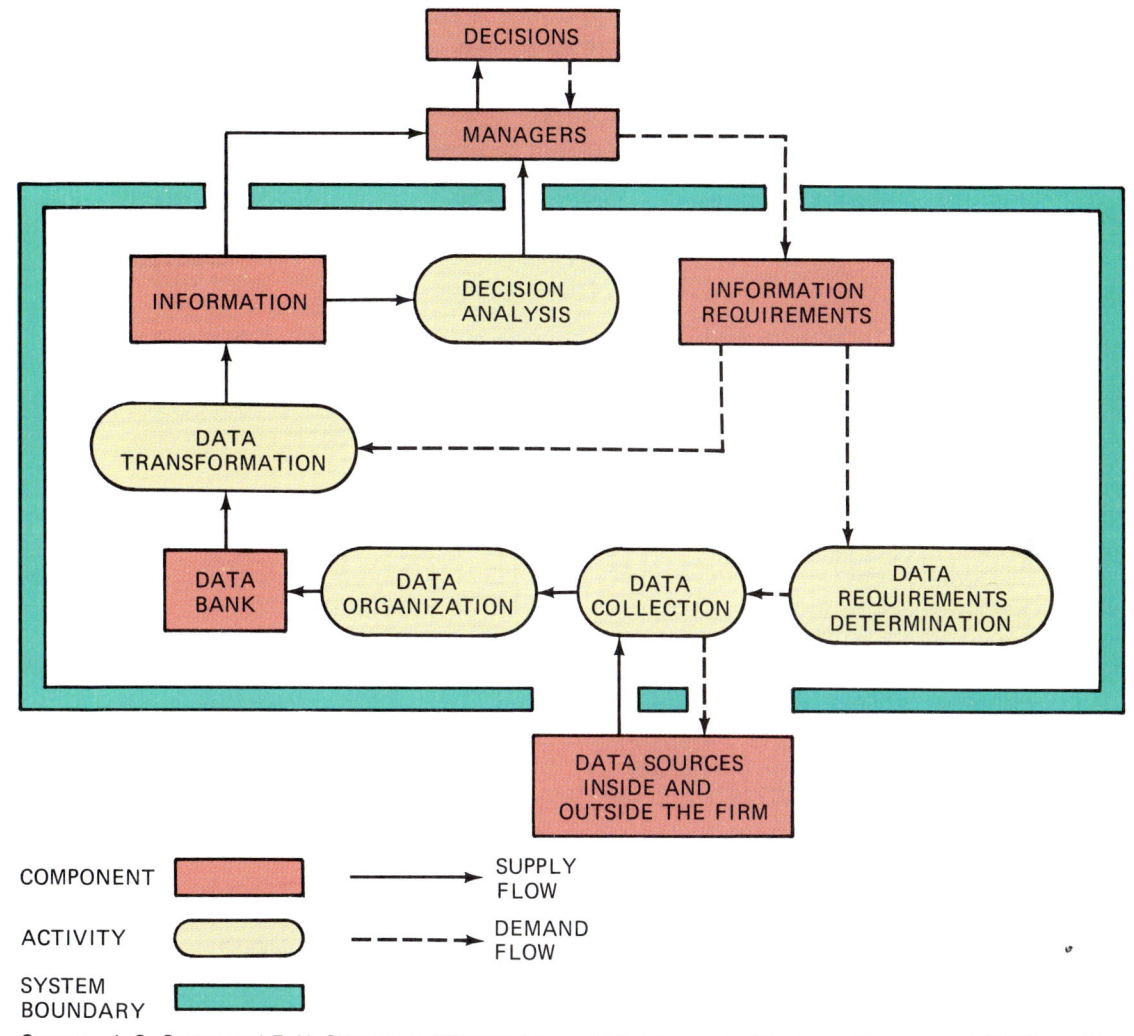

Source: J. C. Carter and F. N. Silverman, "Establishing a MIS," *Journal of Systems Management* (1980), p. 16.

include government regulations, customer demands, or supplier needs. Cost, computer capacity, availability of personnel, and policy considerations are four possible internal constraints.

Once MIS goals and constraints have been identified, the next step is to write a clear statement of information needs. These needs depend on the manager. Some managers desire a sophisticated, computerized system; others want to "keep things simple." Some say, "Get me all the facts"; others say, "Get me only what I need to know." After needs are determined, the sources of the desired information can be found. Some of these sources are considered in the appendix following this chapter.

Finally, the system must be put together. This involves charting the needed flows of information, such as marketing and sales information and reports, and determining how the information is to be stored (data bases), how inputs to the MIS, such as personnel information, will be coded and which type of equipment, such as computers and keypunches, will be needed.

COMPUTERS

In 1952, a new device called the electronic computer predicted that Dwight Eisenhower would win the presidential election by a landslide.

Figure 22-3

Examples of MIS Objectives

Source: Murdick and Ross, p. 147.

Purpose of a MIS	Typical MIS Objective	Related Company Objective
1. Early warning signals	Prevent surprises due to technological break-throughs affecting the firm's products	Avoid crash development programs or loss of market share
2. Decision-assisting information	Supply financial trends and ratios to management	Make good cash and capital investment decisions
3. Programmed decision making	Allocate advertising expenditures among selected magazines	Provide economic and broad support for sales force
4. Automation of routine clerical operations	Automate payroll computations	Timely and accurate pay of employees at minimum cost

Viewing the prediction with disbelief, the programmers changed the results. But the computer was right—Eisenhower was a landslide winner. The public was awed. Here was a machine that was smarter than humans. The computer had captured the people's imagination. Society and business would never be the same.

Computers are now used in virtually every area of business. Business and government spend an estimated $50 billion a year for computer equipment, materials, and staff. In the future, an inability to deal effectively with computers may even be seen as a sort of illiteracy.

What is a Computer?

A **computer** is a machine that can carry out complex and repetitious operations at very high speeds. It receives data and instructions, processes the data into desired information, and provides results in a form that can be read by a person or another machine.

Figure 22-4

Objectives for MIS Subsystems

Source: Murdick and Ross, p. 149.

Subsystem	Objective
Inventory	Optimize inventory costs through the design of decision rules specifying optimum reorder points, safety stock levels, and reorder quantities, each capable of continuous and automatic reassessment.
Accounts Payable	Pay 100 percent of invoices before due date.
Purchasing	Provide performance information on buyer's price negotiations with suppliers in order that purchase variance can be controlled within set limits.
Production Control	Identify cost and quantity variances within one day in order to institute closer control over these variables.
Project Control	Identify performance against plan so that events, costs, and specifications of the project can be met.

CONTROVERSIAL ISSUES

Computer Technology—Time to Slow It Down!

Early computers were built one at a time, with specific customers and purposes in mind. Such custom-built engineering demanded intense research efforts. Today computers are mass-produced, and they are rapidly entering all aspects of our personal lives and our businesses. Is it time for the computer companies to slow down computer research and improve the marketing, pricing, and versatility of computers before they invent more sophisticated models?

Pro

Yes, the computer industry has failed to keep up with its own technology. Today computers can perform calculations with incredible speed and store unbelievable quantities of data. But the industry has yet to find a way to protect these data from illegal users. "Computer crime" is already commonplace. Employees often waste company time to run private programs that can't be recognized because of limitations in computer developments.

A basic flaw in the entire computer industry has been that investors have expected the computer companies to be star performers. Sooner or later, investors will decide that there are better high-technology stocks to invest in, and many computer companies will find themselves stranded with high-growth, high-research-oriented policies that don't work when investors aren't willing to provide the necessary funds.

Pricing then becomes the crux of the problem. American computer manufacturers are being challenged by foreign competitors. Everywhere prices on computer equipment are plummeting, and companies have to maintain very high sales to keep their profits up. Computers have entered the stage of their life cycle where competition is intense and pricing becomes essential to survival in the market. And competitive pricing means that a company has to have low production costs as well.

So far, computer companies have made little attempt to manufacture their products as cheaply as possible. Instead they have charged premium prices, claiming that new features justify the prices. Well, the industry must learn that buyers don't care about sophisticated features when they can't afford the product in the first place.

Buyers want and need highly versatile, easy-to-use, and affordable computers. To take advantage of the new demand, computer companies must provide versatile, easy-to-use and *less expensive* computers. It's that simple!

Con

No, the mistake made in the argument above is in misinterpreting the product life cycle of the computer. Computers are still in a rapid growth stage where demand still exceeds supply, and prices are still a bit too high. It's easy to be trapped into thinking that the product life cycle is just a smooth curve that rises, evens out, and then drops. In fact, the life cycle of computers is highly complex, with all kinds of plateaus, rises, and dips. This happens because there are many different kinds of computer products, not all of which are subject to the same demand. For example, old tube-type computers are worthless today, and the early transistorized computers of the 1960s are little more than scrap. Even today, many highly sophisticated and expensive computer systems can have lifetimes of only two or three years—all because the quality of computers is improving so fast. At the same time, new markets are opening for computers—personal computers, for example—and new and special demands for sophisticated, ultra-high-performance computers are appearing—military guidance systems, for example.

The computer industry needs to keep its emphasis on research and technological development. After all, computer experts are saying that what they have created so far hardly begins to touch what they will have in another five or ten years. We need to keep ahead of the competition in technological research and we need to find new computer products to satisfy markets as yet unrecognized. Meanwhile, the computer industry must produce large quantities of low-cost and low-priced computers to satisfy mass demand in business and at home. Otherwise, the United States will be a has-been in the computer industry.

Profile—
Dr. An Wang

Dr. An Wang is chairman of the board and president of Wang Laboratories, Inc., a research and development based manufacturer of computers and word processing equipment.

Dr. Wang's recognition in the scientific community came in the early 1950s after his invention of the magnetic pulse controlling device, the principle upon which the magnetic core memory is based. For over 20 years, the core memory was a basic component of the modern computer.

In 1940, Wang received a bachelor of science degree from Chiao Tung University, Shanghai, China. In 1945 he came to the United States, where he earned a Ph.D. in applied physics at Harvard University. In 1951, he began his electronic instrument development company, Wang Laboratories, in Boston. Increasing business necessitated moving the company several times, finally establishing its headquarters in Lowell, Massachusetts, in 1976. Wang Laboratories is presently ranked 341 in the Fortune 500 and employs more than 19,000 people all over the world.

In 1962, Dr. Wang developed the first electronic typesetter justifying system, the LINASEC, which was then produced by another company. Wang Laboratories introduced a desktop computer called LOCI in 1965. This first of the Wang electronic scientific desk calculators offered the user the unique feature of generating logarithms with a single keystroke. Every year since the production of the first LOCI, the Wang staff has generated a steady progression of innovations in the field of office automation. In 1972, the company introduced its first word processing products.

In 1980, Wang Laboratories identified six technologies that comprise the automated office: data processing, word processing, image processing, audio processing, networking, and human factors. The company then defined office automation as people using these technologies to manage and communicate information more effectively.

The company integrates the various technologies into single systems and families of systems. All new product developments must address genuine customer needs and must enhance the return on investment of existing customers, offering a family of systems, a clear upgrade path, and compatibility. Further, new product developments must offer a reasonable ratio between development and time required to reach the market.

This approach has made Wang Laboratories the leading worldwide supplier of computer-based office automation systems, with 1982 revenues exceeding $1 billion, net earnings over $100 million, and sales offices in over 70 countries.

There are two types of computers—analog and digital. The **analog computer** uses electrical circuits to simulate the behavior of other types of physical systems. For instance, an appropriate electrical circuit could be used to create the likeness of a physical system of masses and forces. The **digital computer** computes with digits, that is, with numbers. Since the analog computer is almost always used for engineering rather than for business applications, we will focus in this chapter on the digital computer.

Why Use Computers?

Computers have at least five advantages over the human decision maker. First, computers are fast: The speed of some modern computers is measured in nanoseconds (billionths of a second!). Second, they can perform operations that are far too complex for human minds. Travel into space would probably have been impossible without them. Third, computers have a vast memory capacity. Even the computers now being bought for home use are able to store many millions of pieces of information. Fourth, computers are unemotional when performing mathematical calculations or analyzing decision alternatives. Computers will not put off making a decision and will not distort facts to build a case. Finally, computers don't get bored. They find the same challenge in adding two numbers as in guiding the space shuttle.

These strengths of computers suggest the kinds of tasks for which they are most useful: tasks demanding fast completion; very complex jobs, with many tricky computations; repetitive, boring tasks. We'll see, though, that a computer is really a very fast, efficient simpleton. It can only follow orders spoken in the simplest possible language. At least for now, it lacks any real creativity.

Computers Big and Small

Modern computers are electronic. That is, they rely entirely on electronic pulses to function. Early electronic computers used vacuum tubes. Because the vacuum tubes were bulky and generated quite a bit of heat, the computers were often huge and had to be kept in air-conditioned rooms.

The first big electronic computer, ENIAC (Electronic Numerical Integrator and Calculator) was built in 1946. It took up 1,500 square feet of floor space, weighed 30 tons, contained 18,000 vacuum tubes, ate 140,000 watts of electricity, and cost a fortune. It was quickly made obsolete by the development of the transistor. Transistors allowed computers to be smaller, more reliable, and easier to maintain and repair. Computers also became faster, had greater memory capacity, and could use a variety of languages.

Most computers now use integrated circuits, called microprocessors, instead of transistors. **Microprocessors** are tiny wafer-shaped chips that can hold as many as 128 million pieces of information. A single chip of this type is more powerful than its ancestor, ENIAC. Unimaginable a few decades ago, these chips are now a part of our lives; such everyday products as digital watches, pocket calculators, and video games could not have been built without them. There's more good news: these products are not only getting more sophisticated, they're getting cheaper too. Pocket calculators selling for $400 in 1970 retailed (in fancier versions) for about $10 a decade later. It has been estimated that if automobile technology had improved as quickly as computer technology, a Rolls-Royce would cost less than $70 today.

The computer chip—the cornerstone of a revolution in product development.

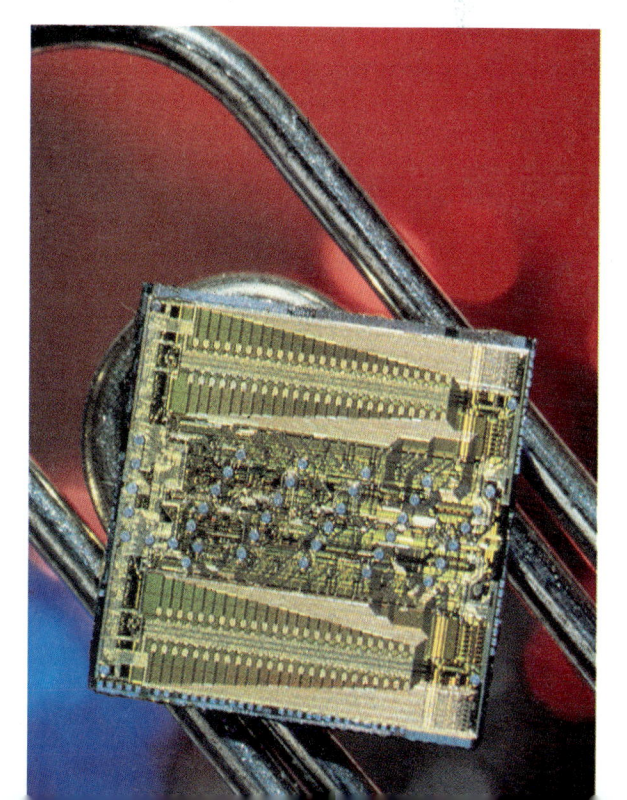

Computers still come in all sizes, including huge "supercomputers." However, microprocessors have made it possible to develop small yet powerful **minicomputers** and even the typewriter-sized **microcomputers** that are finding extensive use in businesses and homes. Complete microcomputer systems capable of performing statistical analyses, text editing, and many other business-related chores are now available for under $2,000.

COMPUTER HARDWARE

The computer and its support equipment are called **hardware**. This is the collection of metal, nuts, and bolts that we see when we look at a computer. As shown in Figure 22-5, the hardware includes input units, processing units, and output units. As a group, input and output units are referred to as **peripheral equipment**.

Input Units

Data and programs are entered into a computer system through **input units**. Before this happens, however, the data and programs are put in "machine-readable" form on punched cards, paper tape, magnetic tape, disk, or other **storage media**. Card readers, paper tape readers, and magnetic tape drives are all examples of input units. Generally, data are collected for some period of time, such as an hour or a day, and then processed all at the same time. This is called **batch processing**.

Nearly everyone has seen **visual display terminals** in offices, airports, or banks. Visual display terminals use a **cathode ray tube (CRT)**—a screen much like that of a television—to show input and output. As data and instructions are entered on a typewriter-like keyboard, they appear on the screen. Visual display terminals allow for **on-line processing**—all input and output units are hooked directly to the processing unit for instant input and output. Such terminals also permit **time-sharing**, in which many different terminals are hooked to the same main computer. Because the main computer processes data so quickly, each user gets very rapid response.

HAL, the computer in the movie *2001: A Space Odyssey*, communicated with two humans by speaking and listening. Some computers now have this voice input capability. One computer has been developed that can even tell the difference between a Texas drawl and a proper English accent. United Parcel Service has a sorting computer that interprets spoken destination codes and then directs a mechanical arm to move packages accordingly. Figure 22-6 shows some input media and devices.

Figure 22-5

Typical Computer Hardware Components

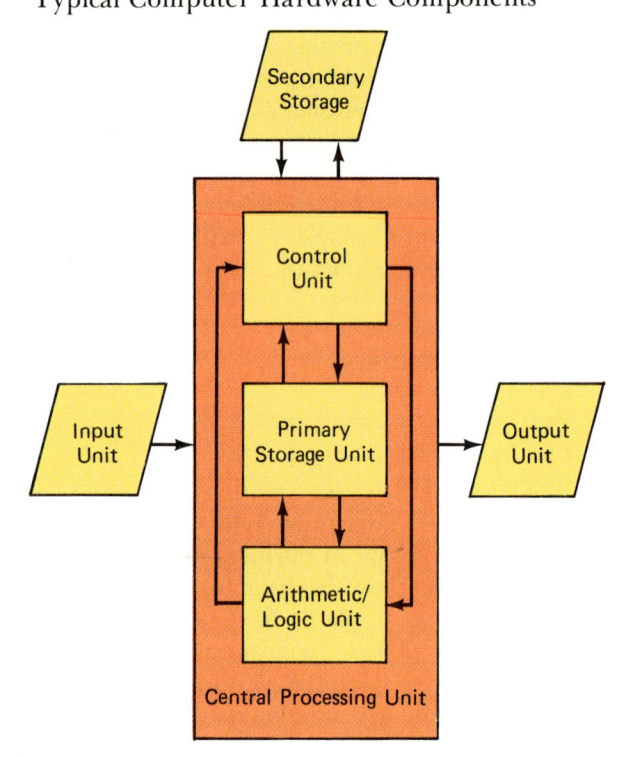

Processing Unit

The **central processing unit (CPU)** is the "brain" of the computer. It does its thinking and memorizing. The CPU has three main parts: the arithmetic/logic unit, the control unit, and the primary storage unit. The **arithmetic/logic unit** performs the mathematical (such as adding and subtracting) and logical (such as comparison) operations on the data. The **control unit** directs what happens within the computer. For instance, it indicates where data should be stored. The **primary storage unit** is the computer's main **memory**, storing data and program instructions.

Output Units

Output units present the results of computer operations to the user. Sometimes, results are presented in a form that can be read by the user, such as on a computer printout. Other times, they are put in a form that is easy to store or to use for further operations. Examples include punched cards or magnetic tape.

Secondary Storage

Secondary storage is extra memory outside the primary storage unit of the central processing unit. Magnetic tapes and disks are examples of secondary storage devices.

COMPUTER SOFTWARE

As shown in Figure 22-7, **software** refers to computer programs and supporting hardware for their use. Software must be prepared before the computer is used. Without it, hardware is useless. Typically, software preparation involves flowcharts, programs, and documentation.

Flowcharts

A **program flowchart** is a graph showing the sequence of operations to be performed by the computer. Suppose we would like to write a program instructing the computer to figure a weekly paycheck. We might first draw a flowchart such as the one shown in Figure 22-8. Then, we would use the flowchart as the basis for writing a computer program.

Computer Programs

A **computer program** is a precise set of instructions, usually written from the program flowchart. The set of instructions is coded in a

Figure 22-6

Some Input Media and Devices

438   Part 6 • Management Control and Information Systems

Figure 22-7

Software and supporting hardware. The bottom photo shows the Cray-1S computer system.

language that the computer can understand. Computers can read any of several languages; none of them, unfortunately, is "simple" English.

Machine Language. Machine language, popular among programmers in the early days of computers and still used by some, is based on the **binary system**, that is, on only two digits—0 and 1. These digits (called **bits** from BInary DigiTs) are combined into strings (called **bytes**). Bytes, in turn, are used to represent alphabetical characters. Digital computers operate by turning on and off many electrical circuits. Turning a circuit on represents a "1," turning a circuit off represents a "0."

Since machine language is hard to learn and use, other "higher level" languages have been developed. These higher level languages are called symbolic languages because they are made up of many symbols, such as +, ×, DO, and /. Inside the computer, a language translator, called a **compiler**, translates symbolic language into machine language so that it can be understood by the computer. Let's take a look at a few of the more popular symbolic programming languages.

BASIC. As its name suggests, the **BASIC** language (short for Beginners All-Purpose Symbolic Instruction Code) is easy to learn. BASIC is the language most often used on small computers. Since small computers have been adopted by many organizations, a knowledge of BASIC is very useful. Figure 22-9 shows what BASIC looks like. It is based on the flowchart drawn in Figure 22-8.

COBOL. COBOL (COmmon Business-Oriented Language) was developed so that data could be processed in a language something like English. Despite being rather difficult to learn, COBOL is widely used throughout business.

FORTRAN. FORTRAN (from FORmula TRANslator) was developed by IBM in the 1950s and is still widely used for mathematical and statistical applications. FORTRAN is the most widely taught programming language in colleges of business administration. Although similar to BASIC, and somewhat more flexible, it is a bit harder to use.

Canned Programs. Happily, using a computer does not always mean starting from scratch and

Figure 22-8

A Flowchart for Computing Weekly Pay

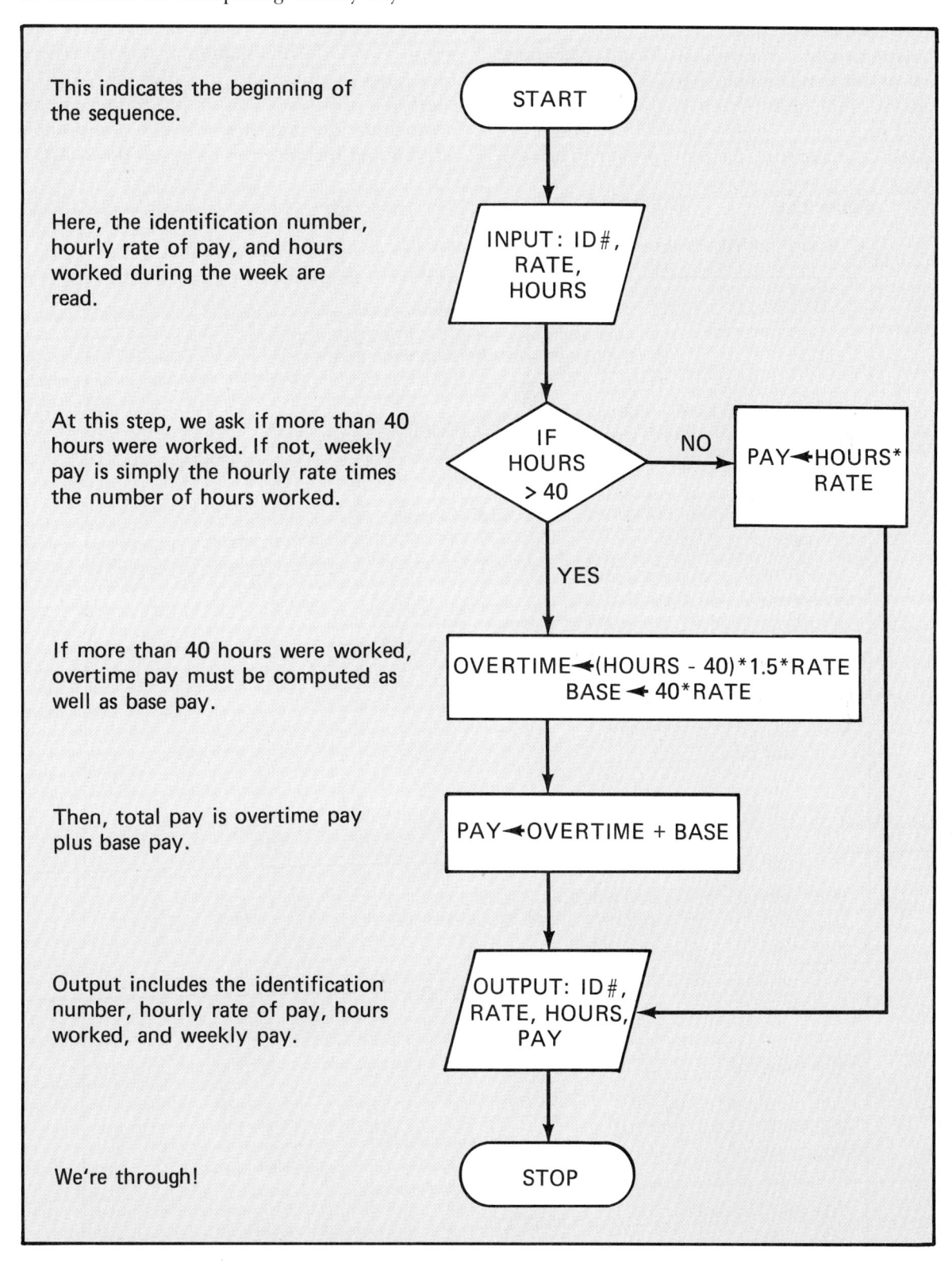

Annotation	Flowchart
This indicates the beginning of the sequence.	START
Here, the identification number, hourly rate of pay, and hours worked during the week are read.	INPUT: ID#, RATE, HOURS
At this step, we ask if more than 40 hours were worked. If not, weekly pay is simply the hourly rate times the number of hours worked.	IF HOURS > 40 — NO → PAY ← HOURS*RATE
If more than 40 hours were worked, overtime pay must be computed as well as base pay.	OVERTIME ← (HOURS - 40)*1.5*RATE BASE ← 40*RATE
Then, total pay is overtime pay plus base pay.	PAY ← OVERTIME + BASE
Output includes the identification number, hourly rate of pay, hours worked, and weekly pay.	OUTPUT: ID#, RATE, HOURS, PAY
We're through!	STOP

writing a program in BASIC, COBOL, or FORTRAN: Many **canned (or packaged) programs** are available. These programs may perform statistical analyses, find optimal solutions to a problem, provide a convenient form for keeping track of records, or help perform any of hundreds of other tasks. Often, they are reasonably priced and have already been thoroughly "debugged" to make sure that they contain no errors.

Documentation

Documentation refers to the process of providing a permanent record of a computer program. Good documentation makes it easier to find flaws in programs. It is also crucial to new users of a previously written program. Generally, documentation indicates why the program was written and includes the program flowchart, the

Figure 22-9

A "Basic" BASIC Program to Compute Weekly Pay

These statement numbers tell the computer the order in which the statements are to be executed.

This statement serves as a reminder of the purpose of the program.	10 REM PROGRAM TO COMPUTE WEEKLY PAY
Identification number, hourly rate of pay, and hours worked are read.	20 READ ID, R, H
This IF-THEN statement allows branching. If hours worked are greater than 40, it branches to statement 60. If not, it moves on to the next statement.	30 IF H>40.0 THEN 60
If no more than 40 hours were worked, this statement computes pay.	40 P = H * R
This statement tells the program to go to statement 90. (Otherwise, pay would be computed again).	50 GO TO 90
Here, overtime pay is computed. (Notice that we get here only if more than 40 hours were worked).	60 OV = (H − 40) * 1.5 * R
Base pay for 40 hours is figured here.	70 B = 40 * R
Total pay is overtime pay plus base pay.	80 P = OV + B
This statement prints out the identification number, hourly rate of pay, hours worked, and pay.	90 PRINT ID, R, H, P
The end. That wasn't too bad, was it?	100 END

program, sample input and output, and comments.

BUSINESS APPLICATIONS OF THE COMPUTER[5]

As stated earlier, computers are being used today in virtually every area of business. Here, we'll survey some of the more notable examples in manufacturing, marketing, accounting and finance, banking and credit, word processing, and data processing.

Manufacturing

Computers now design products, run production lines, check product quality, control machine loads, and automatically guide machines. As discussed in Chapter 11, computers are essential to Material Requirements Planning. Two additional applications are computer assisted design and computer-controlled production.

Computer Assisted Design. To produce many of the special effects in the 1982 science fiction movie, *TRON*, the dimensions of real objects were fed into a computer. The computer then displayed on a screen an image of each object from any distance and from any perspective. Figure 22-10 shows an example of this procedure. These processes are what computer assisted design (CAD) is all about. CAD is a popular tool with automakers and architectural firms for speeding up design projects and reducing the number of needed drafters.

Computer Controlled Production. Many businesses use computers to run and control manufacturing processes. For example, **numerical control** is a system that relies on punched tape or some other automatic control mechanism to direct machine operations. Lathes, looms, and riveting machines are often run by numerical control. Computers have been used extensively in chemical production, oil refining, and other industries

---

[5] Certain of these examples are drawn from H. J. Watson and A. B. Carroll, *Computers for Business: A Managerial Emphasis,* Revised Edition (Dallas: Business Publications, Inc., 1980).

Figure 22-10

An Example of Computer Assisted Design

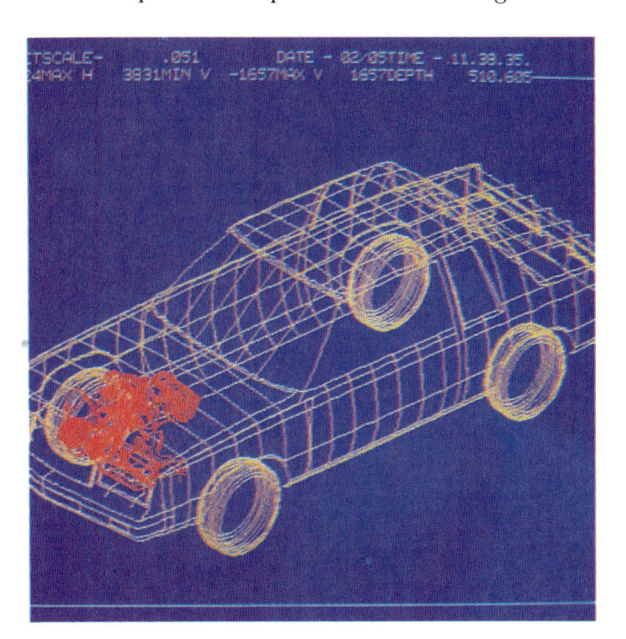

that involve large-volume processing. Computers also put a layer of dye only a few 10,000ths of an inch thick on Polaroid film.

Marketing

Computers have been applied to many routine marketing activities, such as processing customer orders and compiling and reporting sales data. Recently, some more refined applications have been developed.

Sales Analysis. With a computer, sales data can be readily analyzed in terms of product line, territory, customer, and salesperson. Salespersons for Hoffmann-La Roche, Inc., a pharmaceutical firm, take terminals with them on sales calls to help answer doctors' questions.

Sales Forecasting. Because computers are able to process data quickly and to detect and analyze relationships among variables, they are well-suited to sales forecasting. Past relationships among variables can first be evaluated and then extended into the future. Detailed, individualized forecasts, often for many products and different sales regions, can be generated instantly.

"We *can't* sell it -- it knows too much."

Source: From *The Wall Street Journal*, Permission-Cartoon Features Syndicate.

Accounting and Finance

In most companies, the accounting department was the first one to adopt computer technology. Accountants found the computer ideal for storing and processing the vast amounts of data for which they were responsible. Payroll preparation, accounts receivable processing, and customer billing are examples. Two more recent applications are in the areas of financial simulation and securities trading.

Financial Simulation. It is often helpful to determine what a company's financial situation would be like if certain events, such as a jump in sales or an increase in the price of raw materials, were to occur. A financial simulation involves the development of a mathematical model of the firm's financial flows. The model typically includes such factors as costs, revenues, income, and cash flows. Once the model is completed, the numerical values of any of these factors can be changed to see their impact on the values of the other factors. For instance, the impact of a 2 percent sales increase on profits could be assessed.

Securities Trading. Another financial application is in the area of securities trading. Stock price quotations, news items, and data on mergers are all transmitted by computerized equipment. Computerized trading systems are already having a far-reaching impact on securities markets. The International Futures Exchange, or Intex, is a Bermuda-based computerized market that will let participants enter orders from their homes or offices anywhere in the world.

Banking and Credit

Banks also were early to reap the benefits of computers. Many banks computerized their accounting and bookkeeping operations in the early 1960s. Once that was done, many other applications became possible.

On-Site Computers. A wide range of bank processes have been computerized; the processing of checks and handling of time deposits, installment loans, and real estate loans are all examples. Also, many banks make their computers available to small businesses.

Electronic Funds Transfer. A variety of computer applications, grouped under the name of **electronic funds transfer (EFT)**, are changing the way people conduct financial transactions. In this regard, let's discuss automated teller machines, point-of-sale terminals, and automated clearinghouses.

Thousands of **automated teller machines (ATMs)** in shopping centers, bank lobbies, and elsewhere give out cash, take deposits, and report account balances. An even larger number of **point-of-sale terminals** are used in retail stores to verify checks. And dozens of **automated clearinghouses** around the country handle such large-volume transactions as payrolls, transferring funds without the use of checks. Citibank, a leader in electronic banking, has already spent well over $100 million on electronic funds transfer.

It now costs about 30 cents to process a check. Potentially, electronic funds transfer systems could cut that figure by 80 percent.

Word Processing

Microcomputers are increasingly used for word processing. With a word processing system, a person can input, output, and store written information in one easy operation. Corrections can be made easily, and words or sections inserted, deleted, or shifted around. Figure 22-11 shows a

Figure 22-11

Introduction to Business in Floppy Disk Form

computer designed for word processing applications. The "floppy disk" shown contains the information in this chapter.

Data Processing

Another important application of computers is for data processing. **Data processing** is another term for information handling. The information could be of many types, such as names of customers, prices of products, economic indicators, or units in inventory. Let's consider some of the operations that may be performed on data.

Computation. **Computation** refers to the adding, subtracting, multiplying, or dividing of numbers. For instance, to calculate gross profit for each of a company's 200 products, the computer subtracts selling costs for each product from its total sales revenue. This type of repetitious task is efficiently and accurately done by a computer.

Classifying. Many times, it is useful to classify ideas, objects, or people into groups. For example, we might want to group employees by their job classifications, such as sales clerk, district manager, or personnel manager. This process, called **classifying**, is an ideal application for computers.

Sorting. Sometimes, sales orders, inventory items, or the like may need to be put in a sequence. **Sorting** is the arranging of a list of numbers into a desired order. For instance, we might want to sort the numbers 3, 8, 6, 2, 1 into the ascending order 1, 2, 3, 6, 8. Arranging invoices according to their due dates is another task for which computers are ideal.

Merging. **Merging**, or **collating**, refers to the combining of two or more sorted files into a single file in the same sequence. Table 22-1 shows two sorted files and the file into which they were merged.

Moving and Editing. The modifying of data into a more useful form is called **moving** and **editing**. For instance, data may be moved from disk storage to an output device, or the figure 001765 in

Table 22-1

Merging of Files

Territory A Customer Numbers	Territory B Customer Numbers	Merged Customer Numbers
116	86	86
188	112	112
245	181	116
312	356	181
		188
		245
		312
		356

storage may be edited to $17.65 when it is displayed.

COMPUTER-ASSISTED DECISION MAKING

Computers are now relied upon to improve decision making. Such applications include interactive decision making, modeling, and artificial intelligence.

Interactive Decision Making

Many people are concerned that computers will take over decision making, leaving out the human element. Actually, though, the computer is more frequently an aid to human decision making rather than a substitute for it. For example, **interactive computing** permits the user to interact with the computer, reading the information it provides and responding to its questions on a conversational basis, rather than just feeding in data and waiting for an answer. The result is a team effort, drawing on the strengths of people and computers.

How comfortable we feel with computers depends on how "friendly" the computer is programmed to be. In his science-fantasy story, "I Sing the Body Electric," Ray Bradbury wrote of an "electric grandmother," a computerized robot designed to look, talk, and act like a warm, supportive grandmother. In the future, interactive programs will almost certainly be made more "grandmotherly."

Modeling the Decision Maker

People in organizations occasionally face the same routine decisions day after day. An admissions officer selecting people for a college program, a bank officer deciding whether to approve a loan, or a production manager considering schedules for daily production runs are all examples.

Decision makers often say, "These decisions are no challenge to me; they are important but they take up all my time and are routine. I'm responsible for them, so I can't just turn them over to someone else." Wouldn't it be nice if they

FROM THE FILE

Fritz felt that in the 15 years he had been working at Amatex, things had become less and less personal. Computers were making credit decisions, designing products, churning out sales forecasts, and doing just about everything else. It seemed that if you didn't use terms such as "simulation," "byte," and "data bank," nobody listened to you. Fritz wondered if humans would soon become obsolete at Amatex. He could envision the day when computers, programmed with "artificial intelligence," would be the new office workers, gathering around the oil dispenser on their breaks and swapping inside stories about the new microprocessor in the Accounting Department. How would you advise Fritz to deal with this situation?

could have these decisions made as they would like to have them made, but without actually doing it themselves? This can be done by building a **model of man**, that is, by designing a computer model of the decision maker. The model is designed to behave as the decision maker behaves. Once the model is constructed and tested for accuracy, it can replace the decision maker. In "borderline" cases, the model could leave the decision up to the manager.

Artificial Intelligence

The goal of **artificial intelligence** is to design computers to process information like human beings do. The first step in developing artificial intelligence is to study the human brain. For instance, how the brain processes information, draws analogies, and solves puzzles might be examined. Then, the computer is programmed to work in the same way as the brain. When so programmed, the computer, in a sense, is thinking. Because the computer is faster, more reliable, and more objective, it might be expected to make vastly superior decisions.

Programs have been developed that mimic the human brain to play backgammon, to make generalizations, and even to draw inferences and make analogies. Although real learning and creativity are currently beyond the ability of computers, some researchers believe that they are within reach.

PROBLEMS WITH COMPUTERS

Inevitably, any new development with great potential for good also has great potential for bad. This is certainly the case with computers. Let's take a look at four problems commonly associated with computers.

Malfunctions

All of us have heard about computer malfunctions. A computer error caused false alarms on the Air Force's NORAD missile detection system, moving us to the brink of war. On a smaller scale, computer malfunctions can be devastating for businesses. Often, though, computers are blamed for human mistakes.

Invasion of Privacy

In his frightening book, *1984*, George Orwell portrayed computers as all-seeing intruders into people's private lives. Our government now has billions of records on individuals, stored on thousands of data systems. Personal finances, health, travels abroad, and traffic violations are among the data that are available from government computers. Because of fears that such systems could be misused, plans to develop even larger networks of computers, such as a massive network called FEDNET tying together all government computers, have been scrapped.

Businesses also have vast quantities of sensitive information. Medical records, past arrest records, or military discharge information could prove harmful to employees if made public. In response to such concerns, firms such as Cummins Engine Company have refused to computerize their personnel files. Others, including IBM, have removed much information from their files to guard employee privacy. General Electric, Eastman Kodak, and Caterpillar Tractor allow employees access to their files.

Computer Crime

A 25-year-old computer terminal operator used computer trickery to receive pension checks under 30 different names. An accountant working for a fruit wholesaler used a computer to inflate prices on invoices and to send the extra money to dummy vendors. He amassed $1 million over six years. In the infamous Equity Funding fraud, computers were used to build a confusing pyramid of fake assets. By the time the fraud was uncovered in 1973, $185 million in fake assets had been created.

Computers have spawned a whole new class of criminals. Often computer experts, these criminals take advantage of flaws in systems or of access to files to steal an estimated $300 million a year. The FBI figures that, while the average armed bank robbery nets about $10,000, computer crimes often bring in more than $1 million.

Negative Human Reactions to Computers

People's reactions to computers run to extremes. Some view them as all-knowing. They treat anything coming out of a computer as "truth," beyond challenge. In fact, of course, what the computer produces is no better than what is put into it and how it is instructed to process it. This "garbage in—garbage out" idea is too often forgotten.

Other people fear the computer, believing that it will threaten their jobs, either by replacing them or by requiring skills that they don't have. Others fear that we will become too dependent on computers. For still others, the computer represents change and the unknown. Each of these sources of fear may lead to resistance.

Still interested in computers after hearing about these problems? If so, take a look at Figure 22-12, which lists some important factors to consider when buying a computer.

Figure 22-12

Selecting a Computer

There is more to choosing a computer system than just picking the one that is biggest, fastest, or most expensive. Instead, a careful assessment of your needs should first be undertaken. Then, selection criteria can be set up. These might include:
- Service level—the ability of the system to work quickly and reliably.
- Flexibility—whether the system can be used for a variety of applications.
- System support—the quality of maintenance and emergency service.
- Ease of use of hardware and software.
- Cost of installation and operation.
- Quality of supplier management.
- Delivery time, space requirements, and compatibility with equipment now in use.

SUMMARY POINTS

1. A Management Information System is an integrated system to provide managers with information which will enhance the effectiveness of their decision making.
2. Computers have certain advantages relative to human decision makers that make them useful for complex or routine problems, but they are unlikely to replace human decision makers in the foreseeable future.
3. For many business applications, large mainframe computers are being replaced by smaller, more flexible minicomputers and microcomputers.
4. Hardware, the "nuts and bolts" of the computer, includes input units, output units, and processing units.
5. Software preparation involves flowcharting, programming, and documenting. Computers understand only machine language, but higher level languages which are easier to use can be translated by a compiler.
6. Computers have many applications in manufacturing, marketing, accounting and finance, banking and credit, word processing, and data processing.
7. Computers can improve decision making in several ways, including interactive decision making, models of man, and artificial intelligence.
8. Some of the problems associated with computers are malfunctions, invasion of privacy, computer crime, and negative human reaction in the workplace.

KEY TERMS AND CONCEPTS

information
Management Information System
demand flow
supply flow
computer
analog computer
digital computer
microprocessor
minicomputers
microcomputer
hardware
peripheral equipment
input units
storage media
batch processing
visual display terminals

cathode ray tube
on-line processing
time-sharing
central processing unit
arithmetic/logic unit
control unit
primary storage unit
memory
output units
secondary storage
software
program flowchart
computer program
machine language
binary system
bits
bytes
compiler
BASIC
COBOL

FORTRAN
canned (packaged) programs
documentation
numerical control
electronic funds transfer
automated teller machines
point-of-sale terminals
automated clearinghouses
data processing
computation
classifying
sorting
merging
collating
moving
editing
interactive computing
model of man
artificial intelligence

REVIEW QUESTIONS

1. What is information? Why is it important?
2. What is a Management Information System? What are its components?
3. List four purposes of a Management Information System.
4. Give five advantages of computers relative to human decision makers.
5. What is a microprocessor? Why is it important?
6. List three types of computer input units; three types of output units; the three main parts of the central processing unit.
7. What is the difference between software and hardware?
8. List four computer languages.
9. Give applications of computers in manufacturing; marketing; accounting and finance; banking and credit; word processing; data processing.
10. Explain three ways computers can be used to improve decision making.
11. Discuss four problems with use of computers.

DISCUSSION QUESTIONS

1. In what ways is information management similar to the management of other resources? In what ways is it different?
2. Do you think computers are a threat to business? to society? Why or why not?
3. What might be some potential problems with electronic funds transfer?
4. Can you think of business decisions for which computers would *not* be helpful? What might be the characteristics of such decisions?
5. Do you think computers can ever really have artificial intelligence? Why or why not?

CASE 22-1

Computer Courses

There is a large market today for many different kinds of courses designed to teach people about computers and to make them more comfortable with computers. Experts recognize that computers seem very strange to many people. In fact, many people are simply afraid of computers. One expert has estimated that 100 million Americans will need to receive some kind of computer instruction before 1990 if personal computers are to become as widespread as the industry wants them to be. Further, a marketing research company has estimated that computer education will pick up about $3 billion of the total $14 billion that will be spent on personal computers by 1986.

The problems with teaching computer skills have magnified just in the past year or two. In 1980, there were only a very few major computer brands on the market, with even fewer software packages among them. Today, there are literally hundreds of computer brands, each with several different options on software for every possible use. The IBM Personal Computer, for example, has available Easywriter and Easywriter II, plus Easyfiler, Easyspeller and other word processing packages; and other companies offer Wordstar and countless additional word processing packages for the same IBM computer. Education courses on the computer must be able to teach all of these different packages, not just one or two. Also, as equipment becomes more and more sophisticated and purchasers have more choices about memory, disk drives, color graphics, and so on, the problems in teaching about hardware become equally difficult.

One marketing executive has indicated a fear that the personal computer market is already three years behind because it can't train the people who want to buy personal computers. It is clear that the problem is due to get worse before it gets any better.

1. Of the advantages for computers discussed in the text, which are likely to be of most importance to the average individual or family buying a personal computer for personal use? Why?
2. Do potential personal computer purchasers need course instruction in software? in hardware? in both? Why?
3. Do you think courses will overcome adverse human reactions to computers? Why or why not?

CASE 22-2

Computers on the New York Stock Exchange

One of the problems that increased the severity of the stock market crash of 1929 was the inability of stockbrokers to keep up with stock transactions when the market was busy. Stockbrokers often worked all night trying to clear up the paperwork from stock transactions of weeks before. As a result of this experience, the Securities and Exchange Commission went to great lengths to make sure that brokers cleared up their paperwork promptly so the market always knew what prices were being negotiated for stock purchases and sales.

During the crash, the largest number of shares traded in any one day was 12.1 million. By 1970, the high volume day of the year recorded 21.3 million shares sold. Once again the stock exchange fell way behind in its paperwork, and the Securities and Exchange Commission again stepped in.

With the market continuing to grow, improvements were definitely needed. On February 13, 1975, the market sold 35.2 million shares, and on November 5, 1980, it sold 84.3 million shares. By 1980, John Phelan, the president of the New York Stock Exchange, had started a campaign among the major stockbrokers to install modern computer equipment. He pointed out that soon the stock market would be so busy that *only* computers could keep up with transactions.

Reluctantly, stockbrokers started buying computers. Their expenses seemed wasted at first, but in 1982, the market "blew up." In August of 1982, the New York Stock Exchange regularly began recording over-100-million-shares-traded days, and on October 7, 1982, recorded an incredible 147.1 million shares traded on a single day.

With computers, the stockbrokers and investors were able to know the going prices for stocks and bonds instantly. The only delay was in the digital-display ticker tape that recorded each transaction briefly on a screen. And the problem wasn't with computers; the human eye simply could not read more than 900 characters a minute, so the ticker tape could not go any faster and still be usable.

Now, the directors of the New York Stock Exchange are talking about 250-million-shares-traded days, and the stockbrokers aren't doubting them any more. They're just putting in larger and more sophisticated computers to handle the load.

1. In the text, the statement was made that "The organizations that will excel in the 1980s will be those that manage information as a major resource." How do you judge the future success of the New York Stock Exchange, using this standard?
2. Explain how the New York Stock Exchange is a Management Information System. In which parts of the system can computers be used to improve efficiency?
3. Which of the selection criteria in Figure 22-12 were important to stock-brokers picking new computers? Why?

Statistical Appendix

Statistics is the field of study that deals with the collection, classification, analysis, interpretation, and presentation of numerical information. In this appendix, we describe how information is gathered, discuss some useful statistical measures, and show how information can be displayed. Finally, we will give some tips on interpreting statistical information.

GATHERING INFORMATION

The solution of nearly all business problems begins with the gathering of information. Without proper information, how can business managers make intelligent decisions about job incentive programs, marketing strategies, or investment planning? All information sources are classified as either secondary or primary.

Secondary Data Sources

Secondary data are currently available data. These data were collected at an earlier time for a project different from the one now being undertaken. Two general secondary data sources are internal records and published information sources.

Internal Records. There is often a wealth of information available in the firm's own internal records. For example, an analysis of purchase orders may give clues as to which market segments are growing or declining. Personnel files may indicate whether the turnover rate for some groups of employees within the firm is higher than for others. Memos, letters, and various records of the firm's inputs and outputs may all prove useful, too.

Published Sources. Much information of use to businesses can be found in the library. Newspapers, magazines, annual volumes of data, and many other sources provide information about every topic of interest to business. Also, for those of you with computers, the *Standard and Poor's Compustat Tapes* provide extensive information about firms and industries. Figure 22A-1 describes some of the more popular sources of business information.

Figure 22A-1

Business Literature

Newspapers

The Wall Street Journal is "must reading" for people in business trying to keep up with daily developments on stocks, bonds, mutual funds, the economy, company and industry developments, and the like. It is an invaluable publication for business people.

Barron's National Business and Financial Weekly presents "Last Week" and "This Week" sections with current developments. It also covers such topics as money management, tax shelters, stocks and bonds, economic and financial indicators, Wall Street developments, and company and industry features.

Magazines

Business Week provides weekly information on a wide range of business topics. The economy, business firms in the news, mergers and acquisitions, legal and financial developments, new products, social issues, and government regulations are just a sampling of these topics. Also, *Business Week* publishes a variety of "Figures of the Week." These include production indicators, price indices, financial market data, imports and exports, and leading indicators.

Money magazine is a monthly presenting information about personal finance. Articles on choosing a financial planner, selecting stocks and bonds, buying life insurance, and managing one's career are typical.

Fortune, another monthly, provides in-depth analyses of such topics as industry developments, the labor market, business policy, international business, and new books and ideas.

The *Monthly Labor Review* presents data on price changes, earnings trends, labor market developments, and labor-management relations, as well as articles and special reports on related topics. It also includes an extensive section cataloging current labor statistics.

Forbes, a biweekly, contains articles on investments, government, economic conditions, mutual funds, and money and investments, and a variety of columns. Special sections include "Faces Behind the Figures," "Thoughts on the Business Life," and "Fact and Comment."

To find journal reports on business topics, look in the *Business Periodicals Index*. This index is available in public and university libraries.

Surveys of Companies

The *Value Line Investment Survey* presents descriptive statistics for each of 1,700 stocks. It ranks stocks on the basis of investment safety, probable price performance over the next 12 months, estimated percent yield over the next 12 months, and appreciation potential in the next 3 to 5 years.

Standard and Poor's Register of Corporations, Directors, and Executives lists the names of nearly 38,000 corporations and includes addresses, phone numbers, names, and titles of key personnel. It also lists corporate sales and number of employees.

Moody's Manuals cover governments, public utilities, transportation, banking and finance, and other bodies, as well as industrial firms. *Moody's Industrial Manual* features data on firms on the New York Stock Exchange, the American Stock Exchange, regional stock exchanges, and international companies. For each firm, data are presented on such topics as history, capital structure, plants

Continued on next page

and subsidiaries, nature of business and products, officers, balance sheets, income statements, and notes from annual reports. Daily commodity price indices, ranges on the New York Stock Exchange Index and Dow Jones Average, and a wealth of data on stocks and bonds are included.

Government Sources

The Department of Commerce, Washington, D.C., publishes the *Survey of Current Business* (monthly), the *U.S. Industrial Outlook*, and the *Census of Manufacturers*.

The *Census of Population*, published every ten years by the federal government, provides population information by sex, race, language, education, employment status, and income. This information is broken down by state, county, city, and census tract (a unit roughly equivalent to a group of city blocks).

A guide to 900 U.S. government publications on business, finance, national resources, demographics, and other topics is available from: CIS, P. O. Box 30056, Washington, D.C. 20014.

Primary Data Sources

The most efficient research procedure is to first use secondary data sources to obtain the needed information. Sometimes, however, the information you need simply is not available in the company's records or in a published data source. As a result, you may have to collect the data yourself. **Primary data**, therefore, are defined as data collected specifically by the researcher for the problem at hand. Primary data can be collected through observation, surveys, or experiments.

Observation and Case Studies. One way to gather information is through observation. When observation is systematic and in writing, it is called a **case study**. The work habits of assembly line workers or the time management practices of executives can be studied in this way. One problem with this method is that it may not be possible to generalize conclusions to other case situations. For example, any conclusions drawn about executive time management practices are usually specific only to the firm studied—they may have nothing to do with the practices of executives in other firms.

Survey Research. A **survey** involves the gathering of data from a number of sources, such as employees in a department, purchasers of a product, or chief executive officers of firms. Sometimes, surveys are concerned with levels of one or more variables. The researchers might ask what the buyers of a product like or dislike about a product, or they might measure employee motivation levels. At other times, the researchers may be concerned with exploring the relationship between variables. For instance, data may be gathered on employee pay levels and satisfaction to see whether or not higher pay is associated, or correlated, with higher satisfaction. Figure 22A-2 discusses this topic of correlation.

Surveys often involve sampling, as discussed in Figure 22A-3. Survey data are generally collected through written questionnaires, personal interviews, or telephone surveys.

Questionnaires. Questionnaires may be handed out to people or sent by mail and returned to the researcher by mail. Questionnaires are not very costly to use, and the people surveyed can often fill out the questionnaires at their convenience. Unfortunately, many people view questionnaires as a waste of time and, as a result, throw them away.

Personal Interviews. Some questions are too complicated to be asked in a questionnaire. For example, how do you ask a person to respond to three printed cologne advertisements, each with a different appeal—one to price, another to fragrance, and the third to image? It is easier to ask such a question in a personal interview. The answer is likely to be better, too.

A second advantage of personal interviews is that people are more likely to talk with an interviewer than they are to fill out a questionnaire. The big problem with personal interviews is that they are expensive, since the firm must hire a large number of trained interviewers.

Figure 22A-2

Correlation

> A **correlation** (from co-relation) is a measure of the degree of association between two variables. If older people tend to buy more aspirin and younger people tend to buy less, we would say there is a positive relationship, or positive correlation, between age and aspirin purchase.
>
> The correlation can vary from −1, meaning the variables move in exactly opposite directions, to +1, meaning they always move in the same direction. A correlation of 0 shows no apparent relationship between the variables.
>
> Since knowledge of relationships among variables is crucial in business, correlations are widely used. We should stress, though, that a correlation shows only association, not causation. For example, if variables A and B are positively correlated, we can say only that they move together, not that one causes the other. In fact, A may cause B, B may cause A, or they may both be caused by something else. For instance, profits may be positively correlated with satisfaction because both go up when the economy is good and both go down when the economy is bad.

Telephone Surveys. Telephone surveys have become quite popular during the last 15 years because most families now have telephones. Telephone surveys are less expensive than personal interviews because little time is wasted between interviews; the telephone interviewer simply dials another number. The problem with collecting information by telephone is, again, the difficulty of asking long or complicated questions. It would be hard, for example, to ask people on the phone to rank order their preferences for nine local shopping centers.

Experiments. In an **experiment**, some variable is changed, and the impact of this change on other variables is then explored. If we want to see the

Figure 22A-3

Sampling

> The terms **population** or **universe** refer to all things in a group, such as all accountants. A **sample** is a portion of the population. So, if we interviewed 25 accountants, we would have drawn a sample. The process of defining and drawing a sample is called **sampling**. The process of examining an entire population is called a **census**, such as the census of the U.S. population which is taken every ten years.
>
> It is generally too expensive and time consuming, if not impossible, to perform a census. So, sampling is done. The idea is that you don't need to try every spoonful of a bowl of soup to know how the soup tastes. If we properly sample from some population, we should be able to draw conclusions about the population. The key word here is "properly." To draw a conclusion about the entire bowl of soup on the basis of a taste, we have to assume that we've chosen a **random sample** from the bowl. That is, the sample must really be **representative** of all the soup in the bowl. If, instead, we just skimmed the top, or dredged the bottom for the solids, we would draw incorrect conclusions if we tried to generalize. In the same way, if only a small percentage of people respond to a questionnaire, or if those in the sample are very different from those in the population, the results should be questioned.

impact of job enrichment on employees, we might actually change the job design and see what happens. Lab experiments take place in artificial, laboratory settings. Field experiments are carried out in the "real world." Lab experiments permit greater control by the experimenter, but they generally give up some realism.

Because experiments involve an analysis of controlled changes and their consequences, they can tell us something about causation. Based on an experiment, we might conclude that improved job design does cause increased employee motivation. Such experiments, however, are expensive and time consuming.

DESCRIPTIVE STATISTICS

As the name says, **descriptive statistics** describe something. They may take many forms, such as averages, frequencies, ranges, index numbers, and so on. Descriptive statistics are crucial to the successful operation of any business.

Measures of Location

We often want to know which value falls in a certain location in a distribution of data, such as the center. Three measures of location are the mean, the median, and the mode.

Mean. The **mean** is the arithmetic average of all values. It is found by adding up all the values and then dividing by the number of values. Table 22A-1 presents the sales in 1981 of the five largest private industrial corporations. The sum of the sales for the five companies is $14.3 billion. Since there are five values, the mean is $14.3 billion/5 = $2.86 billion. This is the "mean" value of sales for the five companies.

The mean is a very useful value for many purposes. However, it can sometimes be misleading. For instance, some people tend to think of the mean as the value which is most likely to occur. In fact, though, the mean may never occur. It may be just a mathematical fiction. And, one or two extreme values can distort the mean. If sales of the Mars corporation in the above example were $40 billion instead of $4 billion the mean for the five firms would have been $50.3 billion/5 = $10.06 billion. This is clearly not a value that is "in the middle" of the distribution. If a "middle" value is needed, the median is a better measure.

Median. A **median** divides a series of data into two equal parts. So, the median of a set of numbers is the middle value—the value that splits the distribution in two. The median of the values shown in Table 22A-1 is $3 billion. There are the same number of values above as below that point. If there are an even number of values, the median is found by averaging the two middle values.

Mode. The **mode** is the value in a series of data that occurs most often. In Table 22A-1, the mode is $2 billion. While the mode is sometimes near the middle of the distribution, this example shows that it may, in fact, fall anywhere.

Frequency Distribution

A **frequency distribution** shows how many times each value occurs. For instance, a frequency

Table 22A-1

The Five Largest Private Industrial Corporations

Rank	Company	Industry	Sales ($ Billions)
1	Mars	Candy	4.0
2	Hughes Aircraft	Aerospace	3.3
3	GHR	Petroleum refining, crude-oil production	3.0
4	Milliken	Textiles	2.0
5	S.C. Johnson & Son	Chemicals, soaps, cosmetics	2.0

Source: FORTUNE (May 31, 1982), p. 111. © 1982 Time Inc. All rights reserved.

distribution might show that 20 of a firm's 100 top executives are between the ages of 60 and 69, that 35 are between the ages of 50 and 59, that 30 are between the ages of 40 and 49, and that 15 are between the ages of 30 and 39.

One common shape for a frequency distribution is the normal distribution. A **normal distribution**, shown in Figure 22A-4, is shaped like a bell. Values near the mean of the distribution occur quite often. Values much above or below the mean, on the "tails" of the distribution, are uncommon.

Measures of Dispersion

Along with location, we sometimes want to know how much variability there is around a value. For example, suppose we learn that the mean dollar return on a particular $500 investment has been $1,000. We may be very tempted to make the investment. However, if we also learn that there's a good chance we'll lose the full $500, we may think twice before investing, despite the desirable average return. Two useful measures of dispersion are the range and the variance.

Range. The range shows the highest and lowest values of a variable. The range in Table 22A-1 is $2 billion to $4 billion.

Variance. One good measure of the degree to which levels of a variable are spread out is the variance. It is found by squaring the difference between each value and the mean, summing up

Figure 22A-4
The Normal Distribution

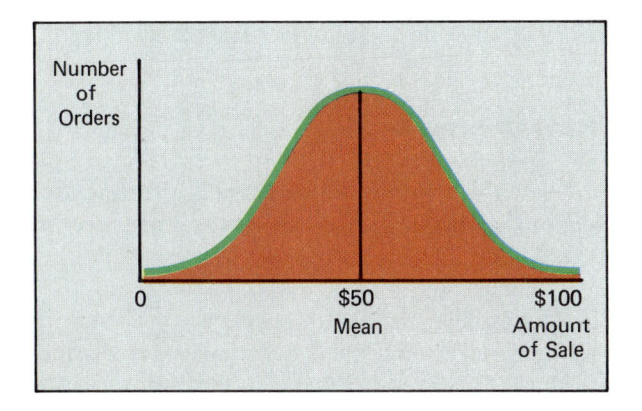

those squares, and averaging them. The variance of the values in Table 22A-1 is $0.598 billion.

Measures of Change Over Time

When the president of a firm tells us that the company's sales were $6 million in 1983, we really cannot say much about the president's performance. However, when we are told that sales have increased 300 percent since 1980, the president's first year as head of the company, we are likely to be impressed indeed. This percentage value is a measure of change over time. Measures of change over time are often much more informative than just a single value for a moment in time, such as the $6 million sales figure for 1983. Three useful measures of change are percentage change, index numbers, and time series.

Percentage Change. As shown in the example above, a percentage change indicates how much a variable, such as sales, profits, or costs, has increased or decreased over a stated period of time. It is a measure of comparison. The interval of time can be anything we want it to be—one week, a month, six months, three years. A percentage change is calculated by subtracting the score on the variable in the base period from its score in the most recent period, and then dividing this difference by the score in the base period and multiplying by 100.

An example will show how simple this percentage calculation is. Let's say that profits for our firm increased from $20,000 in 1982 to $25,000 in 1983. In percentage terms, how much did sales increase over the one-year period? The formula for calculating percentage change is as follows:

$$\frac{\text{Value in the Most Recent Period} - \text{Value in the Base Period}}{\text{Value in the Base Period}} \times 100$$

Using the numbers from our sample problem:

$$\frac{25,000 - 20,000}{20,000} \times 100 = 25\%$$

That is, our firm's sales increased 25 percent between 1982 and 1983.

Any time percentage changes are presented, we should be sure to ask "compared to what?" Almost any value can be made to look good or bad if a suitable comparison point is found. The same figure may be "up 20%" from year X but "down 30%" from year Y. Worse, the basis for comparison may change. For example, suppose we say "Look, times are tough right now, so we're going to have to cut your pay by 50% for a year. They we'll increase it by 50% to even things out." If this sounds reasonable to you, we have a few investment opportunities we would like to discuss with you. In fact, the 50% cut would reduce a $100 check to $50. The 50% raise *on the new base* of $50 would lift pay to only $75, hardly enough to "even things out."

Index Numbers. Index numbers make comparisons over time easier. They are calculated by dividing the value in the current period by the value in the base period and then multiplying by 100:

$$\frac{\text{Value in Current Period}}{\text{Value in Base Period}} \times 100$$

Again, using the numbers from the sample problem:

$$\frac{25,000}{20,000} \times 100 = 125$$

An index number is just another way of showing the percentage change of some variable between the base year and the year in question.

One familiar example is the consumer price index. In relation to the 1967 base year value of 100, the value of the CPI in 1980 was 246.8. That is, what it cost $100 to buy in 1967, it cost $246.80 to buy 13 years later. Index numbers are an especially useful way to show relative change for a long series of annual values.

Time Series. When Sam saw that the produce department's sales were down 15 percent from August to November, he didn't panic. He knew that sales fluctuate month by month for many reasons. **Time series analysis** is a useful way to identify the underlying reasons for change over time. The four components of a time series are trend, cycle, seasonal variation, and random variation.

The **trend** is the long-run direction of the series, such as the pattern of growth or decline for a company, industry, or economy. The growth of the electronics industry and the decline of the rail industry are examples of trends.

The **cycle** refers to a regularly recurring pattern of variation that lasts several years. The business cycle begins with prosperity, a period of high income and employment, and is followed by a period of recession, when income, employment, and production fall. And if recession is severe enough, a depression may occur, bringing a severe drop in business activity. One complete cycle ends when prosperity returns.

A **seasonal fluctuation** is a regular annual variation, often the result of climate or holiday seasons. Sales of fresh corn are higher in August than in December, and sales of toys skyrocket at Christmas.

Finally, **random fluctuations** are the result of such factors as strikes, accidents, or extreme weather. Because they are random, these variations cannot be predicted.

Smart business managers take each of the four components of a time series into account when making forecasts based on past data. Proper use of time series analysis may prevent a manager from interpreting a seasonal fluctuation as a long-term trend, or from ignoring cyclical variations.

DISPLAYING INFORMATION

Confusing facts and figures are made much more understandable when displayed simply and concisely. Statistical data can be displayed in tables, graphs, or statistical maps.

Tables

A **table** is a logically organized, two-dimensional display of numerical information. Table 22A-2 shows hourly earnings by industry for 1980, 1981, and October of 1982.

Charts or Graphs

A **chart** or **graph** is a diagram illustrating the relationship between one variable and another. It can take any of several forms.

Pie Charts. **Pie**, or **circle**, **charts** show a total in the form of a round "pie." Each part's percentage of the pie is represented as a slice of appropriate

Table 22A-2

A Typical Table

Industry	Hourly Earnings by Industry* (dollars)		
	1980 Average	1981 Average	Oct. 1982
Mining	9.17	10.05	11.02
Construction	9.94	10.80	11.82
Manufacturing	7.27	7.99	8.56
Transportation and Public Utilities	8.87	9.70	10.48
Wholesale Trade	6.96	7.57	8.17
Retail Trade	4.88	5.25	5.54
Finance, Insurance, and Real Estate	5.79	6.31	6.97
Services	5.85	6.41	7.05

* Gross averages, production or nonsupervisory workers on private nonagricultural payrolls.
Source: U.S. Department of Labor, Bureau of Labor Statistics.

size. Figure 22A-5 presents a pie chart showing the components of 1981 U.S. nonagricultural employment. Pie charts may require some "lumping together" of categories to make the chart readable. In this case, the categories of mining, construction, and transportation and public utilities were combined into the "other" category.

Figure 22A-5

Pie Chart Showing Components of 1981 U.S. Nonagricultural Employment

- Government 17.54%
- Manufacturing 22.13%
- Finance, Insurance & Real Estate 5.82%
- Services 20.32%
- Wholesale and Retail Trade 22.65%
- Other 11.54%

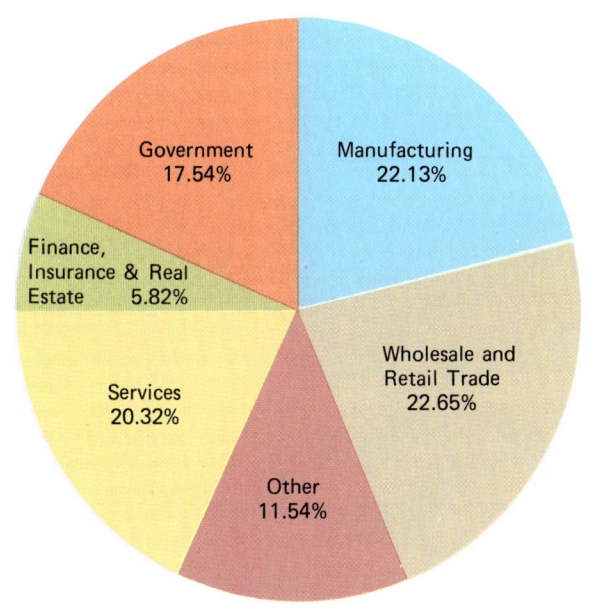

Source: U.S. Department of Commerce, Bureau of the Census.

Bar Charts. A **bar chart** uses horizontal or vertical bars of varying lengths to compare information. Figure 22A-6 shows the labor force participation rate for women by marital status. Of all women, divorced women are the most likely to work (75 percent); widowed women are the least likely (22.3 percent).

Line Charts. When data points are connected by a line or curve, this is called a **line chart**. Figure 22A-7 is a line chart showing how the consumer price index has changed since 1970. Notice that the CPI went up every year.

Statistical Maps

A statistical map uses variations in the concentration of dots, shading, color, or texture to represent quantities. In the sample map shown in Figure 22A-8, different colors represent the various unemployment rate levels by state.

DO STATISTICS LIE?

The famous statesman and novelist, Benjamin Disraeli, said that, "There are three kinds of lies: lies, damned lies, and statistics." A very popular little book—that after 30 years and 34 printings is as relevant as ever—has the title of *How To Lie With Statistics*. It gives example after

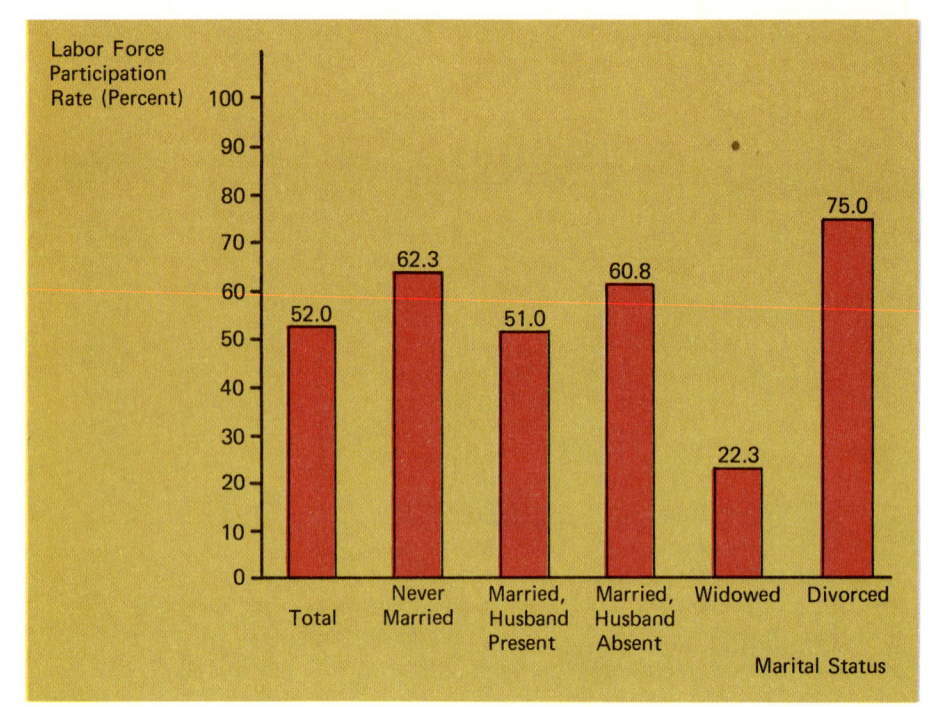

Figure 22A-6

Bar Chart Showing Female Labor Force Participation Rates by Marital Status

Source: U.S. Department of Labor, Bureau of Labor Statistics (March, 1981).

example of how statistics can be distorted, manipulated, and misrepresented to give whatever impression the writer might wish to convey. And yet we've been told since grade school that facts don't lie.

The truth probably is that statistics don't lie, but that the people using them may. Certainly, even well-intentioned people may make mistakes in the use and interpretation of statistics. In a sense, statistics are like a language. If we don't speak the language, we will have trouble challenging it. We may be forced to rely just on a smile and trust. But a smile and trust may not be enough to allow us to survive in the "real world" of business. Figure 22A-9 gives some helpful tips for interpreting statistics.

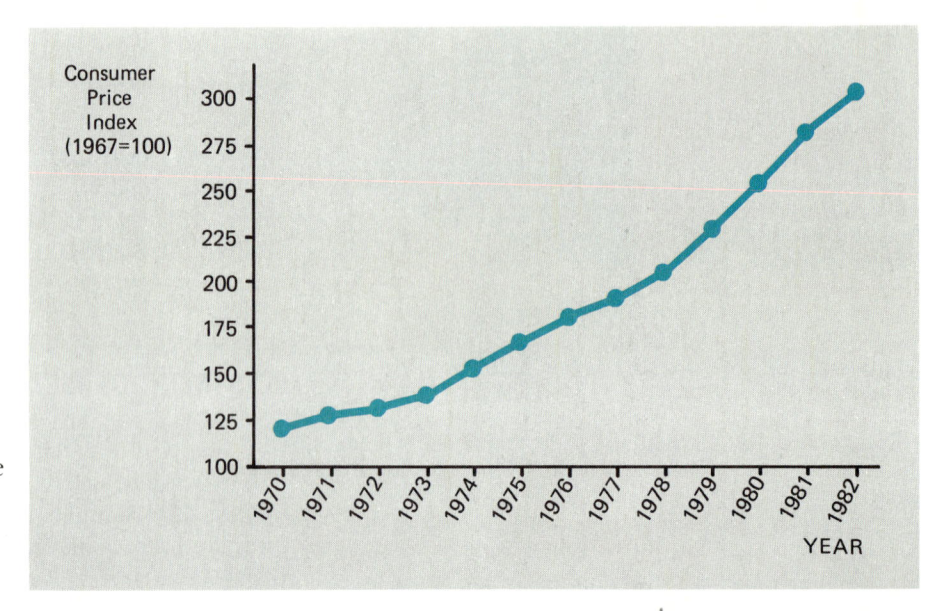

Figure 22A-7

Line Chart Showing the Consumer Price Index

Source: U.S. Department of Labor, Bureau of Labor Statistics.

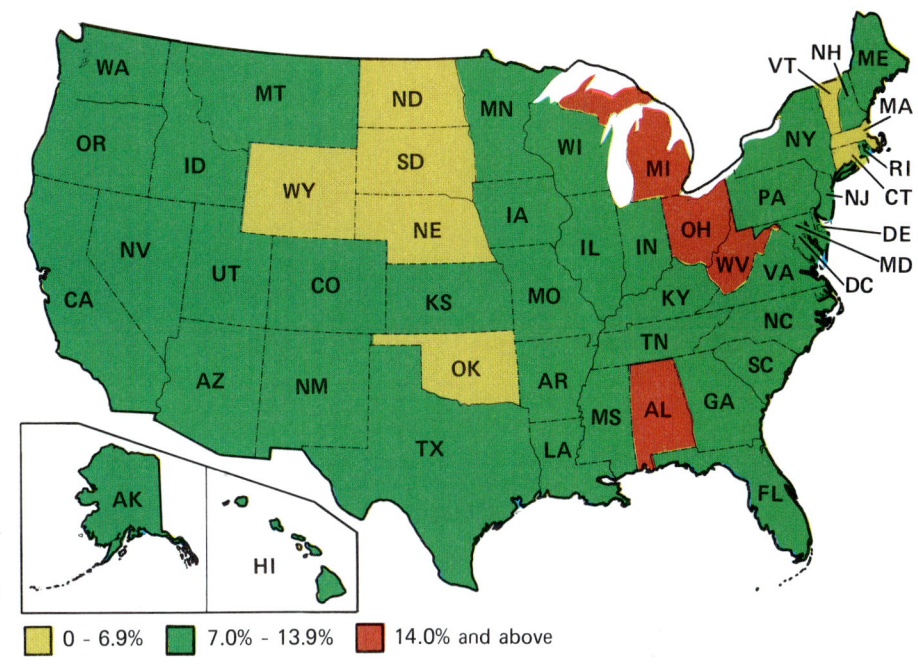

Figure 22A-8

Unemployment Rates by State, November, 1982 (Percent of Labor Force)

Source: U.S. Department of Labor, Bureau of Labor Statistics.

0 - 6.9%   7.0% - 13.9%   14.0% and above

Probabilities

A **probability** is a number indicating how likely it is that some event will occur. Probabilities range from 0, meaning there is no chance the event will happen, to 1, meaning it will definitely happen. Most of the time, people in business do not deal with certainty. That is, the probability of an event occurring is somewhere between 0 and 1. For instance, we do not know for sure whether the economy will improve or whether the oil situation will worsen. Probabilities can help us make good decisions.

Probabilities are often based on frequencies. If in the past 70 percent of all small businesses failed within five years, we could say that the probability that a small business picked at random will fail within five years is .7. This assumes that things haven't changed in important ways since the frequencies were gathered. Sometimes, we have a good idea of the probability of an event occurring just by knowing something about it. For example, the probability of getting a "head" on a flip of a fair coin is .5. When probabilities are based on frequencies or on characteristics of an object, they are called **objective probabilities**.

When objective probabilities are not available, managers may have to estimate their own probabilities. For example, a manager may have to estimate the probability that war will break out in a country where the firm has a large manufacturing installation. Such probabilities—the person's best estimates—are called **subjective probabilities**.

The accuracy of subjective probabilities can decide the fate of many businesses. Witness Chrysler weighing the probabilities of success of various auto designs, or an airline estimating the likelihood that competitors will follow a price reduction on certain key routes.

Figure 22A-9

Some Tips for Interpreting Statistics

- Watch out for overly exact figures. A statement that "72.63% of consumers prefer Brand A" suggests more confidence and precision than "about three fourths of consumers prefer Brand A," but its very precision suggests that we should be on guard.
- Challenge assumptions. Many figures are based on assumptions about the nature of markets, trends, customers, or other variables that may not necessarily be so. If these assumptions are stated, ask whether they seem reasonable. If they're not stated, ask yourself why not.
- Ask if the conclusions really follow from the data. Figures may seem so impressive that their link to conclusions is overlooked. Ask whether the data might, in fact, lead to other conclusions. For instance,

    > You can't prove that your nostrum cures colds, but you can publish (in large type) a sworn laboratory report that half an ounce of the stuff killed 31,108 germs in a test tube in eleven seconds. While you are about it, make sure that the laboratory is reputable or has an impressive name. Reproduce the report in full. Photograph a doctor-type model in white clothes and put his picture alongside.[1]

    The fact that there is a big difference between a test tube and a human body, or that the medication has to be diluted to be taken by humans, or that the germs killed may have nothing to do with colds, may all be overlooked.
- Question why data are presented in a particular way. For instance, the exact same fact can be expressed as a

    > one percent return on sales, a fifteen percent return on investment, a ten-million-dollar profit, an increase in profits of forty percent (compared with 1935-39 average), or a decrease of sixty percent from last year. The method is to choose the one that sounds best for the purpose at hand and trust that few who read it will recognize how imperfectly it fits the situation.[2]

- Ask if it all makes sense. Does it make sense to extend findings from one period of time to another? For example, if the decrease in the birth rate over the past few decades were to continue, there would soon be no people left. Does it make sense for a forward-looking retailer to fold up shop?

---

[1] D. Huff and I. Geis, *How to Lie With Statistics* (New York: W. W. Norton & Company, 1954), pp. 74-75.
[2] Ibid.

Forecasting

This program allows you to make forecasts as far into the future as necessary. The program uses a technique called "least squares regression." The technique basically fits a line through data points and extends that line into the future. You indicate the number of periods for which you have data. For each of those periods, you input the year and the level of your variable (such as sales or earnings). Finally, you indicate the year for which you want a forecast.

Here's the Program

```
10 PRINT
20 PRINT "***********FORECASTING PROGRAM***********"
30 PRINT "HOW MANY POINTS WILL YOU USE TO "
40 INPUT "MAKE THE FORECAST? ";N
50 PRINT
60 J=0:K=0:L=0:M=0:P=0
70 FOR I = 1 TO N: PRINT "ENTER YEAR, A COMMA, & LEVEL FOR POINT ";I
80 INPUT X,Y:J=J+X-1900:K=K+Y:L=L+(X-1900)[2:M=M+Y[2:P=P+(X-1900)*Y
90 NEXT I
100 B=(N*P-K*J)/(N*L-J[2):A=(K-B*J)/N
110 INPUT "YEAR FOR WHICH YOU WANT A FORECAST? ";YR
120 F=A+B*(YR-1900)
130 F=INT(F*100+.5)/100
140 PRINT
150 PRINT "***********FORECAST RESULTS***********"
160 PRINT "THE FORECAST FOR YEAR ";YR;" IS ";F
170 PRINT
180 PRINT "**********************************"
190 PRINT
200 INPUT "FORECAST FOR ANOTHER YEAR? (1=YES; 2=NO) ";G
210 IF G=1 THEN GOTO 110
220 INPUT "WANT ANOTHER RUN? (1=YES; 2=NO) ";G
230 IF G=1 THEN GOTO 10
240 END
```

Here's Sample Output

Two sets of output for this program are provided. In the first, four data points were used to make the forecast. They were: 1975, 24; 1976, 33; 1977, 51; and 1978, 58. A forecast was requested for 1984.

For the second forecast, the same inputs were used, but a forecast for 1987 was requested.

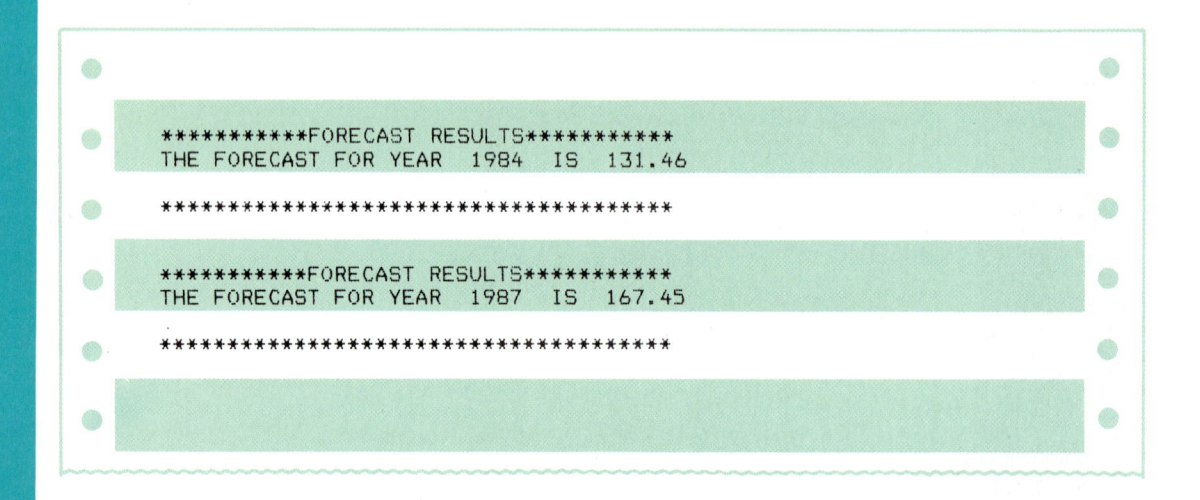

```
***********FORECAST RESULTS***********
THE FORECAST FOR YEAR   1984   IS   131.46

***************************************

***********FORECAST RESULTS***********
THE FORECAST FOR YEAR   1987   IS   167.45

***************************************
```

Questions

1. The forecasting program works by determining a past trend and extending it into the future. What sorts of factors might cause such a forecast to be inaccurate?
2. In the sample runs, how do you think the forecasts would have changed if only the figures for 1975, 1976, and 1977 were used as input? If only the figures for 1976, 1977, and 1978 were used?
3. Suppose you were a sales manager whose departmental sales had increased from 24 units in 1975 to 58 units in 1978, as in the sample runs. Do you think you would accept the sample run forecast of over 167 units in 1987? Why or why not?

7
The Challenge of the Future

23

International Business – A Growing Sector

After studying this chapter, you should be able to:

- Explain why it is important to study international business.
- Identify and analyze the key barriers to international trade.
- Cite five ways a business can enter a foreign market.
- Explain how a firm should decide whether or not to standardize its advertising strategy.
- Discuss the role of multinational corporations (MNCs) in the world economy.
- Discuss the role of international economic communities.

Only a few years ago, most business textbooks did not even mention international business. Not many U.S. corporations had large investments in foreign countries. Few U.S. citizens had been overseas, and even fewer had worked in foreign countries. Today this has all changed. U.S. citizens and corporations now play a major role in many businesses in foreign countries. We begin our discussion of international business by looking at why the study of international business is now so important.

WHY STUDY INTERNATIONAL BUSINESS?

We can think of at least two reasons why it is more important than ever to study international business. The first reason is that the United States, over much of the last decade and a half, has shown a trade deficit with the rest of the world. The second is that total U.S. corporate investment overseas has increased dramatically during this same period of time. Both reasons relate to the increasing interdependence of the U.S. economy and the world economy. The first reason relates to trade flows and the second reason to capital flows.

U. S. Trade Deficits

Before we look at trade deficits and their importance to the study of international business, we need to define exports and imports. Keep in mind that any product made in one country and sold in another is both an export and an import. A product is an **export** from the point of view of the country making and selling it, and an **import** from the point of view of the country buying it. Wheat grown in Kansas and sold to the Soviet Union is an export for the United States and an import for the Soviet Union. All the Toyotas and Datsuns we see on U.S. streets are exports for Japan and imports for the United States.

Each year, all the nations of the world add up their exports and imports to determine their **trade balance**, which is the difference between total exports and total imports. When total exports are greater than total imports, the difference is called a **trade surplus**. When imports are greater than exports, it is called a **trade deficit**. Nations prefer a trade surplus to a trade deficit because it means they are making money in world markets.

Before 1970, the United States consistently showed an end-of-the-year trade surplus. That is, each year, it exported more than it imported. After 1970, however, annual exports exceeded imports only three times. Figure 23-1 shows the difference between total exports and total imports for the period 1960 to 1980. As long as exports exceed imports (the way we would like things to be), the curve is above the zero line. When exports are less than imports, the curve is below the line, indicating that, for those years, the United States ran a trade deficit, and its balance of trade was negative. In those years, foreign countries got more dollars than the United States got in foreign currencies. The law of supply and demand drove the value of the dollar down. As a result, products imported to the United States went up in price.

Foreign Investment

In 1970, the total investment overseas of all U.S. firms was $75.4 billion. This figure climbed to almost $200 billion in the early 1980s. Interestingly, profits on these investments increased much faster than the level of investment itself. Again in 1970, U.S. firms earned $8.2 billion in profits on overseas investments; a decade later, total profits had increased by more than 400 percent. Table 23-1 shows investment levels for U.S. firms in eight foreign countries.

The truth of the matter is that many U.S. business firms make a good percentage of their profits in overseas markets. Many firms, therefore, have little choice but to develop their foreign markets. A classic illustration is Ford Motor Company. Ford is truly an international company. In 1981, the Ford Motor Company lost

Figure 23-1

U.S. Trade Balance, 1960-1980

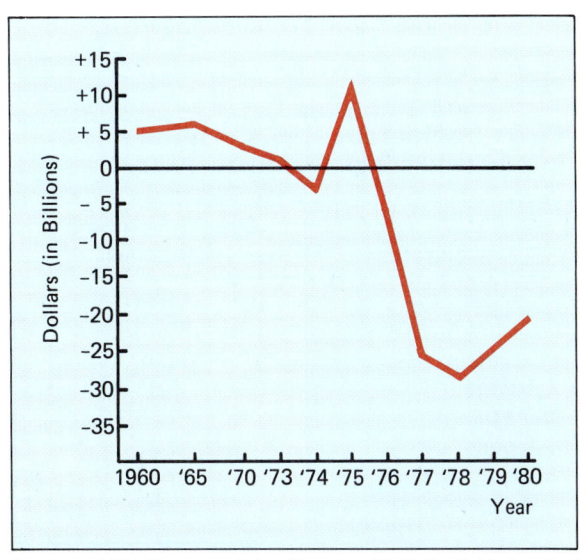

Source: U.S. Bureau of the Census, *Statistical Abstract of the United States, 1981* (102d ed., 1981).

Countries export their own products and import what they cannot produce.

more than a billion dollars. Most of this loss was in the United States. While sales decreased by 2 percent in the U.S., they *increased* by 2 percent overseas. Without its overseas profits, Ford's financial condition would have been much worse. Flows of investment capital to other countries and the resulting profit that is returned to this country, as well as the foreign capital that is invested here, serve to tie the world economy together.

Table 23-1

Direct Investment of U.S. Companies in Selected Foreign Countries, 1980

Countries	Direct Investment ($ Billions)
Canada	44.64
United Kingdom	28.10
Germany	15.39
France	9.35
Brazil	7.55
Japan	6.27
Italy	5.40
Venezuela	1.90

Source: U.S. Bureau of Census, *Statistical Abstract of the United States, 1981* (102d ed., 1981).

BARRIERS TO INTERNATIONAL TRADE

Many businesses are reluctant to enter foreign markets. Sometimes this is due to a lack of knowledge about foreign markets. At other times, it is because of real problems that businesses face abroad. Table 23-2 lists some of these problems. Let's look at them.

Planning Problems

Business managers of firms that sell only in the United States can generally obtain good market information. Also, our government is stable. These are two very strong reasons why some U.S. firms limit themselves to domestic operations only. If the firm's plan does not work, it is usually because the plan was bad or because a competitor had a better one.

A good business plan relies on accurate market information. What kind of people are likely to purchase a new product? How much will they pay for it? How big is the market? Such questions are especially hard to answer in some foreign countries where there may not even be an accurate count of the population. For example,

Table 23-2

Barriers to International Trade

Barriers	Specific Problem
Planning Problems	1. Many Languages 2. Inadequate Market Information 3. Unstable Governments
Tax Controls	1. Import Duties 2. Profit Control
Political Instability	1. Expropriation 2. Civil War
Cultural Factors	1. Advertisements 2. Distribution
Economic Factors	1. Stage of Economic Development 2. Inflation

Saudi Arabia says that its population is about ten million. In fact, the country's population is somewhere between five and ten million. More accurate information than that is needed to estimate the size of a market.

Inadequate market data make planning difficult, but political instability can make it all but impossible. A sudden change in the political leadership of a foreign country can send the value of the local currency plunging. Or it may disrupt the flow of spare parts and machinery into the country.

Tax Controls

Many countries try to limit the amount of goods that they import. These countries assume that both economic growth and employment of the labor force depend on their ability to protect their home industries from foreign competition. As a result, some countries tax many imported goods. Brazil has a tax of almost 200 percent on imported automobiles. The effect of such a tax is to make imported goods more expensive, which discourages people from buying them.

Another type of tax that creates problems for firms doing business abroad is a tax on profits. Many countries encourage U.S. private investment but attempt to limit the flow of earned income back to the United States. Sending profits back home is known as **repatriation**.

Many people believe that these profits should stay in the country where they were earned. Some countries either forbid repatriation of profits or tax them heavily. In Sweden, for example, foreign companies must pay an additional 5 percent in taxes in order to take profits out of the country and send them back home. During its financial crisis of 1982 and 1983, Mexico did not permit any repatriation of profits. To soften the impact of such actions, many countries also offer special loans, tax breaks, and other benefits to foreign corporations so that they will continue to invest there. Denmark has a special banking agency that loans money at low interest rates to foreign companies building factories there. Similarly, Ireland places a hefty tax on repatriated profits, but gives big tax breaks and loan assistance to companies planning to invest in Ireland.

Any company developing an international strategy should consider the effect of tax controls on its business plan. A tax on imports makes it harder to develop overseas markets by making these products more expensive. A foreign firm, such as a U.S. maker of appliances, is therefore at a disadvantage in relation to a domestic manufacturer. A tax on profits may not inhibit market development, but it does restrict the freedom of the firm to send income back to the United States.

Political Instability

We take for granted the stability of our political system, as do the people of Canada and most of the Western world. Unfortunately, this stability tends to be the exception rather than the rule. When the Shah of Iran was forced out of power in the 1970s by the Ayatollah Khomeini, many foreign business people were forced to leave the country within a few days. They lost not only their personal assets but their business assets as well. General Motors operated a major automobile assembly plant in Iran worth well over $60 million. The company may never recover any of this money.

In times of political unrest, it sometimes happens that the host country government takes over the assets of a foreign firm without offering compensation. Called **expropriation without reimbursement**, this does not occur very often, however. Why? Because a country that expropriates the assets of one firm discourages other companies from investing there. Still, the dangers

CONTROVERSIAL ISSUES

The United States Should Impose Strict Trade Barriers.

The United States has long wavered between imposing strict import barriers and accepting any imports freely. Following the Great Depression and World War II, Americans felt little need to protect their businesses from overseas competition. Recently, however, several countries have attempted to flood the American markets with imported goods. The United States, with older and less profitable industrial facilities, is unable to compete effectively either within the United States or abroad. Should we now impose trade barriers on other countries?

Pro

Definitely yes. America has given away billions of dollars in technology and research to countries all over the world. These other countries have used the information to overtake the American businesses that spent the money to develop the technology. American factories are old and need rebuilding, while European and Japanese factories—destroyed during the Second World War—are newly rebuilt (mostly with American money) and obviously better equipped to compete in today's economy. If they choose to bite the hand that fed them, they need the punishment. In particular, Japan has refused to import many American goods, insisting that Japan should industrialize to product these goods itself. Only a few companies who got into Japan right at the end of the war and before barriers were raised—such as Coca Cola, General Foods, and most of the major oil companies—have been able to survive.

The gripe that American industrialists have with Japan is that Japan won't let American companies come into the country to sell competitively with Japanese firms. Americans are becoming more and more irritated that Japan and other countries won't give American products a chance in their countries. If they won't allow our goods in their countries, we should do the same to them.

Con

Trade barriers are not the answer. America has wavered on the use of trade restrictions because every time barriers have been tried, they have failed. Either the American economy suffers in the long run for not having imported products, or political and economic alliances have weakened to America's detriment overseas. For example, in 1973 President Nixon realized that the United States was having a very poor soybean crop and, without warning, embargoed all soybean shipments to Japan. Since soybeans were one of Japan's major foodstuffs, and America was Japan's exclusive supplier, Japan had to find another source. Brazil supplied the beans and, because of the help it got from Japan in 1973, Brazil has been capturing an increasing portion of America's share in the world soybean market. The United States has also unsuccessfully imposed embargoes on iron, steel, beef, grain, oil equipment, and high-technology electronics. The same thing will happen when America denies foreign countries its consumer markets: Japan and other countries will look elsewhere for new markets and forge new trade alliances that leave America out in the cold.

Furthermore, Japan is opening its markets more to American companies. For example, American Express credit cards are now being advertised in Tokyo, and Avon has 160,000 representatives selling American-made cosmetics throughout Japan. Raid bug spray, Glade room deodorant, Bose speakers, IBM computers, and Texas Instruments calculators and watches have all been selling well in Japan. Japanese consumers *want* American goods.

Sometimes American-made products just aren't quite right for foreign consumers. For example, the Japanese never use credit cards to charge purchases, and they rarely write checks, preferring to pay cash. However, American Express discovered that the Japanese loved the idea of a card that they could use to get cash advances, so American Express tailored its credit program to give cash advances, and now American Express cards sell like hotcakes to Japanese consumers.

Those who clamor for trade barriers don't realize that trade barriers just do not work, and that countries like Japan will lower resistance to imports from America with a little pressure and a little time. Let's not impose trade barriers.

of political instability are real, whether expropriation or outright civil war. One need only look at events in Nigeria, Iran, Nicaragua, Argentina, Chile, and El Salvador over the last 15 years to see why business executives are so nervous about investing in foreign countries.

Cultural Factors

Culture is made up of the set of values, ideas, and attitudes that shape human behavior. Cultural attitudes vary dramatically among countries. Many business executives choose not to sell their products in foreign countries because they do not understand the cultures of these countries. Without a cultural understanding, they are likely to make a series of costly mistakes.

There is no question that culture affects business decisions—for example, how a company advertises, distributes, and manufactures its products. Many companies advertise the same product differently in different countries. Renault advertised its new Renault 5 car to buyers in France as a fun car suited to city and highway driving. In Germany, where driving is a very serious matter, the Renault advertisements stressed the car's engineering and its interior comfort. In Italy, flash and speed attract buyers, so the advertisements featured the road performance of the Renault 5.

Culture also affects how a product is distributed. In the United States, Avon and Tupperware use homemakers as a kind of in-home sales force. This approach would not work in Europe because most people there feel that door-to-door sales and gimmicks such as "Tupperware parties" are a violation of personal privacy.

Finally, culture has an influence on how a product is made. Many automobile workers in the United States are more loyal to their union, the United Auto Workers, than to their companies. In Japan, automobile workers feel a personal bond between themselves and their employer.

Economic Conditions

Economic conditions also vary greatly from one country to the next and place certain limits on business activities. The most fundamental of these conditions is the country's state of economic development. In the United States, we are favored with good highways, railroads, and air transport systems. We have a telephone system that works. The benefits of such systems for conducting business are almost immeasurable. Not all countries are similarly favored. When a country lacks basic communication and transportation facilities, known as **infrastructure**, the business executive is severely limited in the options available for developing markets.

Another economic condition is inflation, which was discussed in Chapter 2. It has been a terrible problem for many developing countries. For example, Argentina and Mexico experienced rates of inflation in excess of 100 percent in 1982.

The question for the multinational firm is how best to deal with inflation. There are two basic approaches. First, when inflation rises more rapidly in one nation than in another, the firm can profit by selling merchandise in the high-inflation country that was manufactured in the low-inflation country. By doing so, the firm produces in the country where costs are lower and sells in the country where prices are higher. This widens the profit gap, which is the difference between selling price and costs. The second way to deal with inflation is to invest in material, equipment, and buildings that are expected to increase in value. In a highly inflationary economy, the firm should hold relatively little cash because it loses value quickly.

Sometimes companies must be creative in order to solve distribution problems.

ENTERING FOREIGN MARKETS

Many firms earn large profits without ever operating abroad. More and more U.S. firms, however, now recognize just how profitable foreign markets can be. Figure 23-2 shows five different ways of selling products in foreign markets. Generally speaking, the level of profit from these markets is a function of the level of investment. The greater the investment, the greater the potential profit. But it is also true that the greater the investment, the greater the risk involved. If the overseas operation falls apart, the firm suffers a big loss. The firm is also more vulnerable to such political actions as expropriation. Let's look at each of the five ways of entering foreign markets.[1]

Exporting

The simplest way to enter foreign markets is to export products. A Chicago-based machine tool company might manufacture its products in this country and ship them to Canada, Mexico, Taiwan, and other foreign countries.

Exporting is an attractive strategy because it involves very little risk; the manufacturer has no money invested in plant and facilities abroad. In addition, exports are good for the exporting country because they are a source of foreign exchange. Vigorous export activities also mean jobs for local workers. These are two reasons why our government wants United States-based firms to market products abroad. To encourage exports, the federal government provides information about foreign markets. State Department personnel also help exporters find overseas distributors for their products.

However, business managers frequently encounter two barriers to export activities. First, production and export costs may be too high. Exports compete with domestically made products in the country of interest. Domestic firms may be able to produce and sell more cheaply than the exporter. The exporter also incurs transportation costs in moving the product to the foreign market. Second, as mentioned earlier, the foreign country may place a very high tax on imported products. This makes imported products very expensive in relation to products manufactured domestically.

Licensing

Licensing is another way to sell products in foreign countries. Under this approach, a firm in one country (the licensor) enters into an agreement with a firm from another country (the licensee), whereby the licensor allows the licensee to use its manufacturing process. The licensee then builds a manufacturing plant, sells its products, and pays the licensor a fee for use of its production process. Besides manufacturing skills, the licensor also provides marketing information and other technical and managerial expertise.

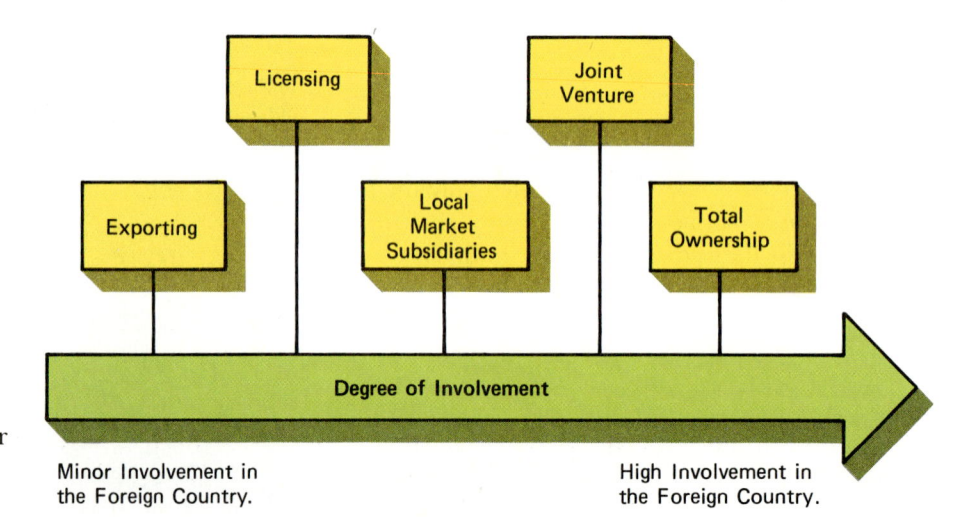

---

[1] This section is adapted from Ruel Kahler and Roland L. Kramer, *International Marketing* (Cincinnati: South-Western Publishing Co., 1977), pp. 80-90.

Figure 23-2
Alternative Methods for Selling Products in Foreign Countries

Profile—
Barbara Webb

In 1979, Webco Lumber Company earned $9 million in revenues and expanded to include a second sawmill. Webco, a family-owned mill company in Oregon, seemed to be going strong. But then a recession hit, housing construction plummeted, and lumber sales all but disappeared. After the company's $9 million year in 1979, Webco's sales dropped to $6 million in 1980, then to $3 million in 1981.

Webco was certainly not alone. Unemployment shot to 50 percent in the Northwest lumber industry, 20 percent of the sawmills closed, and 40 percent of those left were operating far short of capacity. Since that time, however, Webco has begun operating on a full shift with a full crew, has recently added a second shift, and is growing to become one of the best known lumber companies in the Pacific Northwest. Who is responsible for this turnaround? Most observers point to Barbara Webb.

Webb worked at the mill for a while after graduating from college, but then moved to California to pursue a life of her own. She was called back to the company when her family needed her help with administrative problems at the mill. Webb discovered that a manager was defrauding the company. After throwing him out she buried herself in the company and realized that she had the ability to get things done and the skills and knowledge to run the company better than anyone else. From that point on, no one stood in her way.

In early 1981, with Webco shut down and deep in debt, Webb undertook a trade mission to Japan. The lumber market in Japan had just opened to American products but was being overlooked by most American mills. Japanese construction methods demanded lumber dimensions different from those used by American builders, and Japanese construction companies wanted American companies with which they could deal comfortably. Barbara researched the Japanese market. She then had a batch of cards printed with Webco's name and phone number printed in English on the front and in Japanese on the back. Within six weeks, two dozen Japanese buyers visited the mill and, in cooperative arrangements with a lumber exporter in Portland, started purchasing lumber.

However, Webco had to supply wood cut to Japanese dimensions and the quality had to be much higher than that demanded in America. Fortunately, Webco had installed one of Oregon's first computer-variable saws and other new equipment which made it easy for the company to retool its mill to produce the new dimensions. As for quality, the Japanese demanded an excruciating amount of board-by-board inspection of cuts from the most highly priced logs.

Webb's strategy worked. Within two months, Webco had a full production schedule going again. Within a year, sales had doubled. Webb encouraged the Japanese to adopt use of lower grade timber for some of their construction. She has introduced innovations everywhere. Already Webco is the number one imported label in Japan, and some people expect Webco to capture 35 percent of the total Japanese lumber market.

Meanwhile, Webco is expanding to meet the demands of its new markets and to prepare for increased lumber sales in the United States.

Barbara Webb's performance hasn't gone unnoticed. In 1982 she was appointed to the Oregon Advisory Commission of the Oregon State International Trade Commission, becoming the first woman ever to serve on the commission. In August of that year, she was named by the governor to the State Board of Forestry. But her greatest satisfaction comes from the turnaround in her family's company and in the secure employment she can now offer her employees. Today, the sign at the gate of Webco Lumber is written in English, German, and Japanese. Who knows? Perhaps other languages will be added to the sign as well.

U.S. firms license their manufacturing processes because licensing provides extra revenue with few extra costs and virtually no risks. Licensing also sidesteps many tariff laws since the product is now made in the foreign country.

Licensing does have two major problems. First, the licensor is paid out of the profits made by the licensee on the product. Since many licensees lose money, they pay nothing to the licensor. The licensor might have been able to show a profit had it marketed the product itself. Second, the licensee receives the benefit of much production and marketing advice from the licensor. Eventually, licensees can become so skilled in their markets that they can break away and compete directly with the licensor. It's very hard to draw up a contract that will prevent this from happening.

Local Marketing Subsidiaries

A third way to market products abroad is to establish a **local marketing subsidiary**. That is, the firm rents office space in the foreign country, hires and trains a local staff, and sends a few of its executives to manage the facility. It then ships its products to the foreign country, where the staff of the marketing subsidiary directs the selling effort. This approach is more expensive than either exporting or licensing.

Very few firms choose to set up local marketing offices or subsidiaries. The major reason is not the cost involved, which sometimes can be high, but the lack of information about local market conditions. Rather than hire a local distributor, the firm acts as its own marketer under this approach. This means that the firm must learn about its new markets quickly if it is to have any chance of making a profit.

Not all firms are against setting up local marketing subsidiaries. High technology firms are especially concerned about having qualified people sell and service their products. For example, IBM's computer division operates in many foreign markets through a network of local subsidiaries. These subsidiaries sell and service nothing but IBM products. The employees of these subsidiaries, most of whom are nationals of the host country, receive special IBM training. In this way, the company is able to stand behind its computer products sold abroad. Computers are sophisticated devices—they can't be exported as if they were textile products or wheat. Nor does it make much sense to license someone to manufacture them abroad because of the technology and investment involved. Thus, whatever marketing information IBM loses by not hiring a local distributor is more than balanced by greater management control and improved service.

Joint Ventures

Joint ventures are yet another way to enter foreign markets. A **joint venture**, as the name implies, is a partnership between two or more businesses. Most international joint ventures begin when one company, wishing to expand its markets, buys a percentage of a local company operating in the foreign country of interest.

Joint ventures offer several advantages for the company looking at foreign markets. The local partner provides the foreign company with product, promotional, and pricing information about the market. Sometimes, the local partner also has physical facilities, access to a distribution system, a pool of trained labor, and valuable contacts with local officials and businesses. In turn, the foreign company offers managerial, technical, and financial assistance to the local partner.

Unfortunately, there are also some problems with joint ventures. As in any partnership, there is always the possibility that the partners will disagree on an important issue. This is even more likely to happen with an international joint venture because the people involved are often from very different cultures. For example, marketing research is not used very much in less-developed countries. This is partly because market data are hard to collect and partly because many foreign business people have not seen how marketing research can be of use. It is not hard to imagine the U.S. partner in a joint venture insisting on marketing research and the local partner insisting just as strongly that such research is a waste of time. Other potential sources of disagreement might be dividend policy, new products, and the financial contribution of each partner to the joint venture.

Total Ownership

Total ownership involves the greatest commitment to a foreign market. By total ownership we mean 100 percent ownership. One example would be a U.S. manufacturing plant owned by a Swiss corporation. Another example would be a factory in Argentina owned by a U.S. corporation. In short, the multinational firm owns all of the business located in the foreign country. It doesn't just ship the products to the country and sell them through a subsidiary; it manufactures them there as well.

The advantages of total ownership are clear. Compared with a joint venture, total ownership means that neither profits nor decision-making authority need be shared with a foreign partner. Compared with licensing, the company has more managerial control and a greater probability of making a profit.

The advantages of total ownership in comparison to simple exporting are not quite so apparent but are important nonetheless. As we said before, many countries discourage imports. Rather than having foreign companies manufacture products elsewhere and then market them to their people, these countries would prefer that the companies build factories within their borders and make the products there. This creates jobs for the national work force. Often, to encourage such investment, these countries will offer tax incentives, low-interest loans, labor guarantees, and special export arrangements.

There are also several disadvantages to total ownership. The most significant is that the firm loses the knowledge of local market conditions that a good local partner can provide. This can be partially offset by hiring local managers to run the company. Another disadvantage is that total ownership involves a great deal of risk. If the product fails in the foreign market or if the host government is antibusiness, the firm would lose its entire investment. Under total ownership, all the profits belong to the firm—but so do all the risks.

ONE INTERNATIONAL MARKETING STRATEGY?

When a firm decides to sell its products abroad, it must also decide whether to fashion an international marketing strategy. The first step in making the strategy decision is to determine just how big foreign sales are expected to be. If the idea is to sell surplus products abroad on a one-shot basis, it doesn't make much sense to develop an entirely new marketing strategy for the product. But if the idea is to open up new, permanent markets abroad, then the firm should develop an international strategy.

This decision is made more difficult when the firm wants to open up markets in several countries. Should it come up with a separate strategy for each country, or should it use the same strategy in all countries? Since most large firms look to several overseas markets at the same time, we'll confine our attention to this situation. Stated again, the decision is whether or not to standardize the firm's international marketing strategy.

Advantages of Standardization

There are three advantages to using the same marketing strategy, that is, a **standardization strategy**, in each of several foreign markets. They are production cost efficiency, advertising consistency, and efficient idea utilization.

FROM THE FILE

Diana works for the Atlantic Glassware Co. The glass industry has been ailing lately, and the company's U.S. sales have fallen 8 percent in each of the past three years. Atlantic wants to reverse this unfavorable sales trend by expanding into international markets. Diana is to develop a plan for breaking into these overseas markets. The company wants to keep its investment in any such project low, and at the same time maintain a high degree of control over the production and distribution of its products. Diana wonders if these objectives are compatible.

Product Cost Efficiency. Usually, the more of a product a firm manufactures, the lower the unit cost of manufacturing it. As discussed in an earlier chapter, this is brought about by economies of scale. Modern capital-intensive production plants are designed to operate most efficiently at high levels of production. Thus, if the firm can sell basically the same product in each country, it may be able to produce all of its output at one location. The firm sells the same product everywhere, manufactures it cost-efficiently, and relies on the same general marketing strategy from one country to the next. Individually tailored marketing strategies might increase total sales, but the great advantage of a single standardized strategy is that it reduces costs.

Advertising Consistency. When the firm uses the same advertisements in all of its foreign markets—the same, that is, except for language differences—it creates a consistent image for its product. This is important because today many people travel regularly from one country to another. By seeing the same advertisement as they travel, they are more likely to believe that the firm's product claims are genuine. This can lead to higher product sales.

In Europe, advertising consistency is particularly important. Magazines, newspapers, and radio and television broadcasts flow readily across international borders. According to a study by an international advertising agency:

1. Forty percent of Dutch television viewers watch German broadcasts.
2. The magazine *Paris Match* has a circulation of 85,000 in Belgium, 26,000 in Switzerland, and a large readership in Germany and Italy.
3. More than four million French households listen to Radio Luxembourg. It also reaches 620,000 Belgian, 300,000 Swiss, and 100,000 Dutch families.[2]

Such data clearly indicate the advantages, at least in Europe, of a consistent product image.

Efficient Use of Ideas. Marketing ideas that work in one country may work in others. Certain advertising themes that were developed in the United States seem to have a universal appeal. Advertisements for Levi's jeans have a casual flavor wherever Levi's are sold. In the same way, the Marlboro man rides out of the West to sell Marlboro cigarettes in virtually every major language and country of the world. Finally, Coca-Cola relies on a theme stressing the freshness and sparkle of youth in all its advertising. Good advertising ideas are relatively scarce, and if one works in one market, why not try it in another?

Similarly, a new product can be developed and tested in one country, and then produced and sold in many other countries. The Chevrolet

---

[2]As reported in Robert D. Buzzell, "Can You Standardize Multinational Marketing," *Harvard Business Review* (November-December, 1968), pp. 104-106.

Colonel Sanders of Kentucky Fried Chicken—a face recognized around the world.

Chevette is an example. The Chevette was first produced in Brazil. The car was so successful that it was eventually produced in five countries under the names Gemini, Kadett, and Chevette. The car was a good idea in one place, and GM management realized that it might be a good idea in another place.

Disadvantages of Standardization

Standardizing the marketing strategy for a product does pose some problems. The greatest problem is that cultural and social differences across nations may make it all but impossible to rely on a single strategy. Many business managers, unfortunately, don't realize how significant, and sometimes how subtle, the effects of culture can be. Using a single strategy, when a well-reasoned decision would be to use a different strategy for each national market, can lead to disastrous results. For example, IBM has a very successful ad campaign for its personal computers. The ads feature a model dressed up as Charlie Chaplin. In many countries, Charlie Chaplin is unknown, so prospective buyers there would regard the ads merely as "a bum with a computer"—scarcely the right image for IBM to convey.

When to Standardize

When should a firm standardize its marketing strategy? What factors does it consider in making this decision? Ideally, it should consider the type of product involved, the similarity of people and cultures across national markets, the availability of marketing services in each target market, and government restrictions.

Type of Product. Some products have a universal sales appeal: razor blades, ballpoint pens, automobile tires, and electric irons are examples. Each of these products has a specific, obvious function; and the function is the same from one country to the next, and so people buy these products for the same reasons from one country to the next.

What does this mean for the business manager? It means that a standardized marketing strategy is probably the way to go. Can you think of a product for which a standardized strategy would be inappropriate?

Similarity of People and Cultures. The more alike people are across national markets, the more likely they are to buy the same products for the same reasons. For example, the income, education, and even the cultural characteristics of people in Western European countries are quite similar. Therefore, it is sometimes appropriate to use a single strategy for selling products there. However, it probably would not be appropriate to take a strategy developed for Europe and to apply it, without modification, to Venezuela, Brazil, and Peru. As a group, these South American nations are quite different culturally from the Western European nations. Also, the differences among these South American nations may be greater than the differences among the Western European nations.

Availability of Marketing Services. As we said before, not all countries can provide the same level of marketing services and marketing data. A marketing strategy developed in the United States may be based on good marketing research data and on television and radio commercials for advertising. In some countries, however, the government owns the broadcast stations and does not allow commercial advertising. In others, it is nearly impossible to conduct marketing research studies—for example, Burundi, Surinam, Syria, or Mauritania. The greater the differences among nations in terms of the availability of marketing services, the more advisable is a separate marketing strategy for each nation.

Government Restrictions. All nations have laws that regulate the market. These laws determine how products are priced, promoted, and distributed. The greater the differences in these laws among nations, the more advisable, again, are separate marketing strategies.

MULTINATIONAL CORPORATIONS: SAINTS OR SINNERS?

A multinational corporation (MNC) sells its products anywhere in the world where there is a market for them. A multinational corporation may be headquartered in Houston with an English president; manufacture products in Africa and Japan; sell them in Europe, South America, and the United States; and have its stock traded

International companies must understand cultural differences in order to market items effectively. Is there a market here for Levis?

in Hong Kong, London, and New York. Many businesses that we think of as U.S. corporations are really multinational corporations.

Criticisms of MNCs

Multinational corporations and their business practices have been severely criticized over the years: They're too big. They exploit the poor in developing nations. They exploit the poor in developed nations. They export jobs and capital from the U.S. They have contributed to U.S. balance of payment problems. They are loyal to no government. They'll do anything to make a buck. Let's take a closer look at a few of these criticisms.

Morality and Political Influence. In a well-known case, the Lockheed Corporation admitted to spending more than $12 million to influence military purchasing policy in Japan. This action may not have been bribery in the strictest sense, but it was clearly an attempt to affect government policy. What standard of behavior can we reasonably expect from MNCs? Did Lockheed act unethically? In answering these questions, we must distinguish between large-scale payments, or bribes, and so-called "grease" payments. A **grease payment** is a relatively small payment to a local official. These can be very useful in obtaining an import or export license or in moving products rapidly through customs. Many people are troubled by grease payments, but such payments are a standard practice in many countries. Grease payments are often viewed by local citizens as a "tax" to help poorly paid public officials make a living.

We may not approve of grease payments—they are certainly not customary in this country. The tougher question, however, concerns our feeling toward large-scale bribes and whether morality is culturally determined. That is, is it true that what is wrong in one country, such as a bribe in the United States, may be right in another country? People who believe that morality is, in fact, culturally determined argue that the United States has no right to impose its standards on the rest of the world. Outlawing bribery in international business, according to this view, amounts to nothing more than setting up uniform moral standards based on U.S. beliefs and values. Others defend bribery without resorting to arguments about the origin and meaning of morality and suggest that: "If we don't offer a bribe, someone else will." This argument is difficult for many people to accept. It clearly implies that a business firm may operate one way in a foreign country and another way at home.

Impact on Balance of Payments. Many people believe that multinational corporations are responsible for the U.S. balance of payments problem. The charge is that United States-based multinationals are taking money out of the

United States and buying businesses in foreign countries. The facts, however, do not really support this claim. Since 1955, U.S. MNCs have generated more than $3 billion in dollar inflows per year on the basis of only a $2 billion average annual outflow. In addition, the value of U.S. corporation assets in foreign countries has more than doubled during the last ten years, which increases the national wealth of this country. The causes of recent U.S. balance of payments problems are more complex than an explanation based on just MNC-induced cash inflows and outflows.

Exploitation of Cheap Labor. MNCs have been accused of locating operations in foreign countries to take advantage of cheap labor. Wages paid abroad may be lower than U.S. wages, but MNCs are typically among the highest paying firms in foreign countries. They frequently offer fringe benefits, such as free hospitalization and paid vacations, that are not provided by most local employers. IBM and General Electric have also helped bring the races together in South Africa. These firms not only pay their employees well but also refuse to discriminate on the basis of race. There is certainly something good to be said about that. Of course, some MNCs can be faulted—for instance, ITT, which helped to destabilize the democratically elected Allende government in Chile during the early 1970s.

Benefits of MNCs

We've looked at some of the criticisms of MNCs and have attempted to answer them. Now let's look at the other side of the coin. The well-known economist, John Kenneth Galbraith, a frequent critic of business, has said that MNCs have been both economically and socially beneficial. Galbraith's arguments are presented next.[3]

Lessening of Tariffs. MNCs have worked hard for tariff reduction and for the elimination of other trade barriers. High tariffs (import taxes) inhibit the movement of goods and services across borders. High tariffs also lead to higher prices in the country imposing the tariffs. Thus, a lessening of tariffs is generally considered to be a good thing.

Peaceful Influence. During the last century, steel, coal, and shipbuilding industries had a strong interest in creating international tension. The more hostility between countries, the greater the demand for armaments and other war material. Today the opposite is true. MNCs operate in many countries, and a war—or even the threat of war—could cost them a great deal of money in terms of lost trade. Many MNCs, therefore, work to reduce international tensions.

Local Managerial Development. MNCs are not run by their owners or stockholders, but by professional managers. Many times, the authority to make decisions is delegated to local managers who know and understand local conditions. Employing people from the host country not only makes the business more effective but also looks good in the eyes of host country government officials. What has emerged in many less developed nations from such hiring practices is a whole new class of professional managers. For example, in Brazil, General Electric has 10,000 full-time employees, fewer than 20 of whom are U.S. citizens. These employees contribute to their company as well as to the economic growth of their country.

MNCs are clearly not perfect organizations; rather, they are imperfect organizations in an imperfect world. Some are better than others. Some make more money than others. But all of them, in one form or another, contribute to world economic efficiency, raising the standard of living for all. Now let's see how various nations have joined together to promote greater economic cooperation.

INTERNATIONAL ECONOMIC COMMUNITIES

After World War II, several groups of nations decided to form economic alliances, based on the model of the military alliances that they had formed during the war. These economic alliances produced what are called **economic communities**. The members of these communities believe that economic cooperation leads to

---

[3] John Kenneth Galbraith, "The Defense of the Multinational Company," *Harvard Business Review* (March-April, 1978), pp. 83-93.

Dumping

The practice known as dumping is blamed today for many U.S. economic problems. What is dumping? How does it hurt the U.S. economy? Should it be stopped?

Dumping refers to the export and sale of goods to other countries at prices below manufacturing cost or at least far below market prices. All countries dump goods in foreign markets to some extent. When a country industrializes, it either intentionally makes more goods than it can sell inside the country, or it misjudges demand and creates excess inventory that must be sold off quickly. For example, to develop its steel mills, Japan had to produce much more steel than it could consume. The surplus steel was dumped in the United States and other countries. Similarly, Datsun built too many pickup trucks in late 1982 and dumped them in the United States.

The United States has engaged in dumping, too. Many drugs banned by the U.S. Food and Drug Administration have been sold in such countries as Mozambique, where no health laws are in effect.[1] However, the United States has been the most victimized by dumping, with steel and electronics being the industries hardest hit.

How does dumping affect the electronics industry here? The heart of most electronics manufacturing today is the production of tiny semiconductor chips. The semiconductor business is extremely competitive, so prices generally stay low. But research and development costs are very high. As a result, chip manufacturers need to sell a great number of chips so that they can spread R&D costs across large production runs. This is what Japanese firms do. Companies such as Hitachi have sold huge quantities of their chips in Japan and dumped their surplus in the United States. Their U.S. competitors, such as Intel and Motorola, cannot do the same because Japan refuses to open its domestic markets to U.S. companies. Thus, Japan can sell in a market consisting of Japan and the United States, whereas the United States can sell only in the U.S. market.

The consensus here is that dumping is bad. It discourages many companies from introducing new products. They fear that foreign companies might start making the same product and dumping it on the United States. Dumping reduces profits for U.S. companies because they are forced to cut prices to compete.

The U.S. Congress has been trying to force dumping countries to open their markets to U.S. manufacturers. The hope is that the threat of U.S. dumping will discourage other countries from doing the same to us. The government also has taken several dumping cases (particularly in the steel industry) to court, and so far has been winning. Finally, the government has taxed imports at higher rates so that dumped products are more expensive to buy here.

---

[1] "U.S. Drug Dumping in Mozambique," *New Statesman* (August 15, 1980), p. 2.

---

mutual benefit. The first step in establishing an economic community is to create a free trade area among the countries involved. This permits products to flow among member countries without tariff restrictions. Table 23-3 lists six economic communities. Let's look at the most important of these communities—the European Economic Community.

European Economic Community

The European Economic Community (EEC), also known as the Common Market, was established on January 1, 1958. It consisted at that time of six countries: Belgium, the Netherlands, Luxembourg, Germany, France, and Italy. Today, as then, the goal of the EEC is to promote European growth and stability by establishing common economic policies among member nations.

The EEC's first step was to reduce tariffs on industrial goods and to place a common external tariff on all industrial products imported into EEC countries. Today, the EEC has reduced or eliminated virtually all tariffs among its members on industrial and agricultural products. In addition, it has established common transportation, monetary, and antitrust policies.

EEC benefits extend not only to member nations, but also to nations given special treatment. This group of nations, referred to as associate members, consists of former European colonies as well as other European and African nations not given full member status.

Since the establishment of the EEC, there has been talk of making it more of a political organization. Some people have even suggested that the

Table 23-3

Economic Communities

Name and Starting Date	Countries	Level of Integration
European Economic Community (EEC) 1958	Belgium Denmark France Germany Ireland Italy Luxembourg Netherlands United Kingdom	The nations are highly integrated both economically and politically
European Free Trade Association (EFTA) 1960	Austria Iceland Norway Portugal Sweden Switzerland	Free trade area; few political ties among members
Council for Mutual Assistance (COMECON) 1949	Cuba Czechoslovakia East Germany Hungary Poland Romania USSR	No common trade policies
Latin American Integration Association (LAIA), formerly Latin American Free Trade Area (LAFTA) 1960	Argentina Bolivia Brazil Chile Colombia Ecuador Mexico Paraguay Peru Uruguay Venezuela	Some economic integration
Central American Common Market (CACM) 1961	El Salvador Nicaragua Guatemala Costa Rica	Some economic integration
Caribbean Free Trade Association (CARIFTA) 1968	Jamaica Trinidad Tobago Montserrat	Some economic integration

EEC may eventually evolve from an economic organization into a nation state. Although this is possible, EEC member nations so far have not seriously considered becoming one nation.

Economic Communities: Pro and Con

The primary advantage of economic communities to business firms is that these communities open up large markets—markets without tariff and other trade restrictions. This means that a firm should sell its products there for less money because it is able to sell more of them. This has proven to be true for many basic commodities, such as steel and aluminum. For example, a steel maker in England can afford to build a large efficient mill since it can sell steel not only to buyers in England, but also to buyers throughout Europe.

The greatest problem with economic communities from the point of view of firms is that there still exist major cultural barriers among member nations. For example, even within the EEC, traditional national preferences for food remain strong. In the same way, language problems continue to make advertising, labeling, and personal selling difficult in the EEC. It may be called the "Common Market" but it is still necessary for many firms to design separate marketing strategies for each country.[4]

---

[4]Kahler and Kramer, pp. 140-145.

Pepper... and Salt

THE WALL STREET JOURNAL

"Mr. Gottlieb recently read one of those books on Japanese management techniques."

Source: From THE WALL STREET JOURNAL, Permission-Cartoon Features Syndicate.

SUMMARY POINTS

1. It is important to study international business for two reasons: because we need to understand the implications of a trade surplus or trade deficit, and because U.S. businesses have invested large sums of money in foreign markets.
2. Planning is often difficult in foreign countries because of unstable governments and inadequate market information.
3. Foreign countries often use tax controls to keep out imports and to prevent international business from repatriating profits.
4. Cultural attitudes affect how a business manufactures, advertises, and distributes its products.
5. Firms should analyze economic conditions, such as a nation's state of economic development and level of inflation, before entering a foreign market.
6. Exporting is a good way to enter foreign markets because the firm faces little risk and because this approach does not entail much cost.
7. Licensing is an agreement whereby one firm (the licensor) allows another firm in a foreign country (the licensee) to manufacture its products.
8. Very few firms use local marketing offices to enter foreign markets. The major problem is that the seller must learn too much too quickly about selling products in the foreign country.
9. Joint ventures are a partnership between an international firm and a firm in a foreign country.
10. Total ownership involves the greatest commit-

ment to a foreign market. All of the risk and profits go to the international company.
11. There are three advantages to standardizing a firm's marketing strategy—production cost efficiency, advertising consistency, and utilizing good ideas in more than one country.
12. Cultural and social differences among nations may make it all but impossible to standardize an international marketing strategy.
13. In deciding whether to standardize its marketing strategy, the firm should consider the type of product involved, cultural similarities, the availability of marketing services, and government restrictions.
14. Multinational corporations have been accused of bribing local officials, hurting the U.S. balance of payments, and exploiting cheap labor. On the plus side, they have contributed to a reduction in trade barriers, to a lessening of global tensions, and to the development of management talent abroad.
15. The goal of the European Economic Community (the Common Market) is to promote European growth and stability by establishing common economic policies. It has virtually eliminated all tariffs among European countries and has established common transportation, monetary, and antitrust policies.

KEY TERMS AND CONCEPTS

export
import
trade balance
trade surplus
trade deficit
tax controls
repatriation
expropriation without reimbursement
culture
infrastructure
licensing
local marketing subsidiary
joint venture
standardization strategy
multinational corporation (MNC)
grease payment
economic communities
dumping

REVIEW QUESTIONS

1. How do countries determine their trade balance? Why is a trade surplus preferable to a trade deficit?
2. Why do some countries impose taxes on imported goods?
3. What is meant by repatriation of profits?
4. Explain why a country's state of economic development influences a firm's willingness to do business there.
5. Describe two ways that multinational firms deal with inflation.
6. Of the five methods for entering foreign markets, which involves the least amount of risk? Why? Which involves the most risk? Why?
7. What is an international joint venture? List some of its advantages and disadvantages for a firm wishing to market its products overseas.
8. A standardized international marketing strategy has three basic advantages. What are they?
9. What are the factors that should be considered in the decision whether to standardize a marketing strategy across each of several foreign markets?
10. What is an economic community? Why were they established?

DISCUSSION QUESTIONS

1. What are some of the ways that the United States could go about increasing the levels of its exports?
2. How do you think cultural and social differences across nations would affect the marketing of microwave ovens?
3. Evaluate the relationship between risk and potential profit for the five ways of entering foreign markets.
4. On balance, do you think that the MNCs have been a positive or negative force in the international economy? Can you envision a time when the concept of a nation state will be obsolete, having been replaced by the concept of multinational corporate government?
5. What is your attitude toward so-called "grease payments"?

CASE 23-1

The Soviet Trade Balance

The Soviet Union has traditionally been very short on hard currency; that is, it lacks dollars, francs, marks, pounds, and other nonSoviet money with which to buy products from outside its own country. In part, the Soviets have gotten around this problem by creating the Eastern Bloc, including Poland, Czechoslovakia, East Germany, and others. These countries trade extensively with the Soviet Union on a noncurrency basis and supply much of what the Soviet Union needs but cannot produce itself. But the currency problem is still a serious one.

In addition, the Soviet Union has had persistent crop failures. In several successive years, the Soviet Union has had to import as much as 100 million tons of wheat and other grains to feed its people and its animals. Buying this grain has almost wiped out its currency reserves.

The Soviet Union has responded by trying to sell massive quantities of those products it does produce. For example, the Soviet Union is the world's largest producer of natural gas. It is now working on a huge pipeline project to deliver large quantities of this gas to countries throughout Western Europe.

The Soviet Union also controls more than 50 percent of the world's supply of platinum, which it sells when it needs a great deal of hard currency. Although the demand for platinum in the West is very high, the fact that the Soviet Union at times drops large quantities of platinum into the world market has permanently depressed its price.

Similarly, the Soviet Union controls much of the world's gold production. Again, gold is normally in high demand, but when the Soviet Union decides to sell huge quantities to the West, the value drops. When buyers anticipate that more gold will become available from the Soviets, the price stays low.

The Soviets have also flooded the world markets with nickel. Again, the price plummeted and the Soviets found themselves selling thousands of tons of nickel at ridiculously low prices.

1. Given the shortage of hard currency and the excess of marketable products the Soviet Union owns, do you think the Soviets have a trade surplus or a trade deficit? Why?
2. Identify the barriers to international trade that the Soviet Union faces. How might these barriers be eliminated or reduced? How do these barriers produce the Soviet Union's current problems?
3. Why do you think that the United States tightly controls the flow of its dollars to other countries, such as the Soviet Union? Why does the United States want to see very few dollars in the hands of foreign governments?
4. When the Soviet Union sells massive quantities of platinum, gold, or nickel on the world market, what do you think happens to American platinum, gold, and nickel prices? What happens to American companies that produce these metals? to American companies that buy these metals?

CASE 23-2

Thompson International Education, Inc.

Since World War II, the United States has spent vast sums of money providing American technology, military supplies, food supplies, and other products to foreign countries. As the United States realized the importance of oil-producing allies such as Saudi Arabia, Kuwait, Venezuela, and Mexico, large quantities of American aid started flowing to these countries.

America sent squadrons of new sophisticated jet fighters to Saudi Arabia along with technical advisers to instruct Saudi pilots. However, the Saudi pilots knew no English and couldn't understand the advisers. Petroleum engineers sent to Mexico found that many Mexican oil field managers couldn't speak

English. Kuwaiti hospitals received American medical equipment with handbooks and instructions written in English, which Kuwaiti doctors often couldn't read.

To solve this problem, the U.S. State Department put together a program for teaching English to engineers, doctors, military leaders, and other professionals in foreign countries. The program, however, needed an expert. Terry Thompson was working on the project for the State Department at the time, saw the problem, and knew how to solve it. Fluent in Arabic and several other languages, he decided to create a specialized company, marketing English-teaching services to foreign countries. He called his company Thompson International Education, Inc., or TIE.

Thompson reasoned that these countries would be willing and able to foot the bill for a good English-teaching program specially tailored to their needs. He was right. He soon struck a five million dollar contract with Iran. With financial guarantees from the Iranian government, he invested close to a million dollars in salaries, a construction project for an English-teaching college in Iran, and various other materials. The State Department soon handed over authority for similar projects in Libya, Mexico, and Venezuela, and agreements were quickly reached with these countries.

Then, with millions of dollars invested, everything fell apart. Iran's government was toppled and the Ayatollah Khomeini took power. He seized all of Thompson's assets in Iran and severed the contract with Thompson's company. Libya soon followed suit and expelled Thompson's personnel, leaving behind half-completed buildings and funds in Libyan banks. Finally, Mexico and Venezuela began facing a dramatic reversal in their trade surpluses as oil demand decreased, and they told Thompson that they could no longer afford his services. All the investments Thompson had made in these countries were lost. Thompson International Education went bankrupt.

1. Thompson chose total ownership rather than licensing, using a local subsidiary, or a joint venture. What were the risks and opportunities that made him choose total ownership?
2. Thompson standardized his marketing strategy. Was this appropriate? Why or why not?
3. Were cultural or economic barriers important? Why or why not?
4. Why did Thompson International Education fail? How might failure have been averted?

24

The Future of American Business

After studying this chapter, you should be able to:

- Discuss why it is important for businesses to engage in forecasting and prediction.
- Describe current population and income trends both nationally and globally.
- Assess the short-term and long-term prospects for each of several U.S. industries.
- Discuss your role in the future.

It has been said that what distinguishes human beings from other animals is an inclination to take wine with dinner and the ability to think about the future. Today, more than ever before, a concern with the future is essential because of the rapid pace of change and because of our power to influence the direction of change for better or worse.

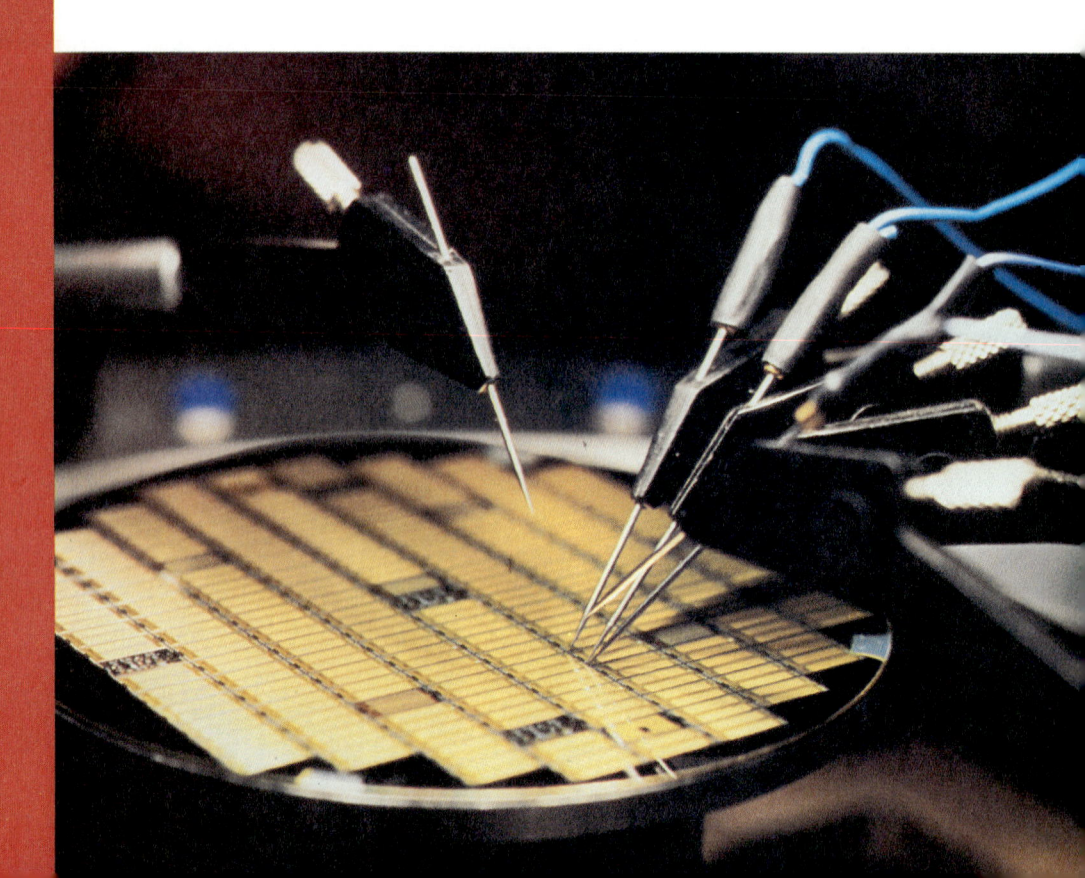

This is an exciting time. Our world may be poised on the threshold of a new industrial revolution as far reaching in its impact on human life as was the first industrial revolution 200 years ago. The first revolution was based on machine power and the production of goods; this next one, on electronics and the production of information and services. In time, our giant factories and office buildings may become all but obsolete, replaced by a new generation of "cottage industries"—small production centers located in the home—linked with one another by computers and electronic communications.

FORECASTING AND PREDICTION

"If you want to know what's going to happen tomorrow, look at what happened yesterday." This is probably the most basic approach to forecasting. When change is the issue, the above statement can be rephrased as, "Expect more of the same, or less of the same, tomorrow."

The Art of Educated Guessing

Forecasting or **predicting** is the art of educated guessing, even when we're just projecting current trends into the future. But when we're trying to predict turning points in trends or technological breakthroughs, forecasting becomes even riskier. In 1970, who would have predicted the Arab oil embargo of 1974 and its impact on gas prices? Similarly, in the late 1970s, who would have predicted the world oil glut of the early 1980s and declining gas prices in 1982 and 1983?

Reducing Uncertainty About the Future

One company that may not have foreseen the oil glut was Exxon. Exxon's synthetic fuels program lost millions of dollars as the price of crude oil started to drop toward $30 a barrel. The production of synthetic fuels is an expensive process and can only be profitable when the price of oil is high. Price cuts in 1982 for imported oil squeezed potential profits out of synthetic fuels production. On the other hand, Exxon diversified into the booming electronic office equipment business. Exxon now markets a line of word processors through its Exxon Office Systems Division.

Despite our mistakes in reading the future, forecasting and prediction are essential activities of all business firms. Our forecasts become more accurate as our understanding of economics, markets, and business conditions increases and as our forecasting techniques improve. The aim of all forecasts is to reduce uncertainty in the environment by telling us something about the future. Thus, forecasting serves as a guide to decision making: "An organization establishes goals and objectives, seeks to predict environmental factors, then selects actions that it hopes will result in attainment of the goals and objectives."[1] With an accurate interest rate forecast, indicating a drop in mortgage rates and an end to a housing slump, a wood products company could gear up production capacity in anticipation of future demand.

INTO THE NEXT CENTURY

In the year 2050, the United States will be a very different place from what it is today. Chapter 2 examined the changing environment of

---

[1] Spyros Makridakis and Steven C. Wheelwright, *Forecasting: Methods and Applications* (New York: John Wiley & Sons, Inc., 1978), p. 5.

Forecasting an event or problem such as this one is vital to business.

business. Let's take a second look at the more important population trends, both nationally and globally, and at where these trends are taking us.

U.S. Population Size

Make no mistake, the population of the United States is growing. Our current population is about 236 million, up from 203 million in 1970. According to census experts, the population will climb to 268 million in the year 2000 and will continue to climb until 2050, at which time it will peak and then begin a decline. These population projections are shown in Figure 24-1. But as Figure 24-2 shows, the *rate* of population growth is already declining and has been since 1950. Whereas the population grew by 11.4 percent during the 1970s, it may grow by as little as 0.3 percent between 2040 and 2050. Could this slowdown in population growth eventually mean an end to unemployment problems? As the size of the labor pool shrinks, will there be fewer people competing for available jobs?

Age Mix

In 1980, at the time of the last population census, the average American was 30 years old. By the end of this century, the average age will be 36, increasing to nearly 42 in the year 2050. Between 1980 and 2000, the proportion of the population 34 years of age or younger will decline from 58 percent to 48 percent. And census experts say that it could drop to 42 percent in 2050.

What does the aging of the population mean for the makers of youth-oriented products? It means that the markets for their products will tighten in years to come. At the same time, the markets for products aimed at middle-aged and elderly people will expand. We can expect to see more demand for home-improvement products, pharmaceutical products, hospital and medical services, financial services, travel services, and fitness services.[2] As we said in Chapter 1, services now play a big part in our economy, and they are likely to play an even bigger part in years to come. Perhaps as much as 80 percent of all employment will be in services by the year 2000.

---

[2] "Where U.S. Is Going: Signposts from Census," *U.S. News & World Report* (November 22, 1982), pp. 51-53.

Family Size and Family Income

As our population grows bigger and bigger, average family size will get smaller and smaller. In 1980, families of five or more persons accounted for 16.6 percent of all U.S. families. But by 1995, as Table 24-1 shows, large families will account for only 9.4 percent of the total. Do you think that small families will continue to be popular into the next century? What factors could bring about a return of the large family?

What about income? On average, will we be better off tomorrow than we are today? Barring a worldwide recession or other economic disaster, families of all sizes should have higher incomes in real terms through the 1990s. Between 1980 and 1995, the proportion of all families earning $50,000 or more should rise from 10 percent to 24 percent. Demographers expect this increase to be greatest for four-person families.

The big reason for these higher incomes is that the output of our economy will continue to grow. Technological innovation will be the driving force behind the increase in national wealth. Also, a greater number of families will be two-career families. In Chapter 2, we observed this trend, and it should continue. Finally, the baby

Figure 24-1

U.S. Population Growth, 1950-2050

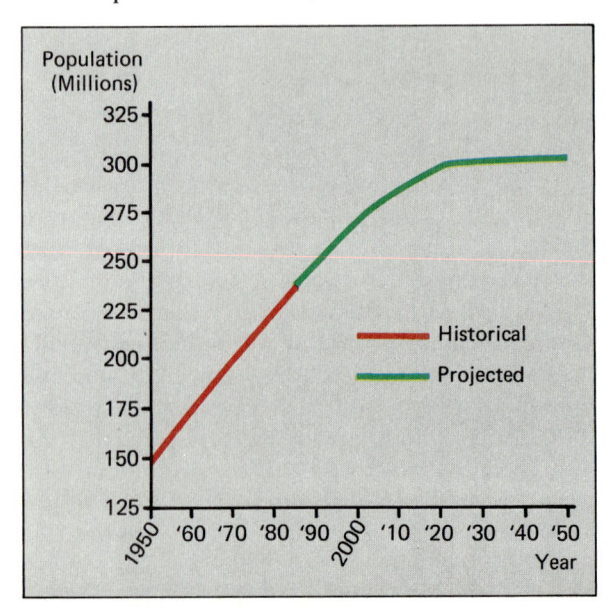

Source: U.S. Department of Commerce, Bureau of the Census, *Current Population Reports*, Series P-25, Projections of the Population of the United States: 1982-2050 (issued October, 1982).

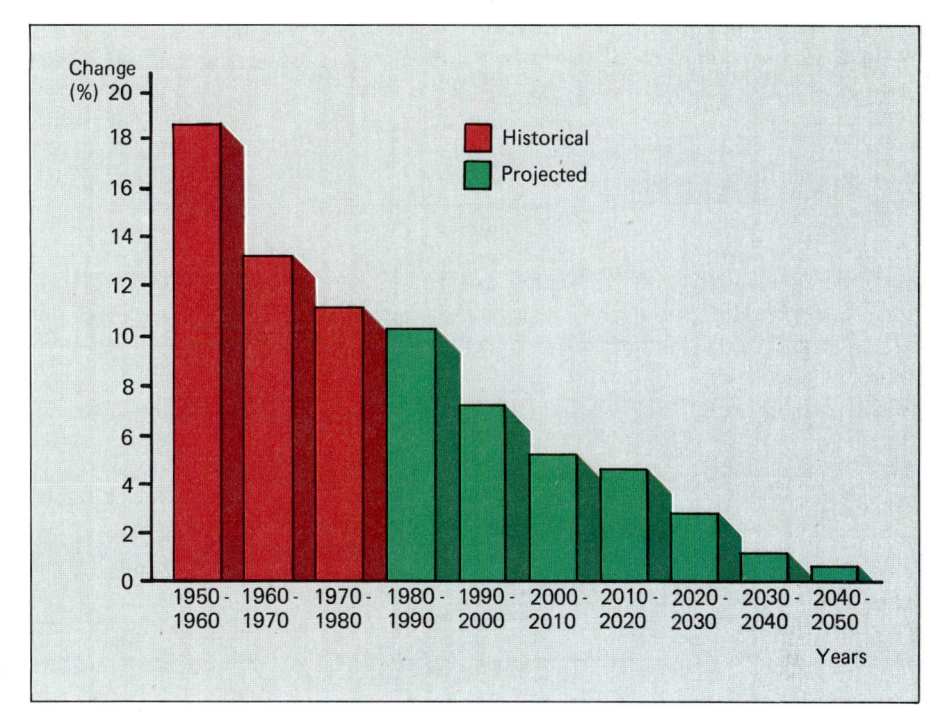

Figure 24-2

Rate of Growth of U.S. Population, 1950-2050

Source: U.S. Department of Commerce, Bureau of the Census, *Current Population Reports*, Series P-25, Projections of the Population of the United States: 1982-2050 (issued October, 1982).

boom generation will have grown up, formed families, and entered the middle-aged years of greatest productivity and earnings.[3]

Global Population and Income Trends

The population and income outlook is much more favorable nationally than globally. Most demographers would now agree that there is little hope that world population growth will be brought under control in the foreseeable future. Between the mid-1980s and the year 2000, world population will increase from 4.6 billion to 6.3 billion, an average increase of about 100 million people a year. Ninety percent of this growth will occur in the **less-developed countries (LDCs)**—the countries least able to provide for growth. Food production in the LDCs is not expected to keep pace with population growth there. If current population growth were to continue indefinitely, the world's population would approach 30 billion by the end of the next century. However, many nations, such as China, the world's biggest, have already made significant strides in slowing the rate of population growth.

Figure 24-3 shows the distribution of world population by region in 1975 and 2000. Compare population growth in the industrialized West with that of less-developed Latin America, Africa, and Asia and Oceania. Given these high rates of growth, what are the chances that such less-developed areas will be able to lift themselves out of poverty?

[3]"Demographic Forecasts: Families by Size and Income," *American Demographics*, Vol. 5 (March, 1983), pp. 50-51.

Table 24-1

Share of Families by Size, 1980-1995

Family Size	1980	1985	1990	1995
Two Persons	39.6%	40.7%	40.9%	36.6%
Three Persons	23.3	24.3	25.0	27.4
Four Persons	20.5	21.9	23.6	26.6
Five+ Persons	16.6	13.0	10.5	9.4

Source: *American Demographics*, Vol. 5 (March, 1983), p. 50.

Figure 24-3

Distribution of the World's Population, 1975-2000

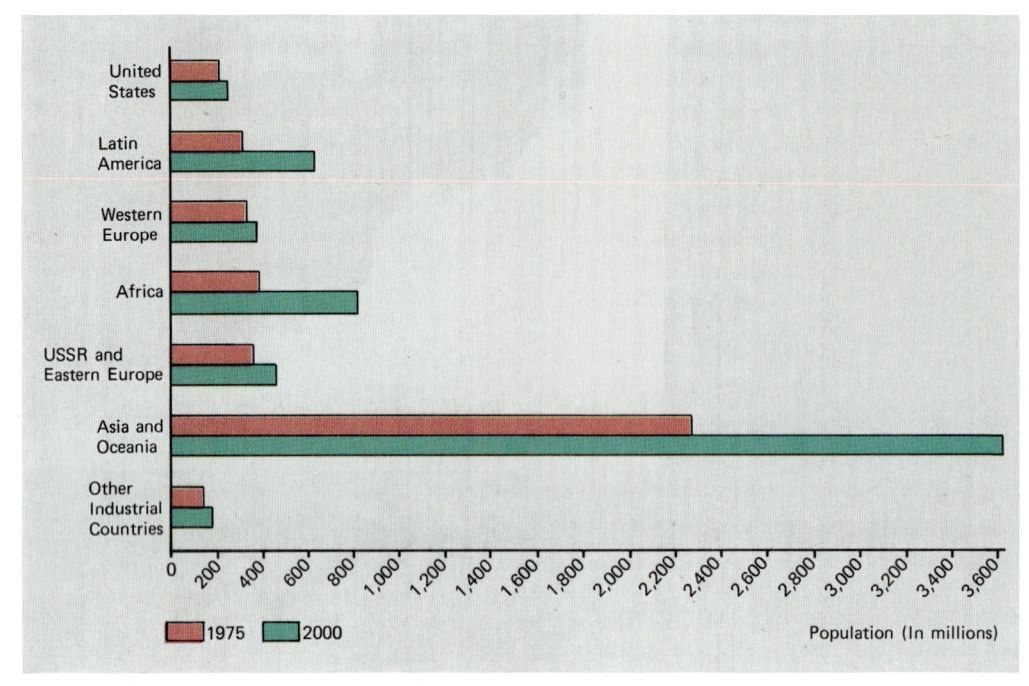

Region	1975	2000
United States		
Latin America		
Western Europe		
Africa		
USSR and Eastern Europe		
Asia and Oceania		
Other Industrial Countries		

Population (In millions)

Source: U.S. Council on Environmental Quality and U.S. State Department, *The Global 2000 Report to the President: Entering the Twenty-First Century* (1981).

Figure 24-4 shows the distribution of per capita gross national product by region. The economies of the LDCs, especially the Latin American countries, are expected to grow faster than those of the wealthier Western nations. One reason is that they are just beginning to undertake widespread industrialization: The early stages of industrialization tend to produce higher rates of national economic growth than the mature stages. The United States and the Western European nations are examples of nations in the mature stage of industrialization. Despite their efforts at industrialization and economic growth, the nations of Africa and Asia will experience only modest gains in per capita wealth. In Africa, for example, per capita GNP will scarcely rise above the equivalent of $600. What sort of pressures will this continuing income gap between the rich and the poor nations place on the world community for a more equitable division of wealth?[4]

[4]U.S. Council on Environmental Quality and U.S. State Department, *The Global 2000 Report: Entering the Twenty-First Century* (1981), pp. 1-16.

INDUSTRIAL OUTLOOK

The trends that are reshaping the industrial composition of our economy are already apparent. The two most important are the decline of basic industries—the so-called "smokestack"

Government and business must work together to ensure a healthy future.

industries—and the rise of high technology industries. The **basic industries** include steel, automobiles, airplanes, chemicals, machinery, rubber, and glass. They employ about one third of the U.S. labor force. The rapid expansion of these industries produced the great economic boom of the postwar period. But now that these industries are in decline, we must look toward the new high technology industries if the United States—and, indeed, all of the industrialized West—is to enter another long period of economic growth.

Bad News and Good News

Tables 24-2 and 24-3 present short-term industrial outlook data. Each year the Department of Commerce publishes forecasts for U. S. industry. The two major industrial trends just mentioned are clearly visible in the data. As the first table shows, the three industries in greatest decline all relate to machinery and machine tools. The percentage growth rates refer to forecasted changes in customer shipments. Other declining industries include agricultural goods and chemicals.

The next table shows ten fast-growing U.S. industries. They include electronic, biomedical, telecommunication, and aerospace technologies. Computers and semiconductors are the leaders among our most vital industries. They should remain strong throughout the rest of the century. Wood pallets and skids hold down second place on the list. The strong showing of this industry is probably only temporary, relating more to the growth in trade and product shipments following economic recovery than to the industry's long-term prospects.

Let's take a closer look at some of the problems of our basic industries, and then we'll examine four high-growth industries.

Basic Industries

The plight of basic industry in this country is best exemplified by the steel industry. During

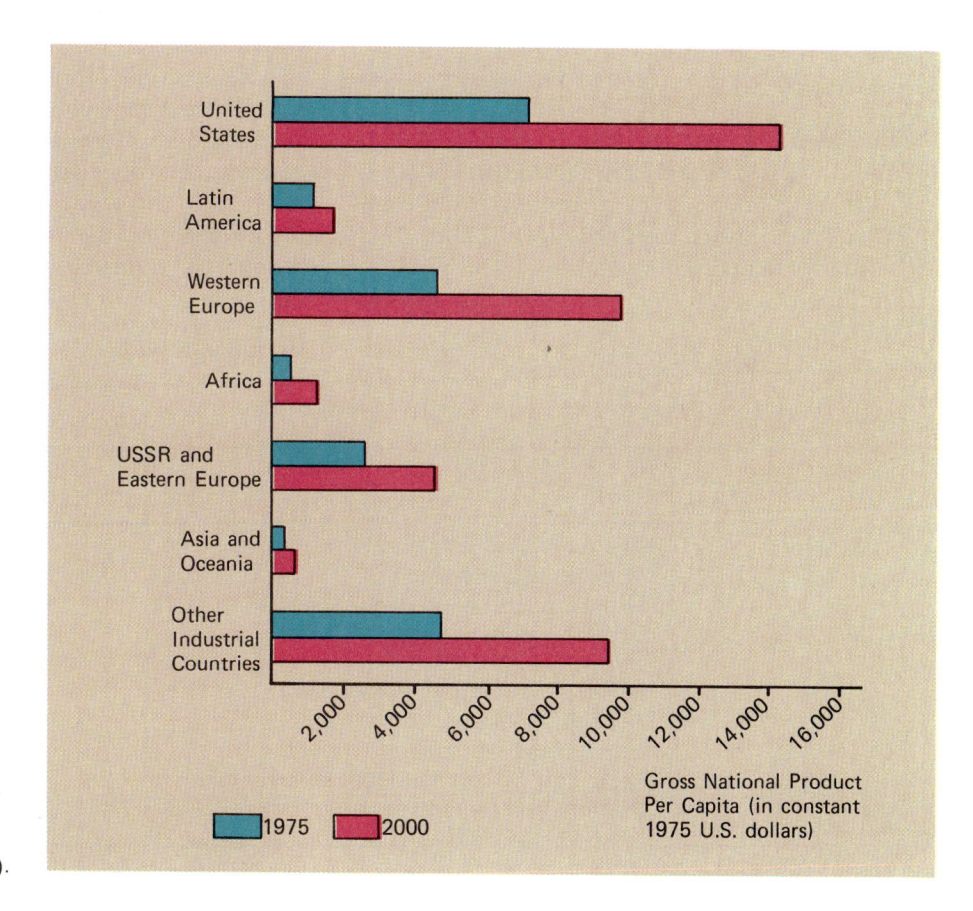

Figure 24-4

Per Capita Gross National Product by Region, 1975-2000

Source: U.S. Council on Environmental Quality and U.S. State Department, *The Global 2000 Report to the President: Entering the Twenty-First Century* (1981).

Table 24-2

Ten Declining Industries in the United States

Rank	Industry	1982-83 Growth Rate
1	Machine tools, metal-cutting types	−33.4%
2	Machine tools, metal-forming types	−28.5
3	Special dies, tools, jigs, and fixtures	−15.6
4	Fine earthenware food utensils	− 9.9
5	Agricultural chemicals	− 7.9
6	Chemical preparations	− 7.7
7	Tobacco stemming and redrying	− 7.4
8	Paper industries machinery	− 7.1
9	Blowers and fans	− 5.3
10	Electron tubes	− 5.1

Source: U.S. Department of Commerce, Bureau of Industrial Economics, *1983 U.S. Industrial Outlook* (January, 1983).

January of 1983, steel mills were operating at only 30 percent of capacity. That is, for every 100 tons of steel that the mills were equipped to produce, they were producing only 30 tons because of slack demand. Unemployment in the industry was running at an astronomical 60 percent. Most analysts believe that, even with aggressive cost cutting, there is not much chance in the short run for steel producers to show profits again.

Labor Costs and Cheaper Imports. Besides the recession, two big reasons for the industry's troubles are high labor costs here and increased competition from foreign steel producers. Labor costs are usually cheaper abroad, and so steel producers in Japan, South Korea, Spain, and other countries are able to undercut the prices of U.S. producers.

Politically, the issue today concerns whether the United States should negotiate trade quota agreements with foreign countries. One such agreement was reached with the European Economic Community in 1982. A quota would set an upper limit on the amount of steel that foreign producers could ship to this country. This would protect the U.S. steel industry from foreign competitors, who often dump their products in U.S. markets, as discussed in the last chapter.

Two Views. In the long run, the problem with many basic industries is the aging of their capital equipment. Two views prevail as to what sort of

Table 24-3

Ten Growing Industries in the United States

Rank	Industry	1982-83 Growth Rate
1	Electronic computing equipment	17.8%
2	Wood pallets and skids	14.9
3	Semiconductors and related devices	14.6
4	Electronic connectors	13.2
5	Electronic components	12.7
6	Games, toys, children's vehicles	9.4
7	Welding apparatus, electric	9.0
8	Surgical and medical instruments	8.5
9	Radio and TV communications equipment	8.2
10	Guided missiles and space vehicles	8.0

Source: U.S. Department of Commerce, Bureau of Industrial Economics, *1983 U.S. Industrial Outlook* (January, 1983).

CONTROVERSIAL ISSUES

Part of the intention behind the massive federal support of NASA's space program during the 1960s and 1970s was to increase the feasibility of starting industrial research and production facilities in space, where many kinds of work can be done that are either too expensive or impossible on Earth. Now that space technology is coming of age, should businesses start investing in space factories and production programs?

Pro

The success of the space shuttle *Columbia* demonstrated that all the tools are available to establish industrial programs of research and production in space. NASA has demonstrated the capability to build permanent space stations. These could house factories engaged in work that is expensive, hazardous, or inefficient on earth. For example, many kinds of drugs are produced in excess by plants and molds when suspended in a weightless environment; thus, space is the perfect environment for new drug factories. Many electronic techniques involving new semiconductor systems require assembly in a vacuum and a far greater dust-free environment than earth's atmosphere can offer; again, space is perfect. A single shuttle flight can deliver enough supplies to construct literally hundreds of millions of dollars worth of products for a shuttle return trip. The prospects are staggering.

Further, consider that in space a factory can obtain almost limitless supplies of energy from the sun. Reductions in expenditures for power may make even further economic efficiencies possible.

American Business Should Invest in Space!

And remember that the American government is still subsidizing much of the cost of space development. Companies who hop on the bandwagon now can get carried into space for very little. The government is even assuming the incredible risks, which means firms don't have to worry about getting Prudential to insure a space factory. (Can you imagine what premiums would be like?)

Most of all, America is the only country with the technological capacity to begin space industry in the near future. As American companies fall behind Japan and other industrialized powers, the advantages gained from space production can vault us back into the lead.

Con

No, space industrialization is not feasible. There are some industrial procedures that are better performed in space, but these methods change from month to month as technology advances; long before space can be developed commercially, scientists will have figured how to improve these techniques for operation on earth.

There will also be economic and political problems. The American government almost scrapped NASA until the shuttle *Columbia* revived interest in space development. What will happen to the space budgets during the next economic downturn? They will be cut. And no company, no matter how large, can afford to go it alone.

Then there's the problem of space politics. For example, to whom will taxes be paid? Will taxes be higher on space-produced products because they have been produced with tax subsidies? In a war, will space stations be protected? International law and political agreements will have to be completely rethought and rewritten; until that's done, producing goods in space will be very risky.

And what about the cost to employees of space life? When the Soviets sent astronauts aloft for three months, they returned home so weak they couldn't even lift a paper cup of orange juice; they had to learn how to walk again; and they were ill and severely disoriented for months. Even if employees are willing to endure these problems, they will expect extra compensation. There's no efficiency in that! If firms try to automate procedures entirely to avoid having employees in space, there will still be horribly expensive breakdowns that will necessitate shipping a repair crew out to fix them.

No, space travel is a tool for the government and for scientific research. Don't try to invest in space industrialization. It isn't worth it.

Profile—
Gilbert Levin

In the 1970s, NASA became involved with discovering life on Mars. It designed and launched several Viking spacecraft to land on Mars, test its atmosphere and soil, and radio back to Earth any information about possible life on that planet. One basic test for life that NASA used was to see if any living organism existed on Mars that could consume different kinds of sugars and other foodstuffs that Earth chemists could devise. One group of sugars that NASA scientists wanted to test was L-sugars. These sugars intrigued scientists because, although they were mirror images of the so-called D-sugars used by humans and all other living organisms on Earth, L-sugars could not be digested by humans (or any other kind of life on Earth). A human could eat L-sugars and could taste the same kind of sweetness one tasted when eating D-sugars, but could not digest them. Therefore, L-sugars gave no nourishment and no calories to the person who ate them.

Gilbert Levin, a researcher who developed the tests for NASA, realized that L-sugars could be the perfect low-calorie sweetener. Genetic engineering had been applied to finding better dietary sweeteners to replace saccharin, which many consumers disliked and some researchers felt caused cancer. In researching the sweetener market, Levin found that the average American eats 125 pounds of sugar and other sweeteners a year, creating a market worth over $50 billion annually. He also realized that artificial sweeteners such as saccharin or aspartame do not give the same taste as sugar, leave a bad aftertaste, cannot be used in cooking as a substitute for sugar, and do not last on the shelf. Levin immediately recognized the potential profit in producing L-sugars as food and drink sweeteners.

His biggest problem was price. When Levin was testing his sugars for NASA, L-sugars cost over $1,000 a pound. However, Boise Cascade has since developed a process to convert waste cellulose from logging and paper-making operations into useful products, one of which is L-sugars. This process lowered the cost to less than $2 a pound.

Levin's company, Biospherics, started a research program at Purdue University to find ways to lower the price still further. At that time, table sugar sold at 30¢ a pound and even aspartame, the new sweetener marketed by the drug company G. D. Searle, cost only 45¢ for an equivalent amount of sweetening power.

Levin still has two problems to face—problems common to many researchers in bioengineering. First, it takes several years for the Food and Drug Administration to approve a new food product; countless tests and studies are needed to prove the product safe for human consumption. Second, to produce L-sugars on a large scale requires money, and Levin is trying to obtain funding from venture capital companies. These are companies that specialize in investing in high-risk enterprises, especially those in high-technology ventures.

Levin is typical of the high-technology entrepreneur today. He found an exciting new application of modern science in the world of business and is pursuing it until it becomes profitable. His efforts embody much of what we've discussed in this book—management, the marketing concept, financial planning, and an optimistic view into the future.

investment policies should be undertaken. One view argues that insufficient investment is the cause of the decline of basic industries. Thus, proponents of this view favor a "reindustrialization" of traditional industries through a combination of tax incentives, import quotas, government-directed investment strategies, and other measures. The other view holds that such policies are badly misguided. Rather than pouring our resources into these "sunset" industries, which are fading as a result of natural economic forces, we should be investing in "sunrise" industries—namely, high technology industries.

One defense of this second view rests on what some economists see in the historical record as the **long wave theory** of economic growth and decline. Each wave, lasting about 50 years or so, is driven by a new cluster of technological innovation. One wave reached its peak around 1920, when the railroads and other early industries produced a period of widespread economic prosperity. The economies of the world went into decline thereafter. Another wave peaked around 1970 and was driven by innovation in such basic industries as steel, chemicals, and transportation. Our economic problems of late, therefore, are the result of the fact that we are on the downside of that wave. What technologies will be behind the next wave? The experts say computers, electronics, space development, biogenetics, and perhaps technologies as yet unimagined.[5]

---

[5]"A Technology Lag That May Stifle Growth," *Business Week* (October 11, 1982), pp. 126-130.

Figure 24-5 illustrates this wave theory. Interestingly, according to this view, we have barely begun the next wave. Most of the benefits of computers and related technologies are still ahead of us. Because this wave pattern of growth and decline operates as almost an unchanging law of history and economics, government attempts to prop up basic industries only postpone the arrival of the next wave. What do you think? Does this interpretation of history make sense to you?

High Technology Industries

However we may feel about the theory of long waves, high technology will certainly play an important role in the future of American business. The effect of technological advance will be twofold: making older manufacturing processes more efficient and creating a whole new array of consumer and producer goods. Figure 24-6 shows the projected growth rates for four high technology industries. Let's survey some of these industries now.

Energy Exploration and Production. Despite the stability of energy prices during the early 1980s, the trend toward development of synthetic fuels and alternative energy sources will certainly continue. Progress in these areas will depend on the pace of technological innovation. In the short run, however, oil and gas producers, despite the industry slump of 1982 and 1983, should enjoy high rates of growth. Economic recovery as well

Figure 24-5

Long Waves of Economic Growth and Decline

Figure 24-6

The Four Big Growth Areas in High Technology

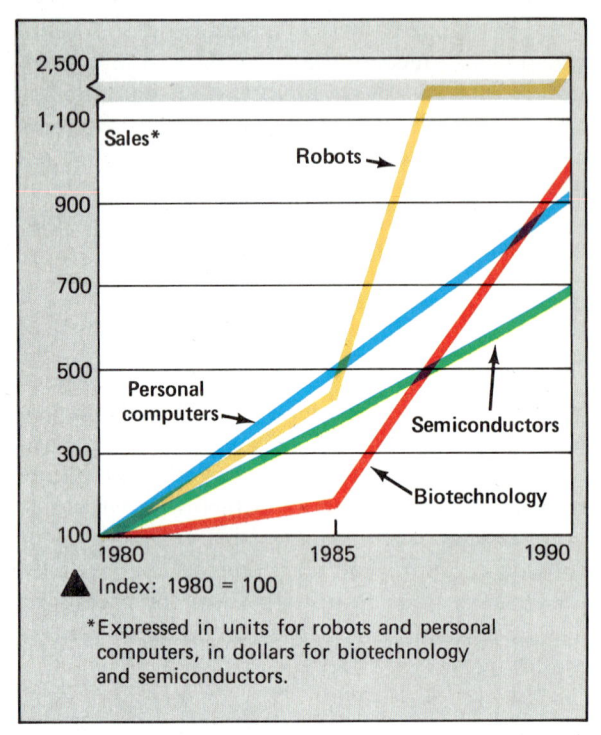

[Chart showing index values from 1980 to 1990, Index: 1980 = 100, for Robots, Personal computers, Semiconductors, and Biotechnology. Y-axis shows values 100, 300, 500, 700, 900, 1,100, 2,500 (Sales*).

*Expressed in units for robots and personal computers, in dollars for biotechnology and semiconductors.]

Source: Reprinted from the June 1, 1981, issue of *Business Week* by special permission, © 1981 by McGraw-Hill, Inc., New York, NY 10020. All rights reserved.

as high energy prices will provide the right conditions for expanded exploration and production activities. Annual sales of exploration and production equipment could surge past the $20 billion mark by 1995, up from $860 million in 1977, the year before the tripling in world oil prices brought about in part by the revolution in Iran. This represents a 2,225 percent increase in sales in less than two decades.[6]

Bioengineering. The newest and perhaps most exciting major industry is bioengineering, also known as recombinant genetics and gene splicing. Only a dream 20 years ago, bioengineering now allows scientists to move genes from one organism to another. Genes are located in the cells of all living organisms and are responsible for the determination and transmission of all hereditary characteristics. By moving them about, geneticists can create new bacteria, yeasts, plants and so on that can benefit mankind. Experts predict that U.S. sales of bioengineered products could exceed $4 billion by the year 1990.

Already in production is a bacterially produced human insulin, a drug used for the treatment of diabetes. Other promising commercial products include human growth hormone, antibodies for fighting viral infections, interferon (an anticancer substance), and aspartame (a sugar substitute). In the long run, recombinant genetics is expected to have a revolutionary impact on the pharmaceutical, medical, food growing and processing, chemical, and petrochemical industries. Eventually, a wealth of new industrial products will be on the market—products that make waste treatment, oil refining, chemical synthesis, and food production more efficient and less costly. The names of some of the new bioengineering firms—Genentech, Inc., Biogen, Cetus Corporation, Genex Corp.—might sound as if they belong in a science fiction novel, but recombinant genetics is one of the brightest areas of our business future.

Robotics. The industrial robots of today bear little resemblance to the mechanical creatures of 1950s science fiction movies. A **robot** can be defined as a machine that can be easily programmed to do a variety of tasks automatically. Some industrial robots are mobile and have many arms, but most are nothing more than a mechanical

Pharmaceuticals—an important industry for the 80s.

---

[6]"The Front-Runners in a Restructured Economy," *Business Week* (June 1, 1981), p. 96.

arm attached to a stationary base. A programmable computing device controls the operation of the arm. Already, robots in U.S. factories are performing such manufacturing tasks as spray painting, arc welding, die casting, assembling, and materials handling. There's not much chance of robots outnumbering human beings any time soon, but by 1990 the robot population in this country could reach 100,000.

Today's industrial robots can be broadly classified into three categories: simple robots, medium-technology robots, and advanced robots. Robots are classified on the basis of flexibility, mobility, intelligence, memory capacity, ability to sense the environment, ease of programming, and ease of integration into computer-controlled work flows. The price of one of these industrial robots ranges from as low as $3,000 to as high as $150,000 or more.

What are the benefits of robot technology to production workers and managers? Two of the most important are greater productivity and improved cost control. Other benefits include more consistent product quality, fewer injuries to workers, around-the-clock output, improved inventory control, and more efficient use of capital equipment. In fact, the health of our basic industries depends in large measure on the successful use of robots. General Motors anticipates a 14,000-machine work force in its plants by 1990.

Someday, these machines may even be able to "see." Through the use of TV cameras and other sensing devices, machine vision will greatly extend the usefulness of robots in manufacturing processes. It is not out of the question that in ten years advanced robots will be working in coal mines, maintaining reactor furnaces, conducting

Robots may not take over the world, but they will increase in number on the business scene.

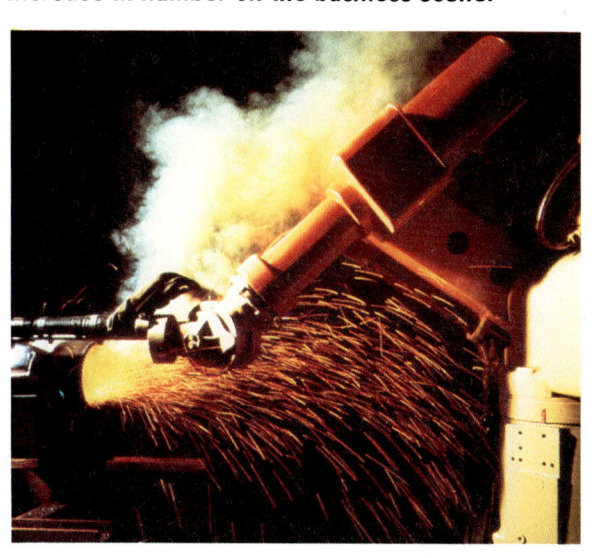

underwater geological surveys, and even digging for minerals on the moon.

Electronics and Computers. In terms of growth in output, productivity, and employment, the high technology sector will lead the way during the 1980s. Within this sector, electronics is our number one glamour industry, as it has been for a decade or more. The vitality of the industry is exemplified by the nearly endless stream of innovations that pour out of its research labs and assembly plants. Each year, microchips get smaller and less expensive. New microelectronics technologies will help bring about the long-imagined integration of computers and telecommunications systems, someday allowing people to

FROM THE FILE

Luis was pondering his new assignment, which is to draw up a series of options for automating several of his firm's production processes. He has read about several new approaches to factory automation, including flexible manufacturing systems (FMS). FMS electronically integrates plant operations through automation and plant redesign. It allows for economies of scale at very low levels of production and for rapid retooling of production lines—two impressive benefits.

Having toured plants using FMS, Luis can see the potential of factory automation. However, he must now identify some of the problems that might arise.

work and shop without leaving their homes. Another reason for the growth of the industry today is the fact that the future of so many manufacturing firms depends on semiconductor technology.

Computers are a particularly bright spot for the electronics industry. Worldwide sales of U.S.-made computers topped $30 billion in 1981, and should increase at an annual rate of 16 percent through 1986. Total sales for personal computers could zoom to more than 1.5 million units in that year. Desktop computers for businesses should experience the fastest rate of growth in sales through the mid-1980s—an annually compounded rate of 40 to 45 percent. Makers of these desktop models currently include Tandy Corp., Apple Computer, Inc., IBM, Commodore International, Atari, Texas Instruments, and Hewlett-Packard. The sales of minicomputers and word processors should also grow rapidly—at a rate of about 20 to 30 percent annually.[7] Figure 24-7 shows some of the applications of microelectronics technologies that we can expect to see as we move into the future.

---

[7]Standard & Poor's *Industry Outlook* (October, 1982), pp. O13-028.

Figure 24-7

The Coming Impact of Microelectronics

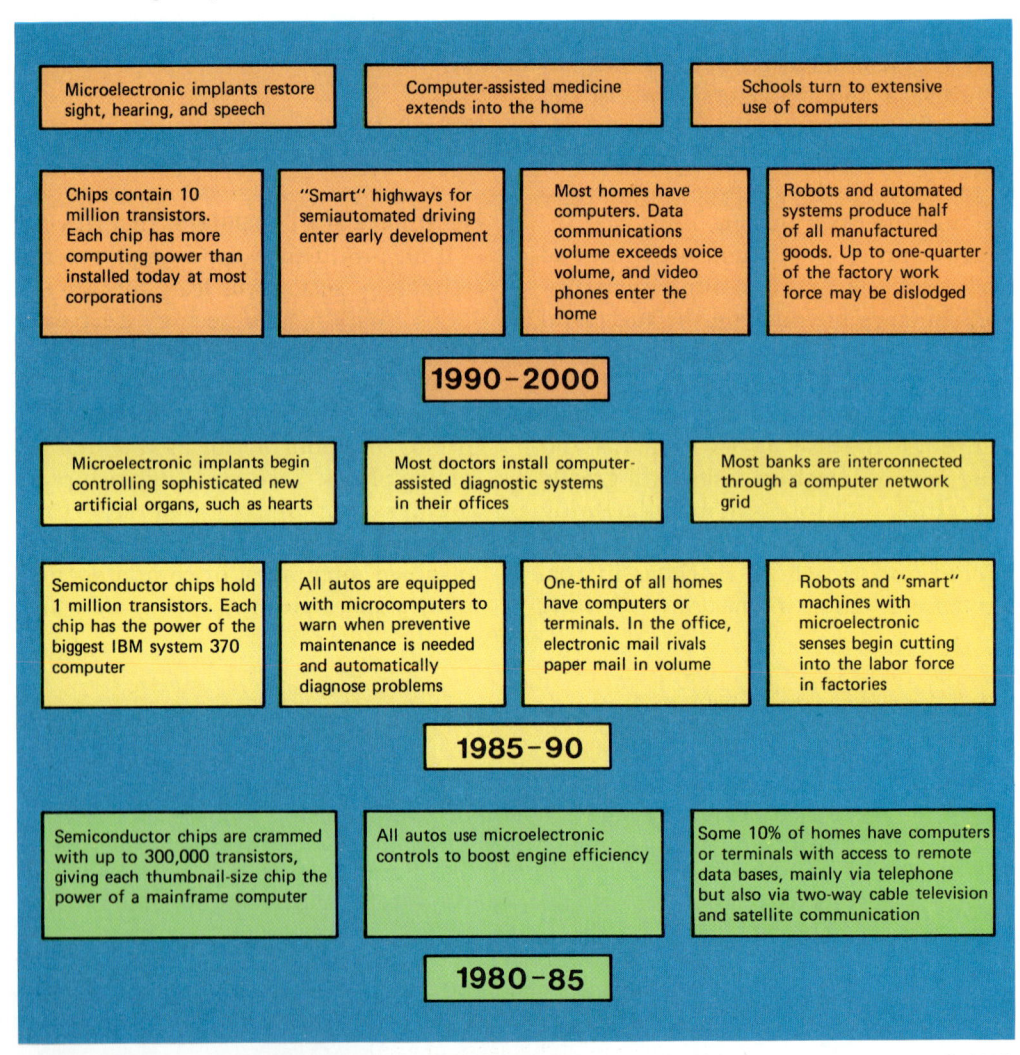

1990–2000

- Microelectronic implants restore sight, hearing, and speech
- Computer-assisted medicine extends into the home
- Schools turn to extensive use of computers
- Chips contain 10 million transistors. Each chip has more computing power than installed today at most corporations
- "Smart" highways for semiautomated driving enter early development
- Most homes have computers. Data communications volume exceeds voice volume, and video phones enter the home
- Robots and automated systems produce half of all manufactured goods. Up to one-quarter of the factory work force may be dislodged

1985–90

- Microelectronic implants begin controlling sophisticated new artificial organs, such as hearts
- Most doctors install computer-assisted diagnostic systems in their offices
- Most banks are interconnected through a computer network grid
- Semiconductor chips hold 1 million transistors. Each chip has the power of the biggest IBM system 370 computer
- All autos are equipped with microcomputers to warn when preventive maintenance is needed and automatically diagnose problems
- One-third of all homes have computers or terminals. In the office, electronic mail rivals paper mail in volume
- Robots and "smart" machines with microelectronic senses begin cutting into the labor force in factories

1980–85

- Semiconductor chips are crammed with up to 300,000 transistors, giving each thumbnail-size chip the power of a mainframe computer
- All autos use microelectronic controls to boost engine efficiency
- Some 10% of homes have computers or terminals with access to remote data bases, mainly via telephone but also via two-way cable television and satellite communication

Source: Reprinted from the November 10, 1980, issue of *Business Week* by special permission, © 1980, by McGraw-Hill, Inc., New York, NY 10020. All rights reserved.

THE FUTURE AND YOU

In this chapter, we have discussed many of the demographic and economic trends that are currently shaping our world. But one key ingredient has been left out of our discussion of the future. You. In our forecasts, we generally focused on the period 1985 to 2000. This is the same period of time during which you will find careers, grow into your most productive years, and, along with the other members of your generation, assume the lead in building the future.

How you will affect the future is largely a function of your choice of a career. The ideas and skills that you learn today, as well as the career decisions that you have already made or will be making shortly, will determine your role in tomorrow's world. In the next chapter of the text, we examine some of the issues involved in career choice and also various careers in business.

SUMMARY POINTS

1. Two essential activities of business firms today are forecasting and prediction. The aim of forecasting and prediction is to reduce uncertainty in the environment by telling us something about the future.
2. The population of the United States is growing, but the rate of population growth is slowing.
3. The population of the United States is gradually getting older. The median age could increase from 30 in 1980 to 42 in the year 2050.
4. In the years ahead, average family size in this country will decrease while average family income will increase.
5. The population of the world's less-developed countries will grow at a faster rate than the population of the industrialized Western countries.
6. Despite efforts at industrialization, the average income for many of the peoples of the world will remain low.
7. The two primary trends reshaping the industrial composition of the U.S. economy are the aging of basic industries and the emergence and growth of high technology industries.
8. Whether the government should encourage a pumping of capital resources into this nation's decaying basic industries is currently a matter of dispute.
9. According to the long wave theory of economic growth and decline, the next wave of technological innovation will be driven by computer, electronics, biogenetics, and space technologies.
10. As long as the price of energy does not continue to fall, oil and gas producers should enjoy a high rate of growth in sales. Eventually, when the price of fossil fuels gets high enough, the developers of synthetic fuels and alternative energy sources should prosper.
11. Bioengineering is based on recombinant genetics and gene splicing. Future applications of bioengineered products will be seen in the areas of waste treatment, oil refining, chemical synthesis, and food production.
12. An industrial robot is a machine that is capable of performing a variety of tasks automatically. A robot can be thought of as a computer with a hand.
13. Today's industrial robots can be classified as simple robots, medium-technology robots, and advanced robots.
14. The electronics and computer industries are probably the central driving forces behind the new technological revolution.

KEY TERMS AND CONCEPTS

forecasting
predicting
less-developed countries (LDCs)
basic industries
long wave theory
robot

REVIEW QUESTIONS

1. How is forecasting useful to a business firm?
2. What is the relationship between forecasting, objectives, and uncertainty?
3. Summarize the major population and income trends taking place in the United States.
4. Which areas of the world are likely to experience the slowest growth in per capita income in the years ahead?
5. What is meant by a basic industry? Give some examples of basic industries.

6. What are some of the reasons for the current problems of our basic industries? How has competition from abroad contributed to these problems?
7. Name four fast-growing high technology industries.
8. What is an industrial robot? List some of the benefits of installing industrial robots in the workplace.

DISCUSSION QUESTIONS

1. Some futurists foresee a world in which nearly all of us will work at home. What problems do you see in such a development? What opportunities?
2. The decline of basic industries has left millions of people out of work. Many of them may never get their old jobs back. What can be done to move these workers into the fast-growing "sunrise" industries?
3. What, in your opinion, is the most likely outcome of the race between population growth and food production? Will we be able to grow enough food to feed everyone? Will we be able to slow the rate of population growth?
4. What potential social and ethical questions does recombinant genetics raise? At a more specific level, do you think that private companies should be able to patent new life forms, just as they are able to patent other inventions?
5. What is the role of private business in building a better tomorrow? Do you think that we will still have private businesses in the twenty-first century, or will all our production facilities be government owned and operated?

CASE 24-1

The Genetic Revolution in Agriculture

In the 1930s, scientists began to understand how the breeding of animals and plants works. Their discoveries finally led to the modern techniques of genetic engineering and cloning.

The results have been astounding! Just through improved breeding practices, milk output of dairy cows has more than doubled. There are fewer than half as many dairy cows today as there were in 1950, but their output of milk is actually greater than the total output in 1950. Scientists at the University of Minnesota expect to push milk production to almost three times its level today; the cows producing such large quantities of milk would be as large as elephants.

Almost every vegetable, fruit, or grain we eat today has similarly been improved. By careful breeding, we now have tomatoes that don't bruise in shipping, oranges with a higher juice content, asparagus that grows on soil with virtually no nutrients, and corn that grows three times the number of ears it grew in 1950 and that is resistant to countless diseases. Scientists are even working on houseplants, creating poinsettia plants that are no longer poisonous to animals and children, holly that has soft spines, and roses that stay fresh for weeks instead of days.

The technology that has made these improvements possible was almost unimaginable a few years ago. Recently, a company in Colorado announced that it can separate the male- and female-producing sperm from cows, so that a dairy farmer can breed 500 calves and know that every one will be a dairy cow and not a steer. In Maryland, researchers have created petunias that no longer need nitrogen fertilizer, and they soon will have corn plants that need no fertilizer and can grow on barren land or sand.

Discoveries are coming so fast that even the researchers cannot keep up with what is happening. But business people and farmers are discovering how profitable this research is going to be for them.

If you were a business person or a farmer trying to make a profit on agricultural genetics, what ways do you see—in the information given above—to make money?

CASE 24-2

The Sardine Industry

While we look at engineering in space, genetic engineering, and factories of the future, we should also realize that many older industries are disappearing. Consider the sardine industry, for example.

Virtually the entire U.S. sardine-packing industry is located in Maine. In 1952, there were 46 sardine-packing plants, but the number has dropped rapidly since then. The table shows how the sardine industry has fared in recent years:

	Number of Canneries	Millions of Cases Packed
1952	46	3.2
1962	32	2.1
1972	18	1.4
1982	14	0.6

Source: Maine Sardine Council (1982).

In 1981, Maine produced $44 million worth of canned sardines, but in 1982, the total sales dropped to $25 million.

What is wrong with this industry? Maine sardine-packers didn't look to the future. They failed to do the market research necessary to tell them what the future of their industry would be like. For example, market surveys showed that many consumers think the canned sardines are raw, that few people know how to cook with them, and that although men like them, their wives won't buy them. In addition, older people tend to like sardines more than do younger people, who are used to fast food and don't bother with canned sardines.

Further, the industry ignored Norwegian imports until it was too late. There's a future to every kind of business—not just engineering and high technology—but it isn't always a rosy one. Most of the Maine sardine industry will disappear, and in the glory of space exploration and genetic engineering, few people will note its passing.

1. How could the Maine sardine industry have been turned around using modern technology of the kind discussed in this chapter?
2. Do all future businesses have to be high technology? Why or why not?

25

You and Your Career

After studying this chapter, you should be able to:

- Explain what a career is and why it is important.
- Identify some sources of information about job opportunities.
- Describe the stages in a job search campaign.
- List the five career stages.
- Discuss the "rules" of success chess.

Each year, more than a third of a million business graduates enter the job market. Fortunately, business is one field that offers both a rich diversity of interesting job opportunities and a favorable job market. Business graduates will take jobs as sales representatives, personnel assistants, research analysts, accountants, purchasing agents, and loan officers. They will earn an average of $17,000 with a bachelor's degree and $24,000 with an M.B.A. degree. In this chapter, we take a look at careers in business. We first consider what careers are and why they are so important.

WHAT IS A CAREER?

Certainly, a career has something to do with getting jobs, and perhaps with moving between jobs, places, and levels of responsibility and challenge. But a career means more than that.

The Protean Career

Proteus was a character in Greek mythology who was able to change his shape in any way he wanted—from fire to lion to dragon to tree. Douglas Hall has drawn on this mythological figure to coin the term **protean career**. The essence of this idea is that there is much more to a career than just moving up the hierarchies of organizations:

> The protean career is a process which the person, not the organization, is managing. It consists of all of the person's varied experiences in education, training, work in several organizations, changes in occupational field, etc. The protean career is not what happens to the person in any one organization. The protean person's own personal career choices and search for self-fulfillment are the unifying or integrative elements in his or her life. The criterion of success is internal (psychological success), not external.[1]

This idea of a protean career is an important one. A career is more than just a promotion, a raise in pay, or an impressive job title. Instead, a career is an ongoing sequence of events, some of which may have little or nothing to do with money or prestige. Also according to this idea, a career extends over the entire work life. What happens in one year or in one corporation is just a small piece of the rich career mosaic. Finally, the decision of whether or not a career is successful is up to the individual. If a person is happy with the way his or her career turns out, how can anyone say that that career was a failure?

Why Are Careers So Important?

Most people would agree that careers are important. Unfortunately, most business students leave college knowing more about how to manage a company than about how to manage their own careers. We can think of at least two reasons why people should be concerned about their careers:

- The career represents a person's entire life in the work setting, and work is a key factor in influencing the quality of a person's life. Work has the potential to directly or indirectly satisfy almost all human needs.
- Work is a way to get social equality and social freedom. For example, the fact that more and more women are entering the work force has changed the way society views women, how much power they have, and the rhythm of family life. Similarly, as more blacks and members of other minority groups obtain high-prestige jobs, their roles in society will change too. Nothing speaks louder than success. A successful career brings recognition, respect, and freedom from economic want.

Managers should understand the career interests of their subordinates. Doing so gives them a better grasp of what motivates their employees, enabling them to manage more effectively.

Quest for the Ideal Job

It would be nice to find a job that's perfect in all ways, but this hope is not very realistic. Instead, we generally have to make trade-offs. We

Business can provide workers with opportunities for social and economic equality.

---

[1] Douglas T. Hall, *Careers in Organizations* (Goodyear Publishing Company, Inc., 1976), p. 201.

may have to take lower pay to get a more "meaningful" job. Or we may have to put up with poor working conditions if we want higher pay.

So you must ask yourself, "What do I really want from a job?" Figure 25-1 presents a list of job characteristics that many people seek. Which one is most important to you? Least important? Do the things you want have anything in common? Would you give up the less important things to get those you have rated most important?

Stages of Job Choice

People's career choices develop over a long period of time. These choices often progress through three stages.[2] The fantasy stage generally occurs between the ages of six and eleven, and is usually not very realistic. It is the stage at which a child wants to be an Indian chief, a firefighter, or the guardian and protector of E.T., the Extra-Terrestrial. The tentative stage usually occurs between the ages of eleven and sixteen. This is the stage when people first realize that they must make important decisions about their future. They start to consider how various professions might fit their abilities, interests, and values. Finally, in the realistic stage, people seriously explore occupational options, firm up their preferences, and make an occupational choice. In this stage, people recognize that they must make compromises between what they want and what is available. This realistic stage often lasts for years—perhaps even for a decade or more.

Self-Analysis: Be Honest

Don't panic if you are still exploring career options, but you should be starting to think about

---

[2] E. Ginzberg, J. W. Ginzberg, S. Axelrod, and J. L. Herma, *Occupational Choice* (New York: Columbia University Press, 1951), pp. 60-72.

A variety of job characteristics are listed below. Rate how important you feel each characteristic is to you by using the following scale:

1	2	3	4	5
Not Important	Slightly Important	Somewhat Important	Quite Important	Crucial

Job Characteristic	Importance Rating
Salary	_____
Challenge and Responsibility	_____
Type of Work	_____
Friendly Coworkers	_____
Opportunity for Promotion	_____
Job Difficulty	_____
Geographical Location	_____
Job Security	_____
Training	_____
Opportunity for Personal Growth	_____
Clear Job Responsibilities	_____
Opportunity to Travel on the Job	_____
Opportunity to Help Others	_____
Work Hours	_____
Opportunity to Participate in Decision Making	_____
Fair Treatment by Employer	_____
Fringe Benefits	_____
Company Reputation	_____
Freedom to Work on Your Own	_____
Job Title	_____

Figure 25-1

What Do You Want From a Job?

CONTROVERSIAL ISSUES

Many bright and competent business students are courted by several companies. Often the firms compete with each other by offering larger and larger salaries. The student has to decide whether to go with the highest paying job or to choose on some other grounds. Is highest pay the best criterion for making this decision?

Several Job Offers? Go for the Money!

Pro

Yes, going after the highest pay is the best way of picking a job. Everyone will tell you that there are lots of things that make a job pleasant and worthwhile besides pay, but in the long run pay is what makes the difference.

Suppose you are offered a lower paying job with more fringe benefits (such as better health insurance programs, more sick leave and vacation time, and an employee swimming pool). Well, all those extra fringes cost the company money that it isn't paying you. While you may value some of those fringes, the chances are small that you will want all of them enough to justify the amount that the company takes out of your paycheck.

There's also the argument that some high-paying jobs are really horrible—you have to deal with complaining customers all day or you have more work than you can possibly do. Some high-paying jobs also include bosses who think that because you are paid so much, you should work evenings and weekends at home. Well, again you have to look at the long run. That position is never going to be filled unless whoever fills it is paid an appropriate amount. How is that "appropriate amount" determined? One economist has said, "You pay people for the unpleasant parts of their job, not for the pleasant parts." The more unpleasantness in your job, the more you are paid. If you don't think you're paid enough, of course, don't take the job. But in the long run, the company will pay just what the market thinks the unpleasantness of the job is worth.

Furthermore, there's always the fact that whatever comforts you miss at work, you'll have more money to buy away from work. For example, you may not like the working conditions at the office, but with a higher salary you will be able to make your home as pleasant and comfortable as you want.

High pay is only given to those employees who must be compensated for unpleasant work. However, since you only spend about 40 hours out of every 168 hours in a week at work, surely you can endure a little unpleasantness as long as it gives you enough extra money to enjoy the rest of the week.

Con

No, high pay is not the best criterion for job selection. Let's look at some of the problems with choosing the highest paying job.

First, fringe benefits can really be worth a lot more than the decrease they make in your paycheck. Many fringes are available at a lower rate to a large group of people—you would have to pay a lot more to buy them for yourself. Consider health insurance. Company health insurance programs are often far cheaper and far more comprehensive than anything you could buy on your own. Furthermore, you don't have to pay taxes on the value of most of the benefits you receive.

Second, being paid a high salary right away sometimes means that you are skipped over the first couple of times for increases on the grounds that you already have a high enough salary. People who started at a lower salary may soon be ahead of you. And in poor economic times, those earning high salaries may be the first to be laid off on the grounds that the company can't afford those high salaries. It may be wiser to accept a slightly lower salary in exchange for greater security against layoffs or firings.

Third, you *don't* get paid just for the unpleasantness in your job! You also get paid for accepting additional responsibility. In fact, many people are willing to work for less if they are given more responsibility or power; they feel the job is more fulfilling and more rewarding that way. So a high-paying job that doesn't give an equivalent amount of responsibility may turn out to be a bad deal.

Finally, employers can usually tell if an employee has taken a job just for the money. When that happens, the employee's loyalty to the company may become suspect. This may even result in fewer promotions later on.

High pay is nice, but there are other things just as important or more important to an employee. Don't pick a job just because it pays the most.

Profile—
Wally (Famous) Amos

Looking for a career? You probably don't want to use Wally Amos, known either as simply Wally or as Famous Amos, as an example. He isn't quite a textbook case on how to plan your way to the top, but he *is* a superb example of how an individual can have a satisfying and enjoyable career with hard work and "smarts."

Amos is the major stockholder of the Famous Amos Chocolate Chip Cookie Corporation. He first tasted chocolate chips when he moved to Harlem, New York at age 12. He fell in love with cooking and attended Food Trades Vocational High School, planning to become a cook. He lost interest in cooking, however; he joined the Air Force for four years, and later was employed for a while at Saks Fifth Avenue in New York City. He then became a mailroom clerk at the William Morris Talent Agency. Amos convinced his supervisors to reorganize the mail room and became an assistant to a company vice president.

Amos was already displaying his unerring sense of talent. He invited his boss to a local club to audition two young singers he had heard—namely, Paul Simon and Art Garfunkel. When the agency set up a rock-and-roll department, Amos managed the Temptations, Dionne Warwick, and other artists. Finally he moved to California and started his own talent agency. Although he acquired an impressive list of clients, Amos really didn't like the Hollywood crowd and the problems of being a talent agent.

Amos had become well known for bringing boxes of chocolate chip cookies as calling cards when he visited with producers and executives in Hollywood. A friend suggested that he start a cookie business. Amos liked the idea and wrote up his financial plans. The Small Business Administration turned down his loan request, but Amos had come to know singer Helen Reddy and her husband, Jeff Wald. Wald and Reddy, along with singer Marvin Gaye and the president of United Artists Records, decided to invest in Amos' business. Amos' store was opened.

Wally Amos was a natural at promoting his cookie. He dropped the tailored banker's suits and started wearing a Hawaiian print shirt, loose-fitting pants, and a gaudy straw hat. Cookie samples were given to passersby in Beverly Hills and Hollywood, and orders were taken for more. Amos then delivered them personally. Soon he opened more stores. He now has stores in California (Los Angeles and Santa Monica) and Hawaii, as well as wholesale baking operations in New Jersey and California. He sells cookies to specialty stores and exclusive department stores throughout the country. Amos plans his marketing strategies around the exclusive reputation his product has acquired. A one-pound bag of cookies costs $5, and a seven-ounce bag selling for $2.50 has been added to the line.

Amos is proud of what he's accomplished: "I feel good. I think my business shows that black people are capable of being successful in the business world in a very big way. You can succeed if you put it in your consciousness. I truly believe that."

Backed by a nonstop promotional campaign consisting mostly of public appearances by Famous Amos and his cookies, the Famous Amos chocolate chip cookie is head and shoulders above any other cookie in the market. In Bloomingdale's and in Neiman-Marcus, Famous Amos chocolate chip cookies can be found alongside Godiva chocolates and Bill Blass truffles. Wally Amos has made a place for himself in the world—a career that anyone would envy.

a realistic job choice. To do this, honest self-analysis is crucial.

Ideally, you will choose a job and career that offers a good fit to your abilities, values, and interests. A job that is really not "right" for you may seem attractive in the short run, but will almost certainly lead to problems. Try to step back from yourself, take an objective look, and assess your abilities, values, and interests.

Your Abilities. It is important to recognize both what you can do well and what you can't do well. Table 25-1 may help you assess your strengths and weaknesses.

Your Values. What is really important to you in life? Some answers might include family, security, status, popularity, love, freedom, power, leisure, wealth, glamour, affection, social welfare, and achievement. What do you really want? What things repel you? Jobs will differ in the extent to which they are consistent with your values.

Your Interests. Interests refer to the things that you like or dislike. Interests often develop from more general values. Some interests are shown in Figure 25-2 on page 507. Think hard about your interests and how various jobs might fulfill them.

EMPLOYMENT OPPORTUNITIES

To make an intelligent career choice, you need information about opportunities for various jobs, about industries, and perhaps about clusters of related jobs. The appendix to this chapter gives detailed information about current and future job opportunities. Throughout the 1980s, some of the jobs expected to be in high demand include those for accountants, actuaries, bank officers and administrators, health services administrators, marketing researchers, purchasing agents, and systems analysts. Other people who will find their skills in less demand include credit managers, securities sales workers, and public utilities managers.

Figure 25-3 on page 507 shows projected employment growth by industry. Services and finance, insurance, and real estate are expected to show the greatest percentage growth, while employment in agriculture is projected to fall by 12 percent.

Career Clusters

Your skills and your knowledge would probably be useful in any of several jobs. So, if opportunities for a particular job dry up, you may be able to find another kind of job elsewhere. The

Your interests, values, and skills can provide important clues in deciding on a career.

Table 25-1

Ability Profile

	Far Below Average	Below Average	Average	Above Average	Outstanding
Intelligence					
Leadership					
Motivation					
Direction					
Self-Confidence					
Energy Level					
Self-Knowledge					
Competitiveness					
Creativity					
Perseverance					
Initiative					
Goal Achievement					
Willingness to Accept Responsibility					
Interpersonal Skills					
Ability to Handle Conflict					
Sensitivity					
Ability to Communicate					
Flexibility					
Writing Skills					
Organizational Ability					
Public Speaking Skills					
Persuasiveness					

Use this checklist to get a better picture of your strengths and weaknesses. It may help you find a job for which you are suited as well as prepare you for job interviews. Also, make a list of the abilities you possess which may be important in particular jobs. Such abilities might include knowledge of electronics, real estate, payroll procedures, or foreign languages.

U.S. Office of Education has identified 15 so-called "career clusters." Each **career cluster** is a group of related jobs. Sample clusters are presented in Figure 25-4 on page 508. When preparing for a career, it may help to think in terms of career clusters as well as in terms of specific jobs.

Employment Information Sources

There are many sources of information about employment opportunities. Here are some to keep in mind:

- College placement services. Most colleges and universities have placement services. Some of

Figure 25-2

Some Interests

Traveling	Helping Others
Working with People	Being Outdoors
Competing	Relaxing
Acting	Using Skills
Speaking	Thinking
Being Alone	Supervising
Working with Data	Solving Puzzles
Writing	Moving
Learning	Organizing

them are very good. Check yours out right away. Ask what services it provides, when you should register your credentials, what percentage of past graduates were placed through the service, and so on.
- Ads. Read the help-wanted ads in newspapers or trade journals. The Sunday edition often has many pages of these ads. Check ads in papers of cities where you might want to work. The *New York Times* and *Wall Street Journal* list many ads for business positions.
- The United States Employment Service (USES). This service has about 2,400 offices throughout the country. You can ask the office in any city or state about opportunities in other locations.
- Private employment agencies. There are about 8,000 private employment agencies in the United States. Some of them specialize in certain types of clients (such as executives) or in particular fields (such as data processing). These agencies charge a fee that is payable when and if the job seeker is hired.
- Local organizations such as the Chamber of Commerce and City Hall. Write to them for information about places that interest you.
- Personal Contacts. Ask friends and relatives about job opportunities. College professors may also have useful suggestions.

HOW TO OBTAIN A POSITION IN BUSINESS

The job search is a challenging, important, and time-consuming process. If done right, it may start you on a rewarding career. Be willing to take the time, effort, and expense to do it right.

Planning the Job Search

A job search should be thought of as a campaign. You are looking for the job which best fits your needs and qualifications. You should plan your job search strategies and tactics and then actively carry them out. Many sources of information are available to help develop your plans. One listing of sources is provided in the appendix to this chapter.

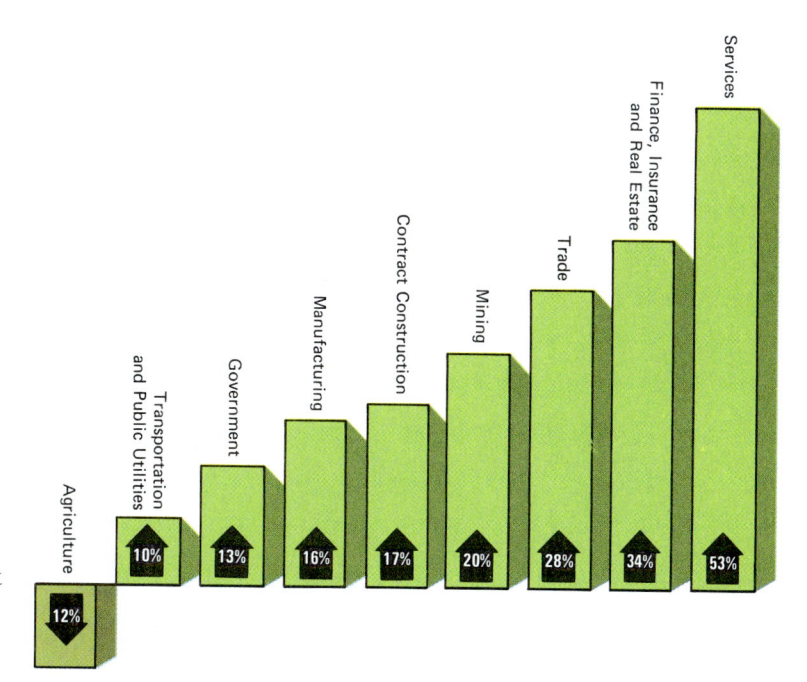

Figure 25-3

Projected Employment Growth by Industry

Source: U.S. Bureau of Labor Statistics

Agriculture 12%
Transportation and Public Utilities 10%
Government 13%
Manufacturing 16%
Contract Construction 17%
Mining 20%
Trade 28%
Finance, Insurance and Real Estate 34%
Services 53%

Figure 25-4

Sample Career Clusters
Source: U.S. Office of Education

> MARKETING AND DISTRIBUTION: Marketing management, marketing research and analysis; purchasing; selling; physical distribution; related business services.
> BUSINESS AND OFFICE: Accounting; computer; secretarial science; management; personnel; finance; insurance; real estate; office (clerical).
> ENVIRONMENT: Pollution prevention and control; disease prevention; environmental planning; resources control.
> HOSPITALITY AND RECREATION: Commercial and noncommercial travel bureaus; travel agencies; transportation; public, private, and industrial recreation; recreation concerned with natural resources.

Preparing a Resume

The **resume** is a written presentation telling the prospective employer who you are, what you know, what you have done, what you can do, and what kind of job you would like. It should provide a complete picture in a compact, convincing way. To write an effective resume:

- Be concise. Keep the resume to one or two pages, if possible. Avoid narrative format.
- Include educational experience and work experience, starting in each case with the most recent.
- When describing your experience, use action verbs, such as:

accomplished	achieved	budgeted
classified	controlled	counseled
designed	evaluated	increased
managed	operated	proposed
researched	sold	trained

- Include a brief career objective. The **career objective** may indicate your area of interest (such as finance or sales), the sort of organization you would like to work for (such as banking or manufacturing), and the level of the position you want. If you have not made up your mind about your career objectives, a more general statement of objectives may be best. Figure 25-5 presents two sample career objectives.
- List relevant personal data. Be selective: omit items that could be misinterpreted, are unnecessary, or do not strengthen your case.
- Point out those skills which are relevant to the positions you are seeking.
- Indicate that references are available on request, or (especially if they are very good) list them.
- Make sure the resume looks good. Work on the layout. Type the resume on white bond paper. Use a carbon ribbon rather than a fabric ribbon. Proofread the resume, have a friend proofread it, and then proofread it again! Have the resume duplicated on "classic laid" bond paper in white or a subdued color.
- Generally, do *not* state salary requirements, do not give reasons for leaving past employers, or indicate your race, religion, or political affiliation. A sample resume is presented in Figure 25-6 on page 510.

Writing the Application Letter

Always include a letter of application when you mail a resume. The **letter of application** should be brief—certainly less than a page—and

Figure 25-5

Two Sample Career Objectives

> *Personnel*—To begin my career in personnel as a personnel assistant with exposure to recruiting, training and development, benefit administration, and compensation administration. Eventually wish to become a personnel manager.
> *Brand Assistant*—Seeking position with responsibility for coordinating and advertising, pricing, packaging, and distribution channels of a consumer goods product line. Eventual goal is to become a product manager.

Special Problems for Women in Business

The number of women in business is growing dramatically. According to the U. S. Bureau of Labor Statistics, the number of female managers and administrators increased by 135 percent between 1970 and 1982, compared to just 20 percent for men.

As we pointed out in Chapter 2, such increases are the result in part of changing cultural norms. Although it was once believed that "a woman's place is in the home," people now recognize that women have an important and legitimate role in the workplace. Also, federal policies and regulations prohibit sex discrimination in organizations.

CURRENT STATUS OF WOMEN IN BUSINESS. To date, the results of these changing norms and regulations have been mixed. Women with business degrees, such as the M.B.A., are earning higher starting salaries than men with comparable degrees, but their salary increases do not then keep up with those of men. Women are increasingly moving into management positions, but they are being confined to entry-level and some middle-level ranks. It is still unusual to find women in upper management.

When women do advance to top management, they often find themselves in areas that are "suitable" for females. The stereotype persists that women are sensitive and understanding, while men are self-reliant, aggressive, and forceful. As a result, positions in personnel, consumer affairs, public relations, and corporate social responsibility are increasingly being offered to women. Unfortunately, such jobs tend to be staff positions, with less power than line positions in functional areas such as finance and production.

Women also face other problems. For example, many have heavy family responsibilities, such as child care. Others find that their bosses are not willing to delegate much responsibility to them. Finally, many male executives are more comfortable dealing with other men; therefore, they conduct some of their important business discussions in informal settings such as on the golf course or in the locker room.

WHAT IS BEING DONE? Many companies are making sincere efforts to improve the status of their female employees. Most are undertaking active hiring programs. In addition, some companies now have supportive programs, such as provision of child care facilities, use of flexible working hours, and financial support for further education and training. Special training programs that help women become more assertive or develop valuable interpersonal networks are also becoming popular. And, of course, women are taking their destinies into their own hands. They are becoming more determined, confident, politically astute, and competent.

---

carefully constructed. It should be typed on quality paper of the same type as your resume. It should be addressed to a specific person. Keep a copy of the letter for your files. A sample letter of application is shown in Figure 25-7 on page 511.

Obtaining Letters of Recommendation

Letters of recommendation are an important part of the job application process. Your letters of recommendation should be favorable, of course, and should be written by people who are in re-

cathy
by Cathy Guisewite

Source: Copyright, 1983, Universal Press Syndicate. Reprinted with permission. All rights reserved.

> **PERCIVAL R. MESSMER**
>
> 18102 Regent Street, Apt. 602
> Madison, WI 53702
> (608) 281-0527
>
> **JOB OBJECTIVE**
>   Wish to join the audit staff of a public accounting firm with the eventual goal of becoming a partner.
>
> **EDUCATION**
>   University of Wisconsin-Madison
>   Earned the Bachelor of Business Administration degree in May 1981.
>   Majored in Accounting and Finance.   3.1 GPA
>
> **WORK EXPERIENCE**
>   <u>Jerred & O'Day, CPAs</u>, Madison, Wisconsin
>   Accounting Clerk (20 hours/week)   June 1980 - Present
>   Maintain accounts payable and accounts receivable. Supervise payroll and payroll tax reporting functions. Assist staff accountants with client work when time permits.
>
>   <u>Leonies' Restaurant</u>, Madison, Wisconsin
>   Part-time Bartender (25 hours/week)   September 1978 - May 1980
>
>   <u>Baraboo Inn</u>, Baraboo, Wisconsin
>   Desk Clerk   Summers 1976, 1977, 1978
>
> **ACTIVITIES**
>   Active member of Beta Alpha Psi, Delta Sigma Pi, and the Hoofer Ski & Sailing Club.
>
> **SKILLS AND INTERESTS**
>   Have well-developed writing and public speaking skills. Speak German and French fluently. Enjoy traveling, reading, and sailing.
>
> **REFERENCES**
>   Professor Jon Smart, Accounting Department, University of Wisconsin-Madison, 1155 Observatory Drive, Madison, WI 53706 (608) 252-1111
>
>   Professor Helen Smith, Mathematics Department, University of Wisconsin-Madison, 1155 Observatory Drive, Madison, WI 53706 (608) 252-1234
>
>   Mr. James Jones, Manager, Jerred & O'Day, CPAs, 202 West Washington Avenue, Madison, WI 53702 (608) 255-9988

Figure 25-6

A Sample Resume
Source: School of Business, University of Wisconsin-Madison, *Placement Manual.* Used with permission.

spected positions and who know you reasonably well. College professors and past employers are natural choices. Make sure that they have copies of your resume and of any other materials that will help them write better informed and more complete letters.

Preparing for the Job Interview

The initial interview may be held on your college campus or in the company's offices. If it goes well, you may be offered a visit to the potential employer, or even a job. If it goes badly, your chances of getting the job are poor.

Make sure that you carefully prepare for the interview. Read everything you can find that might be useful. Thoroughly research the industry and company. Check company annual reports, and look in the *Business Periodicals Index.* Also, anticipate questions that you may be asked, such as those in Figure 25-8. Work out answers for them and practice them. Finally, put together an "interview folder" to take to your interviews. Include extra copies of your resume, questions you have about the company and position, any information you've gathered on the company, a copy of your transcript, and a pen and paper. A few interviewing tips are listed in Figure 25-9.

Visiting Your Prospective Employer

If an employer offers you a visit to the company, you know that you have been evaluated favorably. Such visits are typically for one day. Expect to meet some people in management positions.

During the visit, try to act natural and relaxed. Dress well. Ask questions which you prepared in advance. Keep track of the names of the people you meet. Near the end of the visit, ask what you should do next and what actions the employer will take next. When you get home, write thank-you letters to the employer and others you met during the visit.

Analyzing Job Offers

If you're lucky, you may get a variety of job offers. If so, you have a tough decision. Don't look just at starting salary. Job security, potential for growth and challenge, the sorts of people you

---

1130 Odana Road
Madison, WI 53711
September 30, 1981

Mr. John Jones
Director of Personnel
XYZ Company
1800 Main Street
Monroe, WI 53566

Dear Mr. Jones:

Opening paragraph: Attract attention -- state the position you are applying for and mention how you learned about it. Make the employer want to read on!

Second paragraph: Indicate when and from where you will be graduating. State why you are interested in working for the company (avoid excessive flattery) and specify your reasons for desiring this type of work.

Third paragraph: Refer the reader to your personal resume. Point out college or work experiences which might be of particular interest to the company. Do not repeat what is on the resume!

Closing paragraph: Show appreciation and ask for action, i.e., request an interview and state when you would be available. Mention if you are going to be in the area at a particular time. Remember to include your telephone number. Try to portray a tone of modest confidence without being overbearing.

Sincerely,

Percival R. Messmer
Percival R. Messmer

Enclosure

Figure 25-7

A Sample Letter of Application

Source: School of Business, University of Wisconsin-Madison, *Placement Manual.* Used with permission.

Figure 25-8

Some Typical Interview Questions

> - What are your strengths? Your weaknesses?
> - Tell me about yourself.
> - Why should we hire you?
> - What are your hobbies and interests?
> - Why do you want to work for our company?
> - Are you willing to travel or relocate?
> - What do you want to be doing in two years? Five? Twenty?
> - How will you choose among the various job offers you receive?
> - Why did you choose your major? Do you wish you had chosen differently? Which courses did you like? Dislike? Why?
> - What kinds of extracurricular activities have you participated in? Which did you enjoy the most?
> - What percentage of your college expenses did you earn?
> - Do you plan to further your education? Why or why not?
> - Does your gradepoint average reflect your intelligence? Your potential? Your motivation? Why or why not?
> - What questions do you have about our company?

would be working with, and many other factors should also be considered. Look back at the job characteristics listed in Figure 25-1, and the importance you attached to each. Then ask yourself how much of each of these factors you are likely to get from each job prospect, using the following scale:

1	2	3	4	5
None	Very Little	Some	A Moderate Amount	Very Much

Now multiply each job factor importance weight by the amount of that factor you are likely to get from the job. Add these up across all the job factors. The job prospect with the highest total is probably your best bet.

CAREER STAGES

All careers may be different, but they do have a few things in common. A person's career development typically occurs in distinct stages. Let's look at these stages now.[3]

Preparatory Period

In the preparatory stage, an individual's early experiences and adjustments in school, at home, and in the community help develop mental and physical maturity. For instance, hearing one of your parents talk about a day at work over the dinner table may give you an idea of what to expect when you get a job.

Initial Work Period

The initial work period is characterized by part-time and occasional jobs. It usually begins when an individual seeks a first job while still in school. In this stage, the job is seen as temporary.

Trial Work Period

During the trial work period, people, usually in their 20s or early 30s, take a regular full-time

---

[3] D. C. Miller and W. H. Form, *Industrial Sociology* (New York: Harper and Row, 1964), pp. 541-545.

Figure 25-9

Interviewing Tips

> - Be on time for the interview.
> - Be positive. Show interest and enthusiasm.
> - Speak clearly and maintain good eye contact.
> - Listen to what is being said and follow the interviewer's lead.
> - Think before speaking.
> - Be well groomed.
> - Show a knowledge of the company. Ask only questions that couldn't have been answered by reading the recruiting literature. Ask about such things as training programs, opportunities for advancement, structure of the organization, and fringe benefits. Don't make it seem that you're only concerned with money.
> - Don't act evasive if asked about unfavorable parts of your record.
> - Don't act conceited, overbearing, or overly aggressive.

job and begin to settle into a stable field of work. This stage sees people moving between jobs and finding out what they like.

Stable Work Period

When employees become "old-timers" or "fixtures," they have probably entered the stable work period. In this period, people feel they have found the jobs they will stick with for the rest of their careers.

Retirement

Retirement is seen as a blessing by some people and as a curse by others. Those happiest in retirement are those who have prepared for it over a period of time and who have made plans for the retirement years.

Some people go through all these stages. Others may skip stages or may never get beyond the trial work period. It is important to understand that when you start your career, you probably won't enter the stable work period right away. A lot of job searching—and soul searching—will probably take place first.

SUCCESS CHESS

Managing a career is like playing a complex, high-stakes game of chess, probably against some very tough opponents. Eugene Jennings set down nine rules designed to help people win that game. His rules of **success chess** are summarized as follows:[4]

- *Rule No. 1.* Maintain the widest possible set of options. Don't get stereotyped. Don't stay in technical work too long. And while it may be necessary to get staff experience, a good line reputation is also necessary.
- *Rule No. 2.* Don't get trapped in a "dead-end" position. Try not to work under a superior who hasn't moved in more than three years. Check to see that there are job routes open upward. If there are not, try to get out of the situation.
- *Rule No. 3.* Become a crucial subordinate to a mobile superior. A crucial subordinate is one that the boss needs as much as that person needs the boss. A crucial subordinate will move when the boss moves.
- *Rule No. 4.* Always try for increased exposure and visibility. Exposure refers to how often you are seen by those above you in the organization.

---

[4] E. E. Jennings, *Routes to the Executive Suite* (New York: McGraw-Hill, 1971), pp. 304–318.

Do you see yourself here? Your career may begin with part-time work. Later, you will probably settle into a more permanent job. Good luck!

FROM THE FILE

Susan had been a "shooting star" at Unipac, with four promotions over a period of nine years. Now, though, she felt stymied. Her new boss had been in the same position for almost a decade and seemed unlikely to move. Susan felt that her route to the top of the organization was blocked. She could leave the firm, but that would mean losing some valuable contacts. She could try to get a transfer within the firm, but there didn't seem to be any higher level jobs available. Susan was afraid that a move to another job at the same level would mar her unblemished record of promotions. And she knew that it was unlikely that she would simply be offered such a transfer—she would have to ask for it, and that wasn't the way she liked to operate. She wondered what action she should take—if any.

Visibility is how often *you* can see those above you. Decades ago, people were told that the best way to get to the top was to have a desk near the boss's door. This advice—that you don't get promoted if you aren't noticed—is still valid.

- *Rule No. 5.* Be willing to practice self-nomination. That is, let people in power know when you want a job. Generally, at least two moves in a career span are due to self-nomination. Don't just wait for your boss or someone else to determine your options.
- *Rule No. 6.* If you decide to leave a company, do it at your convenience. Leave on the best of terms. Don't wait for the situation to get really bad or for a nasty face-off to occur. Quit while you're ahead.
- *Rule No. 7.* Rehearse before quitting a job. Don't leave in a state of high emotion. Write out your resignation and wait a week. Think the decision through. Tell your family, take a week-long vacation, and bring your biographical data sheet up to date. After a week, decide whether or not to actually quit. But don't just keep on rehearsing; one way or the other, make up your mind.
- *Rule No. 8.* Think of the corporation as a marketplace for skills. Learn which skills are in demand in a particular company or industry at a particular time. Read business periodicals, such as *The Wall Street Journal* or *Business Week,* to find out which companies need your skills.
- *Rule No. 9.* Don't let success cut off your options. Successful people in one area often can be successful in other areas. Consider new careers. Don't spend your life in a rut.

SUMMARY POINTS

1. Business offers a rich diversity of job opportunities and a favorable job market. An understanding of careers in business can help you find the position for which you are best suited.
2. A career extends over the entire work life; it is more than just money and promotions—it concerns satisfaction as well.
3. The "ideal" job is a fiction. Instead, trade-offs are usually required. By considering which job characteristics you find most important, you can make these trade-offs more intelligently.
4. Realistic job choice begins with self-analysis, that is, an assessment of your abilities, values, and interests.
5. Some jobs and industries offer greater opportunities than others. Greatest growth in employment is projected for the service industry and the finance, insurance, and real estate industries.
6. Career clusters are groups of related jobs which may require similar skills and knowledge.
7. Sources of information about employment opportunities include college placement services, private and public employment agencies, want ads, local organizations, and personal contacts.
8. The job search can be thought of as a campaign; proper handling of the resume, letter of application, job interview, and visit to the prospective employer may help you get the job that you want.
9. Following the rules of "success chess" may lead to more successful career management.

KEY TERMS AND CONCEPTS

career
protean career
career cluster
resume

career objective
letter of application
interview
success chess

REVIEW QUESTIONS

1. What is meant by the term "protean career"?
2. Describe the three stages of career choice.
3. What is a career cluster?
4. List five things you should include in your resume.
5. What are some questions you are likely to be asked at an employment interview?
6. How can letters of recommendation help you get a job?
7. What are the characteristics of the five career stages?
8. List five rules of success chess.

DISCUSSION QUESTIONS

1. Do you think organizations should take an active role in managing their employees' careers? Why or why not?
2. What is your own definition of career success?
3. How well do you think your abilities, values, and interests would fit with each of the following jobs: bank teller, personnel manager, salesperson, securities analyst, and purchasing agent?
4. Do you disagree with any of Jennings' rules of success chess? Why or why not?
5. What do you think can be done to improve the status of women in business?

CASE 25-1

The Recession and Your Career

In the last recession, Daniel Sartorius was an executive at a major, but financially troubled, farm products manufacturing company. He was offered several better paying and higher status jobs with other companies. After turning down three such offers, he finally accepted the fourth one.

Daniel's position in the recession was somewhat unusual. He had been successful, and his skills were in demand among other companies. In deciding whether to take a new job, he looked at the types of jobs that were available during a recession.

The first thing he found was that production managers and financial managers (such as controllers, auditors, and tax experts) have much more likelihood of getting a job in a recession than do marketing and advertising managers. He also found that experience is a real plus. Someone looking for a first job during a recession has a harder time than someone with experience and a successful record. During a recession, employers want people who are cost-cutters, profit-makers, and action-oriented.

He also discovered that people in technical areas are hired at the entry-level (or beginning) positions throughout a recession. In 1974, a recession year, companies stopped hiring entry-level people. When the economy improved, these companies found they didn't have the personnel they needed to operate. Many of those companies suffered severely because of this misjudgment.

Daniel was also impressed by the value of education. More than anything else, hiring consultants commented that "the woods are full of people looking, but a lot of them aren't properly educated." Daniel was glad that he had spent the extra year in school taking business courses and that he had attended community college courses in finance and management even after he had started his job. He felt that these courses were crucial to his getting offers at a time when many coworkers were being laid off with no prospects of jobs at other companies.

1. Why do you think that production managers and financial managers are more in demand in a recession than advertising and marketing managers? Do you think this is wise?
2. If you were offered a job that offered low pay but a lot of valuable experience, do you think it would be worth the loss in pay in the long run? Why?
3. How did Daniel fit into the career stages model described in this chapter?

CASE 25-2

How Executives See Women in Management

On June 28, 1982, *Business Week* published the findings of a poll conducted by Louis Harris & Associates, Inc. This poll sought to find how managers felt about women in business.

Traditionally, of course, one would have expected to hear every kind of sexist comment: "They just get a job to find a man and marry." "They only work a year or two and then quit to marry." "They aren't as competitive as men." "They just don't fit in." And so on.

According to this Harris poll, that kind of view is ending, if not already dead. A summary of some of the results is given below. (Managers were asked whether they agreed or disagreed with the statements made.)

	Agree	Disagree
1. Contributions of women executives in the company are more positive than negative.	94%	2%
2. Women executives are performing on the job as well as or better than expected.	86%	5%
3. Quite a number of women use sex and guile to get ahead.	7%	87%
4. Some men now can't get ahead in certain jobs because the jobs are being saved for women.	8%	89%

Managers were still hesitant to promote women to higher level positions, in part because they felt that neither men nor women like to take orders from women. However, even these views are changing rapidly.

1. If you are a woman, write down the personality characteristics that you *personally* display that might make someone hesitant to promote you. Write down your abilities, strengths, and weaknesses, and comment next to each one on whether you will honestly be able to become a manager. If you decide you won't be able to, describe what you will become instead, and whether you will be happy in that role.
2. If you are a man, give your own comments to the statements cited above. Then assume that you are put in a position where a woman is your manager and can determine whether you are promoted, fired, and so on. Write down how you would treat her, realizing that she is a woman in a hard-earned managerial position and expects to be treated and respected just as a man in that position would be. Do you think you could cope with that role? Where might you have problems coping with a woman manager?

(These are answers that should be written down, but there is no "correct" answer. It is that time in this course when you need to perform some honest evaluation of yourself and decide just what kinds of job roles you could handle and what kinds you couldn't. One way to adjust to new roles is to think about them ahead of time and change your ideas or needs gradually so you are ready when your job starts.)

Careers Appendix

In this appendix, we provide a variety of information to further aid in your career planning. First, we present a listing of qualities bosses say they look for when hiring college graduates. Next, we identify and describe a sampling of jobs in business, including number of people employed, growth prospects, and salary information. We then give some suggestions for additional career reading. Finally, we provide the addresses of organizations from which you can request additional career information.

WHAT DO BOSSES WANT?

Executives of over 400 of the nation's largest corporations were asked which qualities they considered most important when hiring college graduates. Seventy qualities were provided for the executives to rank. Fifteen of the more and less important appear on the following list. Do any of the rankings surprise you? How do you think you rate on the important qualities?

Quality	Ranking
Ability to Get Things Done	1
Common Sense	2
Honesty/Integrity	3
Dependability	4
Initiative	5
Enthusiasm	9
Intelligence	13
Maturity	22
Writing Skills	26
Personality	28
Academic Major	42
Sense of Humor	43
Grade-Point Average (Overall)	51
Extracurricular Activities	56
Recommendations from Politicians	67

Source: J. Shingleton, Michigan State University.

JOBS IN BUSINESS

In this section, we identify and describe a sampling of jobs within several areas of business. To give you an idea of opportunities, we then provide the number of people employed, the probable growth rate through 1990, and 1980 salary information for each job.

The figures and job summaries in this section are adapted from the *Occupational Outlook Handbook*, 1982-83 Edition, prepared by the Bureau of Labor Statistics of the U.S. Department of Labor. Often there are several more specific job titles in each job category we describe. Salaries and duties may vary substantially within each category and may sometimes be outside the range we give as typical. We suggest you consult the *Occupational Outlook Handbook* for more detailed information.

Jobs in Management

Management careers are ideal for individuals with leadership ability and the desire to work with other people. Typically, they also require some experience. Managers may find their skills to be useful in many business, health care, and governmental organizations. Managerial positions are found at all organizational levels. Since management positions are found in each of the functional areas, we list just a few here.

Supervisors of blue-collar workers direct the activities of workers who perform such tasks as assembling television sets, unloading ships, or servicing autos. These supervisors may make work schedules, keep production and employee records, and handle discipline. About 1,300,000 blue-collar supervisors were employed in 1980, and average growth is expected. Average annual earnings for those working full time were about $21,000.

Health services administrators direct the various functions that make health organizations—from large teaching hospitals to storefront clinics—run smoothly. They have overall responsibility for many management decisions, such as preparing budgets; establishing rates; directing hiring and training; and directing and coordinating the activities of the medical department, nursing department, physical plant, and other departments. About 220,000 persons worked in some phase of health administration in 1980, and faster than average growth is expected. Most chief administrators earned in excess of $25,000 annually, and some earned more than $50,000.

Hotel and motel managers are responsible for operating their establishments profitably. They may determine room rates and credit policy; direct the food service operation; and manage the housekeeping, accounting, maintenance, and security departments. There were about 84,000 hotel and motel managers in 1980, and faster than average growth is expected. Hotel general managers earned $20,000 to $80,000 in 1981.

Jobs in Finance, Banking, and Insurance

Careers in finance, banking, and insurance offer exciting opportunities to deal with financial resources. Historically, they have served as excellent routes to the top of an organization.

Actuaries assemble and analyze statistics to calculate probabilities of death, sickness, injury, disability, unemployment, retirement, and property loss from accident, theft, fire, and other hazards. They use this information to determine the expected insured loss. There were 8,000 actuaries employed in 1980, and faster than average growth is expected. Salaries began at about $13,000 annually and reached over $50,000 with experience and expertise.

Bank clerks handle paperwork in banks. Duties may include sorting checks, totaling debit and credit slips, and preparing monthly statements for depositors. Banks employed nearly 1,000,000 clerks in 1980, and faster than average growth is expected. Earnings were between $6,700 and $8,300 annually.

Bank officers and managers usually include: a president who directs operations; vice presidents who act as general managers or are in charge of departments; comptrollers or cashiers who are responsible for bank property; and perhaps other officers. Banks employed over 400,000 officers and managers in 1980, and faster than average growth is expected. Starting salaries for trainees ranged from $13,200 to $28,800, depending on qualifications, and salaries of senior officers were often several times as high.

Bank tellers cash bank customers' checks, process their deposits and withdrawals from checking accounts, and may perform specialized duties such as handling foreign currencies. Banks employed 480,000 tellers in 1980 and faster than average growth is expected. Salaries began at about $6,700 annually and rose to as much as $12,000 with increased responsibilities.

Claim representatives investigate insurance claims, negotiate settlement with policyholders, and authorize payment. About 210,000 people worked as claim representatives in 1980, and faster than average growth is expected. Annual salaries from $15,000 to $21,000 were typical.

Collection workers, often called bill collectors or collections agents, help keep a company's delinquent and bad debts to a minimum. Their primary job is to persuade people to pay their bills. There were about 89,000 collection workers in 1980, and an average growth rate is expected. Salaries averaged $9,000 for beginners and increased to $15,000 for experienced collectors.

Credit managers generally have the final authority to accept or reject credit applications by individuals and businesses. They collect and analyze a variety of information in making their judgments. About 55,000 people worked as credit managers in 1980, and slower than average growth is expected. Annual salaries ranged from $12,000 to $14,000 for college-educated trainees and from $22,000 to $25,000 for experienced credit managers.

Economists try to determine the costs and benefits of making, distributing, and using resources in particular ways. They may be concerned with issues such as energy costs, inflation, business cycles, unemployment, tax policy, or farm prices. Economists who work for businesses may provide managers with information to use in making pricing, production, or diversification decisions. About 44,000 people worked as economists in 1980, fewer than one third of them in private industry, and faster than average growth is expected. The median base salary of business economists was $38,000.

Insurance agents and brokers sell insurance policies, provide advice about financial planning and insurance needs, prepare reports, maintain records, and help settle policyholders' claims. About 325,000 agents and brokers sold insurance in 1980 and average growth is expected. Most agents are paid on a commission basis. Agents with 5 or more years of experience had a median income of $22,000, though some earned much more.

Securities sales workers put the "market machinery" into operation when investors want to buy or sell stocks, bonds, shares in mutual funds, or other financial products. They may provide financial counseling, relay orders, and provide price quotations. There were about 63,000 securities sales workers in 1980, and faster than average growth is expected. While trainees' salaries averaged about $11,000 to $14,000 annually, experienced securities sales workers who serviced individual investors averaged over $40,000. Those servicing institutional accounts averaged over $88,000.

Underwriters appraise and select the risks their insurance companies will insure. They analyze various types of information in deciding whether a risk is acceptable. About 76,000 persons worked as underwriters in 1980, and average growth is expected. Average annual earnings ranged from about $16,000 to $24,000.

Jobs in Marketing

The many jobs involved in creating time and place utility make marketing a diverse and fascinating field. Marketing jobs often provide unique opportunities for creativity, personal accomplishment, and financial reward.

Advertising managers recommend amounts that should be spent on advertising, goals the advertising should meet, and the advertising agency that would be most effective. After selecting an agency, the advertising manager monitors and supervises the agency's efforts. Average growth is expected. Most advertising managers earned well over $25,000 annually.

Advertising workers handle a variety of tasks—such as copywriting, graphic art, layout, purchase of media space or time, and handling of accounts—in advertising agencies. There were about 100,000 advertising workers in 1980, and average growth is expected. Beginning advertising workers averaged $10,000 to $18,000 a year, and in 3 to 4 years averaged $18,000 to $25,000.

Automobile sales workers assist potential car buyers in making a selection and then go through the steps associated with making a sale and handling necessary paperwork. About 157,000 people were employed as automobile sales workers in 1980, and faster than average growth is expected. Earnings, based primarily on commissions, averaged $18,000 annually.

Buyers purchase goods for their stores. They seek goods that will satisfy customers and generate a profit. About 150,000 buyers worked for retail firms in 1980, and average growth is expected. Most salaries were between $19,000 and $28,000.

Manufacturers' sales workers sell manufacturers' products to other businesses (factories, banks, wholesalers, and retailers) and to other institutions. They visit prospective customers, prepare reports on sales prospects or customers' credit ratings, and handle correspondence. There were nearly 440,000 manufacturers' sales workers in 1980 and average growth is expected. Annual salaries ranged from $13,900 to $15,400 for beginners and from $21,000 to $24,400 for experienced workers. Sales supervisors averaged between $32,400 and $37,400.

Market research analysts analyze the buying public and its wants and needs, thus providing the information on which marketing decisions can be based. They plan, design, implement, and analyze the results of surveys. There were about 29,000 market research analysts in 1980, and faster than average growth is expected. Salaries of beginning market researchers ranged from $12,000 to $17,000 a year, and experienced workers averaged about $27,000.

Public relations workers help businesses and other institutions to maintain a positive public reputation. They inform the public of their organization's policies, activities, and accomplishments and keep management aware of public attitudes. There were 87,000 public relations workers in 1980, and average growth is expected. Beginning salaries ranged from $10,000 to $13,000 in 1980, and top public relations workers had a median salary of $38,000.

Real estate agents and brokers help people to buy and sell homes and other real estate. They provide information about the housing market and act as a medium for price negotiations between buyer and seller. Brokers are independent businesspeople who not only sell real estate owned by others, but also rent and manage properties, make appraisals, and develop new building projects. Agents generally are independent sales workers who contract their services with a licensed broker. 580,000 persons sold real estate as their primary occupation in 1980, and faster than average growth is expected. Full-time agents earned $14,700 a year and brokers earned nearly $29,000.

Retail trade sales workers sell such things as furniture, clothing, and appliances in retail stores. They may also perform such tasks as making out sales slips, receiving cash payments, and handling returns. In 1980, more than 3.3 million sales workers were employed in retail businesses, and average growth is expected. Median earnings, including bonuses and commissions, ranged from $8,312 to $14,203 for full-time sales workers.

Travel agents are specialists who have the information and know-how to make the best possible travel arrangements with their clients' tastes and budgets in mind. There were about 52,000 travel agents in 1980, and very fast growth is expected. About one fourth of travel agents are self-employed. Their earnings come from commissions from airlines and other carriers, tour operators, and lodging facilities. Salaried travel agents earned from $9,500 to $18,000 a year.

Wholesale trade sales workers help move goods from the factory to the consumer. They represent wholesalers that distribute to stores selling directly to the consumer. They visit buyers for retail, industrial, and commercial firms and institutions such as schools and hospitals. They may demonstrate products, perform services for retailers, and handle various paperwork related to sales. About 1.1 million persons were employed in wholesale sales in 1980, and average growth is expected. Median annual earnings of wholesale trade sales workers ranged from $23,000 to $30,800.

Jobs in Accounting

Many accounting careers are important, challenging, and rewarding. As managers increasingly rely on accounting information to make business decisions, the demand for skilled accounting personnel will continue to grow.

Accountants and auditors prepare and analyze financial reports that provide managers with the up-to-date financial information they need to make decisions. They may work in such areas as taxation, budgeting, costs, or investments. There were 900,000 accountants and auditors in 1980, and faster than average growth is expected. Experienced accountants and auditors earned from about $18,000 to $30,000.

Bookkeepers and accounting clerks maintain systematic and up-to-date records of accounts and business transactions. They also prepare periodic financial statements showing all money received and paid out. About 1,700,000 persons worked as bookkeepers and accounting clerks in 1980, and average growth is expected. Earnings of experienced accounting clerks averaged from $11,431 to $13,454 annually.

Jobs in Production Management

Individuals pursuing careers in production management are responsible for the many tasks needed to keep the modern production facility running properly. Jobs in production management require considerable mathematical and mechanical skill.

Engineering and science technicians have knowledge of science, mathematics, industrial machinery, and technical processes. They apply technical knowledge to all phases of business—from research and design to manufacturing, sales, and customer service. There were 885,000 persons working as engineering and science technicians in 1980, and faster than average growth is expected. Senior technicians earned an average of $22,300 a year.

Industrial engineers determine the most effective ways for an organization to use the basic factors of production—people, machines, and materials. They design data processing systems and control systems, do plant location surveys, and apply mathematical concepts to production. There were about 115,000 industrial engineers employed in 1980, and faster than average growth is expected. Starting salaries averaged $19,860, and many industrial engineers earn substantially more.

Purchasing agents see that the firm has the right materials, supplies, and equipment when they are needed. They obtain goods and services of the quality required at the lowest possible cost. About 172,000 persons worked as purchasing agents in 1980, and average growth is expected. Experienced agents purchasing standard items earned an average of $20,300 a year.

Jobs in Human Resource Management

Individuals with careers in human resource management make sure that organizations get, keep, and develop the best possible employees and use them in productive and satisfying ways. Dealing with people is a challenging task, and considerable training is required for most human resource management positions.

Affirmative action coordinators maintain contact with women and minority employees and they investigate and resolve Equal Employment Opportunity (EEO) grievances. They also examine corporate practices for possible violations, and compile and submit EEO reports. Average growth is expected. Starting salaries averaged $17,100 in 1980, and those with over 5 years of experience earned $25,000 to $27,000.

Compensation managers establish and maintain a firm's pay system. They devise ways to ensure that pay rates in the firm are fair and equitable and that they meet legal requirements. Average growth is expected. Salaries for compensation managers ranged from $24,200 to $38,400.

Employee-welfare managers handle the company's benefits program, notably its insurance and pension programs. Average growth is expected, and starting salaries averaged $18,000 in 1980.

Industrial and organizational psychologists apply psychological techniques to personnel administration, management, and marketing problems. They are involved in policy planning, training and development, psychological testing research, counseling, and organizational development and analysis. Average growth is expected. Psychologists with doctorates who worked in business averaged $36,700 in 1980.

Job analysts collect and examine information about job duties and prepare job descriptions. Average growth is expected. Starting salaries averaged $16,100 in 1980, and those with over 5 years experience averaged $25,000.

Labor relations specialists advise management on all aspects of union-management relations. When a collective bargaining agreement is up for negotiation, they provide background information for management's bargaining position. Average growth is expected. Salaries ranged from $29,400 to $35,000.

Sociologists study human society and social behavior by examining the groups that people form. Industrial sociologists are concerned with many issues relevant to business, such as group decision making, leadership, and power. About 21,000 people were employed as sociologists in 1980, and slower than average growth is expected. Sociologists with doctorates working in business and industry earned an average of $33,600.

Training specialists are responsible for a broad range of employee education and training activities. Average growth is expected. Starting salaries averaged $19,000, and those with over 5 years experience earned from $25,000 to $27,000.

Jobs in Information Management, Computers, and Statistics

Careers in information management, computers, and statistics offer individuals the chance to deal with the crucial information resources of the organization. They are among the most rapidly growing, dynamic, and exciting fields.

Computer operating personnel perform such functions as entering data and instructions, operating the computer, and retrieving results. About 558,000 persons worked in such computer operating jobs as console, auxiliary equipment, and keypunch operators in 1980, and very fast growth is expected. Most computer operating personnel in businesses earned from $10,440 to $19,500 annually.

Mathematicians are engaged in a wide variety of activities, ranging from the creation of new theories to the translation of scientific and managerial problems into mathematical terms. Applied mathematicians use mathematics to develop theories, approaches, and techniques to solve practical problems. There were about 40,000 persons working as mathematicians in 1980, with about one fourth in business and government. Slower than average growth is expected. Starting salaries of mathematicians with bachelor's, master's, and Ph.D. degrees averaged $17,700, $20,200, and $26,400, respectively.

Programmers write detailed instructions, called programs, that list in a logical order the steps a computer must follow to organize data, solve a problem, or do some other task. In 1980, about 228,000 persons worked as computer programmers, and faster than average growth is expected. Average salaries for experienced programmers ranged from $20,800 to $24,440.

Statisticians devise, carry out, and interpret the results of surveys and experiments. They may use statistical techniques to predict economic conditions, develop quality control tests, or evaluate the results of new management programs. About 26,500 persons worked as statisticians in 1980, and average growth is expected. The average salary for statisticians in the federal government was about $29,300, and salaries in private industry were comparable.

Systems analysts plan efficient methods of processing data and handling the results. To develop a new system, they may determine what new data must be collected, the equipment needed for computation, and the steps to be involved in processing the information. About 205,000 persons worked as systems analysts in 1980, and very fast growth is expected. Beginning systems analysts averaged $17,160 annually, and experienced workers earned from $20,280 to $23,920.

Other Jobs in Business

There are many other jobs needed to keep organizations running effectively. A few of them are presented in the following paragraphs.

Lawyers link the legal system and society. As advocates, lawyers represent opposing parties in criminal and civil trials by presenting arguments in a court of law. As advisors, they counsel their clients as to their legal rights and obligations and suggest courses of action. As we have indicated throughout the text, the legal environment of a firm is becoming increasingly important. About 425,000 persons worked as lawyers in 1980, and faster than average growth is expected. Beginning annual salaries in private industry averaged $21,000, and most experienced lawyers in private industry earned over $60,000.

Receptionists greet customers and other visitors, determine their needs, and refer callers to the person who can help them. About 635,000 persons worked as receptionists in 1980, and faster than average growth is expected. Full-time receptionists earned from $9,204 to $10,296 annually.

Secretaries perform a variety of administrative and office duties. They schedule appointments, give information to callers, organize and maintain files, fill out forms, and record and transcribe dictation. Nearly 2.5 million secretaries were employed in 1980, and faster than average growth is expected. Secretaries' annual salaries averaged from $12,818 to $14,586.

Stenographers take dictation and then transcribe their notes on a typewriter. They may take shorthand or use a stenotype machine. About 280,000 persons worked as stenographers in 1980, and that number is expected to decline. Stenographers in private industry earned $13,191.

Typists produce typewritten copies of handwritten, printed, and recorded words. Nearly 1.1 million persons worked as typists in 1980, and average growth is expected. Beginning typists had average earnings of $9,959, and those with experience averaged $12,358.

SUGGESTIONS FOR ADDITIONAL READING

Bolles, Richard. *What Color Is Your Parachute?* Berkeley, CA: Ten Speed Press, 1982.

Figler, H. *The Complete Job Search Handbook.* New York: Holt, Rinehart & Winston, 1980.

Fox, M. R. *Put Your Degree to Work: Job-Hunting Success for the New Professional.* New York: W. W. Norton & Co., 1979.

Irish, R. K. *Go Hire Yourself an Employer.* Garden City, NY: Anchor Books, 1978.

Hennig, M., and A. Jardim. *The Managerial Woman.* New York: Pocket Books, 1977.

Jackson, T. *Guerrilla Tactics in the Job Market.* Toronto: Bantam Books, 1978.

Jackson, T., and D. Mayleas. *The Hidden Job Market for the Eighties.* New York: Times Books, 1981.

Jackson, T. *The Perfect Resume.* Garden City, NY: Anchor Books, 1981.

Medley, H. A. *Sweaty Palms: The Neglected Art of Being Interviewed.* Belmont, CA: Lifetime Learning Books, 1978.

Shingleton, J., and R. Bao. *College to Career.* New York: McGraw-Hill, Inc., 1977.

Ulrich, H., and R. Conner. *The National Job-Finding Guide.* Garden City, NY: Anchor Books, 1981.

SOURCES OF ADDITIONAL CAREER INFORMATION

To learn more about opportunities in the various fields of business, we suggest that you write to the following sources. In your letter, indicate that you would like career information.

Accounting

American Accounting Association
650 South Orange Avenue
Sarasota, FL 33577

American Institute of Certified
  Public Accountants
1211 Avenue of the Americas
New York, NY 10036

Data Processing

American Society for
  Information Science
1010 Sixteenth Street, N.W.
Washington, DC 20036

Association for Computing Machinery
1133 Avenue of the Americas
New York, NY 10036

Finance

American Bankers Association
1120 Connecticut Avenue, N.W.
Washington, DC 20036

Bank Administration Institute
303 South Northwest Highway
Park Ridge, IL 60068

Institute of Chartered
  Financial Analysts
Post Office Box 3668
University of Virginia
Charlottesville, VA 22903

New York Stock Exchange
11 Wall Street
New York, NY 10005

Insurance

American Council of Life Insurance
277 Park Avenue
New York, NY 10017

Insurance Information Institute
110 William Street
New York, NY 10038

Marketing

American Advertising Federation
1225 Connecticut Avenue, N.W.
Washington, DC 20036

American Marketing Association
222 South Riverside Plaza
Chicago, IL 60606

Production and Materials Management

National Association of
  Purchasing Management
11 Park Place
New York, NY 10007

American Society for Quality Control
161 West Wisconsin Avenue
Milwaukee, WI 53203

American Production and
  Inventory Control Society
Suite 504 Watergate Building
2600 Virginia Avenue, N.W.
Washington, DC 20037

Human Resource Management

American Society for
  Personnel Administration
19 Church Street
Berea, OH 44017

Industrial Relations
  Research Association
Social Science Building
University of Wisconsin
Madison, WI 53706

National Employment Association
1835 K Street, N.W.
Washington, DC 20006

Management

American Management Association, Inc.
135 West 50th Street
New York, NY 10020

Small Business Management

Chamber of Commerce of
  the United States
1615 H Street, N.W.
Washington, DC 20006

U.S. Small Business Administration
1441 L Street, N.W.
Washington, DC 20416

Future Balance

Suppose you would like to have a certain amount of money at some time in the future—such as $500 in five years. You tell this program the amount you want, the time you want it, the interest rate, and the number of compounding periods per year, and it determines the amount you would have to invest now to reach your goal. Try a few different interest rates and compounding periods to see how your required initial investment changes.

Here's the Program

```
10 PRINT
20 PRINT "******FUTURE BALANCE PROGRAM*****"
30 PRINT
40 INPUT "DESIRED FUTURE BALANCE ";A
50 INPUT "NOMINAL INTEREST RATE (%): ";I
60 INPUT "LENGTH OF INVESTMENT (YEARS): ";Y
70 INPUT "NUMBER OF COMPOUNDING PERIODS/YEAR: ";N
80 J=I/N/100
85 REM ON APPLE USE A CARET INSTEAD OF [ ON LINE 90
90 P=A/(INT((J+1)[(N*Y)*100+.51)/100)
100 P=INT(P*100+.51)/100
110 PRINT
120 PRINT "*************************************************"
130 PRINT "DESIRED FUTURE BALANCE........$";A
140 PRINT "LENGTH OF INVESTMENT (YEARS)...";Y
150 PRINT "# OF COMPOUNDING PERIODS/YEAR..";N
160 PRINT "NOMINAL INTEREST RATE (%)......";I
170 PRINT "-------------------------------------------------"
180 PRINT "REQUIRED INITIAL INVESTMENT...$";P
190 PRINT "-------------------------------------------------"
200 INPUT "DO YOU WANT ANOTHER RUN? (1=YES;2=NO) ";K
210 IF K=1 THEN GOTO 10
220 END
```

COMPUTER AWARENESS

Here's Sample Output

Two sets of the future balance program are provided. All inputs are summarized in the output.

```
**********************************************
DESIRED FUTURE BALANCE........$ 1000
LENGTH OF INVESTMENT (YEARS)... 10
# OF COMPOUNDING PERIODS/YEAR.. 365
NOMINAL INTEREST RATE (%)...... 15
---------------------------------------------
REQUIRED INITIAL INVESTMENT...$ 223.21
---------------------------------------------
**********************************************
DESIRED FUTURE BALANCE........$ 1000
LENGTH OF INVESTMENT (YEARS)... 10
# OF COMPOUNDING PERIODS/YEAR.. 365
NOMINAL INTEREST RATE (%)...... 10
---------------------------------------------
REQUIRED INITIAL INVESTMENT...$ 367.65
---------------------------------------------
```

Questions

1. Give an example of a situation in which a firm might want to have a certain amount of money at a specified time in the future.
2. In the sample runs, a cut in interest rate from 15 percent to 10 percent (a drop of about 33 percent) caused an increase in the required initial investment from $223.21 to $367.65 (a jump of almost 65 percent). Why was the percentage increase in the required initial investment so much greater than the percentage drop in interest rate?
3. How would the required initial balance be affected by an increase in each of the following? Why?
   a) Nominal interest rate
   b) Length of investment
   c) Number of compounding periods per year

GLOSSARY

A

ability test. A test which measures how well a job applicant is able to perform the tasks required in a job.

acceptance. An expression of willingness, on the part of a party to a contract, to be bound by the terms of the offer.

accounting equation. Assets = Equity, or Assets = Liabilities + Owners' Equity, or Assets − Liabilities = Owners' Equity.

accounts payable. Short-term obligations, namely bills, due within a year.

accounts receivable. The amount of money owed to a firm as a result of the sale of its products on credit.

accrued expenses. The amount of money owed for services; to be paid after their performance.

acid-test ratio. A ratio calculated by dividing a firm's current assets which can be quickly converted to cash by the firm's total liabilities.

acquisition. The purchase of one company by another.

administrative expenses. Business costs that do not vary with the level of production and that are not traceable to production. Such costs include the salaries of management and other indirect costs relating to the management of a business.

administrative law. The rules and regulations issued by the many governmental boards, commissions, and agencies.

advertising. "Any paid form of nonpersonal presentation and promotion of ideas, goods and services."

advertising objectives. The immediate objectives of advertising are to increase the frequency of product use, to introduce complementary products, or to enhance corporate image; ultimately, the objective is to sell more of a firm's products or services.

advertising spiral. Three distinct stages of an advertising campaign which correlate with the five stages of the product life cycle.

affirmative action. An employer's active recruitment, hiring, and promotion of members of minority groups if such groups are underrepresented in the firm.

agreement. The basic element of a contract, composed of an offer and an acceptance.

allowances. Partial refunds to the customers of a firm. These refunds are deducted from gross revenue on the income statement.

analog computer. A type of computer using electrical circuits to simulate the behavior of other types of physical systems.

analytic transformation. A type of production process by which material is broken down into one or more final products.

arbitration. The process wherein an experienced, neutral person listens to the arguments of labor and management, weighs the merits of each argument, and then makes a binding judgment.

arithmetic/logic unit. The part of the central

processing unit which performs the mathematical and logical operations on the data.

articles of partnership. An agreement signed by each co-owner of a business, defining the role of each in the operation of the business.

artificial intelligence. The processing of information in a way that imitates the processes of the human mind.

assessment center. A center where psychologists and other experts on human behavior provide a variety of procedures to evaluate prospective employees.

assets. The properties owned by a business firm.

authorization card. A card signed by a worker which designates a union as the worker's bargaining agent.

authorized shares. The total number of shares of common stock that a corporation may sell to the public.

automated teller machines (ATMs). A computer that serves the function of a bank teller, conveniently located in shopping centers, bank lobbies, and elsewhere.

automation. The substitution of machine tools for human laborers in production processes.

B

balance sheet. A financial "snapshot" of a business at a particular moment in time, based on the accounting equation, and used by creditors in deciding whether to lend money to the business. It indicates the general health of a business.

banker's blanket bond. A type of insurance that protects a financial institution from losses resulting from employee fraud or dishonesty as well as from robbery, burglary, and theft.

bankruptcy. A condition whereby a firm is forced out of business as a result of debt and often required to sell its remaining assets in order to pay off its creditors.

bargaining unit. The group of employees which a union will represent if it receives a majority of votes.

BASIC (Beginner's All-Purpose Symbolic Instruction Code). A beginner's computer language most often used on small computers.

basic industries. Steel, automobile, airplane, chemical, machinery, rubber, glass, and other heavy manufacturing industries.

batch processing. The collection of data for a period of time so that they may be processed all at the same time.

bits (BInary DigiTs). The basic elements of machine-readable computer language; two digits, 0 and 1.

blanket bond. A type of fidelity bond that protects a business against losses caused by any of its employees.

board of directors. A group of individuals elected by corporate stockholders to represent their interests, to set corporate policy, and to assume ultimate management of the corporation.

bodily injury liability. A type of automobile insurance that protects a policyholder against claims from injuries to pedestrians, passengers, or people in other cars.

bond. A contract between the bond's issuer and the bond's buyer, the purchase price of which represents a loan to the issuing firm.

bond fund. A type of mutual fund characterized by conservative investment policies and a fairly stable rate of return.

bond indenture. The terms of a bond's lending agreement.

bond ratings. Published evaluations of bonds, indicating where each bond stands as regards its safety/risk as an investment.

bonds payable. The obligation on the books of the issuing firm to repay long-term bonds.

boycott. Union action to exert pressure on a

company during which union members and sympathizers refuse to purchase or handle the company's goods or services.

brand. Any name, symbol, or design which identifies a firm and its products.

break-even analysis. An approach to cost pricing which shows how alternative prices affect a firm's profit position.

break-even point. The volume of sales in units at which total revenue exactly equals total cost.

business. An individual or a group of people whose goal is to make a profit by selling products or services.

business ethics. Rules and standards of conduct governing the behavior of businesses and their employees.

business-interruption insurance. A form of loss-of-earning power insurance that protects a business against losses caused by a temporary disruption of its regular operations.

buying on the margin. A practice whereby an investor finances part of a stock purchase with borrowed money.

bytes. A combination of bits used to represent alphabetical characters.

C

call. An option to buy a specified stock at a specified price within a designated period of time.

call price. The price at which an issuer buys back a bond.

callable. A quality of some bonds whereby they may be retired before the maturity date stated on the indenture agreement.

canned (packaged) programs. Ready-made computer programs.

capital. Long-term money, or the long-lived productive assets of a firm.

capital structure. The term used to describe a company's long-term financing mix.

career. A chosen pursuit or life's work.

career cluster. A group of related jobs.

career objective. A statement that indicates a person's area of interest, the type of organization in which the person would like to work, and the level of the position desired.

cash discount. A price reduction offered when a buyer pays for a product within a designated period of time.

cathode ray tube (CRT). A screen, much like that of a television, which shows computer input and output.

cease-and-desist order. A ruling by the FTC requiring a company to stop an unfair business practice.

central processing unit (CPU). The "brain" of the computer which does the thinking and memorizing.

chain. A group of stores owned by one individual or firm.

channel intermediaries. The individuals and businesses through which goods and services flow from producers to end users.

channel of distribution. A group of marketing institutions which links together the manufacturer and the consumer.

check. A piece of paper legally authorizing a bank to withdraw the specified amount of money from the account and to pay it to the person or organization to whom the check is written.

checking account. A type of deposit account offered by a bank on which no interest is paid.

checkoff. An automatic deduction of union dues from a worker's paycheck.

Civil Rights Act. Legislation passed by Congress in 1964 making it illegal to discriminate in hiring and training on the basis of race, color, sex, religion, or national origin.

classical view. A view about the social responsibility of business which argues that business firms, when they produce goods and services in the most efficient way possible, are led as if by an "invisible hand" to maximize the social welfare of all.

classifying. The process of arranging or organizing according to class or category.

Clayton Act. Legislation passed by Congress (1914) for the purpose of making the Sherman Act more effective; outlawed tying agreements and exclusive agreements.

closed-end trust. A mutual fund with restricted membership.

COBOL (COmmon Business-Oriented Language). A simplified computer language used widely in business applications.

code of ethics. A listing of principles and standards of appropriate behavior within a given company.

cold calls. Business calls made by salespeople in which no advance warning is offered.

collating. See merging.

collective bargaining. The process whereby representatives of labor and management formulate an agreement governing pay scales and terms of work.

collision insurance. A type of automobile insurance that pays for damage to the policyholder's car in the event of an accident.

commercial bank. A financial insitution, chartered by either the state or the federal government, that channels money from savers to investors by offering demand deposits and other accounts and by lending money to individual and corporate borrowers.

commercial paper. Unsecured, short-term promissory notes issued by large corporations and state and municipal governments.

commercialization. The sixth stage in a new product development process, during which the product is made available to the market.

commission. A form of compensation whereby a salesperson's pay is tied to how much he or she sells.

commission broker. The person on the floor of a stock exchange who walks over to the trading area and fulfills the instructions of a stockbroker's customer.

common law. The body of decisions, which have the force of law, made by court judges in cases brought before them.

common stock. A certificate indicating a share of ownership in a corporation but not specifying an annual dividend.

communication strategy. A plan of action through which a firm communicates with its market(s).

competitive stage. The second stage of the advertising spiral in which the advertiser stresses the unique features of its product and the advantages of the product in relation to competing goods.

compiler. A language translator inside a computer which translates symbolic language into machine language which can then be read by the computer.

comprehensive insurance. A type of automobile insurance that covers expenses resulting from the theft of an automobile and from a variety of other losses.

computer. A machine that can carry out complex and repetitious operations at very high speeds.

computer program. A precise set of computer instructions, usually written from the program flowchart.

congeneric merger. A business combination in which one company buys another that is in a different industry but that performs a related activity.

conglomerate merger. A business combination in which one company buys another that is in a different industry and that performs an unrelated activity.

consideration. That which each party to a contract gives up or promises to do. Consideration can refer to a promise of payment or to a pledge to perform a certain action.

constrainers. Supporters of a view on social responsibility which sees business enterprises as essentially indifferent to the social consequences of their actions, therefore requiring legal and political constraints on their actions.

consumer price index (CPI). The average price changes of a group of goods and services that make up a typical consumer's budget.

consumer product. A good produced for sale to an individual or family for personal consumption.

consumer sovereignty. The idea that consumers determine through the purchase decisions they make in the marketplace what goods and services will be produced.

consumerism. A popular social movement which began in the 1960s, the aim of which is to give consumers more power in relation to the makers of consumer goods.

continuous manufacturing. The production of a flow of goods at a predetermined rate.

contract. An agreement between two or more people which defines the relationship between these people in the performance of a specified action.

contract administration. In labor-management relations, the process whereby a contract is interpreted and followed on a daily basis.

contractual capacity. The eligibility of an individual to enter into a legally binding contract.

control unit. The part of a central processing unit that directs the internal operations of the computer.

control chart. A diagram, usually used in conjunction with statistical quality control, showing the upper and lower control limits of a production system so as to ensure quality maintenance.

controlling. The monitoring of job or task performance to make sure that it is in line with intended performance, and if unfavorable deviations are observed, the correcting of those deviations.

convenience good. A good purchased frequently, immediately, and with little shopping effort.

convenience store. A minisupermarket offering a limited selection in terms of brands and package sizes.

convertible bond. A bond that can be converted into shares of stock at the option of the bondholder.

convertible term insurance. Life insurance that allows a policyholder to switch to another type of coverage without being required to pass a physical examination.

cooling-off rule. An FTC rule which protects the consumer from making unwise purchases at home.

cooperative. An incorporated business concern owned by its user-members for the collective operation of production and/or distribution activities.

corporation. A group of persons granted a charter by the state which legally recognizes them as a separate entity with its own rights, privileges, and liabilities.

corrective action. Action taken by management (such as the scheduling of overtime or shifting work to other machines) when a production delay occurs.

corrective advertising. Advertising sometimes required by the FTC when a sponsoring firm has misled many consumers.

cost of goods sold. The amount of money spent by a seller on merchandise sold.

cost-of-living adjustment (COLA). A key issue in collective bargaining situations whereby labor seeks wage adjustments that track changes in the consumer price index over the life of the contract.

cost-plus pricing. See markup pricing.

cost pricing. Establishing the price of a product in relation to the cost of producing or purchasing it.

coupon. A piece of paper entitling its holder to a discount on a particular product.

credit union. A type of savings institution

which functions as a cooperative owned by its members rather than by stockholders.

critical path. The sequence of in-series production activities requiring the longest time for completion.

culture. The set of values, ideas, and attitudes that shape human behavior.

cumulative preferred stock. A preferred stock issue whose dividends are carried forward to the next year if not paid in one year.

current assets. "Liquid" assets that a firm expects to use, sell, or turn into cash within one year.

current liabilities. The legal obligations of a firm that must be paid within a year.

current ratio. A ratio calculated by dividing a firm's total current assets by its total current liabilities.

D

data processing. A term for information handling, primarily through mechanical or electronic computing devices.

debenture. A bond that does not include a pledge of specified assets as a guarantee of repayment.

debt capital. Borrowed long-term funds.

debt-to-net-worth ratio. A measure of the amount of money owed by a firm to its creditors relative to the equity value of a company, or Total Liabilities ÷ Owners' Equity.

decline stage. The fifth stage in the product life cycle in which consumers begin to switch to new products, and the product in question eventually disappears from the market.

definite and measurable risk. A principle of insurance by which the insurance company protects against quantifiable losses that result directly from a specific event at a specific moment in time.

demand. The quantity of a product that buyers are willing to buy at a specified price.

demand curve. The fundamental tool of economic analysis which shows the relationship between the price of a product and the amount of the product that consumers are willing to buy at that price.

demand deposit. A checking account at a commercial bank.

demand pricing. A firm's consideration of the level of demand for a product in making its pricing decisions.

demanders. Supporters of a view on social responsibility which holds businesses accountable to act responsibly because of their resources and power, and which claims that the public has a right to expect a level of social involvement proportionate to the amount of power held.

demographic segmentation. A method of defining submarkets using population, age, income, and other socioeconomic variables as the segmenting criterion.

demography. The statistical study of the characteristics of human populations.

demotion. A movement down in title, responsibility, or benefits.

department store. A store selling a wide assortment of merchandise.

departmentalization. The division of a large organization into smaller units or departments.

depreciation. The amount of a property's decline in value since its purchase.

differential pricing. A demand-pricing technique which considers the differences in demand among various market segments in determining the price of a product.

digital computer. A type of computer that computes with digits, that is, numbers.

directing. A set of management activities the aim of which is to encourage subordinates to work toward the achievement of the company's goals.

discount. The difference between the list price

and the selling price of a good.

discount brokers. Stockholders offering only a few services to their customers and charging considerably lower fees for handling stock transactions than full service brokers.

discount rate. The interest rate charged on short-term money that a bank borrows from its regional Federal Reserve bank.

discount store. A store whose merchandise lines are limited to the most popular items and colors, which operates long hours and is usually open Sundays, and which operates on a self-service basis.

dispatching. The process of preparing and issuing work orders.

diversification. The purchase of a variety of stocks and bonds in many different companies representing many different industries.

dividends. The after-tax earnings of a corporation, when distributed to shareholders.

division of labor. The breaking down of complex jobs into simpler, smaller tasks.

documentation. The permanent, step-by-step record of a computer program.

double-entry bookkeeping. A method of financial record keeping based on the accounting equation, showing two entries in the book for each transaction.

dumping. The sale of domestically produced goods abroad at prices below their production costs.

duress. Coercion illegally applied.

E

earnings per share. A profitability measure calculated by dividing net income after taxes by the number of shares of common stock outstanding.

economic analysis. The third stage of a new product development process during which the expected profitability of the product is estimated.

economic communities. Alliances formed by several member nations for the purpose of mutual economic benefit.

editing. The process of modifying data into a more useful form.

electronic funds transfer (EFT). A variety of computer applications to financial transactions, including automated teller machines and automated clearinghouses.

employment. The state of holding a job, or the number of people holding jobs.

endowment insurance. Life insurance that allows the insured, rather than a beneficiary, to collect the face value of the policy upon maturity or to collect that value in annual payments.

environmental protection. The preservation and conservation of the nation's air, land, and water resources for future generations.

Equal Employment Act. Legislation passed in 1972 which supplemented the 1964 Civil Rights Act, making it illegal to discriminate in hiring and promotions.

equity. The rights or claims to the properties owned by a business firm.

equity capital. Long-term funds provided by the sale of ownership shares, such as common stock.

exchange function. That function of a marketing system concerned with the centralization of the exchange of goods and services so as to increase distribution efficiency.

exclusive agreement. An illegal trade agreement in which the seller, as a condition of the sale, forbids the buyer from purchasing for resale the products of competing sellers.

exclusive distribution. A retailing approach whereby a product is made available through one or only a few stores in a geographic market.

expectancy theory. A theory of motivation focusing on employees' desires and expectations.

export. A good or service produced in one country and then sold to another.

express warranty. Any "fact or promise" made by the seller to the buyer concerning a product.

expropriation without reimbursement. The appropriation of the assets of a foreign firm by the host country's government without compensation to the firm.

extended coverage. The inclusion of other risks — besides fire damage — against which a business will be protected under a fire insurance policy.

external auditors. CPAs who audit the books of a firm but who are not salaried members of that firm.

external expansion. The process whereby a firm grows by purchasing another company.

extinction. The disappearance of a certain behavior.

extrinsic reward. A reward, such as a pay raise or a promotion, given to the employee by someone else—usually by someone in management.

F

factor. A financial institution that buys accounts receivable from a firm in need of short-term cash.

factoring accounts receivable. The process of selling accounts receivable to a factor so as to raise needed cash.

family brand. A brand name that covers most or all of a firm's products.

Federal Reserve System. The central bank of the United States, serving as a bank for bankers.

Federal Trade Commission (FTC). The federal agency established in 1914 for the purpose of enforcing the Clayton Act, and entrusted with the authority to define "unfair methods of competition."

fidelity bond. An employee insurance that protects an employer from losses resulting from a dishonest employee.

financial leverage. The use of high levels of debt to make the total cost of financing lower.

financial manager. The person whose responsibility is to make sure that the firm has enough cash to meet its obligations, and to obtain this cash from the least costly sources.

financial reward. A monetary symbol of recognition.

finished goods. Products that are ready for shipment or sale to a buyer.

first-in, first-out (FIFO). A method of inventory valuation in which current sales revenue is matched against the cost of the first items purchased.

fixed assets. "Long-lived" or permanent assets not sold during the ordinary course of operation.

fixed costs. Costs that do not vary with the level of production or sales.

fixed price. A price that is not negotiable between the buyer and seller.

flextime. A way of scheduling employee work time in which the arrival and departure times of workers are varied but in which all workers are on the job during a core work period in the middle of the day.

FOB-destination pricing. A geographic pricing approach whereby the seller pays all transportation costs.

FOB-factory pricing. A geographic pricing approach whereby the seller adds shipping costs to the price of a product.

follow-up. The process of keeping track of work completed and any time lags or delays that may have occurred.

foreboders. Supporters of a view on social responsibility which argues for business' contribution to social improvements in order to alleviate social problems and to eliminate the need for government intervention.

forecasting. The prediction of future trends, cycles, or occurrences.

form transformation. The processing or conversion of raw and semifinished materials into finished products.

FORTRAN (FORmula TRANslator). A computer language used widely for mathematical and statistical applications.

forward buying. In materials purchasing, the buying of more of a good than is immediately needed for production.

franchisee. The person or group who obtains the right to use the franchising organization's name and trademark.

franchising. A business agreement whereby the franchisor allows the franchisee to sell the franchisor's products under a strict set of rules, to display the franchisor's sign, and to call upon the franchisor for assistance.

franchisor. The corporation granting the franchise license, along with exclusive territorial distribution, use of its emblem, and whatever other benefits are offered to the franchisee.

fraud. A willful misrepresentation of fact.

frequency. The number of times a person is exposed to an advertisement.

fringe benefit. A benefit received by employees in addition to their regular salary.

full-service merchant wholesaler. A wholesaler that offers a broad range of services to its customers, and that takes title to and possession of the products it sells.

full-service stockbrokers. Stockbrokers who not only buy and sell stock, but who also provide research and other services to their customers.

G

Gantt Chart. A schedule chart providing managers with information on the flow of materials through a production process or the flow of work through a job shop as well as the status of work performed relative to the work scheduled.

general overhead. See administrative expenses.

generic product. A nonbranded, nonadvertised product.

geographic segmentation. A method of defining submarkets using geographic location or place of residence or work as the segmenting criterion.

giveback. In labor-management bargaining, a reduction in wages and benefits, or a delay in receiving wage and benefit increases granted to labor earlier.

goods available for sale. The money value of inventory available for sale during an accounting period, for example, a year.

grease payment. A relatively small payment to a local official by a foreign business, or its representative, in order to facilitate business operations.

grievance procedure. A set of steps to be followed should a dispute over contract provisions arise.

gross national product (GNP). The total annual value of all goods and services produced in a country.

gross profit. The difference between net sales and cost of goods sold.

gross sales. Income received from the sale of a firm's products or services, including cash sales and sales made on account or charged.

growth fund. A type of mutual fund composed of stock from companies with excellent growth potential.

guaranty loan. A loan in which a third person undertakes to fulfill the obligation of repayment should the borrower responsible for the loan be unable to do so.

H

hardware. A computer and its support equipment.

health insurance. An insurance plan offered by many businesses to their employees and families, or purchased by people for themselves, covering most or all the cost of hospitalization, surgical procedures, physician office visits, and diagnostic tests.

hierarchy of authority. A ranking of people according to their authority in an organization.

hiring. The final selection of the best job candidate for the position available.

holding costs. The expense of storing, or holding, an inventory in the firm's warehouse or on its stock shelves.

horizontal merger. A form of business combination in which one company buys another that is in the same industry and that performs the same function.

human change. A type of organizational change involving employee attitudes, skills, or knowledge.

hypermarket. A type of large discount store that developed in Germany.

I

idea generation. The first stage of a new product development process during which many new product ideas originate.

implied warranty. The guarantee by the seller that the product sold is at least of "average quality" and is "adequately packaged and labeled."

import. A good or service of foreign production which is purchased by another country.

in-basket. An assessment approach where a job recruit's performance is evaluated in terms of how well and how quickly the recruit organizes a series of tasks and makes decisions concerning them.

income bond. A bond on which the issuing firm is required to pay interest only when it earns enough money to do so.

income rights. The right of common stockholders to receive a share of a corporation's after-tax earnings.

income statement. A financial statement showing all of a firm's revenues and expenses occurring over an interval of time.

income tax payable. The estimated amount of money owed to the government on income already earned.

individual fidelity bond. A type of fidelity bond that protects a business against losses brought about by one or more named individuals.

industrial advertising. Advertising carried out by the makers of industrial goods in order to reach other firms that may use these goods in the manufacture of their products.

industrial development bond. A bond issued by state and local governments under the auspices of an industrial development agency, the purpose of which is to raise money for an industrial project of benefit to the local economy.

industrial products. Goods and services which are sold to private business firms or public agencies, and which are later used in the production of their goods and services.

inflation. A rise in prices.

inflationary expectations. A cause of inflation characterized by the belief, on the part of various segments of the population, that prices will continue to rise.

information. Knowledge that is passed along in order to enlighten or to inform.

information function. That function of a marketing system concerning the back-and-forth flow of market information from producers to consumers.

injunction. A court order requiring striking workers to return to work or face a penalty.

input units. The means through which data and programs are entered into a computer.

inspection. The comparison of products against established manufacturing standards, the approval of those that meet the standards, and the rejection of those that do not.

institutional advertising. Advertising that extols the advertiser itself, rather than a particular product or product line.

insurable interests. A principle of insurance by which the buyers of insurance policies show that they would suffer financial loss, not gain, from an accident of the type covered by the policy.

insurance. An arrangement by which many in a society share the losses of a few.

intangible assets. Assets, such as patents, licenses, trademarks, and goodwill, none of which in itself is a physical object.

intensive distribution. A retailing approach whereby a product is made available through as many stores as possible.

interactive computing. A relationship between the computer and the user characterized by a sequence of actions (or statements) and responses rather than by the simple inputting of data by the user.

interest rate. The price paid for the use of money over a stated period of time.

interest rate ceiling. The maximum amount that a financial institution, by law, may pay on an account of a given type.

interest test. A test measuring a person's likes and dislikes for various activities.

intermittent manufacturing. A type of merchandized manufacturing process in which a product is processed in lots rather than in a continuous flow.

internal expansion. The process whereby a business grows by increasing its sales and capital investment each year.

interview. A meeting between an employer and a job applicant, during which the employer asks several questions regarding the applicant's qualifications and interests.

infrastructure. A country's basic communication, transportation, and other public facilities.

intrinsic reward. A reward related to the job itself and the pleasure and sense of accomplishment that it gives an employee.

inventory financing. Inventories used as collateral for short-term loans.

inventory function. That function of a marketing system concerned with balancing the relationship between supply and demand throughout an economy.

inventory turn-over ratio. A measure of how many times a year a firm sells off or "turns over" its merchandise inventory.

investment bank. A bank that helps firms raise needed capital in the securities markets by underwriting the sale of new stock or bond issues.

investor. The person or organization that buys long-term debt and equity securities.

issued shares. All shares of common stock held by the public, or held by the issuer as treasury stock.

J

job analysis. The systematic study of a job to determine its characteristics.

job description. A short summary of the basic tasks making up a job.

job enrichment. A way to improve product quality by restructuring the job to make it more meaningful to the worker.

job evaluation. A process whereby the relative worth of a job in the firm is determined.

job shop. A type of intermittent manufacturing whereby products are manufactured or assembled to a customer's purchase order or specification.

job specification. A summary of the qualities needed in a worker for a specific job.

joint venture. An agreement between two or more business concerns, usually corporations, for the joint production or distribution of a good or service.

K

kanban. A method of inventory control whereby a firm maintains very small inventories.

L

labor union. An organization composed of workers from the same industry or sharing similar occupational characteristics, who have united to achieve their goals.

last-in, first-out (LIFO). A method of inventory valuation in which sales revenue is matched against the costs of the most recently purchased items.

law of effect. A law stating that rewarded behavior tends to be repeated while punished behavior does not.

law of large numbers. A statement of the assumption that the true likelihood of an event occurring can be predicted from an examination of the past rate of occurrence of the event, given many occurrences of that event.

lead time. The time from order placement to delivery.

learning theory. A theory of motivation which states that the consequences of an act determine whether it is repeated.

less developed countries (LDCs). Those countries, predominantly in Asia, Africa and Latin Amercia, whose economic and social indicators place them at the lower end of the development spectrum, but whose population growth rates are among the highest in the world.

letter of application. A letter that accompanies a mailed resume, stating an interest in being considered for a job opening.

leverage. The amount of risk a company assumes in order to increase its earnings for stockholders.

liabilities. The rights of creditors, viewed as debt to a business firm.

licensing. An agreement between a firm of one country (the licensor) and a firm of another country (the licensee), whereby the licensor allows the licensee to use its manufacturing process to manufacture and sell products in its country.

life insurance. Insurance paying a cash benefit to a surviving person or firm in the event of the death of the person insured.

limit order. A type of stock order whereby the customer tells the commission broker to buy or sell a stock when it reaches a certain price.

limited liability. A feature of common stock stipulating that the stockholders cannot be sued by the corporation's creditors for recovery of their claims.

limited life policy. A form of whole life insurance in which the policyholder pays premiums only until the policy is paid.

limited partnership. An association of one or more general co-owners who assume unlimited liability and act as managers of a project or business, and one or more limited partners who supply investment money but do not act as managers.

limited-service merchant wholesaler. A wholesaler that offers only a few services to its customers, and takes title to and possession of its merchandise.

line of credit. An agreement between a bank and a borrower which specifies how much the bank is willing to lend the borrower over a specified period of time.

line position. A job in the direct chain of command that begins with the board of directors and ends with the production people.

liquidity. The ease with which an asset can be converted into spendable cash.

list price. A publicly stated price for which the firm or store expects to sell each of its products.

load fund. A type of mutual fund in which the manager is paid an annual operating fee by the other members of the fund, and which involves the payment of a sales commission at the time the stocks comprising the fund are purchased.

loading. The process of determining how long it takes to perform a particular operation at a machine or work station, and then adding that amount of time to the time for work already scheduled there.

local marketing subsidiary. An office staffed by residents of the host country, but managed by executives from a firm's home office abroad, established to market goods or services in the local market.

lockout. A company's shutdown of its operations, thus preventing union members from working.

long-term debt. Debt with a maturity date of ten years or more.

long-term financing. Money contributed by the owners of a business, or money from lenders who do not expect immediate repayment.

long-term liabilities. Debts that do not have to be repaid for at least 12 months.

long wave theory. A theory of economic growth which distinguishes 50-year "waves" of global economic prosperity fluctuating with 50-year waves of economic decline.

loss leader. A product that is sold below cost in order to stimulate the sales of other products.

loss-of-earning-power insurance. A form of insurance that protects a business against loss-of-earning-power because of some unusual event.

M

machine language. A computer language based on the binary (or two-digit) system, where the digits (bits) combine into strings (bytes) that are in turn used to represent alphabetical characters.

macromarketing. The study of how goods and services are distributed from buyers to sellers.

management. "The art of getting things done through people."

Management By Objectives (MBO). A method of improving employee motivation whereby general areas of responsibility important to the firm are identified, the employer and employee agree upon specific objectives that the employee will meet during a certain period of time, and at the end of that period, they meet to review performance relative to goals.

Management Information System. An integrated system of information flows designed to enhance decision-making.

management process. The totality of a manager's planning, organizing, staffing, directing, and controlling functions, all of which are interrelated in the pursuit of a common goal.

management-rights clause. A list of the areas of operation in which management may take actions without having to obtain permission from a union.

management science. The science concerned with the development and application of mathematical models to business problems.

manufacturer-owned wholesaler. A manufacturer that also acts as its own wholesaler.

marine insurance. An insurance policy that protects ship owners against damage to the ship and its cargo, or one that protects against damage to property being transported by ship, truck, or train.

markdown. A discount designed to encourage customers to buy a product that they might not otherwise want at the time.

market. The total of all sales for a given kind of good among all buyers and sellers.

market coverage. The extent to which a product is readily available to consumers.

market development stage. The first stage in the product life cycle in which the product is introduced to the market, and sales pick up slowly.

market order. A type of stock under which the commission broker is authorized to buy or sell a stock at the best possible price.

market segmentation. The process of identifying smaller markets and modifying a product or a firm's selling strategies to match the characteristics of each smaller market.

market structure. The manner in which buyers and sellers interact and the degree to which there is competition involved in a private enterprise economy.

market value. The current selling price of a common stock.

marketing concept. A contemporary philosophy of business that sees marketing as a customer-oriented activity.

marketing mix. The totality of marketing decisions covering the key elements of product, distribution, price, and communication.

marketing research. "The systematic gathering, recording and analyzing of data about problems related to the marketing of goods and services."

markup. The amount in dollars added to production or purchase cost in order to determine the good's selling price.

markup pricing. The practice of establishing price by adding a predetermined percentage to the cost of manufacturing or purchasing the product.

materials requiring planning (MRP). A recent inventory control technique that relies on computer programs to coordinate information about customer orders, the amount of various materials on hand, and the sequencing of production operations.

matrix departmentalization. A flexible organizational design of departments in which each employee has a boss "higher up" in his or her functional area, and another boss for the particular project being worked on.

maturity. The length of time between the issuance of a debt instrument and the date at which repayment of the debt is due in full.

maturity stage. The fourth stage in the product life cycle in which sales rise and fall with the health of the economy.

mechanistic organizational design. A view of organizational design characterized by a tight compartmentalization of jobs, heavy reliance on rules, and strict adherence to the chain of command.

mediation. The process whereby an experienced and knowledgeable neutral person assists the union and management in reaching an agreement.

medical payments insurance. A type of automobile insurance that covers medical expenses resulting from an automobile accident injury.

medium of exchange. The primary function of money.

meeting or matching competition. A pricing practice whereby a firm raises or lowers its prices in response to the actions of its competitors.

memory. See primary storage unit.

merchandise agent. A wholesaler that does not take title to its merchandise and hold it for resale, but rather is paid a fee to bring buyer and seller together.

merchandise inventory. The finished goods, work-in-process, and raw materials listed as current assets on a balance sheet.

merger. A type of acquisition in which the company purchased ceases to exist as a separate entity.

merging. In data processing, the combining of two or more sorted files into a single file in the same sequence.

microcomputer. A typewriter-sized computer.

micromarketing. The process of planning and carrying out a product development, distribution, pricing, and communication strategy that enables a firm to earn a profit.

microprocessors. Tiny wafer-shaped chips that can hold up to 128 million pieces of information.

migration. The movement of people (population shifts) from one area of a country to another.

minicomputer. A cabinet-sized computer.

model of man. A computer model of a human decision maker.

money. That which is generally accepted as payment for goods and services.

money market account. An account at a commercial bank or other financial institution requiring a minimum deposit, with no interest rate ceiling or fixed maturity.

money market funds. Virtually risk-free funds made up of short-term, high-yield government notes, commercial paper, and negotiable certificates of deposit.

money supply. The total currency in circulation plus checking account balances at commercial banks.

monopolistic competition. A type of market structure characterized by many buyers and sellers, some measure of product differentiation, imperfect information, and government regulation.

monopoly. A type of market structure characterized by little or no competition, given the presence of only one selling firm and many small buyers.

mortgage bond. A bond that is secured with a fixed asset.

motivation. The attempt to satisfy a need.

multinational corporation (MNC). A corporation with direct investments in several countries and which sells its goods or services anywhere in the world where there is a demand for them.

mutual company. A private insurance company that is organized as a nonprofit organization owned by insurance policyholders.

mutual fund. An association of many small investors who pool their earnings to buy stock or bonds.

mutual savings banks. Financial institutions similar to savings and loan associations, whose deposits consist mostly of small savings accounts and whose funds are invested primarily in real estate mortgages.

N

name advertising. Advertising whose objective is to put the name of the product, or the company's trademark, in front of as many people as possible.

national advertising. Advertising paid for by manufacturers and directed at consumers, using mass media as the means of communication.

national banks. Commercial banks that receive their operating charters from the federal government.

need for achievement. One of McClelland's three needs; the need to do well in pursuit of any chosen goal.

need hierarchy. Maslow's ranking of five needs in a hierarchy of importance.

negotiable certificate of deposit (CD). A bank savings account held by a corporation or person in an amount usually in excess of $100,000.

negotiated price. A price agreed upon by the buyer and the seller.

net income after taxes. The "bottom line" on an income statement, representing the result of all a business' operations after taxes have been deducted, or the amount of money a firm earned during a year.

net income before taxes. The figure that represents the result of all operations of a business before taxes have been netted out.

net period. The length of time for which the seller has extended credit to a buyer.

net sales. Gross sales minus returns and allowances.

new product. A product that performs an entirely new function for the buyer.

no-fault insurance. A new type of automobile insurance under which the parties to an accident recover their medical and hospital expenses, as well as any losses in income, from their own insurance companies.

no-load fund. A type of mutual fund in which no payment of a sales commission is made at the time the stocks comprising the fund are purchased.

nonfinancial reward. A nonmonetary reward given to an employee for a job well done.

note payable. The equivalent of a transaction loan, as it appears on the borrower's books.

note receivable. The equivalent of a transaction loan, as it appears on the lender's books.

NOW (Negotiable Order of Withdrawal) Account. An account offered by a commercial bank which combines features of both a checking account and a passbook savings account; a checking account that pays interest.

numerical control. A manufacturing process relying on an automatic control mechanism to direct machine operations.

O

Occupational Safety and Health Administration (OSHA). Federal agency established in 1970 for the purpose of ensuring safe and healthful working conditions.

odd lots. Trading units of less than 100 shares of stock.

offer. A proposal to enter into a contractual relationship.

oligopoly. A type of market structure characterized by the presence of a few large sellers, any of whom may affect the prices of the products sold in a particular market, and by the presence of many small buyers.

ombudsman. A person hired by management to investigate and resolve employee complaints.

on-line processing. The direct hook-up of all input and output units to the same main computer.

on-the-job training. Training conducted while employees perform job-related tasks.

open account. See open book credit.

open book credit. An informal trade credit arrangement whereby a buyer makes purchases from a supplier and pays for them later.

open-end trust. A mutual fund that is open to new investors into the investment pool at its current per share value.

open market operations. The buying and selling of U.S. government securities on the open market.

operating expenses. All costs that a business incurs in its normal operations.

operating income. The income from business operations; gross profit minus total operating expenses.

operating leverage. The use of high fixed costs to make the total cost of production lower.

operations research. See management science.

option. The right to buy or sell a specified stock at the current market price for a certain period of time.

ordering costs. The expenses involved in placing an order.

order cycle. The length of time between the placing of a purchase order and the delivery of the merchandise to the buyer.

organic organizational design. A view of organizational design characterized by flexibility of the organizational structure so as to ensure maximum adaptability to a changing environment, and a freer atmosphere of communication among all levels of the organization.

organization chart. A formal representation of a firm's hierarchy.

organizing. The manner in which work is arranged and distributed among members of a firm.

orientation. The process whereby new employees are introduced to their jobs and their new company.

other expenses. All expenses that cannot be directly associated with the operations of a firm.

other income. Revenue from sources other than the primary activity of a firm.

output units. The means by which computer operations are presented to the user.

outstanding shares. The number of shares of a corporation held by the public; issued shares minus the number of shares held as treasury stock.

over-the-counter market (OTC). A market in which unlisted securities are bought and sold.

owners' equity. The claims of owners on the assets of a business firm.

P

participating. A feature of preferred stock allowing its stockholders to share along with common stockholders in the corporation's operating profits.

partnership. An association of two or more co-owners to operate a business.

par value. The face value of a common stock.

passbook account. A type of deposit account offered by commercial banks and other financial institutions on which interest is paid.

penetration pricing. The practice of introducing a product to the market at a low price.

perfect competition. A type of market structure characterized by many small buyers and sellers (none of whom is large enough to have any effect on the price of the product being traded), identical products, perfect information to all buyers and sellers, and lack of government regulation.

performance appraisal. The measurement of employee performance.

performance standards. The definition of goals to be achieved by a worker over a specified period of time.

periodic inventory. A physical count of an inventory at the end of each accounting period.

peripheral equipment. The combined input and output units of a computer.

perpetual inventory. A running count of inventory levels.

personal selling. Direct face-to-face encounters between salespeople and potential buyers.

personality test. A test that measures the strengths or weaknesses of personality characteristics that might be important on the job.

PERT (Project Evaluation and Review Technique). A chart developed by a production manager which depicts each activity involved in the completion of a project, the sequencing of these activities, and the time allotted for each activity.

Peter Principle. An informal principle of organizational behavior stating that managerial workers are ultimately promoted to positions for which they are not qualified; that is, in the movement up the organizational hierarchy, workers in time reach their level of incompetence.

physical distribution. The movement of a product from the manufacturer to the final buyer.

picket. The marching back and forth of striking workers in front of the entrances to their workplace, carrying signs listing their grievances which precipitated the strike and their demands.

piece-rate system. A system of compensation in which total wages paid are tied directly to output.

pioneering stage. The first stage of the advertising spiral in which the advertiser introduces the product to the public.

place utility. A measure of the degree to which a product is available where the customer wants it.

placement. The process by which a person is matched to a specific job.

planning. The advance determination of which tasks need to be performed in order to achieve a particular goal.

pledging. The use of accounts receivable as security, or collateral, for short-term financing.

point-of-purchase displays. Visual displays that direct the attention of the buyer to the product.

point-of-sales terminals. Computer terminals used to verify checks, particularly in retail stores.

post trading. A system of stock trading utilized by most exchanges in which each stock traded is assigned to a "post" or trading area.

positioning. The use of advertising to establish in the mind of the consumer an association between the product advertised and an already popular product or type of product.

precedents. Past court decisions which provide guidelines in settling future court controversies.

predicting. See forecasting.

preferred stock. Stock on which dividend payments are stated, and which rank above common stock in the claims of creditors and owners in the event of dissolution of a firm.

prepaid expenses. Expenses paid in advance.

prestige pricing. A demand pricing tactic that refers to the association between quality, higher price, and desirability of purchase.

price. What a seller feels a buyer is willing to pay for a product.

price lining. The practice of pricing products within certain price ranges.

price skimming. The strategy of pricing a new product at an artificially high price.

primary boycott. A union's refusal to patronize a business involved in a dispute with labor.

primary market. The securities markets.

primary storage unit. The part of a central processing unit which serves as the computer's main memory, storing data and program instructions.

prime rate. The minimum interest rate that a bank charges its best customers.

private enterprise. An economic system in which business is free to organize and operate for profit and to function in a competitive system, and in which government intervention is limited to a regulatory role.

privilege pay. A type of nonfinancial reward involving the amount of say an employee has in a management decision.

process departmentalization. The organization of departments on the basis of similar skills.

product demand stimulation. The generation of interest in a product, or the creation of a perceived need for a product.

product demonstration. A promotional device in which an advertiser shows the customer how and how well a certain product works.

product evaluation. The second stage of a new product development system during which company analysts inexpensively and quickly screen new product ideas.

product life cycle. A marketing concept based on the idea that products pass through several stages from the time they are introduced to the market to the time they disappear.

product or service liability. A form of liability insurance that covers damages caused by a product defect, a breach of product warranty, and any danger caused by the use of a product.

production. The process whereby raw materials and other inputs are converted into intermediate or finished goods.

production management. The process of handling and managing all aspects of a production facility.

productivity. Output per worker-hour.

profit. The earnings remaining in a business after its operating costs have been deducted.

profit margin. The difference between a product's cost and its selling price.

profit motive. The incentive to make money.

profit-sharing plan. A bonus plan in which employees are given bonuses if a company's profits increase.

pro forma income statement. An estimate of future sales, expenses, and expected profit; useful for entrepreneurs and lenders in anticipating future cash requirements.

program flowchart. A graph showing the sequence of operations to be performed by a computer.

promissory note. Trade credit in the form of a note drawn up by the buyer, indicating the amount of money owed to the seller and the payment date.

promotion. A job move up. A move up an organizational hierarchy in terms of pay, prestige, benefits, job title, and responsibility.

property damage liability. A type of automobile insurance that pays the cost of damage to another person's property resulting from an automobile accident.

property insurance. An insurance policy that protects a business building and its contents against financial losses caused by fire or other mishap.

protean career. "A process consisting of all a person's varied experiences in education, training, work in several organizations, and changes in occupational field."

prototype. A physical model or a first, custom-made version of a product.

proxy. A right to vote given to the managers of a corporation by a stockholder who cannot vote in person.

public liability. A form of liability insurance that covers the normal forms of business risk, typically the ownership and maintenance of property.

puffery. Innocent exaggerations used to sell a product.

pure risk. The characteristic of situations in which the only possible outcomes are loss or no loss, thus making such situations insurable.

purpose departmentalization. The organization of departments on the basis of similarity of purpose.

purpose or task change. A type of organizational change in which the goal of the organization is changed.

put. An option to sell a specified stock, at a specific price, within a designated period of time.

Q

quality circles. A type of quality improvement program using a committee of workers who analyze and solve problems relating to quality.

quality control. The process of setting manufacturing standards and measuring products against these standards.

quantity discount. A reduction offered on a large order.

quick ratio. See acid-test ratio.

R

rapid growth stage. The second stage of the product life cycle in which sales increase as the market discovers the product's existence.

raw materials. The inputs from which a firm makes its products.

reach. A measure of how many people see or hear an advertisement in a given medium.

real GNP. Gross national product minus the effect of price changes.

realistic job preview. The totality of printed and visual information which a company uses in order to give job recruits an accurate picture of what the job and company are like.

recruiting. The process of finding and putting together a group of job applicants from which to choose.

reorder point. The point in the inventory order cycle at which an order is placed.

reorder quantity. The size of the addition to inventory.

repatriation. The return of profits earned by firms doing business abroad to their countries of origin.

replanning. In production management, the development of new routing, loading, and scheduling.

reserve requirements. The percentage of total demand and time deposits that a bank must hold as cash in a vault or as deposits in the regional Federal Reserve bank.

resume. A written presentation informing a prospective employer of a person's education and employment records, personal, educational and professional honors, and desired career objective.

retail advertising. Advertising performed by retail stores.

retailer. Anyone involved in selling goods to consumers.

retailing. All activity involving firms which sell their products to final consumers for their own use.

retained earnings. The amount of money left at year-end after all expenses, interest payments, taxes, and dividends have been paid.

retentive stage. The third stage of the advertising spiral in which the advertiser attempts to foster brand loyalty.

return. The gain realized on investment.

return on equity. A profitability measure that tells how effective a firm has been in earning money on the invested capital of owners; calculated by dividing net income by total owners' equity.

return on sales. A profitability measure calculated by dividing net income by net sales; represents the amount of profit generated by each dollar of sales.

returns. Products that customers returned to the business and for which they received full refunds.

revolving credit agreement. An agreement between a bank and a borrower under which the bank is obligated to extend funds to the borrower up to a specified credit limit.

risk. In finance, the probability that an issuing firm will not be able to meet its periodic financial obligations over the life of a bond; or in insurance, the uncertainty of loss.

risk reduction. A way of managing pure risk which involves steps taken to reduce or protect against it.

robotics. A field of study concerned with the construction, maintenance, and application of automatically controlled mechanisms to production processes.

role playing. An approach to selection and hiring that calls for job applicants to pretend to be a corporate manager in a problem-solving or decision-making situation so that their abilities can be evaluated.

round lots. Trading units, each of 100 shares of stock.

routing. In production management, the process of determining work flows from one operation to the next.

S

sales contract. A written agreement between two or more parties involving the sale of goods valued at $500 or more.

sales promotion. A form of advertising which makes use of purchase displays, free samples, coupons, gifts, and product demonstrations.

sample. A promotional device, usually free, to introduce a consumer to a new product.

satisfaction. The condition of need fulfillment.

savings and loan associations. Thrift institutions that accept savings deposits from individual savers and businesses and that make primarily home mortgage loans.

Scanlon Plan. A bonus plan in which groups of employees suggest to management how productivity might be improved, and when productivity is up, each worker is rewarded with a bonus.

schedule chart. In production management, a planning diagram indicating when each of a series of job orders is to be performed at each machine, work station, or department.

scheduling. In production management, the process of determining when an operation is to be performed at a machine or work station.

Scientific Management. The first (1911) major research on managing human beings, stressing the importance of finding the best person for a given job and the "one best way" to perform a task.

scoring approach. An approach to evaluation and selection in which each choice alternative is assigned a score, with the alternative with the highest number of points as the one selected.

screening approach. An approach to evaluation and selection in which unsatisfactory choice alternatives are sorted out, leaving only the satisfactory ones for further consideration.

seasonal discount. A price deduction based on the time of year.

secondary boycott. A union's efforts to persuade third parties to stop dealing with a company with which the union is in dispute.

secondary market. All trading of debt or equity securities that takes place between investors.

secondary storage. The extra memory outside the primary storage unit of a computer's central processing unit.

selection. The evaluation of job candidates and choice of the best one for the position available.

selective distribution. A retailing approach whereby a product is made available through several—but not all—retailers in a market.

self-insurance. A way to reduce pure risk which involves putting money aside each month to pay for unexpected losses.

selling expenses. All costs that result directly from a firm's sales efforts.

selling short. A speculative stock trading tactic involving the sale of a stock before its purchase.

seniority. The number of years an employee has spent with the company or organization.

share draft account. An account offered by a credit union which serves the same function as a NOW account.

shareholders. The owners of a firm.

Sherman Act. The first (1890) of the government's antitrust legislation which declared illegal "every contract, combination . . . or conspiracy in restraint of trade or commerce."

shopping goods. Goods that elicit careful consideration of the buyer, as regards price, quality, style, and value, before a decision to purchase is made.

short-term financing. Debts with a maturity date of one year or less.

sinking fund. A savings account at a financial institution into which a bond issuer periodically makes cash payments, enabling the issue to be redeemed in full at its maturity date.

small business. A business independently owned and operated and not dominant in its field of operation.

Small Business Administration (SBA). The principal government agency concerned with the financing, operation, and management of small businesses.

social audit. A step-by-step examination of all the activities comprising the firm's social programs.

social responsibility. Business' concern for the social and economic effects of its decisions.

social security. Required insurance that is provided by the federal government, which includes benefits to the elderly and disability insurance to workers between the ages of 50 and 64.

software. The computer programs and supporting materials for their use.

sole proprietorship. A business owned by one person.

sorting. In data processing, the arranging of a list of numbers into a desired order.

span of control. The number of employees under the direct supervision of a manager.

spatial transformation. A production process involving the movement of goods from one place to another, such as the movement of freight on a railroad from a point of origination to a destination.

specialty fund. A type of mutual fund composed of stock from companies in the same industry.

specialty goods. Goods for which shoppers have a distinct brand preference before the need or the desire for the good arises.

specialty store. A store selling a narrow range of goods and meeting the needs of a well-defined market segment.

speculative risk. The characteristic of a situation in which the possible outcomes are gain or loss.

speculator. A person willing to accept greater risk in the investment market if it means a potentially greater profit.

staff position. A job in an organization that is ancillary to the chain of command and that involves the provision of advice or other specialized services.

staffing. Bringing new people into an organization and ensuring that they serve as valuable additions to the work force.

standard of value. That function of money involving the comparison of the value of objects in terms of their respective worth in dollars.

standardization strategy. The application of the same marketing strategy in each of several foreign markets.

state banks. Commercial banks receiving their operating charters from the states in which they are located.

statistical quality control. A method of monitoring production quality that assumes that flaws in manufacturing systems, not errors by production workers, are the primary cause of quality problems.

status pay. A type of nonfinancial reward involving some status symbol.

statutory law. The legal rules and regulations enacted by legislative bodies, such as the U.S. Congress and the 50 state legislatures.

stock certificate. A written proof of ownership of a share of a company.

stock company. A private insurance company, highly regulated by state insurance agencies and laws, which is organized to provide insurance for policyholders and profit for stockholders.

stock dividend. The distribution of additional shares of stock received, rather than cash, by an investor.

stock exchange. An association of corporations to facilitate the buying and selling of ownership shares in corporations.

stock fund. A type of mutual fund made up of equity securities.

stock market indicators. Indexes of the performance of the stock market; used by investors to evaluate the performance of particular stocks against the market; examples include the Dow Jones Industrial Average, Standard & Poor's 500 Index, the NYSE Composite Index, and the ASE Market Value Index.

stock split. The distribution of one or more new shares of stock for every share currently held.

stockbroker. The person who initiates the buying or selling of a stock by wiring an investor's instructions to a commission broker on the floor of an exchange.

stockout costs. The expenses incurred when a firm runs out of inventory.

stop order. A type of stock order that instructs the commission broker to protect a stock price gain or to minimize a price loss.

storage media. The "machine readable" form on which data and programs are stored for the purpose of computer processing at a later time.

store of value. The measure of the savings function of money.

straight life insurance. A form of whole life insurance in which the policyholder pays premiums for life.

stress. A feeling of strain or pressure.

strike. A work stoppage called by workers.

structural change. A type of organizational change involving an alteration of the firm's formal authority structure or its job definitions.

subordinated debentures. Unsecured bonds, the claims of which are subordinated to those of other debenture issues in the event of the issuer's default.

success chess. Eugene Jennings' nine rules designed to help people manage their careers.

supermarkets. Large food stores offering a broad selection of brands and product sizes.

supply. The quantity of a product a firm or industry is willing to produce at a specified price.

synthetic transformation. A type of production process by which basic parts, components, or chemicals are combined to form a finished product.

T

target market share. A pricing objective according to which prices are set so as to achieve a specified share of the market for a good.

target return on investment. A pricing objective according to which prices are set so as to achieve a specified, or target, yield on investment.

target segments. Smaller markets within the overall market to which businesses direct their selling efforts.

tax controls. The imposition of taxes on the goods or services imported by a country as a means of protecting its home industries from foreign competition.

technological change. A type of organizational change resulting from the introduction of new production processes and equipment.

temporal transformation. A production process involving the storage of goods, such as rented warehouse space.

term life insurance. Life insurance that has no cash value upon expiration of the policy.

terms of trade. The short-term financing conditions given by a seller to a buyer.

test marketing. The fifth stage in the new product development process, during which the marketing research staff evaluates the product.

Theory X. A theory of management that regards people as lazy and self-indulgent, as requiring constant supervision, and as working only because they get paid.

Theory Y. A theory of management that regards workers as responsible individuals who like their work and who want intrinsic rewards.

time deposit. A savings account at a financial institution stipulating the minimum amount of time that money must be left in the account if an interest penalty is to be avoided.

time-sharing. In data processing, the hook-up of many different terminals to the same main computer.

time utility. A measure of the degree to which a

product is available when the buyer wants it.

trade acceptance. A form of trade credit, drawn up by the seller and signed by the buyer, which indicates the amount of money owed and the repayment date.

trade advertising. Informative, detailed advertising whose purpose is to communicate with members of the channels of distribution, including wholesalers and retailers.

trade balance. The difference between a nation's total exports and its total imports.

trade credit. Supplier financing of a purchase by giving the buyer 30 days or more to pay.

trade deficit. A negative trade balance.

trade surplus. A positive trade balance.

trademark. A brand granted legal protection so that it cannot be used by anyone else.

transaction loan. Credit extended by a bank for a specific purpose.

treasury stock. Shares of common stock which have been repurchased by the issuing corporation.

Truth-in-Lending Act. Legislation empowering the Federal Reserve Board to specify how interest rates on consumer purchases are to be calculated and reported to the consumer.

turbulence stage. The third stage in the product life cycle in which competition stiffens, and product sales increase at a slower rate than before.

tying agreement. An illegal trade agreement between a buyer and a seller in which the seller agrees to sell a product on the condition that the buyer also purchases other merchandise from the seller.

U

uncontrollable variables. Uncertain political, social, and economic forces affecting the business environment but over which business firms have no control.

Uniform Commercial Code. A comprehensive set of business laws governing commercial transactions so as to achieve uniformity of business law among the various jurisdictions in the United States.

uniform-delivered pricing. A geographic pricing approach whereby the seller charges its customers the same delivered price regardless of where the customers are located or how much it costs to ship the merchandise.

uninsured motorist coverage. A type of automobile insurance that pays the car owner and any family member for medical expenses resulting from an accident caused by an uninsured motorist or by a hit-and-run driver.

union steward. A member of a local union who represents the local in a plant.

universal life insurance. Life insurance designed to give the buyer the protection of term insurance and the opportunity to earn a high yield on funds invested with the insurance company.

unlimited liability. Liability under which all business and personal assets are subject to the claims of creditors.

V

validity. A term for describing the effectiveness of a test—specifically, whether the test in fact measures what it was designed to measure.

value added. The sales dollar value of output minus the cost of all raw materials and semifinished inputs bought from other manufacturers.

value analysis. In materials purchasing, the systematic appraisal of a purchase requisition.

variable costs. Costs varying with the level of production or sales of a product.

vertical merger. A business combination in which one company buys another that is in the same industry but that performs a different production or distribution activity.

visual display terminal. In computer processing, a form of peripheral equipment that uses a screen, or cathode ray tube, and which permits the input of data to the computer and/or the output of information to the user.

voting rights. The rights of common stockholders to participate in certain corporate decisions or elections.

W

whistleblowers. Employees who report to the press or other organization any illegal activity occurring within their firms.

whole life insurance. A form of life insurance that gives lifetime protection to the insured person.

wholesaler. Any firm that helps a manufacturer sell its products to other businesses (usually to retailers) for eventual resale to final consumers.

wholesaling. The entirety of marketing activities of firms selling to retailers, industrial firms, and all other commercial users.

work in process. Products that need to move through one or more stages in the manufacturing process.

work sample test. In selection and hiring, a test measuring how well applicants perform selected job tasks.

workers' compensation. Insurance that protects employees from financial losses due to job-related accidents and illnesses.

Z

zone-delivered pricing. A geographic pricing approach whereby the seller assigns each customer to a geographic zone and charges the customers within each zone the same delivered price for the good.

INDEX

A

ability test, 160
acceptance of contract, 101
accountant, role of, 403
accounting:
   private, 403-404
   public, 403
   users of, 404
accounting, as key business activity, 4
accounting, concepts of:
   accounting equation, 404-405
   double-entry bookkeeping, 405-406
accounting equation, 404-405
accounts payable, 316, 409
accounts receivable, 320, 406
accrued expense, 409
acid-test, 418
acquisition, of business, 72
acts:
   Age and Discrimination Act of 1978, 51
   Child Protection and Toy Safety Act (1969), 109
   Cigarette Labeling Act (1966), 109
   Civil Rights Act of 1964, 111
   Civil Service Reform Act, Title VII (1978), 181
   Clayton Act (1914), 104
   Clean Air Act (1970), 31
   Consumer Credit Protection Act (1968), 109
   Consumer Education Act (1978), 109
   Consumer Product Safety Act (1972), 109
   Depository Institutions Deregulation and Monetary Control Act of 1980, 326
   Equal Employment Act of 1972, 111
   Equal Pay Act, 113-114
   Fair Labor Standards Act (1938), 106-107
   Fair Packaging and Labeling Act (1966), 109
   Federal Trade Commission Act (1914), 104, 109
   Federal Water Pollution Control Act (1972), 31
   Flammable Fabrics Act (1953), 109
   Food and Drug Act (1906), 109
   Foreign Corrupt Practices Act of 1977, 55
   Garn-St. Germain Depository Institutions Act, 326
   Landrum-Griffin Act (1959), 181
   Magnuson-Moss Warranty/Federal Trade Commission Improvement Act (1975), 109
   National Environmental Policy Act (1969), 31
   Norris-LaGuardia Act (1932), 181
   Sherman Act (1890), 104
   Small Business Act of 1953, 80
   Social Security Act (1935), 107
   Taft-Hartley Act (1947), 181
   Truth-in-Lending Act (1969), 105
   Wagner Act (1935), 181
   Wheeler-Lea Act (1938), 109
   Whistleblowers' Protection Act, 57-58
administrative expense, 413
administrative law, 100-101
advertising:
   corrective, 106
   defined, 290
   industrial, 293
   leading national advertisers, 1981, 290
   measuring effectiveness of, 300-301
   national, 296-297
   objectives of, 293
   and the product life cycle, 297-300
   puffery, 105
   retail, 296
   spiral of, 297-300
   trade, 293; illus., 296
advertising, newspaper, as source of job applicants, 157
advertising spiral:
   competitive stage, 299
   defined, 297
   pioneering stage, 299
   retentive stage, 299
affirmative action, 114
age, as basis for discrimination, 113
age, change in, 37
Age and Discrimination Act of 1978, 51
agency shop, 176
Agency's Management Assistance Program, of SBA, 86
agreement, of contract, 101
airlines, as carriers of goods, 265
air pollutant emissions, by source, illus., 32
allowances, 411
Aluminum Company of America (ALCOA), case study of, 115-116
American Federation of Labor-Congress of Industrial Organizations (AFL-CIO), 180
American Institute of Certified Public Accountants, 403
American Stock Exchange (AMEX), 361
analog computer, 435
analystic transformation, 196
annual report, how to read an, 420-421
applicant, sources of, 157-158
application blank, 158-159
approach, in sales, 304
arbitration, 186
arithmetic/logic unit, 436
articles of partnership, 67
artificial intelligence, 445
ASE Market Value Index, 374
assessment center, 163
asset:
   current, 406-409
   defined, 404
   fixed, 409
   intangible, 409
Atari, case study of, 250-251
authorization card, 180

authorized share, of common stock, 347
automated clearing-house, 442
automated teller machines (ATMs), 442
automation, 197

B

balance sheet:
    assets, 406-409
    defined, 406
    liabilities, 409-411
    owner's equity, 411
banker's blanket bond, 388
bank failure, during Great Depression, 19
bankruptcy, 113
bankruptcy, as basic freedom, 10
Banquet Foods Corporation, case study of, 153-154
bar chart, 457; illus., 458
bargaining unit, 181-182
BASIC (Beginners All-Purpose Symbolic Instruction Code), 438
basic industry, 489
batch processing, 436
behavioral approach, of appraising performance, 167
benefit segmentation, 229
binary system, 438
bioengineering, 494
bits, 438
blanket bond, 390
board of directors, in corporation, 70
Board of Governors, of the Federal Reserve System, 327
bodily injury liability, 387
bond, 337
bond, classification of:
    debentures, 338
    income, 341-342
    industrial development, 342-343
    mortgage, 341
    subordinated debenture, 338
bond, published ratings of, 344
bond, repayment and retirement of:
    callable bond, 343
    convertible bond, 343-344
    sinking fund, 344
bond, risk and return of, 344
bond fund, 371
bond indenture, 338
bonds payable, 411
boycott, by labor, 187
brand, 240
branding, of products:
    characteristics of a good brand name, 242-243

family brands vs. individual brands, 242
    new product sales, 240
    repeat sales, 240
break-even analysis, 273
break-even point, 274
Budweiser, case study of, 231-232
business:
    defined, 3
    key activities of, 3-5
    new morality for, 33
    new product opportunities, 33
    objectives of, 5-9
    pollution control expenditures, 32
    project delays, 33
    small, 80
business, changing environment of:
    age mix, 486
    family size and income, 486
    global population and income trends, 487-488
    U.S. population trend, 486
business, small:
    advantages, 84
    buying, 85-87
    characteristics of, 80
    defined, 80
    disadvantages, 84-85
    as employer, 81
    federal loans to, 80
    franchising, 91-95
    by industry, illus., 81
    reasons for failure, 85
    share of GNP, 80
    as source of new ideas, 81
    sources of capital, illus., 89
    starting, 87-91
    types of, 81-84
business ethics:
    code of, 55-56
    defined, 55
    demand for, 55
    encouragement of, 57
    Gulf Oil Statement of, 57
    whistleblowers, 57
business-interruption expense, 390
buying goods, as key business activity, 4
buying on the margin, 368
buying services, as key business activity, 4
bytes, 438

C

call, 369
callable bond, 343
call price, of bond, 343
Camps, Frank, 57
canned program, 438-440

capital, 335
capital structure, 351
career, 501
career, stages of, 512-513
career cluster, 505-506; illus., 508
career information, sources of, 523-524
career objective, 508
Caribbean Free Trade Association (CARIFTA), 480
case law, 100
case study, 452
cash, 406
cash discount, 278
cathode ray tube (CRT), 436
cease and desist order, 104
census, 453
Central American Common Market (CACM), 480
central processing unit (CPU), 436
certificates of deposit, 325
Certified Internal Auditor (CIA), 404
Certified Public Accountant (CPA), 403
Cessna Aircraft Company, case study of, 376-377
chain, of retail stores, 261
channel of distribution, 219
chart, 456
check, 323
checking account, 324
checkoff, of union dues, 182
child labor, 107
Child Protection and Toy Safety Act (1969), 109
Cigarette Labeling Act (1966), 109
circle chart, 456
Civil Aeronautics Board, 101
Civil Rights Act of 1964, 111
Civil Service Reform Act, Title VII (1978), 181
classical organizational design, 127
classical view, of business, 47
classifying, 443
Clayton Act (1914), 104
Clean Air Act (1970), 31
closed-end trust, 370
closed shop, 176
closely held corporation, 69
COBOL (COmmon Business-Oriented Language), 438
code of ethics, 55-56
cold calls, in sales, 303
collating, 443
collective bargaining:
    compensation, 182
    defined, 182
    fringe benefits, 182
    give-and-take of contract, 184
    hours of work, 182-184
    job security, 182

management rights, 182
negotiation, 185
prenegotiation, 185
quality of work life, 184
safety and health, 184
union security, 182
collision insurance, 387
commercial banking:
 money, 322-324
 national banks, 321
 state banks, 321
 twenty largest U.S. commercial banks, illus., 322
 types of accounts, 324-325
commercialization, of new product, 247
commercial paper, 318
commission, in sales, 302
commission broker, 363
common law, 100
common market, 478-480
common stock:
 authorized shares, 347
 defined, 344
 income right, 346
 issued shares, 347
 limited liability, 345-346
 market value of, 347
 maturity, 346
 outstanding share, 347
 par value of, 347
 stock dividend, 348
 stock split, 348-349
 treasury stock, 347
 voting rights, 346
communication, in marketing mix, 220
communication strategy, developing a:
 communication program analysis, 289-290
 positioning analysis, 289
 product analysis, 289
community, responsibility of business to, 51
comparative analysis, 417
compensation of employees:
 under collective bargaining agreements, 182
 job analysis, 168
 job description, 168
 labor market conditions, 168
 pay systems, 168-171
competition:
 monopolistic, 11
 monopoly, 14
 oligopoly, 12
 perfect, 11
competition, regulation of:
 Clayton Act (1914), 104
 Federal Trade Commission Act (1914), 104

Sherman Act (1890), 104
competitive parity, 52
competitive stage, of the advertising spiral, 299
compiler, 438
comprehensive insurance, 387
computation, 443
computer:
 advantages of, 435
 analog, 435
 defined, 432
 digital, 435
 Electronic Numerical Integrator and Calculator (ENIAC), 435
 human reactions to, 446
 invasion of privacy by, 445
 malfunctions of, 445
 in manufacturing, 197
 microcomputer, 436
 microprocessor, 435
 minicomputer, 436
computer, business applications of:
 computer assisted design, 441
 computer controlled production, 441
 data processing, 443
 electronic funds transfer (EFT), 442
 financial simulation, 442
 material requirements planning, 441
 on-site computers, 442
 sales analysis, 441
 sales forecasting, 441
 securities trading, 442
 word processing, 442-443
computer assisted design (CAD), 441
computer courses, case study of, 447-448
computer crime, 445
computer hardware:
 defined, 436
 input units, 436
 output unit, 437
 processing unit, 436
 secondary storage, 437
computer program:
 BASIC, 438
 canned (or packaged) program, 438-440
 COBOL, 438
 defined, 437
 FORTRAN, 438
 machine language, 438
computer software:
 computer program, 437-440
 defined, 437
 documentation, 440-441
 program flowchart, 437

computers on the New York Stock Exchange, case study of, 448-449
congeneric merger, 74
conglomerate merger, 75
consideration, in contract, 102
constrainer, 48
consumer, interest in social responsibility of business, 49
Consumer Credit Protection Act (1968), 109
Consumer Education Act (1978), 109
consumerism, 42, 49
consumer price, change in, 27-28
consumer price index (CPI), 24
consumer price index, percentage change in, illus., 25
consumer product, 235
Consumer Product Safety Act (1972), 109
Consumer Product Safety Commission, 42, 101
consumer sovereignty, 18
continuous manufacturing, 196
contract:
 acceptance, 101
 agreement, 101
 capacity, 101-102
 consideration, 102
 defined, 101
 elements of, 101-102
 fraud and duress, 102
 legality, 102
 offer, 101
 written and oral, 102-103
contract administration, 186
contractual capacity, 101-102
control chart, in quality control, 207
Control Data Corp. (CDC), case study of, 154
controlling, as function of management, 130-131
control unit, 436
convenience good, 235
convenience store, 261
convertible bond, 343-344
convertible term life insurance, 397
Cooling-Off Rule (1974), 105
cooperative, 73
corporation:
 advantages of, 70-72
 closely held, 69
 defined, 69
 disadvantages of, 72
 features of, 69
 five largest in U.S. according to 1981 sales, 69
 publicly held, 69
 structure of, 70

corrective action, in production, 203
corrective advertising, 106
corrective maintenance, 208
correlation, 453
cost of goods sold, 411
cost of inventory, 199
cost-of-living adjustments (COLAs), 182
cost-plus pricing, 273
cost pricing:
   break-even analysis, 273-274
   cost-plus pricing, 273
   markup pricing, 273
Council for Mutual Assistance (COMECON), 479
coupon, as sales promotion, 305
credit extension, as key business activity, 5
credit union, 326-327
critical path, 204
culture, 469
cumulative preferred stock, 349
current asset, 406-409
current liability, 409-410
current ratio, 418
cycle, 456

D

data processing, 443
debenture, 338
debt capital, 336
debt to net worth ratio, 419
decision making, managerial:
   difficulties in, 131
   stages of, 131-133; illus., 132
Decker Hotel, case study of, 44
decline stage, of product life cycle, 239
definite and measurable risk, 380
demand, as related to price determination, 11
demand deposit, 323
demander, 48
demand flow of information, 429
demand pricing:
   demand curve, 275
   differential pricing, 276
   prestige pricing, 275-276
demographic segmentation:
   age, 225
   ethnic background, 225
   income, 224
demography:
   age, 37
   declining fertility rates, 37-38
   defined, 33
   employment, 34
   population changes, 34
   relevance of changes, 38-39
   shifts in, 33-39

demotion, of employees, 164
departmentalization:
   defined, 123
   matrix, 124
   process, 123-124
   purpose, 124
department store, 261-262
Depository Institutions Deregulation and Monetary Control Act of 1980, 326
depreciation, 409
descriptive statistics:
   defined, 454
   frequency distribution, 454-455
   measures of change over time, 455
   measures of dispersion, 455
   measures of location, 454
differential pricing, 276
digital computer, 435
direct cost, 283
directing, as function of management, 130
direct loan, 86
disability-income insurance, 391
discount, 277
discount broker, 367
discount rate, 329-330
discount store, 262
discrimination, in employment:
   affirmative action, 114
   Equal Pay Act, 113-114
   fairness in testing, 113
   major provisions against, 111-112
   Equal Employment Opportunity Commission (EEOC), 111
   Equal Employment Act of 1972, 111
   Civil Rights Act of 1964, 111
dispatching, in production, 203
dispute between labor and management:
   arbitration, 186
   contract administration, 186
   mediation, 186
   negotiating behaviors, illus., 185
   strike outcome, 186
distribution, channels of:
   defined, 253
   functions of, 254
   intermediaries, 254-256
   kinds of, 253-254
distribution, in marketing mix, 219
dividend, 346
division of labor, 123
diversification, 359
documentation, 440
double-entry bookkeeping, 405-406

double taxation, 72
Dow Jones Industrial Average, 372-373
dumping, 478
duress, 102

E

earnings per share, 419-420
economic analysis of new product, 246
economic community, 477
Economic Order Quantity (EOQ), 200
editing, 443
educational institution, as source of job applicants, 158
electronic funds transfer (EFT), 442
employee, compensation of, 167-171
employee, impact of labor union on, 177
employee, protection of:
   child labor, 107
   discrimination, 111-114
   Fair Labor Standards Act (1938), 106-107
   Occupational Safety and Health Administration, 106, 108-111
   social security, 107
   unemployment benefits, 107-108
employee insurance:
   disability-income, 391
   fidelity bonds, 390
   health, 391
   workers' compensation, 391
employee interest in social responsibility of business, 49
employee purchase of companies, 189
employer, small business as, 81
employment opportunities:
   career clusters, 505-506
   information sources, 506-507
endowment insurance, 393
energy:
   conservation of, 30
   crisis of 1973-74, 28
   crisis of 1979, 28
   demand of, 29
   impacts of scarcity, 31
   supply of, 29
Environmental Protection Agency (EPA), 31, 101
Equal Employment Act of 1972, 111
Equal Employment Opportunity Commission (EEOC), 111
Equal Pay Act, 113-114

equity, 404
equity capital, 336
European Economic Community (EEOC), 478-480
European Free Trade Association (EFTA), 480
exchange function in macromarketing, 218
exclusion of property in bankruptcy, 113
exclusive distribution, 263
expansion of business:
  external, 72
  internal, 72
expectancy theory of motivation, 143
export, 465
express warranty, 103
expropriation without reimbursement, 467
external auditor, 403
external expansion, 72
extinction of behavior, 142
extra-expense insurance, 390
extrinsic rewards of employee, 143

F

factor, 321
factoring accounts receivable, 321
Fair Labor Standards Act (1938), 106-107
Fair Packaging and Labeling Act (1966), 109
family brand, 242
Federal Communication Commission, 101
Federal Crime Insurance (1970), 382
Federal Crop Insurance Corporation (1938), 382
Federal Deposit Insurance Corporation (FDIC), 321
federal environmental laws, restricting use of private property, 9
Federal Flood Insurance (1968), 382
Federal Home Mortgage Loan Insurance (1934), 382
Federal Mediation and Conciliation Service, 181, 186
Federal Reserve Board, 101
Federal Reserve System:
  check-clearing, 330
  controlling the money supply, 327
  discount rate, 329-330
  open market operations, 328-329
  reserve requirements, 327
  structure of, 327
Federal Trade Commission, 100-101, 104
Federal Trade Commission Act (1914), 104, 109
Federal Water Pollution Control Act (1972), 31
federation of labor unions, 180
fertility rates, change in, 37
fidelity bond, 390
financial leverage, 342
financial manager, 313
financial statements, interpreting, 416-423
finished good, 409
Firestone Tires, case study of, 249-250
first-in, first-out (FIFO), method of inventory valuation, 416
fixed asset, 336, 409
fixed cost, 273
fixed price, 271
Flammable Fabrics Act (1953), 109
flextime, as motivation, 150
FOB-destination pricing, 282
FOB-factory pricing, 282
follow-up, 203
Food and Drug Act (1906), 109
Ford Foundation, case study of, 59
foreboder, 48
forecasting, 485
Foreign Corrupt Practices Act of 1977, 55
foreign market, entering the:
  exporting, 470
  joint venture, 472
  licensing, 470
  local marketing subsidiary, 472
  total ownership, 472-473
form transformation, 196
FORTRAN (FORmula TRANslator), 438
franchising:
  company-owned systems, 94-95
  defined, 92
  franchisee, 92
  franchisor, 92
  fraudulent practices of, 95
  pros and cons of, 93-94
franchisee, 92, 93-94
franchisor, 92, 93
fraud, 102
freedoms, basic, in U.S.:
  bankruptcy, 10
  private property, 9
  profits, 9
free market system, 9
frequency distribution, 454
frequency in advertising, 301
fringe benefit, 182
full-service merchant wholesaler, 258
full-service broker, 367

G

Gala Cosmetics, Inc., case study of, 173-174
Galbraith, John Kenneth, 477
Gantt chart, 203; illus., 204
Garn-St. Germain Depository Institutions Act, 326
genentech, case study of, 355-356
General Electric, case study of, 355-356
General Motors work rules, case study of, 191-192
general overhead, 413
generic product, 260
genetic revolution in agriculture, case study of, 498
geographic pricing:
  FOB-destination, 282
  FOB-factory, 282
  uniform-delivered, 282
  zone-delivered, 283
geographic segmentation, 225-227
Ghiselli Self Description Inventory, 160
gift, as sales promotion, 306
giveback, 182
Global Marine, Inc., case study of, 45
goods available for sale, 413
governmental limitations on private ownership, 9
graph, 456
grease payment, 476
Great Depression, 19
grievance procedure, 186
Grinberg Telecommunictions Systems, Inc., case study of, 333-334
gross margin, 264
gross national product (GNP), 3; illus, 15
gross national product (GNP), share of small business, 80
gross profit, 413
gross sales, 411
growth fund, 371
guaranty loan, 86
Gulf Oil, Statement of Basic Business Principles, 57

H

handicapped, discrimination against, 113

558 Index

handicapped, responsibility of business to, 51
hardware, of computer, 436
health insurance, 391
hierarchy of authority, 122-123
hiring employees, as key business activity, 3
hiring of job candidates, 158
holding costs, 199
horizontal merger, 74
housing costs, as related to inflation, 26
how executives see women in management, case study of, 516-517
human change in organization, 134
hypermarket, 262

I

idea generation of new product, 245
illustrations:
 accounting information, need for, 405
 advertising and the product life cycle, 299
 age distribution of U.S. population, 1980-2000, 227
 application, letter of, 511
 AT&T profits and dividends, 1970-1982, 338
 automobile information network, 218
 backward-bending demand curve associated with prestige pricing, 276
 banks create money, 325
 BASIC program to compute weekly pay, 440
 "Big Eight" accounting firms, 403
 bond certificate, 338
 bond interest rates, 1960-1982, 346
 break-even analysis, 275
 business, key activities of, 4
 business, 12 steps for starting a new, 88
 business activities and short-term money needs for a Christmas card manufacturer, 313
 business literature, 451-452
 capital for entrepreneurs, sources of, 89
 career clusters, 508
 check, collection of, 330
 commercial paper outstanding, 1970-1982, 318
 communication strategies, developing, 289

computer assisted design, 441
computer hardware components, 436
consumer price index, percentage change in, 25
consumer prices around the world, change in, 28
contract, give-and-take of, 184
control chart, 207
convenience, shopping, and specialty goods, 236
corporate bonds, highly rated, 346
corporation structure, 70
correlation, 453
crime, statistics of, 388
daily trading volume of New York Stock Exchange, 361
decision process, steps in, 132
departmentalization by function, 124
departmentalization by purpose, 125
differential pricing, 277
dividends per share of IBM, 1970-1982, 360
Dow Jones Industrial Average, 372
economic growth and decline, 493
employees and positions, matching, 156
employment growth by industry, 507
energy demanded, 29
energy supplies, sources of future, 30
exchanges in decentralized and centralized markets, 219
explanation of a stock quotation as reported daily in The Wall Street Journal, 364
failure of new products, causes of, 248
federal agencies, 101
Federal Reserve controls the economy, 329
Federal Reserve System, 328
fertility rates, by age of mother, 1950-1979, 38
fixed and variable costs, 273
flowchart for computing weekly pay, 439
freight transportation costs, 265
Gantt chart, 204
generic products, 262
gross national product, 15
growth rates in population, 1978-2000, 35
high technology, four growth areas in, 494
housing costs, 1969-1981, 26

information flows in the channel of distribution, 256
input media and devices, 437
insurance, types of, 386
international trade, barriers to, 467
interregional migration, 34
inventory levels, 200
inventory valuation, 417
job description, 169
largest life insurance companies, 1981, 392
largest retailing companies ranked by sales, 261
largest U.S. commercial banks, 322
largest U.S. corporations ranked in terms of number of employees, 5
life insurance programs, comparisons of, 395
long-term money, sources and uses of, 337
management information system, 431
management, levels of, 121
management process, 131
managing by objectives, 151
marketing mix for automobile batteries and men's shaving cream, 220
marketing variables, interaction of, 220
market structures, differences among, 12
markup calculation, 273
Maslow's need hierarchy, 141
matrix organization structure, 127
MBO program, possible objectives in, 151
median family income, 15
mental ability test items, 161
microelectronics, coming impact of, 496
MIS, basic meaning of, 430
MIS objectives, 432
MIS subsystems, objectives of, 432
money supply movement, 1974-1982, 324
name advertising, 301
nation's output, changing composition of, 1950-1980, 17
negotiating behaviors, 185
new product, ways it is "new", 243
new product development process, 246
no-fault automobile insurance states, 387
NOW accounts, growth of, 326

Index

obsolete products and their replacements, 223
open market transactions, 329
organization chart, 123
orientation program characteristics and cautions, 164
ownership, other forms of, 73
partnership agreement, provisions of, 68
per capita gross national product by region, 1975-2000, 489
percentage of men and women more than 16 years of age employed in the U.S., 39
PERT chart, 205
posted price per barrel (of oil) in dollars, Jan. 1 of year, 1970-1981, 28
preemployment inquiries, unfair, 159
price skimming, 281
pricing objectives of ten large firms, 272
production management trade-offs, 199
product life cycle, 238
profit, as percentages of GNP, sales, and return on investment, 4
recessions and the rate of business failures, 1920-1976, 84
resume, 510
sales process, 303
sales promotion advertisement, 305
sampling, 453
selling products in foreign countries, 470
short-term interest rates, 1950-1982, 317
small business by industry, 81
software and supporting hardware, 438
span of control, 129
staffing mix, balancing the, 157
Standard & Poor's and Moody's bond ratings, 345
steelworkers' union, structure of, 178
stock prices for Ford, General Motors, and Chrysler, 1970-1982, 361
stocks, buying and selling of, 364
stressful jobs (most and least), 147
Texas Tile balance sheet, 408
total value of assets held by mutual funds and sales of mutual funds, 1971-1980, 371
transformation process, 195
two-for-one stock split, 349
union security, forms of, 176
U.S. population growth, 1950-2050, 486
U.S. trade balance, 1960-1980, 465
voluntary federal insurance programs, 382
wage determination process, 170
whole life insurance, types of, 394
world's population, 1975-2000, 488
implied warranty, 104
import, 465
in basket, 163
income, as employees' business objective, 7
income bond, 341-342
income right of common stock, 346
income statement:
    cost of goods sold, 411
    defined, 411
    federal income taxes, 414
    gross profit, 413
    gross sales, 411
    income from operations, 414
    net income after taxes, 415
    net income before taxes, 414
    net sales, 411
    operating expenses, 413-414
    operating income, 414
    other expenses, 414
    other income, 414
income tax payable, 411
independence, as owners' business objective, 6
index numbers, 456
indirect cost, 283
individual fidelity bond, 390
industrial advertising, 293
industrial development bond, 342-343
industrial product, 236-237
industry, trends of:
    basic industries, 489-490
    ten declining U.S. industries, 490
    ten growing U.S. industries, 490
    high technology industries, 493
inflation:
    defined, 24
    causes of, 24-25
    in post-World-War-II America, 24
    responses to, 26
    worldwide, 26
inflationary expectations, 24-25
information, 429
information function in macro-marketing, 217
infrastructure, 469
injunction, 188
inland waterways as carriers of goods, 266
input unit, 436
inspection, in quality control, 205
Institute of Internal Auditors, 404
institutional advertising, 293; illus., 295
insurable interest, 381
insurance:
    automobile, 387
    defined, 380
    employer, 390-391
    liability, 388-390
    life, 391-395
    loss-of-earning power, 390
    property, 385-388
insurance, principles of:
    accidental loss, 380
    definite and measurable risk, 380
    insurable interests, 381
    law of large numbers, 380
    loss not subject to catastrophic hazard, 381
insurance, sources of:
    federal government, 381-384
    private insurance companies, 384-385
intangible asset, 409
intensive distribution, 263
interest rate, 317
interest rate ceiling, 325
interest test, 160
intermediary, in distribution channels, 254-256
Interminco, case study of, 397-398
intermittent manufacturing, 196
internal auditor, 403
internal expansion, 72
Internal Revenue Service, 101
international business:
    foreign investment, 465
    U.S. trade deficits, 465
international economic community:
    defined, 477
    European Economic Community (EEC), 478-480
    pro and con, 480
International Futures Exchange (Intex), 442
internationalization, of economy, 18
international marketing strategy:
    advantages of standardization, 473-474
    disadvantages of standardization, 475
    when to standardize, 475

international trade, barriers to:
  cultural factors, 469
  economic conditions, 469
  planning problems, 466-467
  political instability, 467
  tax controls, 467
interview, 159
intrinsic reward, of employee, 143
inventory, control of:
  costs, 199
  Economic Order Quantity (EOQ), 200
  Kanban approach, 200
  keeping track of, 200
  levels of; illus., 200
  materials requirement planning (MRP), 202
  reorder point, 199
  reorder quantity, 199
inventory, valuation of:
  first-in, first-out (FIFO), 416
  last-in, first-out (LIFO), 416
  problem of, 415-416
inventory financing, 320
inventory function in macromarketing, 218
inventory-turnover ratio, 419
investment bank, 358
investor, 336
involuntary bankruptcy, 113
issued share, of common stock, 347

J

Jan Stuart Natural Skin Care for Men, case study of, 96-97
job, dissatisfaction with:
  inferior products, 147
  stress, 146
job analysis, 168
job choice, stages of, 502
job description, 168; illus., 169
job enrichment, as motivation, 149-150
job evaluation, 168
job interview, preparing for, 510-511
job preview, realistic, 158
job search, planning the, 507
job security, 182
job specification, 168
job shop, 196
jobs:
  in accounting, 520-521
  in finance, banking, and insurance, 518-519
  in human resource management, 521-522
  in information management, computers, and statistics, 522

  in management, 518
  in marketing, 519-520
  in production management, 521
John Deere, case study of, 268
joint venture, 73, 472

K

Kanban approach, in inventory control, 200
Kuder Vocational Preference Record, 160

L

labor, division of, 123
labor, negotiating strength of:
  boycott, 187
  picket, 187
  political influence, 187
  strike, 187
labor law:
  Civil Service Reform Act, Title VII (1978), 181
  Landrum-Griffin Act (1959), 181
  Norris-LaGuardia Act (1932), 181
  Taft-Hartley Act (1947), 181
  Wagner Act (1935), 181
labor market condition, as related to employee compensation, 168
labor union:
  defined, 176
  forms of union security, illus., 176
  ten largest, illus., 177
  organizing, 180-182
  role in economy, 176-177
  source of job applicants, 158
  structure, 177-180
labor union, structure of:
  federation, 180
  local, 180
  national, 177-180
Landrum-Griffin Act (1959), 181
last-in, first-out (LIFO), method of inventory valuation, 416
Latin American Integration Association (LAIA), 480
law:
  administrative, 100-101
  defined, 100
  common, 100
  statutory, 100
law of effect, in learning theory, 142
law of large numbers, 380
lead time, in ordering, 199

learning theory, of motivation, 142-143
legality of contract, 102
less-developed country (LDC), 487
letter of application, 508-509
letter of recommendation, 509-510
leverage, 342
liability:
  current, 409-411
  defined, 404, 409
  long-term, 411
liability insurance:
  product or service, 388
  public, 388
licensing, in foreign markets, 470
life insurance:
  endowment, 393
  evaluation of, 394
  term, 392
  types of whole life, illus., 394
  universal, 393-394
  whole, 392-393
limited liability, 10, 72, 345-346
limited-life policy, 393
limited partnership, 73
limited-service merchant wholesaler, 258
limit order, 364
line chart, 457; illus., 458
line of credit, 316-317
line position in organization, 125
liquidity, 359
list price, 277
load chart, 202
load fund, 370-371
loading, 202
local marketing subsidiary, 472
local union, labor, 180
lockout, by management, 188
Loeb & Company, Inc. v. Schreiner, case study of, 116
long-term debt, 313
long-term financing:
  bonds, 337-344
  common stock, 344-349
  defined, 335
  preferred stock, 349-350
  retained earnings, 336-337
  sources of, 336
  sources of funds, pros and cons of, 351
  uses of, 336
long-term liability, 411
long wave theory, 493
loss-of-earning power insurance:
  business-interruption, 390
  extra-expense, 390
  rain, 390
loss leader, 278
Louisville, Kentucky, case study of, 192-193
Lubella Furniture Company, case study of, 210-211

Index 561

M

machine language, 438
macromarketing:
   defined, 217
   exchange function, 218
   information function, 217
   inventory function, 218
Magnuson-Moss Warranty/Federal Trade Commission Improvement Act (1975), 109
maintenance-of-membership shop, 176
maintenance policy, 208
management:
   defined, 121
   impact of labor union on, 177
   levels of, illus., 121
   lower level of, 122
   middle level of, 122
   top level of, 121
management, negotiating strengths of:
   agreements and organizations, 188
   business as usual, 188
   employee relations programs, 188-189
   injunction, 188
   lockout, 188
Management By Objectives (MBO):
   appraising performances, 151
   defined, 150
   evaluation of, 151; illus., 151
   planning strategies, 151
   setting new strategies, 151
   setting objectives, 150
Management Information System (MIS):
   components of, 429
   defined, 429
   design of, 429-431
management process, 129; illus., 131
management-rights clause, 182
management science, 197
manager, function of:
   controlling, 130-131
   directing, 130
   management process, 129
   organizing, 129-130
   planning, 129
   staffing, 130
manufacturer-owned wholesaler, 258
manufacturing, characteristics of:
   computers and mathematical models, 197
   mechanization, 196
   transformation process, 195-196

Manville Corporation, case study of, 60
markdown, 278
market, 11, 229
market coverage:
   defined, 262
   exclusive, 263
   intensive, 263
   selective, 263
market development, as stage of product life cycle, 238
marketing, as key business activity, 5
marketing concept:
   belief in competitive substitutes, 223
   concern with profit, not sales, 223
   defined, 222
   Schlitz Brewing Company, 222-223
marketng mix, elements of:
   communication, 220
   defined, 219
   distribution, 219
   price, 219
   product, 219
marketing research:
   defined, 227
   evaluation of promotional strategies, 229-230
   evaluation of sales potential, 229
   limitations of, 230
market order, 364
market segmentation:
   defined, 223
   demographic, 224-225
   geographic, 225-227
   Volkswagen's strategy, 223-224
market share of U.S. auto makers and all imports, 1971 and 1981, illus., 14
market structures:
   differences among the four, illus., 12
   illus., 12
   monopolistic competition, 11
   monopoly, 14
   oligopoly, 12
   perfect competition, 11
market study, as key business activity, 5
market value, of common stock, 347
markup, 273
markup method of setting prices, 283
markup pricing, 273
Marshall Field & Company, case study of, 232-233
Maslow, Abraham, 141

Maslow's need hierarchy, 141
materials, purchasing of, 197
materials requirement planning (MRP), in inventory control, 202
mathematical model, in manufacturing, 197
maturity, of common stock, 346
maturity stage, of product life cycle, 239
matrix departmentalization, 124; illus., 127
McClelland, David, 141
mean, 454
mechanistic organizational design, 127; illus., 130
median, 454
median family income, illus., 15
mediation, 186
medical insurance (Medicare), 382
medical payments insurance, 387
medium of exchange, 322
memory, 436
Mendel's Book Stores, case study of, 307-308
merchandise agent, 258-260
merchandise inventory:
   finished goods, 409
   raw materials, 409
   work in process, 409
merger:
   congeneric, 74
   conglomerate, 75
   defined, 72
   horizontal, 74
   vertical, 74
merging, 443
microcomputer, 436
micromarketing:
   defined, 219
   elements of the marketing mix, 219-220
   marketing mix interaction, 220-222
microprocessor, 435
minicomputer, 436
minority groups, responsibility of business to, 50
Mississippi Band of Choctaw Indians, case study of, 77
Mississippi Power Company, case study of, 424-425
mode, 454
model of man, 445
money:
   creation of, 323-324
   defined, 322
   functions of, 322-323
   supply of, 323
money market account, 325
money market fund, 371-372
monopolistic competition, 11

monopoly, 14
Moody's Investors Service, Inc., 344
mortgage bond, 341
motivation, 140
motivation, job:
   expectancy theory, 143
   Hawthorne Studies, 140
   Maslow's need hierarchy, 141
   learning theory, 142
   need for achievement, 141-142
   Scientific Management theory, 140
   use of flextime, 150
   use of job enrichment, 149-150
   use of Management By Objectives (MBO), 150-152
moving, 443
mutual funds:
   bond funds, 371
   how mutual funds work, 370
   load funds, 370-371
   money market funds, 371-372
   no-load funds, 370-371
   reasons for popularity of, 370
   stock funds, 371
multinational corporation (MNC):
   benefits of, 477
   criticisms of, 476-477
mutual company, 73
mutual insurance company, 384-385
mutual savings banks, 326

N

name advertising, 299
national advertising, 296-297
National Association of Manufacturers, 188
National Association of Securities Dealers Automated Quotations (NASDAQ), 362
national bank, 321
National Environmental Policy Act (1969), 31
National Labor Relations Board (NLRB), 100, 181
national union, labor, 177-180
nation's output, 1950-1980, changing composition of, illus., 17
need, as related to job motivation, 140
need for achievement, as related to job motivation, 141-142
negotiable certificate of deposit, 317
negotiated price, 271
negotiation, in collective bargaining, 185

Nestle', case study of, 136-137
net income after taxes, 415
net income before taxes, 414
net period, 316
net sales, 411
new product development:
   attributes of new product, 243
   reasons for, 245
   stages of, 245-247
New York Stock Exchange (NYSE), 361
New York Stock Exchange (NYSE), Composite Index, 373-374
Nike, Inc., case study of, 332-333
no-fault insurance, 387
no-load fund, 370-371
normal distribution, 455
Norris-LaGuardia Act (1932), 181
note payable, 317, 409
note receivable, 409
NOW account, 324-325
Nuclear Energy Liability Insurance (1957), 382
numerical control, 441

O

objective probability, 459
objectives of business:
   of employees, 6-7
   of owners, 6
   of society, 7
Occupational Outlook Handbook, 1982-83 Edition, 518
Occupational Safety and Health Act (1970), 108-111
Occupational Safety and Health Administration, 106, 108-111
odd lot, 367
offer, of contract, 101
older people, responsibility of business to, 50
oligopoly, 12
ombudsman, 189
on-line processing, 436
on-the-job training, 167
open book account, 314
open-end trust, 370
operating expense, 413-414
operating income, 414
operating leverage, 342
operations research, 197
option, 369
order, delivery of in purchase cycle, 197
order, monitoring of in purchase cycle, 197
order, placement of in purchase cycle, 197
order cycle, 264
ordering costs, 199

ordinary (or straight) life contract insurance, 393
organic organizational design, 127; illus., 130
organization, design of:
   classical or mechanistic, 127
   departmentalization, 123-124
   division of labor, 123
   hierarchy of authority, 122-123
   line and staff relationships, 125
   organic, 127
   organization chart, 122-123
   span of control, 125
organizational change managing:
   overcoming resistance to, 134
   types of, 133-134
organization chart, 122-123
Organization of Petroleum Exporting Countries (OPEC), as related to inflation, 25
organized labor, challenges for, 189-190
organizing, as function of management, 129-130
organizing campaign, of labor union, 180
orientation, of new employees, 163
other expenses, 414
other income, 414
outcome approach, 167
out of control manufacturing system, 205-206
output unit, 437
outstanding share, 347
over-the-counter (OTC) market, 362
owners' equity, 404, 411
ownership, forms of:
   corporation, 68-72
   other, illus., 73
   partnership, 65-68
   sole proprietorship, 63-65

P

Panaeros Airlines, case study of, 137-138
paper plates, case study of, 285-286
participating preferred stock, 349-350
partnership:
   advantages of, 67-68
   articles of, 67
   defined, 67
   disadvantages of, 68
   features of, 67
   provisions of agreement, illus., 68
par value, 347
passbook account, 324

pay system:
    group performance, 169-170
    individual performance, 169
    plant-wide productivity, 170
    profit-sharing plans, 170-171
    seniority, 168-169
penetration pricing, 281; illus., 282
percentage change, 455
perfect competition, 11
performance, appraising:
    behavioral approach, 167
    outcome approach, 167
    reasons for, 167
    trait approach, 167
performance appraisal, 167
performance standards, 168
periodic inventory, 200
peripheral equipment, 436
perpetual inventory, 200
personal growth, as employees' business objective, 7
personality test, 160
personal selling:
    career opportunities, 302
    defined, 302
    financial rewards, 302
    freedom from direct control, 302
    roles and responsibilities of salespeople, 302-303
    sales process, 303-304
Peter Principle, 163
physical distribution:
    defined, 263
    and marketing, 264-265
    modes of, 265-266
    total cost approach, 265
picket, 187
piece-rate system, 169
pie chart, 456; illus., 457
pioneering stage of the advertising spiral, 299
pipelines, as carriers of goods, 266
placement, of job personnel:
    defined, 163
    demotion, 164
    orientation, 163
    promotion, 163-164
place utility, 217
planning, as function of management, 129
plant location decisions, 206
pledging, 320
Plenum Publishing Company, case study of, 97-98
point-of-purchase display, 305
point-of-sale terminals, 442
pollution:
    and air quality, 31
    business impacts, 32-33
    and energy development, 31
    and environmental reforms, 31
pollution control, expenditures for, 32-33
population, 453
population, growth rates in, illus., 35
population, migration of, illus., 34
positioning, 289
post office, insurance of, 382
post trading, of stock, 363
precedent in law, 100
predicting, 485
predictive maintenance, 208
preferred stock:
    cumulative, 349
    defined, 349
    participating, 349-350
prenegotiation, 185
prepaid expense, 409
presentation in sales, 304
prestige pricing, 275
preventive maintenance, 208
price, discounts of:
    cash, 278
    promotional, 278
    quantity, 277
    seasonal, 277-278
price, setting of:
    cost pricing, 273-274
    demand pricing, 274-276
price determination, 11
price in marketing mix, 219
price lining, 278
price of product:
    defined, 271
    fixed vs. negotiated, 271
    stimulation function, 271
    used in comparing value, 271
    used to ration goods, 271
price skimming, 278; illus., 281
pricing, objectives of:
    achieving target market share, 272
    achieving a target return on investment, 272
    meeting or matching the competition, 272
    geographic pricing, 282-283
    new product pricing, 278-281
    price discounts, 277-278
    price lining, 278
primary boycott, 187
primary data:
    defined, 452
    experiment, 453-454
    observation and case study, 452
    survey research, 452-453
primary demand stimulation, 299
primary market, 358
primary storage unit, 436
prime rate, 317
Prince Tennis Rackets, case study of, 308
private employment agency, as source of job applicants, 158
private enterprise, 2-3
private enterprise system, 9
private insurance:
    mutual company, 384-385
    stock company, 384
private property, as basic freedom, 9
privilege pay, 145
promotional discount, 278
probability, 459
process departmentalization, 123-124
product, classification of:
    consumer, 235-236
    convenience good, 235
    industrial, 236-237
    shopping good, 235
    specialty good, 236
product, new, 243
product, success of, 247-248
product development of new product, 246
product evaluation of new product, 245-246
product demonstration, as sales promotion, 306
product in marketing mix, 219
production, 195
production, as key business activity, 5
production, management of, 195
production, planning and controlling process of:
    corrective action, 203
    dispatching, 203
    follow-up, 203
    loading, 202
    PERT and the critical path, 203-204
    replanning, 203
    routing, 202
    schedule charts, 203
    scheduling, 202
productivity, 24, 140
product life cycle:
    decline, 239
    defined, 237
    forecasting sales, 239-240; illus., 238
    introducing new products, 240
    managing products, 240
    market development, 238
    maturity, 238-239
    rapid growth, 238
    stages of, 238-239
    turbulence, 238
product or service liability, 388

profit:
  as basic freedom, 9
  defined, 3
  government controls on, 10
  for the ten most profitable U.S. businesses in 1981, illus., 10
  motive, 3
  as percentage of GNP, illus., 4
  as percentage of sales, illus., 4
  as percentage return on stockholders' investment, illus., 4
  role in competitive economy, 3
profit margin, 235
profit-sharing plan, 170-171
pro forma income statement, 88
program flowchart, 437
Project Evaluation and Review Technique (PERT) chart, 204; illus., 205
promissory note, 314-316
promotion, regulation of:
  advertising, 105-106
  personal selling, 105
promotion of employees, 163-164
property damage liability, 387
property insurance:
  automobile, 387
  burglary, robbery, and theft, 387
  extended coverage, 385
  fire, 385
  marine, 385
prospecting, 303
protean career, 501
prototype, 246
proxy, 346
public disclosure, 72
public employment agency, as source of job applicants, 158
public liability, 388
publicly held corporation, 69
puffery, 105
Pure Food and Drug Administration, 101
pure risk:
  defined, 379
  insurance, 380
  pay for loss out of current income, 380
  risk reduction, 379
  self-insurance, 379
purpose change in organization, 133
purpose departmentalization, 124; illus., 125
put, 369

Q

quality circle, 205
quality control:
  control chart, 207
  defined, 205
  inspection, 205
  monitoring the quality of supplies, 207-208
  statistical, 205
quality of work life, 184
quantity discount, 277
quick ratio, 418

R

race, as basis for discrimination, 111
railroads, as carriers of goods, 266
rain insurance, 390
raising money, as key business activity, 4
random fluctuation, 456
random sample, 453
random variation, 205-206
range, 455
rapid growth, as stage of product life cycle, 238
ratio analysis:
  acid-test, 418
  current ratio, 418
  debt net worth ratio, 419
  earnings per share, 419-420
  inventory-turnover ratio, 419
  quick ratio, 418
  return on equity, 421-423
  return on sales, 420
raw material, 409
reach in advertising, 300
real GNP (gross national product), illus., 15
realistic job preview, 158
recruiting of job applicants, 157
referral, as source of job applicants, 157-158
reference of job applicant, 159
regional exchange, 362
reorder point, 199
reorder quantity, 199
repatriation, 467
replanning, 203
representation election campaign, 182
representative, 453
requisition, 197
reserves, of banks, 327
resume, 508; illus., 510
retail advertising, 296
retailer, 260
retail store, kinds of:
  convenience, 261
  discount, 262
  hypermarket, 262
  speciality, 261
  supermarket, 260
retained earnings, 336-337
retentive stage of the advertising spiral, 299
retirement security as owners' business objective, 6
return on bond, 344
return on equity, 421-423
return on sales, 420
returns, 411
Revco, case study of, 268-269
revolving credit agreement, 317
reward, employee:
  classes of, 143-145
  extrinsic, 143
  financial, 145
  giving out, 145-146
  intrinsic, 143
  nonfinancial, 145
right-to-work law, 181
risk, 379
risk, of bond ownership, 344
risk reduction, 379
robot, 189, 494
robotics, 494-495
role playing, 163
round lot, 367
routing in production, 202

S

safety-deposit boxes, case study of, 398
sales contract, 103
salespeople, roles of:
  credit reviewer, 302-303
  external consultant, 303
  glad handler, 303
  team manager, 303
sales process:
  approach, 304
  follow-up, 304
  presentation, 304
  prospecting, 303
  questions and objections, 304
  the sale, 304
sales promotion:
  coupons, 305
  defined, 304
  gifts, 306
  point-of-purchase displays, 305
  product demonstrations, 306
  reasons for, 304-305
  samples, 305
sample, as sales promotion, 305
sample, statistical, 453
sampling, 453
sardine industry, case study of, 499
satisfaction, as related to job motivation, 140
savings and loan association, 326
scabs, 188
Scanlon Plan, 170
schedule chart, 203
scheduling in production, 202

Schlitz Brewing Company, marketing concept of, 222-223
Scientific Management, 140
scoring approach, 132
screening approach, 132
scrambled merchandising, 264
seasonal discount, 277-278
seasonal fluctuation, 456
secondary boycott, 187
secondary data:
 defined, 450
 internal records, 450
 published sources, 450
secondary market, 358
secondary storage, 437
secured loan, 320
Securities and Exchange Commission, 100-101, 367
securities market, perspective of the firm:
 new issues, 358
 outstanding issues, 358-359
securities market, perspective of the investor:
 appreciation in value, 360
 freedom from care, 360
 liquidity, 359
 maintenance of purchasing power, 360
 safety of principal, 359
 stability of income, 359-360
security, as employees' business objective, 7
security for short-term loans, 320-321
selection, of job candidates, 158
selection and hiring of job personnel:
 application blanks, 158-159
 assessment center, 163
 interview, 159
 references, 159
 testing, 160
 unfair preemployment inquiries, illus., 159
selective distribution, 263
self-analysis in career choice, 504-505
self-insurance, 379
selling, personal:
 Cooling-Off Rule (1974), 105
 regulation of, 105
 Truth-in-Lending Act (1969), 105
 selling expense, 413
 selling short, 368
 seniority, 168-169
 sex, as basis for discrimination, 111
 shareholder, interest in social responsibility of business, 49

shareholder, limited liability of, 10
Sherman Act (1890), 104
Shipowners' Mutual Strike Insurance Association, 188
shopping good, 235
short-term financing:
 defined, 313
 reasons for, 313
 sources of short-term funds, 314-321
short-term funds, sources of:
 commercial paper, 318
 factoring accounts receivable, 321
 secured borrowing, 320-321
 trade credit, 314-316
 unsecured bank loans, 316-318
simple-recognition shop, 176
sinking fund, 344
small business, 80
Small Business Act of 1953, 80
Small Business Administration (SBA), 80, 86
Smith Pipe and Supply, Inc., case study of, 172-173
social audit of business responsibility:
 defined, 53
 conducting and reporting on, 54
social responsibility of business:
 benefits of, 51-52
 classical view of, 47-48
 to community, 51
 comparing benefits and costs of, 52
 competitive parity, 52
 costs of, 52
 current views of, 48
 defined, 47
 to handicapped, 51
 to minority groups, 50
 to older people, 50-51
 social audit of, 52-54
 to women, 50
Social Security:
 benefits of, 382-384
 costs of, 384
Social Security Act (1935), 107
Softsel Computer Products, case study of, 76-77
sole proprietorship:
 advantages of, 64-65
 defined, 63
 disadvantages of, 65
 features of, 63-64
sorting, 443
Soviet trade balance, case study of, 482
span of control, 125; illus., 129
spatial transformation, 196
specialty fund, 371

specialty good, 236
specialty store, 261
speculative risk, 379
speculative trading tactics:
 buying on the margin, 368
 selling short, 368
 trading on the options market, 369-370
speculator, 359
staffing:
 defined, 156
 placement, 163-165
 recruiting, 157-158
 selection and hiring, 158-163
staffing, as function of management, 130
staff position, 125
Standard and Poor's Compustat Tapes, 450
Standard and Poor's Corporation (S&P), 344
Standard and Poor's 500 Index, 373
standardization strategy, 473
standard of value, 322
state bank, 321
statistical data, display of, 456-457
statistical map, 457; illus., 459
statistical quality control, 205
statistics, 450
statistics, tips for interpreting, 460
status pay, 145
statute, 100
statutory law, 100
stimulation function of price, 271
stock, buying and selling of:
 limit order, 364
 market order, 364
 odd lots, 367
 post trading, 363
 price setting, 363
 round lots, 367
 role of stockbroker, 363
 stop order, 364-367
 transaction costs, 367
 trading specialists, 367
stockbroker, 363
stock certificate, 345
stock exchange:
 American Stock Exchange (AMEX), 361
 New York Stock Exchange (NYSE), 361
 over-the-counter (OTC) market, 362
 regional exchanges, 362
stock dividend, 348
stock fund, 371
stockholder, 6, 70
stock insurance company, 384
stock market, indicators of:

ASE Market Value Index, 374
Dow Jones Industrial Average, 372-373
NYSE Composite Index, 373-374
Standard & Poor's 500 Index, 373
stock market crash of 1929, 19
stockout costs, 199
stock ownership, 6
stock split, 348-349
stop order, 364-367
storage media, 436
store of value, 322
stress, as related to job dissatisfaction, 146
strike, 187
strikebreakers, 188
structural change in organization, 133-134
subjective probability, 459
subordinated debenture, 338
success chess, 513-514
supermarket, 260
supplier selection, 197
supply, as related to price determination, 11
supply flow of information, 429
survey, 452
synthetic transformation, 196

T

table, as used to display statistical information, 456; illus., 457
tables:
    ability profile, 506
    air pollutant emissions, by source, 1979, 32
    average hourly wage rates for selected jobs by city, 170
    consumer protection laws, 109
    cost comparisons between two full service and one discount brokerage firms, 368
    declining industries in the United States, 490
    differences in true interest as a result of payment schedules, 106
    distribution of U.S. population by age, 1950-1980, 37
    earnings by occupation, 1981 weekly medians, 40
    economic communities, 479
    failures (of small businesses), causes of, 85
    families, by size, 1980-1995, 487
    federal loans to small businesses, 1970-1980, 80
    (ten) growing industries in the United States, 490
    high pressure sales tactics, 105
    (ten biggest) imports and exports in 1981, 18
    income and income taxes, 415
    labor force unemployed for selected states and localities, 1980-82, 37
    leading national advertisers, 1981, 290
    long term financing for ten large U.S. Companies, 352
    market share of U.S. auto makers and all imports, 1971 and 1981, 14
    mortality table, 381
    price changes during Great Depression, 19
    profits and federal income taxes for the ten most profitable U.S. businesses in 1981, 10
    securities traded on leading U.S. stock exchanges in 1981, value of, 362
    shareholders for five largest U.S. industrial corporations, ranked according to 1981 sales, 69
    Small Business Administration's definition of a small business, 80
    social security tax rates, 1980-1985, 384
    stock, buying on margin, 369
    stock prices, high and low for nine large U.S. corporations, 1971-1982, 348
    unemployment during Great Depression, 19
    U.S. labor unions, ten largest in terms of total membership, 177
    wholesalers, functions of, 258
Taft-Hartley Act (1947), 181
target market, 223
task change in organization, 133
Taylor, Frederick W., 140
Teamsters Union, 177
technological change in organization, 133
temporal transformation, 196
term life insurance, 392
terms of trade, 316
testing of job applicant, 160
test marketing of new product 246-247
Texaco, case study of, 426-427
Theory X, as related to employee rewards, 143
Theory Y, as related to employee rewards, 143
the recession and your career, case study of, 515-516
The Wall Street Journal, how to read, 372
Thompson International Education, Inc., case study of, 482-483
time deposit, 325
time series analysis, 456
time-sharing, 436
time utility, 217
total cost approach, 265
trade acceptance, 316
trade advertising, 293; illus., 296
trade balance, 465
trade credit, types of:
    open book account or open account, 314
    promissory note, 314-316
    trade acceptance, 316
trade deficit, 465
trademark, 240
trade surplus, 465
trading on the options market, 369
training, of employees:
    case studies, 165
    determining needs for, 165
    group discussion, 165
    on-the-job, 167
training employees, as key business activity, 3
trait approach of appraising performance, 167
Trammell Crow Co., case study of, 354-355
transaction loan, 317
transformation process:
    analytic, 196
    form, 196
    spatial, 196
    synthetic, 196
    temporal, 196
treasury stock, 347
trend, 456
trucks, as carriers of goods, 265-266
Truth-in-Lending Act (1969), 105
turbulence stage, of product life cycle, 238

U

uncontrollable variables, 24
unemployment benefits, 107-108
unemployment statistics, illus., 41
Uniform Commercial Code (UCC), 103
uniform-delivered pricing, 282
uninsured motorist coverage, 387

union shop, 176
United Automobile Workers, 177
United Mine Workers (UMW), 178
United States Employment Services (USES), 507
United Steelworkers' of America, structure of, 178
universal life insurance, 393-394
universe, 453
unlimited liability:
    of partnership, 68
    of sole proprietorship, 65
unsecured bank loan:
    interest rates, 317
    line of credit, 316-317
    revolving credit agreement, 317
    transaction loan, 317
unwritten law, 100

V

validity of job testing, 160
value added, 195
value analysis, 197
Vandivier, Kermit, 57
variable cost, 273
variance, 455
vertical merger, 74
visual display terminal, 436
Volkswagen and market segmentation, 223-224
voluntary bankruptcy, 113
voting right of common stock, 346

W

wage parity, 24
Wagner Act (1935), 181
warranty:
    express, 103
    implied, 103
Washington State Human Rights Commission, 158
WD-40 Company, case study of, 21
Weis Markets, case study of, 21, 22
Wham-O, case study of, 286-287
Wheeler-Lea Act (1938), 109
whistleblower, 57
Whistleblowers' Protection Act, 57-58
whole life insurance, 392-393
wholesaler, 256
wholesalers, kinds of:
    full-service merchant, 258
    limited-service merchant, 258
    manufacturer-owned, 258
    merchandise agent, 258-260
wholesaling industry, size of, 256
Williams Greenhouses, case study of, 211-212
women:
    changing role of, 39
    implications for business, 40
    problems in business, 509
    responsibility of business to, 50
    treatment in the workplace, 40
work, hours of, 182-184
work in process, 409
worker's compensation insurance, 391

Z

zone-delivered pricing, 283
zoning laws, 9

PHOTO CREDITS

Part Openers | Credit

Part 1	The Signal Companies, Inc.
Part 2	Capitol photo, Washington, D.C. Convention and Visitors Bureau
Part 4	Santa Fe Railway Photograph
Part 5	Chicago Mercantile Exchange
Part 6	Boise Cascade Corporation
Part 7	Bell Laboratories

Chapter Openers | Credit

Chapter 1	Queen City Metro, Cincinnati, Ohio
Chapter 2	Arizona-Sonora Desert Museum
Chapter 5	© 1983 Joel Gordon
Chapter 6	National Park Service Photo by Mishi Kamiya
Chapter 9	Alcoa
Chapter 11	The Lehigh Press, Inc.
Chapter 13	Color Tile Supermart, Inc.
Chapter 14	H.J. Heinz Company
Chapter 16	Queen City Metro, Cincinnati, Ohio
Chapter 18	Parker Pen Company

Chapter Openers | Credit

Chapter 22	Ramtek
Chapter 23	H.J. Heinz Company
Chapter 24	Bell Laboratories

Table of Contents Photos | Credit

Page

viii (top)	Sperry New Holland
(center)	Air Products and Chemicals, Inc.
(bottom)	Boise Cascade Corporation
x (top)	Cyclops Corporation
(bottom)	The Lehigh Press, Inc.
xi (top)	Santa Fe Railway Photograph
(bottom)	The Goodyear Tire & Rubber Co.
xii (bottom)	Florida Department of Commerce/Division of Tourism
xiii (bottom)	The Lehigh Press, Inc.
xiv	IBM Corporation

Internal Photos | Credit

Page

6 (left)	AETNA Life & Casualty Company
(2nd from left)	Florida Department of Commerce/Division of Tourism
(2nd from right)	Courtesy of Evans Products Company, Portland, Oregon
(right)	Deere & Company
9	Steven Green/Chicago Cubs
11	Ralston Purina Co.
16 (Figure 1-7)	Virginia State Travel Service
17	IBM Corporation
28	United States Department of Energy
32	Odessa, Texas, Chamber of Commerce
35 (lower right)	Texas State Department of Highways and Public Transportation

Internal Photos Credit

Page

37		© 1981 Tom McCarthy
48		Atlantic Richfield Company
51		U.S. Fish and Wildlife Service photo by Phil Norton
55		Ballet West, Salt Lake City, Utah, photo by Jack Mitchell
63	(left)	© Dr. E.R. Degginger
	(right)	Springs Industries, Inc.
65		Cessna Aircraft Company
67		Sears, Roebuck and Co.
69		Hershey Foods Corporation
81		Burt Glinn/Magnum Photos, Inc.
82		Las Vegas News Bureau
91		Environmental Communications
92		Bundy American Corporation/RENT-A-WRECK
103		Dana Duke Photography
107		The Bettman Archive, Inc.
111		Cyclops Corporation
122		© 1983 William B. Folsom/UNIPHOTO
127		NASA
133		Four by Five, Inc.
142	(left)	Photo courtesy of Celanese Corporation
	(2d from left)	French Government Tourist Office
	(2d from right)	Circus World
	(right)	Cosmos Soccer Club, Inc.
143	(left)	Courtesy of Verbatim Corporation
147		The Bettman Archive, Inc.
149		Saab-Scandia of America, Inc.
157		Walgreen Company
160	(left)	© Victoria Beller-Smith
	(right)	Rockwell International Corporation
163		Four by Five, Inc.
180		The Kentucky Horse Park
186		Santa Fe Railway Photograph

Internal Photos   Credit

Page

190	American Iron and Steel Institute
196 (top)	Photo Courtesy of Georgia-Pacific Corporation
(center)	Crown Zellerbach
200	Norton Simon Inc.
207	NASA
217	New York Convention and Visitors Bureau, Inc.
222 (left)	Castle & Cooke, Inc.
(right)	Valvoline Oil Company
224 (left)	H.J. Heinz Company
(center)	Texas State Department of Highways and Public Transportation
(right)	Department of Housing and Urban Development
225 (2d from right)	Boise Cascade Corporation
(right)	Springs Industries, Inc.
237	Pontiac Motor Division/General Motors Corporation
243	Ford Motor Company
245	The Bettman Archive, Inc.
255	DeLong Sportswear
260	Texas State Department of Highways and Public Transportation
266	Association of American Railroads
271	Brazilian Tourism Authority/Embratur
274	Standard Oil Company of California
277	Cosmos Soccer Club, Inc.
294 (top)	Chevrolet Motor Division/General Motors Corporation
(bottom)	AT&T Long Lines
295	Boise Cascade Corporation
296	Mead Corporation
297	Courtesy of Cincinnati Milacron
298	McAlpin's
300	Franklin Computer Corporation
301	The Coca Cola Company
305 (right)	The Coca Cola Company/Foods Division

Photo Credits

Internal Photos		Credit

Page

314		Bronner's Christmas Decorations/Division of Bronner Display & Sign Advertising, Inc.
320	(left)	Courtesy of the Nielsen Lithographing Co.
	(center)	The Lehigh Press, Inc.
	(right)	The Lehigh Press, Inc.
336		Boeing Photo
338		Crocker National Bank
359		New York State Department of Commerce
361	(left)	Courtesy of Cincinnati Milacron
	(center)	Falconbridge Limited
	(right)	Courtesy of Exxon Corporation
363		Minneapolis Grain Exchange
380		© John Kasinger/West Stock
385		© Bill Staley/West Stock
392		North Dakota Economic Development Commission
404		The Bettman Archive, Inc.
414		Balloons-N-Tunes, Cincinnati, Ohio
416		Used with the permission of Alexander & Alexander Services, Inc.
435		IBM Corporation
437	(left)	Atari Incorporated
	(right top)	NCR Corporation
	(right bottom)	NCR Corporation
438	(top)	Courtesy of Apple Computer, Inc.
	(2d from bottom)	Courtesy of Apple Computer, Inc.
	(bottom)	Cray Research, Inc.
441		Chrysler Corporation
466	(left)	Sperry New Holland
	(right)	Brazilian Tourism Authority/Embratur
469		Fred Ward/Black Star, Courtesy of Richardson-Vicks, Inc.
474		Courtesy Kentucky Fried Chicken
476	(left)	Globus-Gateway
	(right)	French Government Tourist Office

Internal Photos

Page

	Credit
485	Queen City Metro, Cincinnati, Ohio
488	Brazilian Tourism Authority/Embratur
494	Photo Courtesy of Pfizer, Inc.
495	Courtesy of Cincinnati Milacron
505 (Center)	Boise Cascade Corporation
513 (right)	Digital Equipment Corporation

Profiles

	Credit
Chapter **4**	The Bettman Archive, Inc.